CONTENTS

PREFACE

There have been significant advances in the use of information technology to support decision making during the past few years. These changes have been driven by business needs and the emergence of new hardware and software technology. Traditional decision support systems (DSS), the maturing of expert systems (ES) and executive information systems (EIS), and the emergence of group decision support systems (GDSS) have resulted in a rich and varied set of computer applications that can be used to support decision making and other managerial and professional work. Because of these rapid changes, there has been an abundance of news articles, journal articles, conferences, and seminars describing the changes in the decision support field. Unfortunately for students and faculty, many of these resources are not readily available in the formal literature. News articles are brief and sketchy, carefully prepared journal articles frequently require several years to come into print, conference proceedings are expensive and not widely circulated, and seminars are seldom documented.

We have prepared this book specifically to deal with this problem. Articles from the trade literature and conference proceedings have been chosen and organized to characterize recent developments. In some instances, we have commissioned the writing of selections specifically for the book. We have sought out readings that give life to the theory and concepts in order to enrich the understanding and learning of students.

In addition, we have provided several valuable resources. A listing of decision support software products and vendors is provided. Many of these vendors have university support programs, which makes their products available at affordable prices. A cross- referenced bibliography is provided to help students and faculty who wish to pursue some topics in more depth.

THE USE OF THE BOOK

This book can be used in several ways:

As the main text in a DSS course. Many DSS courses include hands-on DSS building experiences with software products such as IFPS. This book of readings would be appropriate as the main text in a course that takes this approach. It would also be useful in those courses that are based on current literature alone.

As a supplementary text in a DSS course. The book of readings could be used with another DSS text to provide broader DSS perspective, such as Sprague and Carlson, *Building Effective Decision Support Systems* (Prentice Hall, 1982).

As a supplementary text in an MIS course. Many management information systems (MIS) textbooks provide only limited coverage of decision support applications. This book of readings could be used to enhance this coverage.

CHANGES TO THE THIRD EDITION

In this third edition, we have continued the philosophy of drawing on the best literature to provide an up-to-date treatment of this dynamic field. The overall result is twenty-seven readings, of which eleven are new to this edition. Several of the readings continued from the second edition have been revised by the authors to keep them up to date. We also paid particular attention to comprehensive coverage of the field. In several cases, we have sought out the best authors in an important topic and commissioned a selection for this book. "Group Decision Support Systems" by Gray and Nunamaker, "A Technology Infrastructure for Document-Based Decision Support Systems" by Fedorowicz, and "Intelligent Support Systems' Art, Augmentation, and Agents" by King fall into this category.

In addition to comprehensive coverage, we have tried to provide a consistency of style and philosophy that is uncommon in readings books. In fact, close to half of the readings were authored, coauthored, or commissioned by us. This is not just bias on our part, but a desire to provide the consistency and coverage that allow the book to be used as a primary text on the subject.

EIS, GDSS, and ES have evolved to the point that they merit special emphasis, and separate parts of the book are now devoted to each of these types of systems. They represent much of the "new news" in the decision support field. The reader should gain a better understanding of the constellation of possible decision support applications. Furthermore, the possible combining of applications should be better appreciated.

ACKNOWLEDGMENTS

We would like to express our appreciation to the authors of the selections in this book, especially those who were gracious enough to accommodate our suggested changes, and to the publishers of the articles for allowing us to reprint them. Also, we would like to thank Doug Campbell Stephanie Hatcher, and Maggie O'Hara for their assistance in developing materials for the book.

Ralph H. Sprague, Jr.
Hugh J. Watson

Introduction to Decision Support Systems: Putting Theory into Practice

Decision support systems (DSS) first appeared in the 1970s. In the early part of the decade, academicians conceptualized about what they were and their potential, the first commercial software appeared, and a few leading-edge companies began developing them. By the end of the decade, a large number of organizations was actively engaged in DSS work.

DSS was both an evolution and a departure from previous types of computer support for decision making. Its precursors included management information systems (MIS) that provide scheduled reports for well-defined information needs, demand reports for ad hoc information requests, and the ability to query a database for specific data, and operations research/management science (OR/MS) which employ mathematical models to better analyze and understand specific problems. Each was lacking, however, with regard to focus, development methodology, handling of data, use of analytic aids, or dialogue between user and system.

As is often the case with new developments, there were different conceptualizations initially about what decision support systems were. Not only did academicians give different definitions, but vendors, quick to pick up on anything to help sell their products, applied the DSS label very loosely. One popular interpretation was provided by Steven Alter, who viewed any system that supported decision making as being a DSS [1]. Although this understanding has an intuitive appeal, it does not differentiate between the variety of systems that can support decision making. As a consequence, and quite important, it does not provide sufficient guidelines and focus for DSS developers and researchers.

An alternative understanding, and the one that prevails today, was set forward in a seminal DSS book by Ralph Sprague and Eric Carlson [3]. They define DSS as

- computer- based systems
- that help decision makers
- confront ill-structured problems
- through direct interaction
- with data and analysis models

Also in their book, and in an earlier article by Ralph Sprague [2], a framework for thinking about and developing DSS was provided. Some of the key concepts from this framework include the following:

1. The technology for DSS must consist of three sets of capabilities in the areas of dialog, data, and modeling, what Sprague and Carlson call the DDM paradigm. They make the point that a good DSS should have *balance* among the three capabilities. It should be *easy to use* to support the interaction with nontechnical users, it should have access to a *wide variety of data,* and it should provide *analysis and modeling* in a variety of ways. Many systems claim to be DSS when they are strong in only one area and weak in the others.

2. Three *levels* of technology are useful in developing DSS. This concept illustrates the usefulness of configuring *DSS tools* into a *DSS generator* which can be used to develop a variety of *specific DSS* quickly and easily to aid decision makers.

3. DSS are not developed according to traditional approaches but require a form of *iterative development* that allows them to evolve and change as the situation changes.

4. Effective development of DSS requires an organizational strategy to build an *environment* within which such systems can originate and evolve. The environment includes a group of people with interacting roles, a set of hardware and software technology, and a set of data sources.

While the 1980s saw the institutionalization of DSS in many organizations, there were important new developments on the decision support scene. One of these was expert systems (ES), which capture the experience, knowledge, training, and judgment of a human expert in a computer program. Expert systems date back to the dawn of computers and interest in artificial intelligence. To illustrate, Alan Turing [4] in 1950 wrote the classic article, "Can a Machine Think." For many years, however, work on expert systems was confined to high-profile research laboratories, conducted by highly skilled professionals, supported by multimillion dollar budgets and specialized hardware and software, on "rocket scientist" types of applications. It is only recently that expert systems have entered the mainstream of computer applications. Not all organizations are currently developing expert systems, but nearly all of them understand and have an interest in their potential use.

The late 1980s also saw the emergence of executive information systems (EIS) which are designed to support the information needs of a firm's senior executives. Heretofore, the occupants of "mahogany row" received little computer-generated information of value to support them in performing their job responsibilities. A number of factors has fueled EIS development: executives' need for information, a growing understanding of the nature of executives and executive work, the increasing number of EIS success stories, and hardware and especially software advances. Today, EIS is the fastest growing computer application in corporate America.

The newest "star" in "the constellation of decision support applications" is group decision support systems (GDSS). These systems, also known as collaborative work systems, group support systems, electronic meeting systems, or simply as groupware are designed to bring computer support to teams of people working together. Given the large amount of time that people spend working in groups, it is easy to see why systems that have the potential for improving the efficiency and effectiveness of groups are attracting considerable attention. At the present time, Lotus Notes is the most recognized group support product, but many others are working their way into the marketplace.

As can be seen, there are many types of decision support applications. Each has similarities and differences when compared to the others. In practice, a particular application may combine features from several of them. For example, an EIS may contain a DSS capability. Because each kind of decision support application has evolved to the point where it merits significant attention, this book is structured to accommodate this fact.

A major criterion that we have employed when selecting and organizing the readings for this book is to be at the cutting edge of what is going on. Although there is a certain amount of foundation, or baseline, material that must be learned, it is what's new in DSS that excites us the most and that we cover in this book. We want you to be on top of emerging DSS trends.

STRUCTURE OF THE BOOK

The readings in the book are organized into seven parts.

- Part 1 contains two selections that provide the conceptual foundation for understanding DSS.
- Part 2 deals with developing and using DSS. Specific topics include management's roles in developing and operating a DSS, how a DSS expenditure is evaluated, the iterative design methodology for DSS, and two detailed DSS examples.

- Part 3 treats the architecture of DSS, showing developments in each area of the dialog, data, and model paradigm. Special attention is devoted to the inclusion of documents and intelligent agents in DSS.

- Part 4 contains four selections on creating an organizational environment where DSS can flourish. The main focus is on organizing and staffing the DSS support group and the selections include three examples from different organizations. Selecting DSS software is also included in this part of the book.

- Part 5 contains four EIS selections that include a detailed EIS example, a framework for developing an EIS, advice on how to avoid an EIS failure, and discussions with three CEOs about how they use their EIS and what the payoffs are.

- Part 6 explores GDSS by covering what a GDSS is, how a GDSS might be used, what has been learned from GDSS research and practice, and what are the possible future directions for GDSS.

- Part 7 contains four selections on EIS. Specific topics include what an expert system is, how they are developed and used, organizational strategies for introducing expert systems, and a detailed ES example.

Following Part 7 are some resources that we think will be valuable in pursuing the subject of DSS further. First is a listing of decision support software products. Many vendors make them available to educational institutions at reduced cost. Hands-on experience is quite valuable to students in learning and understanding how the systems can be developed and used. The bibliography, cross-referenced by topic, will help the reader who wants to pursue a specific decision support topic in more detail.

REFERENCES

1. ALTER, S. "A Taxonomy of Decision Support Systems," *Sloan Management Review,* 19, no. 1 (Fall 1977), 39–56.

2. SPRAGUE, R. H., and E. D. CARLSON *Building Effective Decision Support Systems.* Englewood Cliffs, N.J.: Prentice Hall, 1982.

3. SPRAGUE, R. H. "A Framework for the Development of Decision Support Systems," *MIS Quarterly,* 4, no. 4 (1980), 1–26.

4. TURING, A. M. "Can a Machine Think?," in *The World of Mathematics,* ed. J. R. Newman, 2099–123. New York: Simon & Schuster, 1956.

PART 1

The Conceptual Foundation for DSS

In the late 1960s and early 1970s, the first decision support systems (DSS) began to appear. They were the result of a number of factors: emerging computer hardware and software technology; research efforts at leading universities; a growing awareness of how to support decision making; a desire for better information; an increasingly turbulent economic environment; and stronger competition pressures, especially from abroad. During the rest of the decade, there was a growing body of DSS research from the academic community, and an increasing number of organizations began to develop decision support systems. These experiences provided the conceptual foundation for DSS.

Ralph Sprague's article, "A Framework for the Development of Decision Support Systems" (Reading 1), played a major role in establishing DSS's conceptual foundation. It identifies the characteristics of a DSS, especially in contrast to the characteristics of electronic data processing (EDP) and management information systems (MIS). It also defines the various levels of DSS technology and the different organizational roles associated with DSS. The unique development approach for DSS is discussed. The DSS performance objectives from a user's perspective are stated. The technical capabilities from a builder's point of view are identified. The underlying DSS technology from the toolsmith's perspective is discussed. And in conclusion, the article considers issues associated with the future development of DSS.

A few years later, Sprague expanded the framework by arguing that the context of DSS and its applicability are often too narrowly viewed. His "DSS in Context" (Reading 2) argues that the boundaries of decision-making activities are difficult to define and that DSS are useful in supporting a wide range of activities that are goal-directed and process-independent—not defined in advance as a series of steps. Reading 2 also shows that the field of DSS lies at the convergence of evolutionary developments in EDP/MIS and management science.

1

A FRAMEWORK FOR THE DEVELOPMENT OF DECISION SUPPORT SYSTEMS

Ralph H. Sprague, Jr.

INTRODUCTION

We seem to be on the verge of another "era" in the relentless advancement of computer based information systems in organizations. Designated by the term "decision support systems" (DSS), these systems are receiving reactions ranging from "a major break-through" to "just another 'buzz word.'"

One view is that the natural evolutionary advancement of information technology and its use in the organizational context has led from EDP to MIS to the current DSS thrust. In this view, the DSS picks up where MIS leaves off. A contrary view portrays DSS as an important subset of what MIS has been and will continue to be. Still another view recognizes a type of system that has been developing for several years and "now we have a name for it." Meanwhile, the skeptics suspect that DSS is just another "buzz word" to justify the next round of visits from the vendors.

The purpose of this reading is to briefly examine these alternative views of DSS, and present a framework that proves valuable in reconciling them. The framework articulates and integrates major concerns of several "stakeholders" in the development of DSS:

Reprinted by special permission of the *MIS Quarterly*, Volume 4, Number 4, December 1980. Copyright 1980 by the Society for Information Management and the Management Information Systems Research Center.

executives and professionals who use them, the MIS managers who manage the process of developing and installing them, the information specialists who build and develop them, the system designers who create and assemble the technology on which they are based, and the researchers who study the DSS subject and process.

DEFINITION, EXAMPLES, CHARACTERISTICS

The concepts involved in DSS were first articulated in the early '70s by Michael S. Scott Morton under the term "management decision systems" [32]. A few firms and scholars began to develop and research DSS, which became characterized as *interactive* computer based systems, which *help* decision makers utilize *data* and *models* to solve *unstructured* problems. The unique contribution of DSS resulted from these key words. That definition proved restrictive enough that few actual systems completely satisfied it. Some authors recently extended the definition of DSS to include any system that makes some contribution to decision making; in this way the term can be applied to all but transaction processing. A serious definitional problem is that the words have a certain "intuitive validity"; any system that supports a decision, in any way, is a "Decision Support System."

Unfortunately, neither the restrictive nor the broad definition helps much, because they do not provide guidance for understanding the value, the technical requirements, or the approach for developing a DSS. A complicating factor is that people from different backgrounds and contexts view a DSS quite differently. A manager and computer scientist seldom see things in the same way.

Another way to get a feeling for a complex subject like a DSS is to consider examples. Several specific examples were discussed in The Society for Management Information Systems (SMIS) Workshop on DSS in 1979 [35]. Alter examined fifty-six systems which might have some claim to the DSS label, and used this sample to develop a set of abstractions describing their characteristics [1, 2]. More recently, Keen has designated about thirty examples of what he feels are DSS and compares their characteristics [26].

The "characteristics" approach seems to hold more promise than either definitions or collections of examples in understanding a DSS and its potential. More specifically, a DSS may be defined by its capabilities in several critical areas—capabilities which are required to accomplish the objectives which are pursued by the development and use of a DSS. Observed characteristics of a DSS which have evolved from the work of Alter, Keen, and others include:

- they tend to be aimed at the less well structured, underspecified problems that upper level managers typically face;
- they attempt to combine the use of models or analytic techniques with traditional data access and retrieval functions;
- they specifically focus on features which make them easy to use by noncomputer people in an interactive mode; and
- they emphasize flexibility and adaptability to accommodate changes in the environment and the decision making approach of the user.

A serious question remains. Are the definitions, examples, and characteristics of a DSS sufficiently different to justify the use of a new term and the inference of a new era in information systems for organizations, or are the skeptics right? Is it just another "buzz word" to replace the fading appeal of MIS?

DSS VERSUS MIS

Much of the difficulty and controversy with terms like "DSS" and "MIS" can be traced to the difference between an academic or theoretical definition and "connotational" definition. The former is carefully articulated by people who write textbooks and articles in journals. The latter evolves from what actually is developed and used in practice, and is heavily influenced by the personal experiences that the user of the term has had with the subject. It is this connotational definition of EDP/MIS/DSS that is used in justifying the assertion that a DSS is an evolutionary advancement beyond MIS.

This view can be expressed using Figure 1.1, a simple organizational chart, as a model of an organization. EDP was first applied to the lower operational levels of the organization to automate the paperwork. Its basic characteristics include:

- a focus on data, storage, processing, and flows at the operational level;
- efficient transaction processing;
- scheduled and optimized computer runs;
- integrated files for related jobs; and
- summary reports for management.

In recent years, the EDP level of activity in many firms has become a well-oiled and efficient production facility for transactions processing.

The MIS approach elevated the focus on information systems activities, with additional emphasis on integration and planning of the information systems function. In *practice,* the characteristics of MIS include:

FIGURE 1.1 The Connotational View

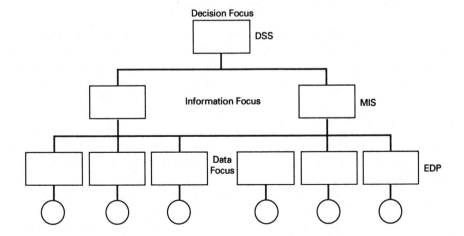

- an information focus, aimed at the middle managers;
- structured information flow;
- an integration of EDP jobs by business function, such as production MIS, marketing MIS, personnel MIS, etc.; and
- inquiry and report generation, usually with a database.

The MIS era contributed a new level of information to serve management needs, but was still very much oriented to, and built upon, information flows and data files.

According to this connotational view, a DSS is focused still higher in the organization with an emphasis on the following characteristics:

- decision focused, aimed at top managers and executive decision makers;
- emphasis on flexibility, adaptability, and quick response;
- user-initiated and -controlled; and
- support for the personal decision making styles of individual managers.

This connotational and evolutionary view has some credence because it roughly corresponds to developments in practice over time. A recent study found MIS managers able to distinguish the level of advancement of their application systems using criteria similar to those above [27]. Many installations with MIS type applications planned to develop applications with DSS type characteristics. However, the "connotational" view has some serious deficiencies, and is definitely misleading in the further development of a DSS.

- It implies that *decision support* is needed only at the top levels. In fact, *decision support* is required at all levels of management in the organization.
- The decision making which occurs at several levels frequently must be coordinated. Therefore, an important dimension of *decision support* is the communication and coordination between decision makers across organizational levels, as well as at the same level.
- It implies that *decision support* is the only thing top managers need from the information system. In fact, decision making is only one of the activities of managers that benefits from information systems support.

There is also the problem that many information systems professionals, especially those in the Society for Information Management (SIM), are not willing to accept the narrow connotational view of the term "MIS." To us, MIS refers to the entire set of systems and activities required to manage, process, and use information as a resource in the organization.

THE THEORETICAL VIEW

To consider the appropriate role of a DSS in this overall context of information systems, the broad charter and objectives of the information systems function in the organization are characterized:

- Dedicated to improving the performance of knowledge workers in organizations through the application of information technology.
- Improving the performance is the ultimate objective of information systems—not the storage of data, the production of reports, or even "getting the right informa-

tion to the right person at the right time." The ultimate objective must be viewed in terms of the ability of information systems to support the improved performance of people in organizations.

- Knowledge workers are the clientele. This group includes managers, professionals, staff analysts, and clerical workers whose primary job responsibility is the handling of information in some form.
- Organizations are the context. The focus is on information handling in goal seeking organizations of all kinds.
- The application of information technology is the challenge and opportunity facing the information systems professional for the purposes and in the contexts given above.

A triangle was used by Robert Head in the late 1960s as a visual model to characterize MIS in this broad comprehensive sense [22]. It has become a classic way to view the dimensions of an information system. The vertical dimension represented the levels of management, and the horizontal dimension represented the main functional areas of the business organization. Later authors added transactional processing as a base on which the entire system rested. The result was a two-dimensional model of an MIS in the broad sense—the total activities which comprise the information system in an organization. Figure 1.2 is a further extension of the basic triangle to help describe the concept of the potential role of a DSS. The depth dimension shows the major technology "subsystems" which provide support for the activities of knowledge workers.

Three major thrusts are shown here, but there could be more. The structured reporting system includes the reports required for the management and control of the organization, and for satisfying the information needs of external parties. It has been evolving from efforts in EDP and MIS, in the narrow sense, for several years. Systems to support the communication needs of the organization are evolving rapidly from advances in telecommunications with a strong impetus from office automation and word processing. DSS seems to be evolving from the coalescence of information technology and operations research/management science approaches in the form of interactive modeling.

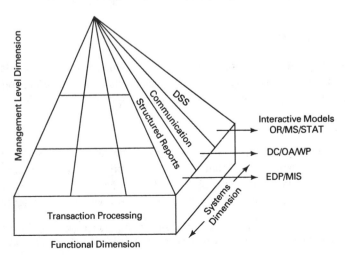

FIGURE 1.2 The Complete View

To summarize this introductory section, a DSS is not merely an evolutionary advancement of EDP and MIS, and it will certainly not replace either. Nor is it merely a type of information system aimed exclusively at top management, where other information systems seem to have failed. A DSS is a class of information system that draws on transaction processing systems and interacts with the other parts of the overall information system to support the decision making activities of managers and other knowledge workers in the organizations. However, there are some subtle but significant differences between a DSS and traditional EDP or so-called MIS approaches. Moreover, these systems require a new combination of information systems technology to satisfy a set of heretofore unmet needs. It is not yet clear exactly how these technologies fit together, or which important problems need to be solved. Indeed, that is a large part of the purpose of this article. It is apparent, however, that a DSS has the potential to become another powerful weapon in the arsenal of the information systems professional to help improve the effectiveness of the people in organizations.

THE FRAMEWORK

The remainder of this reading is devoted to an exploration of the nature of this "thrust" in information systems called "DSS." The mechanism for this exploration is another of the often maligned but repeatedly used "frameworks."

A framework, in the absence of theory, is helpful in organizing a complex subject, identifying the relationships between the parts, and revealing the areas in which further developments will be required. The framework presented here has evolved over the past two years in discussions with many different groups of people.[1] It is organized in two major parts. The first part considers: (a) three levels of technology, all of which have been designated as a DSS, with considerable confusion; (b) the developmental approach that is evolving for the creation of a DSS; and (c) the roles of several key types of people in the building and use of a DSS. The second part of the framework develops a descriptive model to assess the performance objectives and the capabilities of a DSS as viewed by three of the major stakeholders in their continued development and use.

THREE TECHNOLOGY LEVELS

It is helpful to identify three levels of hardware/software which have been included in the label "DSS." They are used by people with different levels of technical capability, and vary in the nature and scope of task to which they can be applied.

Specific DSS

The system which actually accomplishes the work might be called the *Specific DSS*. It is an information systems "application," but with characteristics that make it significantly different from a typical data processing application. It is the hardware/software that allows a specific decision maker or group of decision makers to deal with a specific set of related

---

[1]This reading grew out of the workshop on DSS at the 1979 Annual Meeting of SIM in Minneapolis [35]. Portions of the material were presented at two conferences in the summer [40, 41] and are included herein by permission.

problems. An early example is the portfolio management system [20] also described in the first major DSS book by Keen and Scott Morton [23]. Another example is the police beat allocation system used on an experimental basis by the City of San Jose, California [9]. The latter system allowed a police officer to display a map outline and call up data by geographical zone, showing police calls for service, activity levels, service time, etc. The interactive graphic capability of the system enabled the officer to manipulate the maps, zones, and data to try a variety of police beat alternatives quickly and easily. In effect, the system provided tools to *amplify* a manager's judgment. Incidentally, a later experiment attempted to apply a traditional linear programming model to the problem. The solution was less satisfactory than the one designed by the police officer.

DSS Generator

The second technology level might be called a *DSS Generator*. This is a "package" of related hardware and software which provides a set of capabilities to quickly and easily build a Specific DSS. For example, the police beat system described above was built from the Geodata Analysis and Display System (GADS), an experimental system developed at the IBM Research Laboratory in San Jose [8]. By loading different maps, data, menu choices, and procedures or command strings, GADS was later used to build a Specific DSS to support the routing of IBM copier repairmen [42]. The development of this new "application" required less than one month.

Another example of a *DSS Generator* is the Executive Information System (EIS) marketed by Boeing Computer Services [6]. EIS is an integrated set of capabilities which includes report preparation, inquiry capability, a modeling language, graphic display commands, and a set of financial and statistical analysis subroutines. These capabilities have all been available individually for some time. The unique contribution of EIS is that these capabilities are available through a common language which acts on a common set of data. The result is that EIS can be used as a DSS Generator, especially for a Specific DSS to help in financial decision-making situations.

Evolutionary growth toward DSS Generators has come from special-purpose languages. In fact, most of the software systems that might be used as Generators are evolving from enhanced planning languages or modeling languages, perhaps with report preparation and graphic display capabilities added. The Interactive Financial Planning System (IFPS), marketed by Execucom Systems of Austin, Texas [18], and EXPRESS, available from TYMSHARE [44], are good examples.

DSS Tools

The third and most fundamental level of technology applied to the development of a DSS might be called *DSS Tools*. These are hardware or software elements which facilitate the development of a specific DSS *or* a DSS Generator. This category of technology has seen the greatest amount of recent development, including new special-purpose languages, improvements in operating systems to support conversational approaches, color graphics hardware and supporting software, etc. For example, the GADS system described above was written in FORTRAN using an experimental graphics subroutine package as the primary dialogue handling software, a laboratory-enhanced rasterscan color monitor, and a powerful interactive data extraction/database management system.

Relationships

The relationships between these three levels of technology and types of DSS are illustrated by Figure 1.3. The DSS Tools can be used to develop a Specific DSS application directly, as shown on the left half of the diagram. This is the same approach used to develop most traditional applications with tools such as a general-purpose language, data access software, subroutine packages, etc. The difficulty with this approach for developing DSS applications is the constant change and flexibility which characterize them. A DSS changes character not only in response to changes in the environment, but to changes in the way managers want to approach the problem. Therefore, a serious complicating factor in the use of basic tools is the need to involve the user directly in the change and modification of the Specific DSS.

APL was heavily used in the development of Specific DSS because it proved to be cheap and easy for APL programmers, especially the APL enthusiasts, to produce "throwaway" code which could be easily revised or discarded as the nature of the application changed. However, except for the few users who became members of the APL fan club, that language *did not* help capture the involvement of users in the building and modification of the DSS. The development and use of DSS Generators promises to create a "platform" or staging area from which Specific DSS can be constantly developed and modified with the cooperation of the user, and without heavy consumption of time and effort.

EVOLVING ROLES IN *DSS*

All three levels of technology will probably be used over time in the development and operation of a DSS. Some interesting developments are occurring, however, in the roles that managers and technicians will play.

Figure 1.4 repeats part of the earlier diagram with a spectrum of five roles spread across the three levels.

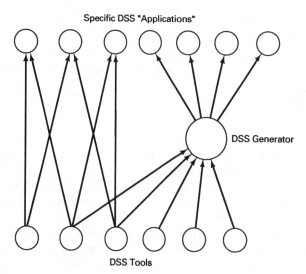

FIGURE 1.3   Three Levels of DSS Technology

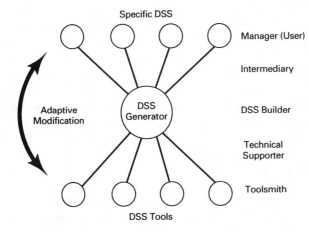

FIGURE 1.4   Three Levels of DSS with Five Associated Roles for Managers and Technicians

- The *manager or user* is the person faced with the problem or decision—the one that must take action and be responsible for the consequences.
- The *intermediary* is the person who helps the user, perhaps merely as a clerical assistant to push the buttons of the terminal, or perhaps as a more substantial "staff assistant" to interact and make suggestions.
- The *DSS builder* or facilitator assembles the necessary capabilities from the DSS Generator to "configure" the specific DSS with which the user/intermediary interacts directly. This person must have some familiarity with the problem area and also be comfortable with the information system technology components and capabilities.
- The *technical supporter* develops additional information system capabilities or components when they are needed as part of the Generator. New databases, new analysis models, and additional data display formats will be developed by the person filling this role. It requires a strong familiarity with technology, and a minor acquaintance with the problem or application area.
- The *toolsmith* develops new technology, new languages, new hardware and software, improves the efficiency of linkages between subsystems, etc.

Two observations about this spectrum of roles are appropriate. First, it is clear that they do not necessarily align with individuals on a one-to-one basis. One person may assume several roles, or more than one person may be required to fill a role. The appropriate role assignment will generally depend on:

- the nature of the problem, particularly how narrow or broad;
- the nature of the person, particularly how comfortable the individual is with the computer equipment, language, and concepts; and
- the strength of the technology, particularly how user oriented it is.

Some managers do not need or want an intermediary. There are even a few chief executives who take the terminal home on weekends to write programs, thereby assuming the upper three or four roles. In fact, a recent survey of the users of IFPS shows that more than one third of them are middle and top level managers [45]. Decisions which require group consensus or systems design (builder) teams are examples of multiple persons per role.

Second, these roles appear similar to those present in traditional systems development, but there are subtle differences. The top two are familiar even in name for the development of many interactive or online systems. It is common practice in some systems to combine them into one "virtual" user for convenience. The user of the DSS, however, will play a much more active and controlling role in the design and development of the system than has been true in the past. The builder/technical support dichotomy is relatively close to the information specialist/system designer dichotomy discussed in the ACM curriculum recommendations [3]. Increasingly, however, the DSS builder resides in the functional area and not in the MIS department. The toolsmith is similar to a systems programmer, software designer, or computer scientist, but is increasingly employed by a hardware or software vendor, and not by the user's organization. The net result is less direct involvement in the DSS process by the information systems professional in the EDP/MIS department. (Some implications of this trend are discussed later.) Moreover, the interplay between these roles is evolving into a unique development approach for a DSS.

THE DEVELOPMENT APPROACH FOR *DSS*

The very nature of a DSS requires a different design technique from traditional batch, or online, transaction processing systems. The traditional approaches for analysis and design have proven inadequate because there is no single comprehensive theory of decision making, and because of the rapidity of change in the conditions which decision makers face. Designers literally "cannot get to first base" because no one, least of all the decision maker or user, can define in advance what the functional requirements of the system should be. A DSS needs to be built with short, rapid feedback from users to ensure that development is proceeding correctly. It must be developed to permit change quickly and easily.

Iterative Design

The result is that the most important four steps in the typical systems development process—analysis, design, construction, implementation—are combined into a single step which is iteratively repeated. Several names are evolving to describe this process including breadboarding [31], L'Approache Evolutive [14], and "middle out" [30]. The essence of the approach is that the manager and builder agree on a small but significant subproblem, then design and develop an initial system to support the decision making which it requires. After a short period of use, for instance, a few weeks, the system is evaluated, modified, and incrementally expanded. This cycle is repeated three to six times over the course of a few months until a *relatively* stable system is evolved which supports decision making for a cluster of tasks. The word "relatively" is important, because although the frequency and extent of change will decrease, it will never be stable. The system will always be changing, not as a necessary evil in response to imposed environmental changes, but as a conscious strategy on the part of the user and builder. In terms of the three level model presented earlier, this process can be viewed as the iterative cycling between the DSS Generator and the Specific DSS as shown in Figure 1.4. With each cycle, capabilities are added to, or deleted from, the Specific DSS from those available in the DSS Generator. Keen depicts the expansion and growth of the system in terms of adding verbs which represent actions managers require [24]. Carlson adds more dimension by focusing on representations, operations, control, and memories as the elements of expansion and modification [11]. In another paper, Keen deals substantively with the interaction between the user, the builder, and the technology in this iterative, adaptive design process [25].

Note that this approach requires an unusual level of management involvement or management participation in the design. The manager is actually the iterative designer of the system; the systems analyst is merely the catalyst between the manager and the system, implementing the required changes and modifications.

Note also that this is different from the concept of "prototyping"; the initial system is real, live, and usable, not just a pilot test. The iterative process does not *merely* lead to a good understanding of the systems performance requirements, which are then frozen. The iterative changeability is actually *built into* the DSS as it is used over time. In fact, the development approach *becomes the system*. Rather than developing a system which is then "run" as a traditional EDP system, the DSS development approach results in the installation of an adaptive process in which a decision maker and a set of information system "capabilities" interact to confront problems while responding to changes from a variety of sources.

The Adaptive System

In the broad sense, the DSS is an adaptive system which consists of all three levels of technology in place and operating with the participants (roles), and the technology adapting to changes over time. Thus, the development of a DSS is actually the development and installation of this adaptive system. Simon describes such a system as one that adapts to changes of several kinds over three time horizons [34]. In the short run, the system allows a *search* for answers within a relatively narrow scope. In the intermediate time horizon, the system *learns* by modifying its capabilities and activities, i.e., the scope or domain changes. In the long run, the system *evolves* to accommodate much different behavior styles and capabilities.

The three level model of a DSS is analogous to Simon's adaptive system. The Specific DSS gives the manager the capabilities and flexibility to search, explore, and experiment with the problem area, within certain boundaries. Over time, as changes occur in a task, the environment, and the user's behavior, the Specific DSS must *learn* to accommodate these changes through the reconfiguration of the elements in the DSS Generator, with the aid of the DSS builder. Over a longer period of time, the basic tools *evolve* to provide the technology for changing the capabilities of the Generators out of which the Specific DSS is constructed, through the efforts of the toolsmith.

The ideas expressed above are not particularly new. Rapid feedback between the systems analyst and the client has been pursued for years. In the long run, most computer systems are adaptive systems. They are changed and modified during the normal system life cycle, and they evolve through major enhancements and extensions as the life cycle is repeated. However, when the length of that life cycle is shortened from three to five months, or even weeks, there are significant implications. The resulting changes in the development approach and the traditional view of the systems life cycle promise to be one of the important impacts of the growing use of a DSS.

PERFORMANCE OBJECTIVES AND CAPABILITIES

Most of the foregoing discussion has dealt with some aspects of the technological and organizational contexts within which a DSS will be built and operated. The second part of the framework deals with what a DSS must accomplish, and what capabilities or characteristics it must have. The three levels of hardware/software technology and the corresponding three major "stakeholders" or interested parties in the development and use of a DSS can be used to identify the characteristics and attributes of a DSS.

At the top level are the *managers or users* who are primarily concerned with what the Specific DSS can do for them. Their focus is the problem solving or decision making task they face, and the organizational environment in which they operate. They will assess a DSS in terms of the assistance they receive in pursuing these tasks. At the level of the DSS Generator, the *builders* or designers must use the capabilities of the Generator to configure a Specific DSS to meet the manager's needs. They will be concerned with the capabilities the Generator offers, and how these capabilities can be assembled to create the Specific DSS. At the DSS tool level, the *"toolsmiths"* are concerned with the development of basic technology components, and how they can be integrated to form a DSS Generator which has the necessary capabilities.

The attributes and characteristics of a DSS as viewed from each level must be examined. From the manager's view, six general performance objectives for the Specific DSS can be identified. They are not the only six that could be identified, but as a group they represent the overall performance of a DSS that seems to be expected and desirable from a managerial viewpoint. The characteristics of the DSS Generator from the viewpoint of the builder are described by a conceptual model which identifies performance characteristics in three categories: dialogue handling or the man-machine interface, database and database management capability, and modeling and analytic capability. The same three part model is used to depict the viewpoint of the "toolsmith," but from the aspect of the technology, tactics, and architecture required to produce those capabilities required by the builders.

Manager's View: Performance Objectives

The following performance requirements are phrased using the normative word "should." It is likely that no Specific DSS will be required to satisfy all six of the performance requirements given here. In fact, it is important to recall that the performance criteria for any Specific DSS will depend entirely on the task, the organizational environment, and the decision maker(s) involved. Nevertheless, the following objectives collectively represent a set of capabilities which characterize the full value of the DSS concept from the manager/user point of view. The first three pertain to the type of decision making task which managers and professionals face. The latter three relate to the type of support which is needed.

1. *A DSS should provide support for decision making, but with emphasis on semistructured and unstructured decisions.* These are the types of decisions that

have had little or no support from EDP, MIS, or management science/operations research (MS/OR) in the past. It might be better to refer to "hard" or under-specified problems, because the concept of "structure" in decision making is heavily dependent on the cognitive style and approach to problem solving of the decision maker. It is clear from their expressed concerns, however, that managers need additional support for certain kinds of problems.

2. *A DSS should provide decision making support for managers at all levels, assisting in integration between the levels whenever appropriate.* This requirement evolves from the realization that managers at *all* organizational levels face "tough" problems as described in the first objective above. Moreover, a major need articulated by managers is the integration and coordination of decision making by several managers dealing with related parts of a larger problem.

3. *A DSS should support decisions which are interdependent as well as those that are independent.* Much of the early DSS work inferred that a decision maker would sit at a terminal, use a system, and develop a decision *alone*. DSS development experience has shown that a DSS must accommodate decisions which are made by groups or made in part by several people in sequence. Keen and Hackathorn [24] explore three decision types as:

Independent. A decision maker has full responsibility and authority to make a complete implementable decision.

Sequential Interdependent. A decision maker makes part of a decision which is passed on to someone else.

Pooled Interdependent. The decision must result from negotiation and interaction among decision makers.

Different capabilities will be required to support each type of decision—personal support, organizational support, and group support, respectively.

4. *A DSS should support all phases of the decision making process.* A popular model of the decision making process is given in the work of Herbert Simon [33]. He characterized three main steps in the process as follows:

Intelligence. Searching the environment for conditions calling for decisions. Raw data is obtained, processed, and examined for clues that may identify problems.

Design. Inventing, developing, and analyzing possible courses of action. This involves processes to understand the problem, generate solutions, and test solutions for feasibility.

Choice. Selecting a particular course of action from those available. A choice is made and implemented.

Although the third phase includes implementation, many authors feel that it is significant enough to be shown separately. It has been added to Figure 1.5 to show the relationships between the steps. Simon's model also illustrates the contribution of MIS/EDP and MS/OR to decision making. From the definition of the three stages given above, it is clear that EDP and MIS, in the narrow sense, have made major contributions to the intelligence phase, while MIS/OR has been primarily useful at the choice phase. There has been no substantial support for the design phase, which seems to be one of the primary potential contributions of a DSS. There also has been very little support from traditional systems for the implementation phase, but some early experience has shown that a DSS can make a major contribution here also [42].

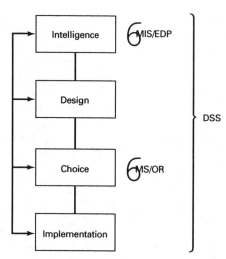

FIGURE 1.5   Phases of Decision Making

5. *A DSS should support a variety of decision making processes, but not be dependent on any one.* Simon's model, though widely accepted, is only one model of how decisions are actually made. In fact, there is no universally accepted model of the decision making process, and there is no promise of such a general theory in the foreseeable future. There are too many variables, too many different types of decisions, and too much variety in the characteristics of decision makers. Consequently, a very important characteristic of a DSS is that it provide the decision maker with a set of capabilities to apply in a sequence and form that fits each individual cognitive style. In short, a DSS should be process independent, and user driven or controlled.

6. *Finally, a DSS should be easy to use.* A variety of terms have been used to describe this characteristic including flexibility, user friendly, nonthreatening, etc. The importance of this characteristic is underscored by the discretionary latitude of a DSS's clientele. Although some systems which require heavy organizational support or group support may limit the discretion somewhat, the user of a DSS has much more latitude to ignore or circumvent the system than the user of a more traditional transaction system or required reporting system. Therefore, a DSS must "earn" its users' allegiance by being valuable and convenient.

THE BUILDER'S VIEW: TECHNICAL CAPABILITIES

The DSS Builder has the responsibility of drawing on computer based tools and techniques to provide the decision support required by the manager. DSS Tools can be used directly, but it is generally more efficient and effective to use a DSS Generator for this task. The Generator must have a set of capabilities which facilitate the quick and easy configuration of a Specific DSS and modification in response to changes in the manager's requirements, environment, tasks, and thinking approaches. A conceptual model can be used to organize these capabilities, both for the builders and for the "toolsmith" who will develop the technology to provide these capabilities.

The old "black box" approach is helpful here, starting with the view of the system as a black box, successively "opening" the boxes to understand the subsystems and how they are interconnected. Although the DSS is treated as the black box here, it is important to recall that the overall system is the decision *making* system, consisting of a manager/user who uses a DSS to confront a task in an organizational environment.

Opening the large DSS box reveals a database, a model base, and a complex software system for linking the user to each of them as shown in Figure 1.6. Opening each of these boxes reveals that the database and model base have some interrelated components, and that the software system is comprised of three sets of capabilities: database management software (DBMS), model base management software (MBMS), and the software for managing the interface between the user and the system, which might be called the dialogue generation and management software (DGMS). These three major subsystems provide a convenient scheme for identifying the technical capability which a DSS must have. The key aspects in each category that are critical to a DSS from the Builder's point of view, and a list of capabilities which will be required in each category must now be considered.

THE DATA SUBSYSTEM

The data subsystem is thought to be a well understood set of capabilities because of the rapidly maturing technology related to databases and their management. The typical advantages of the database approach, and the powerful functions of the DBMS, are also important to the development and use of a DSS. There are, however, some significant differences between the Database/Data Communication approach for traditional systems,

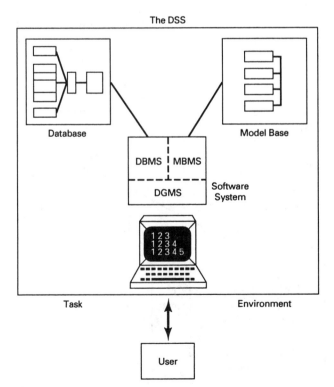

FIGURE 1.6   Components of the DSS

and those applicable for a DSS. Opening the Database box summarizes these key characteristics as shown in Figure 1.7.

First is the importance of a much richer set of data sources than are usually found in typical non-DSS applications. Data must come from external as well as internal sources, since decision making, especially in the upper management levels, is heavily dependent on external data sources. In addition, the typical accounting oriented transaction data must be supplemented with non-transactional, non-accounting data, some of which has not been computerized in the past.

Another significant difference is the importance of the data capture and extraction process from this wider set of data sources. The nature of a DSS requires that the extraction process, and the DBMS which manages it, be flexible enough to allow rapid additions and changes in response to unanticipated user requests. Finally, most successful DSS's have found it necessary to create a DSS database which is logically separate from other operational databases. A partial set of capabilities required in the database area can be summarized by the following:

- the ability to combine a variety of data sources through a data capture and extraction process;
- the ability to add and delete data sources quickly and easily;
- the ability to portray logical data structures in user terms so the user understands what is available and can specify needed additions and deletions;
- the ability to handle personal and unofficial data so the user can experiment with alternatives based on personal judgment; and
- the ability to manage this wide variety of data with a full range of data management functions.

FIGURE 1.7   The Data Subsystem

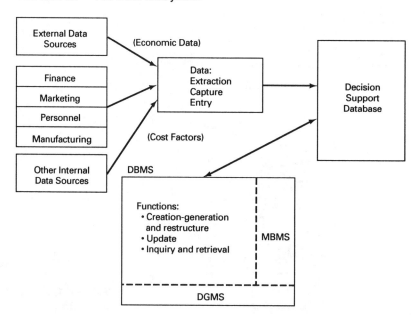

THE MODEL SUBSYSTEM

A very promising aspect of a DSS is its ability to integrate data access and decision models. It does so by imbedding the decision models in an information system which uses the database as the integration and communication mechanism between models. This characteristic unifies the strength of data retrieval and reporting from the EDP field and the significant developments in management science in a way the manager can use and trust.

The misuse and disuse of models have been widely discussed [21, 28, 36, 39]. One major problem has been that model builders were frequently preoccupied with the structure of the model. The existence of the correct input data and the proper delivery of the output to the user was assumed. In addition to these heroic assumptions, models tended to suffer from inadequacy because of the difficulty of developing an integrated model to handle a realistic set of interrelated decisions. The solution was a collection of separate models, each of which dealt with a distinct part of the problem. Communication between these related models was left to the decision maker and intellectual process.

A more enlightened view of models suggests that they be imbedded in an information system with the database as the integration and communication mechanism between them. Figure 1.8 summarizes the components of the model base "box." The model creation process must be flexible, with a strong modeling language and a set of building blocks, much like subroutines, which can be assembled to assist the modeling process. In fact, there are a set of model management functions, very much analogous to data management functions. The key capabilities for a DSS in the model subsystems include:

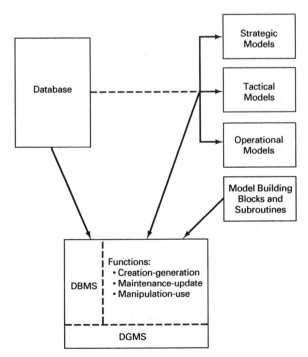

FIGURE 1.8 The Models Subsystem

- the ability to create new models quickly and easily;
- the ability to catalog and maintain a wide range of models, supporting all levels of management;
- the ability to interrelate these models with appropriate linkages through the database;
- the ability to access and integrate model "building blocks;" and
- the ability to manage the model base with management functions analogous to database management (e.g., mechanisms for storing, cataloging, linking, and accessing models).

For a more detailed discussion of the model base and its management see [37, 38, 46].

The User System Interface

Much of the power, flexibility, and usability characteristics of a DSS are derived from capabilities in the user system interface. Bennett identifies the user, terminal, and software system as the components of the interface subsystem [5]. He then divides the dialogue or interface experience itself into three parts as shown in Figure 1.9:

1. *The action language*—what the user *can do* in communicating with the system. It includes such options as the availability of a regular keyboard, function keys, touch panels, joy stick, voice command, etc.
2. *The display or presentation language*—what the user *sees.* The display language includes options such as character or line printer, display screen, graphics, color, plotters, audio output, etc.

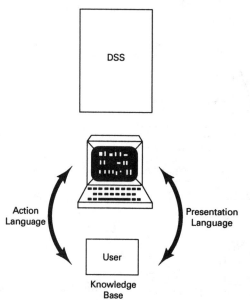

FIGURE 1.9   The User System Interface

3. *The knowledge base*—what the user *must know.* The knowledge base consists of what the user needs to bring to the session with the system in order to effectively use it. The knowledge may be in the user's head, on a reference card or instruction sheet, in a user's manual, in a series of "help" commands available upon request, etc.

The "richness" of the interface will depend on the strength of capabilities in each of these areas.

Another dimension of the user system interface is the concept of "dialogue style." Examples include the questions/answer approach, command languages, menus, and "fill in the blanks." Each style has pro's and con's depending on the type of user, task, and decision situation. For a more detailed discussion of dialogue styles see [13].

Although this just scratches the surface in this important area, a partial set of desirable capabilities for a DSS Generator to support the user/system interface includes:

- the ability to handle a variety of dialogue styles, perhaps with the ability to shift among them at the user's choice;
- the ability to accommodate user actions in a variety of media;
- the ability to present data in a variety of formats and media; and
- the ability to provide flexible support for the users' knowledge base.

THE TOOLSMITH VIEW: THE UNDERLYING TECHNOLOGY

The toolsmith is concerned with the science involved in creating the information technology to support a DSS, and the architecture of combining the basic tools into a coherent system. The same three part model can be used to describe the toolsmith's concerns because the tools must be designed and combined to provide the three sets of capabilities.

Each of the three areas—dialogue, data handling, and model handling—has received a fair amount of attention from toolsmiths in the past. The topic of DSS and the requirements it imposes have put these efforts in a new perspective revealing how they can be interrelated to increase their collective effectiveness. Moreover, the DSS requirements have revealed some missing elements in existing efforts, indicating valuable potential areas for development.

Dialogue Management

There has been a great deal of theoretical and some empirical work on systems requirements for good man/machine interface. Many of these studies are based on watching users' behavior in using terminals, or surveying users or programmers to ascertain what they want in interactive systems [10, 16]. A recent study examines a series of interactive applications, many of which are DSS's, to assess the *type* of software capabilities required by the applications [43]. This study led directly to some creative work on the software architecture for dialogue generation and management systems (DGMS) as characterized in the model of the previous section [12]. This research uses a relation as the data structure for storing each picture or "frame" used in the system, and a decision table for storing the control mechanism for representing the potential users' option in branching from one frame to another.

Data Management

Most of the significant work in the database management area during the past several years is aimed at transaction processing against large databases. Large DBMS's generally have inquiry/retrieval and flexible report preparation capabilities, but their largest contribution has been in the reduction of program maintenance costs through the separation of application programs and data definitions. On the other hand, DBMS work has generally had a rather naive view of the user and the user's requirements. A DSS user will not be satisfied merely with the capability to issue a set of retrieval commands which select items from the database, or even to display those selected items in a report with the flexible definition of format and headings. A DSS user needs to interact repeatedly and creatively with a relatively small set of data. The user may only need 40–100 data variables, but they must be the *right ones;* and what is right may change from day to day and week to week. Required data will probably include time series data which are not handled comprehensively by typical DBMS's. Better ways are needed to handle and coordinate time series data as well as mechanisms for capturing, processing, and tagging judgmental and probabilistic data. Better ways are also needed for extracting data from existing files and capturing data from previously non-computerized sources. The critical area of data extraction with fast response, which allows additions and deletions to the DSS database from the large transaction database, was a major contribution of the GADS work [8, 29]. In short, the significant development in database technology needs to be focused and extended in some key areas in order to directly serve the needs of a DSS.

Model Management

The area of model creation and handling may have the greatest potential contribution to a DSS. So far, the analytic capability provided by systems has evolved from statistical or financial analysis subroutines which can be called from a common command language. More recently, modeling languages provide a way of formulating interrelationships between variables in a way that permits the creation of simulation or "what if" models. As we noted earlier, many of the currently viable DSS Generators have evolved from these efforts. Early forms of "model management" seem to be evolving from enhancements to some modeling languages, which permit a model of this type to be used for sensitivity testing or goal seeking by specifying target and flexibility variables.

The model management area also has the potential for bringing some of the contributions of artificial intelligence (AI) to bear on a DSS. MYCIN, a system to support medical diagnosis, is based on "production rules," in the AI sense, which play the role of models in performing analytic and decision guidance functions [15]. A more general characterization of "knowledge management" as a way of handling models and data has also been tentatively explored [7]. More recent work proposes the use of a version of semantic networks for model representation [17]. Though this latter work is promising, AI research has shown the semantic network approach to be relatively inefficient with today's technology. Usable capabilities in model management in the near future are more likely to evolve from modeling languages, expanded subroutine approaches, and, in some cases, AI production rules.

ISSUES FOR THE FUTURE

At this stage in the development of the DSS area, issues, problems, and fruitful directions for further research/development are plentiful. At a "task force" meeting this summer, thirty researchers from twelve countries gathered to discuss the nature of DSS's and to identify issues for the future. Their list, developed in group discussions over several days, was quite long [19]. The issues given here, phrased as difficult questions, seem to be the ones that must be dealt with quickly, lest the promise and potential benefits of DSS's be diluted or seriously delayed.

What's A DSS?

Earlier it was noted that some skeptics regard DSS as "just another buzz word." This reading has shown that there is a significant amount of content behind the label. The danger remains, however, that the bandwagon effect will outrun our ability to define and develop potential contributions of a DSS. The market imperatives of the multi-billion dollar information systems industry tend to generate pressures to create simple labels for intuitively good ideas. It happened in many cases, but not all, of course, with MIS. Some companies are still trying to live down the aftereffects of the overpromise/underdelivery/disenchantment sequence from the MIS bandwagon of the late '60s. Eventually, a set of minimal capabilities or characteristics which characterize a DSS should evolve. In the short range, a partial solution is education—supplying managers with intellectual ammunition they can use in dealing with vendors. Managers should and must ask sharp, critical questions about the capabilities of any purported DSS, matching them against what is really needed.

What Is Really Needed?

After nearly two decades of advancements in information technology, the real needs of managers from an information system are not well understood. The issue is further complicated by the realization that managers' needs and the needs of other "knowledge workers" with which they interact are heavily interdependent. The DSS philosophy and approach has already shed some light on this issue by emphasizing "capabilities"—the ability for a manager to do things with an information system—rather than just "information needs" which too often infer data items and totals on a report.

Nevertheless, it is tempting to call for a hesitation in the development of DSS's until decision making and related managerial activities are fully understood. Though logically appealing, such a strategy is not practical. Neither the managers who face increasingly complex tasks, nor the information systems industry which has increasingly strong technology to offer, will be denied. They point out that a truly comprehensive theory of decision making has been pursued for years with minimum success.

A potential resolution of this problem is to develop and use a DSS in a way that reveals what managers can and should receive from an information system. For example, one of Scott Morton's early suggestions was that the system be designed to capture and track the steps taken by managers in the process of making key decisions, both as an aid to the analysis of the process, and as a potential training device for new managers.

The counterpart of the "needs" issue is the extent to which the system meets those needs, and the value of the performance increase that results. Evaluation of a DSS will be just as difficult, and important, as the evaluation of MIS has been. The direct and constant involvement of users, the ones in the best position to evaluate the systems, provides a glimmer of hope on this tough problem. Pursuit of these two tasks together may yield progress on both fronts with the kind of synergistic effect often sought from systems efforts. The iterative design approach and the three levels of technology afford the opportunity, if such a strategy is developed from the beginning.

Who Will Do It?

A series of organizational issues will revolve around the roles and organizational placement of the people who will take the principal responsibility for the development of DSS's. Initiative and guidance for DSS development efforts frequently come from the user area, not from the EDP/MIS area. Yet current technology still requires technical support from the information systems professional. The DSS builder may work for the vice president of finance, but the technical support role is still played by someone in the MIS department. To some extent, the demand for a DSS supports the more general trend to distribute systems development efforts out of the MIS department into the user department. The difference is that many DSS software systems, or generators, specifically attempt to directly reach the end user without involvement of the MIS group. The enlightened MIS administrator considers this a healthy trend, and willingly supplies the required technical support and coordination. Less enlightened DP administrators often see it as a threat. Some companies have set up a group specifically charged with developing DSS type applications. This strategy creates a team of "DSS Builders" who can develop the necessary skills in dealing with users, become familiar with the available technology, and define the steps in the developmental approach for DSS's.

How Should It Be Done?

One of the pillars on which the success of DSS rests is the iterative development or adaptive design approach. The traditional five to seven stage system development process and the system life cycle concept have been the backbone of systems analysis for years. Most project management systems and approaches are based on it. The adaptive design approach, because it combines all the stages into one quick step which is repeated, will require a redefinition of system development milestones and a major modification of project management mechanisms. Since many traditional systems will not be susceptible to the iterative approach, a way is also needed for deciding when an application should be developed in the new way instead of the traditional way. The outline of the approach described earlier is conceptually straightforward for applications that require only personal support. It becomes more complicated for group or organizational support when there are multiple users. In short, DSS builders will need to develop a set of milestones, checkpoints, documentation strategies, and project management procedures for DSS applications, and recognize when they should be used.

How Much Can Be Done?

The final issue is a caveat dealing with the limitations of technical solutions to the complexity faced by managers and decision makers. As information systems professionals, we must be careful not to feel, or even allow others to feel, that we can develop or devise a technological solution to all the problems of management. Managers will always "deal with complexity in a state of perplexity"—it is the nature of the job. Information technology can, and is, making a major contribution to improving the effectiveness of people in this situation, but the solution will never be total. With traditional systems, we continually narrow the scope and definition of the system until we know it will do the job it is required to do. If the specification/design/construction/implementation process is done right, the system is a success, measured against its original objectives. With a DSS, the user and his systems capabilities are constantly pursuing the problem, but the underspecified nature of the problem insures that there will never be a complete solution. Systems analysts have always had a little trouble with humility, but the DSS process requires a healthy dose of modesty with respect to the ability of technology to solve all the problems of managers in organizations.

SUMMARY

The "Framework for Development" described above attempts to show the dimensions and scope of DSS in a way that will promote the further *development* of this highly promising type of information system.

1. The relationships between EDP, MIS, and DSS show that DSS is only one of several important technology subsystems for improving organizational performance, and that DSS development efforts must carefully integrate with these other systems.
2. The three levels of technology and the interrelationships between people that use them provide a context for organizing the development effort.
3. The iterative design approach shows that the ultimate goal of the DSS development effort is the installation of an *adaptive system* consisting of all three levels of technology and their users operating and adapting to changes over time.
4. The performance objectives show the types of decision making to be served by, and the types of support which should be built into, a DSS as it is developed.
5. The three technical capabilities illustrate that development efforts must provide the DSS with capabilities in dialogue management, data management, and model management.
6. The issues discussed at the end of the article identify some potential roadblocks that must be recognized and confronted to permit the continued development of DSS.

In closing, it should now be clear that DSS is more than just a "buzz word," but caution must be used in announcing a new "era" in information systems. Perhaps the best term is a "DSS Movement" as user organizations, information systems vendors, and researchers become aware of the field, its potential, and the many unanswered questions. Events and mechanisms in the DSS Movement include systems development experience in organizations, hardware/software developments by vendors, publishing activities to report experience and research, and conferences to provide a forum for the exchange of ideas among interested parties.

It is clear that the momentum of the DSS Movement is building. With appropriate care and reasonable restraint, the coordinated efforts of managers, builders, toolsmiths, and researchers can converge in the development of a significant set of information systems to help improve the effectiveness of organizations and the people who work in them.

QUESTIONS

1. What characteristics of a DSS differentiate it from an EDP or an MIS?
2. Discuss the three levels of DSS technology. Give examples of each level.
3. Compare and contrast iterative design with the more traditional approaches (e.g., systems development life cycle).
4. Discuss the components of a DSS from a builder's perspective.

REFERENCES

1. ALTER, S. "A Taxonomy of Decision Support Systems," *Sloan Management Review,* 19, no. 1 (Fall 1977), 39–56.
2. ALTER, S. *Decision Support Systems: Current Practice and Continuing Challenges.* Reading, Mass.: Addison-Wesley, 1980.
3. ASHENURST, R. L. "Curriculum Recommendations for Graduate Professional Programs in Information Systems," *ACM Communications,* 15, no. 5 (May 1972), 363–98.
4. BARBOSA, L. C., AND R. G. HIRKO "Integration of Algorithmic Aids into Decision Support Systems," *MIS Quarterly,* 4, no. 1 (March 1980), 1–12.
5. BENNETT, J. "User-Oriented Graphics, Systems for Decision Support in Unstructured Tasks," in *User-Oriented Design of Interactive Graphics Systems,* ed. S. Treu, 3–11. New York: Association for Computing Machinery, 1977.
6. BOEING COMPUTER SERVICES c/o Mr. Park Thoreson, P.O. Box 24346, Seattle, Wash. 98124.
7. BONEZEK, H., C. W. HOSAPPLE, AND A. WHINSTON "Evolving Roles of Models in Decision Support Systems," *Decision Sciences,* 11, no. 2 (April 1980), 337–56.
8. CARLSON, E. D., J. BENNETT, G. GIDDINGS, AND P. MANTEY "The Design and Evaluation of an Interactive Geo-Data Analysis and Display System," *Information Processing—74.* Amsterdam: North Holland Publishing, 1974.
9. CARLSON, E. D., AND J. A. SUTTON "A Case Study of Non-Programmer Interactive Problem Solving," *IBM Research Report RJ1382,* San Jose, Calif., 1974.
10. CARLSON, E. D., B. F. GRACE, AND J. A. SUTTON "Case Studies of End User Requirements for Interactive Problem-Solving Systems," *MIS Quarterly,* 1, no. 1 (March 1977), 51–63.

11. CARLSON, E. D.   "An Approach for Designing Decision Support Systems," *Proceedings, 11th Hawaii International Conference on Systems Sciences,* Western Periodicals Co., North Hollywood, Calif., 1978, 76–96.

12. CARLSON, E. D., AND W. METZ   "Integrating Dialog Management and Data Management," *IBM Research Report RJ2738,* February 1, 1980, San Jose, Calif.

13. CARLSON, E. D.   "The User-Interface for Decision Support Systems," unpublished working paper, IBM Research Laboratory, San Jose, Calif.

14. COURBON, J., J. DRAGEOF, AND T. JOSE   "L'Approache Evolutive," *Information et Gestion No. 103,* Institute d'Administration des Enterprises, Grenoble, France, January–February 1979, 51–59.

15. DAVIS, R.   "A DSS for Diagnosis and Therapy," *DataBase,* 8, no. 3 (Winter 1977), 58–72.

16. DZIDA, W., S. HERDA, AND W. D. ITZFELDT   "User-Perceived Quality of Software Interactive Systems," *Proceedings, Third Annual Conference on Engineering (IEEE) Computer Society,* Long Beach, Calif., 1978, 188–95.

17. ELAM, J., J. HENDERSON, AND L. MILLER   "Model Management Systems: An Approach to Decision Support in Complex Organizations," *Proceedings, Conference on Information Systems,* Society for Management Information Systems, Philadelphia, December 1980.

18. EXECUCOM SYSTEMS CORPORATION   P.O. Box 9758, Austin, Tex. 78766.

19. FICK, G., AND R. H. SPRAGUE, JR., EDS.   *Decision Support Systems: Issues and Challenges.* Oxford, England: Pergamon Press, 1981.

20. GERRITY, T. P., JR.   "Design of Man-Machine Decision Systems: An Application to Portfolio Management," *Sloan Management Review,* 12, no. 2 (Winter 1971), 59–75.

21. HAYES, R. H., AND R. L. NOLAND   "What Kind of Corporate Modeling Functions Best?" *Harvard Business Review,* 52 (May–June 1974), 102–12.

22. HEAD, R.   "Management Information Systems: A Critical Appraisal," *Datamation,* 13, no. 5 (May 1967), 22–28.

23. KEEN, P. G. W., AND M. S. SCOTT MORTON   *Decision Support Systems: An Organizational Perspective.* Reading Mass.: Addison-Wesley, 1978.

24. KEEN, P. G. W., AND R. D. HACKATHORN   "Decision Support Systems and Personal Computing," Department of Decision Sciences, Wharton School, University of Pennsylvania, Working Paper 79-01-03, Philadelphia, April 3, 1979.

25. KEEN, P. G. W.   "Adaptive Design for DSS," *Database,* 12, nos. 1 and 2 (Fall 1980), 15–25.

26. KEEN, P. G. W.   "Decision Support Systems: A Research Perspective," in *Decision Support Systems: Issues and Challenges.* Oxford, England: Pergamon Press, 1981.

27. KROEBER, H. W., H. J. WATSON, AND R. H. SPRAGUE, JR.   "An Empirical Investigation and Analysis of the Current State of Information Systems Evolution," *Journal of Information and Management,* 3, no. 1 (February 1980), 35–43.

28. LITTLE, J. D. C.   "Models and Managers: The Concept of a Decision Calculus," *Management Science,* 16, no. 8 (April 1970), B466–85.

29. MANTEY, P. E., AND E. D. CARLSON   "Integrated Geographic Data Bases: The GADS Experience," IBM Research Division, *IBM Research Report RJ2702,* San Jose, Calif., December 3, 1979.

30. NESS, D. N.   "Decision Support Systems: Theories of Design," presented at the Wharton Office of Naval Research Conference on Decision Support Systems, Philadelphia, November 4–7, 1975.

31. SCOTT, J. H.   "The Management Science Opportunity: A Systems Development Management Viewpoint," *MIS Quarterly,* 2, no. 4 (December 1978), 59–61.

32. SCOTT MORTON, M. S.   *Management Decision Systems: Computer Based Support for Decision Making,* Division of Research, Harvard University, Cambridge, Mass., 1971.

33. SIMON, H.   *The New Science of Management Decision.* New York: Harper & Row, 1960.

34. SIMON, H.   "Cognitive Science: The Newest Science of the Artificial," *Cognitive Science,* 4 (1980), 33–46.

35. Society for Management Information Systems,   *Proceedings of the Eleventh Annual Conference,* Chicago, September 10–13, 1979, 45–56.

36. SPRAGUE, R. H., AND H. J. WATSON   "MIS Concepts Part I," *Journal of Systems Management,* 26, no. 1 (January 1975), 34–37.

37. SPRAGUE, R. H., AND H. J. WATSON   "Model Management in MIS," *Proceedings, 7th National AIDS,* Cincinnati, November 5, 1975, 213–15.

38. SPRAGUE, R. H., AND H. J. WATSON   "A Decision Support System for Banks," *Omega—The International Journal of Management Science,* 4, no. 6 (1976), 657–71.

39. SPRAGUE, R. H., AND H. J. WATSON   "Bit by Bit: Toward Decision Support Systems," *California Management Review,* XXII, no. 1 (Fall 1979), 60–68.

40. SPRAGUE, R. H.   "Decision Support Systems—Implications for the Systems Analysts," *Systems Analysis and Design: A Foundation for the 1980's.* New York: Elsevier-North Holland, 1980.

41. SPRAGUE, R. H.   "A Framework for Research on Decision Support Systems," in *Decision Support Systems: Issues and Challenges,* ed. G. Fick and R. H. Sprague. Oxford, England: Pergamon Press, 1981.

42. SUTTON, J.   "Evaluation of a Decision Support System: A Case Study with the Office Products Division of IBM," San Jose, Calif.: *IBM Research Report FJ2214,* 1978.

43. SUTTON, J. A., AND R. H. SPRAGUE   "A Study of Display Generation and Management in Interactive Business Applications," San Jose, Calif.: *IBM Research Report No. RJ2392,* IBM Research Division, November 9, 1978.

44. TYMSHARE   20705 Valley Green Drive, Cupertino, Calif. 95014.

45. WAGNER, G. R.   "DSS: Hypotheses and Inferences," Internal Report, EXECUCOM Systems Corporation, Austin, Tex., 1980.

46. WILL, HART J.   "Model Management Systems," in *Information Systems and Organizational Structure,* ed. E. Grochia and H. Szyperski, 467–83. New York: Walter de Gruyter, 1975.

2

DSS IN CONTEXT

Ralph H. Sprague, Jr.

INTRODUCTION

The theme of the papers in this issue is to establish some perspective on the progress of DSS during the past 10 years. This paper contributes to that theme by considering DSS in a broad context—one that includes other efforts in information systems and management science. Over the past decade we have seen information systems evolve under a variety of names. Electronic Data Processing was augmented by management information systems, office automation, management reporting (or support) systems, executive information systems, and of course, decision support systems. Meanwhile, many of the analysis efforts established initially under titles such as management science, operations research, quantitative techniques, and statistical analysis have been brought under the information systems function because so much analysis is now computer-based.

There have been a variety of models and paradigms to explain how these various systems and analysis efforts relate to each other. They usually include variables such as

Ralph H. Sprague, Jr., "DSS in Context," *Decision Support Systems*, 3 (1987), pp. 197–202.

the level of management served, the nature of the transaction, the type of data used, response times (batch or on-line) whether they are done by the data processing center or at the user's desk, whether they are based primarily on data or primarily on models, etc. This paper proposes a characteristic which promises to be more helpful than these traditional measures for organizing the way information systems are built and used.

The initial section reexamines the overall objective or mission for information systems in organizations. The next section introduces the concept of Type I and Type II information handling activities which are to be supported or improved through the use of information systems. A third section contains a retrospective of some key developments during the past decade viewed in this new context. Finally, the paper suggests future developments we should expect, or pursue, to enhance the contribution of DSS to the overall mission.

THE OVERALL MISSION

In the frenetic, fast changing world of information systems, it is sometimes hard to keep perspective on the true objective or mission of information systems in organizations. New terms (buzz words?) are created, new systems proposed, and new products are developed with confusing rapidity. It sometimes seems that the true objective is to enlarge the power base of the IS department, or enhance the reputation of certain academics, or increase the market share of IS vendors. These may be somewhat legitimate outcomes, but they are by-products of a more important objective. I suggest that the ultimate mission of IS in an organization is *to improve the performance of information workers in organizations through the application of information technology.*

This mission is admittedly not very specific—with ambiguous words such as "improve" and "performance"—but there are two important implications nevertheless. First, it establishes people as the target of IS. Systems should be built to serve people. The kind of people—information workers—are those whose job is primarily handling information. The United States Bureau of Labor Statistics shows that more than 50 percent of the employees in the country are information workers. In some industries, such as banks, the percentage is above 90.

Second, information systems should increase performance. Merely producing reports, or supporting activities, or even "getting the right information to the right person at the right time" falls short unless the result is performance improvement. Certainly there will be problems defining "performance" and "improvement," but at least the general objective is clear.

SUPPORT FOR INFORMATION WORKERS

How can performance be improved? The generic word "support" has been used to infer the concept of using IS as a resource to leverage the activities of managers (Management Support Systems, Decision Support Systems). With information workers as the majority of employed people in the U.S. and most other advanced societies, it is clear that IS can be used in a multitude of ways to support a multitude of activities performed by information workers. In fact, some form of segmentation of information workers and their activities is required to better focus information system efforts to support them.

Type I and Type II Work

Several recent articles have explored an intuitive dichotomy labeled Type I and Type II information activity [1, 2]. The key characteristics of this dichotomy include:

1. Transactions: Type I work consists of a large volume of transactions with a relatively low value (or cost) connected with each. Type II work consists of fewer transactions, but each is more costly or valuable.
2. Process: Type I work is based on well defined procedures, while Type II work is process-independent.
3. Output: The output from Type I work is more easily measured because it is defined by quantities of procedural iteration. The focus is on performing the necessary process or procedure quickly, efficiently, and usually many times. Type II output is not easily measured because it consists of problem solving and goal attainment. You can assign a Type I task to an information worker by explaining the sequence of steps required to accomplish it. With a Type II task, you must specify the desired outcome. Figuring out the necessary steps in the sequence is part of the job, and may be significantly different for different people.
4. Data: Type I work uses data in relatively well structured form, whereas Type II work deals primarily with concepts which are represented in less well structured form, usually with a great deal of ambiguity.

At first glance this dichotomy looks similar to the "clerical" versus "managerial-professional" breakdown that has been used for many years. Upon closer examination, however, it is clear that clerical personnel, especially secretaries, frequently have process-independent tasks defined only by their outcome. Likewise, most managers and professionals have a certain proportion of their work which is process defined.

It can be argued that the nature of the task, according to this two-way classification, is the most important characteristic in determining what kind of support is required from information systems. It should be clear that most uses of information systems in the past have been for supporting Type I tasks. It is easiest and most natural to use a process engine (computer) to support process driven tasks. It is also clear that the challenge of the future is to use information systems to support Type II tasks. The nature of the tasks is different, the mentality required to do it is different, and so the information support must be different from the traditional Type I approaches.

Supporting Type II Work

There have been several attempts to support Type II work with information systems. In most cases, however, it has been done by providing Type II workers with better access to tools that have been used for Type I tasks.

For example, consider a typical breakdown of Type II functions.

1. Tracking, monitoring, alerting.
2. Problem-solving, analysis, design.
3. Communication.

Systems to support each one of these clusters of activities have evolved under the names Management Information Systems, Management Science (including Operations Research, statistics, and mathematics), and Office Automation respectively. But they tend to be separate and diverse, poorly linked, and built on completely different structures. Note also that the Type II task we have called decision making, usually requires an intermixture of all three functions.

What is needed, then, is a system effort specifically focused on supporting Type II activities. To be specific, we should broaden our concept of DSS to include tracking-monitoring-alerting and communicating as well as the more traditional intelligence-design-choice view of decision making. This can be accomplished by merging the systems development in several areas into an amalgam of systems capabilities under the control of information workers performing Type II activities.

DSS AS INTEGRATOR

The DSS movement has become one of the most substantive on-going efforts to deal with support for Type II activities. Until recently, however, even this effort was based on using tools designed originally for Type I purposes. Traditional data base and modeling tools were integrated in a system with a facile interface to the user. The user contributed the mental capability to deal with the Type II task, while the system tools leveraged those mental skills.

A significant contribution of the DSS movement, however, was the merging and integration of previously separate tool sets into a unified whole more valuable than the sum of the parts. In fact, current DSS can be viewed as computer-based systems that lie at the intersection of two major evolutionary trends—*data processing* which has yielded a significant body of knowledge about managing data, and *management science* which is generating a significant body of knowledge about modeling. The confluence of these two trends forms the two major resources with which decision makers interact in the process of dealing with ill-structured tasks.

Data, models, and interaction support-(dialog) (the dialog-data-model paradigm) has become a popular way to categorize the sets of capabilities required in a DSS. (See Figure 2.1.) Let us consider how evolutionary developments in data processing and management science have led to the data base and model base capability of DSS [3].

The Data Processing Evolution

A helpful way to define the stages in the evolution of data processing is the following:

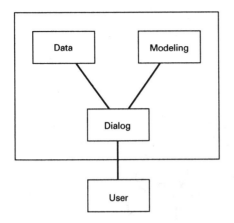

FIGURE 2.1   The DDM Paradigm

1. *Basic data processing*—characterized by stand-alone EDP jobs, mostly for transaction processing, with each program having its own files. Data handling was limited to such classic data processing functions as sorting, classifying, summarizing, etc.
2. *File management*—integrated EDP jobs for related functions, sometimes sharing files across several programs. This stage included attempts to develop common software for handling files (utilities), and prescribed ways to insure data security, integrity, backup, etc.
3. *Data base management*—a major capability of the MIS era, with particular emphasis on the software system for dealing with data separate from the programs that use it. The major impact of DBMS at this stage was the reduction of program maintenance, since data files could be modified without recompiling all the programs that used it. At this stage, DBMS software began to use data "models" to represent the way data were logically related.
4. *Query, report generation*—the addition of flexible report generators and "English-like" query languages to facilitate ad hoc requests and special reports. Emphasis here was on the direct access to data bases by non-technical people such as end users.

Figure 2.2 represents the steps in this evolution, from left to right. Note that each stage contributed a major capability that is still valuable in today's systems. In other words, we have not evolved beyond the need for the contribution of each stage, but have added capabilities to increase the value.

Throughout the EDP evolution, emphasis has been on manipulating data, initially in predefined ways to accomplish structured tasks, and later in flexible ways to accommodate ad hoc requests and preferences by individual users. Sophisticated ways of manipulating data (models) were embedded in the data processing system for some well-structured problems, for example inventory management, but modeling was generally considered a separate type of application. Users dealt with less well-structured problems by querying the data base, getting special reports, and then using their judgment.

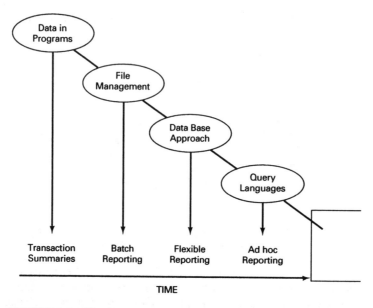

FIGURE 2.2   The Data Processing Evolution

In general, the data base approach evolving from the EDP tradition seemed to be characterized by the following objectives:

1. to effectively manage a large amount of data,
2. to establish independence between the data and the programs that used it,
3. to separate the physical and logical structures of data and deal with them separately,
4. to provide flexible, easy access to data by non-programmers.

The problems and limitations of this approach were related to its dominantly accounting-oriented historical data, and its focus on information flows and summaries. Unfortunately, for an important set of problems and decisions, getting "the right information to the right person" was necessary but not sufficient. That data often needed to be analyzed, interpreted, and extended with the use of some decision models being developed from Management Science/Operations Research efforts.

The Modeling Evolution

While data processing professionals were strengthening their ability to store and handle data, management scientists and operations researchers were increasing their ability to create "models" of a problem or situation and manipulate them to shed light on how to handle that problem. A similar sequence of evolutionary steps in the development of modeling might include the following:

1. *Symbolic models*—The early stages of modeling were characterized by heavy use of linear and nonlinear equations, sometimes in large sets of simultaneous equations.

2. *Computers as a computational engine*—The computer first became important to modeling as number crunchers to reduce large amounts of data to coefficient estimates for the equations, or as computational engines for solving sets of equations.

3. *Computer models*—Eventually, the computer took on a subtly different role. Rather than a device to compute a mathematical model, the computer program *became* the model. Computer variables became the symbols which were manipulated by the computer program instead of by mathematical operations. This approach led to a popular class of models that were not "solved" but rather "run" over time to observe the behavior of the model and thus shed light on the modeled situation.

4. *Modeling systems*—The computer became so important to modeling efforts that software systems were developed to handle classes of models. The software generally provided common data input formats, similar report formats, and integrated documentation. Modeling systems for statistical programs (for example SPSS) and mathematical programming (for example MPSX) are good examples.

5. *Interactive modeling*—As computers became more available in "time sharing" mode, interactive modeling became more feasible. Mini-computers and main-frames dedicated to on-line usage generally had libraries of models which could be called to do a variety of analyses. Unfortunately, it was common for the models to be stand-alone programs with different data requirements and formats and little if any linkage between the models.

Figure 2.3 graphically represents the stages in this modeling evolution, from right to left. Again, as before, each stage yielded knowledge or capability that contributed a valuable part of the tools available for dealing with problem solving decision making. Also, as before, the evolution led to the modeling capabilities utilized in DSS to help decision makers deal with Type II problems.

In summary, modeling evolution led to an increasingly close relationship between the models and computers, but continued to be separate from the data which they used. This seemed to reflect model builders' preoccupation with the model as the focus of attention and their hesitance to get intimately involved with data sources and structures. In general, the modeling efforts needed major contributions from the data base efforts of systems professionals.

Evolutions Converge

Figure 2.4 (on page 37) represents the convergence of these two trends into the data and modeling components of DSS. This figure can also be used to represent the range of systems that have been called DSS. Alter discussed "data oriented" versus "model oriented" DSS as those which depended more on data query or interactive modeling respectively [4]. Those DSS with a "balance" of capabilities occupy the center of the figure.

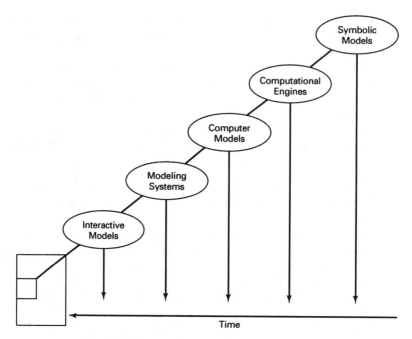

FIGURE 2.3   The Modeling Evolution

Each of the two development tracks—in data base and in modeling—were useful in their own right. They were each significantly lacking, however, in helping information workers deal with Type II tasks. Developments in Decision Support Systems allowed each set of capabilities to realize their potential in this area. DSS extended and combined both the data base technology and the modeling technology, and gave non-technical users access to them. The data and models were intimately linked, and both were linked with the user.

Conversely, DSS makes demands on the data base and the modeling capability that were not necessary before. Specifically, DSS makes model management capabilities necessary. Without the integration requirements of DSS, modeling systems or libraries of interactive models would probably suffice. So as the need for model management capabilities became apparent, it was the DSS builders and researchers who began working on its development.

THE FUTURE

We are now positioned to continue this development track into the future. Viewing DSS in the broad context of supporting Type II information work will guide these developments to better integrate mechanisms to support monitoring-tracking-alerting as well as better integration of communication support systems. New developments from artificial intelligence will make major contributions to all three of the DSS capability sets. Data

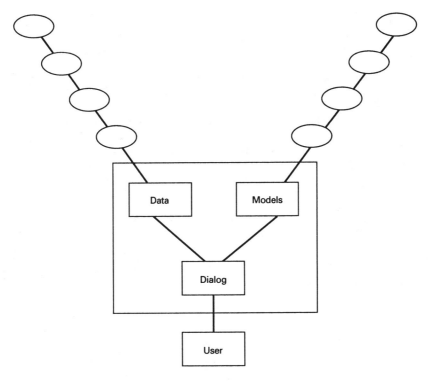

FIGURE 2.4   Evolutions Converge

base management will benefit from infusion of library science as well as AI to create better ways to organize and manage text-based data. Developments in model management are leading to better ways of defining and manipulating models. Dialog will profit significantly from the inclusion of natural language processing techniques and voice recognition.

In summary, with a broad view of DSS's role in the overall mission of information systems in organization, the future is exceedingly bright. The DSS "movement" has made a major contribution during the past decade. The evolving DSS "discipline" promises to be even more significant in the next decade.

QUESTIONS

1. What is the difference between Type I and Type II information work?
2. Why is the distinction important to the design and use of DSS?
3. Trace the stages of the data processing and MIS evolution. What is likely to be the next stage?
4. Trace the stages of the management science evolution. What is likely to be the next stage?
5. Explain how parts of each of these evolutions have converged in DSS. What is likely to be the next stage in DSS?

REFERENCES

1. PANKO, R., AND R. H. SPRAGUE   DP Needs New Approach to Office Automation, *Data Management* (1984).

2. PANKO, R., AND R. H. SPRAGUE   Towards a New Framework for Office Support, ACM Conference on Office Automation Systems (Philadelphia, PA, 1982).

3. An earlier version of this section is included in: KONSYNSKI, B., AND SPRAGUE, R. H. Future Research Directions in Model Management, *Decision Support Systems,* 2, no. 1 (1986).

4. ALTER, S.   A Taxonomy of Decision Support Systems. *Sloan Management Review,* 19, no. 1, 39–56.

PART 2

Developing and Using DSS

A number of activities are required before a DSS is available to support decision making. The organization must plan and organize both computer and human resources. Decisions must be made as to what hardware and software are required and where these resources will come from. Decisions must be made as to what roles will be assumed by various organizational personnel: Who will build the DSS? Who will support the DSS? While the answers to these and other questions are likely to evolve over time, it is important that they be carefully thought out. As with most organizational endeavors, thoughtful planning and organizing is an important key to success.

Once the planning and organizing for DSS has been accomplished, the development of specific decision support systems can begin. As was suggested in the first part of the book, the development approach for DSS differs from most other types of computer applications. It is important that these differences be clearly understood if DSS efforts are to be successful.

Once the DSS has been created, it can be put into use. This is when the payoff from the DSS is received. It should support all phases of the decision-making process and enhance the decision maker(s)' effectiveness.

This part contains four readings. Each reading should make a contribution to your understanding of how decision support systems are developed and used.

Management becomes involved with a DSS in a variety of ways: as approver and administrator, developer, operator, and user of output. A number of issues related to these responsibilities are explored by Jack Hogue in "A Framework for the Examination of Management Involvement in Decision Support Systems" (Reading 3). The findings from a study of eighteen organizations with DSS help answer such questions as: What methods are used in evaluating the desirability of creating a DSS? How are managers involved in developing a DSS? Who are the hands-on users of a DSS? Are all phases of the decision-making process supported by a DSS?

A DSS can involve a substantial commitment of organizational resources. Peter Keen, in "Value Analysis: Justifying Decision Support Systems" (Reading 4), explores how a proposed DSS should be evaluated. He argues that typical methods such as cost-benefit and return-on-investment analyses are inappropriate for DSS. For the typical DSS, the costs and especially the benefits are difficult or impossible to quantify. As a method of analysis, Keen recommends "value analysis." This approach is consistent with the less formal approaches most managers seem to use in assessing technical innovations.

It is widely believed that decision support systems require a unique development approach. The names *iterative, evolutionary,* and *adaptive design* are all used to describe this approach in which requirements analysis, design, development, and implementation are all combined into a single phase which is reiterated in a short period of time. Maryam Alavi and Al Napier's reading, "An Experiment in Applying the Adaptive Design Approach to DSS Development" (Reading 5), discusses and illustrates this development approach for DSS.

The final reading in this part is an example of a DSS and its usage in a real problem-solving situation. We felt it was important at this early stage of the book to examine a real, valuable, fully implemented system, before continuing to discuss additional DSS characteristics and attributes. Train dispatchers route trains along the section of tracks for which they are responsible. Richard Sauder and William Westerman in "Computer Aided Train Dispatching: Decision Support through Optimization" (Reading 6) describe a highly successful train dispatching DSS at Southern Railway. They describe the conditions that led to the creation of the DSS, how the system was developed, its architecture, and the benefits that are being realized.

3

A FRAMEWORK FOR THE EXAMINATION OF MANAGEMENT INVOLVEMENT IN DECISION SUPPORT SYSTEMS

Jack T. Hogue

INTRODUCTION

The evolution of computer-based information system (CBIS) applications in organizations has been noted and studied in the literature [15]. Applications that have evolved are often organized into one of the categories of transaction processing system (TPS), management information system (MIS), or decision support system (DSS) [13, 22, 25]. Both TPS and MIS are directed toward structured information flows in support of lower and middle organizational processes.

Decision support systems have a very specific purpose—the assistance of middle or upper level management decision makers with decisions of significant importance. Mann and Watson [17, p. 27] provide the following definition of a DSS:

Reprinted from the *Journal of Management Information Systems,* Vol. 4, No. 1, 1987, pp. 96–110. By permission of M. E. Sharpe, Inc., Armonk, NY.

A decision support system is an interactive system that provides the user with easy access to decision models and data in order to support semi-structured and unstructured decision-making tasks.

A particularly significant difference between the TPS and MIS, on one hand, and DSS on the other, is that a variety of information supporting a specific decision is available in a variety of formats with a DSS. With the TPS and MIS, the available information is quite inflexible.

In order to evaluate the necessary levels and types of management involvement in DSS, a framework for such an investigation will be proposed. This framework is derived both from a logical, intuitive categorization of processes and from the existing literature. First, a framework for the examination of management involvement in DSS will be proposed and related to specific speculations/research in the literature. Then, results from a field study of 18 DSS will be used to examine and reinforce the framework.

FRAMEWORK FOR INVESTIGATION

Based upon and extending beyond existing research and speculation in the literature, this work proposes that the involvement of management in DSS separates logically into four areas. The manager, in relation to the DSS, serves as a(an):

I.   approver and administrator
II.   developer
III. operator
IV.   user of output

It is with this fourfold conceptual taxonomy of roles that the involvement of management is to be examined. The basic fourfold taxonomy is proposed as a logical segmentation of management task with regard to DSS.[1] These four roles would appear to apply also to other categories of information systems (i.e., TPS and MIS); however, no such extension is being proposed in this research. Much of the subclassification of issues for the "developer" role and the "user of output" role is derived from the work of Sprague [22]. In the following sections, issues relevant to management's involvement in DSS with regard to the approver, developer, operator, and user roles will be presented, along with any supporting evidence from the literature. These specific issues will then be related directly to findings of a study of specific DSS.

Approver and Administrator

As an approver, the manager is functioning in a way quite consistent with other planning activities. It is generally the responsibility of management to judge the relative merits of alternative organizational investments and to accept these investments when it is to the benefit of the organization. In addition, DSS become an additional organizational entity requiring a position within the organization's structure and requiring relationships to other interacting organizational units.

With regard to the approver role, there are three basic issues to be investigated. First, how and by whom are DSS policy issues determined within the organization? The question of who sets policy has not been previously examined.

- DSS planning should be incorporated into corporate planning processes— Sprague and Carlson [23].
- In planning for implementation of the DSS into the organization, the political impact on power should be examined—Ahn and Grudnitski [1].

Second, how does management evaluate the DSS in terms of their benefit/cost to the organization?

- Financial evaluation of DSS is difficult and infrequent—Alter [2], Keen [12], McCosh and Scott Morton [18].
- DSS evaluation should be based upon both value-addition—Keen [12]—and cost-reduction—Meador and Keen [19].
- A "portfolio" approach should be utilized which considers risk and reward— Gremillion and Pyburn [8].

Third, how are DSS related to other organizational functions, specifically the more traditional CBIS functions?

- Some DSS resources are shared, and some are separate from other CBIS resources and controlled by user management—Blumenthal [5], Locander, Napier, and Scamell [16], Sprague [22].

Developer

Once a DSS has been approved it must be brought into being; that is, it must be developed. Given that the function of the DSS is to support the manager's decision-making responsibilities, and given that decision making is a difficult task to specify or structure, it should not seem illogical that the manager would need to play a substantial role in the DSS development process.

There are four subconcerns relevant to the manager's role as DSS developer. First, at what points in the DSS development process is management involvement required?

- Management involvement should be heavy throughout development—Alter [3], Bahl and Hunt [4], Ginzberg [7], McCosh and Scott Morton [18], Sprague [22].
- Management should provide leadership in DSS development—Keen and Scott Morton [13], Keen and Wagner [14], Locander, Napier, and Scamell [16].
- DSS development is often promoted and fostered by the advocacy of an "organizational champion"—Curley and Gremillion [6], Hayes and Nolan [9], Sprague and Olson [24].
- DSS development should include a fostering of cooperation and coordination between user/managers and technical designers—Ahn and Grudnitski [1].
- User-led development approaches often lead to improved DSS performance—Kasper [11].

Second, how much time is required of management in developing the DSS? While no one has addressed this issue specifically, length of the total development effort has been examined.

- Total development time is short (1 day to 20 weeks)—Keen [12].

Third, how are the personal needs and style of the manager/decision maker incorporated into the DSS?

- The DSS should be developed to include the personal decision-making style of the manager—Keen [12], McCosh and Scott Morton [18].

Finally, what technology is used (or not used) by managers in developing the DSS? Very little research has been performed in this area.

- The nominal level of available DSS technology has a significant impact on the extent of user and manager involvement—Mann and Watson [17].

Operator

The actual operation of the DSS requires skills perhaps most dissimilar to those typically required of managers. There are differing "levels" of technical sophistication in DSS which require differing amounts of ability for use. It is expected that some amount of operational ability and actual operation of the DSS may be desired by managers.

Of managerial interest with regard to system operation are two general subissues. First, how much will management operate the DSS? There has been no prior examination of the frequency of management operation.

- Managers prefer to turn operation of the DSS over to their staff—Wagner [26].
- There is a "significant" number of upper managers sitting at terminals—Keen and Wagner [14].

Second, how is a manager's personal decision-making style maintained during operation of the DSS, if by other than the manager (e.g., an intermediary)? This issue has not been previously examined.

User of Output

In making decisions, managers typically make use of a variety of sources of information. Depending on the manager's own personal style (e.g., Simon's intuitive-rational dichotomy [21]), the emphasis placed on different information will, of course, vary. The entire purpose of the DSS is to support the manager in his decision-making process by attempting to supply information the manager requests. In the final analysis it is with the outputs of the DSS that management is most interested.

The last of the four roles, user of output, contains four subconcerns. First, how is DSS output utilized by management vertically throughout the organization?

■ The DSS should be used in support of managerial decision making at all levels of the organization—Keen and Scott Morton [13], McCosh and Scott Morton [18], Sprague [22].

Second, is DSS output used for decision making at the discretion of the user manager? This issue has not been examined. Third, does the DSS support managers in both individual and group decision making?

■ The DSS should support both individual and group ("sequential interdependent" and "pooled interdependent") decision making—Keen and Scott Morton [13], Sanders and Courtney [20], Sprague [22], Huber [10].

Fourth, how does the DSS support management in the different phases of decision making (i.e., intelligence, design, choice)?

■ The DSS should be able to assist the manager with all phases of the decision process—Keen and Scott Morton [13], McCosh and Scott Morton [18], Sprague [22].

THE STUDY

Study Methodology

The objective of this study is to investigate a large number of issues, many of which have been examined only to a limited degree (e.g., single case situations). Questionnaire study offers limited viability when examining a relatively new discipline such as DSS. The primary difficulty is in developing unambiguous questions. For these reasons, the in-depth personal field interview method was chosen. This permits individual explanations and clarifications when required and the ability to probe to varying levels of detail as issues of interest present themselves. Alter [2] has conducted a study with a similar approach; however, many of Alter's cases would not be considered DSS by today's standards.

Sample Selection

In order to facilitate the location of a sufficient number of DSS, the Dallas-Fort Worth-Atlanta areas were chosen as the study site. This was due to two factors. First, these areas host a high percentage of high-level corporate policy-making organizations. This was desirable since DSS applications are most relevant for upper level policy decision making. Second, these areas provided a necessary convenience sample.

Selection of companies (see Table 3.1) was accomplished via telephone interviews with corporate personnel involved at high levels of both the CBIS function and other corporate areas (e.g., finance, marketing, planning). These initial conversations served to locate other corporate personnel involved with DSS applications. Of 109 total companies contacted, a sample of 18 separate companies was selected. These 18 were the only companies which had DSS which satisfied all of the essential criteria and most of the additional criteria (derived from Keen and Scott Morton [13] and Sprague [22]) listed below.

ESSENTIAL CRITERIA FOR A *DSS*

- Supports but does not replace decision making.
- Directed toward semistructured and/or unstructured decision-making tasks.
- Data and models organized around the decision(s).
- Easy to use software interface.

ADDITIONAL CRITERIA FOR A *DSS*

- Interactive processing.
- DSS use and control is determined by the user.
- Flexible and adaptable to changes in the environment and decision maker's style.
- Quick *ad hoc* DSS building capacity.

Conduct of the Interview

For each of the 18 companies in the sample, a 2- to 3-hour interview was conducted with the individual in the company who had the highest level of interaction with the development and use of the DSS. In all cases the interviewee was either a high ranking management decision maker (president or vice president) or a high ranking assistant to the decision maker (senior financial analyst or middle manager).

STUDY FINDINGS

This study examines numerous issues related to the involvement and role of management in decision support systems. Space does not permit an exhaustive presentation and discussion of all results. For this reason, study findings are first provided through a list of generalizations believed to be most relevant. These generalizations are intended to be brief and to the point. Each statement is accompanied by the percentage of total cases (n = 18) which was found to be in evidence for the generalization. These statements are hardly intended to be considered as fact, but rather as evidence to be evaluated in seeking to shed light on the issues. These generalizations are then condensed and examined in relation to the framework recommended. This is done in the examination-of-findings section of the paper.

Approval and Administration of the DSS

1. Administration of the DSS is localized to specific individuals within the company/department (73%).
2. Administration of the DSS usually is at the departmental level (73%), but occasionally company-wide steering committees are utilized (27%).
3. Administration of the DSS is by middle and/or upper management (100%).

TABLE 3.1 Companies Studied for Decision Support Systems

COMPANY NAME	DECISION SUPPORT SYSTEM AREA	INDUSTRY	SCOPE OF BUSINESS	SALES ($)
American Airlines	Price and route selection	Transportation	International	3.5 million
American Petrofina	Corporate planning and forecasting	Oil & mining	National	2.1 billion
Central and Southwest Corporation	Corporate planning and forecasting	Utility	Regional	1.7 billion
Champlin Petroleum	Corporate planning and forecasting	Oil & mining	National	2.5 billion
First United Bancorporation	Investment evaluation	Financial	State	190 million
Frito-Lay, Inc.	Pricing, advertising, and promotion	Manufacturer	International	6 billion
General Dynamics	Price evaluation	Manufacturer	International	4.74 billion
Gifford-Hill & Company	Corporate planning and forecasting	Construction	International	560 million
Lear Petroleum	Evaluation of potential drilling sites	Oil & mining	National	90 million
Mercantile Texas Corporation	Corporate planning and forecasting	Financial	State	520 million
National Gypsum	Corporate planning and forecasting	Manufacturer	International	840 million
Southern Railway	Train dispatching and routing	Transportation	Regional	1.5 billion
Texas-New Mexico Power	Corporate planning and forecasting	Utility	Regional	216 million
Texas Oil & Gas Corp.	Evaluation of potential drilling sites	Oil & mining	National	1.6 billion
Texas Utilities Company	Corporate planning and forecasting	Utility	State	278 million
The LTV Corporation	Terms of real estate	Diversified	International	8 billion
The Western Company	Corporate planning and forecasting	Oil services	International	500 million
Zale Corporation	Evaluation of potential store sites	Retail	International	830 million

4. Administrative policy for the DSS is usually informal (72%).
5. DSS master plans rarely exist from either the organizational or departmental level (0%).
6. Evaluation of DSS benefit is either nonexistent (39%) or based upon intuitive value of qualitative benefits (45%).
7. Quantification of costs varies considerably with no analysis (50%), complete analysis of all factors (28%), or partial analysis of factors (22%).
8. Resource support for the DSS varies as to source, but usually:
   a. Hardware is provided by the data processing department or vendor (78%).
   b. System software is provided by data processing or vendor (72%).
   c. Communications linkage is provided by data processing or vendor (78%).
   d. Data are prepared and input by DSS user/operators (100%—one case shared responsibility with data processing).
   e. Logic is determined by DSS user/managers (94%—two cases shared responsibility with data processing).
   f. Development personnel are from the DSS user department managers and staff (94%) and frequently data processing or vendor (60%).

Development of the DSS

9. Involvement at some point in DSS development is very likely for both middle (83%) and upper (89%) management. See Table 3.2 for more specific points and levels of involvement.
10. Lower management is rarely involved with DSS development (22%).
11. Middle management is usually involved with all phases/stages of DSS development (72%).

TABLE 3.2   Management Involvement in the Development of the Decision Support System

		Management Level		
STAGES*	LOWER (%)	MIDDLE (%)	TOP (%)	ALL** (%)
Idea	0	61	61	100
Information requirements	0	78	61	100
Building	11	72	6	78
Testing	11	72	6	83
Demonstration	11	78	28	89
Acceptance	0	72	67	100

*Traditional stage labels were easy for respondents to relate to. With few exceptions, development evolved several times through the stages.
**Combines management involvement from all three managerial levels.

TABLE 3.3   Personnel Involved with the Different Decision Support Systems Levels of Technology

TYPE OF EMPLOYEE	SPECIFIC DSS, PERCENTAGE OF COMPANIES	DSS GENERATOR, PERCENTAGE OF COMPANIES	DSS TOOLS, PERCENTAGE OF COMPANIES
Management			
Lower	17	6	6
Middle	56	33	22
Upper	22	6	6
Intermediary	83	37	39
Staff (decision maker)	6	0	0
Staff (builder)*	0	22	72

*A staff builder is, in all cases, a technician who appears in none of the other categories; this individual builds only for others to use.

12. Upper management is involved with DSS development primarily for idea generation, stating needs, and approval (72%).
13. DSS development is often accompanied by a strong organizational advocate for the DSS (44%).
14. Formal management approval is usually required at one or more points during development (72%).
15. Development time for the DSS varies considerably (near a uniform distribution from 1 week to 4 years).
16. Management time required during DSS development averages 38% (for upper and middle management), but with considerable variation (from 0% to 100% of time).
17. Personal user style is usually provided for by including capabilities into the DSS to interact with multiple approaches of different users (100%).
18. Management utilization of tools for development (33%) is slightly less than utilization of generators for development (45%). See Table 3.3.

Operation of the Physical Components of the DSS

19. Operation of the DSS is usually performed by both management (72%) and staff (89%) from the user area.
20. Operation of the DSS by all personnel (management and staff) is rarely less than once per week (11%); however, management often uses the DSS less than once per week (56%).
21. Decision maker style/approach is maintained by the intermediary (when intermediaries are used—95% of managers at least occasionally use intermediaries) through the following:

TABLE 3.4   Users of the Decision Support System for Decision-making Purposes

DECISION MAKER	PERCENTAGE OF COMPANIES
Management	
Upper	89
Middle	67
Lower	11
Middle and/or upper	100
Staff	11

a. Easy access of intermediary to decision maker (100%).
b. Easy access of intermediary to DSS (83%).
c. Fast turnaround time on DSS output (89% less than 1 minute).

Use of Output Generated by the DSS

22. Decision-making support is provided by the DSS primarily for middle and/or upper management (100%). Use by others is only occasional (17%). See Table 3.4.
23. Decision makers are rarely compelled to rely upon output from the DSS (6%).
24. Independent decisions are rarely made by managers when utilizing DSS output (6%). See Table 3.5.
25. Both pooled interdependent (67%) and sequential interdependent decisions (33%) are supported by DSS. See Table 3.5.
26. The intelligence phase of the decision-making process is almost always supported by the DSS (100%). See Table 3.6.
27. The design phase is supported via either a what- if capability (100%) or a goal-seeking capability (60%). See Table 3.6.
28. The choice phase of the decision-making process is often supported by the DSS (33%). See Table 3.6.

**TABLE 3.5   Form of Interaction between Decision Makers involving
Decision Support System Output**

FORM OF INTERACTION	PERCENTAGE OF COMPANIES
None	6
Shared interpretation of output	94
Sequential interdependent	33
Pooled interdependent	67

TABLE 3.6   **Phases of the Decision-making Process Supported
by the Decision Support System**

PHASE	PERCENTAGE OF COMPANIES
Intelligence	100
Design	
What-if	100
Goal-seeking	60
Choice	33

EXAMINATION OF FINDINGS

The fourfold framework presented in this article has provided a useful basis for examining and classifying issues relevant to management involvement in DSS. The framework has also provided a good means for examining the "conventional wisdom" in the existing DSS literature. In this section of the paper the conventional wisdom is compared with study findings in an attempt to draw generalizations, where the two verify each other, and to point to departures from the conventional wisdom, where the two do not coincide.

In relating the literature with these study findings, it is important to be able to demonstrate that the findings are derived from essentially successful DSS. This is particularly important given the relatively limited sample size. Several mechanisms for evaluation of MIS success have been suggested, however; Welsch [27] has utilized a set of measures, specifically for evaluation of DSS success. These measures focus on three major issues: satisfaction of users with the "final" product, acceptability of the DSS to users, and frequency of use (if use is voluntary).

In this study user satisfaction was measured on a seven-point scale. Respondents were asked to indicate their satisfaction/dissatisfaction with the DSS. Table 3.7 demonstrates the high level of perceived satisfaction with the DSS. Acceptability of the DSS to the user was evaluated through an open-ended question asking the respondent to comment on acceptance of the DSS. None of the systems was described in any way other than "highly acceptable" or, "after some initial skepticism the system is now quite acceptable."

Frequency of use has often been recommended as a measure of information system success, if use of the system is voluntary. For all but one of the 18 cases, use of the DSS is completely voluntary, and for this one case, use is only occasionally dictated to the user. Use of the DSS was found to be quite high. All but two DSS are used at least once per week, and the majority are used at least ten times per week.

Approver and Administrator

■   DSS planning should be incorporated into corporate planning processes.

TABLE 3.7   **Satisfaction/Dissatisfaction of the User with the Decision Support System**

RANKING	PERCENTAGE OF COMPANIES
1–3	0
4	11
5	22
6	50
7	17
	───
	100

Note: Measurement was on a 7-point scale with 1 = very dissatisfied, 4 = indifferent, and 7 = very satisfied.

It appears that formal planning for DSS is not the rule. While DSS are occasionally administered by a corporate steering committee, no master plan exists and policies are usually informally set by middle and/or upper managers within the user group.

- Financial evaluation of DSS is difficult and infrequent, but should still be based upon value-addition and cost reduction.

In providing approval for DSS it is apparent that management is conducting relatively little formal evaluation of costs or benefits. The cost factors, which are typically easiest to measure, generally are only partially measured or not measured at all. While benefits are often examined, measurement is primarily intuitive.

- Resource support for DSS and for other information system activities is shared in some cases and separate in some cases.

There appears to be a distinct segmentation between "technical" resource support and the "application" itself. Most technical support resources to include hardware (usually mini or mainframe), operating system capabilities, and communication linkages are provided and administered by formal information system personnel. The actual application itself is administered by management in the using area(s). This includes data input, application logic, and application maintenance.

Development of the DSS

- Management involvement should be heavy throughout development and should be in the form of a leadership role for the project.

Both middle and upper management are heavily involved in the projects, with middle management providing a strong leadership role throughout the process. Initiation of the project, as well as maintenance of support, is often accomplished through a middle or upper management advocate. Involvement thus appears to be quite heavy.

- The DSS should be developed to include the personal decision-making style of the manager.

None of the DSS in this study attempted to formally model the manager's decision-making process as a way of accommodating a personal approach to the decision. Decision style was accommodated (for multiple potential managers) by building the capability into the DSS to interact with a variety of approaches or styles (e.g., variation in detail of output, tabular and graphical display).

- The type of available DSS technology will have an impact on the extent of user and manager involvement in DSS development.

Findings are quite inconclusive here. While there was more involvement from managers when a DSS generator was used/available (43% vs. 33%), this would not seem to have been significant in affecting management involvement.

Operation of the DSS

- There is a "significant" number of upper managers operating the DSS, but many (most) prefer to turn operation over to their staff.

In contrast to the literature, this study finds that a fairly high percentage of user managers operate the DSS directly. In most of the cases the managers often turn operation over to an intermediary, but still operate the DSS on occasion. The manager's own approach is maintained by the operating intermediary through frequent and easy access of the intermediary to both the manager and the DSS.

User of Output

- The DSS should be used in support of managerial decision making at all levels of the organization.

Findings indicate that the DSS do support all managerial levels; however, there are significant differences in frequency. While middle and upper management are almost always supported, lower management was only rarely supported. Support is found to be at the discretion of the manager in all but one of the 18 cases.

- The DSS should support both individual and group decision-making processes of managers.

The DSS were found to support individual decision making in but one case. All other DSS (and their supported decisions) appear to involve at least one other person in a negotiable process. These decisions may be made sequentially (one individual after another, which is nearly individual decision making) or in a group process.

- The DSS should be able to assist the manager with all phases of the decision process.

Both intelligence and design were found to be supported in almost all cases. Choice was supported in one-third of the cases. This is likely due to the need for manager interaction to enable a choice to be made, since decision processes were not modeled.

CONCLUSIONS

The framework presented in this writing has provided a useful model for examining existing research/speculation in the DSS literature relating to management's role in DSS. By comparing the existing literature with results of a study of 18 DSS, we have found it possible to shed light upon certain aspects of the conventional wisdom in the field. This framework may further serve as a reference for future studies of management role in DSS.

While much of the conventional wisdom has been further supported by comparison with the case studies presented herein, much has been contradicted. In particular, corporate planning and administration of the DSS may be viewed as desirable, but have a long way yet to go. Further, approval processes need to focus on more specific cost and benefit measurements.

It appears that few DSS are actual models of decision maker processes. This may be true, and necessary, since most DSS appear to support multiple decision makers. It is difficult to draw conclusions about the level of technology (generator or tools) most appropriate for management. There is much intuitive appeal to facilitating manager involvement with a user-friendly generator, but this study did not bear this out. It could well be that a needed DSS will be built with whatever technology is made available (as in the study), but that significant improvements could be realized with a generator. This is a subject for further research.

Managers do operate the DSS, but less frequently than their intermediaries. This suggests the need for multiple interface "levels." This is needed to accommodate the infrequent, novice user and the frequent, expert user. Shared decisions appear to be the rule rather than the exception. There has been recent interest in "group decision support systems" for support of group decision making [22]. The study presented here would tend to indicate that specialized DSS for groups may not be essential, given a "conventional" DSS.

Management involvement in DSS is extensive in both breadth and depth. Management's role cuts across each of the areas of approval and administration, developer, operator, and user. This involvement must be expected and planned for. To date the most neglected aspect of DSS activity is planning for its approval and administration in the organization. Much additional research is needed in this area.

QUESTIONS

1. Briefly summarize how DSS are approved and administered.
2. Briefly describe how DSS are developed.
3. Briefly discuss how DSS are operated.
4. Briefly describe how the output from a DSS is used.

REFERENCES

1. AHN, T., AND GRUDNITSKI, G.   Conceptual perspectives on key factors in DSS development: A systems approach. *Journal of Management Information Systems,* 2, 1 (Summer 1985), 18–32.
2. ALTER, S.   A study of computer aided decision making in organizations. Unpublished Ph.D. dissertation, Massachusetts Institute of Technology, Cambridge, Mass., 1975.
3. ALTER, S.   Development patterns for decision support systems. *MIS Quarterly* (September 1978), 33–42.
4. BAHL, H. C., AND HUNT, R. G.   Problem solving strategies for DSS design. *Information and Management,* 8, 2 (February 1985), 81–88.
5. BLUMENTHAL, M.   Rift cited between MIS, decision support. *Computerworld,* 15, 6 (February 9, 1981), 28.
6. CURLEY, K., AND GREMILLION, L.   The role of the champion in DSS implementation. *Information and Management,* 6, 4 (1983), 203–209.
7. GINZBERG, M.   Redesign of managerial tasks: A requisite for successful decision support systems. *MIS Quarterly,* 2, 1 (March 1978), 38–52.
8. GREMILLION, L., AND PYBURN, P.   Justifying decision support and office automation systems. *Journal of Management Information Systems,* 2, 1 (Summer 1985), 5–17.
9. HAYES, R., AND NOLAN, R.   What kind of corporate modeling functions best. *Harvard Business Review,* 52, 3 (May–June 1974), 102–112.
10. HUBER, G.   Issues in the design of group decision support systems. *MIS Quarterly,* 8, 3 (September 1984), 195–204.
11. KASPER, G.   The effect of user-developed DSS applications on forecasting decision-making performance in an experimental setting. *Journal of Management Information Systems,* 2, 2 (Fall 1985), 26–39.
12. KEEN, P.   Decision support systems: Translating analytic techniques into useful tools. *Sloan Management Review,* 22, 3 (Spring 1980), 33–44.
13. KEEN, P., AND SCOTT MORTON, M.   *Decision Support Systems: An Organizational Perspective.* Reading, Mass.: Addison-Wesley, 1978.
14. KEEN, P., AND WAGNER, G.   DSS: An executive mind-support system. *Datamation,* 25, 11 (November 11, 1979), 117–122.
15. KROEBER, D., WATSON, H., AND SPRAGUE, R.   An empirical investigation and analysis of the current state of information systems evolution. *Information and Management,* 3 (1980), 35–43.
16. LOCANDER, W., NAPIER, A., AND SCAMELL, R.   A team approach to managing the development of a decision support system. *MIS Quarterly,* 3, 1 (March 1979), 53–63.
17. MANN, R., AND WATSON, H.   A contingency model for user involvement in DSS development. *MIS Quarterly,* 8, 1 (March 1984), 27–38.
18. McCOSH, A., AND SCOTT MORTON, M.   *Management Decision Support Systems.* New York: John Wiley and Sons, 1978.
19. MEADOR, M. J., AND KEEN, P. G.   Setting priorities for DSS development. *MIS Quarterly,* 8, 2 (June 1984), 117–129.
20. SANDERS, G. L., AND COURTNEY, J. F.   A field study of organizational factors influencing DSS success. *MIS Quarterly,* 9, 1 (March 1985), 77–93.

21. SIMON, H. *The New Science of Management Decision.* New York: Harper & Row, 1960.

22. SPRAGUE, R. A framework for the development of decision support systems. *MIS Quarterly,* 4, 4 (December 1980), 1–26.

23. SPRAGUE, R., AND CARLSON, E. *Building Effective Decision Support Systems.* Englewood Cliffs, N.J.: Prentice-Hall, 1982.

24. SPRAGUE, R., AND OLSON, R. The financial planning system at Louisiana National Bank. *MIS Quarterly,* 3, 3 (September 1979), 35–46.

25. SPRAGUE, R., AND WATSON, H. MIS concepts: Part II. *Journal of Systems Management,* 26, 2 (February 1975), 25–30.

26. WAGNER, G. Optimizing decision support systems. *Datamation,* 26, 5 (May 1980), 209–214.

27. WELSCH, G. M. Successful implementation of decision support systems: Preinstallation factors, service characteristics, and the role of the information transfer, specialist. Unpublished Ph.D. dissertation, Northwestern University, Evanston, Illinois, 1980.

The author is indebted to Hugh Watson at the University of Georgia for his insights into the role of management in DSS.

4

VALUE ANALYSIS: JUSTIFYING DECISION SUPPORT SYSTEMS

Peter G. W. Keen

INTRODUCTION

Decision support systems (DSS) are designed to help improve the effectiveness and productivity of managers and professionals. They are interactive systems frequently used by individuals with little experience in computers and analytic methods. They support, rather than replace, judgment in that they do not automate the decision process nor impose a sequence of analysis on the user. A DSS is in effect a staff assistant to whom the manager delegates activities involving retrieval, computation, and reporting. The manager evaluates the results and selects the next step in the process. Table 4.1 lists typical DSS applications.

Traditional cost-benefit analysis is not well-suited to DSS. The benefits they provide are often qualitative; examples cited by users of DSS include the ability to examine more alternatives, stimulation of new ideas, and improved communication of analysis. It is extra-

Reprinted by special permission of the *MIS Quarterly,* Volume 5, Number 1, March 1981. Copyright 1981 by the Society for Information Management and the Management Information Systems Research Center.

TABLE 4.1   Examples of DSS Applications[1]

DSS	APPLICATIONS	BENEFITS
GADSPI Geodata Analysis Display System	Geographical resource allocation and analysis; applications include sales force territories, police beat redesign, designing school boundaries	Ability to look at more alternatives, improved teamwork, can use the screen to get ideas across, improved confidence in the decision
PMS Portfolio Management System	Portfolio investment management	Better customer relations, ability to convey logic of a decision, value of graphics for identifying problem areas
IRIS Industrial Relations Information	*Ad hoc* access to employee data for analysis of productivity and resource allocation	*Ad hoc* analysis, better use of "neglected and wasted" existing data resource, ability to handle unexpected short term problems
PROJECTOR	Strategic financial planning	Insight into the dynamics of the business, broader understanding of key variables
IFPS Interactive Financial Planning System	Financial modeling, including mergers and acquisitions, new product analysis, facilities planning and pricing analysis	Better and faster decisions, saving analysts' time, better understanding of business factors, leveraging managing skills
ISSPA—Interactive Support System for Policy Analysts	Policy analysis in state government; simulations, reporting, and *ad hoc* modeling	*Ad hoc* analysis, broader scope, communication to/with legislators, fast reaction to new situations
BRANDAID	Marketing planning, setting prices and budgets for advertising, sales force, promotion, etc.	Answering "what-if?" questions, fine-tuning plans, problem finding
IMS Interactive Marketing System	Media analysis of large consumer database, plan strategies for advertising	Helps build and explain to clients the rationale for media campaigns, *ad hoc* and easy access to information

[1]Detailed descriptions of each DSS shown in Table 4.1 can be found in the following references:
GADS: Keen and Scott Morton [12], Carlson and Sutton [6]
PMS: Keen and Scott Morton [12], Andreoli and Steadman [2]
IRIS: Berger and Edelman [3]
PROJECTOR: Keen and Scott Morton [12]
IFPS: Wagner [19]
ISSPA: Keen and Gambino [11]
BRANDAID: Keen and Scott Morton [12], Little [14]
IMS: Alter [1]
Other DSS referred to in this article are:
AAIMS: Klass [13], Alter [1]
CAUSE: Alter [1]
GPLAN: Haseman [9]

ordinarily difficult to place a value on these. In addition, most DSS evolve. There is no "final" system; an initial version is built and new facilities are added in response to the users' experience and learning. Because of this, the costs of the DSS are not easy to identify.

The decision to build a DSS seems to be based on value, rather than cost. The system represents an investment for future effectiveness. A useful analogue is management education. A company will sponsor a five-day course on strategic planning, organizational development, or management control systems on the basis of perceived need or long-term value. There is no attempt to look at payback period or ROI, nor does management expect a direct improvement in earnings per share.

This article examines how DSS are justified and recommends Value Analysis (VA), an overall methodology for planning and evaluating DSS proposals. The next section illustrates applications of DSS. Key points are:

1. a reliance on prototypes,
2. the absence of cost-benefit analysis,
3. the evolutionary nature of DSS development, and
4. the nature of the perceived benefits.

The section on the Dynamics of Innovation relates DSS to other types of innovation. It seems clear that innovation in general is driven by "demand-pull"—response to visible, concrete needs—and not "technology push."

The Methodologies for Evaluating Proposals section briefly examines alternative approaches to evaluation: cost-benefit analysis, scoring techniques, and feasibility studies. They all require fairly precise estimates of, and tradeoffs between costs and benefits and often do not handle the qualitative issues central to DSS development and innovation in general. The final part of the article defines Value Analysis.

The overall issue this article addresses is a managerial one:

1. What does one need to know to decide if it is worthwhile to build a DSS?
2. How can an executive encourage innovation while making sure money is well spent?
3. How can one put some sort of figure on the value of effectiveness, learning, or creativity?

It would be foolish to sell a strategic planning course for executives on the basis of cost displacement and ROI. Similarly, any effort to exploit the substantial opportunity DSS provide to help managers do a better job must be couched in terms meaningful to them. This requires a focus on value and a recognition that qualitative benefits are of central relevance. At the same time, systematic assessment is essential. The initial expense of a DSS may be only in the $10,000 range, but this still represents a significant commitment of funds and scarce programming resources. The methodology proposed here is based on a detailed analysis of the implementation of over twenty DSS. It is consistent with the less formal approaches most managers seem to use in assessing technical innovations. Value analysis involves a two stage process:

1. *Version 0:* This is an initial, small-scale system which is complete in itself, but may include limited functional capability. The decision to build Version 0 is based on:

      a. An assessment of benefits, not necessarily quantified;

      b. A cost threshold—is it worth risking this amount of money to get these benefits?

In general, only a few benefits will be assessed. The cost threshold must be kept low, so that this decision can be viewed as a low-risk research and development venture, and not a capital investment.

    2. *Base System:* This is the full system, which will be assessed if the trial Version 0 has successfully established the value of the proposed concept. The decision to develop it is based on:

      a. Cost analysis: What are the costs of building this larger system?

      b. Value threshold: What level of benefits is needed to justify the cost? What is the likelihood of this level being attained?

A major practical advantage of this two stage strategy is that it reduces the risks involved in development. More importantly, it simplifies the tradeoff between costs and benefits, without making the analysis simplistic. It is also a more natural approach than traditional cost-benefit analysis; until value is established, *any* cost is disproportionate.

DECISION SUPPORT SYSTEMS

The DSS applications shown in Table 4.1 cover a range of functional areas and types of tasks. They have many features in common:

    1. They are *non-routine* and involve frequent *ad hoc* analysis, fast access to data, and generation of non-standard reports.

    2. They often address "what-if?" questions; for example, "What if the interest rate is X%?" or "What if sales are 10% below the forecast?"

    3. They have no obvious correct answers; the manager has to make qualitative tradeoffs and take into account situational factors.

The following examples illustrate the above points:

    1. **GADS.** In designing school boundaries, parents and school officials worked together to resolve a highly charged political problem. A proposal might be rejected because it meant closing a particular school, having children cross a busy highway, or breaking up neighborhood groups. In a previous effort involving redistricting, only one solution has been generated, as opposed to six with GADS over a four day period. The interactive problem solving brought out a large number of previously unrecognized constraints such as transportation patterns and walking times, and parent's feelings.

    2. **BRANDAID.** A brand manager heard a rumor that his advertising budget would be cut in half. By 5:00 p.m. he had a complete analysis of what he felt the effect would be on this year's and next year's sales.

    3. **IFPS.** A model had been built to assess a potential acquisition. A decision was needed by 9:00 a.m. The results of the model suggested the acquisition be made. The senior executive involved felt uneasy. Within one hour, the model had been modified and "what if" issues assessed that led to rejection of the proposal.

4. **ISSPA** and **IRIS**. Data which had always been available, but not accessible, were used to answer *ad hoc,* simple questions. Previously, no one bothered to ask them.

These characteristics of problems for which DSS are best suited impose design criteria. The system must be:

1. *Flexible* to handle varied situations.
2. *Easy to use* so it can be meshed into the manager's decision process simply and quickly.
3. *Responsive* because it must not impose a structure on the user and must give speedy service.
4. *Communicative* because the quality of the user-DSS dialogue and of the system outputs are key determinants of effective uses especially in tasks involving communication or negotiation. Managers will use computer systems that mesh with their natural mode of operation. The analogy of the DSS as a staff assistant is a useful one.

Many DSS rely on prototypes. Since the task the system supports is by definition non-routine, it is hard for the user to articulate the criteria for the DSS and for the designer to build functional specifications. An increasingly popular strategy is thus to use a flexible DSS "tool" such as APL, or a DSS "Generator" [15]. These allow an initial version of a "Specific DSS" to be delivered quickly and cheaply. It provides a concrete example that the user can react to and learn from. It can be easily expanded or modified. The initial system, Version 0, clarifies the design criteria and specifications for the full DSS. Examples of this two phase strategy include:

1. **ISSPA**—built in APL. Version 0 took seventy hours to build and contained nineteen commands. The design process began by sketching out the user-system dialogue. New user commands were added as APL functions. Ten of the forty-eight commands were requested by users, and several of the most complex ones were entirely defined by users.
2. **AAIMS**—an APL-based "personal information system" for analysis of 150,000 time series. The development was not based on a survey or user requirements, nor on any formal plan. New routines are tested and "proven" by a small user group.
3. **IRIS**—a prototype was built in five months and evolved over a one year period. An "Executive language" interface was defined as the base for the DSS and a philosophy was adopted of "build and evaluate as you go."
4. **CAUSE**—There were four evolutionary versions. A phased development was used to build credibility. The number of routines was expanded from 26 to 200.

There have been several detailed studies of the time and the cost needed to build a DSS in APL. A usable prototype takes about three weeks to deliver. A full system requires another twelve to sixteen weeks.[2]

---

[2] See Grajew and Tolovi [8] for a substantiation of these figures. They built a number of DSS in a manufacturing firm to test the "evolutive approach" to development.

TABLE 4.2   IFPS Development Process

	DATA PROCESSING	STAFF ANALYST	MIDDLE MANAGEMENT	TOP MANAGEMENT
Who requested the application	0	4	30	66
Who built it	3	53	22	22
Who uses the terminal	0	70	21	9
Who uses the output	0	6	42	52

End-user languages similarly allow fast development. One such DSS "generator" is Execucom's IFPS (Interactive Financial Planning System), a simple, English-like language for building strategic planning models. The discussion below is based on a survey of 300 IFPS applications in 42 companies.[3] The models included long range planning, budgeting, project analysis, evolution of mergers, and acquisitions.

The average IFPS model took five days to build and contained 360 lines (the median was 200). Documented specifications were developed for only 16%. In 66% of the cases, an analyst simply responded to a manager's request and got something up and running quickly. Cost-benefit analysis was done for 13%, and only 30% have any objective evidence of "hard" benefits. 74% of the applications replace manual procedures. Given that most of the responding companies are in the Fortune 100, this indicates the limited degree to which managers in the planning functions make direct use of computers.

Most DSS are built outside data processing, generally by individuals who are knowledgeable about the application area. Table 4.2 gives figures on where requests for IFPS applications came from and how they are built.

The IFPS users were asked to identify the features of the language that contributed most to the success of the DSS. In order of importance, these are:

1. speed of response,
2. ease of use,
3. package features (curve-fitting, risk analysis, what-if?),
4. sensitivity analysis, and
5. time savings.

The evolutionary nature of DSS development follows from the reliance on prototypes and fast development. There is no "final" system. In most instances, the system evolves in response to user learning. A major difficulty in designing DSS is that many of the most effective uses are unanticipated and even unpredictable. Examples are:

1. **PMS**—the intended use was to facilitate a portfolio based rather than security based approach to investment. This did not occur, but the DSS was invaluable in communicating with customers.
2. **GPLAN**—the DSS forced the users (engineers) to change their roles from analysts to decision makers.

---

[3]IFPS is a proprietary product of Execucom, Inc., in Austin, Texas. The survey of IFPS users is described in Wagner [19].

TABLE 4.3   Relative Use of DSS Operators (PMS)

	Percentage of Use by Each Manager						
OPERATOR	A	B	C	D	E	F	PERCENTAGE OF USE BY ALL USERS
Table	22	22	38	22	76	57	47
Summary	40	10	30	8	0	38	17
Scan	0	26	5	24	0	0	4
Graph	14	4	13	30	5	0	8
Directory	2	0	0	0	1	4	1
Others	22	38	14	16	18	1	23

3. **PROJECTOR**—the intended use was to analyze financial data in order to answer preplanned questions and the actual use was as an educational vehicle to alert managers to new issues.

Usage is also very personalized, since the managers differ in their modes of analysis and the DSS is under their own control. For example, six users of PMS studied over a six month period differed strongly in their choice of operators (see Table 4.3).[4]

The benefits of DSS vary; this is to be expected given the complex situational nature of the tasks they support and their personalized uses. The following list shows those frequently cited in DSS cases studies, together with representative examples.[5] Table 4.4 summarizes the list.

1. INCREASE IN THE NUMBER OF ALTERNATIVES EXAMINED

■ Sensitivity analysis takes 10% of the time needed previously.

■ Eight detailed solutions generated versus one in previous study.

■ Previously took weeks to evaluate a plan; now takes minutes, so much broader analysis.

■ Users could imagine solutions and use DSS to test out hypotheses.

■ "No one had bothered to try price/profit options before."

2. BETTER UNDERSTANDING OF THE BUSINESS

■ President made major changes in company's overall plan, after using DSS to analyze single acquisition proposal.

■ DSS alerted managers that an apparently successful marketing venture would be in trouble in six months' time.

■ DSS is used to train managers; gives them a clear overall picture.

---

[4] See Andreoli and Steadman [2] for a detailed analysis of PMS usage.

[5] This list is taken verbatim from Keen, "Decision Support Systems and Managerial Productivity Analysis" [10].

TABLE 4.4   DSS Benefits

	EASY TO MEASURE?	BENEFIT CAN BE QUANTIFIED IN A "BOTTOM LINE" FIGURE?
1. Increase in number of alternatives examined	N	N
2. Better understanding of the business	N	N
3. Fast response to unexpected situations	Y	N
4. Ability to carry out *ad hoc* analysis	Y	N
5. New insights and learning	N	N
6. Improved communication	N	N
7. Control	N	N
8. Cost savings	Y	Y
9. Better decisions	N	N
10. More effective teamwork	N	N
11. Time savings	Y	Y
12. Making better use of data resource	Y	N

- "Now able to see relationships among variables."

3. FAST RESPONSE TO UNEXPECTED SITUATIONS

- A marketing manager faced with an unexpected budget cut used the DSS to show that this would have a severe impact later.
- Helped develop legal case to remove tariff on petroleum in New England states.
- Model revised in twenty minutes, adding risk analysis; led to reversal of major decision made one hour earlier.

4. ABILITY TO CARRY OUT *AD HOC* ANALYSIS

- 50% increase in planning group's throughput in three years.
- The governor's bill was published at noon "and by 5 pm I had it fully costed out."
- "I can now do QAD's—quick-and-dirties."
- System successfully used to challenge legislator's statements within a few hours.

5. NEW INSIGHTS AND LEARNING

- Quickened management's awareness of branch bank problems.
- Gives a much better sense of true costs.
- Identified underutilized resources already at analysts' disposal.

- Allows a more elegant breakdown of data into categories heretofore impractical.
- Stimulated new approaches to evaluating investment proposals.

6. IMPROVED COMMUNICATION

- Used in "switch presentations" by advertising agencies to reveal short comings in customer's present agency.
- Can explain rationale for decision to investment clients.
- Improved customer relations.
- "Analysis was easier to understand and explain. Management had confidence in the results."
- "It makes it a lot easier to sell (customers) on an idea."

7. CONTROL

- Permits better tracking of cases.
- Plans are more consistent and management can spot discrepancies.
- Can "get a fix on the overall expense picture."
- Standardized calculation procedures.
- Improved frequency and quality of annual account reviews.
- Better monitoring of trends in airline's fuel consumption.

8. COST SAVINGS

- Reduced clerical work.
- Eliminated overtime.
- Stay of patients shortened.
- Reduced turnover of underwriters.

9. BETTER DECISIONS

- "He was forced to think about issues he would not have considered otherwise."
- Analysis of personnel data allowed management to identify for the first time where productivity gains could be obtained by investing in office automation.
- Increased depth and sophistication of analysis.
- Analysts became decision makers instead of form preparers.

10. MORE EFFECTIVE TEAM WORK

- Allowed parents and school administrators to work together exploring ideas.
- Reduced conflict—managers could quickly look at proposal without prior argument.

11. TIME SAVINGS

- Planning cycle reduced from six man-days spread over twenty elapsed days to one half day spread over two days.

- "Substantial reduction in manhours" for planning studies.
- "(My) time-effectiveness improved by a factor of 20."

12. MAKING BETTER USE OF DATA RESOURCE

- Experimental engineers more ready to collect data since they knew it would be entered into a usable system.
- "More cost-effective than any other system (we) implemented in capitalizing on the neglected and wasted resource of data."
- Allows quick browsing.
- "Puts a tremendous amount of data at manager's disposal in form and combinations never possible at this speed."

Table 4.4 adds up to a definition of managerial productivity. All the benefits are valuable but few of them are quantifiable in ROI or payback terms.

In few of the DSS case studies is there any evidence of formal cost-benefit analysis. In most instances, the system was built in response to a concern about timeliness or scope of analysis, the need to upgrade management skills, or the potential opportunity a computer data resource or modeling capability provides. Since there is little *a priori* definition of costs and benefits, there is little *a posteriori* assessment of gains. A number of DSS failed in their aims, but where they are successful, there is rarely any formal analysis of the returns. Many of the benefits are not proven. In managerial tasks there is rarely a clear link between decisions and outcomes, and a DSS can be expected to *contribute* to better financial performance, but not directly cause it. In general, managers describe a successful DSS as "indispensable" without trying to place an economic value on it.

THE DYNAMICS OF INNOVATION

DSS are a form of innovation. They represent:

1. a relatively new concept of the role of computers in the decision process;
2. an explicit effort to make computers helpful to managers who on the whole have not found them relevant to their own job, even if they are useful to the organization as a whole;
3. a decentralization of systems development and operation, and often a bypassing of the data processing department; and
4. the use of computers for "value added" applications rather than cost displacement.

There is much literature on the dynamics of technical innovations in organizations.[6] Its conclusions are fairly uniform and heavily backed by empirical data.

Surveys of the use of computer planning models support these conclusions. In nine cases studied[7] the decision to adopt planning models was based on:

1. comparison with an ongoing system which involves examining either a manual or partially computerized system and deciding that some change is desirable;

---

[6] See Tornatzky et al. [16].

[7] See Blanning, "How Managers Decide to Use Planning Models [4], *Long Range Planning,* Vol. 13, April 1980.

2. comparison with a related system, such as a successful planning model in another functional area;

3. initiation of a low cost project; and

4. comparison with competitors' behavior resulting in the use of a "reference model" which reduces the need to estimate the impact of a model not yet constructed on improved decisions and performance.

Even in traditional data processing applications, the emphasis on value rather than cost is common. A survey of all the proposals for new systems accepted for development in a large multinational company found that even though cost-benefit analysis was formally required, it was used infrequently.[8] The two main reasons for implementing systems were:

1. mandated requirements, such as regulatory reports, and

2. identification of one or two benefits, rarely quantified.

Traditional cost-benefit analysis is effective for many computer-based systems. It seems clear, however, that it is not used in innovation. This may partly be because innovations involve R&D; they cannot be predefined and clear specifications provided. There is some evidence that there is a conflict in organizations between groups concerned with performance and those focused on cost. In several DSS case studies, the initiators of the system stress to their superiors that the project is an investment in R&D, not in a predefined product.

Surveys of product innovations consistently find that they come from customers and users rather than centralized technical or research staff. Well over three-quarters of new products are initiated by someone with a clear problem looking for a solution.[9] Industrial salesmen play a key role as "gatekeepers" bringing these needs to the attention of technical specialists. Even in the microprocessor industry, the majority of products are stimulated in this way by "demand-pull," not by "technology-push."[10]

Case studies indicate that DSS development reflects the same dynamics of innovation as in other technical fields. Table 4.5 states the same dynamics of innovation as in other technical fields.

Methodologies for Evaluating Proposals

There are three basic techniques used to evaluate proposals for computer systems in most organizations:

1. cost-benefit analysis and related ROI approaches—this views the decision as a *capital investment,*

2. scoring evaluation—this views it in terms of *weighted scores,* and

3. feasibility study—this views it as *engineering.*

Each of these is well-suited to situations that involve hard costs and benefits, and that permit clear performance criteria. They do not seem to be useful—or at least used—for evaluating innovations of DSS.

[8] See Ginzberg [7].
[9] See Utterback [17].
[10] See von Hippel [18].

TABLE 4.5 Dynamics of DSS Innovation

Innovations are value-driven	Main motivation for DSS is "better" planning, timely information, *ad hoc* capability, etc.
Early adopters differ from late adopters	DSS are often initiated by line managers in their own budgets; once the system is proven other departments may pick it up.
Informal processes are central	DSS development usually involves a small team; key role of intermediaries knowledgeable about the users and the technology for the DSS; data processing rarely involved; frequently DSS are "bootleg" projects.
Cost is a secondary issue	Costs are rarely tracked in detail; DSS budget is often based on staff rather than dollars; little change out of systems (this may reflect item below).
Uncertainty reduced by trial-ability, ease of understanding, clear performance value	Use of prototypes, emphasis on ease of use.

Cost-benefit analysis is highly sensitive to assumptions such as discount rates and residual value. It needs artificial and often arbitrary modifications to handle qualitative factors such as the value of improved communication and improved job satisfaction. Managers seem to be more comfortable thinking in terms of perceived value and then asking if the cost is reasonable. For example, expensive investments in training are made with no effort at quantification. The major benefits of DSS listed in Table 4.4 are mainly qualitative and uncertain. It is difficult to see how cost-benefit analysis of them can be reliable and convincing in this context.

Scoring methods are a popular technique for evaluating large-scale technical projects, such as the choice of a telecommunications package, especially when there are multiple proposals with varying prices and capabilities. Scoring techniques focus on a list of desired performance characteristics. Weights are assigned to them and each alternative rated. For example:

CHARACTERISTIC	WEIGHT	ALTERNATIVE	WEIGHTED SCORE
response time	.30	15	4.5
ease of use	.20	20	4.0
user manual	.10	17	1.7

Composite scores may be generated in several ways: mean rating, pass-fail, or elimination of any alternative that does not meet a mandatory performance requirement. Cost is considered only after all alternatives are scored. There is no obvious way of deciding if alternative A, with a cost of $80,000 and a composite score of 67, is better than B, with a cost of $95,000 and a score of 79.

Feasibility studies involve an investment to identify likely costs and benefits. They tend to be expensive and to focus on defining specifications for a complete system. They rarely give much insight into *how* to build it, and assume that the details of the system can be laid out in advance. DSS prototypes are a form of feasibility study in themselves. They are a first cut at a system. Some designers of DSS point out that Version "0" can be literally thrown away. Its major value is to clarify design criteria and establish feasibility, usefulness, and usability. The differences between a prototype and a feasibility study are important:

1. The prototype moves the project forward, in that a basic system is available for use and the logic and structure of the DSS already implemented.
2. The prototype is often cheaper, if the application is suited to APL or an end-user language.
3. The feasibility study is an abstraction and the prototype is concrete. Since DSS uses are often personalized and unanticipated, direct use of the DSS may be essential to establishing design criteria.

There is no evidence that any of these methods are used in evaluating DSS, except occasionally as a rationale or a ritual. More importantly, almost every survey of the dynamics of innovation indicates that they do not facilitate innovation and often impede it.

VALUE ANALYSIS

The dilemma managers face in assessing DSS proposals is that the issue of qualitative benefits is central, but they must find some way of deciding if the cost is justified. What is needed is a systematic methodology that focuses on:

1. value first, cost second;
2. simplicity and robustness—decision makers cannot, and should not have to, provide precise estimates of uncertain, qualitative future variables;
3. reducing uncertainty and risk; and
4. innovation, rather than routinization.

The methodology recommended here addresses all these issues. It relies on prototyping which:

1. factors risk, by reducing the initial investment, delay between approval of the project, and delivery of a tangible product; and
2. separates cost and benefit, by keeping the initial investment within a relatively small, predictable range.

If an innovation involves a large investment, the risk is high. Since estimates of costs and benefits are at best approximate, the decision maker has no way of making a sensible judgment. Risk is factored by reducing scope. An initial system is built at a cost below the capital investment level; the project is then an R&D effort. It can be written off if it fails. By using the DSS one identifies benefits and establishes value. The designer is also likely to learn something new about how to design the full system. The prototype accomplishes the same things as a feasibility study, but goes further in that a real system is built.

The benefit of a DSS is the incentive for going ahead. The complex calculations of cost-benefit analysis are replaced in value analysis by simple questions that most managers naturally ask and handle with ease:

1. What exactly will I get from the system?
   - it solves a business problem;
   - it can help improve planning, communication, and control; and
   - it saves time.
2. If the prototype costs $X, do I feel that the cost is acceptable?

Obviously the manager can try out several alternatives—"If the prototype only accomplishes two of my three operational objectives, at a lower cost of $Y, would I prefer that?" The key point is that value and cost are kept separate and not equated. This is sensible only if the cost is kept fairly low. From case studies of DSS, it appears that the cost must be below $20,000 in most organizations for value analysis to be applicable.

The first stage of value analysis is similar to the way in which effective decisions to adopt innovations are made. It corresponds to most managers' implicit strategy. The second stage is a recommendation; there is no evidence in the literature that it is widely used, but it seems a robust and simple extension of Version "0." Once the nature and value of the concept has been established the next step is to build the full DSS. The assessment of cost and value now needs to be reversed:

1. How much will the full system cost?
2. What threshold of values must be obtained to justify the cost? What is the likelihood they will occur?

If the expected values exceed the threshold, no further quantification is required. If they do not, then there must either be a scaling down of the system and a reduction in cost, or a more detailed exploration of benefits.

Value analysis follows a general principle of effective decision making—simplify the problem to make it manageable. A general weakness of the cost-benefit approach is that it requires knowledge, accuracy, and confidence about issues which for innovations are unknown, ill-defined, and uncertain. It therefore is more feasible to:

1. Establish value first, then test if the expected cost is acceptable.
2. For the full system, establish cost first, then test if the expected benefits are acceptable.

Instead of comparing benefits against cost, value analysis merely identifies relevant benefits and tests them against what is in effect a market price: "Would I be willing to pay $X to get this capability?" It is essential that the benefits be accurately identified and made operational. The key question is how would one know that better planning has occurred? The prototype is in effect an experiment in identifying and assessing it.

Figure 4.1 illustrates the logic and sequence of value analysis. The specific details of the method are less important than the overall assumptions, which have important implications for anyone trying to justify a DSS whether as a designer or user. Marketing a DSS requires building a convincing case. Figure 4.1 can be restated in these terms:

1. Establish value—the selling point for a DSS is the specific benefits it provides for busy managers in complex jobs.
2. Establish cost threshold—"trialability" is possible only if the DSS is relatively cheap and installed quickly. If it costs, say, $200,000, it is a capital investment, and must be evaluated as such. This removes the project from the realm of R&D and benefits as the focus of attention to ROI and tangible costs and inhibits innovation.
3. Build Version "0"—from a marketing perspective this is equivalent to "strike while the iron is hot." Doing so is possible only with tools that allow speedy development, modification, and extension.

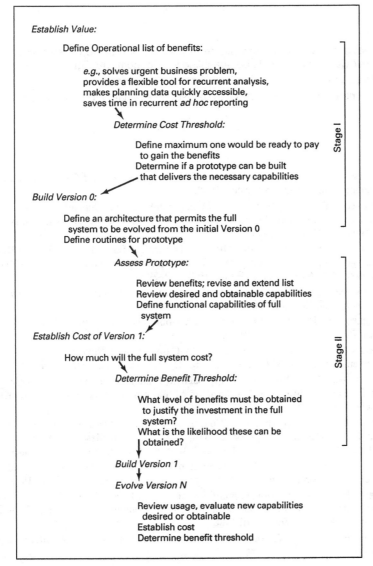

FIGURE 4.1
Value Analysis

4. Assess the prototype—for the marketer this means working closely with the user and providing response service.

Two analogies for DSS have been mentioned in this article: the staff assistant and management education. The strategy used to justify DSS depends upon the extent to which one views such systems as service innovations and investments in future effectiveness as opposed to products, routinization, and investment in cost displacement and efficiency. The evidence seems clear—DSS are a potentially important innovation. Value is the issue, and any exploitation of the DSS approach rests on a systematic strategy for identifying benefits, however qualitative, and encouraging R&D and experimentation.

QUESTIONS

1. What are the possible benefits from a DSS? Are these benefits easy to measure? Can these benefits be quantified in a "bottom line" figure?
2. Discuss the ways in which a DSS represents an innovation.
3. Describe how value analysis can be used to evaluate a proposed DSS.

REFERENCES

1. ALTER, S.   *Decision Support Systems: Current Practice and Continuing Challenges.* Reading, Mass.: Addison-Wesley, 1980.
2. ANDREOLI, P., AND J. STEADMAN   "Management Decision Support Systems: Impact on the Decision Process," Master's thesis, Sloan School of Management, Massachusetts Institute of Technology, 1975.
3. BERGER, P., AND F. EDELMAN   "IRIS: A Transaction Based DSS for Human Resources Management," in "Proceedings of a Conference on Decision Support Systems," ed. E. D. Carlson, *Data Base,* 8, no. 3 (Winter 1977), 22–29.
4. BLANNING, R.   "How Managers Decide to Use Planning Models," *Long Range Planning,* vol. 13, April 1980.
5. CARLSON, E. D., ed.   "Proceedings of a Conference on Decision Support Systems," *Data Base,* 8, no. 3 (Winter 1977).
6. CARLSON, E. D., AND J. A. SUTTON   "A Case Study of Non-programmer Interactive Problem Solving," IBM Research Report, RJ13H2, San Jose, Calif., 1974.
7. GINZBERG, M. J.   "A Process Approach to Management Science Implementation," Ph.D. dissertation, Sloan School of Management, Massachusetts Institute of Technology, 1975.
8. GRAJEW, J., AND J. TOLOVI, JR.   "Conception et Mise en Oeuvre des Systems Interactifs d'aide a la Decision: l'approche Evolutive," Doctoral dissertation, Université des Sciences Sociales de Grenoble, Institut d'Administration des Entreprises, France, 1978.
9. HASEMAN, W. D.   "GPLAN: An Operational DSS," in "Proceedings of a Conference on Decision Support Systems," ed. E. D. Carlson, *Data Base,* 8, no. 3 (Winter 1977), 73–78.
10. KEEN, P.G.W.   "Decision Support Systems and Managerial Productivity Analysis," paper presented at the American Productivity Council Conference on Productivity Research, Houston, Tex., April 1980.
11. KEEN, P.G.W., AND T. GAMBINO   "The Mythical Man-Month Revisited: Building a

Decision Support System in APL," paper presented at the APL Users Meeting, Toronto, Canada, September 1980.

12. KEEN, P.G.W., AND M. S. SCOTT MORTON *Decision Support Systems: An Organizational Perspective.* Reading, Mass.: Addison-Wesley, 1978.

13. KLAAS, R. L. "A DSS for Airline Management," in "Proceedings of a Conference on Decision Support Systems," ed. E. D. Carlson, *Data Base,* 8, no. 3 (Winter 1977), 3–8.

14. LITTLE, J.D.C. "BRANDAID," *Operations Research,* 23, no. 4 (May 1975), 628–673.

15. SPRAGUE, R. H., JR. "A Framework for the Development of Decision Support Systems," *MIS Quarterly,* 4, no. 4 (December 1980), 1–26.

16. TORNATAZKY, L. G., et al. "Innovation Processes and Their Management: A Conceptual, Empirical, and Policy Review of Innovation Process Research," National Science Foundation Working Draft, October 19, 1979.

17. UUTTERBACK, J. M. "Innovation in Industry and the Diffusion of Technology," *Science,* vol. 183, February 1974.

18. VON HIPPEL, E. "The Dominant Role of Users in the Scientific Instrument Innovation Process," *Research Policy,* July 1976.

19. WAGNER, G. R. "Realizing DSS Benefits with the IFPS Planning Language," paper presented at the Hawaii International Conference on System Sciences, Honolulu, January 1980.

5

AN EXPERIMENT IN APPLYING THE ADAPTIVE DESIGN APPROACH TO DSS DEVELOPMENT

Maryam Alavi
H. Albert Napier

INTRODUCTION

Decision support systems (DSS) are computer based systems designed to enhance the effectiveness of decision makers in performing semistructured tasks. With such tasks, the decision maker is uncertain about the nature of the problem/opportunity, the alternative solutions and/or the criteria or value for making a choice. Hence, the primary role of a DSS is to aid the judgment processes as the decision maker contends with poorly defined problems.

The way of designing a DSS is different from that of a transaction processing system. A fundamental assumption in the traditional "life cycle" approach is that the requirements can be determined prior to the start of the design and development process. However, Sprague [14] stated that DSS designers literally "cannot get to first base"

Maryam Alavi and H. Albert Napier, "An Experiment in Applying the Adaptive Design Approach to DSS Development," *Information & Management,* Vol. 7, No. 1, 1984.

because the decision maker or user cannot define the functional requirements of the DSS in advance. Also, as an inherent part of the DSS design and implementation process, the user and designer will "learn" about the decision task and environment, thereby identifying new and unanticipated functional requirements.

Generally, DSS designers have recognized that this circumstance calls for a departure from tradition: we suggest adaptive design. This is an emerging concept, and published empirical work in this area is very limited.

This article focuses on the adaptive design approach. First, conceptual issues of adaptive design are explored and discussed. Then a case study is presented. The empirical findings of this provide some insight into the application and the effectiveness of the approach. Some areas for future research are also identified.

THE ADAPTIVE DESIGN PROCESS

In an adaptive design approach, the four traditional system development activities (requirements analysis, design, development, and implementation) are combined into a single phase, which is iteratively repeated in a relatively short time [14]. The process is described in the context of the framework of Keen [9]. According to this framework, the major components of adaptive design include the builder, the user, and the technical system (DSS). During the design process, these elements interact with ("influence") each other. Hence, three adaptive links are established in this framework: the user-system, the user-builder and the builder-system.

In this framework, the user is either the manager or individual faced with a problem or opportunity. The user is responsible for taking action and its consequences. In some cases, the user may not directly interact with the technical system. Then, an intermediary provides the interface between the user and the system. The intermediary may play a clerical role (interact with the terminal to obtain user specified outputs) or play the role of a "staff assistant" (interact with the user and make suggestions) [14].

The DSS builder is the individual who develops the specific DSS with which the user or intermediary interacts. The builder should be knowledgeable about information systems technology and capabilities, and become familiar with the task for which the DSS is being designed. In some cases the builder may also play the role of user intermediary.

In the adaptive design framework, the technical system is the hardware/software provided to the user. A technical system is "configured" from DSS generator and/or DSS tools. A generator is a "package" which provides a set of capabilities to build a specific DSS quickly and easily [14]. An example of a DSS generator is the Executive Information System (EIS) marketed by Boeing Computer Services [4]. EIS capabilities include report generation, graphics, inquiry, and modeling languages which are available through a common command language. DSS tools are hardware and software elements applied to the development of a specific DSS or a DSS generator. Examples of DSS tools include general purpose programming languages, database management systems, and financial planning languages. Many early DSS were developed by direct application of DSS tools.

User-System Interactions

The user-system link deals with the effect of a user's characteristics on the system utilization. Research by Dickson, Chervany and Senn [6] established that some individual characteristics, such as problem solving style, experience, background and skills, influence the quality and quantity of system utilization. Alavi and Henderson [1] showed that individuals with an "analytical problem solving" style are more willing and inclined to use DSS than "intuitive" individuals.

This link reflects user learning as a result of using the system. It is argued that through interaction with the DSS, the user's understanding and perception of the decision task and potential solutions are enhanced. Case studies [9] have shown this.

The builder-system link occurs as the builder adds new capabilities and functions to the system. System evaluation and change is feasible only if system architecture is flexible; i.e., new capabilities can be added with little expenditure of time and resources. The system-builder link concerns the demand placed on the builder for system evolution resulting from user and builder learning and changes in the decision environment.

User-Builder Interactions

User-builder interactions involve communication and collaboration between the user and builder during the DSS development process. Through these interactions, the user learns about the capabilities and possibilities for decision support and the designer learns about user requirements and builds credibility. Effective communication and collaboration between user and builder are key aspects of adaptive design.

A CASE STUDY

Background

The system discussed here has been implemented in a southwestern U.S. real estate development and management firm which had revenues of about 50 million dollars in 1982. Prior to development and implementation of the system, the firm had some experience related to computers, but none with DSS. The firm had an in-house IBM System 34 computer that was used primarily for transaction processing applications. The company purchased this computer in 1979.

Elements of Adaptive Design   The elements of adaptive design: The user, builder, and DSS in the case are depicted in Figure 5.1.

THE USERS.   The primary users of the decision support system, a corporate cash flow analysis and projection system, are the chief executive officer (CEO), the controller, the

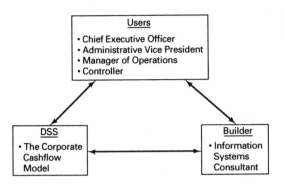

FIGURE 5.1   The Elements of Adaptive Design in the Case

administrative vice president and the manager of operations. The CEO uses the system through an intermediary (the controller). Summary cash flow projection reports and sensitivity analysis results are used by the CEO for support of financial decisions, such as: identifying times when cash is needed and when surpluses are available, making "hold" or "sell" decisions for existing properties, and in making investment decisions for new real estate development projects. The controller is a "hands- on" user; the system outputs and its "what-if" capability is used to assist in activities such as the determination of the timing of construction draws and major cash payment and tax planning. The administrative vice president and the manager of operations use the system in budgeting activities for individual projects. Clerical staff personnel perform the role of intermediary for the vice president and the manager. Some demographic characteristics of these users are summarized in Table 5.1. Prior to the implementation of the DSS, the users had no familiarity with decision support systems.

THE BUILDER.   The DSS builder was an information systems consultant. The builder configured a cash flow model (the specific DSS) from a DSS generator, the Interactive Financial Planning System (IFPS) marketed by Execucom systems Corporation [8]. In

TABLE 5.1   Parameters of the DSS Users

ORGANIZATIONAL TITLE	NUMBER OF YEARS IN THE CURRENT POSITION	EDUCATIONAL BACKGROUND	AGE	DSS UTILIZATION MODE
1. Chief Executive Officer	19	Engineering	45	Through an intermediary (the controller)
2. Administrative Vice President	4	Engineering	48	Through an intermediary (a clerk)
3. Manager of Operations	7	Mathematics	37	Through an intermediary (a clerk)
4. Controller	7	Accounting	32	"Hands-on"

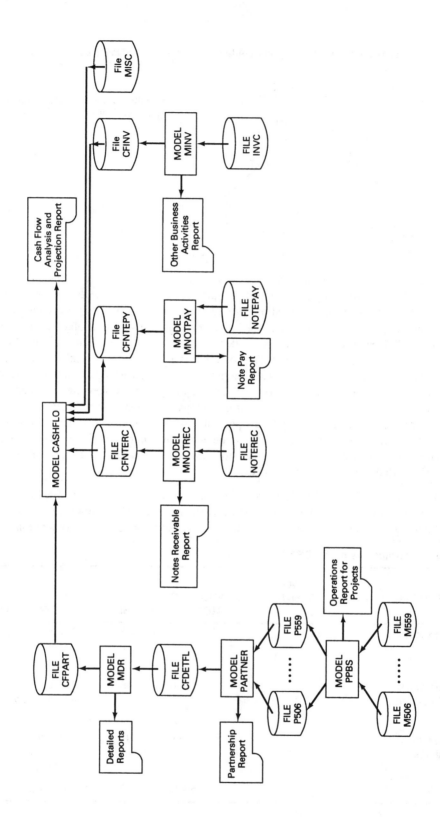

FIGURE 5.2 The DSS: Corporate Cash Flow System

the early stages of the project, the builder also acted as an intermediary to the CEO and the controller.

THE DSS: THE CORPORATE CASH FLOW SYSTEM.   The corporate cash flow system consists of seven models and a set of datafiles, as illustrated in Figure 5.2. The DSS was developed using the IFPS modeling language and is processed on the Control Data Corporation (CDC) Cybernet timesharing system.

Model PPBS (Project Planning and Budgeting System) is used to project the cash flow operations for each real estate project. The datafiles for the model are prepared by the vice president of administration and the manager of operations. An intermediary, in this case a secretary, inputs the various datafiles and processes the Model PPBS using these files. Model Partner is processed for each property and a partnership report is printed.The datafiles for Model Partner are prepared by the controller. This requires the controller to obtain information from various operations personnel. After the datafiles are prepared, an intermediary, the controller's secretary, enters the data and processes Model Partner using the datafiles. The Model for Detailed Reports (MDR) generates detailed management reports and schedules for sources and uses of cash. The data for Model MDR is generated automatically by Model Partner. This model also generates the datafile CFPART, which is an input to the corporate cash flow model. Model Notes Receivable (MNOTREC) generates a note receivable report and a datafile (CFNTREC) of the totals by month for notes receivable. The input file to Model MNOTREC is the datafile NOTEREC. This input file is prepared by the accounting department and contains payment amounts for the notes receivable accounts. The controller's secretary enters this data and processes Model MNOTREC. The Model MNOTPAY generates a notes payable report. The accounting department prepares datafile (NOTEPAY), containing relevant payments to other organizations and individuals. The totals by month for notes payable are stored in file CFNTEPY which is used as input for the Corporate Cash flow model. The controller's secretary enters this data and processes Model NOTEPAY. Model Investment (MINV) produces a detailed report for other company financial activities. Totals by month for projected sales and projected costs and expenses are stored on datafile CFINV. The input file to Model MINV is datafile INVC which contains the projected revenues and expenses for the relevant business interests. The datafile is prepared by the accounting department. Again, the secretary of the controller acts as an intermediary by entering the datafile and processing Model MINV.

The Model Cash Flow (CASHFLO) provides a projection of cash flow and a report on sources and applications of cash. The cash flow model is developed with input files generated by the other 6 models contained in the system. In addition to these input files, the datafile MISC provides other necessary input to the cash flow model. The controller prepares and inputs the datafile MISC, and processes Model CASHFLO.

It should be noted that as the various models and datafiles were initially being developed, the DSS builder and user (the controller) did most of the data entry and all the model processing. After the system was well defined and procedures developed, more intermediaries were used by the controller. Furthermore, after each of the various key processing steps occurred (completion of Model PPBS for all projects, processing of Model Partner for all projects, etc.) the controller and personnel responsible for various operations reviewed the reports and data to make sure it was correct before going to the next step in processing the system.

The cash flow system is processed monthly. Additional cash flow reports are run, as necessary, to facilitate decision making using various parameters. These additional reports are processed using the "what-if" capability of IFPS. This decision support system evolved in an iterative fashion over a period of 2 1/2 months.

Application of Adaptive Design Approach

Prior to development and implementation of the DSS, cash flow analysis and projections were performed manually. The process was time consuming, error prone, and did not provide opportunities for sensitivity analysis. The DSS development process was initiated by the CEO, who approached the builder and expressed the need for improving the effectiveness and timeliness of the cash flow projections. During an informal session with the builder that lasted about one hour, the CEO briefly described the dynamics of real estate financing, the characteristics of his business and his perceived need for timely, accurate information and the ability to perform sensitivity analysis.

Based on the chief executive officer's basic requirements, the builder developed a simple cash flow projection model. This model served two primary purposes:

- It demonstrated the potential for decision support and the essential features of a DSS.
- It enhanced the builder's understanding of the user's business and the environment.

Through the use of the simple cash flow model, with the builder acting as the intermediary, the chief executive officer quickly learned about the possible capabilities and features of the system. For example, the IFPS "What-If" and "Goal Seeking" commands were demonstrated by making various changes in model assumptions and parameters. After trying the initial system and entering some "What-If" commands, the chief executive officer perceived that a DSS could be built to assist in the projection and analysis of cash flow for his organization. The builder was then asked to develop and implement a cash flow system for the firm.

First Iteration   After the decision to build the cash flow system was made, but prior to initiating the development process, a 3-hour seminar providing an overview of financial planning and IFPS capabilities was conducted by the builder.

At the outset of the development process, the controller was somewhat hesitant about the attainment of the potential benefits and capabilities of the system. She also thought that the use of such a system might require more work than the manual system. To overcome this hesitancy, during the initial stage of the development process, the builder also assumed the role of educator. Specific examples of the potential capabilities and features of the system were provided to illustrate time savings and sensitivity analysis. The controller assumed a proactive role during the design process by providing information and input about the financial operations of the firm and the desired features of the system. Through this collaborative effort, with the builder providing the modeling expertise and the user (controller) providing the business expertise, the first version of the corporate cash flow system was created. The first version consisted of the following components:

1. The model CASHFLO, which generated the summary cash flow reports and projections for the CEO.
2. Models MNOTREC, MNOTPAY, MINV, and PARTNER and the associated datafiles.

The CEO was closely involved in the development of the first version of the cash flow system by monitoring the progress of the development effort and evaluating the system outputs. The first iteration of the cash flow model required 49 hours of the DSS builder's time, 25 hours of the controller's time and 10 hours of the chief executive officer's time. The first iteration of the system was completed in one month of elapsed time.

Second Iteration   All the users (the chief executive officer, the controller, the vice president of administration and manager of operations) actively participated in the second iteration of the system. This phase involved the development of Model PPBS and creation of the input files which contained detailed operational and financial data on individual properties. The level of effort spent in this phase was 31.5 hours of the DSS builder's time, 15 hours each of the vice president and the manager's time and 10 hours of the controller's time. The CEO spent 5 hours during the second iteration.

The CEO's role at this time involved monitoring the project activities and progress. The controller, vice president of administration, and manager of operations assisted in defining the output reports and the processing logic. They also developed the necessary input datafiles.

Third Iteration   At the completion of the second iteration, the functional requirements were all satisfied. However, operational use of the system indicated that the approach taken in the creation of the detailed reports (using model MDR) needed modification and refinement. A single model with a large matrix size was used to create the detail reports. If some of the detail reports had to be regenerated due to an error, the large model had to be reprocessed and all the detail reports regenerated. This was highly inefficient in terms of user time and computing resources. Hence, in the third iteration, the single large model was replaced by a set of 12 models that collectively generated the detailed report datafiles. These smaller models were more efficient. Furthermore, if one report had to be regenerated, only one small model had to be processed. "Command" files which automated the processing of the various processing segments were also developed to enhance the operation of the DSS.

The third iteration phase of the system was concluded by documenting the system and the operational procedures. The level of the effort spent at this iteration consisted of 60 hours of the builder's time and 20 hours of the controller's time.

Case Summary

The case involved the actual design and implementation of a decision support system for cash flow projections and analysis. The user group consisted of four decision makers: the CEO, the controller, the vice president of administration, and the manager of operations.

The design process can be best characterized as an iterative cycling between the DSS generator (IFPS) and the specific corporate cash flow system. With each cycle, the cash flow system was enhanced and new components were added. In each iteration, the typical systems development steps (analysis, design, construction and implementation) were united.

The user group was closely involved in the process of development and implementation. The total level of user effort was 90 person-hours. The cash flow system has been in operation for the past 1 1/2 years. The system is operated solely by the users and is under their control.

The users are satisfied with the system and perceive it as a valuable and beneficial tool for use in cash flow decisions. Their perceived benefits of the system include: obtaining better control over the operations; ability to respond to environmental changes (e.g., in the interest rates) in a timely manner; and increased capability for decision analysis.

OBSERVATIONS ON THE CASE STUDY

During the development of the corporate cash flow decision support system, the following observations were made on the effectiveness and requirements of the adaptive design approach.

1. The adaptive design approach requires a high level of user participation and involvement. In this project, the users spent 90 person-hours in the development process compared to 140.5 person-hours spent by the builder. User involvement and cooperation seem to be a necessary condition for effective application of the approach. Hence, it may not be applicable to those design situations in which the user is unable or unwilling to participate actively in the design process.

2. During the early stages of the development process, there was rapid progress toward defining the user requirements and developing DSS capabilities to meet them. There were cycles of discussion, development, review of the output, and further development. Such rapid progress resulted in positive user attitudes. Furthermore, providing quick and tangible output in early stages established credibility for the DSS builder and helped in obtaining user cooperation.

3. Availability of a program generator and interactive computing resource were critical factors in the application of the approach. Capabilities provided by IFPS (self- documentation, ease of coding and making changes, data storage and retrieval, report generation, etc.) allowed rapid response to requirements and the iterative and modular development process used to develop the cash flow system.

4. Except for a 3-hour introductory seminar on financial planning languages and IFPS conducted at the outset, no other formal user training programs were needed. The interactions among the user, builder, and system, and the proactive role of the users in the design process decreased the requirements for formal user training.

5. The perceived need and usefulness of the system seemed to be the incentive for its adoption. No attempts at an explicit and formal cost/benefit analysis were made. Perceived value was established at the outset by using and evaluating a prototype cash flow system.

SUMMARY

The adaptive design approach seems to be useful and effective for DSS development. However, further experimentation and evaluation are required before suggesting it is universally applicable. The following are some areas in which research or investigation must be conducted to increase understanding of the approach and its applicability:

1. What are the advantages and disadvantages of the adaptive design approach relative to others?
2. What contextual variables (e.g., organizational and task) seem to impact the process of adaptive design? What variables enhance or constrain its application?
3. What is the impact of the adaptive design approach on the user? Is there user-related psychological satisfaction or dissatisfaction derived from this approach?
4. What is the impact of the adaptive design approach on the DSS builder?
5. What training and skills are required of the builder for successful application of the approach?
6. What technological tools and resources are required?

Adaptive design may only be effective given certain contingencies: it may work well in one environment but not in another. However, preliminary findings from this case study suggest that the approach has high potential for developing effective decision support systems.

QUESTIONS

1. What is it about DSS applications that requires an adaptive rather than a traditional development approach?
2. Describe the activities of the organizational personnel who were involved in the development of the corporate cash flow system. Discuss how the organizational roles of manager, intermediary, DSS builder, technical supporter, and toolsmith were filled.
3. Discuss the three iterations in the development of the corporate cash flow system.

REFERENCES

1. ALAVI, M., AND J. C. HENDERSON "An Evolutionary Strategy for Implementing a Decision Support System," *Management Science,* 27, no. 11 (November 1981).
2. BALLY, L., J. BRITTAN, AND K. H. WAYNER "A Prototype Approach to Information System Design and Development," *Information & Management,* 1 (1977), 21–26.
3. BERRISFORD, T., AND J. C. WETHERBE "Heuristic Development: A Redesign of Systems Design," *MIS Quarterly,* March 1979, 11–19.
4. BOEING COMPUTER SERVICES c/o Mr. Park Thoreson, P.O. Box 24346, Seattle, Wash. 98124.
5. BOLAND, R. J., JR. "The Process and Product of System Design," *Management Science,* 24, no. 9 (1978), 887–98.

6. DICKSON, G. W., N. L. CHERVANY, AND J. A. SENN   "Research in Management Information Systems: The Minnesota Experiments," *Management Science,* 23, no. 9 (May 1977).

7. HAWGOOD, J., ED..   *Evolutionary Information Systems,* Proceedings of the IFIP TC 8 Working Conference on Evolutionary Information Systems, Budapest, Hungary, September 1-3, 1981 (Amsterdam: North Holland Publishing, 1982; ISBN: 0-444-86359-1).

8. IFPS USERS MANUAL, EXECUCOM SYSTEMS CORPORATION   P.O. Box 9758, Austin, Tex. 78766.

9. KEEN, P. G. W.   "Adaptive Design for DSS," *Database,* 12, nos. 1 and 2 (Fall 1980), 15–25.

10. KEEN, P. G. W.   "Value Analysis: Justifying Decision Support Systems," *MIS Quarterly,* March 1981, 1–15.

11. LIVARI, J.   "Taxonomy of the Experimental and Evolutionary Approaches to the Systemeering," in J. Hawgood, *Evolutionary Information Systems,* Proceedings of the IFIP TC 8 Working Conference on Evolutionary Information Systems, Budapest, Hungary, September 1-3, 1981 (Amsterdam: North Holland Publishing, 1982; ISBN 0-444-83539-1).

12. LUCAS, H. C.   "The Evolution of an Information System: From Key-Man to Every Person," *Sloan Management Review,* Winter 1978.

13. NAUMAN, J. G., AND M. A. JENKINS   "Prototyping: The New Paradigm for Systems Development," *MIS Quarterly,* 6, no. 3 (September 1982), 29–4.

14. SPRAGUE, R. H., JR.   "A Framework for the Development of Decision Support Systems," *MIS Quarterly,* December 1980, 1–26.

15. ZMUD, R. W.   "Individual Differences and MIS Success: A Review of the Empirical Literature," *Management Science,* 25, no. 10 (1979).

6

COMPUTER AIDED TRAIN DISPATCHING: DECISION SUPPORT THROUGH OPTIMIZATION

Richard L. Sauder,
William M. Westerman

A mini-computer based information system with on-line optimal route planning capability was developed to assist dispatchers on the complex northern portion of Southern Railway's Alabama Division. The routing plan is revised automatically as conditions change. Since implementation in September 1980, train delay has been more than 15 percent lower, reflecting annual savings of $316,000.

The dispatching support system is now being expanded to all other Southern Railway operating divisions with $3,000,000 annual savings expected from reduced train delay.

Southern Railway Company operating throughout the southeastern United States is one of the nation's largest railroads. For years it has been a leader in profitability in

Reprinted by permission of Richard L. Sauder and William M. Westerman, "Computer Aided Train Dispatching: Decision Support Through Optimization," *Interfaces,* Vol. 13, No. 6, December 1983. Copyright 1983 The Institute of Management Sciences.

the industry. In 1981 Southern's after tax profits totaled $212 million from revenues of $1.87 billion.

In June 1982, Southern Railway and the Norfolk and Western Railway merged to form the Norfolk Southern Corporation. The combined system provides efficient single system service throughout the South, East, and Midwest. The Norfolk Southern Corporation is now the nation's fifth largest and most profitable railway system. Had it existed in 1981, it would have produced revenue of $3.59 billion and realized profits of $500 million. Even in the 1982 recession year, after tax profits, on a pro forma basis, amounted to $411 million.

Southern Railway and the Norfolk and Western operate as autonomous organizations whose activities are coordinated at the holding company level. Each railroad is divided into two operating regions, and each region, headed by a general manager, contains five operating divisions.

Daily operations are controlled at the division headquarters level. Although movement of trains between divisions is coordinated through a centralized operations control center, the responsibility for the safe and efficient movement of trains over the division lies principally in the division dispatching office. Directly accountable to the division superintendent, the dispatching office is headed by an assistant superintendent, the "Super Chief"; reporting to him is a chief dispatcher and a staff of train dispatchers.

Dispatching trains is complex and demanding. In a typical eight hour shift, a train dispatcher will control the movement of 20 to 30 trains over territories spanning three to six hundred miles. In most cases, these trains operate over single tracks and opposing trains must meet at strategically placed passing sidings. The dispatcher arranges these "meets" with safety the paramount consideration. He also must safely coordinate movements of roadway maintenance gangs, signal maintenance crews, industrial switch engines, and motor car inspection crews.

The dispatcher is also in constant contact with yard personnel at freight terminals who report essential information regarding trains that will move over the division. Once trains reach their destinations, they report operating and delay statistics for the dispatcher to record. Federal law requires that the dispatcher maintain this "train sheet." Finally, the train dispatcher interacts and coordinates with other dispatchers, as well as the chief dispatcher, giving and taking information about the operation of his territory.

Southern Railway's Alabama Division (Figure 6.1) is a complex operating division. Headquartered at Birmingham, Alabama, its most heavily traveled routes extend from Atlanta through Birmingham to Sheffield, Alabama, near Memphis. It interfaces with other operating divisions at each of these locations. Other major routes extend from Birmingham south to Mobile and from Birmingham southeast to Columbus, Georgia. Altogether, mainline trackage exceeds 800 miles and 80 to 90 trains operate daily. The division employs more than 1,200 persons, mostly in train and engine service.

Two train dispatchers are on duty around the clock at the Birmingham headquarters. One controls the high density Birmingham-Sheffield corridor (the North Alabama District) and the line south to Mobile. The other controls the Birmingham-Atlanta route (the East End District) and the line into southwest Georgia.

Both the North Alabama and the East End Districts operate under Centralized Traffic Control (CTC). This provides a failsafe system of signals and switches in the field controlled

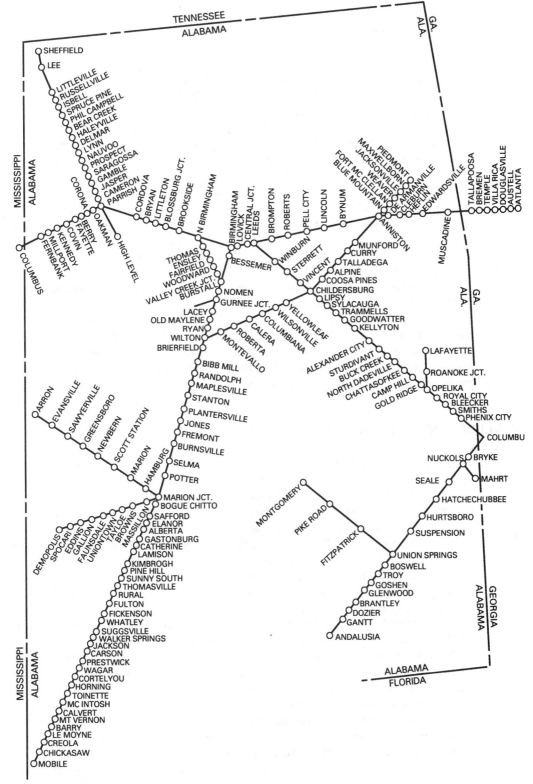

FIGURE 6.1 Southern Railway's Alabama Division

centrally by the dispatcher who monitors all field activity on an electronic display board. The other lines on the division have no signal control. In these "dark" territories, train movement is controlled solely by the dispatcher issuing stringent orders to train crews.

Until the mid-1970s, the operation of the Alabama Division was not overly complex; in fact, there was no centralized traffic control whatsoever. Then in 1974 with the opening of a large freight yard facility at Sheffield, merchandise traffic levels began to grow steadily, making the North Alabama District a major gateway to and from the Midwest. A coal loading facility near Sheffield was opened in 1977, further congesting the line. Unit trains (trains with up to seven locomotives and 96 loaded coal cars) began operating to key power plants in Georgia and Alabama. These trains operate on 40 hour "cycles," that is, moving loaded to their destination, unloading, and returning empty over the reverse route for reloading. Up to four such trains operate concurrently.

Management foresaw the need for centralized traffic control to assist dispatchers and began installation in 1976.

The research and development project to provide computer assistance for the dispatcher was in progress independently during this same period. As the CTC installation neared completion and as the R&D project began to show promise, it became clear that the Alabama Division was a logical location for determining how computer aided dispatching could further improve performance.

DEVELOPMENT OF THE SUPPORT SYSTEM

Southern Railway's operations research staff (which is now the Norfolk Southern Corporation's OR staff) has existed since the mid-1960s. Originally oriented toward computer model development, the operations research group by the early 1970s had become a corporate consulting staff providing *applications* support using tested analytical techniques, on one hand, and supporting *research and development* on the other.

The development staff began to investigate computer aid for the train dispatcher in 1975. Information systems for yard and terminal operations were already in place at many locations on the railroad. Extensions to this system requiring chief dispatchers to report realtime status of key trains were already envisioned. No other division-level systems were then being contemplated.

Concurrently, several signal manufacturers started selling turn-key systems to support CTC operations, providing features such as automatic "OS-ing (On Station reporting of the time a train passed a key location). Some systems permitted automated record keeping. One system even incorporated a rudimentary planning capability, tracing the routes of two opposing trains to determine when they would meet.

Operations research personnel reviewed a number of these systems and rejected them as being too inflexible. They saw the potential for automating the vast amount of division level information being manually recorded and for integrating this with other information systems. With extensive experience using simulation models to analyze line changes, they also foresaw the real possibility of on-line predictive planning aids for the dispatcher. They proposed that a computerized physical simulator be developed to explore these possibilities. Southern's top management computer usage committee approved the R&D project in late 1976.

The mini-computer based simulator, built and thoroughly tested over a three-year period, emulated a centralized-traffic-control- office environment and permitted designers and dispatchers alike to play and replay real-life scenarios, refining features that could eventually be installed in a division office. The simulator contained a bank of four color CRT's. Two displayed the track layout of the territory being studied. A simulation model was written to emulate movement of trains over the territory and it displayed movement of trains on the two track-layout CRT's based on route decisions interactively keyed by the "dispatcher."

A third CRT served as a work sheet for updating automated train-data files. A specially designed function keyboard permitted screen formats to be displayed which allowed dispatchers to update train sheets, reports of delay, locomotive failures, weather conditions, and many other records, all of which were then kept manually at division offices. The computerized system did not change what was being recorded; it merely changed the manner in which data was being recorded. A fourth CRT was reserved for displaying how trains should be routed—a capability which was being developed at the same time.

The potential for an on-line planning algorithm lay in considering all feasible future train meets throughout the territory and advising the dispatcher of that combination which would minimize total train delay. This "meet/pass plan," as it was labeled, had to account for all realistic operating conditions: travel times between sidings based on power and tonnage, speed limits, speed restrictions, train length compared with siding length, the ability of a train to start once stopped in a siding, train adherence to schedule, special cargo requiring special handling, work locations, and so forth. It also had to respond to dynamically changing conditions and display its latest recommended plan of action to the dispatcher in a manner he could readily comprehend.

The time-distance graph shown in Figure 6.2 is a standard method for displaying train meeting points and associated delay. Even in this simplified example involving five sidings and four eastbound and five westbound trains, there are thousands of meet combinations that could occur. The meet-pass plan was designed to reevaluate the combination at any time conditions changed and to display this new plan starting at the current time (8:30 am in the Figure 6.2 example) and projecting six to eight hours into the future.

Also incorporated was the ability for the dispatcher to override the plan by stating specific meet locations, by taking track out of service and by forcing trains in one direction to be stopped in sidings prior to the arrival of an opposing train. This permitted dispatcher experience and judgment to be reflected in the plan. It also formed the basis for a "what if" planning capability!

The first attempt to model the process evaluated feasible train routes with a decomposition approach incorporating a shortest path algorithm and a linear programming formulation. Although optimal solutions were obtainable, more often than not, convergence time was excessive and suboptimal solutions resulted. This method was subsequently replaced with a branch-and-bound technique enumerating all feasible meet locations and this approach did insure optimal results in a highly responsive fashion.

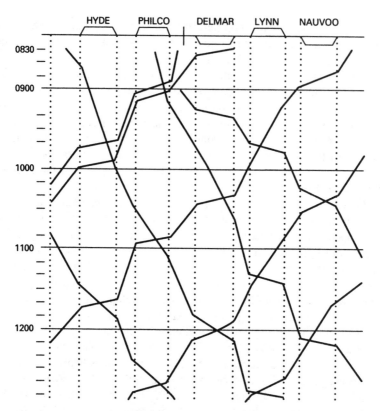

FIGURE 6.2   A time-distance graph displaying train movement through a five siding network in a four and one-half hour time frame. Four eastbound trains move diagonally from left to right meeting five westbound trains where the lines intersect.

The meet/pass plan was integrated into the simulator, and its use for on-line tactical planning was evaluated in detail. Possibly its most significant use was predicting the impact of the system operating in a real environment. During a periodic review of the project's status, the computer usage committee directed the operations research group to evaluate the potential of the system on the North Alabama District.

Operation was simulated both with and without computer-aided planning, and the impact on resulting train delay was measured. Train sheets for the North Alabama line were reviewed, and a typically heavy, yet normal, day of operation was selected. Train-meet delay for the first eight-hour shift on that day had amounted to 457 minutes. An Alabama Division dispatcher operated that same shift of operation in the simulator. The session began with train locations shown and information available concerning oncoming trains. The dispatcher worked the entire shift with no planning assistance, and the delay recorded at the conclusion of the session amounted to 455 minutes—a two minute difference.

The dispatcher then replayed the shift, this time following meets recommended by the plan. The resulting delay, 300 minutes, reflected a reduction of 34 percent.

Reductions in other scenarios subsequently simulated ranged from 22 to 38 percent. When the OR group presented these findings, the committee, perceiving that if even half of these benefits could be realized they would create a significant performance impact, immediately approved the project. The North Alabama pilot project was underway.

IMPLEMENTATION AND ITS IMPACT

Interfacing the mini-computers and the CTC system was the only significant task involved in converting from a simulated to an on-line environment. CRT's were added to the North Alabama dispatcher's work station to complement the CTC display board: two "work" CRT's were installed to provide flexibility and backup, and a third CRT was installed solely for meet/pass plan display.

Installation and parallel testing of the North Alabama system began in January 1980. On September 15, 1980, the system was placed in production and the dispatcher's manual train sheets were removed. Six weeks later, instructions were issued to dispatchers to utilize the computer-generated plan.

Earlier in 1980, groundwork had been laid for installing a second, independent system to support the East End Alabama Division dispatcher. In the meantime, Data General Corporation, the mini computer system manufacturer, announced an advanced operating system that would permit a *single* minicomputer, with additional internal memory, to support a large number of users and work stations simultaneously. The desirability of such a single system that could support two or more dispatchers and any others needing access to the system was evident.

Conversion of the system started in mid-1981, with East End operations added to the dispatching system in March 1982. A final system supporting all territories on the Alabama Division became a reality in September. What had begun as a system to support a single train dispatcher had now evolved into one supporting all division operations.

Auditing operating performance as the system gained acceptance and comparing it with prior performance experience was a vital step in measuring the impact of computer-aided dispatching. The improvement predicted in the simulator experiment now had to be verified. For two full years since implementation, performance statistics have been compiled daily reflecting the total numbers of trains operating, train meets, and the total delay caused by these meets. Reviewing manual train sheets for a full year of operation starting in September 1979 provided similar data for pre-implementation comparison.

Forty weeks of operations in each of these periods were then selected for a comparison study (a choice made necessary to compensate for a ten-week coal strike in 1981). Corresponding weeks were used for the year before implementation (the base period) and the year after. In the second year of operation, the first 40 contiguous weeks, beginning September 15, 1981, were used, thereby eliminating from consideration a period when business took a sharp downturn during the latter half of 1982.

Stringent guidelines were developed for analyzing delay reports to insure consistent measurement across periods:

1. Only delay within the limits controlled by the dispatcher was included.
2. Only delay that the dispatcher's planning would influence was considered.

TABLE 6.1   North Alabama District Operating Statistics for the Three- Year Period Starting September 15, 1979

	PERIOD A	PERIOD B	PERIOD C
	Year Prior to Implementation	First Year since Implementation	Second Year since Implementation
Average Weekly Meet Delay (Minutes)	8893	8290 (−6.8%)	6645 (−25.3%)
Trains Operated (Weekly)	147.4	156.9 (+8.5%)	147.7 (+0.2%)
Train Meets (Weekly)	245.9	262.1 (+6.6%)	226.3 (+8.0%)
Meets Per Train Operated	1.67	1.67	1.53
Delay Per Train (Minutes)	60.3	52.8 (−12.4%)	45.0 (−25.4%)
Delay Per Meet (Minutes)	36.2	31.6 (−12.7%)	29.4 (−18.8%)

3. Days reflecting highly abnormal operation, such as during a derailment, were excluded and replaced with an average for the same day in the four previous weeks. The operating statistics for the three measured periods are summarized in Table 6.1.

By comparing the first year of implementation with the previous year, traffic increased nearly nine percent, yet delay per train operated and delay per meet were down more than twelve percent. Traffic in the second year of operation returned to pre- implementation levels. The average number of trains operating weekly is nearly identical in the two periods, yet delay is more than 25 percent less in the 1981–1982 period.

Of the two measures, delay/train and delay/meet, the latter is more meaningful because division personnel have some control in scheduling trains to avoid meets but have little control over the numbers of trains operating. This ability to plan and control meets is evident in the figures for the second year of operation when delay per meet was reduced 18.8 percent. Overall, combining the 80 weeks of measured operation since computer-aided dispatching was placed on line, delay per meet has improved 15.5 percent. In addition, as Figure 6.3 shows, the operation is more consistent. In the year prior to implementation delay per meet ranged from 31.0 to 44.4 minutes. In the first year after implementation, it ranged from 26.6 to 40.2 and in the second, from 26.2 to 33.7 minutes.

Optimal planning together with information availability has improved performance significantly, and the resulting operation is a more consistent one. Several of the reasons are:

1. *A cleaner, neater, more professional operation.* Information is mechanically and electronically recorded, replacing hand-scrawled and often altered massive documents.

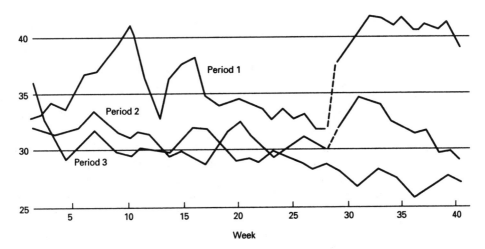

FIGURE 6.3   Minutes of Delay per Meet, a Three-Week Moving Average

2. *A readily accessible information base.* Information recorded by the dispatcher is readily available and functional in inquiry form to all division personnel. Train information can also be transferred from one dispatcher's territory to another, reducing manual recording.

3. *An optimal plan clearly reflecting management policy.* The meet/pass plan considers management directives regarding key priorities for dispatching trains. The continually updated nature of the plan ensures compliance with this policy under dynamic conditions.

4. *An equitable attitude toward dispatcher responsibility and action.* As should be expected, dispatchers are severely criticized for delays caused by poor planning or inattention, for example if a high-priority train is delayed because a low-priority opposing train blocks its movement. A common dispatching solution had been to clear the low-priority train into a siding far in advance to minimize possibility of delaying the hot train. Computer aided dispatching has virtually eliminated this waste. Dispatchers are encouraged to use the plan and are not hauled on the carpet if they follow it, even should a delay occur.

In addition to freeing the dispatcher from complex, diversionary, time-consuming calculations and risks, this computerized system has ancillary benefits. For instance, train crews now make their runs in consistently less time, giving them more time at home and substantially improving morale. By the same token, locomotive fuel and equipment requirements are cut, thereby effecting a measurable reduction in mechanical costs.

Reduction in train delay translates directly to cost savings. One hour of train operation equates to more than $240 using a formula which considers fuel consumption, crew costs, locomotive availability and utilization, freight car ownership costs, revenue producing potential, and a variety of other factors. The more than 15 percent reduction in delay experienced in the 80 measured weeks of performance directly reflects savings of $316,000 in each of the first two years of operation.

What are the anticipated division wide savings now that the system does in fact support all operating districts on the division? It is reasonable to expect similar percentage savings on the East End CTC line between Atlanta and Birmingham. On the non-CTC portion of the division, some lesser improvement will occur from better planning and train scheduling. On this basis, future savings for the Alabama Division, when traffic returns to pre-1982 levels, are estimated at $675,000 annually. In addition, a proposed new passing siding on the North Alabama line, at a cost of $1,500,000, has been postponed indefinitely as a direct result of the greater dispatching efficiency.

Another monetary saving which cannot be easily quantified is additional track time for various types of maintenance crews. The dispatcher can now more quickly and efficiently allocate working time, because he can adjust the locations of train delays to accommodate these crews. Using the meet/pass plan's "what-if" capability, he can determine the best times to allocate, maximizing on-track working time yet minimizing train delay.

BEYOND THE BASIC SYSTEM

On the same basis that expected division wide savings were estimated for the Alabama Division, implementation of the computer-aided dispatching system on all Southern Railway divisions will produce cost savings of $3,000,000 annually in train delay reduction alone.

On September 27, 1982, a memo sent to the Executive Vice President for Administration, Norfolk Southern, from the President of the Southern Railway read in part:

> I am very much interested in extending this system to other divisions. I feel the results on the Alabama Division have been even better than we anticipated, and I believe we should move now to the north end of the Georgia Division between Chattanooga and Atlanta...

Computer hardware to support the Georgia Division operation was delivered in the last week of December. Starting in early January, operations research analysts, working with Georgia Division personnel, "defined" the division, using interactive file definition programs. On January 27, the Georgia Division support system was put on-line to begin dispatcher training and no computer program changes were required to transfer the existing Alabama Division support system to the Georgia Division.

Training continued through February, and on March 18 manual train sheets for the north end of the Georgia Division, Atlanta to Chattanooga, were removed. The total conversion effort required less than six operations-research man weeks, and less than three Georgia Division man weeks, including system support and training.

Systems for three additional Southern Railway divisions are budgeted for the remainder of 1983. In January of 1983, the President of Southern Railway convened a task force representing transportation, engineering, operations research, and data processing to produce an implementation plan that considers real installation costs matched against previously derived benefits. At the present time, it is expected that total installation cost at each division, except for one that requires new building facilities, will be less than $300,000.

The system described to this point is in operation and results have been demonstrated. The need for some new features became evident in working with the implemented system and they will be implemented soon.

First is formal planning assistance for the chief dispatcher. Improved efficiency in his duties has already been achieved through the information processing capabilities of the system. The meet/pass plans now used by the train dispatchers are tactical plans that consider trains now on the territory and trains whose arrival is imminent. In a new approach, appropriately dubbed "SUPERPLAN," the individual meet/pass plans for each dispatching territory will provide input to a division-wide planning process and allow the chief dispatcher to adjust train schedules and work assignments to avoid unnecessary train meets and traffic congestion.

A second innovation provides information transfer among division offices. This step ties together each of the divisions through Southern Railway's central computer complex in Atlanta. This feature, first of all, eases the chief dispatcher's clerical effort in reporting key train movements. More important, it provides the basis for "SUPERPLAN-II"—optimal planning among divisions. The ultimate capability, now a potential reality, is vastly improved planning among divisions, at the general manager level and at the system control and coordination level. What was once a blue-sky dream of optimizing system-wide operation is now within reach because the basic building block, the division-level computer-aided dispatching system, works!

SUMMARY

Today the working computer-aided dispatching system continues to demonstrate significant dollar impact. Direction to expand the application to other territories testifies to the faith management has in the future benefits of the system. From a management scientist's viewpoint, the dispatching system is a marriage of information processing and management science. It is a distributed system and a decision support system. Proven management science optimization techniques form the basis of the system which around the clock provides dispatchers and managers alike the real time key to improving productivity and expanding profitability.

QUESTIONS

1. Describe the responsibilities of a train dispatcher.
2. Describe the development approach for the train- dispatching DSS at Southern Railway.
3. Does Southern Railway's train-dispatching DSS support or automate decision making? Discuss.
4. Discuss the benefits that have resulted from the implementation of Southern Railway's train-dispatching DSS.

PART 3

The Architecture for DSS

Even though decision support systems can differ significantly, there are similarities. There is a software interface through which the user directs the actions and receives the output from the DSS. This is frequently referred to as the dialog between the user and the system. Then there is the database component which serves such functions as providing information in response to queries from the user; supplying data for the building, updating, and running of models; and storing intermediate and final results from analyses that are made. And finally there is the model base component. This component includes permanent models as well as modeling capabilities for building and updating models.

The software interface, database, and model base can be thought of as the architecture for a DSS. This part of the book provides one or more readings for each of these three components.

The first selection (Reading 7), by the editors of this book, deals with the data-dialog-modeling components of the DSS architecture in more detail. Each of the three architectural components provides capabilities and functions beyond that which is first apparent. The dialog component can be broken down into what the user can do (action language), must know (knowledge base), and can see (presentation language). Specific combinations of attributes for each of these functions form a "dialog style" that specifies how the system and the user interact. The data component must deal not just with traditional data, but a full range of information resources. And the modeling component goes beyond traditional models to incorporate advanced techniques from the field of artificial intelligence. Subsequent readings in this part of the book explore these richer aspects of the architectural components of DSS in additional depth.

Decision support systems can be categorized as being ad hoc or institutional, depending on a number of characteristics, including whether they are used infrequently or on a repetitive basis. Carleen Garnto and Hugh Watson, in "An Investigation of Database Requirements for Institutional and Ad Hoc DSS" (Reading 8), describe the database component of two institutional and ad hoc DSS and suggest database differences that seem to exist between these two types of decision support systems. An understanding of these differences can facilitate the design of a DSS database.

An important new aspect of the database/data management component is the growing use of document data. It is easy to see how the data and information contained in documents, reports, memos, and even phone messages can be an extremely important resource for DSS. New technologies are now evolving that will make it possible to manage this data resource better, as explained by Jane Fedorowicz in Reading 9.

The final selection in this part was prepared especially for this book by David King, Director of Artificial Intelligence Research for Comshare (Reading 10). It provides a look at the important developments in the field of AI and the impact they are likely to have in the future on DSS. These impacts will be significant both in the modeling and the dialog components of the DSS architecture.

7

THE COMPONENTS
OF AN ARCHITECTURE
FOR *DSS*

Hugh J. Watson,
Ralph H. Sprague, Jr.

INTRODUCTION

A useful way of thinking about the component parts of a decision support system (DSS) and the relationships among the parts is to use the dialog, data, and models (D,D,M) paradigm [7, 8]. In this conceptualization, there is the *dialog* (D) between the user and the system, the *data* (D) that support the system, and the *models* (M) that provide the analysis capabilities. While the components differ somewhat from application to application, they always exist in some form. Figure 7.1, adapted from [7], provides a pictorial representation of the component parts of a DSS.

For users and DSS builders, it is important to understand how each component can be designed. For users, it creates an awareness of what can be requested in a DSS. For DSS builders, it suggests what can be delivered.

This reading was written especially for this book, and revised in 1992 for the third edition.

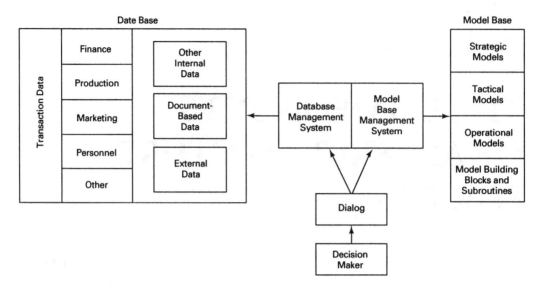

FIGURE 7.1   The Components of a DSS

New technology continues to affect the dialog, data, and models components. For example, icon-based, touchscreen systems provide new options for directing the system. Relational database technology, and more recently object oriented databases, are influencing how data are stored, updated, and retrieved. Drawing from artificial intelligence advances, there is the potential for representing and using models in new ways.

Our purpose in this reading is to explore the component parts of a DSS. We will attempt to describe the richness of what is currently possible, and suggest emerging technologies that will continue to expand this domain.

THE DIALOG COMPONENT

An appreciation of the importance of the dialog component is gained by recognizing that from the user's perspective, the dialog is the system. What the user has to *know in order to use the system,* the options for *directing the system's actions,* and the alternative *presentations of the system's responses* are what is important. Bennett [1] refers to these dialog components as the *knowledge base,* the *action language,* and the *presentation language,* respectively. Unless they affect the dialog, the user typically has little interest in such considerations as the hardware and software used, how data are stored in memory, and the algorithms employed by the models. Such factors are often transparent to the user; that is, they are neither seen nor recognized.

General Considerations

When designing the DSS dialog, it is important to recognize who the potential users are. In some instances, there is a single user; more typically, the DSS has multiple users [4]. While much of the writing on DSS emphasizes its usefulness for supporting the poorly structured decision-making tasks of top management [7], the reality is that middle management and especially professional staff (e.g., financial planners, marketing researchers) are the hands-on users of DSS [4]. This does not mean that DSS is not used by top management. Rather, what often happens is that senior executives request information from a staff assistant who uses a DSS to obtain the information. Operating this way, the assistant is an extension of the DSS. As will be seen, this arrangement has important implications for dialog design.

It should be recognized that a dialog involves *simplicity* versus *flexibility* trade-offs. Dialogs that are simple to use typically offer less flexibility. For example, the old *question-answer* approach requires the user to respond to questions. While this approach is simple and is often appropriate for novice users performing well-structured tasks, it does not provide flexibility beyond what was planned by the system's designers. In this situation, the system is largely in control. *Menu*-oriented systems impose the same kind of structure on the user even though they provide a different dialog approach. By way of contrast, *command languages* place the user more in control but require additional knowledge to use the system. Command languages normally employ a verb-noun syntax (e.g., RUN SIMULATION, PRINT REPORT). Most DSS generators use variations of the command language approach. While DSS generators simplify the development and operation of a DSS, they require training and a frequency of use sufficient to remember their syntax. It is for these reasons that most top managers are not hands-on DSS users. They are unwilling or unable to take the time to be trained properly and have job responsibilities that do not allow frequent use.

When a DSS supports several uses, multiple dialog options can be designed for the system. This is sometimes referred to as a *tiered* dialog approach because there are several levels of dialog options. Novice users can employ the system in one way and more experienced ones can use it in another way. The availability of multiple dialog options also supports differences in cognitive style among users. A person's *cognitive style* refers to the systematic and pervasive way that data are perceived and analyzed. For example, a *systematic* person processes data in a structured, step-by-step process, whereas an *intuitive* person may jump from one analysis process to another. A systematic person may feel comfortable with a menu-oriented dialog, but an intuitive person may want the flexibility offered by a command language.

Another dialog consideration is whether the DSS will be operated by the decision maker or an intermediary (sometimes called the *chauffeur*). With chauffeur-driven systems, the emphasis can be on the power and flexibility of the dialog. Ease-of-use features that might be critical to nonspecialists can be omitted, resulting in systems with less software "overhead."

The Knowledge Base

The knowledge base includes what the user knows about the decision and about how to use the DSS. Note that this is not the definition of *knowledge base* that is prevalent in the field of artificial intelligence. It is, rather, Bennett's term to represent what knowledge the user must bring to the system in order to interact with it in dealing with the problem area or making the necessary decisions.

The user's knowledge of the problem is largely learned external to the DSS. The DSS allows the user to understand better the decision, but much about the problem must already be known. A notable exception is when a DSS is used to train new decision makers. In this case, the DSS is an educational vehicle.

Users can be trained in the use of a DSS in multiple ways [8]. The *one-on-one tutorial* is commonly employed with senior executives. *Classes* and *lectures* are efficient when many users require training. *Programmed* and *computer-aided instruction* are economical approaches when the DSS is expected to have a long life span and serve many users. A *resident expert* can respond to specific requests for help.

The DSS can include features that make it easier to use. Instruction manuals can be made available online. Any time during a session, a user can receive help by pressing a single key. The help can be made *context sensitive;* that is, depending on where the decision maker is in the use of the DSS, the system provides help that is customized for the situation.

Command or *sequence files* are useful to novice or infrequent users. These files contain preprogrammed instructions that are activated by a few simple keystrokes. Consequently, a user does not have to know any of the underlying commands, only how to execute the command file. As an example of a command file, at the end of each month, a senior manager may want to compare projected versus actual cash flow. Such an analysis is common with many financial DSS but often requires the user to enter a series of commands. In order to make it easy for the manager to obtain the analysis, the required commands might be put into a command file.

Comprehensive DSS generators usually support the creation and use of command files. Some have a "capture" feature, which functions by recording and saving all commands entered. The user issues a command to evoke the capture feature, enters the commands to be saved, and provides an appropriate filename.

The Action Language

The actions that the user can take to control the DSS can be described in a variety of ways, depending on the system's design. Question-answer, menu-oriented, and command language approaches have already been discussed. Other options exist, and additional attractive alternatives continue to appear.

Some DSS use an input-output form approach. The user is provided an input form and enters the required data. After all the data are input, the DSS performs the analysis and presents the results.

The visual-oriented interfaces developed originally by Xerox, and later adapted by Apple for the Macintosh are growing in popularity. These interfaces use "icons," or pictorial symbols to represent familiar objects, such as a document, file folder, outbasket, or trash bin. The action language is usually implemented by using a mouse to move icons or to perform actions on them by selecting choices from a menu.

Voice input is the ultimate in ease of use. While important advances in voice input are being made, currently it is not a popular option for DSS. Existing technology supports only a limited vocabulary, must be typically calibrated to the user's voice, and offers discrete rather than continuous speech recognition. These limitations tend to make voice input only appropriate for individual DSS that are used in a highly structured manner. As the technology improves, however, more voice-oriented systems can be expected.

The physical actions required to direct a DSS have also undergone change. Keyboard input is no longer the only choice. Touchscreen and especially mouse-driven systems are common. These are attractive alternatives for executives who do not want to type.

The Presentation Language

The PC used on a stand-alone basis or as an intelligent terminal connected to a mainframe has significantly expanded and enhanced how output from a DSS is presented. Printed reports are no longer the only output option. In fact, in many instances there is no hard copy output. Instead, the output is presented on the screen, internalized by the decision maker, and discarded. The DSS can be rerun if the user needs to see the output again.

One of the greatest contributions of the PC is its superior *graphics* capabilities. Used with graphics software, a variety of graphs, in three dimensions and in color, are easily created. The current research on chip technology promises to improve graphics quality even more, providing nearly perfect resolution. Even though research has not clearly established the superiority of graphics over tabular output [5], its popularity speaks for its perceived usefulness.

Animation is beginning to be used for DSS output, especially for applications that involve the simulation of physical systems. A research group at Delft University of Technology, for example, has developed several DSS projects using automation. One shows the flow of trucks, goods, and the required paperwork for a shipping and loading application at the Port of Rotterdam. Watching the trucks and ships move on the screen while the documents are processed in the offices gives the decision maker a sense of the dynamics of the problem that would not be possible without the animation. See for example, reference [6].

Voice output is also a possibility, even though it is not currently being used for DSS. As an example of its potential, consider a financial DSS where not only exception reports are provided, but a voice overlay describes or explains the exceptions.

Dialog Styles

Combinations or sets of options for implementing the knowledge base, the action language, and the presentation language, taken together, can be called a "dialog style." For example, one dialog style results in a system that requires users to keep a reference card (knowledge base) and to remember which commands to enter with a keyboard (action language) in order to obtain a printed report (presentation language). Quite another dialog style results from using a mouse to access pull-down menus and move icons on a color screen to get a graphical presentation of analysis results. The latter dialog style, popularized by the Apple Macintosh, revolutionized the dialog component in recent years. The explosive growth of Microsoft's Windows 3 for the PC/DOS environment, X-Windows for the Unix environment, and Globalview by Xerox for their Sun-based workstations have made this dialog style the dominant "standard" for end user computing.

Much of its popularity results from basing all the elements of the dialog around a familiar metaphor—the virtual desktop. The display screen represents a desktop, icons represent familiar objects on a desk (documents, file folders, etc.), and the mouse is used to move things around, open and close files and documents, and choose actions from the menu. The success of this dialog style suggests that most systems for DSS will eventually have a dialog component with a similar design.

THE DATA COMPONENT

Data play an important role in a DSS. Data are either accessed directly by the user or are an input to the models for processing. Care must be taken to ensure their availability.

Data Sources

As the importance of DSS has grown, it is becoming increasingly critical for the DSS to use all the important data sources within the organization, and from external sources also. Indeed, the concept of data sources must be expanded to *information sources—* moving beyond traditional access to database records, to include documents containing concepts, ideas, and opinions that are so important to decision making.

To characterize the full scope of information sources relevant to DSS, and to explore some of its ramifications, it is helpful to consider four types of information. First, there are two types of information generated and managed internally in the organization: (1) information based on data records such as is found in data files, and (2) document-based information such as reports, opinions, memos, and estimates.

The first type of internal information pertains primarily to entities, such as individual employees, customers, parts, or accounting codes. Well-structured data records are used to hold a set of attributes that describes each entity. The second category of information pertains primarily to *concepts*—ideas, thoughts, and opinions. Less-structured documents or messages, with a wide variety of information forms, are used to describe these.

The same two types of information are also generated externally to the organization. There is external record-based information, such as government data on economic and financial conditions, stock price quotations, and airline schedules. There is also external document-based information, such as opinions about economic forecasts or rumors. Figure 7.2 shows these four types of information in a simple matrix along with the information management activity that has characterized each in the past. Internal record-based information has been the focus of attention of information systems because that is the type of information computer-based application systems generate and manage easily. External record-based information has become more popular recently in the form of public databases; end users themselves have generally handled the procurement of this data, often using outside time-sharing services. Until recently, practically no attention has been given by DSS builders or vendors to document-based information, either internal or external, as an information resource for DSS. Those areas have been the responsibility of either the administrative vice president or the corporate library. Reading 9, later in this part of the book, discusses the increasing availability of document resources for DSS.

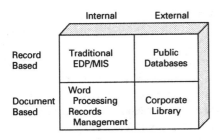

FIGURE 7.2   Four Types of Information

Few DSS need data at the transaction level. Summarized data are more typically required and can be obtained in several ways. One way is to have the database management system (DBMS) for the transaction processing system extract the transaction data, summarize them, and make the data available to the DSS. Another option is to extract the data but have the processing done external to the DBMS. While this is ideally a computerized process, some DSS rely on manual processing. This may be appropriate when the processing requires little effort or when the DSS is needed quickly and a more "elegant" solution cannot be implemented in a timely manner.

Some organizations only give end users access to *extract files*. These are files maintained externally to the DBMS and are created specifically to meet the data needs of end users. Extract files are used for security, ease of access, and data integrity reasons. In organizations with extract files, the DSS obtains data from these files.

The previous comments suggest that the database for a DSS may be separate from the transaction processing database, and, for several reasons, this indeed is the case in most organizations. The same line of thinking that leads to extract files also supports the idea of a separate DSS database. Many people believe that it is best to not intermix the rather different worlds of end-user and information systems computing. Also, most DBMS for handling transaction data (e.g., IBM's IMS, and later DB/2) were created for information systems specialists rather than end users and require considerable training. Also end users expect fast response times, and this may be a problem when they are competing with transaction processing applications for machine cycles. Because of the need for fast response times, organizations often dedicate a specific machine for end-user applications.

In addition to transaction data, *other internal data* may be needed. For example, subjective estimates from managers and engineering-related data may be needed. These kinds of data are seldom available from normal data processing activities. In order to have other internal data available, they must be collected, entered, and maintained. The collection effort may be difficult and time consuming because it requires a special initiative. If the data must be available on an ongoing basis, specific methods and procedures must be developed for keeping the data up to date. A good DBMS is required to support the entering, maintenance, and extraction of data.

External data may also be needed, especially for decision support at the upper managerial levels. Examples of external data include national and regional economic data, industry data, and competitive data. Like internal data, making external data available requires special efforts. Unlike internal data, external data may be purchased. For example, marketing data can be purchased from firms such as A. C. Nielson, Market

Research Corporation of America, and Brand Rating Index Corporation. The data are extracted from the commercial database, communicated to the user's organization, and entered into the organization's database.

Researchers and organizations are exploring how to include yet another type of data in a DSS: *document-based data.* Organizations have a wealth of data contained in documents such as memos, letters, contracts, and organization charts. If the contents of these documents can be electronically stored (e.g., videodisc) and then retrieved by key characteristics (e.g., topic, date, location), a powerful new source of information for decision support can be supplied to decision makers.

Vendor Contributions

Vendors are providing products with better database capabilities. At the PC level, products that make it easier to create, maintain, and use a database are very popular. Other products support downloading corporate data to the PC. Mainframe DSS generators have improved their database capabilities. Nearly all of the major vendors have "pipeline" software that extracts data from a DBMS, reformats the data, and places the data in the DSS generator's database. Two of the primary vendors of DSS software, Pilot and Comshare, have announced capabilities that allow their DSS to retrieve documents, based on the content as represented by the text, from E-mail messages and other document collections.

THE MODEL COMPONENT

Models provide the analysis capabilities for a DSS. Using a mathematical representation of the problem, algorithmic processes are employed to generate information to support decision making. For example, a linear programming model of a production blending problem might reveal the cheapest way to blend a product while meeting product specifications.

Types of Models

There are many different types of models and various ways that they can be categorized. Important distinctions can be made on the basis of their *purpose, treatment of randomness,* and *generality of application.*

The purpose of a model can be either optimization or description. An *optimization model* is one that seeks to identify points of maximization or minimization. For example, management often wants to know what actions will lead to a profit or a revenue maximization or a cost minimization. Optimization models provide this information. A *descriptive model* describes the behavior of a system. In a sense, any model is a descriptive model if it is a valid representation of reality. But a descriptive model *only* describes the system's behavior; it does not suggest optimizing conditions.

Regarding randomness, nearly all systems are probabilistic. That is, the behavior of the system cannot be predicted with certainty because a degree of randomness is present.

A *probabilistic model* attempts to capture the probabilistic nature of the system by requiring probabilistic data inputs and by generating probabilistic outputs. Even though most systems are probabilistic, most mathematical models are *deterministic*. *Deterministic models* employ single-valued estimates for the variables in the model and generate single-valued outputs. Deterministic models are more popular than probabilistic ones because they are less expensive, less difficult, and less time consuming to build and use, and they often provide satisfactory information to support decision making.

In terms of generality of application, a model can be developed for use with only one system (a *custom-built* model) or a model may be applicable to many systems (*ready-built* models). In general, custom-built models describe a particular system and, consequently, provide a better description than a ready-built model. However, they are generally more expensive for the organization, because they have to be built "from the ground up."

Model Base

The models in a DSS can be thought of as a *model base*. As Figure 7.1 shows, a variety of models can be included: strategic, tactical, and operational models and model-building blocks and subroutines. Each type of model has unique characteristics.

The *strategic models* are used by top management to help determine the objectives of the organization, the resources needed to accomplish those objectives, and the policies to govern the acquisition, use, and disposition of these resources. They might be used for company objectives planning, plant location selection, environmental impact planning, or similar types of applications. Strategic models tend to be broad in scope with many variables expressed in compressed, aggregated form. Much of the data required to fuel the models are external and subjective. The time horizons for the models are often measured in years, as are top management's strategic planning responsibilities. The models are usually deterministic, descriptive, and custom-built for the particular organization.

The *tactical models* are commonly employed by middle management to assist in allocating and controlling the use of the organization's resources. Applications include financial planning, worker requirements planning, sales promotion planning, and plant layout determination. The models are usually only applicable to a subset of the organization, like production, and there is some aggregation of variables. Their time horizon varies from one month to less than two years. Some subjective and external data are needed, but the greatest requirements are for internal data. The models tend to be deterministic, and in comparison to strategic models are more likely to provide optimality information and to be ready-built.

The *operational models* are usually employed to support the short-term decisions (e.g., daily, weekly) commonly found at lower organizational levels. Potential applications include credit scoring, media selection, production scheduling, and inventory control. Operational models normally use internal data in their operation. They are typically deterministic, often ready-built, and provide optimization information.

In addition to strategic, tactical, and operational models, the model base contains *model-building blocks and subroutines*. They might include linear programming, time-series analysis, regression analysis, and Monte Carlo sampling procedures. In form and size, these tools might range from a subroutine for calculating an internal rate of return to a packaged set of programs for exploring a generic class of problems (e.g., SAS for statistical analysis problems). The model-building blocks and subroutines can be used separately for ad hoc decision support, or together to construct and maintain more comprehensive models.

Problems with Traditional Modeling

From a historical perspective, organizations' experiences with models are mixed. While there are many successes, there are often many failures. With hindsight, it is possible to identify the problems that lead to failure:

- Difficulties in obtaining input data for the models.
- Difficulties in understanding how to apply the output from models.
- Difficulties in keeping the models up to date.
- Lack of confidence in the models by users; therefore, the models are not trusted.
- Little integration among models.
- Poor interaction between the models and users.
- Difficult for users to create their own models.
- The models' little explanation for their output.

The DSS Approach to Modeling

The DSS approach to modeling attempts to minimize the traditional modeling problems by emphasizing that a *system* (e.g., dialog, data, and models working together) to support decision making is required.

The database is important to solving many of the problems. It provides the data required to build, use, and maintain the models. The output from the models is placed in the database, thus making the output accessible to other models and providing integration among the models.

A well-designed dialog enhances the likelihood that users will be able to develop their own models, operate the system successfully, keep it up to date, and apply the output to decision-making tasks. These considerations, along with high levels of involvement during the system development process, lead to greater confidence in the models.

The models in a DSS are likely to be useful because they are adequately supported by the data and dialog components. An interesting new development in modeling is the inclusion of artificial intelligence capabilities through which the models explain the factors that led to the output. For example, it might be explained that a decrease in profits is due to the drop in market share in the western region.

The DSS approach to modeling requires a model base management system (MBMS) with capabilities analogous to a DBMS. The most important capabilities include:

- A flexible mechanism for building models.
- Ease of use of the models to obtain needed decision support.

- Methods for saving models that will be used again.
- Procedures for updating models.
- Methods for making output from a model available to other models as input.

Unlike a DBMS, a MBMS is not commercially available as a stand-alone product. Rather, it exists as a component capability of DSS generators. Consider, IFPS as an example. It has an English-like syntax with built-in functions that facilitate the building and updating of models (e.g., VALUE = INFLOWS – OUTFLOWS). Specifications for directing model execution are easily understood (e.g., SOLVE, MONTE CARLO). Models can be saved for future use (e.g., SAVE).

Considerable research is being conducted in MBMS. One stream of research focuses on applying and extending the relational model for DBMS to MBMS [2]. Another approach is to apply artificial intelligence concepts to model management [3]. Reading 10, later in this section, by Dave King, provides a good survey of the emerging technologies from the field of artificial intelligence, and their contribution to model management and other capabilities of DSS.

CONCLUSION

The dialog, data, and models paradigm provides a powerful conceptual model for understanding the components and relationships in a DSS. Each is critical if a DSS is to live up to its decision support potential. The D,D,M paradigm is useful in understanding and assessing the capabilities of DSS generators, and to some extent has influenced the evolution of these products. Current DSS research can also be understood in the context of the D,D,M model.

QUESTIONS

1. What is meant by "From the user's perspective, the dialog is the system"? Do you agree with this statement? Discuss.
2. What information sources may be required by a DSS? To what extent are the data machine-readable? Discuss.
3. Compare and contrast the traditional and DSS approaches to modeling.

REFERENCES

1. BENNETT, J. "User-Oriented Graphics, Systems for Support in Unstructured Tasks," in *User Oriented Design of Interactive Graphics Systems,* S. Treu (ed.). New York: Association for Computing Machinery, 1977.
2. BLANNING, ROBERT W. "A Relational Theory of Model Management," in *Decision Support Systems: Theory and Application,* Clyde W. Holsapple and Andrew Winston (eds.). Berlin: Springer-Verlag, 1987.
3. ELAM, JOYCE J., AND BENN KONSYNSKI "Using Artificial Intelligence Techniques to Enhance the Capabilities of Model Management Systems," *Decision Sciences* (Summer 1987), 487–502.

4. HOGUE, JACK T. "A Framework for the Examination of Management Involvement in Decision Support Systems," *Journal of Management Information Systems,* no. 1 (1987), 96–110. (Reprinted as Reading 3 in this book.)

5. JARVENPAA, SIRKA L., GARY W. DICKSON, AND GERARDINE DESANCTIS "Methodological Issues in Experimental IS Research: Experiences and Recommendations," *MIS Quarterly* (June 1985), 141–56.

6. SCHRIJVER, P. R., AND H. G. SOL "A Fleet Management System for Road Transportation," *Proceedings of the Second International Conference on Applications of Advanced Technologies in Transportation Engineering,* Minneapolis, 1991.

7. SPRAGUE, RALPH H. "A Framework for the Development of Decision Support Systems," *MIS Quarterly* (December 1980), 1–26.

8. SPRAGUE, RALPH H., AND ERIC D. CARLSON *Building Effective Decision Support Systems* (Englewood Cliffs, N.J.: Prentice Hall, 1982).

8

AN INVESTIGATION OF DATABASE REQUIREMENTS FOR INSTITUTIONAL AND AD HOC *DSS*

Carleen Garnto,
Hugh J. Watson

INTRODUCTION

A growing number of organizations have developed decision support systems (DSS). The applications include financial planning [19], portfolio management [6], marketing-mix decision making [13, 14], plant capacity planning [17], and joint venture analysis [12]. As one studies various DSS applications, it becomes clear that decision support systems can differ considerably. They can be used for operational control, management control, or strategic planning. They can vary in the structuredness of the decision-making task which they support. They can be used for one time or recurring decision making. Because of the variations which exist, one might expect to find differences in their component parts, including the database component.

The authors recently investigated four decision support systems developed for budgeting and resource allocation, train dispatching, pricing, and acquisition applications.

Carleen Garnto and Hugh J. Watson, "An Investigation of Data Base Requirements for Institutional and Ad Hoc DSS," *DATABASE,* Summer 1985.

Two of the DSS studied are used on a recurring basis while the other two were used for a one-time decision. Donovan and Madnick [4] refer to these as institutional and ad hoc DSS, respectively. The primary area of investigation was whether there are differences in the database component of the DSS based on the institutional and ad hoc distinction. This study suggests that there are differences with practical implications for DSS designers.

THE CONCEPTUAL FRAMEWORK

Gorry and Scott Morton [7] combined Anthony's [2] categories of managerial activity (that is, operational control, management control, and strategic planning) with Simon's [15] concepts of structured and unstructured decision making to provide a framework for viewing information systems. This framework has proven useful in understanding information requirements and the type of information system needed to support decision making. For example, information requirements vary with managerial activity. Keen and Scott Morton [11] identify accuracy, age of information, level of detail, time horizon, frequency of use, source, scope of information, and type of information as aspects of information requirements which vary with managerial activity. In another example, the type of information system needed that is, electronic data processing (EDP), management information system (MIS) or (DSS) is related to the structuredness of the decision-making task. While EDP and to a great extent MIS are recognized as useful for supporting structured decisions, DSS are appropriate for supporting semistructured and unstructured decision making. And as a final example, the type of information system needed is related to managerial activity. Most frequently, EDP best serves operational control, MIS is oriented to management control, and DSS supports strategic planning.

While Gorry and Scott Morton's framework suggests useful generalizations, there are many exceptions. Of particular interest to this study is that DSS can be used for operational control, management control, or strategic planning. This being the case, it follows that different types of DSS may be appropriate for various managerial activities. The work of Donovan and Madnick supports this contention. They suggest that DSS can be divided meaningfully into two categories: institutional DSS which deal with decisions of a recurring nature, and ad hoc DSS which deal with specific decisions which are not usually anticipated or recurring. The characteristics of each type of DSS are summarized in Table 8.1. Donovan and Madnick suggest that these characteristics of institutional and ad hoc DSS lead to the conclusion that institutional DSS are most appropriate for operational control applications, ad hoc DSS are most useful for strategic planning applications, and there is an area of overlap in regard to management control applications.

Keen and Scott Morton indicate that just as information requirements vary with managerial activity, so do data requirements. Because institutional and ad hoc DSS tend to be associated with different managerial activities, it might be expected that the database component would differ. While DSS database requirements have been considered in a variety of contexts, no research has been conducted on the specific database requirements for institutional and ad hoc DSS. Given that the institutional and ad hoc DSS dichotomy seems to be a useful way of looking at DSS, such research might potentially

TABLE 8.1   Comparison of Institutional and Ad Hoc Decision Support Systems

	INSTITUTIONAL DSS	Ad Hoc DSS
Number of decision occurrences for a decision type	many	few
Number of decision types	few	many
Number of people making decisions of same type	many	few
Range of decisions supported	narrow	wide
Range of users supported	narrow	wide
Range of issues addressed	narrow	wide
Specific data needed known in advance	usually	rarely
Problems are recurring	usually	rarely
Importance of operational efficiency	high	low
Duration of specific type of problem being addressed	long	short
Need for rapid development	low	high

SOURCE: J. Donovan and S. Madnick, "Institutional and Ad Hoc DSS and Their Effective Use," *DATABASE*, 8, no. 3 (Winter 1977), 82.

provide helpful guidelines for DSS database design. Sprague and Carlson [16] have developed a list of general requirements common to DSS databases which is presented in Table 8.2. It is used in this study as a basis for exploring the database requirements for institutional and ad hoc DSS.

TABLE 8.2   General Requirements for DSS Databases

■ Support for Memories	■ Varying Degrees of Accuracy
■ Data Reduction	■ Set Operations
■ Varying Levels of Detail	■ Random Access
■ Varying Amounts of Data	■ Support for Relationships and Views
■ Multiple Sources	■ Performance
■ Catalog of Sources	■ Interface to Other DSS Components
■ Wide Time Frame	■ End-User Interface
■ Public and Private Data Bases	

SOURCE: Ralph H. Sprague, Jr., and Eric D. Carlson, *Building Effective Decision Support Systems* (Englewood Cliffs, N.J.: Prentice Hall, 1982).

THE STUDY METHOD

Purpose

The purpose of this study was to gather and analyze data about the database component of institutional and ad hoc DSS based on the general requirements proposed by Sprague and Carlson. This information is used to suggest generalizations about database requirements for institutional and ad hoc DSS. The findings should prove helpful to interested researchers and to those considering the development of decision support systems.

Research Methodology

The research method selected for this study was the field study. A structured interview was conducted with a knowledgeable individual in the company about a specific application of an institutional or ad hoc DSS in order to gain information related to each of the database requirements identified by Sprague and Carlson.

Sample Selection

Four companies in Atlanta, Georgia, who are developing and using DSS participated in the study. The criteria for including a specific DSS in the study was the same as that used by Hogue and Watson [9] in their study of management's role in the approval and administration of DSS. Each of the four companies had developed a DSS which met the following essential criteria:

- Supports but does not replace decision making.
- Directed toward semistructured and/or unstructured decision-making tasks.
- Data and models organized around the decision.
- Easy to use software interface.

In addition, each of the four DSS satisfied most of the following additional criteria:

- Interactive processing.
- DSS use and control determined by the user.
- Flexible and adaptable to changes in the environment and decision maker's style.
- Quick ad hoc DSS building capabilities.

The DSS was judged to be either institutional or ad hoc based on the characteristics provided by Donovan and Madnick. For the purpose of the study, two institutional and two ad hoc systems were identified. Each was considered successful by users and developers.

The Interview

Interviews were conducted at each organization with a member or members of the DSS development team. The interviews were tape recorded so that the information could be carefully analyzed and categorized.

The interviews consisted of two parts. The first part was designed to gather background information on the company and on the development and use of the DSS. It included questions related to the corporate business sector, conditions that led to the creation of the DSS, developmental history, and usage patterns. The second part of the interview focused on the database component of the DSS. Specific questions were designed to obtain information related to each of the general requirements proposed by Sprague and Carlson. This information was used to prepare case studies, descriptions, and summary tables regarding institutional and ad hoc database requirements.

FOUR CASE STUDIES

Brief descriptions follow for the four DSS, two institutional and two ad hoc, selected for this study of database requirements. All DSS met the requirements for DSS as defined by Hogue and Watson, each could be classified as institutional or ad hoc based on the characteristics set forth by Donovan and Madnick, and each was considered successful.

Collectively, the systems support all of Anthony's levels of managerial activity. The train dispatching system aids in the area of operational control, while a majority of AIMS capabilities focus on managerial control. Both ad hoc systems, the pricing model and the acquisition model, support strategic planning.

Train Dispatching System

The train dispatching system used by the Norfolk Southern Corporation is an example of an institutional DSS. It is an on-line, real-time, operational DSS that is used daily by train dispatchers of the Norfolk and Southern Railroad. It was developed to assist dispatchers on the northern portion of the Alabama Division and is now being expanded to include the nine other divisions of the Norfolk and Southern Railway.

Each dispatcher is typically responsible for the movement of twenty to thirty trains over three to six hundred miles of track. Most of this is single track and requires that the routes of opposing trains be safely coordinated so that the trains meet at strategically placed passing sidings. In addition, the dispatcher must safely coordinate the movement of work and inspection crews along these same tracks. The dispatcher is also in constant contact with freight terminals for information regarding trains that will move over the division and for information on trains that have arrived at their destination. The system developed by the operations research staff was designed to assist the dispatchers with these activities.

The train dispatching system now in use provides for more accurate and timely entry of federal reporting information directly into the system by the dispatchers and allows the dispatchers ready access to the information needed for train and work crew dispatching.

Specialized algorithms and models were developed by the operations research staff specifically for train dispatching and related decisions. The models take into account thousands of possible meet/pass combinations that could occur for the trains and suggest the optimal solution. As information is entered regarding changes in track or train conditions, a new optimal solution is displayed along with projections of future conditions over a six-to-eight hour period. All train information is current and changes as conditions change. While the system offers an optimal solution for each dispatching decision, the dispatcher has the ability to override each plan to reflect his experience and judgment. His decision can be entered into the system which results in new projections.

The minicomputer based system involved approximately three years of prototype work. The system at a division office includes four color CRTs. Two display track layout and the movement of trains along the tracks. A third CRT displays screen formats which serve as work sheets for updating the train data by the dispatchers. The fourth CRT displays how trains should be routed based on calculations of the models.

Automated Information Management System (AIMS)

In January 1984, BellSouth began operation as the parent company for Southern Bell and South Central Bell. This brought the two divisions which supply local telephone service to the southern United States under a single managing body separate from American Telephone and Telegraph. This proved to be a great opportunity and challenge for BellSouth. Top management saw the need for an extensive management support system to aid largely in management control decision making. As a result, a systems analysis group was formed at BellSouth to develop such a system. The first prototype of the Automated Information Management System (AIMS) was installed approximately six weeks later. AIMS is a corporate planning model used for budgeting, resource allocation, and strategic planning. It utilizes forecasting, graphics, and spreadsheet packages along with a sophisticated database management package to provide needed information and analysis capabilities at different managerial levels. It has approximately 4000 users at the district, state, and headquarters level and combines features of office automation and information resource management as well as decision support.

At the district level, managers use the system to evaluate daily operations. They can analyze present performance in terms of past performance and can view projected performance generated from preprogrammed models. This information is used to keep service to customers in line with company standards and to see that budget restrictions are maintained. The district data is used by managers at the state level to prepare preliminary budgets and to forecast resource needs using additional models.

At the corporate level managers consolidate the state budgets and develop a corporate budget and corporate resource forecasts. They serve as intermediaries for the CEO by preparing reports, identifying problem areas, and exploring "what if" performance and budgeting scenarios. These budgets and reports are stored in a private database accessible only by the CEO and used at his discretion for strategic planning decisions.

Pricing Model

Coca-Cola® USA is the producer and marketer of all Coca-Cola domestic beverages. Rather than marketing a finished product, however, Coca-Cola USA supplies the beverage syrup and sweetening agent to individual bottling franchises and fountain operations where it is then mixed for bottling and final sale.

In early 1983 Coca-Cola USA geared for the introduction of Diet Coke, a new diet product, into the market. All market research and testing had been completed for the product, but the Vice President of Strategic Planning faced a problem. What price would bottlers be charged for the Diet Coke syrup and Aspartame sweetener? Would the syrup be priced at the Tab rate, the rate for Coca-Cola USA's other diet product, or would it be priced, as the bottlers hoped, at the rate for original Coke? There were also questions about the pricing of the sweetener Aspartame. The Vice President for Strategic Planning also had to consider how the pricing of the Diet Coke syrup and sweetener would affect Tab's market share.

To assist him in making the pricing decision, the Vice President requested the creation of a model that would allow him to manipulate the model's parameters in order to evaluate possible pricing combinations. As a result of working with the model, a pricing proposal would then be prepared and presented to the bottlers. A three-person, in-house team was selected to develop the model. The group was composed of a financial analyst, a builder/intermediary, and the Vice President for Strategic Planning. The Vice President was important in determining the parameters necessary for the decision and was the ultimate user of the information provided by the model. The financial analyst determined the financial relationships necessary for the model, and the builder/intermediary actually created and coded the model using available tools. The builder intermediary also operated the model to obtain results for the Vice President.

The model was created using EXPRESS, a DSS generator equipped with a high level, non-procedural programming language, financial and statistical analysis capabilities, graphics, and database management capabilities. The initial creation of the model took approximately one week. The model was refined as new parameters were identified and as additional considerations were raised by the bottlers.

Acquisition Model

Since its founding in 1933, Gold Kist, Inc., has become the leader in the Southeast's agribusiness industry. At the present time, Gold Kist is considering adding to its holdings through the acquisition of a company in a related area of business. The Executive Committee instructed the Director of Corporate Planning and Economic Research to recommend the best company for such an acquisition. The Executive Committee provided the Director with basic parameters the selected company should meet, including the price range Gold Kist would pay to acquire the company, the volume of business the company should maintain, and the company's contribution to the Gold Kist profit picture. Even with these guidelines the Director faced a big job. Many companies met the requirements specified by the Executive Committee. Selecting the one best company from as many as twenty-five possibilities would require careful analysis of each company's performance based on information from knowledgeable individuals at all levels within the company, as well as financial information.

The Director wanted financial information that reflected the company's future performance should an acquisition by Gold Kist take place. This information could be easily identified and analyzed once basic fundamental reports such as balance sheets and income statements had been prepared. Therefore, the Director wanted a model that would formulate these reports for each company under study. Using PROFIT II, a DSS generator that combines a high level programming language with financial and statistical analysis capabilities, graphics, and data management capabilities, the Director set out to develop such a model. After one week, the Director had a working model that produced an income statement, cash flow statement, working capital statement, and source and use of funds statement, as well as financial ratios and forecasting ratios for each company being considered.

FINDINGS AND DISCUSSION

As was expected, differences were found in the database component of the four DSS studied. In general, the differences can be explained by the institutional and ad hoc DSS distinction. Of course, the differences are also related to the managerial activity supported by the DSS. Consider now the database differences using the general DSS database requirements suggested by Sprague and Carlson.

Multiple Sources

Data for the train dispatching system is largely transaction data gathered as a result of daily dispatching operations. The remainder of the data is also internal. The data for AIMS comes from a variety of sources. It includes transaction data obtained from operations, internal data from corporate personnel databases and from corporate planning, and external population data purchased outside of the organization. All the data for Coca-Cola USA's pricing model was internally generated and gathered by different departments within the company. This data reflected external factors such as consumer preferences, market demand, and economic conditions. The data was prepared to reflect total corporate performance before its inclusion in the database. Likewise, all data included in Gold Kist's acquisition model was based on information gained from external sources. This external information was modified during planning and evaluation. The internally generated results were then included in the database.

The use of transaction, other internal, and external data by the institutional and ad hoc DSS is presented in Table 8.3. The general impression is that institutional DSS rely primarily on transaction and other internal data while ad hoc DSS employ non- transaction internal data and external data. The data requirements for the four DSS also correspond with what one would expect based on Anthony's levels of managerial activity.

Wide Time Frame

While all data in Gold Kist's acquisition model was based on historical data, the actual data included in the database were projections of performance. A similar situation existed for Coca- Cola USA's pricing model, however, one time period of historical data was included for projection purposes. The train dispatching system relies exclusively on current data, while AIMS uses data from all three time frames: historical, current, and projected.

The time frame for the data used in the four DSS does not appear to be strongly related to the type of DSS. However, as can be seen in Table 8.4, both ad hoc DSS

TABLE 8.3   Sources of Data for Each System

	TRANSACTION	INTERNAL	EXTERNAL
Institutional			
Train Dispatching System	X	X	
AIMS	X	X	X
Ad hoc			
Pricing Model		X	X
Acquisition Model		X	X

employ projected data. There seems to be a stronger relationship between the data's time frame and the level of managerial activity.

Data Reduction

Based on Sprague and Carlson's definition, very little data reduction took place in the ad hoc systems studied. In the pricing model and the acquisition model all data reduction manipulations were performed on the data before their inclusion in data files. The data management capabilities of the DSS generators serve to limit the extent to which these features can be included in the ad hoc systems.

On the other hand, the institutional systems studied rely heavily on data reduction. AIMS aggregates data at each level of use, while the train dispatching system relies on sub-setting and combination to represent the movement of all trains over a division. These capabilities necessitate the use of packaged or in-house created database management systems.

Various Levels of Detail

It follows from the data reduction requirements that institutional and ad hoc systems would vary in the level of detail of data necessary to support the systems. For the ad hoc systems no attempt was made to maintain detailed data in the database. A request for this type of information was beyond the scope of each of the ad hoc systems.

TABLE 8.4   Time Frame for Data for Each System

	HISTORICAL	CURRENT	PROJECTED
Institutional			
Train Dispatching System	X		
AIMS	X	X	X
Ad hoc			
Pricing Model	X		X
Acquisition			X

The institutional DSS studied do maintain data at different levels of detail. With AIMS, if a question arises regarding a figure in the corporate budget, the data used to arrive at that figure can be traced to the district level through data maintained in the database. Likewise, a question about a division's performance can be investigated by viewing data on each train dispatched in the division during a specific shift. In both cases, the decisions supported by the systems call for this type of capability. The institutional systems have a commitment of resources and technology that make these levels of data easier to maintain.

Varying Amounts of Data

Varying amounts of data are also maintained and used in institutional and ad hoc DSS. This follows from the previous requirements regarding data reduction and varying levels of detail. The ad hoc systems studied maintained only those data which were actually used for the decision-making process. In contrast, the institutional systems maintained a large amount of data. Both AIMS and the train dispatching system maintain a large volume of potentially relevant data in varying levels of detail. As mentioned earlier, this facilitates the explanation of aggregate data should a question arise. It also results in much data being maintained which is seldom used.

Varying Degrees of Accuracy

Absolute accuracy was not required of the data included in the ad hoc systems. It is difficult to verify the accuracy of the data for these systems since both relied on aggregate, projected data.

Related to accuracy is the idea of currency of the data. For both ad hoc systems, all data included were based on historical data. With Gold Kist's acquisition model, data were based on the latest financial reports available for a company. In many cases these were as much as a year old. This data was, therefore, subject to a certain amount of inaccuracy due to the lack of currency of the historical data. The increasing age of the information on which the projections were based would tend to decrease the accuracy.

By the same argument, the institutional systems tended to have a much higher degree of accuracy. The long-range projections included in AIMS and short-range, shift projections included in the train dispatching system are based on current information. The operational natures of the dispatching decision for Norfolk and Southern and district service for BellSouth require a high degree of accuracy.

Support for Memories

Sprague and Carlson suggest four kinds of memory aids that the DSS database should support. Table 8.5 illustrates the types of memory aids that are found in the database component of each of the systems studied.

Both the institutional and ad hoc systems were organized around the "scratch pad" concept. All four systems provided workspaces where calculations could be performed and displayed. Each system also provided libraries for saving intermediate results for later use.

The institutional database components provide additional memory support in the form of links and triggers. With the train dispatching system, a particular train can be identified

TABLE 8.5   Memory Aids Provided by Each System

	WORKSPACES	LIBRARIES	LINKS	TRIGGERS
Institutional				
Train Dispatching System	X	X	X	X
AIMS	X	X	X	X
Ad hoc				
Pricing Model	X	X		
Acquisition Model	X	X		

from a list of those dispatched during a shift. All information relevant to that train can be stored in link memory for use with another workspace. A blinking asterisk also appears in the corner of the display screen if changing track conditions result in a new meet/pass plan. This triggers a new decision situation for the dispatcher. Similarly, with AIMS, blinking, reverse screen figures indicate when a budgetary or service figure is out of range.

Support for Relationships and Views

While both types of systems provided support in this area, the ad hoc systems tended to provide the best support for relationships and views. The "what if" capabilities of the DSS generators used by each of the ad hoc systems allowed the managers to test alternate scenarios quickly and with relative ease. This flexibility was essential due to the ill-defined nature of the ad hoc decisions.

The institutional systems studied, on the other hand, do not exhibit this degree of flexibility. Due to the better defined nature of the decision, alternate relationships and ways of viewing the data were designed at the time of system development. While "what if" scenarios may be carried out on AIMS by certain skilled managers at the headquarters level, "what if" options beyond those originally developed for the train dispatching system must be handled by the OR development team.

Random Access

Database components of both the ad hoc and institutional DSS were found to support random access. This access proved to be more sophisticated for the institutional DSS. Their database management capabilities allowed access to data that the decision maker did not expect to need and to data that was not related to the data currently being used.

Security and Private Databases

No specific measures were taken to protect the data included in the database component of either of the ad hoc systems studied. Both systems were designed for personal support for a single user. Therefore, data security was not a primary concern.

The institutional systems studied, on the other hand, are accessible by many people. As a result, measures were taken to secure certain data. While any dispatcher can access and view any train information during his shift, only certain dispatchers can alter specific train data. Likewise, AIMS provides a private database, accessible only by the CEO, where sensitive budgets and reports are stored.

End-User Interface

Differences were observed in the end-user interface for the institutional and ad hoc DSS. The interfaces for the institutional systems were designed to be "transparent" to the user. Users need know nothing of the internal structure of the DSS. Both DSS employ menus and function keys which facilitate the use of each system by many users.

In contrast, no special end-user interfaces were designed for the ad hoc systems studied other than the standard prompt interfaces provided by each DSS generator.

CONCLUSION

Based on the characteristics of the database components of the systems studied, generalizations can be proposed for the specific database requirements for institutional and ad hoc systems. Table 8.6 summarizes these requirements as they apply to the general database requirements for DSS.

From these requirements we see that the nature of the decision, whether or not it is recurring, does indeed affect the type of DSS support chosen and the database requirements for the DSS. Recurring, well-defined decisions call for institutional systems. These are developed by highly technical and experienced development teams using a sophisticated collection of DSS tools. Institutional DSS provides organizational support to a large number of users. Consequently, considerable time and money are spent making the system as complete and easy to use as possible. This is illustrated by the data requirements for memory aids, varying amounts of data, public and private databases, and easy to use end-user interface. As a result, flexibility to change and to create new views of the data is limited.

The one-shot decisions are difficult to anticipate and define and call for ad hoc support. This support must be provided quickly and cost effectively. As a result, the ad hoc system is normally developed by a small development team using a DSS generator. The system's data management capabilities are limited to the data management capabilities of the DSS generator. Therefore, much preparatory work is usually done on the data before it is included in the database.

Ad hoc systems tend to provide personal support to single users. Consequently, only data handling features essential for the decision are included in the system. The user's familiarity with the system or an intermediary to operate the system for the decision maker reduces the data management features necessary, as well as the development time. The DSS generator does provide a great deal of flexibility for making changes and viewing data in many ways. The ill-defined nature of ad hoc problems makes this essential.

The database components for these two types of DSS are different. These differences reflect the nature of the decision involved as well as characteristics of the system

TABLE 8.6   Database Requirements for Institutional and Ad Hoc DSS

	INSTITUTIONAL	AD HOC
Multiple sources	internal	external
Wide time frame	no relationship found	
Data reduction	extensive	minor
Varying levels of detail	many	few
Varying amounts of data	large	small
Varying degree of accuracy	high	low
Security & private databases	common	rare
Support for memories	broad	narrow
Support for relationships and views	limited	extensive
Random access	complex	simple
End-user interface	fixed	variable

itself. These requirements facilitate the storage and transformation of data for decisions unique to each type of system.

QUESTIONS

1. What are the differences between institutional and ad hoc DSS?
2. Describe the general requirements for a DSS database.
3. Describe the database component of the train dispatching DSS at Southern Railway, the automated information management system (AIMS) at BellSouth, the pricing model at Coca-Cola USA, and the acquisition model at Gold Kist.
4. Discuss the differences in database requirements for institutional and ad hoc DSS.

REFERENCES

1. ALTER, STEVEN L. *Decision Support Systems: Current Practices and Continuing Challenges.* Reading, Mass.: Addison-Wesley, 1980.
2. ANTHONY, R. N. *Planning and Control Systems: A Framework for Analysis,* Harvard University Graduate School of Business Administration, Boston, 1965.
3. BENNETT, JOHN L., ED. *Building Decision Support Systems.* Reading, Mass.: Addison-Wesley, 1983.
4. DONOVAN, J., AND S. MADNICK "Institutional and Ad Hoc DSS and Their Effective Use," *Data Base,* 8, no. 3 (Winter 1977), 79–88.
5. FICK, GLORIA, AND RALPH H. SPRAGUE, JR., EDS. *Decision Support Systems: Issues and Challenges.* London: Pergamon Press, 1980.

6.   GERRITY, THOMAS P.   "Design of Man-Machine Decision Systems: An Application to Portfolio Management," *Sloan Management Review,* 12, no. 2 (Winter 1971), 59–75.

7.   GORRY, G. A., AND M. S. SCOTT MORTON   "A Framework for Management Information Systems," *Sloan Management Review,* 12, no. 1 (Fall 1971), 55–70.

8.   HACKATHORN, RICHARD D., AND PETER G. W. KEEN   "Organizational Strategies for Personal Computing in Decision Support Systems," *MIS Quarterly,* 5, no. 3 (September 1981), 21–26.

9.   HOGUE, JACK T., AND HUGH J. WATSON   "Management's Role in the Approval and Administration of Decision Support Systems," *MIS Quarterly,* 7, no. 2 (June 1983), 15–25.

10. KEEN, PETER G. W.   "Interactive Computer Systems for Managers: A Modest Proposal," *Sloan Management Review,* 18, no. 1 (Fall 1976), 1–17.

11. KEEN, PETER G. W., AND MICHAEL S. SCOTT MORTON   *Decision Support Systems: An Organizational Perspective.* Reading, Mass.: Addison-Wesley, 1978.

12. KEEN, PETER G. W., AND GERALD R. WAGNER   "DSS: An Executive Mind-Support System," *Datamation,* 25, no. 12 (November 1979), 117–22.

13. LITTLE, JOHN D. C.   "BRANDAID: A Marketing-Mix Model, Part I: Structure," *Operations Research,* 23, no. 4 (July–August 1975), 628–55.

14. LITTLE, JOHN D. C.   "BRANDAID: A Marketing-Mix Model, Part 2: Implementation, Calibration, and Case Study," *Operations Research,* 23, no. 4 (July–August 1975), 656–73.

15. SIMON, HERBERT A.   *The New Science of Management Decision.* New York: Harper & Row, 1960.

16. SPRAGUE, RALPH H., JR., AND ERIC D. CARLSON   *Building Effective Decision Support Systems.* Englewood Cliffs, N.J.: Prentice Hall, 1982.

17. SPRAGUE, RALPH H., JR., AND HUGH J. WATSON   "Bit by Bit: Toward Decision Support Systems," *California Management Review,* 22, no. 1 (Fall 1979), 60–68.

18. SPRAGUE, RALPH H., JR., AND HUGH J. WATSON   "MIS Concepts: Part II," *Journal of Systems Management,* 26, no. 2 (February 1975), 35–40.

19. SPRAGUE, RALPH H., JR., AND RON L. OLSEN   "The Financial Planning System at the Louisiana National Bank," *MIS Quarterly,* 3, no. 3 (September 1979), 1–11.

9

A TECHNOLOGY INFRASTRUCTURE FOR DOCUMENT-BASED DECISION SUPPORT SYSTEMS

Jane Fedorowicz

INTRODUCTION

> ...the online portion of a typical organization's total information resource is only 2 percent. (Wallace, 1990, p. 120)

Incalculable amounts of information are generated, disseminated, and stored away in organizations daily. Yet, with all the technological advances and large corporate expenditures made with the goal of improving accessibility to information, very little of an organization's information base is actually computerized. An even smaller percentage of this information is accessible online by managers and decision makers.

This reading was written especially for this book, and revised in 1992 for the third edition..

Why is this? Part of reason can be ascribed to the fact that the information needed by managers is not predisposed to a generic definition. That is, it is not easily molded or manipulated in the simple record format required by most information systems. Although decision support systems (DSS) were conceived to provide decision-making support to managers faced with semistructured problems, the data model underlying their databases comprises a series of well-defined fields and relationships. It is the analytical engine, or model base, that provides the user with greater flexibility of analysis. In spite of this limitation on the type of data with which DSS can work, DSS have become very powerful tools in a decision maker's arsenal.

The information needs of senior-level managers and executives, in particular, do not conform to the traditional concept of database querying. Much of their information acquisition activity is driven by what information is accessible. Artificial intelligence (AI) will aid us in improving the ability of technology to understand, interpret, and classify the information itself. The technological demands of a DSS must be determined in light of advances in many related research areas. A document base will require different internal representation and access schemes. This will become possible with new techniques in AI, object-oriented database management, group decision support systems, information retrieval, electronic mail, and storage standards.

In these and other areas, technological advances are now emerging to enable the management of document-based data in DSS, making it accessible to managers, executives, and other decision makers. In this reading, we examine advances in hardware, software, and application areas that are leading in that direction.

HARDWARE

Decreased cost and increased processing speed are obvious technology indicators for pursuing document-based support systems (DDSS), which inherently process large amounts of stored data. But these alone will not suffice for handling the volume of documents that a document base will contain. Indeed, because not all documents are accumulated using traditional keyboarding options, alternative input and access mechanisms are required. Key to DDSS success are accompanying improvements in storage technology, and standards for inputing and storing this type of data.

New storage options based on optical disks are burgeoning in the marketplace (Bhatt, 1991). The technologies include CD-ROM (compact disk read-only memory), WORM (write once read many), and laser disks, all of which enable large amounts of information to be stored relatively cheaply. CD jukeboxes increase the amount of data that can be stored and retrieved efficiently.

CD technology is not limited to storing traditional textual data (Strothman, 1991; Maguire, 1992). CD-I provides a standardized multi-media format that combines video, audio, and graphics. A related technology marketed by Intel and others is DVI (Digital Video Interactive), which mixes motion video, still frames, audio, graphics, databases, retrieval schemes, and interactive processes onto a CD. It can store full-motion video as well.

Imaging technology, initially marketed in the desktop publishing arena, will enable the DDSS user to incorporate pictorial or textual documents (Edelstein, 1991). Image scanners can copy any image into the PC. An appealing aspect of some of these scanners is that they will input a textual document in a format manipulable by word processing software and pictorial images in a form that can be accessed by "painting" programs. Thus, any printed document can be included in the DDSS as if it had been input by hand. Although few products exhibit acceptable scanning quality today, advances in intelligent character recognition (ICR) (such as Xerox's ScanWorX) will make this an imperative component of a "paperless" environment.

All of these technologies provide high-volume data, but at a slower rate than magnetic disk technology. Few of them can be rewritten or changed after data are initially placed on them, so that historic and reference data are better suited for their use than data that change frequently. The low cost of reproducing large quantities of CDs promotes regular or frequent updates of data that do not change in real time.

Real-time stock market quotations, for example, are still better suited to magnetic disk or remote access. Now, recent advances in circuit board technology and compression standards permit compression of digitized images, including video, enabling them to be stored and updated quickly on a hard disk. This technology has the potential for supporting real-time updating and access needs.

A DDSS must integrate a variety of storage and processing technologies to provide complete document retrieval. Magnetic disks or newer content-addressable storage mechanisms, whether at a workstation or on a server, could be used for time-sensitive corporate data. On-line database services could be tied in to gather timely external information. Graphics, audio, and video images could be linked to more conventional databases. CDs can be used for historical records, including minutes of meetings, digitized voice, videotapes or teleconferences, copies of memos, external databases and search algorithms, and other documents that a decision maker might normally retain.

These storage and input technologies, in conjunction with powerful workstation processing and telecommunications, are vital components for DDSS. They provide the ease of use, flexibility, and speed of access that decision makers demand. The next sections present an overview of the software advances that make the system feasible.

ON-LINE DATABASES

Competitive analysis through environmental scanning has become an essential element in the strategy of today's organizations (Weston, 1991). These are formal methods of monitoring the competitive environment to assess an organization's posture in the marketplace. One way to obtain this intelligence is by searching the data available on external databases. These are a key source of external information favored by managers and executives.

Not surprisingly, then, is a study of Information Market Indicators Inc. that indicates that U.S. businesses increased their on-line database expenditures by 117% in 3 years, (Jenkins, 1986a, 1986b). Companies are retrieving more and more information from databases such as Dow Jones News Retrieval, Compuserve, Dialog Information

Service, and Mead Data Central. For individuals, Prodigy has brought cheap and easy database access into the PC.

The increased reliance on external market indicators and improved sources of information have dramatically boosted the demand for online database services. Telecom estimates that demand for its services is growing at 25% per year or more (Reed, 1989). One source estimates that there are over 7000 on-line databases available worldwide (Reed, 1989). Another survey identified 5043 on-line databases, compared with only 1000 in 1982 (Nicholls, 1991).

Typically, users of these systems are trained librarians who provide a service within their company, or PC users, who tie into general-purpose databases. Most of the time, the results of the search are hard copy reports of bibliographic, or financial, or other stored information. Some DSS and Executive Information System products such as Pilot's EIS or Metaphor/IBM's Data Interpretation System provide links to external databases and display the results of prespecified searches on the screen.

A low-cost alternative for accessing these databases has evolved with the increasing number of CD/ROM installations. A 1990 survey of databases title listings showed 1025 CD/ROM databases, with an expectation of a doubling of that number by mid-1991. The relatively low price and easy accessibility of this option appears to compensate for the fact that many of these databases (in fact, more than half) are only updated once or twice a year. This medium also permits the storage of multimedia titles. About 15% of all CD-ROM databases include multimedia documents.

The mechanisms for searching textual databases have improved over time. Techniques for information retrieval are the subjects of the next sections.

INFORMATION RETRIEVAL

Document bases have their roots in the field of bibliographic information retrieval. Bibliographic searching to produce lists of citations and abstracts based on keyword selection has been successfully applied to large indexed files for approximately 25 years. These mechanisms provide the sorting and searching techniques used in querying large, external databases.

Commonly in information retrieval, keywords are linked by Boolean operators (e.g., AND, OR, NOT) to detect the documents that best match the characterization specified by the searcher. These services had been the domain of librarians, as they have been used predominantly as a research support mechanism for academics, corporate researchers, and practitioners who want to be apprised of new developments in their field.

Bibliographic retrieval research comprises a number of issues related to document management, including effective and efficient index term assignment, keyword search schemes, free text search algorithms, inverted file design, specification of adjacency conditions for free text terms, and the use of truncation and synonyms to improve the efficiency of retrieval (Salton, 1986; Fedorowicz, 1987). Recently, improvements in retrieval effectiveness have been attained through the application of probabilistic indexing (Kwok, 1985), clustering of documents (van Rijsbergen, 1979), non-Boolean tree configurations of keywords (Appleton, 1992), signature files (Zezula et al., 1991), and cognitive modeling of users. Cognitive models are a user- profiling technique that may simplify the interaction of individuals with DDSS.

Cognitive modeling has been incorporated into a number of expert systems that adapt knowledge about a user into a personalized retrieval tool (Daniels, 1986). Models can be explicit, demanding answers to a list of questions by the user before the retrieval process can begin. Alternatively, implicit user modeling is based on the answers to a few preliminary questions, after which the system reverts to knowledge about stereotypical users. GRUNDY (Rich, 1979), for example, constructs a user model in this way, and incorporates feedback from the user to update the user profile and hypotheses. User models, in any case, will need to encompass static models reflecting permanent information about the user, and dynamic models, which depend on the particular interaction with the system.

Additionally, AI techniques have been advanced as a way to increase the effectiveness of the retrieval process. For example, fuzzy set theory has been applied to documents to represent the extent that a document is "about" an index term (Buell, 1985).

Vickery et al. (1985) proposed a prototype expert systems that assigns each index term entered by the user to one of about two dozen categories. The system presumes a set of dependency relations between categories. These are used to guide the system to try to amplify the user's query and to eliminate terms by reformulating the request (Vickery, 1986).

Other expert systems have also been developed to provide intelligent interfaces for document retrieval systems. Vickery and Brooks (1987) review a number of them, including EXPERT, which uses production rules to select which database to search, and provides advice on how to select synonyms and how to combine terms in a query.

A project underway at Indiana University of Pennsylvania combines hypermedia with an expert system to monitor results from a traditional user query of a database of citations, and helps the user to broaden or narrow the search. To expand a query that is too narrow, a natural language component aids in suggesting additional keywords or classifications. An overly broad search is reduced in scope by using various classifications or subdivisions of subfields (Micco, 1991).

Advances in information retrieval will prove invaluable for DDSS search activities. Frustration with current DDSS centers on the difficulty of identifying relevant documents (Appleton, 1992). A DDSS will probably consist of large-scale collections of bibliographic, encyclopedic, reference, historical, informal notes or other types of text, image and audio documents. Combined, these would be available in online databases. For example, current financial data, interoffice memos, and newspaper clippings could be retrieved using artificially intelligent keyword profiles and user models. Multimedia documents would require the more sophisticated indexing of signature files.

If user profiles were sufficiently sophisticated, passive retrieval activities could be incorporated to provide environmental scanning facilities for executives. (A simple but extremely effective version of this type of facility is available through the Prodigy system.) New concerns could be added or modified from existing profiles when new opportunities or problems arise, making this an active support tool as well.

HYPERMEDIA

Recent advances in hypertext and multimedia have combined to make DDSS a commercially viable opportunity. Multimedia employs imaging, digital, and audio technology to store and retrieve graphics, photography, full-motion video, sound, and animation along with more traditional text and data. Hypertext is the web that connects these disparate documents together in a way that imitates human cognitive maps.

Hypertext links together various computer documents based on user-specified associations. Thus, a phone memo pertaining to a stored report could be linked together by associative labeling, so that one could easily recall one when referring to the other. Graphs and drawings on the same subject could also be tied in, in line with the user's thought processes. The ability to associate different types of documents in a free-form manner provides the flexibility many decision makers need for ad hoc information retrieval.

Hypertext-based products, such as Lotus Development Corp.'s Agenda and Executive Technologies' Search Express, are PC-based applications that can be integrated with other PC products. Search Express is marketed as an information-retrieval enhancement, featuring fast access to up to one million documents. Agenda provides a way of managing various types of user-input documents by cross-referencing and labeling documents stored by assorted software packages. Both incorporate artificial intelligence with hypertext retrieval to aid the user in the assignment and selection of document-level associations.

Hypermedia results from coupling hypertext with multimedia. Multimedia computing allows for efficient collection and distribution of organizational documents of all types. Without a governing mechanism such as hypertext, these documents are retrievable only after time-consuming indexing and keyword assignment activity. Although effective for structured forms of data, indexing and keywords suffer from the bias of the coder, the need for prespecification of the aspects of interest in the document, and limitations of the keyword vocabulary.

Hypertext and hypermedia packages for microcomputers are relatively inexpensive, ranging in price from free (e.g., Hyper Rez by MaxThink) to $995 and up. Table 9.1 lists some valuable PC products.

More sophisticated retrieval techniques (as outlined earlier), coupled with the flexibility of hypertext links, will lead to increased growth in the multimedia market. With 1990 sales estimated at $3.7 billion, the multimedia market is forecast to grow to $13.6 billion in 1994 (Wallace, 1990). In the United States, the installed based of multimedia systems on business personal computers is expected to grow from 792,000 in 1991 to 7,500,000 in 1995 (Strothman, 1991). Table 9.2 lists some of the multimedia software packages currently available.

Hypermedia is a fast-growing product area, as it is the preeminent technique for integrating assorted documents in a way that will make them accessible to, and therefore usable by, decision makers in organizations. The ability to annotate and transport these documents provides the expanded capabilities needed by executives and other decision makers who feel limited by current database support. Hypermedia will also augment traditional methods of communication in the organization, by allowing individuals to

TABLE 9.1   Some Hypertext and Hypermedia Products for the Microcomputer

PRODUCT	VENDOR	PLATFORM
Aldus Supercard	Aldus Corp.	Macintosh
askSam V 5	Seaside Software	IBM
Asymetrix ToolBook	Asymterix Corp.	IBM
AUTHORWARE	Authorware	Macintosh, IBM
Black Magic	INTERGAID	IBM
Folio Views 2.1	Folio Corp.	IBM
GUIDE	OWL, International	Macintosh, IBM
Hyper BBS	MaxThink	IBM
Hyper LAN	MaxThink	IBM
Hyper Rez	MaxThink	IBM
HyperCARD 2.1	Claris Corp.	Macintosh
HyperPAD	Brightbill-Roberts & Co.	IBM
Hyperties 3.0	Cognetics Corp.	IBM
Hyperwriter 3.0	INTERGAID	IBM

Source: Derived from Shim (1992).

append notes to formal reports, audio messages to written documents, and pictures to text. Video clips will give a better sense of product dynamics than any spreadsheet ever will. In short, the ability to cut, paste, and link up a variety of source documents will make computer-supported analysis and communication an organizational imperative.

ELECTRONIC MAIL

In order for documents to be disseminated and shared in a timely manner, a DDSS must include a suitable communications component. It is not enough, however, to tie decision makers to a central server or to put them on an electronic mail network. The shear amount of information content in organizational documents will require the DDSS to sort and route documents to those who need them, and also prevent them from burdening those who do not.

Electronic mail provides a medium for sending mail messages privately over a local area network, or worldwide using a public-access network. Many companies have adopted internal E-mail systems, with many turning to the mainframe IBM offering, PROFS, and to PC products such as cc:Mail. These systems do not permit receivers of mail to sort messages based on the meaning of their contents prior to reading them. A

TABLE 9.2   Available Multimedia Software Tools and Authoring Packages

PRODUCT	VENDOR
MetaWindows	MetaGraphics
Knowledge Pro	Knowledge Garden
Toolbook	Asymetrix
Guide	Owl International
Director	MacroMind
SuperBase 4	Precision Software
Professional	Authorware
Quest	Allen Communications
TenCORE	Computer Teaching Corp.
Icon Author	AimTech

Source: Adapted from Duhms (1991).

number of development projects are currently under way to augment these systems with the capability of filtering messages based on their content or header information.

Chang and Leung (1987) propose a knowledge-based message management system in which messages may contain graphic documents, image documents, and voice documents as well as text. The messages are stored in a relational database. A linguistic message filter culls out junk messages, and user-defined "alerter rules" process relevant messages. The message filter considers network traffic, message rate, message length, and message relevance. Alerter rules can trigger database retrievals, office activities, filing activities, and mailing actions.

The LENS project at MIT is designed to disseminate information "...so that it reaches those people to whom it is valuable without interfering with those it is not" (Malone et al., 1987, p. 390). Dissemination is accomplished through a process of filtering. The researchers on this project have proposed three mechanisms that can be used in filtering messages. Social filtering is based on the organizational relationship between sender and receiver. Economic filtering relies on the cost to the sender of transmitting a message, and proposes a cutoff to the receiver based on the trade-off between quality and personalization. The third type of filtering is the one emphasized in the LENS project. Cognitive filtering is based on sophisticated heuristics combining message contents with the information needs of the receiver. Future extensions to the project include connections to external information sources, natural-language processing, advanced information-retrieval techniques, and forms processing.

Beyond Mail, from Beyond, Inc., is an electronic mail product that filters messages, and is based on the rules in the LENS prototype. Another message-filtering system, WIJIT by Agility Systems Corp., is expected to be released soon (Higgins, 1990).

The electronic mail projects are important because they provide mechanisms to manipulate the contents of documents based on the meaning of the messages rather than solely manipulating the descriptive information defining their fields (or slots). These systems demonstrate the application of AI techniques as a way of providing a meaningful interpretation of document contents in a DDSS. The filtering techniques can be adapted to other types of documents as well, and extended to applications not normally found in the electronic mail area. They can be viewed as a type of personal search profile, or at least as a part of a more generic profile. They also demonstrate that multiple types of documents can be supported with a single representational structure.

DOCUMENT-BASED SYSTEMS

Several commercial database vendors have begun to provide capabilities for storing and retrieving documents, and some can also handle images and voice. These multimedia databases are typically upgraded versions of relational databases. One of the earliest competitors in this arena is Empress Software, which has combined multimedia, relational, and object-oriented database management capabilities in a distributed environment.

Many other existing database or document-processing products are beginning to incorporate document-retrieval mechanisms. Among these are RdB from Digital Equipment Corporation, Informix from Informix Software, Hewlett Packard's NewWave Office software, NCR's Cooperation office automation system, IBM's OfficeVision, SQL Text from Oracle, and Lotus Notes. Comshare is taking a slightly different approach by integrating the capability within its executive information system offering (Appleton, 1992).

The most common method of providing this increased functionality is by incorporating sophisticated search capabilities into existing products that themselves have been extended to include multimedia documents. Leading competitors in the area of search and retrieval software are TOPIC by Verity Inc., Ful/Text by Fulcrum Technologies, and products by Excalibur Technologies Corp., Gescan International, and Information Dimensions. TOPIC provides object-oriented, "concept-based" searches ranked by relevance to a search. It incorporates hypertext links to multimedia documents. User profiles filter and distribute feeds from online database services. These products are an important first step toward comprehensive DDSS.

In addition to these commercial document-based systems, a number of projects are in the works that support interactive storage and manipulation of multimedia documents. The MINOS project (Christodoulakis et al., 1986, 1987) uses an object-oriented model of a document that is composed of attributes, text, images (line graphs, bit maps), and voice. Another prototype, MULTOS, employs signature files to aid in creating, modifying, and deleting documents in an office systems application (Zezula et al., 1991).

Similarities exist among MINOS, MULTOS, and hypertext-based systems. All allow for multiple types of documents to be represented. Linkages can be made among relevant objects or documents, so that associative browsing among documents and document types is supported. New documents can be constructed from bits and pieces of existing documents, again permitting generation of multiformatted output. All can incorporate artificial intelligence to carry out these complex activities. AI governs the storage and retrieval patterns of the document-based systems.

The role of these systems in DDSS is obvious. The ability to integrate and link multimedia documents is vital to the success of a DDSS. These technological advancements demonstrate the intricacies and magnitude of a DDSS project. These systems permit the active access and reconstruction of many types of documents. In combination with advanced information-retrieval profiling mechanisms that promote system-generated associations within and between documents, the document-based systems will become the basis of a valuable decision support tool. The addition of analytical capabilities, communications, and group support mechanisms would expand their usefulness beyond the "office system" world, to supporting higher-level decision makers and teams.

CONCLUDING REMARKS

Where do we go from here? It is apparent that commercial efforts to produce a document-based management system are well under way, and that a document-based decision support environment is not far behind. The hardware technology, long a stumbling block for large document databases needing fast retrieval time, has progressed to a point where storage and microcomputer systems are inexpensively available, and are linked together in client/server configurations. Information-retrieval techniques have advanced as well, with sophisticated search algorithms and expert system components providing efficient and effective searching. Electronic mail and hypermedia systems provide the technological foundations for augmenting passive retrieval techniques.

The missing element in successfully deploying DDSS is not the technology. It is the knowledge of how to effectively employ the technology in such a way that managerial decision makers will benefit from it. Further study is needed to ascertain whether managers have not used available technology because it has been cumbersome and inappropriate to their needs, or if the inherent "impersonalness" of an information system as a source of information will persist as a deterrent to its use (Trevino et al., 1987). Only after determining its potential usefulness and, ultimately, its role in the decision-making process can a DDSS be successfully designed.

QUESTIONS

1. Why is it important to include document-based data in the database for DSS?
2. In what ways do hardware advances assist in the process of information retrieval?
3. What is the value of hypertext in DDSS?
4. Develop a decision-making or problem-solving scenario in which the decision maker uses one or more of the features of a DDSS. Explain how each feature is used and why it is valuable.

REFERENCES

INFORMATION PREFERENCES

FEDOROWICZ, J. "The Future of Decision Support: An Examination of Managers' Decision Making Needs," in *Proceedings of the Twenty-Second Annual Hawaii International Conference on Systems Sciences*, Kona, Hawaii, January 1989, IV, 167–174.

FEDOROWICZ, J. AND P. J. GUINAN "Information Acquisition Behavior: A Pilot Study of EIS User," *DSS-91 Transactions*, Manhattan Beach, CA, June 1991, 33–43.

TREVINO, L. K., R. LENGEL, AND R. L. DAFT "Media Symbolism, Media Richness, and Media Choice in Organizations: A Symbolic Interactionist Perspective," *Communication Research*, 14, no. 5 (October 1987).

HARDWARE

BHATT, K. "Optical Storage Unraveled," *Management Services*, 35, no. 1 (January 1991), 34–37.

DUHMS, M. *Motion Video and Multimedia: The Encounter with Imaging*, prepared by New Media Graphics, Inc., 1991.

MAGUIRE, J. G. "Movies on Your Screen," *Computer Graphics World* (February 1992), 51–56.

WETMORE, T. "The Multimedia Challenge," *Information Week* (January 13, 1992), 22–30.

ONLINE DATABASES

JENKINS, A. "Firms Work To Control On-line Database Charges," *PC Week* (March 11, 1986a), 41–42.

JENKINS, A. "On-line Databases," *PC Week* (March 11, 1986b), 83–84.

NICHOLLS, P. T. "A Survey of Commercially Available CD-ROM Database Titles," *CD- ROM Professional, 4, no. 2, (March 1991), 23–28.*

NICHOLLS, P. T. *CD-ROM Collection Builder's Toolkit* (Weston, CT:Pemberton Press, 1990).

REED, N. "On-line Databases: Can They Help Your Business?," *Australian Accountant*, 59, no. 8 (September 1989), 70–72.

TURNER, T. L. "On-line Databases: The Professional Edge," *Communication World*, 6, no. 10 (October 1989), 34–37.

WESTON, D. M. *Best Practices in Competitive Analysis*, SRI International, Spring 1991.

INFORMATION RETRIEVAL

APPLETON, E. L. "Smart Document Retrieval," *Datamation*, 38, no. 2 (January 15, 1992), 20–23.

BUELL, D. A. "A Problem in Information Retrieval With Fuzzy Sets," *Journal of the American Society for Information Science*, 36, no. 6 (November 1985), 398–401.

DANIELS, P. J. "Cognitive Models in Information Retrieval—An Evaluative Review," *Journal of Documentation*, 24, no. 4 (December 1986), 272–304.

FEDOROWICZ, J. "Database Performance Evaluation in an Indexed File Environment," *Transactions on Database Systems*, 12, no. 1 (March 1987), 85–110.

KWOK, K. L. "A Probabilistic Theory of Indexing and Similarity Measure Based on Cited and Citing Documents," *Journal of the American Society for Information Science*, 36, no. 5 (September 1985), 342–351.

MICCO, M. "The NeXT Generation of Subject Access Systems: Hypermedia for Improved Access," *Information Today*, 8, no. 7 (July/August 1991), 36.

RICH, E.   "User Modelling via Stereotypes," *Cognitive Science*, 3 (1979), 329–354.

SALTON, G.   "Another Look at Automatic Text-Retrieval Systems," *Communications of the ACM*, 29, no. 7 (July 1986), 648–656.

VAN RIJSBERGEN, C. J.   *Information Retrieval*, 2d ed. (London: Buttersworth Publishers, 1979).

VICKERY, B. C.   "Knowledge Representation: A Brief Review," *Journal of Documentation*, 42, no. 3 (September 1986), 145–159.

VICKERY, A., AND H. BROOKS   "Expert Systems and Their Applications in LIS," *Online Review*, 11, no. 3 (1987), 149–163.

VICKERY, B. C., H. BROOKS AND B. A. ROBINSON   *Expert Systems for Referral, Final Report for the First Phase of the Project* (London: University of London, Central Information Service, 1985).

ZEZULA, R., F. RABITTI, AND P. TIBERIO   "Dynamic Partitioning of Signature Files," *ACM Transactions on Information Systems*, 9, no. 4 (October 1991), 336–369.

Executive Technologies, Inc.   *SearchExpress* Marketing literature, August 1987.

FIELD, A. R., et al.   "PC Software That Helps You Think," *Business Week* (November 2, 1987), 142.

SHIM, J. P.   "Living Up to the 'Hype,'" *OR/MS Today* (February 1992), 34–45.

STROTHMAN, J. E.   *Interactive Multimedia: Promises and Pitfalls*, a white paper presented for Comdex, Fall 1991.

WALLACE, S.   "Desktop Spectaculars," *CIO Magazine* (October 1990) 114–120.

ELECTRONIC MAIL

CHANG, S. AND L. LEUNG   "A Knowledge-Based Message Management System," *ACM Transactions on Office Information Systems*, 5, no. 3 (July 1987), 213–236.

HIGGINS, S.   "Startup Looks Beyond Messaging Horizon," *PC Week*, 7, no. 50, December 17, 1990, pp. 1, 8.

MALONE, T. W., K. R. GRANT, F. A. TURBAK, S. A. BROBST, AND M. D. COHEN   "Intelligent Information-Sharing Systems," *Communications of the ACM*, 30, no. 5 (May 1987), 390–402.

DOCUMENT-BASED SYSTEMS

CHRISTODOULAKIS, S., M. THEODORIDOU, F. HO, M. PAPA, AND A. PATHRIA   "Multimedia Document Presentation, Information Extraction, and Document Formation in MINOS: A Model and System," *ACM Transactions on Office Information Systems*, 4, no. 4 (October 1986), 345–383.

CHRISTODOULAKIS, S., AND T. VELISSAROPOULAKIS   "Issues in the Design of a Distributed Testbed for Multimedia Information Systems (MINOS)," *Journal of Management Information Systems*, 4, no. 2, (Fall 1987), 8–33.

10

INTELLIGENT SUPPORT SYSTEMS: ART, AUGMENTATION, AND AGENTS

David King

INTRODUCTION

Everywhere and everyday, corporations confront accelerating change—change brought about by new alliances, downsizing, the growth of the global marketplace and the quickening pace at which competitors, products, problems, and opportunities come and go. This "chaos" [1] requires senior management and their staffs to monitor, digest, access, and understand an increasing volume of data. This flood of data has heightened the desire for computerized assistance with decision-making and problem-solving processes.

Historically, database management systems (DBMS) and decision support systems (DSS) have been at the core of this computerized assistance. It has been the role of DBMS to serve as a collection point for corporate data and to provide tools for describing past and present status. DSS have been used not only to describe the past and present, but also to examine potential futures, i.e., to assess the impacts of potential decisions, to evaluate alternative courses of action, and to measure trade-offs among different situations. In recent years, expert systems (ES) have been added to the core. ES permit the application of business expertise to the discovery of opportunities and problems and to the construction of diagnoses and recommendations for attacking these opportunities and problems.

Because no single system is capable of addressing the full range of management support requirements, many theoreticians, researchers and practitioners have called for the integration of the separate systems [2, 3, 4, 5, 6, 7]. In so doing, a variety of architectures has been proposed along with a variety of terms to label the resulting architectures. Although there are certainly differences among the individual proposals, two basic approaches are discernible—*expert support systems* (ESS) [8] and *intelligent support systems* (ISS). The two approaches are predicated on different conceptions of managers and the tasks they confront, have substantially different system architectures, and, as a consequence, result in different types of applications. Although this reading considers both approaches, the focus is on the latter. In particular, the reading describes the conceptual underpinnings and actual and potential uses of ISS, especially those employing software agents.

NAVIGATORS OF OLD

In the preface to her book on human–machine communication, Lucy Suchman [9] references Thomas Gladwin's [10] description of the difference between the European and Trukese navigators of old:

> the European navigator begins with a plan—a course—which he has charted according to certain universal principles, and he carries out his voyage by relating his every move to that plan. His effort throughout his voyage is directed to remaining "on course." If unexpected events occur, he must first alter the plan, then respond accordingly. The Trukese navigator begins with an objective rather than a plan. He sets off toward the objective and responds to conditions as they arise in an ad hoc fashion. He utilizes information provided by the wind, the waves, the tide and current, the fauna, the stars, the clouds, the sound of the water on the side of the boat, and he steers accordingly. His effort is directed to doing whatever is necessary to reach the objective. If asked, he can point to his objective at any moment, but he cannot describe his course.

In today's organizations, there are counterparts to the navigational styles of the Europeans and the Trukese. The stereotype of the European navigator corresponds to the stereotype of the *rational* manager. Here, management is a *science* and *decisions* are made *by the numbers*. On the other hand, the stereotype of the Trukese navigator corresponds to the stereotypical *intuitive* manager. In this case, management is an *art* and *problems* are solved by *gut feel*. Clearly, the two types of managers rely on different tools. The rational manager needs a set of tools for setting and staying on course. The intuitive manager needs tools that will enhance his senses.

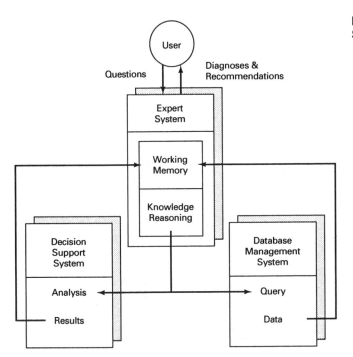

FIGURE 10.1 Expert Support System

EXPERT SUPPORT SYSTEMS

Expert support systems provide decision making support for rational managers. As shown in Figure 10.1, an ESS takes a set of numbers and qualitative measures as input, utilizes DSS models, knowledge-base structures and inferencing to analyze these inputs, and produces diagnoses and recommendations as its output.

At the executive level, the types of problems an ESS is designed to handle are illustrated quite succinctly by Edward Rensi, CEO and President of McDonald's USA [11]

> In the business environment, quick access to critical data is essential to making correct decisions. Although quick access to data currently exists in most corporations, computer assistance usually stops at this point. The near future, however, promises a computer management system that will not only give the executive raw information, but will also identify problems and negative trends quickly, list probable causes, and recommend probable cures/remedies as well. In our case, we could have a system that is constantly monitoring the profit plan. Any deviations would be pointed out as soon as they occur (e.g. food costs 1% higher than projected). The computer could quickly analyze the entire McDonald's system to see if the problem is within specific regions or across the country. The next step would be to identify the raw products that caused the increase in food costs, as well as the cause of the increase. Finally, the system would recommend options to take to resolve the problem. Keep in mind that this is advice based on history, and the final decision will and should always be made by the manager or executive.

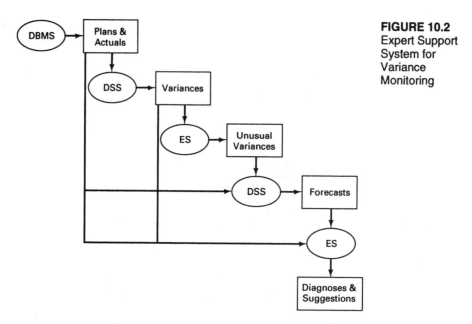

FIGURE 10.2
Expert Support
System for
Variance
Monitoring

However, imagine starting your decision-making process with the appropriate information and recommendations, rather than starting from scratch.

Figure 10.2 displays the dataflow components of an ESS that fulfill Rensi's wishes. In this system numeric database values delineate planned performance and capture actual results. A DSS model extracts these values and computes variances from plan. An ES monitors the variances in an effort to locate opportunities and problems. Based on the ES results, a DSS then simulates new forecasts. Utilizing these forecasts along with the original plans and results, a second ES produces a series of diagnoses and recommendations.

Payne and McArthur [12] provide a detailed description of this architecture, which they call the "Analytical Paradigm," and also describe a number of domains in business and finance where the architecture can be fruitfully employed. For example, Toys-R-Us utilizes an architecture of this sort for inventory control [13]. In this case, point of sales data (POS) are feed directly into a database. The actual sales figures are matched against projected sales figures. The variances are then used as a base for forecasting demand. In turn, the forecasts are used to determine how much inventory to carry in a particular store. Toys-R-Us claims that the system enabled them to project increasing demand for the Cabbage Patch doll and dwindling demand for Trivial Pursuit. A number of other retail operations employ similar systems [14].

Many ESS implementations are ill-suited for executives and managers. The systems (1) tend to rely on expert terminology; (2) utilize poor interfaces; (3) are narrowly focused on a single domain; and (4) don't encourage experimentation because the "rules" and "logic" are inaccessible to the end user [15]. In other words, ESS emphasizes the "expert" in expert systems. These "sins of commission" can be overcome by making appropriate adjustments in the user interface (e.g., hooking up the system to an EIS rather than utilizing a standard ES interface), by opening up the rules and logic to "what-ifing" in the same manner than a DSS model is open, and by focusing on "generic" problems like "exception analysis" rather than domain-specific problems like "mergers and acquisitions" or "credit scoring."

But, what about the "sins of omission?" Critics suggest that the focus and underlying assumptions of an ESS are all wrong for managers and executives [16, 17, 18, 19]. Like most DSS, ESS are designed to support specific decisions where goals are quantifiable and the alternative scenarios and potential outcomes are well known in advance. Yet, as these critics point out, most enterprises are "open" systems undergoing continuous change. In such an environment, decision making is not a rational activity, but a "situated" action emerging in response to this change. Indeed, decision making per se (i.e., the selection of a action from a delineated set of actions) is difficult at best because of the problems associated with specifying alternatives in advance. Additionally, decision making represents only a minor component of the organizational roles performed by managers and executives.

MANAGEMENT AS AN ART

The complex, emerging collection of activities that make up the roles of a manager and executive have been given a variety of names, including "problem-management processes" [20], "mess management" [21], "problem-working processes" [18], and "decision-working processes" [22]. Conceptually, all these names suggest that [21]

> Executives can be said to be primarily involved with defining and largely intuitively directing a dynamically changing agenda or network of "concerns," what Ackoff has described as "managing a mess."

More specifically, as El Sawy and El Sherif [23] have noted, the problem-and decision-working tasks facing an executive or manager are

- murky and ill-structured and can be drawn out over weeks and months
- usually a group effort rather than an individual one
- involve a substantial amount of environmental scanning for early warnings about potential discontinuities, surprises, threats, and opportunities
- takes place in an emergent rather than a deliberate fashion
- revolve around soft information such as verbal communication and written documents, memos, etc.

Concomitantly, this suggests that rather than "expert decision support," executives and managers require intelligent assistance with a variety of tasks including

- Scanning the environment for problems and opportunities
- Representing and managing a variety of entities including concerns and issues, resources, schedules, and agendas

■ Monitoring and tracking plans and actions with respect to schedules, agendas, preferences, and other patterns and conditions.

■ Handling small chunks of qualitative and quantitative data and information.

■ Summarizing and inferring underlying patterns, generalities, and solutions from these chunks.

■ Communicating and collaborating with other organizational participants.

Intelligent support systems (ISS) are designed to assist with these tasks.

AUGMENTATION

ISS is "a generic term for computer-based systems which act as tutors, critics, consultants or advisors" [24]. While ISS and ESS both have ties to the world of artificial intelligence, ISS are based on a entirely different metaphor than ESS. The human counterpart of an ESS is an "expert." In large part, ESS are designed to "replace" human expertise with machine expertise. The human counterpart of an ISS, on the other hand, is an "assistant." ISS are designed to "augment or amplify" the memory and intelligence of humans and groups.

The notion of "augmenting" human and group activities with computer systems originated in the work of Doug Englebart [25]. Englebart is credited with a number of innovations that have gradually evolved into today's desktop processors. Included among them are the mouse, multiwindow displays, WSYWIG text editors, composite text–graphics screens, outline and idea processors, shared-screen teleconferencing, integrated help systems, and full-scale electronic mail, to name just a few. To Englebart, these innovations were all seen as "tools" designed to "augment" the capabilities of humans and organizations, especially the way they "think, formulate, conceptualize, portray, manipulate, communicate and collaborate."

Although the major offshoot of Englebart's innovations has been the development of the "desktop" metaphor with its emphasis on the direct manipulation of office objects (e.g., the folders and trashcan found in the Apple Macintosh interface), this is not the illusion underlying ISS. Instead, ISS focus on background services rather than foreground manipulations. Nicholas Negroponte, Director of the MIT Media Lab, couches the ISS vision in the following terms [26]:

> Direct manipulation has its place, and in many regards is part of the joys of life: sports, food, sex, and for some, driving. But wouldn't you prefer to run your home and your office life with a gaggle of well-trained butlers, maids, secretaries, accountants, brokers, and on some occasions, cooks, gardeners, and chauffeurs when there are too many guests, weeds, or cars on the road?

The key element in an ISS is an computerized assistant working individually, or in unison with other assistants, to perform some time-consuming, tedious, or complex task on behalf of the user or simply to supplement the user's short- or long-term memory. These computerized assistants go by a variety of colorful names. Knowbots [27], daemons, triggers, notifiers [28], dynadots [26], and smartifacts [29] are some examples. However, the most commonly used term is *software agents*.

Like many other computer concepts, software agents can trace their origins to the late 1950s when John McCarthy, the father of the LISP programming language, introduced the concept of the "Advice Taker." What McCarthy had in mind [30, 31] was a system that, when given a goal, could perform appropriate actions, and could ask for and receive advice from the user when it reached a dead end. It would be a *soft robot* living and working in a computerized network of information utilities.

Today, there is a tendency to both personify and magnify the abilities of software agents. In reality, most software agents perform rather mundane tasks. The discussion that follows describes the system architecture of a typical software agent and examines some of its more important uses to date.

Technically, a software agent is an intelligent background process that is implicitly activated by a system event. Figure 10.3 depicts the operation of an agent. Basically, an agent lies idle, waiting for some system event to occur. The event might be a key stroke, the passage of time (measured by the system's internal clock), or perhaps a message stream flowing across a communication port. When something of interest occurs, the agent is awakened. At this time, the agent invokes a set of pattern-matching rules that are tested against external data. Based on the test, the agent performs an action.

A simple example of an agent like utility is Lotus Agenda's "conditions." Lotus Agenda is a personal information manager [32]. Without going into too many details, a user enters various "items" into an Agenda database. The items can refer to virtually anything. The items can also be placed in one or more "categories" that are arranged in different "views." For instance, suppose you're in charge of a project and want to keep track of the tasks to be performed by various project members by certain dates. You might establish a series of categories like the person responsible for the task, the type of task to be performed (e.g., calls to be made, documents to be written, etc.), and the scheduled date of completion. In this way, you could view the tasks by person, by type,

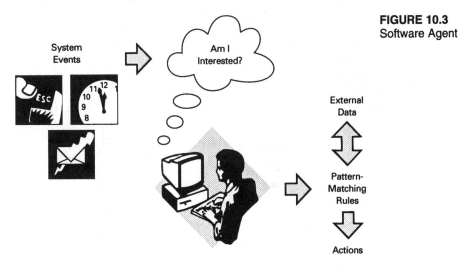

FIGURE 10.3
Software Agent

or by due date. If you were using a standard database to track the tasks, you might create a set of records with the following format:

FIELD NAME	FIELD TYPE AND LENGTH
TaskName	Text(30)
TaskDescription	Text(80)
PersonResponsible	Text(30)
TaskType	Text(30)
DueDate	Date

Anytime you entered a task, you would have to explicitly enter each of the fields. In Agenda, however, you would first establish a list of people who might be responsible and a list of task types. You wouldn't need to enter the list of dates because Agenda already knows about dates. Now, when you entered an item, e.g., "Have Joe call about the meeting room by next Tuesday," the "condition" facility would automatically assign values for the person, type, and date categories based on the contents of the item.

In other words, the "condition" facility is an agent that watches keystroke events (Figure 10.4). When an item is entered (signaled by the F9 key), the "condition" agent wakes up. It then examines the text of an item word by word (external data). Each word is checked against the category lists (pattern-matching rules). When a word matches a word in the list (or a synonym or alias), it is assigned the appropriate value (action).

Although Agenda's "condition" facility captures the essence of the agent concept, as well as the underlying notion of augmentation, most researchers and practitioners have

FIGURE 10.4   Agenda's "Condition" Agent

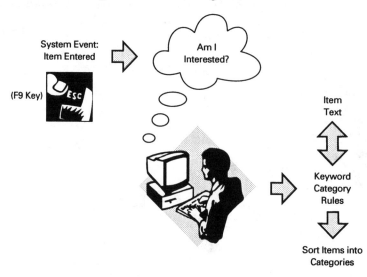

grander visions for the potential applications of agent-based ISS, especially in the executive suite. The following quotes exemplify these visions:

In science fiction terms, you'd almost have a companion—really a complete extension of your memory—that you'd have extremely ready access to (Ken McCready, CEO, TransAlta [33]).

When Ann and I were playing chess last night, we started to move the rook and the computer asked, "Are you sure?" It prompts me and takes its power and my creativity and builds the two together. That is what I'd like in a business scenario as well (Thomas Stephens, CEO, Manville [33]).

You may have an agent that follows particular kinds of news for you and automatically generates a personal newspaper... (Ester Dyson, [34]).

In other words the (Executive Information) system can be expected to interrupt the executive (perhaps via an executive secretary just like staff members do) when an important event occurs (Allan Paller [35]).

While we go to a meeting or perform other work, the "software agent lives on after you leave and keeps working" (David Nagel, Senior VP Apple Computer, [36]).

Information-filtering tools will be developed to help screen out any unwanted information. Intelligent agents will be deployed across the network to search for and retrieve any interesting information (Mitch Kapor, [34]).

Inside the soul of the computer will be an intelligent software "agent." The agent is your surrogate, the ultimate observer. It will wander around throughout dozens of databases, pulling together whatever it thinks you, the user, are interested in. You won't have to search through stacks of libraries—the world's largest libraries will exist on your desktop or lap. (John Sculley, CEO Apple [37]).

The following is a list of activities that an agent might perform on behalf of or in concert with an executive:

Navigate	Schedule
Browse	Remind
Retrieve	Suggest
Sort	Guide
Organize	Advise
Enlist	Teach
Filter	Critique
Summarize	Explain
Alert	Broadcast
Store	Distribute
Monitor	Solicit

AGENT APPLICATIONS

Agents have already been employed in a variety of ISS applications. Five of these applications—intelligent electronic mail (E-mail), competitive intelligence, active documents, personalized newspapers, and hypertext guides—are described in what follows.

Intelligent E-Mail

One of the best known, and most often cited, examples of an agent-based system is the Information Lens [38]. The Information Lens assists the senders and readers of electronic mail messages. The Information Lens employs artificial-intelligence rules and a graphical user interface to create intelligent assistants that can sort and store incoming messages, alert readers when urgent messages arrive, search for specified information, and automatically respond to messages.

The basic assumption underlying the operation of the Lens rests on the idea that E-mail messages are "semistructured." That is, some parts of a message can be prespecified (e.g., the list of people we send a message to is fairly regularized), whereas other parts cannot (e.g., the body of the text usually varies from message to message, although we often use common terms within the messages). The fact that the messages are semistructured means that (1) a series of templates or forms with a specified list of choices for many of the fields can be established for sending messages, and (2) a series of rules can be constructed for deciding what to do with incoming messages based on the contents of the various slots. The types of rules that can be created with the Information Lens are illustrated in what follows (note this is not the exact syntax that is used in the system):

> IF Subject is "Weekly Meeting"
> THEN Store in Meetings

> IF From is "Kirk"
> THEN Alert

> IF Date is Between(Next Monday and Next Friday)
> THEN Store in Temp. and Send Vacation_Msg to From

> IF Subject is "Miscellaneous"
> THEN Delete

For instance, the first rule says that if the "Subject" field in the E-mail message contains the text "Weekly Meeting," then store the message in a file labeled "Meeting_Folder." Similarly, the third rule says that if an E-mail message arrives (is Dated) between next Monday and next Friday, then store the message in a file called "Temp" and send a reply titled "Vacation_Msg" to the person who sent the mail (i.e., the person whose name appears in the "From" field of the E-mail).

In addition to templates and rules, the Information Lens also contains a "public mailbox" where users can post messages on any topic of interest. This public mailbox serves the same functions as a computer-mediated conference or bulletin board. Just like other mail messages, rules are used to retrieve and manage postings in the public mailbox.

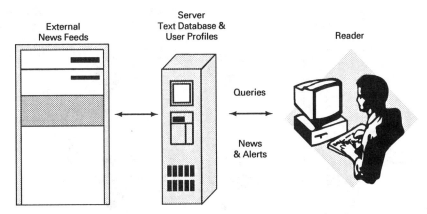

FIGURE 10.5   Text Retrieval and Alerting for Competitive Analysis

The basic features in the Information Lens are rapidly making their way into the marketplace [39]. To date, Beyond Mail is the only commercially available E-mail system with these features. Dun and Bradstreet and DEC have also licensed the technology and are using it in a variety of development projects. In the near future, virtually all E-mail systems will contain agent-based facilities of this sort.

Competitive Intelligence

Many businesses keep tabs on their competitors, gleaning data about new product developments, new plant investments, promotional activities, managerial changes, sales force activity, pricing information, and the like. Much of the information about competitors comes from publicly available, online databases (e.g., Dow Jones, Dialog, NEXIS, NewsNet, etc.). Most executive information systems (EIS) provide a graphical user interface (GUI) to these soft information sources. The problem is that most of these facilities are *keyword* driven and relatively *passive* in nature. It's up to the user to know the right keywords and to periodically access the data.

Newer, proactive systems are appearing. These systems are based on the premises that (1) keyword searches are too imprecise for large text databases, and (2) there is often a mismatch between those who know something about a competitor and those who need to know something about a competitor. Three elements are essential to these systems (Figure 10.5): (1) a database that supports retrieval of text by "meaning" rather than solely by keywords or Boolean queries; (2) a list of users along with their profiles of interests; and (3) an agent-based utility that periodically searches the database for articles of interest, distributes the articles to interested users, and alerts users when an important or urgent story appears.

An example of this type of system is a prototype news retrieval service currently being tested by Comshare Inc. The prototype integrates three separate products (Figure 10.6). The first product is the Dow Vision *news server*, which receives continual updates from the Dow Jones news service. The second product is a real-time *text database* called Verity Topic [40], which acts as the storage tank and filter for Dow Jones stories. Stories are

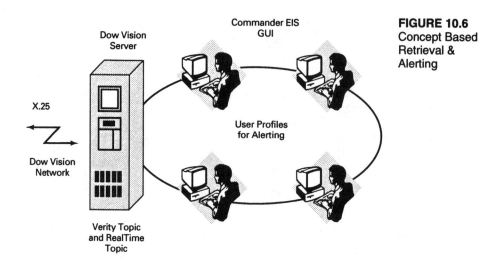

FIGURE 10.6
Concept Based
Retrieval &
Alerting

filtered on the basis of a set of "topics" that are of interest to corporate users. Again, without going into the details, a "topic" query retrieves stories based on concepts rather than by keywords. For example, suppose you were interested in stories about IBM. Simply telling the computer to retrieve stories about "IBM," or it might mention "John Akers," IBM's CEO, without mentioning "IBM." So, "IBM" is not really a word but a general "topic" of interest that is represented by a large number of intertwined concepts, words, and phrases. The final product is Comshare's Commander EIS, which serves as the GUI front end to the news stories and provides the agent utilities that periodically retrieve stories of interest to a particular executive and immediately alert the executive when urgent stories appear in the Verity database (what is "urgent" is defined by the executive or the corporation).

The following is a list of other commercial products (C) and prototypes (P) that provide analogous forms of text retrieval and in some cases alert the user when important entries appear:

CONTENT-BASED RETRIEVAL

C–Construe-TIS [41]
C–grapeVine [42]
C–WAIS [43]
P–Coder [44]
P–InfoNotebook/Dow Quest [45]
P–InfoScope [46]
P–Internet Browser [47]
P–Knowledge Cache [48]

Active Documents

An "active" document is one that knows how to compose itself, store itself, and to automatically move itself from desktop to desktop depending on either its content, some predetermined schedule, or some predetermined route. For example, if data indicate that corporate sales are off in a particular week or quarter, this event could trigger the construction of a report, complete with graphics, and automatically distribute the report to the appropriate executives and sales personnel. Interleaf Release 5.0 and ArborText are both commercially available document-processing systems that support the active document concept.

Active documents can also be implemented using off-the-shelf components such as Microsoft's Excel and Word for Windows products. As an example, consider the Marketing Workbench system developed at Duke University's Fuqua School of Business by John McCann and John Gallagher [49]. The system is a low-cost substitute for the "COVERSTORY" system implemented by Information Resources Inc. [14]. The primary function of the system is to track and analyze sales data generated by UPC (universal product code) scanners and to generate a report recommending strategies for increasing the distribution of one or more products of interest to its end users (sales personnel). The operation of the system is outlined in Figure 10.7.

Basically, a series of Excel macros drive the analysis of the UPC data, which are accessed from a Q+E (SQL) database. Depending on what the analysis reveals, Excel produces appropriate chunks of text and graphics to reflect the underlying "story." A set of Word macros are then used to pull chunks of text and graphics into a formatted report and to print it. Although the system produces printed reports, Word macros could also be used to activate a communications or E-mail package to distribute an electronic version of the report to interested parties.

The Marketing Workbench straddles the fine dividing line between ISS and ESS. In this system, there is virtually no human intervention involved in the construction of the report. Instead, the Excel and Word macros serve as expert systems analyzing the data and composing the report without human aid. The macros embody McCann and Gallagher's analytical and reporting skills. Indeed, one aim of the system is to create

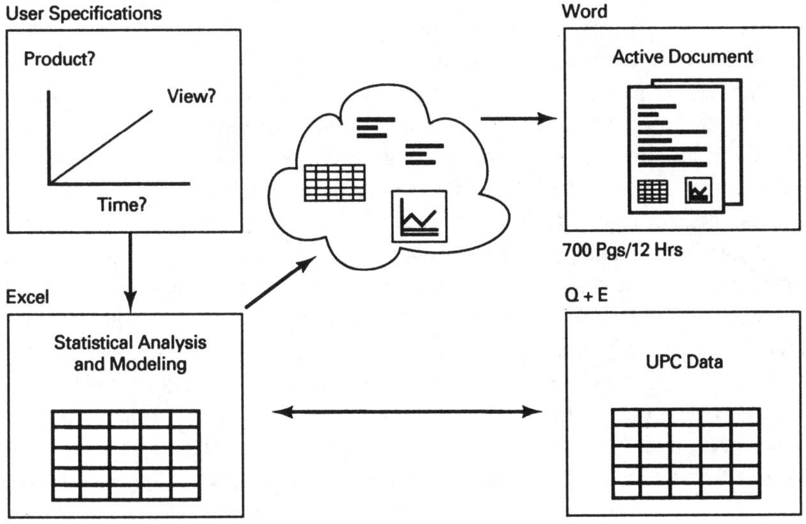

FIGURE 10.7   McCann and Gallagher's Marketing Workbench

automated reports that are as readable and as intelligible as those produced by human analysts. This is expert support. On the other hand, intelligent support might come into play if the system were capable of determining the recepients of the document based on its content.

Because documents (and forms) are key to any large organization, active documents are central to most "workflow" products cropping up in the "groupware" marketplace. "Workflow" is a relatively new product category, although its roots can be traced to earlier work done in the field of Office Automation. AT&T's Rhapsody, Dec's TeamRoute, NCR's Coordination, IBM's Officevision, and HP's NewWave are some of the products that fit in this category. Although automated documents composition is important, automated document routing is equally, if not more, important. After all, it is the routing or movement of work that defines its "flow." Automated routing enables an active document to determine when it should move and where in the network it should move to next. Like intelligent E-mail, routing is usually accomplished with ES-like rules that can move a document based on its content or on the basis of a predetermined schedule or route. Suppose, for instance, that a group of people is writing a document, where each section is assigned to a different person and where each section is dependent on the previous section. Further suppose that each section needs to be completed by a certain date. An active document could, for example, watch the calendar. If a particular section was behind schedule, then the document could inform the writer and urge him or her on. Additionally, the document would know who to forward itself to when the section was complete.

Personalized Newspapers

For some time, pundits have been predicting the emergence of "personalized" newspapers. As early as 1966, a study conducted by TRW [50] forecasted that by 1978, newspapers would be printed on home facsimile machines, and by 1980, these machines would print newspapers with information tailored to the individual's needs. While the fax version never came to pass, there are prototypes and commercially implemented applications that deliver electronic versions of personalized newspapers.

One example is a newspaper that is electronically assembled and distributed to employees at the headquarters of Lincoln National Corporation, a Fort Wayne, Indiana, financial services and banking firm. Making the editorial choices for this automatic newspaper is a text retrieval and "intelligent correlation package" called Metamorph from Thunderstone Software [51]. The software is based on software developed for U.S. government intelligence analysis. The software scans the full text of all news stories as they are transmitted by the major wire services and then pulls out only those items that contain information of interest. This information is combined along with various E-mail messages and reports of public interest into the newspaper, which is distributed by E-mail.

Another, often cited, example is the NewsPeek prototype developed by MIT Media Lab [52]. Again, this prototype draws information from Dow Jones, Nexis, XPress, the wire services, and TV newscasts. Unlike Lincoln National's newspaper, a NewsPeek newspaper is personalized to reflect the interests of the individual reader. The newspaper also supports the inclusion of videodisk images, as well as audio and video clips from TV news stories. The headlines, graphical images, and certain highlighted words in the various stories act as *hot spots* that, when touched by the user, link to underlying detail or retailed stories.

At MIT, one of the future aims is to create "prescient" agents that will learn about user preferences and interests by watching the user as he or she reads the paper. Negroponte [53] provides a simple example of the process:

> Suppose you are reading this electronic paper on line. The system could infer from the time you dwell on particular stories how much of an interest you have in various subjects. So maybe you've been reading articles about government policy toward advanced television research. You might find that the system starts feeding you stories about rulings by the Federal Communications Commission, even though you never explicitly exhibited interest in the FCC. And over time, it would learn more and more about you and so get better and better at figuring out what you want.

Fischer and Stevens [46] have implemented prescient agents in their Infoscope system, which is a graphical front end for browsing messages in Usenet newsgroups. As they note, these agents are loosely based on Anderson's *Rational Analysis of Human Memory* [54]. His analysis forms the base for a series of indicators that are employed to measure the probability of future usage based on prior usage patterns. Of particular importance are the measures of frequency, recency, and spacing. Frequency refers to the number of times a particular item or type of item is needed within a given time period. Recency refers to the amount of elapsed time since a particular item or type of item was needed. Spacing refers to the distribution across time of exposure to a particular item or type of item. The probability that a particular type of item will be needed in the future increases when the frequency is high, when recency is high, and when usage is evenly distributed. By keeping track of these measures, prescient agents in the InfoScope system can adjust the types of messages that are shown to a user and the grouping or location of the messages in the browser. Similar measures could also be employed with personal newspapers to adjust the types of stories that were being displayed, the location of the stories (e.g., moving certain types from the front page to later pages), and the linkages among the stories.

Hypertext Guides

Hypertext has been defined in a variety of ways. From a surface perspective, hypertext has been defined as "nonlinear" text to contrast it with standard text. Nonlinear text allows the reader to easily move from one point of interest to the next in a nonsequential fashion, whereas linear text encourages readers to move from top to bottom and from beginning to end. From a systems perspective, hypertext has been defined as a network database where the database consists of a set of nodes along with a set of links connecting the nodes. Each node contains a chunk of information that might include text, images, graphics, video, audio, or some combination of these. Within each chunk, there is usually one or more buttons, labels, or hot spots representing links to other nodes. When the buttons, labels, or hot spots are touched by the user (usually with a mouse), the linked node appears.

Hypertext is both an authoring tool and a reading tool, although the emphasis is traditionally on reading. As an authoring tool, hypertext has been used for the following:

1. Constructing multimedia documents and presentations (e.g., hypertext reference books, training manuals, games, and product demos).
2. Structured thinking and design in the same way that outline programs have been used for these purposes (e.g., the Notecard system from Xerox is often used by individuals to write plans, papers, and other research documents).
3. Structured communication and collaboration among the members of a team or work group (e.g., gIBIS is a graphical, hypertext system for capturing the issues and arguments raised by various team members during the software design process).

As a reading tool, hypertext is used to browse and navigate the hypertext nodes created in each of these authoring situations.

In the case of multimedia documents and presentations, the links typically serve "functional" roles. That is, a link can

- transfer the user to a new topic
- display a reference
- provide auxiliary information (e.g., a footnote or definition)
- display a graphic image
- activate a video or audio clip
- display an index
- run a program

On the other hand, with structured thinking, communication and collaboration, the links serve not only "functional" roles, but also "conceptual" or "semantic" roles. Here, the nodes in the network represent ideas, issues, arguments, observations, propositions, and the like, and the links represent semantic associations between the nodes. Finally, the resulting network portrays the flow of thought from node to node or the flow of conversation among a group of participants. Semantic networks of this sort have been used, for example, to support the development of mental models in the strategic planning process [55], to support conversations for crisis management [56], and to aid readers of analytical reports based on DSS analysis [57]. Indeed, Murray Turoff, a leading authority on computer conferencing, has boldly claimed that [56]

> Every computer mediated communication system that has ever been implemented may be viewed as a specific tailored version of the Hypertext concept. The concepts of mail, conferences, comments, replies, notifications are all specified linking structures designed to support human communication.

Similar claims have been made by David Friend and Wayne Burkan, two authorities on executive information systems, that "hypertext is the metaphor for EIS in the 1990s."

In general, most of the links in a hypertext system are hard coded by hand. This means that any time a reader activities a button or hot spot, the same (linked) node appears. The following observations pinpoint some of the problems of hard-coded links among nodes [58]:

1. Equally skilled or intelligent readers may use the same information in different ways.
2. The same reader may want to use the same document in different ways at different times.
3. Readers can arrive at the same nodes from radically different routes.
4. Readers have different interests and different skills and may wish to proceed in different ways depending on these attributes.
5. Readers can make mistakes, stumbling down the wrong paths.

One way to overcome the problems with hard-coded links is to produce an *adaptable network*. The key to adaptation is "programmable" links (see the last functional role described before), so that the actions of a button or hot spot can be modified depending on the interests, attributes, or usage patterns of the user. Littleford [58] calls these programmable links "localized" agents. Their primary function is to help readers navigate through the system and to avoid the problem of either feeling or actually being "lost in hyperspace." The feeling arises when readers become disoriented about "where they are" in the network. In large networks, the feeling is manifested, for example, by the tendency of readers to keep revisiting nodes or pathways [59]. One way to assist the reader is to provide prespecified tours or overview maps of the network. Another is to provide the reader with guides (i.e., localized agents) strategically placed at various nodes and links in the network.

One metaphor that has been used to describe these hypertext guides is that of a "park ranger" [60]. In this metaphor, the network is viewed as a set of trails in a large national park. The reader is like a hiker who is trying to wind his way through the trails. Ranger stations are placed at strategic points throughout the park. It is the function of the rangers to assist the hiker when he is lost or to suggest interesting trails to explore. The type of advice provided by the ranger depends on his perceptions of the hiker's interests (he wouldn't send a novice hiker down a difficult trail) and the hiker's interests (he wouldn't send a hiker interested in fauna down a barren path). Similarly, we can think of a "local agent" as an intelligent guide situated at a particular link, waiting for the reader to click the associated button or hot spot. The guide's job is to determine or suggest which node or type of node the reader should visit next by combining knowledge about the user's attributes, interests and usage patterns with knowledge of the organization, and content of the document. The following are some examples of the types of rules a guide might use:

If the reader is interested in an "overview," then guide the reader through sections 1, 5 and 10.

If the reader is an expert, then link to "Advanced Examples" section; otherwise link to "Basic Examples" section.

If the reader asks for suggestions, recommend the path chosen most frequently by previous readers.

If the reader is at a dead end, move the reader back to the nearest "landmark" position.

If the reader has selected this link before, inform and suggest another link.

The use of local agents or guides places a heavy burden on the author. Not only must the author write the text, but the author must also program the rules and create a set of programs (i.e., prescient agents) for tracking the attributes and usage patterns of the reader. Nielsen [59] provides some examples of how this is done. Besides the sweat and toil of the author, the major requisite for constructing adaptable networks is an authoring tool based on an event-driven, expert system or AI-based programming language. The following shows some sample tools that meet this requisite:

HYPERTEXT PROGRAMMING LANGUAGES

HyperBase (Cogent Software—Prolog-based programming language)
1st Class HT (AI Corp.)
KnowledgePro Windows (Knowledge Garden)
Level5 Object (Information Builders)
Nexpert Object (Neuron Data)
Notecards (Xerox—Lisp-based programming language)
Hypercard (Clarion Software)
Visual Basic (Microsoft)

The Future of Intelligent Executive and Decision Support

Many observers begin their comments about agent-based intelligent support systems with the phrase "in the future...." This implies that today's agents are viewed as "limited editions" of future generations [61]. Although there are exceptions, the agents that appear in today's intelligent support systems tend to (1) work alone, not in concert with other agents; (2) focus on single and relatively simple tasks; (3) employ basic reasoning capabilities (i.e., rule-based reasoning); and (4) exhibit only modest learning capabilities. Work on distributed and decentralized artificial intelligence, common sense reasoning and machine learning will certainly enhance the capabilities of coming generations of agents.

Yet, there's always a danger in extrapolating from the present to the future—in saying that the future of intelligent executive and decision support will be more of the same, only better. As Stan Davies and Bill Davidson remind us in their book *2020 Vision*, economies, industries, businesses, products and technologies—like people—have life cycles [62]. As one era matures, the seeds of another begin. Often, the slow demise of the old era and the appearance of the new era is imperceptible. This makes it difficult to predict the future because it's not more of the same.

Alan Kay [30, 31] tells us that "agents" had their origin in the late 1950s and have been on the rise over the past ten years. The examples explored in this reading show some of the ways that agents have been and will be used to assist executives and managers with their decision-making and problem-solving processes. But, if Davis and Davidson are correct, our ideas about agent-based intelligent support and our ideas about executive and decision support in general are already moving toward maturity. More important, the beginnings of a new paradigm are already in progress. The question is: What does this new future look like?

Many commentators have observed that the following organizational and technological changes, among others, will shape the future of executive and decision support systems [63, 64]:

- focus on teams, work groups, and other distributed, decentralized organizational structures
- emphasis on time-based competition and shortened product life cycles
- blurring of the boundaries between enterprises and their environments
- increased use of computers for purposes of communication rather than computation, and the concomitant rise of global computer networks
- rapid rise in the use of object-oriented methodologies, languages, end- user tools, databases, and operating systems
- widespread use of microprocessors in all kinds of technological artifacts

These observations conjure up a number of interesting possibilities:

1. Organizational structures and computer network structures may become coterminious. In fact, some organizations may only exist on the network [65]. Current experiences with EDI (electronic data interchange) [66] and experiences with Lucas Film's Habitat cyberspace experiment [67] provide some indications of the way in which these organizations might operate and the problems they might confront.

2. Executive support and decision support may cease to exist as independent, software categories. The same fate may await most types of software. The demise of these categories is reflected in the rapid eradication of the boundaries between several types of software including: hypertext, GUI front-end tools, spreadsheet, word and document processing, e-mail, conferencing, Imaging, forms, text databases and groupware. In today's windowing environments, it is often very difficult to tell on the surface the underlying tools used to create particular applications. EIS applications, for instance, have been created from EIS software, spreadsheets, GUI front-end tools and word processing programs, to name a few. Because of the increasing use of object oriented methodologies and tools, the distinctions may become even cloudier in the future.

3. "Intelligence" may cease to be an important distinction among applications, systems and programs. In fact, applications, systems and programs (as we know them) may even cease to exist. Instead, everything in the network will probably be an Independent object with the ability to communicate with every other object. Even end-users will be represented by objects. The distinctions among

objects will be found in the services they provide and the types of actions they can perform. In the context of this discussion, becausse objects and agents share virtually the same properties, agency will no longer be a unique property. Insead, everything will be an agent. Additionally, when we want to accomplish a particular communication or computational task, we will organize these agents or objects into goal directed collections in much the same way that we organize teams and workgroups. Again, there are several examples that illustrate the ways in which a purely object oriented world might operate ([68], [69], [70], [71], [72]).

4. Gradually, computers and computer networks may "fade into the woodwork." The services and intelligence currently provided by networked computers will become "ubiguitous" ([29], [53]). Whiteboards, desks, telephones, TVs, light switches, eyeglasses and even kitchen appliances will have embedded intelligence. A network of these "smartifacts," as Mountford [29] calls them, will become the support system of the future.

When these possibilities are viewed in a combined light, the overall result is what Mark Sefik [73] has labeled an *Interactive Knowledge Media*—Information networks encompassing semi autonomous services for the generation, distribution and consumption of knowledge. As Johansen and Saffo (1990) recommend, instead of viewing a system as a collection of autonomous agents, "a knowledge media aproach argues in favor of making the entire communication system an intelligent agent like device."

QUESTIONS

1. What is the difference in the underlying metaphors for expert support systems and intelligent support systems? Why is it an important difference?
2. What is a software agent? What does it do in general? How does it work?
3. Identify some applications for software agents. Describe what the agent accomplishes in each case.
4. Describe hypertext. Why is it viewed as so important?

REFERENCES

1. PETERS, T.   *Thriving on Chaos*. New York: Knopf, 1987.
2. FEDEROWICZ, J., AND M. MANHEIM   "A Framework for Assessing Design Support and Expert Systems," *Transactions of the Sixth International Conference on Decision Support Systems*, 116–127. Washington, D.C., 1986.
3. JARKE, T. AND Y. VASSILIOU   "Coupling Expert Systems with Database Management Systems," *Artificial Intelligence Applications for Business*, ed. W. Reitman, 65–95. Norwood, N.J.: Ablex, 1984.
4. PARSAYE, K., M. CHIGNELL, S. KHOSHAFIAN, AND H. WONG   *Intelligent Databases: Object- Oriented, Deductive, Hypermedia Technologies*. New York: 1989.
5. SCHUR, S.   "Intelligent Databases," *Database Programming and Design* (June 1988), 46–55.

6. TURBAN, E., AND D. KING "Building Expert Systems for Decision Support," *Transactions of the Sixth International Conference on Decision Support Systems*, 96–115. Washington, D.C., 1986.

7. TURBAN, E., AND P. WATKINS "Integrating Expert Systems and Decision Support Systems," *MIS Quarterly* (June 1966):

8. LUCONI, F., T. MALONE, AND M.S.S. MORTON "Expert Systems: The Next Challenge for Managers," *Decision Support Systems: Putting Theory into Practice*, 2d Ed., ed. R. Sprague and H. Watson, 320–334. Englewood Cliffs, N.J.: Prentice Hall, 1989.

9. SUCHMAN, L. *Plans and Situated Actions*. New York: Cambridge University Press, 1987.

10. BERREMAN, G. "Anemic and Emetic Analysis in Social Anthropology," *American Anthropologist*, 68 (1066), 347.

11. RENSI, E. "Computers at McDonalds," *Strategies...Senior Executives Speak Out*, ed. J. McLimore and L. Larwood, 166–167. New York: Harper and Row, 1988.

12. PAYNE, E., AND R. McARTHUR *Developing Expert Systems*. New York: John Wiley, 1990.

13. MILLS, D. Q. *Rebirth of the Corporation*. New York: John Wiley, 1991.

14. SCHMITZ, J., G. ARMSTRONG, AND J. LITTLE "COVERSTORY—Automate d News Finding in Marketing," *Transactions of the Tenth International Conference on Decision Support Systems*, 46–54. Boston, 1990.

15. KING, D. "Intelligent Decision Support: Strategies for Integrating Decision Support, Database Management, and Expert System Technologies," in *Expert Systems with Applications*, Vol. 1, 23–38. 1990.

16. EL SAWY, O. AND T. PAUCHANT "Triggers, Templates and Twitches in Tracking of Emerging Strategic Issues," *Strategic Management Journal*, 9 (September 1988), 46–473.

17. MINYZBERG, H. *Mintzberg on Management*. New York: Free Press, 1989.

18. MANHEIM, M. AND D. ISENBERG "A Theoretical Model of Human Problem Solving and its Use for Designing Decision Support Systems," *Proceedings of the Twentieth Hawaii International Conference on Systems Sciences*, Vol. 1, 614–627. 1987.

19. VAIL, P. *Managing As a Performing Art*. New York: Jossey-Bass, 1989.

20. WEBER, S., AND B. KONSYNSKI 1987.

21. YOUNG, L. 1987.

22. HUBER, G. "The Nature and Design of Postindustrial Organizations," *Management Sciences*, 30 (1964), 926–951.

23. EL SAWY, O. AND H. EL SHERIF "Issue-Based Decision Support Systems for the Egyptian Cabinet," in *Decision Support Systems: Putting Theory into Practice*, 2d Ed., ed. R. Sprague and H. Watson, 206–230. Englewood Cliffs, N.J.: Prentice Hall, 1989.

24. FISCHER, G. *Intelligent Support Systems*, Tutorial. Austin: ACM SIGCHI, 1989.

25. ENGLEBART, D. "The Augmentation Sytem Framework," in *Interactive Multimedia*, ed. S. Ambron and K. Hooper. Redmond, Wash.: Microsoft Press, 1988.

26. NEGROPONTE, N. "HOSPITAL CORNERS," IN *The Art of Human-Computer Interface Design*, ED. B. LAUREL, 352. NEW YORK: ADDISON-WESLEY,

27. DAVISS, B. "Knowbots," *Discover* (April 1991), 21–23.

28. TUROFF, M. "Computer- Mediated Communication Requirements for Group Support," *Journal of Organization Computing*, 1 (1991), 85–113.

29. MOUNTFORD, S. J. 1991.

30. KAY, A. "Computer Software," *Scientific American*, 251 (September 1984), 52–59.

31. KAY, A. "User Interface: A Personal View," in *The Art of Human- Computer Interface Design*, ed. B. Laurel, 191–207. New York: Addison-Wesley,

32. KAPLAN, S. J., M. KAPOR, E. BELOVE, R. LANDSMAN, AND T. DRAKE "Agenda: A Personal Information Manager," *CACM*, 33 (July 1990), 105–116.

33. BOONE, M. *Leadership and the Computer*. New York: Prima, 1991.

34. FISHER, S. "Networking: Promises and Problems," *Byte Special Edition: Outlook '92* (1991), 117–121.

35. PALLER, A. *The EIS Book*. Homewood, Ill.: Dow Jones Irwin, 1990.

36. BARTIMO, J. "Crystal Ball," *Wall Street Journal* (May 20, 1991), R31.

37. SCULLEY, J. *Odyssey*. New York: Harper and Row, 1987.

38. MALONE, T., K. GRANT, F. Turbak, S. Brebet, and M. Cohen "INTELLIGENT INFORMATION SHARING SYSTEMS," *CACM*, 30 (MAY 1987),

39. ROBINSON, M. "Through the Lens Smartly," *Byte* (May 1991), 177–187.

40. APPLETON, E. "Smart Document Retrieval," *Datamation* (January 15, 1992), 20–23.

41. HAYES, P. AND S. WEINSTEIN "Construe-TIS: A System for Content-Based Indexing of a Database of News Stories," in *Innovative Applications of Artificial Intelligence*, ed. A. Rapport and R. Smith, Cambridge, Mass.: MIT Press, 1991.

42. BROOKES, C. "A Corporate Intelligence System for Soft Information Exchange," in *Knowledge Representation for Decision Support System*, ed. L. Methlie and R. Sprague, 161–166. New York: Elsevier, 1985.

43. STEIN, R. "Browsing Thru Terabytes," *Byte* (May 1991, 157–164.

44. FOX, E., O. CHEN, AND R. FRANCE "Integrating Search and Retrieval with Hypertext," in *Hypertext/Hypermedia Handbook*, ed. E. Berk and J. Devlin, 329–356. New York: Intertext, 1991.

45. ERICKSON, T. AND G. SALAMON "Designing a Desktop Information System: Observations and Issues," *CHI Conference Proceedings: Human Factors in Computing Systems*, 49–54. ACM Press, 1991.

46. FISCHER, G., AND P. STEVENS "Information Access in Complex, Poorly Structured Information Spaces," *CHI Conference Proceedings: Human Factors in Computing Systems, 63–70. ACM Press, 1991.*

47. RATZAN, L. "Building An Internet Browser," *Unix Review* (January 1992), 25–29.

48. ELOFSON, G., AND B. KONSYNSKI "Supporting Knowledge Sharing in Environmental Scanning," *Proceedings of the Twenty-Third Hawaii International Conference on System Sciences*, Vol. IV, 261–266. 1990.

49. McCANN, J., AND J. GALLAGHER *Databases and Knowledge Systems in Merchandising*. New York: Van Nostrand Reinhold, 1991.

50. SCHNAARS, S. *Megamistakes: Forecasting and the Myth of Rapid Technological Change*. New York: Free Press, 1989.

51. KONSTADT, P. "Informed Sources," *CIO* (November 1990), 73–80.

52. BRAND, S. *The Media Lab: Inventing the Future at MIT*. New York: Viking, 1987.

53. BRODY, H. "Machine Dreams: An Interview with Nicholas Negroponte," *Technology Review*, 95, (January 1992), 33–40.

54. ANDERSON, J. *The Adaptive Character of Thought*. Hillsdale, N.J.: Lawrence Erlbaum Associates, 1990.

55. CARLSON, D., AND S. RAM "HyperIntelligence: The New Frontier," *CACM* (May 1990), 311–322.

56. TUROFF, M., U. RAO, AND S. HILTZ "Collaborative Hypertext in Computer Mediated Communications," *Proceedings of the Twenty-Fourth Hawaii International Conference on System Sciences*, Vol. IV, 357–366. 1991.

57. KIMBROUGH, S., C. PRITCHETT, M. BIEBER, AND H. BHARFAVA "An Overview of the Coast Guard's KSS Project: DSS Concepts and Technology," *Transactions of the Tenth International Conference on Decision Support Systems*, Cambridge, Mass., May 1990, 63–77.

58. LITTLEFORD, A. "Artificial Intelligence and Hypermedia," in *Hypertext/Hypermedia Handbook*, ed. E. Berk and J. Devlin, 357–380. New York: Intertext, 1991.

59. NIELSEN, J. *Hypertext and Hypermedia*. New York: Academic Press, 1990.

60. STEINBERG, D., AND H. ZIV "Software Visualization and Yosemite National Park," *Proceedings of the Twenty-Fifth Hawaii International Conference on System Sciences*, Vol. II, 607–618. 1992.

61. JOHANSEN, R. *Groupware: Computer Support for Business Teams*. New York: Free Press, 1988.

62. DAVIS, S., AND B. DAVIDSON *2020 Vision*. New York: Simon & Schuster, 1991.

63. HUBER, G. "Organizational Learning: The Contributing Processes and Literatures," *Organizational Science*, 2 (1991), 88–115.

64. OPPER, S., AND H. WEISS *Technology for Teams: Enhancing Productivity in Networked Organizations*. New York: Van Nostrand Reinhold, 1992.

65. MALONE, T., AND J. ROCKERT "Computers, Networks and the Corporation," *Scientific American*, 265, (September 1991), 92–99.

66. KIMBROUGH, S., AND S. MOORE "Message Management Systems: Concepts and Motivations," *Proceedings of the Twenty- Fifth Hawaii International Conference on System Sciences*, Vol. IV, 654–665. 1992.

67. MORNINGSTAR, C., AND F. FARMER "The Lessons of LucasFilm's Habitat," *Cyberspace: First Steps*, ed. M. Benedikt, 273–302. Cambridge, Mass.: MIT Press.

68. CARR, R., AND D. SHAFER *The Power of Penpoint*. New York: Addison-Wesley, 1991.

69. DEJONG, S. P. *Ubik: A Framework for the Development of Distributed Organizations*. Ph.D. dissertation, Massachusetts Institute of Technology, Cambridge, Mass., August 1989.

70. LAI, K., T. MALONE, AND K. YU "Object Lens: A Spreadsheet," *ACM Transactions on Office Information Systems*, 6 (October 1988),

71. TSICHRITZIS, D. "Objectworld," in *Office Automation*, ed. by D. Tsichritzis. New York: Springer Verlag, 1985.

72. GELERTNER, D. *Mirror Worlds*. Oxford: Oxford University Press, 1991.

73. STEFIK, M. "The Next Knowledge Medium," *AI Magazine*, 7 (Spirng 1986), 34–46.

PART 4

Creating the DSS Environment

DSS activity can begin in a variety of ways in an organization. At one extreme, an individual champion may build decision support systems on an entrepreneurial basis, and at the other extreme, the organization may commit itself to supporting and encouraging DSS as part of its corporate strategy. Whatever approach is taken, there normally comes a time when management realizes that a systematic approach must be used in order to create an appropriate DSS environment. This endeavor is a major undertaking that involves human as well as physical resources.

This part of the book contains four readings on creating the DSS environment. It ranges from broad selections such as how to develop an organizational environment for DSS to narrower ones such as how to select DSS software. It includes both conceptual ideas and actual illustrations of how organizations are creating an environment for DSS. The end result should be an enhanced understanding of how to develop a setting in which DSS activities can flourish.

An important part of the DSS environment is the organizational environment within which the DSS will be developed and revised. Hugh Watson and Houston Carr in Reading 11 discuss the principal elements of this organizational environment and explain how the DSS support team can be organized for maximum effectiveness. They also describe how DSS support is being provided at the Oglethorpe Power Corporation.

Another important environment is the political, cultural, and problem-solving environment, which is especially important for the support of high-level strategy formulation and policy setting. In their award-winning article, "Issue-Based Decision Support Systems for the Egyptian Cabinet," Omar El Sawy and Hisham El Sherif in Reading 12 show how a DSS can be structured to provide valuable support in an environment characterized by turbulence and ambiguity.

The software environment for DSS is crucial because it provides the ability to create DSS applications quickly and change them frequently. Louis Le Blanc and Tawfik Jelassi, in Reading 13, offer an approach to selecting the heart of the software environment—the DSS generator—using an expanded set of evaluation criteria. Their approach allows for the possibility of building the software environment without a generator, and building specific DSS directly from DSS tools.

Some firms have changed their information systems organization structure to better accommodate end-user computing, office automation, and decision support systems. The Mead Corporation is one of these firms. Ralph Sprague and Barbara McNurlin, in "The Mead Corporation" (Reading 14), describe how Mead has organized its information systems activities and what services are provided. They also discuss the benefits and problems of Mead's organization structure.

11

ORGANIZING FOR DECISION SUPPORT SYSTEM SUPPORT: THE END-USER SERVICES ALTERNATIVE

Hugh J. Watson,
Houston H. Carr

INTRODUCTION

Decision support systems (DSS) are being used in an increasing number of organizations, and with this development comes the need to support DSS efforts. This includes helping users evaluate hardware and software products, providing access to data, and participating in application development. First, however, it must be decided which organizational unit(s) is (are) responsible for DSS support. This decision has a potentially significant impact on the success and direction of DSS efforts in an organization. It is not an easy decision because there are many alternatives, there is no conventional wisdom, an organization's past history influences the choices, and organization structure decisions are frequently difficult to make.

Our purpose is to explore the issue of where to locate DSS support. We will discuss the evolution of DSS, especially in regard to how organizations have handled it. We

Reprinted from the *Journal of Management Information Systems,* Vol. 4, No. 1, 1987. By permission of M. E. Sharpe, Inc., Armonk, NY.

will also examine the evolution of end-user computing (EUC) because it has many parallels with DSS and offers an emerging placement alternative. In order to evaluate the placement alternatives, their advantages and disadvantages are considered. Given this background, we will explore the end-user services alternative and describe how one company, the Oglethorpe Power Corporation of Atlanta, Georgia, is organized. The discussion and case study should help senior-level information systems managers and executives understand the issues and alternatives which exist and stimulate researchers to investigate this relatively unexplored area.

DSS AND *EUC*: PARALLEL LINES OF EVOLUTION

DSS activity can be traced to the late 1960s when the first decision support systems began to appear [9]. Their emergence can be associated with hardware and software advances (e.g., timesharing terminals) and the realization that traditional management information systems (MIS) or operations research/management science (OR/MS) approaches to supporting poorly structured decision making were unlikely to succeed. During the early to mid 1970s there were further hardware and, especially, software advances (e.g., DSS generators) and the conceptual foundation (e.g., iterative design) for DSS was laid. From the late 1970s to the present, hardware and software advances (e.g., PCs, integrated software packages) facilitated DSS application development and an increasing number of books, articles, and conferences spread the DSS doctrine.

Today, DSS activity may be found in most large organizations. This activity can have a variety of origins, it can change over time, and different organizational units may be involved with it. However, as DSS activity spreads in an organization, there is normally a growing awareness that DSS efforts need formal organizational support. This typically results in one or more organizational units assuming DSS responsibilities. Independent of which choice(s) is (are) made, responsibility for the activities listed in Table 11.1 needs to be assumed. The importance of supporting these activities by one or more groups tends to change over time as DSS activity in an organization moves through the stages of growth [3, 5].

TABLE 11.1   Responsibilities of a Decision Support System (DSS) Group

- Plan, organize, staff, direct, and control DSS activities
- Provide hardware, software, and data
- Promote the use of DSS
- Build DSS for end users
- Conduct training programs
- Provide DSS consulting services
- Evaluate DSS hardware and software products
- Provide technical support

During the same timeframe, end-user computing was developing. The first end users were in engineering where direct access to the computer made it possible to avoid the delays and backlogs of formal development. The engineering departments had a well-defined organizational structure and charter, an established power base, access to financial resources, and trained personnel and could often acquire their own computing equipment. The engineers also had the aptitude and inclination to support themselves.

Business-oriented EUC did not appear until the early 1970s. At this point, the backlog of requests was intolerable, hardware and software advances were such that business end users were better able to address their own needs, and colleges were producing more computer literate graduates. Even so, business-oriented EUC did not advance rapidly due to the nature of the end users. They often did not have the attitude, aptitude, and training to support themselves as did the engineers.

Near the end of the 1970s, software and hardware developments, as well as vendor attitudes, combined to make resources, support, and training available. This occurred at a time when the data services department and company management began to recognize the value of EUC and as data services became less and less able to respond to the demand for application development. Not all users gained access and support through the usual path to the firm's computer. Many sought faster routes through the purchase of packaged software, the use of outside timesharing services, and the departmental purchase of personal computers. In each case, the user's objective was to gain access to the computer and computer-resident data to make queries, analyze data, and generate reports.

The establishment of formal EUC support groups did not occur until the early 1980s. Unlike that of DSS, EUC support customarily comes from designated members of the application development department, who work with technical services and data administration for the users. Part of the impetus to formally support end users was to reduce the expenditures for outside timesharing services and to control the purchase of personal computers. As formal EUC support developed, both of these practices have either declined or been more generally controlled [4]. Table 11.2 lists the responsibilities of an EUC support group.

Many organizations are making EUC support groups full-fledged brothers to technical support, application development, and operations. There are many advantages to this organizational arrangement. It provides a central, visible place where end users can go for

TABLE 11.2   Responsibilities of an End-User Computing Group

- Plan, support, market, and control end-user computing

- Provide consulting and troubleshooting services

- Conduct end-user training

- Support end users in interfacing with other data processing departments

- Help provide access to corporate data

- Perform hardware and software evaluations

- Assist in acquiring and installing hardware

- Promote aspects of security

a variety of support. When end users seek support, they find personnel with the right mix of education, experience, and personal attributes. The existence of an EUC support group naturally separates those development tasks which are large, complex, lengthy, and costly and which are best handled by IS development from those which are small, simple, quick, or hard to cost-justify and which can be best handled by end users given appropriate support. It also reduces interruptions to other IS personnel by end users.

As one considers the responsibilities of DSS and EUC groups, many similarities are seen in the support services that each provides. These similarities suggest the possibility that both types of support might be provided by a common organizational unit. Though this general concept has its merits, the differences between DSS and EUC groups must be considered before any support is organized. These issues are discussed next as the various placement alternatives for DSS support are explored.

DSS ORGANIZATIONAL PLACEMENT

Organizations use a variety of organizational placements for DSS. Some placements remain where they began originally. At the other extreme, some placements reflect careful thought and consideration. For example, one company's financial planning group used a financial planning language for application development and became the major source of DSS support in the organization. At another company, a decision support systems unit was created to lead the organization's DSS efforts.

There is no organizational placement for DSS which is best for all organizations. Each alternative has pros and cons which need to be considered in light of an organization's past and current situation. As with many organizational structure decisions, a number of alternatives can be used if appropriate care is taken.

An organization can choose to centralize or distribute DSS responsibilities. In the first case, a single organizational unit is charged with the responsibility for formally supporting DSS. In the latter case, DSS responsibilities are spread over several organizational units. Once again, each alternative is potentially viable. However, a danger with distributing DSS responsibilities is that important DSS activities may be neglected.

Sprague and Carlson [10] suggest a number of origins for DSS groups in organizations:

1. a special purpose team of applications systems analysts,
2. a reoriented tools group,
3. management science or operations research group,
4. a planning department, and
5. a staff analysis group from one of the functional areas.

Each of these origins can become an organization's primary DSS support group. There are also other possibilities:

6. a formally chartered DSS group,
7. the information center, and
8. a DSS group within end-user services.

There is some evidence that shows which alternatives are most common in organizations. In view of empirical data and the authors' own observations, a planning department or specialized staff analysis group seems to be the most popular choice [6]. There is no reason to believe, however, that the most popular current placements will remain the same over time given the speed with which computer-related activities change.

There are advantages and disadvantages to the various placement alternatives. Several of the alternatives are grouped together because of their similarities. Only the most distinguishing advantages and disadvantages are discussed in order to highlight the differences among the alternatives.

Alternatives 1–2: Applications Systems Analysts and Reoriented Tools Groups

Alternatives 1–2 involve placing DSS support in the hands of data-processing professionals. There are several advantages to this choice. Personnel in these groups are skilled in the use of computer hardware and software technology, are experienced in developing computer applications, and are capable of providing strong technical support.

There are also disadvantages with this selection. Data-processing professionals tend to be oriented toward traditional information systems methods and applications, and their training and experience may have limited transferability to DSS work. Also the group does not contain the mix of personnel with the skills needed for supporting DSS activities. They may only have a limited understanding of the nature of the decisions faced by managers and functional area personnel. They may speak in jargon alien to many potential users. For these reasons, they do not enjoy the confidence of management and functional area users. For most organizations, the disadvantages of alternatives 1–2 outweigh the advantages.

Alternative 3: Operations Research/Management Science Groups

Operations research/management science (OR/MS) groups are highly skilled in modeling and providing computer-based decision support. Unfortunately, many OR/MS groups are not held in high regard by management. The OR/MS people and their methods seem remote from the problems and decisions in the functional areas. In fact, the trend in many organizations is to distribute rather than centralize OR/MS talent [12]. Traditional OR/MS approaches are best suited for structured decision making rather than the semi-structured and unstructured decision making which characterizes DSS. Their organizational ties to data services may be loose, and OR/MS personnel also are frequently criticized for their specialized jargon.

Once again the disadvantages outweigh the advantages. However, we should point out that the OR/MS field is reconsidering its usefulness and organizational role. These deliberations may produce a new orientation more closely associated with the DSS approach. If this happens, the disadvantages associated with the OR/MS alternative would decrease.

Alternatives 4–5: Planning Departments and Staff Analysis Groups

Alternatives 4–5 (planning departments and staff analysis groups) are similar in that both are specialized staff groups. Both are also popular choices for housing DSS activities. They have the advantage of being where many of the potential DSS applications are located. They have frequent contact with management and functional area personnel. Their mindset is that of an end user, and they speak in the language of potential DSS users.

There are also disadvantages associated with this choice. The interest of planning departments and staff analysis groups in DSS may be greater in their own applications than in the applications of other potential users. They may have trouble perceiving themselves as a DSS support group and, hence, ready to accept the full range of DSS support responsibilities. They are likely to be relatively weak in their ability to provide technical support and may have only weak ties to the data services department.

Though these are popular choices for housing DSS work, there are significant problems with these alternatives. The most serious are a possible lack of support for DSS efforts outside of the group and the group's low visibility as a focal point for DSS activities.

Alternative 6: Formally Chartered DSS Groups

Some organizations have created new, formally chartered organizational units responsible for DSS activities. This approach has a number of appeals. A staff can be assembled with the correct combination of skills necessary for DSS work, including the ability to communicate effectively with users. A range of DSS support responsibilities is easily assigned to the group, and they can take an organization-wide approach to DSS.

The disadvantages are less obvious than with the other alternatives, but they do exist. As a new, small, specialized staff group, they may not have a strong base of political support. Depending on their placement in the organization's structure, they may not be highly visible to potential users. In an ideal arrangement for fostering DSS, the DSS group should be placed high in the organization's structure and support upper management. However, this arrangement is not always easy to sell to top management because management may be uncertain about what DSS has to offer and may feel that DSS is just another set of computer applications. Also, the appealing nature of their work and their potential contacts with top management and other important organizational personnel may foster resentment from the data services group.

The separate DSS group has considerable appeal. Safeguards need to be installed, however, to minimize disadvantages.

Alternative 7: Information Centers

Many organizations have created information centers (IC) to formally support end-user computing. Their responsibilities are similar to those listed for an EUC group. Both groups have administrative responsibilities, provide consulting services, supply technical support, evaluate hardware and software products, and provide training. Consequently, it makes sense to consider placing DSS activities in the information center. There are other points in favor of this placement alternative. It is more efficient to have a single group. Information centers are well received, highly visible, and familiar with organization-wide information needs. They tend to be service-oriented and capable of serving a variety of computing and information needs.

The use of the information center has disadvantages that, like those of the formally chartered DSS group, may not be obvious immediately. Information centers tend to be understaffed relative to the amount of work and customer base they support. The backgrounds, educational levels, and training of IC and DSS groups differ. IC staff support to top management may be limited, and they may be more familiar with tools than with potential applications.

Information centers ultimately may be an attractive home for DSS activities. To date, there is little evidence about how well this alternative is working. There is another alternative, however, that has the advantages of the IC but fewer of the disadvantages.

Alternative 8: A DSS Group within End-User Services

The last alternative, and one that we believe has great potential, is the end-user services (EUS) group. With this organizational arrangement, the DSS group becomes a department within EUS along with the IC and other user support staffs. This alternative has many advantages, overcomes most of the disadvantages associated with the other alternatives, and is compatible with current trends in providing computer services. EUS advantages include high visibility, accessibility, a formal organization charter, support for fast application development, a management and a functional area orientation, a firm base of support, and close ties to data services.

Separating DSS from the IC eliminates many of the disadvantages of an IC placement. The DSS group would not be affected by the existing workload of IC staffs. The DSS staff would have the right mix of education, skills, and experience. This staff could possess an exceptionally strong management and functional area orientation. They would have the time, opportunity, and charter to stay current with DSS developments.

There are some disadvantages to this placement alternative. Because placement of an end-user services group in the overall organization structure is relatively low, upper management may not fully perceive and utilize this support. This problem might be reduced, however, by aggressive promotion of DSS services. Another potential problem is how the data services group treats the DSS group. There may be jealousy within the application development department because of the attractiveness of DSS work and the contacts that such work provides throughout the organization. Data services management might fail to recognize the contribution of DSS to the organization because of the difficulty of measuring many of the benefits of DSS. One key to managing this potential problem is to make data services management understand the role and value of DSS to an organization. Another is to protect the DSS group.

The following case study illustrates the value of an end-user services group for the support of DSS as well as more generic end-user computing activities.

THE OGLETHORPE POWER CORPORATION

Oglethorpe Power Corporation (OPC) is a not-for-profit power supply cooperative formed in 1974 to provide electricity to 39 of Georgia's 42 consumer-owned Electric Membership Corporations (EMCs). These EMCs serve businesses, farms, homes, and institutions in many of Georgia's rural and suburban areas. Oglethorpe Power's member-EMCs provide electricity to more than 1.6 million Georgians living in about 71% of the state's geographic area.

The corporation employs more than 400 people, 40 of whom are in the MIS department. The end-user services group is a relatively recent addition to the MIS organization. It is a result of splitting the systems development group to provide better management and control of both operational and end-user-developed applications and to formally acknowledge the difference in these applications. End-user services contains three separate functions: corporate model, decision support systems, and the information center. The corporate model and decision support systems groups support OPC's efforts at modeling the demand and supply of electrical energy and translating this analysis into financial terms. The information center provides the classic (i.e., the IBM concept) set of IC services. Figure 11.1 shows the present organization structure for supporting EUC.

Corporate Models

Work on a corporate planning model was begun in 1977. A team of financial planners, engineers, and consultants used SIMPLAN in creating it. The model was first used by the planning department in 1979.

The corporate model unit consists of three people who assist in support and development. The model is updated on a project basis using a team consisting of EUS personnel and staff from the user department. The model is especially important to the functioning of the planning department.

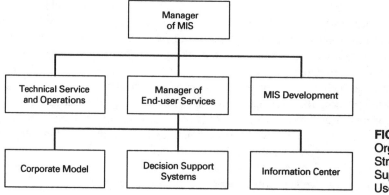

FIGURE 11.1
Organization Structure for Supporting End-User Computing

Decision Support Systems

The three members of the DSS staff support the development of DSS by end users. Personnel from planning, contracts, and finance are the primary users of DSS. Most of the DSS applications are for planning purposes. As the manager of MIS has said, "Planning is our major emphasis."

A variety of services are provided by the DSS staff. Most DSS applications at OPC are detailed, complex, and mainframe-oriented. This requires that the DSS staff works closely with end users who are the primary DSS developers. Training must be provided for the use of products such as XSIM, Easytrieve, SIMPLAN, Tel-a-graph, SAS, and Megacalc. Many of the DSS applications utilize large amounts of historical data, and users frequently need assistance in accessing this data. The DSS staff provides technical support in utilizing the mainframe. It also assists in model development.

Information Center

The information center is staffed by two individuals who provide classic IC services. Most of the IC work is PC-oriented and requires no support for modeling efforts. Much of the staff's time is spent answering end users' questions. Lotus 1-2-3, Symphony, dBase III, and a variety of specialized software are used, and training is provided on the use of these products. Users frequently require assistance in obtaining needed data. The IC is expanding in size and scope, and the IC staff is responsible for managing this growth. New products must be evaluated, purchased, installed, and implemented.

How It Is Working

The organizational arrangements at OPC for supporting DSS are working out well. Both the manager of MIS and end users feel that strong DSS support is being provided. The DSS group has an organizational charter to help users develop their own DSS applications. An appropriate range of DSS services is being provided. The group is visible within the organization. Its separation from the IC staff allows the group to focus its attention on DSS activities. The EUS staff is received well by the user community. In a recent survey, EUS in general and DSS in particular received good grades from the people they support.

CONCLUSION

Many organizations are reorganizing for the delivery of information systems products and services. This change is the result of growing awareness that the role of the data services organization is moving from that of a provider of products to a supplier of products *and* services. With the likelihood that end-user computing will become the dominant form of computing in the 1990s [7], this added attention to the service dimension is entirely appropriate. In order to better accommodate EUC, many organizations are adding end-user computing support groups to the systems development, operations, and technical support departments within the data services department.

Information systems applications can be categorized as operational, end-user-developed, and third-environment [7]. Operational applications are company wide, use corporate data, and serve many users. These are the types of applications developed by IS professionals. End-user-developed applications are found in organizational subunits, use private as well as corporate data, and serve one or only a few users. Third-environment applications are departmental, employ data from one or only a few departments, and serve users at the same level. The development of these applications is jointly shared by end users and IS professionals.

End-user services groups within data services support EUC and third-environment application development. In order to provide this support, several departments may be placed within EUS. The most common, of course, is the information center. Other logical candidates include office automation and decision support systems because of the nature of the applications they support.

Eight organization placement alternatives for DSS have been discussed. The major advantages and disadvantages associated with each alternative are summarized in Table 11.3. We have argued for placing DSS in a separate department within data services, called end-user services. This alternative currently is being used quite well by the Oglethorpe Power Corporation, as the case study showed.

The placement of DSS support in a separate group within end- user services is a new development. Not only does it suggest an interesting option for MIS managers, but it also provides a new area for MIS researchers. In a few years we should better understand how this placement alternative is working out.[*]

TABLE 11.3   The Advantages and Disadvantages of Decision Support Systems (DSS) Organization Placement Alternatives

DSS ALTERNATIVES 1–2: APPLICATIONS SYSTEMS ANALYSTS AND REORIENTED TOOLS GROUPS

Advantages	Disadvantages
Skilled in the use of computer hardware and software technology	Oriented toward traditional IS applications and methods
Experienced in application development	Staff does not have an appropriate mix of backgrounds and experiences
Capable of providing strong technical support	Not familiar with many potential applications

DSS ALTERNATIVE 3: OPERATIONS RESEARCH/MANAGEMENT SCIENCE GROUPS

Advantages	Disadvantages
Skilled in the use of models	May be more oriented toward providing solutions rather than supporting decision making

[*]The authors would like to thank Margaret Schultz, manager of MIS at Oglethorpe Power Corporation, for providing the information on which this case is based.

Table 11.3   (Continued)

DSS ALTERNATIVE 3: OPERATIONS RESEARCH/MANAGEMENT SCIENCE GROUPS (Continued)

Advantages	Disadvantages
Experienced in providing computer-based support	May not have the confidence of management and functional area users
	May not communicate in terms understandable to managers and functional area users
	Has only loose ties to IS

DSS ALTERNATIVES 4–5: PLANNING DEPARTMENTS AND STAFF ANALYSIS GROUPS

Advantages	Disadvantages
Many DSS applications are located here	May not be as interested in other DSS applications as in their own
High level of contact with management and functional area users	May not perceive themselves as having responsibility for the full range of DSS support responsibilities
Communicates in the language of managers and functional area users	May offer only weak technical support

---

DSS ALTERNATIVE 6: FORMALLY CHARTERED DSS GROUPS

Advantages	Disadvantages
The staff has the appropriate mix of skills for performing DSS work	May not have a firm base of support
Understands the role and nature of DSS Fully responsible for supporting DSS activities	May not be highly visible in the organization May be resented by IS
Can take an organization-wide approach to supporting DSS	

DSS ALTERNATIVE 7: INFORMATION CENTERS (ICs)

Advantages	Disadvantages
High visibility with management and functional area users	May be understaffed for supporting DSS
Many of the responsibilities of ICs correspond with DSS responsibilities	The staff typically does not have the appropriate mix of background and experiences
Very accessible to managers and functional area users	May have limited contact with top management
Good technical support for DSS	Staff may be unfamiliar with potential applications

Table 11.3   (Continued)

DSS ALTERNATIVE 7: INFORMATION CENTERS (ICs)

Advantages	Disadvantages
Familiar with organization-wide information needs	
Has a service orientation	

DSS ALTERNATIVE 8: A DSS GROUP WITHIN END-USER SERVICES

Advantages	Disadvantages
High visibility with management and functional area users	May be too much under the influence of data services
Many of the responsibilities of EUC correspond with DSS responsibilities	Low organization placement may limit its use by top management
Very accessible to managers and functional area users	
A firm base of support	
Good technical support for DSS	

QUESTIONS

1. It appears that the responsibilities of the DSS and end-user support groups are very similar. What are the important characteristics that differentiate them?
2. Eight alternatives are given for the support of DSS in an organization. One view is that the groups can be placed on a continuum ranging from a technical to a managerial orientation. Draw this continuum and place the eight groups in their proper places. (If appropriate, you may wish to place some of them at a vertical distance from the horizontal continuum line to show an additional dimension.)
3. Discuss the advantages and the disadvantages of the organization structure shown in Figure 11.1.
4. Potentially, DSS could be developed at any level of the organization—that is, operational, management control, or strategic. Would different qualities or resources be required to support the building of DSS at these different levels? If so, what would they be?

REFERENCES

1. ALLOWAY, R. M., AND J. A. QUILLARD   User managers' systems needs. *MIS Quarterly,* 7, 2 (June 1983), 27–41.
2. EDELMAN, F.   The management of information resources—A challenge for American business. *MIS Quarterly,* 5, 1 (March 1981), 17–27.

3.   GIBSON, C. F., AND R. L. NOLAN   Managing the four stages of EDP growth. *Harvard Business Review*, 52, 1 (January–February 1974), 76–88.

4.   HARRAR, G.   Information center, the user's report. *Computerworld* (December 26, 1983–January 2, 1984), 70–74.

5.   HENDERSON, J. C., AND M. E. TREACY   Managing end user computing. CISR working paper No. 114. Massachusetts Institute of Technology Center for Information Systems Research, Cambridge, MA, May 1984.

6.   HOGUE, J. T., AND H. H. WATSON   Management's role in the approval and administration of decision support systems. *MIS Quarterly*, 7, 2, (June 1983), 15–26.

7.   ROCKART, J. F., AND L. S. FLANNERY   The management of end user computing—A research perspective. CISR working paper No. 100, Massachusetts Institute of Technology, Cambridge, MA, February 1983.

8.   ROSENBERGER, R. B.   The productivity impacts of an information center on application development. *Proceedings GUIDE 53*. Dallas, TX, 1981, 918–932.

9.   SCOTT MORTON, M. S.   Management decision systems: Computer based support for decision making. Division of Research, Harvard University, Cambridge, MA, 1971.

10.   SPRAGUE, R. H., JR., AND E. D. CARLSON   *Building Effective Decision Support Systems*. Englewood Cliffs, NJ: Prentice Hall, 1982.

11.   TARGLER, R.   Information center. *Information Processing*, 2, 1 (March 1983), 12–14.

12.   THOMAS, G., AND J. A. DA COSTA   Sample survey of corporate operations research. Interfaces (August 1979), 103–111.

12

ISSUE-BASED DECISION SUPPORT SYSTEMS FOR THE EGYPTIAN CABINET

Omar A. El Sawy,
Hisham El Sherif

THE CHALLENGE OF PROVIDING INFORMATION AND DECISION SUPPORT FOR STRATEGIC DECISION-MAKING PROCESSES

The effectiveness of strategic decisions can have enormous impacts on organizations and their successful functioning. Consequently, it is a critical priority for information systems professionals to effectively provide organizations with information and decision support systems that support and enhance the strategic decision-making process. The process of managing the design and delivery of such systems is what we report and examine in this article.

Information systems professionals generally agree that—despite the advances in the design and implementation of decision support systems (DSS) in the last decade,

Reprinted by special permission of the *MIS Quarterly,* Volume 12, Number 4, December 1988. Copyright 1988 by the Society for Information Management and the Management Information Systems Research Center.

despite the rapid strides in information technology capabilities, despite the relatively widespread acceptance of DSS by professionals and middle managers, and even despite the recent emergence of executive information systems (EIS)—the provision of effective DSS for strategic decision making remains a challenge that we have yet to overcome. While there are examples of successful DSS used for strategic decision making by top managers in such decision contexts as mergers and acquisitions, plant location, and capital expenditures, they tend to focus on limited well-structured phases of specific decisions. However, when it comes to supporting the whole strategic decision-making process over time with competing and changing strategic issues, multiple decisions, and changing participants, we have made much less progress. Our motivation here is to contribute one more step toward overcoming that challenge.

A large part of the challenge comes from the messy and complex nature of the strategic decision-making process itself and the accompanying encumbrances that it brings to the DSS design and delivery situation:

- Strategic decision making is a murky, ill-structured process that can be drawn out over weeks and months, yet often requires very rapid response capabilities in crisis situations.

- Strategic decision making is usually a group effort rather than an individual one, and it involves activities such as cooperative ideation, cooperative problem solving, conflict resolution, negotiation, crisis management, and consensus building (Gray, 1988).

- Strategic decision making in turbulent and dynamic environments is accompanied by a large environmental scanning component which has its own information requirements for early warning about potential discontinuities, surprises, threats, and opportunities (El Sawy, 1985).

- A strategic decision involves multiple stakeholders with different implicit assumptions that need to be surfaced and made explicit (Mason and Mitroff, 1981).

- Strategy formation in dynamic environments takes place in a somewhat less deliberate and a much more emergent fashion than conventional descriptions of strategic management suggest, bringing with it a large serendipitous discovery component whose support requirements are difficult to forecast (Mintzberg and Waters, 1985).

- Since a large proportion of information needed for strategic decision making comes from a virtually unlimited external environment, the key problem that the decision maker faces is information overload with multiple and conflicting interpretations, rather than solely the absence of relevant information (Zmud, 1986).

- Much of the information that is used for strategic decisions is qualitative, verbal, and poorly recorded.

- Because the stakes in strategic decision making are very high, there is much more situational vulnerability to both political maneuvering and stressed emotional behavior, which may call for additional considerations in DSS implementation.

Another part of the challenge comes from the nature of the decision maker who typically engages in the strategic decision- making process as one of the central participants. He or she is usually:

- A top manager, executive, or policymaker whose time is very valuable.
- Older and more resistant to technological change.
- Comfortable relying on intuition and gut feeling.
- Unwilling to spend time learning to personally use computer-based DSS.
- Powerful enough to require and enforce quick response to his or her demands.

The call for designing and delivering DSS for such a demanding class of decision-making situations and decision makers has not gone unheeded in the information systems community. Various efforts have been made to advance the state of the art, each of which has moved us closer toward overcoming that challenge. These include:

- Focusing on the decision maker and providing generalized support tailored to senior executives in the form of EIS (see Houdeshel and Watson, 1987, for a description of the MIDS system at Lockheed-Georgia; Rockart and DeLong, 1988).
- Focusing on the provision of EIS generators with user-seductive technology platforms suited to executives with fancy graphics, pop-up menus, touchscreens, and optical mice (Paller, 1988; typical examples include products from software vendors such as Comshare, Execucom, and Pilot).
- Focusing on better understanding of the decision context (see Stabell, 1983, who advocates "bringing the D back into DSS").
- Focusing on information requirements determination methodologies that foster the fit between the executive decision maker and the strategic decision context (Henderson, Rockart, and Sifonis, 1987).
- Focusing on the structuring of fit between the decision context and the decision makers by building decision rooms and group decision support systems (Gray, 1987).
- Focusing on the simultaneous advancement of the "squeakiest wheels" in DSS design and implementation (see Keen, 1987, and his call to action for "a redressing of the balance between D, S, and S").

The approach that we take in this work builds on the experiences gained from the above. However, our approach tries to make progress toward overcoming this challenge through focusing on the process of *managing* the design and delivery of DSS while preserving the fit among the decision makers, the form of support provided, and the technologies used in the context of an ongoing strategic decision-making context. Our application context is the cabinet of Egypt.

DECISION MAKING IN THE EGYPTIAN CABINET

The Egyptian Cabinet comprises the prime minister, thirty-two ministers, and four sectoral ministerial committees assisted by staff. Decision making at the cabinet level addresses a variety of national socioeconomic and infrastructural concerns, such as reducing the deficit in the balance of payments and national budget, debt management, performance improvement of public sector organizations, ways of promoting the development of small- and medium-scale private industries, and the allocation of resources to solve urban housing problems and overpopulation.

Depending on the scope, urgency, and criticality of an issue, it is addressed either through the ministerial committees or by the full cabinet. The decision-making process involves much debate and group discussion, requires much preparation of position papers and studies, and is subject to public accountability and media attention. A simplified view of the cabinet decision-making process showing key participants, deliberation forums, and information flows is shown in Figure 12.1.

As is the case with any decision-making setting, the cabinet has its own jargon and mental constructions. Labels indicative of deliberate structured logic (such as objectives, outcomes, directives, and decrees) and rational decision making (such as decisions, alternatives, choices, problems, and solutions) are used in both written and oral communica-

FIGURE 12.1   The Cabinet Decision-Making Process before IDSC

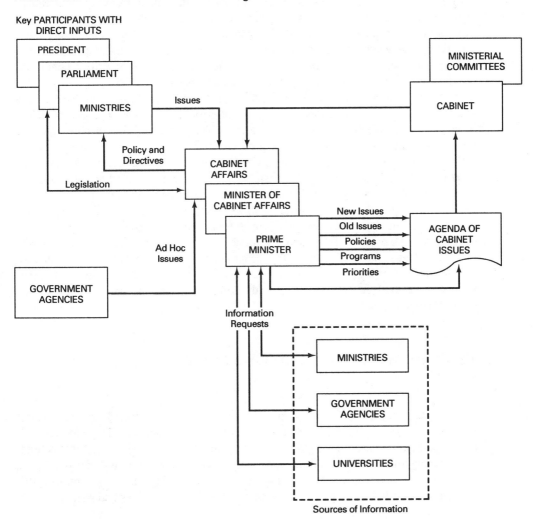

tion. However, a closer examination of those reveals that the decision-making process is best and most comfortably viewed by the participants as a process of attention to sets of *issues* with varying and shifting priorities; the cabinet world is chunked primarily into issues, rather than decisions. As indicated in Figure 12.1 by the closed loops, sets of issues circulate continuously and are managed over time. They enter and exit circulation through the key participants. When some of them are resolved (or dissolved) by decisions, actions, political maneuvering, or environmental shifts, they fade from circulation. Similarly, they can reappear and also become more salient. Of course, decisions are made, but the focal point of deliberation is the issue rather than the one of many decisions made around it.

The decisions around issues considered by the cabinet are usually complex, ill-structured, interdependent, and multisectoral, with strategic impacts at the national, regional, and international levels. The nature of the information environment can be characterized as one that is data rich but information poor, in which there is an overload of information of questionable reliability, which often yields multiple and murky interpretations, and which is often qualitative and disjointed. The cabinet is the epitome of strategic decision making at the group level under complex and turbulent conditions which cries out for information and decision support systems (IS/DSS).

After Egypt's peace agreement with Israel, the cabinet of Egypt embarked on a program of economic revival and was faced with formidable infrastructural and socioeconomic development challenges in the early 1980s. In addition, the turbulence of the regional and international economy and politics was causing major shifts in Egypt's traditional sources of GNP such as Suez Canal revenues, remittances from Egyptians working in oil-rich countries, and tourism. This created a heightened awareness of the increasing complexity of the environment and the vulnerability of static plans and slow decision making at the strategic level. It also brought into focus the critical importance of making available in an integrated form the information needed for supporting the decision-making process of the cabinet through the use of the most appropriate information technologies and services. In 1985, as part of a broader intensive national plan for administrative development, an information systems project for the cabinet was initiated, and it has evolved into what is now the Information and Decision Support Center (IDSC) for the cabinet.

THE CABINET INFORMATION AND DECISION SUPPORT CENTER (*IDSC*)

Since its inception, the IDSC was guided by three strategic objectives. First and foremost was the development of information and decision support systems (IS/DSS) for the cabinet and top policymakers in Egypt. Second was to support the establishment of end-user–managed information and decision support centers in the individual ministries. Third and more indirect was to encourage, support, and initiate informatics projects that would accelerate the development of Egyptian government ministries and agencies.

To achieve these strategic objectives, a trilevel architecture for information infrastructure and decision support was conceived:

■ IDSC level	Building of IDSC base at the cabinet to provide a focal point for cabinet issues support, information and decision support, multisectoral analysis, and integration.
■ National nodes level	Linking to and/or supporting the building of local sources level of information and decision support at ministries and national agencies.
■ International level	Extending telecommunications access to international levelsources of information and major databases worldwide.

As of November 1985, the IDSC started providing information and decision support services for the cabinet and developing this trilevel architecture. Figure 12.2 shows the positioning of the IDSC as a facilitative conduit, integrator, and expediter of information from various sources to the cabinet. New information sources such as sectoral information centers and international databases have been added, and since then, the computer-based component has been growing.

The IDSC has evolved rapidly from a three-person start-up with a handful of personal computers to an organization of over 150 people in mid-1988, which provides an array of information and decision support services specifically targeted to the strategic decision-making level. It has since implemented twenty-eight IS/DSS projects. Learning how to effectively provide information and decision support for strategic decisions in the cabinet context while managing rapid growth and response to an impatient and increasing service demand—and simultaneously developing the poor information and technological infrastructure of Egyptian government organizations—provided many managerial, technological, and contextual challenges for the IDSC.

With respect to the design and delivery of IS/DSS for cabinet decision making, the IDSC was convinced that not only was there a need for a process different from that used for traditional DSS, but that it was also important to create an organization design that could facilitate the effective management of such services. Initially, the IDSC thought that the answers were "out there somewhere" and sought comparative information from other countries with similar projects. While these inputs were very helpful, it became painfully obvious to the IDSC that it would have to devise both the design and delivery process and the organizational design through its own contextual learning in the Egyptian cabinet strategic decision-making environment.

To deal with this challenge, the IDSC's strategy had several components. First, to maximize the chances of implementation success, it saw the need to improve the fit among the users in their decision-making context, the form of support provided, and the technologies used (examples of ways that the IDSC used for contextual fit improvement are shown in Table 12.1). Second, it would use an iterative prototyping strategy for IS/DSS design and delivery. Third, the organizational design would emerge and develop as the process for managing the design and delivery of IS/DSS became more apparent.

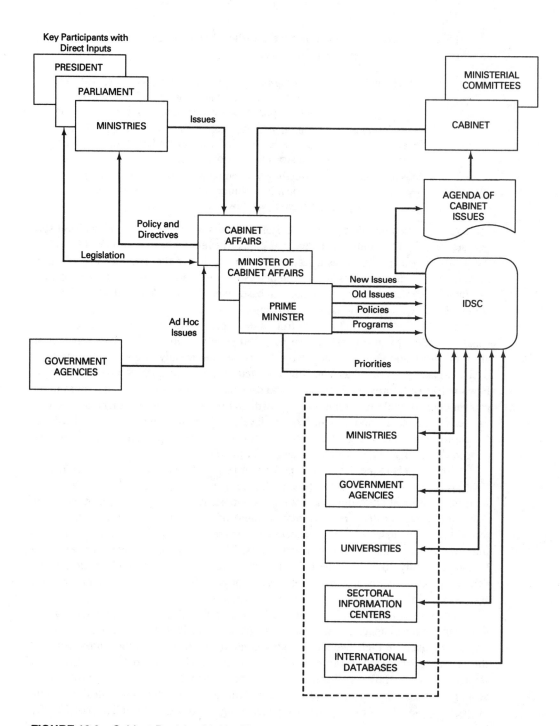

FIGURE 12.2 Cabinet Decision-Making Process after IDSC

TABLE 12.1   Examples of Contextual Fit Improvement Strategies Used by IDSC

DESCRIPTION	EFFECTS
Reverse Distributed Processing	
Approach for developing technology infrastructure which started with islands of personal computers, then linked them together and built a network infrastructure and finally added a mainframe.	Bridged user-technology gap and allowed accelerated implementation of applications. There are now 110 PCs and a data network of national nodes at various ministries.
Two-Tiered Teams	
IDSC design team always includes two two types of members: * One who is technically competent (typically a young college graduate) * Another who is fully experienced with the bureaucracy (an older person with government experience)	Bridged translation gap between DSS builders and typical bureaucrats whose inputs are sought and needed. Improved communication and minimized risk of technical failures.
Arabization of Software	
Linguistic and cultural adaptation of user interfaces to the Egyptian decision-making environment. The IDSC has also championed incentives for a "Pyramids Technology Valley" project for software start-ups.	Bridged user- application gap. Custom applications and many standard tools (such as dBase III, Lotus 1-2-3, FOCUS) are fully Arabized. Bilingual (English/Arabic) electronic mail in beta test.
Chauffeured IS/DSS Use	
Use of staff intermediaries for supporting senior policymakers, rather than having him or her directly online.	Kept focus on providing support for strategic decision making, rather than draining IDSC resources in supporting nonstrategic office applications.

The IS/DSS design and delivery process was initially conceived as shown in Figure 12.3. While deliberation inside the cabinet decision-making forum revolves around issues, formal communications outside it are expressed in terms of policies, programs, and objectives. Thus, IS/DSS project definitions are handed down to the IDSC in either a broad mission-driven form (such as "we need to build a DSS to help formulate, develop, and monitor the industrial sector strategic and tactical plans") or in a directive data-driven form (such as "we want you to establish an information base about all companies in the industrial sector in Egypt"). At the IDSC management level, this is translated through interactions with policymakers to a set of better articulated strategic issues around which IS/DSS are defined. Design, delivery, and institutionalization are carried out at the IDSC builder and implementer level as the process goes through iterative prototyping cycles. The tactical details of this procedure, its requisite management

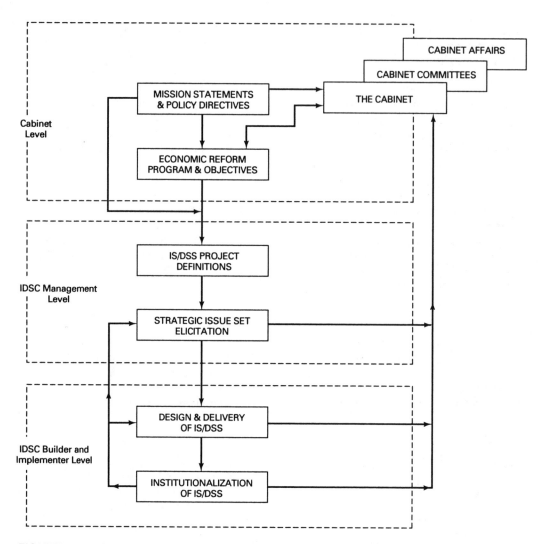

FIGURE 12.3   Supporting and Shaping Cabinet Strategic Decision Making through IS/DSS

processes, and supporting organizational design evolved as more was learned from each successive IS/DSS project.

LEARNING ABOUT THE MANAGEMENT OF DSS FOR STRATEGIC DECISION MAKING THROUGH ILLUSTRATIVE IDSC PROJECTS

Episodes from five example IS/DSS projects from the IDSC experience are presented to illustrate the generic lessons that were learned for managing the design and delivery of DSS for strategic decision making.

Illustrative Case 1: Customs Tariff Policy Formulation DSS

For many years there was much effort by the cabinet to overhaul a complex customs tariff structure that encompassed too many inconsistent regulations. That concerted effort had evolved into initial agreement on a formulation of three broad reform objectives: a homogeneous consistent tariff structure, increasing revenues to the treasury, and minimum impact on low income groups. In early 1986, the "new customs program" was announced as in prefinal form. But six months later, despite initial agreement and good intentions, interministerial debates and conflicts about policy form and perceived sectoral impacts grew. In June 1986, the services of the IDSC were requested by the cabinet.

A joint IDSC/Ministry of Finance crisis team developed an initial PC-based DSS model using the written tariff reform proposal. The team consisted of thirty-two people: two IDSC managers, two undersecretaries, six builders/implementers, and twenty-two data entry/validation personnel. Data were collected from fragmented sources with difficulty. As development progressed, the team shuttled daily to the six most affected ministries and met with senior policymakers to gather input and feedback and build consensus. Initially, conflicts were sharp, discussions heated, and one-sided theories prevailed. For example, the Ministry of Industry, wanting to encourage local manufacturing, sought to raise import tariffs on auto spare parts. The Ministry of Economy agreed because it would reduce foreign currency expenditures, but the Ministry of Finance disagreed because this would reduce a sizable source of customs revenue.

However, as the model became more explicit through the prototyping effort, the strategic issues were better articulated, assumptions were uncovered, and the impacts of various "what-if" scenarios for structural alternatives were demonstrated with numbers rather than abstract opinions. The focus gradually moved from objection to constructive input and considerate accommodation. After one month of intense effort, a consensus was reached and a new customs tariff policy was in place.

Lessons 1 and 2 for the Management of DSS for Strategic Decision Making

Lesson 1:   Structuring and articulating strategic issues is an integral, critical, and very time-consuming portion of the design/delivery of DSS for strategic decisions. It should be labeled as an explicit "rewardable/billable" activity in the design/delivery cycle. It includes conflict resolution and consensus building and may involve shuttle diplomacy.

Lesson 2:   Providing DSS for strategic decision making is most often coupled with both urgency and criticality, making crisis management a frequent mode of operation. This requires an organization design and human resource policy for the support organization that explicitly includes a crisis management component. It is a type of crisis management that has large unexpected variance in tempo and task (i.e., more like a fire department than an overnight package delivery business). The IDSC has added crisis management teams to its organization design (see Figure 12.4). These can be quickly put together in response to crisis requests.

Impacts   The customs tariff DSS facilitated a group decision-making process by reducing conflict and promoting consensus by clarifying the trade-offs and potential impacts of tariff structures on individual sectors and on the overall economy. It has proved to be an excellent negotiation tool, and the decision- making process was conducted with more information and less misplaced emotion. It has also made it possible to provide an equitable uniform tariff structure. Furthermore, the originally estimated £E 500 million increase in customs revenues ($1 = about £E 2) were shown by the DSS "what-if" process to be unlikely and that any realistic scenarios would generate about £E 50 million. A year later the actual increase turned out to be £E 56 million.

Illustrative Case 2: Production IS/DSS

Initiated in late 1985 and developed jointly with the General Organization for Industrialization (GOFI), the project was identified by the cabinet as having two main objectives: establishing an information base about all industrial companies in Egypt and building a DSS to help formulate, develop, and monitor the industrial sector's strategic and tactical plans. The IDSC's data collection efforts from four main data centers (one at GOFI) were met with subject databases with incomparable structures, nonstandardized data definitions, and contradictory definitional assumptions. Furthermore, examination of redundant data indicated uneven updating and unreliable integrity. Rebuilding of an integrated database was a massive effort that detracted from decision support. This prompted the IDSC to have separate decision support.

This prompted the IDSC to have separate decision support services (DSSV) and project development (PD) departments (see Figure 12.4). DSSV provides frontline decision support services to the cabinet, and is staffed by about twenty-five multidisciplinary user consultants. If an IS/DSS project is initiated that requires massive systems development, database building, or infrastructure development at the ministry/agency level, then PD

FIGURE 12.4   Organization Chart for IDSC

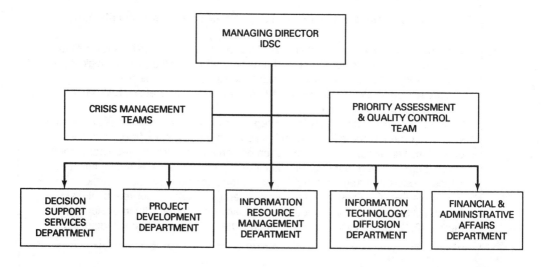

takes over. PD is staffed by project managers, DSS builders/implementers, and application programmers. A third department, information resources management (IRM), provides technical support and manages databases. It comprises technical staff, database administrators, and systems programmers. For better interdepartmental coordination and crisis management peak demands, there is some staff rotation among DSSV, PD, and IRM.

Lesson 3 for the Management of DSS for Strategic Decision Making

Providing information and decision support for strategic decision making often requires much effort in building and integrating databases from diverse extraorganizational sources. The frontline decision support consultants should not get sucked into this activity at the expense of reduced decision support. The organizational design should reflect that.

As the issue-based structuring process moved forward, several other specific strategic issues were articulated. These focused the database building effort on a much smaller extracted database which was built much faster. For example, at one point, the issue of import substitution with local production surfaced as critical and focused database building on imported industrial commodities.

Lesson 4 for the Management of DSS for Strategic Decision Making

The structuring of one strategic issue begets other strategic issues and these can be used to focus the database building effort.

Impacts   A prototype PC-based DSS showed that 248 commodities represented 90 percent ($7 billion) of Egypt's 1985 total commodity imports of which 112 were industrial commodities. That further revealed that ninety-two of these had not been promoted locally by the Ministry of Industry since 1974. Further DSS prototypes showed that eighty-seven commodities out of these ninety-two could be manufactured locally with favorable economics. Based on this diagnosis, the national industrial five-year plan was changed by the cabinet. This diagnostic also resulted in identifying another strategic issue—idle capacity. Using simple bar chart comparisons for each of the eighty-seven commodities that compared local production, idle capacity, and imports, another DSS component allowed the identification of idle and/or underutilized capacities for about 55 percent of public sector industrial companies and the "what-iffing" of many scenarios.

Because of the initial data reliability problems, this project accentuated the importance of having explicit quality indicators for critical information in IS/DSS. It also brought to the IDSC's attention the importance of decision methods that could enhance the effectiveness of information "beyond the information given." Methods such as the examination and surfacing of critical assumptions underlying the information, transforming data from table to chart form, comparing rates of change, and sensitivity analysis of variables needed to be made more salient to users. To accentuate to users the fact that decision-making effectiveness depends on much more than information, the IDSC made a distinction between information services support and decision methods support within its DSSV organization design (see Figure 12.5). Furthermore, to emphasize the importance of surfacing assumptions, the IDSC has integrated them within its IS/DSS designs and includes an "assumption key" (similar to a help key).

Lesson 5 for the Management of DSS for Strategic Decision Making

It is key to articulate explicitly to users that effective decision making depends on more than information. For decisions around strategic issues, information is usually partial and its quality questionable. Rather than just trying to improve information quality, it may often be more useful to use more decision methods/heuristics on it.

Illustrative Case 3: Debt Management DSS

In its massive effort to rebuild the economy, Egypt has accumulated a staggering foreign debt of $33 billion. Servicing this debt involves pegging sources of funds, renegotiating terms and interest rates, managing payment schedules, and monitoring transactions for over 5,000 loans with a large number of creditor countries, banks, and international agencies. Previously, a decision or renegotiation on a loan payment was done on a case-by-case basis (often through telex responses), data related to each loan were fragmented, global planning for matching sources of funds was not possible, and the aggregate debt portfolio details were not accurately known.

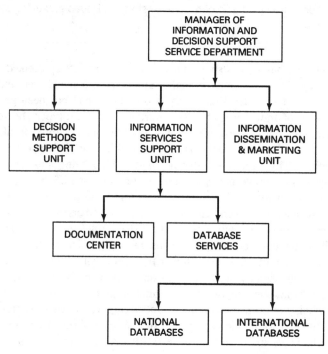

FIGURE 12.5
Organization Chart for Decision Support Services Department

A debt management IS/DSS project was established to centralize and computerize all foreign debt data in the Central Bank of Egypt and to develop a management tool to support and facilitate the registration, control, and analysis of debt. Over eighteen months a comprehensive debt validated database for government loans and a transaction processing system for debt management was built with DSS capabilities for examining the impacts of different scenarios. The DSS includes a multiperiod forward- looking component that provides overall debt status in the future, and includes "what-if" functions for queries related to such things as refinancing. A rescheduling module that allows users to dynamically track and mark status changes on any loan in the total portfolio has also been added.

Lesson 6 for the Management of DSS for Strategic Decision Making

If recurring decisions are to be made around a strategic issue, there is critical need for setting up a management system for tracking and monitoring changes in the critical parameters of the issue.

The rescheduling activities carried out during the last eight months of 1987 showed that it is still difficult to maintain and manage the loans database, especially with dispersed negotiation for 5,000 loans. This project also experienced technical difficulties that eventually were resolved but that caused delay and aggravation. These included a classic transaction processing situation: Off-the-shelf mainframe software is adapted but does not deliver, modification efforts delayed, spaghetti code and inadequate documentation, switch to PC-based system, prototype appears quickly and works but much too slowly.

Lesson 7 for the Management of DSS for Strategic Decision Making

The dynamic tracking component of an issue-based DSS has the usual technical demands of transaction processing systems and requires more demanding technological capabilities.

Impacts   However, technical performance problems, while frustrating, did not hinder the debt management DSS from having strategic impacts. Rescheduling negotiations with fourteen countries have been smoothly managed because of the detailed convincing information support made available to negotiators (such as preemptive assessment of alternatives). A key impact on the strategic decision-making process is that loans are now viewed as part of a dynamic and integrated portfolio rather than being managed on an isolated case-by-case basis.

Illustrative Case 4: Electricity DSS

"I would like to have a computer system on my desk" was the triggering statement by the minister of electricity and energy at a meeting in August 1987 to which the IDSC director was summoned. The seemingly symbolic statement was quickly followed by: "The cost of providing electricity is increasingly contributing to the deficit in the national budget and balance of payments. Most investment in electric power generation requires foreign currency. Besides, the current tariff structure still requires government subsidies."

It was clear that there was a set of strategic issues around which an IS/DSS was needed, and there was a top policymaker who was championing it. Again, the need had been expressed initially around strategic issues rather than specific decisions. Further probing with the minister identified several critical sets of information and decision support needs such as daily information about the production and consumption of electricity in Egypt, ability to assess the impact of tariff changes on different income groups, ability

---

Lesson 8 for the Management of DSS for Strategic Decision Making

The issue-based approach to DSS provides a solid base for easy transition to EIS in the future.

---

to manage debt effectively, monitoring large electricity sector projects, and access to studies and legislation relevant to this sector.

A joint IS/DSS team was quickly formed by the IDSC and the ministry. Because of the multiplicity and diversity of data sources needed for this project, the desire to build an internal information and decision support center inside the Ministry of Electricity and the minister's expressed long-term interest in having EIS-like capabilities, the IDSC saw a much greater need in this project to focus on the process of managing the delivery of the system with its requisite support infrastructure rather than just the design of the IS/DSS itself. However, the process by which this effort would be managed was prototyped and adjusted on the fly: The ministry team would be responsible for gathering data around the issues identified by the minister, and the IDSC team would be responsible for issue structuring, DSS development, hardware selection, training, and managing the process. However, these roles changed as the project progressed and was adapted to the contextual requirements of DSS implementation.

Lesson 9 for the Management of DSS for Strategic Decision Making

It was not only DSS design that could be prototyped; the management of delivery could be prototyped as well.

A working prototype was developed, methods for providing information support services were devised, and decision heuristics to assess the impact of various tariff structures and production and consumption patterns were implemented. As the design and delivery activity proceeded, a related strategic issue of crisis proportions surfaced: Drought in the source regions of the Nile River and its overuse in irrigation was causing peak hydroelectric power generated by the Aswan Dam to drop precipitously; $500 million were needed to quickly build three generating stations. There was now a crisis dimension that had appeared suddenly. Furthermore, the strategic issue had now drawn in the Ministry of Water Resources as a critical stakeholder in DSS design. The process by which the effort was managed also changed at this point: A team of six people were selected from the ministry as a core group for its own information and decision support center, and seven user committees were formed by the ministry's undersecretary to manage data collection and analysis.

Impacts   The DSS is still evolving and so is the process by which it is being managed. The management process had to be changed when two of the six undersecretaries were unwilling to accept the DSS. However, the impacts of the DSS have already been felt, and the water level crisis is in full focus and much better understood. The DSS has also helped to assess the different tariff alternatives and the impact of each on citizens and total revenue, and a new electricity tariff is in place since January 1988.

Case 5: Document-based DSS

Various IDSC projects accentuated the role of textual documents as key sources used in the strategic decision-making process. For example, the legislation and decrees project was initiated to respond to the access problems related to the retrieval and classification of all Egyptian government legislation and decrees since legislation was first passed in Egypt in 1824. The project to date has classified all legislation and decrees from 1957 to 1987. This document database has been used in conjunction with other DSS such as the electricity DSS. The IDSC has established a fully staffed documentation center as part of its information support services unit (see Figure 12.5).

Lesson 10 for the Management of DSS for Strategic Decision Making

Providing decision support for strategic decision making will require many textual and document-based information sources. Organizational design should reflect that capability.

ASSESSING IMPACTS AND VALUE

In general, DSS benefits are often very uncertain and are elusive to assess. In the cabinet case with a prototyping approach where development is evolutionary, and when benefits can appear very early (while structuring an issue) or much later (crisis response in a future negotiation), this is especially the case. The ongoing group strategic decision-making context with multiple interrelated DSS in shifting environments makes it even more so. Orthodox cost/benefit analysis will not work. However, at the strategic level, the leverage of a few big obvious "hits" can also justify the whole effort many times over. Some of the examples presented have illustrated the magnitude of a few "hits." The IDSC has implemented a total of twenty-eight IS/DSS projects for the cabinet, and while some projects may not have been as successful as others, and in some cases the benefits were not as obvious, the cumulative leverage that IS/DSS has provided through the obvious "hits" has been estimated by the cabinet to be at least in the tens and possibly in the hundreds of millions of dollars. For the cabinet, the leverage is now overwhelmingly clear.

However, even without the track record of a few big hits, the *potential* leverage is sufficient to justify the investment in IS/DSS to support strategic decision making. It is difficult to ignore the potential leverage of effective IS/DSS for debt management when negotiating a 1 percent interest rate difference on a $33 billion debt is a whopping $330 million. In contrast, the IDSC's total operating costs (excluding overhead borne by the Ministry of Cabinet Affairs) have been around $2 million. In order to enable IS/DSS for strategic decision making to be delivered successfully in any organization, that balance must be very clear to top management; otherwise, it will be difficult to generate strong and sustained top management commitment. The IDSC project could not have gone forward without that understanding and strong commitment and support from the minister of cabinet affairs. The IDSC director reports directly to him.

The "bottom line" impacts of IS/DSS at the cabinet level have been mediated through process changes and qualitative valuation criteria. In the examples given, the valuation criteria in each case were different, usually qualitative, context-dependent, and in many instances they blurred the difference between process and outcome: quicker and more effective consensus on a group decision, uncovering hidden assumptions, better crisis response, better understanding of the interaction among industry forces, preemptive generation of alternatives for better negotiation, and identification of new strategic issues. Cumulatively, these impacts have also changed the way that the cabinet views the role and value of IS/DSS: There is a deeper realization of its potential leverage for helping the decision-making process, as evidenced by the increasing requests and resulting growth of IDSC services.

Finally, this experience has convinced us that, contrary to stereotypical depictions, computer-based DSS do not necessarily have to move the decision-making process away from emotional deliberation. Rather, the IDSC management process for the design and delivery of issue-based DSS accommodated and took advantage of (rather than denied) the social, visceral, political, and intuitive aspects of the strategic decision-making process. The metaphor used at the IDSC is that the group decision-making forum has changed from "a darkened room to a more illuminated one" where assumptions are more visible, potential impacts are better seen, quality of information is made more explicit, and competing scenarios can be made clearer. This extra illumination still allows emotional views to be aired and the intensity of values and commitments to be expressed and considered; but now it takes place with less misplaced emotion and in an information context in which more effective strategic decision making can be realized.

A PROCEDURE FOR MANAGING THE DESIGN AND DELIVERY OF ISSUE-BASED DSS FOR STRATEGIC DECISION MAKING

This work has resulted in a generalized procedure for managing the design and delivery of issue-based DSS for strategic decision making. It evolved through lessons learned from the IDSC's cumulative experience with twenty-eight cabinet IS/DSS projects. In addition, the procedure was more formally articulated and the process expertise more thoroughly captured through a six-day participative workshop in late 1987 attended by over twenty professional IDSC staff (El Sawy and El Sherif, 1987).

The unconventional nature of the Egyptian cabinet setting has helped to stimulate our approach. Strategic decision making is the major cabinet activity, thus affording an

FIGURE 12.6 Supporting and Shaping Corporate Strategic Decision Making through IS/DSS

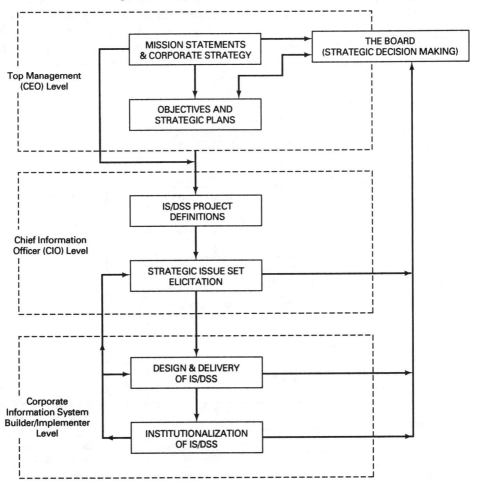

opportunity to observe the process with an intensity that is unequaled in more conventional settings. Coupled with the Egyptian cultural penchant for debate around focal points (rather than talking directly at them), it accentuated the notion that strategic decision making primarily revolved around issues rather than riveted on decisions. The inadequate reliability of the information infrastructure, coupled with the need for crisis response, led to the idea of prototyping the delivery process as well as the design. However, while the setting's cultural and environmental uniqueness helped to shape our approach, we believe that both the tactical essence of the procedure and its underlying concepts are transferable to other types of organizational settings.

Parallels are easily mapped from the cabinet to corporate settings, whether for executive roles, IS management, issue "downloading/uploading" between levels, or potential interaction between strategic decision making and IS/DSS (compare Figure 12.6 to Figure 12.3). The use of issues management is not alien to corporations (King, 1987), and has also been applied to planning for the MIS organization (Dansker et al., 1987). While strategic decision making in the corporate world may be more closely linked to competitive advantage, that does not seem to change any of its process features.

Figure 12.7 shows the basic building blocks of the procedure for managing the design and delivery of issue-based DSS for strategic decision making; Table 12.2 illustrates its tactical essence. The procedure has the following distinctive features:

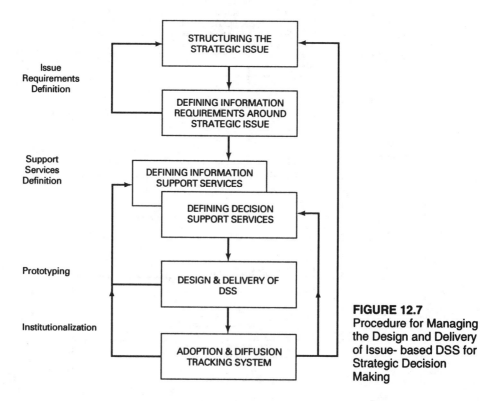

FIGURE 12.7
Procedure for Managing the Design and Delivery of Issue- based DSS for Strategic Decision Making

- It is *based on issues* rather than primarily on decisions.
- It is *a management process* rather than solely a systems development life cycle.
- It has a strategic *issue structuring front-end* that is sizable, explicitly identifiable, and consequently rewardable and billable.
- It explicitly *distinguishes between information support* services *and decision support* services.
- As well as prototyping the DSS design, it also *prototypes the DSS delivery process.* Its "delivery" stance implies a service view of implementation with continuous user support. This maximizes contextual fit and accommodates crisis response.
- As part of the institutionalization process for the DSS, it includes setting up a *dynamic tracking back-end* for monitoring shifts in critical issue parameters. This is key for recurring decisions and also makes transition to EIS much easier.

The procedure, as shown in Figure 12.7 and elaborated in Table 12.2, is highly iterative and consists of both nested and intersecting process loops:

- *Issue requirements definition loop:* Cycles between structuring the strategic issue and defining the requirements around strategic issues.
- *Support services definition loop:* Cycles between defining information support services and decision support services. In combination, this component roughly parallels Sprague and Carlson's (1982) ROMC approach.

TABLE 12.2 Tactical Essence of Procedure for Managing the Design and Delivery of Issue-Based DSS for Strategic Decision Making

OUTCOMES	TYPICAL ACTIVITIES	REPRESENTATIVE METHODS AND TOOLS	TYPICAL KEY PARTICIPANTS
1. Structuring the Strategic Issue			
Reformulated issue	Assumption surfacing	Shuttle diplomacy	Issue stakeholders
Emergent objectives	Negotiation	Interviews	Key decision makers
Issue articulation	Conflict resolution	Group meetings	CIO
Stakeholder consensus	Stakeholder identification	Brainstorming and idea processing tools	
		Empathy	
2. Defining Information Requirements around Strategic Issues			
Critical information	Defining initial information needs	Modified variants of extended CSF methods	Key decisions makers
Critical assumptions	Determining information quality requirements	Delphi methods	DSS user consultants
Decision scenarios	Defining information format requirements	Interviews	Staff intermediaries
Crisis scenarios			

TABLE 12.2   (Continued)

OUTCOMES	TYPICAL ACTIVITIES	REPRESENTATIVE METHODS AND TOOLS	TYPICAL KEY PARTICIPANTS
3. Defining Information Support Services around Strategic Issue			
Scope and type of information support services that need to be provided	Providing access routes to information Integrating information from multiple sources Providing information views	Data dictionaries Bibliographic searches External information utilities	Staff intermediaries DSS user consultants DSS builders
4. Defining Decision Support Services around Strategic Issue			
Scope and type of decision support services that need to be provided	Providing "what-if" analysis capabilities Scenario generation	Modeling software Assumption surfacing tools	Staff intermediaries DSS user consultants DSS builders
5. Prototyping the Design and Delivery of DSS Related to Strategic Issue			
DSS delivery methods Working DSS prototypes	Infrastructure development Database development DSS design and delivery	Prototyping tools	Key decision makers Staff intermediaries DSS user consultants DSS builders Toolsmiths
6. Managing Institutionalization of DSS			
DSS adoption DSS diffusion Dynamic tracking system	Cultural adaptation User support	Training workshops Newsletters Exception reporting	DSS consultants Trainers Staff intermediaries

- ***Prototyping design and delivery loop:*** The design prototyping iterations are nested in a delivery process envelope that is also prototyped. Iterates with support services definition loop.
- ***Institutionalization loop:*** Encompasses both organizational adoption and diffusion, including the setting up of an issue tracking system. Iterates with all other loops.
- ***Evaluation and prioritization envelope*** (not shown in Figure 12.7): The procedure is enveloped by continuous evaluation and prioritization, which enables

TABLE 12.3 Comparing the Conventional and the Issue-Based DSS Approaches

	CONVENTIONAL	*ISSUE-BASED*
Focus:	On decision maker On single decision Decision making Alternative generation	On issue On groups of interacting issues Attention focusing Agenda setting
Favored Domains:	Tactical and operational decisions One-shot decisions Functional applications Departmental applications	Strategic decisions Recurring strategic decisions Cross-functional applications Transorganizational applications

Design and Delivery:	Promotes customization
	    to individual decision maker
	Interaction between decisions
	    not incorporated
	Prototypes design
	Design approach becomes
	    the system
		Promotes consensus around
		    group issue
		Integration and consensus
		    drive process
		Prototypes design and delivery
		Delivery approach becomes
		    the system

EIS Readiness:	No tracking component
	Emphasizes convergent
	    structuring
	Major transformation
		Incorporates tracking component
		Balances divergent exploration
		    and convergent structuring
		Easy transition to EIS

Emerging Leveraging Technologies:	Expert systems	Idea processing and associative
		    aids (hypertext)
		Multimedia connectivity platforms
		    (video conferencing)
		Object-oriented languages

shifting and/or intensifying effort and resources between issues and/or DSSs as appropriate.

COMPARING THE CONVENTIONAL AND ISSUE-BASED DSS APPROACHES

We have shown how the issued-based DSS approach has been successfully implemented in response to the need for supporting strategic decision making at the cabinet level in Egypt. We have also presented a procedure for managing the design and delivery process for such DSS. In Table 12.3 we provide a brief comparison of the conventional and issue-based approaches to DSS. The table may be useful to both information systems practitioners and researchers in clarifying the advantages and limitations of the issue-based approach to various situations and organizational settings. It is also meant to suggest how the issue-based view of DSS may be the missing stepping-stone to advancing the state of the art in the definition, design, and delivery of EIS.

CONCLUSIONS

The use of information and decision support systems has significantly leveraged the strategic decision-making process in the Egyptian cabinet. Ministers and senior policymakers have increasingly realized that information systems and information technologies are not convenient luxuries for times of prosperity, but rather can be vital necessities in times of turbulence and adversity.

Strategic decision making is a very messy process, but it can still be made more effective by information and decision support systems. However, the IDSC cabinet experience suggests that it may be necessary for us to change our conventional views about DSS and our ways of managing them, if we are to make more progress in the strategic decision-making arena. The issue-based view that we have presented and its accompanying design and delivery procedure is one way of doing that.

Finally, we hope that this narrative provides the international information systems profession with a compelling example to show that there are things that can be learned to advance the field and its practice through information systems implementations in international contexts with less advanced technological infrastructures. We also hope that this will encourage SIM to continue to become more international.

QUESTIONS

1. Explain the difference between prototyping the design of a DSS and prototyping the delivery system.
2. What is the most significant impact or value of the ISDC effort? What does this say about efforts to justify or evaluate DSS?
3. Explain how each of the "lessons" evolved from one or more of the projects.

REFERENCES

DANSKER, B., J. S. HANSEN, R. LOFTIN, AND M. VELDWEISCH "Issues Management in the Information Planning Process," *MIS Quarterly,* 11, no. 2 (June 1987), 223–232.

DUTTON, W., AND K. KRAEMER *Modeling as Negotiating: The Political Dynamics of Computer Models in the Policy Process.* Norwood, N.J.: Ablex, 1985.

EL SAWY, O. A. "Personal Information Systems for Strategic Scanning in Turbulent Environments: Can the CEO Go On-line?" *MIS Quarterly,* 9, no. 1 (March 1985), 53–60.

EL SAWY, O. A., AND H. EL SHERIF, "Partnership Workshop on Providing Information and Decision Support Services for Top Level Decision Makers," Information and Decision Support Center, Cabinet of Egypt, Cairo, 1987.

EL SHERIF, H. "The Cabinet Information and Decision Support Systems Project," Ministry of Cabinet Affairs, Cairo, Egypt, 1985.

EL SHERIF, H. "Managing Large Information and Decision Support Systems Projects," IFORS Conference Proceedings, Argentina, August 1987.

GRAY, P. "Group Decision Support Systems," *Decision Support Systems,* 3 (September 1987), 233–242.

GRAY, P. "Using Technology for Strategic Group Decision Making," Working Paper, Claremont Graduate School, Claremont, Calif., January 1988.

HENDERSON, J., J. ROCKART, AND J. SIFONIS "Integrating Management Support Systems into Strategic Information Systems Planning," *Journal of MIS, 4 (Summer 1987), 5–24.*

HOUDESHEL, G., AND H. WATSON "The Management Information and Decision Support (MIDS) System at Lockheed-Georgia," *MIS Quarterly,* 11, no. 1 (March 1987), 127–140.

KEEN, P. G. W. "Value Analysis: Justifying Decision Support Systems," *MIS Quarterly,* 5, no. 1 (March 1981), 1–15.

KEEN, P. G. W. "Decision Support Systems: The Next Decade," *Decision Support Systems,* 3 (September 1987), 253–265.

KEEN, P. G. W. AND H. EL SHERIF "An Accelerated Development Strategy for Applying DSS in Developing Countries," paper presented at DSS-82 Conference, San Francisco, 1982.

KING, W. R. "Strategic Issue Management," in *Strategic Planning and Management Handbook,* ed. W. R. King and D. I. Cleland, pp. 252–264. New York: Van Nostrand Reinhold, 1987.

LASDEN, M. "Decision Support Systems: Mission Accomplished?" *Computer Decisions* (April 6, 1987), 41–42.

MASON, R. O., AND I. I. MITROFF *Challenging Strategic Planning Assumptions.* New York: John Wiley, 1981.

MINTZBERG, H., AND J. WATERS "Of Strategies, Deliberate and Emergent," *Strategic Management Journal,* 6, no. 3 (1985), 257–272.

MOORE, J. H., AND M. G. CHANG "Meta-Design Considerations in Building DSS," in *Building Decision Support Systems,* ed. J. L. Bennett, pp. 173–204. Reading, Mass.: Addison- Wesley, 1983.

PALLER, A. "Executive Information Systems Should Do More than Just Identify Problems," *Information Center,* 4, no. 2 (February 1988), 16–17.

PIEPTEA, D., and E. Anderson "Price and Value of Decision Support Systems," *MIS Quarterly,* 11, NO. 4 (December 1987), 515–528.

ROCKART, J. F., AND D. W. DELONG *Executive Support Systems.* Homewood, Ill.: Dow Jones-Irwin, 1988.

SPRAGUE, R., AND E. CARLSON *Building Effective Decision Support Systems.* Englewood Cliffs, N.J.: Prentice Hall, 1982.

SPRAGUE, R. H., AND H. J. WATSON, EDS. *Decision Support Systems: Putting Theory into Practice.* Englewood Cliffs, N.J.: Prentice Hall, 1986.

STABELL, C. B. "A Decision- Oriented Approach to Building Decision Support Systems," in *Building Decision Support Systems,* ed. J. L. Bennett, pp. 221–260. Reading, Mass.: Addison-Wesley, 1983.

TURBAN, E., AND D. SCHAEFFER "A Comparative Study of Executive Information Systems," in *DSS-87* Transactions, ed. O. A. El Sawy, pp. 139–148. Providence, R.I.: Institute of Management Sciences, 1987.

ZMUD, R. "Supporting Senior Executives through Decision Support Technologies: A Review and Directions for Future Research," in *Decision Support Systems: A Decade in Perspective,* ed. E. R. Mclean and H. G. Sol, pp. 87–101. Amsterdam: Elsevier Science, 1986.

13

DSS SOFTWARE SELECTION: A MULTIPLE CRITERIA DECISION METHODOLOGY

Louis A. Le Blanc,
M. Tawfik Jelassi

INTRODUCTION

The DSS Software Selection Problem

Recent publications devoted to evaluating decision support systems (DSS) software [19, 21, 22, 28, and 32] have identified criteria, especially user-related ones, which are critical in selecting a suitable DSS generator. However, these authors have not suggested how to incorporate multiple user criteria, as well as technical attributes, into a complete and thorough evaluation and selection process. Furthermore, Lynch [16, 17] suggests that inadequate examination of prospective software packages leads to serious difficulties if not failures when implementing information systems.

Although a number of approaches to selecting application software for transaction processing and MIS have been proposed [3, 4, 6, 9, 18, 25, 33], some critical factors

Reprinted by special permission of *Information & Management*, Volume 17, 1989. © 1989 by Elsevier Science Publishers B.V. (North-Holland)

were omitted. These factors include assuring that the selected software package is superi-
or to a custom alternative, or that a screening process is provided to reduce the number of
packages subjected to detailed evaluation.

DSS Terminology

A number of key terms and expressions that will be used throughout the paper are now
defined. A *DSS Generator* is a "package of related hardware and software which provides a set of capabilities to build specific DSS quickly and easily" [26]. Examples of
such generators include IFPS [8], Prefcalc [15], Expert Choice [7], and Lightyear [29]. A
DSS generator constitutes one of the three technological levels that make up the DSS
development framework suggested by Sprague [26]. The other two levels are: *Specific
DSS,* which are systems that actually support the manager (user) to solve specific sets of
related decision problems; and *DSS Tools,* which are hardware and software elements
built by a toolsmith to facilitate the development of both specific DSS and DSS generators (see respectively (1) and (2) in Figure 13.1). Examples of such DSS tools include
procedural programming languages, graphics and color subroutines, and other dialog-
handling software.

Figure 13.1 (adapted from [26]), shows the three technological levels defined
above, the relationships between them, and the manager/technician roles associated with
each level. Notice that specific DSS can be developed either directly from tools or by
adapting the DSS generator to satisfy the application requirements. In the latter case, the
DSS builder may use the *iterative design approach* [5] to add capabilities to the ones
available in the DSS generator (or delete unnecessary features) as needed by the specific
DSS. This approach can be represented by the iterative cycling between the DSS generator and the specific DSS (see (3) in Figure 13.1).

FIGURE 13.1   DSS Technology Levels and Development Framework

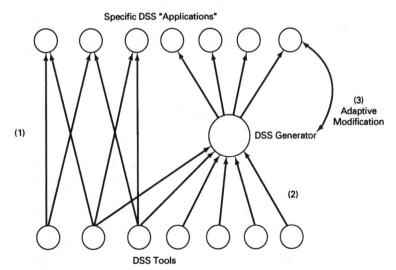

To emphasize the importance of evaluation and selection of DSS software (as compared to that of other information systems), it should be noted that DSS generators are used to develop *multiple* application systems, while MIS software is employed only for a *single* application. To efficiently develop specific DSS using the iterative design approach, a generator needs to be available. Hogue and Watson [10] reported that 50 percent of the firms that they studied developed specific DSS applications with a generator. The very critical software evaluation and selection process for DSS generators should take place prior to any systems analysis and design efforts.

This paper illustrates a method to select the most appropriate DSS generator where multiple criteria exist not only from functional requirements but also from technical and vendor support perspectives. As an essential part of the methodology, an initial stage determines whether a DSS software product is even suitable for a particular enterprise, or should specific DSS be developed from available tools.

The proposed selection process in this paper also ensures that, at each successive stage of the methodology, a DSS generator is superior to a DSS application custom-built from tools. It continually reduces the number of DSS software products under consideration until a final selection of a generator is made or constructing a specific DSS from tools is chosen as the best alternative (see Figure 13.2).

Structure of the Paper

This paper is primarily addressed to academics interested in software selection methodologies as well as practitioners faced with DSS-related problems. The second section outlines DSS developments affecting information systems (IS) planning. In particular, the enterprise software policy and the implications that DSS generators might have are discussed. The third section suggests a multiple criteria methodology for DSS software selection. The three stages of the methodology—DSS software screening, DSS generator evaluation, and specific DSS design—are described. Then, the fourth section presents a case example that demonstrates the applicability of the proposed methodology. The fifth section covers the impact of DSS software on specific DSS development from systems analysis and design, installation, and operating support viewpoints. The sixth section concludes the reading with some final remarks.

DSS DEVELOPMENTS AFFECTING *IS* PLANNING

The increased use and availability of DSS software has greatly influenced IS planning [34]. Questions such as the following ones have been raised. What is the organization's strategy concerning the use of packaged software? What types of criteria should be used? Are packages easy to maintain?

These questions and others must be directly addressed by IS management, since many applications requirements can be effectively satisfied by DSS software packages. One major consideration is the degree to which DSS generators are compatible with the enterprise's technical architecture for information processing. For example, if multiple

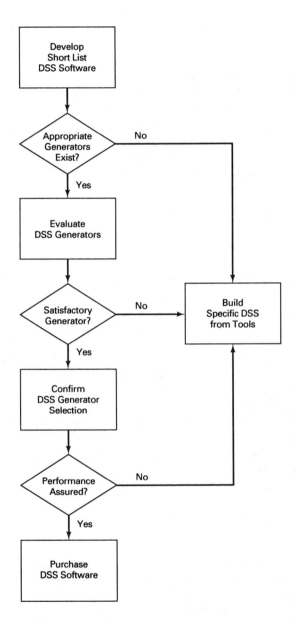

FIGURE 13.2   A Multiple Criteria Decision Methodology for DSS Software Selection

DSS generators and vendors are used, how effectively can a common database be employed throughout the organization?

Implications of DSS Generators

With the greater availability of DSS generator software and its improved quality, it appears that, for most organizations, DSS packages may be preferred over custom development from DSS tools. While there are obvious benefits to using generator packages, they are not necessarily "off-the-shelf" solutions. Generator selection should be a careful and well-organized process to satisfy user requirements and meet generally accepted information processing standards for quality and performance.

The selection of a DSS generator needs to be a disciplined process of matching package options with operating procedures, and reconciling any differences. Modifications to the DSS software should be carefully analyzed before they are made to consider risks and jeopardizing longer-term vendor support.

The use of DSS generators may conflict with the major benefit of adopting a corporate database—that is, sharing data among several users while enforcing a unique way to define it and manipulate it in addition to minimizing and controlling data redundancy. Since generator packages often create and manage their own data, this may lead to having multiple versions of the same data and can be a source of inconsistencies.

Enterprise Software Policy

The importance of an enterprise-wide policy regarding the use of application software cannot be overemphasized. This means a stated "going-in" position concerning the desirability of using DSS generators and the manner in which it should be used. Such a policy statement guides a project team as it considers the compromises that users might have to make to employ DSS technology.

The hardware and software policy of the firm has a direct relationship to the choice of DSS products. Normally, such a policy will have been determined by the enterprise IS strategy. The evaluators of DSS generators will then restrict their search to vendors offering software that will operate in the given technical environment.

The organization needs to determine overall vendor and market criteria for DSS software evaluation. For example, each package must meet 85 percent of the application's functional requirements; and each DSS generator must have been previously installed in at least five organizations.

A DECISION METHODOLOGY FOR DSS SOFTWARE SELECTION

There are three principal stages in the proposed DSS evaluation and selection methodology: (1) screening of prospective candidates and development of a short list of DSS software packages; (2) selecting a DSS generator, if any, which best suits the application requirements; and, (3) matching user requirements to the features of the selected generator and describing how these requirements will be satisfied through the building of prototypes for specific DSS. The detailed procedures involved in each state of the selection process are described in the following sections.

DSS Software Screening

During the first state of the evaluation and selection methodology, three key issues must be addressed: (1) Is there DSS software that can be used or should a specific DSS be developed from tools?; (2) What DSS generators are available?; and, (3) Which DSS software packages should be seriously considered and evaluated in detail? (Examples of commercially available mainframe- and microcomputer-based DSS software packages are given in Table 13.1.

The purpose of developing a short list of generator products is to narrow the field of available DSS software for consideration during Generator Evaluation. A short list of software (two or three) eliminates any unnecessary effort or confusion which might result because too many alternative DSS products are evaluated.

Identify Candidate Software   The project team must first identify available DSS products that operate within the enterprise's specific computer hardware and are compatible with its operating system and database management system (DBMS). To accomplish this task, there are several publications (e.g., Datapro Directory and ICP Directory) which provide profiles of DSS software vendors and the products they offer.

TABLE 13.1   Representative DSS Software Products

PRODUCT	VENDOR
Mainframe Packages	
EXPRESS	Management Decisions, Inc.
IFPS	Execucom Systems, Corp.
SYSTEM W	Comshare, Inc.
SIMPLAN	Simplan Systems, Inc.
INSIGHT	Insight Software
PLATO	OR/MS Dialogue, Inc.
Microcomputer Packages	
FOCUS/PC	Information Builders, Inc.
IFPS/PERSONAL	Execucom Systems, Corp.
NOMAD 2 PC	D&B Computing Services
ENCORE	Ferox Microsystems
PC ANALECT	Dialogue, Inc.
PC EXPRESS	Information Resource, Inc.
PREFCALC	Euro-Decision
ENABLE	Software Publishing Group
SYMPHONY	Lotus Development
FRAMEWORK	Ashton-Tate

Screening Criteria   At this point in the process, since a detailed analysis of user requirements has not likely been performed, screening criteria should be kept to a rather high level. Otherwise, these criteria will become so specific that it might become impossible to meet them with any commercially-available DSS generator. The list of criteria will contain relatively few items and should concentrate on functional requirements not commonly provided by DSS packages and which are very specific to the organization evaluating DSS software.

Some of the screening criteria are requirements that cannot be compromised and are easy to define objectively, such as compatibility with a particular operating system. However, other criteria are less definite, such as a vendor's ability to adequately support the software. Screening criteria can be categorized into four major types: (1) technical requirements; (2) functional requirements; (3) documentation and training; and (4) vendor information.

TECHNICAL REQUIREMENTS.   An organization's hardware and software strategy will likely dictate the high-level criteria in the technical area. To be considered, a package must fit the framework of the proposed system; it must be compatible with the hardware and software direction already identified (usually IS planning). The operating system is clearly a strict technical requirement. Others could include programming languages, peripherals, memory needs, or data communication capabilities. If relatively high transaction and

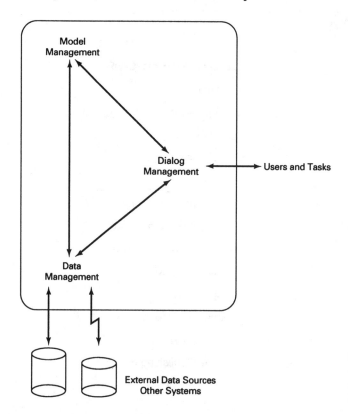

FIGURE 13.3
Functional Components
of a Decision Support
System

report volumes are required, then the technical architecture of the DSS software package must support efficient processing.

FUNCTIONAL REQUIREMENTS. The functional requirements of a DSS generator can be classified according to the following system components (see Figure 13.3 adapted from [2]): (1) Dialog Management; (2) Data Management; and (3) Model Management. The functional requirements associated with each of these three system components readily distinguish DSS generator evaluation and selection from other software appraisal efforts [27], where functional requirements are less unique to the IS type.

The dialog component of a DSS is the software and hardware that provides the user interface for the system. It presents the process outputs to the users and collects the inputs to the DSS. Building a DSS without databases and associated DBMS will be extremely difficult, since this component provides the data needed for decision making. The modeling component gives decision makers the ability to analyze a problem by developing and comparing alternative solutions.

Table 13.2 lists several examples of functional criteria to conduct the first-cut screening according to the DSS components. High-level criteria for the dialog management component would be that the DSS generator offers several dialog (e.g., command language, menu, question/answer, and object oriented) to accommodate different cognitive styles of various users. The data management component could call for both relational and hierarchical DBMS. Model management criteria might require the availability of multiple optimization models, such as linear, dynamic, and integer programming models.

DOCUMENTATION AND TRAINING. DSS software packages normally include the documentation required to install and support the DSS generator. It should be detailed, complete, and easy to understand. Poor documentation makes it more difficult for personnel to understand the package, and would also increase the time to modify it, if necessary. The avail-

TABLE 13.2   High-Level Screening Criteria of DSS Components

DIALOG MANAGEMENT	DATA MANAGEMENT	MODEL MANAGEMENT
Multiple Dialog Styles	Variety of Logical Data Views	Library of Optimization Models
Command Language	Relational DBMS	Linear-Programming
Menu	Hierarchical DBMS	Dynamic Programming
Question/ Answer	Network DBMS	Integer Programming
Object Oriented	File Management System	

ability of vendor-developed training sessions and materials may be very important, especially when the organization's personnel are inexperienced in implementing software.

VENDOR INFORMATION.   A vendor's ability to support its package through training, consultation, installation, and maintenance assistance is an important consideration in evaluating DSS software packages. Whenever the extent of a vendor's support for a generator package is unclear, the vendor should be contacted so the point can be clarified. He should also be able to refer an evaluation team to a user who is willing to talk to them about the DSS package and the accompanying support.

The financial stability of a vendor can also be an important consideration. Financially successful vendors that have been in existence for more than a few years are more likely to adequately support their packages initially and in the future. Such vendors attract and retain competent personnel, so that, in addition to having the funds available for support, they also have the personnel.

It is important to remember, however, that financial success alone does not ensure adequate, continued support. Vendor image, package reputation, the unit price, and the number of installations are also important considerations. Either the vendors themselves or the users to whom they directed the prospective buyer should be able to provide the needed information in these areas. Vendor support should always be carefully investigated.

Pick Finalists   The matching of the screening criteria against the list of DSS software and their capabilities will cause the elimination of many (but hopefully not all) generators. The following are typical reasons to eliminate potential DSS software candidates: (1) a vendor has only three employees and has been in business less than a year; (2) operating systems software and hardware is not supported by a vendor; and, (3) system documentation is inadequate.

By reducing the number of DSS software packages under consideration from as many as twenty to two or three, a project team can more effectively devote its attention to the critical details that can make the difference between selecting an adequate DSS and selecting a superior one. Moreover, by determining what DSS software packages are available for the application, the screening process also determines whether a DSS generator can be used or if a specific decision support system should be constructed from DSS tools (see Figure 13.2).

DSS Generator Evaluation

This second stage focuses on the two or three DSS generators that were identified in the screening of DSS software. The objective is to evaluate in detail the DSS generator finalists and select the one software product that best meets the needs of the organization. The primary tasks of DSS software selection are: (1) to further define the detailed evaluation criteria; (2) obtain generator product information; and, (3) evaluate the DSS software finalists and pick one as the best alternative.

Expand Evaluation Criteria   The screening criteria are expanded in more detail and fall into the same four categories: (1) technical requirements; (2) functional requirements; (3) documentation and training; and (4) vendor information. Although all categories are expanded during generator evaluation, the *functional requirements* receive the majority of attention and are related to the dialog, data, and model management components of the DSS generator.

The purpose of this task is to develop a rather comprehensive functional view of the proposed system and to summarize the requirements that must be satisfied by the DSS. The definition of functional requirements must be detailed enough to provide users and management with a complete view of the proposed system. This task should emphasize how the new system will work in the business environment. As the project team defines the functional criteria, they should also document the levels of importance and need to the user. The following functional requirements for DSS software, identified in [19, 22, and 27], are those for a hypothetical firm: (1) user friendliness; (2) hardware and operating system considerations; (3) variety of dialog styles; (4) data handling functions; (5) management of internal and external databases; (6) logical data models; (7) analysis; (8) forecasting and statistics; and, (9) graphics. These categories represent an outline for the extended functional criteria of the DSS generator. Table 3.3 exhibits an expansion of the above summary list of functional generator requirements categorized by the DSS as dialog, data, and model management components.

TABLE 13.3   Detailed Functional Criteria for DSS Software

Dialog Management Component

User Friendliness
  Consistent, natural language commands
  "Help" command and error messages
  Novice and expert modes

Hardware and Operating System Elements
  Printer and plotter support
  Variety of input device support

Variety of Dialog Styles
  Menu
  Command language
  Object oriented
  Question/Answer

Graphics
  Basic plots and charts
  Multicolor support
  Previewing of output

Data Management Component

Data Handling Functions
  Dictionary
  Creation, deletion, update, and query

TABLE 13.3   (Continued)

Management of Internal and External Databases
    Extraction
    Capture
    Integration of data sources

Logical Data Views
    Record
    Relational, Hierarchical, and Network DBMS
    Rule

Model Management Component

Analysis
    What-if and goal seeking
    Monte Carlo
    Mathematical optimization

Forecasting and Statistics
    Basic statistical functions
    Time series with seasonal adjustment
    Multivariate statistics

Obviously, some criteria are more important or critical to users than others. To reflect the relative importance of each criterion, the users must weight or assign a level of importance (such as "3" for essential, "2" for important, or "1" for optional) to each criterion. To demonstrate this element of the evaluation and selection methodology, an example of the weighting procedure is given below using the "Analysis" criteria from Table 13.3 for a hypothetical enterprise.

ANALYSIS	WEIGHT
What-If	1
Goal Seeking	3
Monte Carlo	2
Optimization	2

The purpose of this weighting process will be discussed in more detail in a later section (Evaluate DSS Generators).

Criticism levied against weighting schemes for software selection decisions [14] can be minimized through the screening process and development of a short list. Naumann and Palvia [20] successfully applied weighting and scoring measures to select a systems development tool from a relatively short list (4) of candidate techniques. By weighting criteria for only two or three packages rather than for a dozen (in which case the aforementioned criticism is probably valid), the proposed evaluation process allows for a very detailed and focused inspection of just the few best alternative DSS software products.

The proposed approach is an efficient, pragmatic, and managerially oriented evaluation and selection procedure. The advantages of using a DSS generator may be reduced significantly by a lengthy evaluation and selection process which often delays the prompt installation of the software and postpones the benefits available from rapidly producing a specific DSS from a generator.

Obtain Package Information   Once the system requirements have been established, and the criteria have been reviewed and weighted, the capability of each DSS generator to satisfy the requirements must be measured. Several techniques may be used to gather enough information to determine how well each package meets the requirements.

In many cases, the project team can meet directly with the vendor sales and support personnel and discuss each requirement. But if requirements are so comprehensive and detailed that a more formal procedure should be followed, a request for proposal (RFP) can be submitted to vendors. In situations where requirements are less detailed and complex, the RFP can be replaced by a less formal and more direct procedure, for example a basic letter of request.

Evaluate DSS Generators   Once the vendors' responses to requirements have been received, the actual evaluation process can begin. The review is very detailed at this point, since the project team is looking for specific strengths and weaknesses of each package.

The project team is searching for deciding factors—not only *what* DSS software packages have and how well they provide it, but also what they *don't* have. Detailed information is desired on the functions of the DSS software and its related processing, including if and how functions that are not included in the DSS generator could be implemented.

EVALUATION MATRIX.   An evaluation matrix should be constructed to organize and assimilate all necessary information. The first step in constructing this matrix is to set up a rating scale that indicates, for each evaluation criterion (i.e., technical, functional, documentation, and vendor-related), how easily each package is able to meet that specific criterion. These rating scores are then multiplied by the weight factor for that criterion. The weights reflect the relative importance of each of the criteria, while the rating scores show how well a given package meets each user criterion.

Using the previous example of the "Analysis" criteria, a project team might employ a scale of 0–3: "3" if the DSS package totally meets the requirements; "2" when the product does not meet the requirement completely but enough so that tailoring is not warranted; "1" if the criterion would be met with some tailoring; and, "0" when the package does not meet the criterion at all. (Other rating, scoring, or evaluation methods (e.g., [23, 24, and 31]) could also be appropriate depending on the particular user requirements.)

Using this scale, two prospective DSS software packages, ABC and XYZ, were scored:

ANALYSIS	ABC	XYZ
What-If	1	3
Goal Seeking	3	3
Monte Carlo	3	2
Optimization	2	3
Subtotal	9	11

These results would indicate that XYZ meets the hypothetical requirements better. However, these may not be accurate! The detailed requirements for "Analysis" (an element of the model management component in the DSS generator) are probably not equal. The weighting factors, which were established earlier, are absent from these calculations.

If the scores are adjusted by multiplying the rating score for each "Analysis" criterion by the corresponding weight factor, then the figures would appear as the following:

ANALYSIS	ABC GENERATOR						XYZ GENERATOR					
	WEIGHT		RATING		TOTAL		WEIGHT		RATING		TOTAL	
What-If	1	×	1	=	1		1	×	3	=	3	
Goal Seeking	3	×	3	=	9		3	×	3	=	9	
Monte Carlo	2	×	3	=	6		2	×	2	=	4	
Optimization	2	×	2	=	4		2	×	3	=	6	
Total					20						22	

Note that the weight scores for each "Analysis" criterion are the same for both DSS generators, reflecting the user's decision about the relative importance of each of the criteria. On the other hand, the rating scores indicate how well each DSS software package meets each criterion established by the users.

A "total possible points" column could represent an ideal package meeting 100 percent of requirements. The "constant" weight factor would be multiplied by the highest possible rating score for each of the "Analysis" criteria. An ideal package would have all of the analysis features (i.e., what-if, goal seeking, Monte Carlo, and optimization) as standard. This would mean a score of "3" in the example.

This scoring by matrix is a small part of the DSS software evaluation process; but this exercise or calculation must be completed for each criterion, such as those listed in Table 13.3. The total points of each criterion for each DSS software package would then be recorded in a large matrix. A partially completed matrix for the hypothetical example follows:

FUNCTIONAL REQUIREMENTS	ABC	XYZ	TOTAL POSSIBLE POINTS
1. User Friendliness	23	21	24
2. Hardware and Operating System Elements	13	13	16
3. Variety of Dialog Styles	20	22	24
4. Data Handling Functions	15	14	18
5. Extraction from Internal or External Data Base	22	20	22
6. Logical Data Views	18	17	20
7. Analysis	20	22	24
8. Forecasting and Statistics	12	10	15
9. Graphics	26	21	30
Subtotal	169	160	193

As established in an enterprise software policy, hurdle scores ensure that DSS generators provide adequate coverage of requirements. A policy for software selection might be that all DSS generators must satisfy at least 80 percent of the requirements. In the prior partial matrix, the "ABC Generator" satisfied 88 percent of the criteria, while "XYZ" covered only 83 percent. Both DSS software packages met the minimum hurdle.

In this instance, where both packages exceed the hurdle percentage scores, an index would be constructed by dividing the cost of each respective package by its score, giving the price in dollars per requirement point. For example, if the ABC package sold for $100,000 and XYZ costs $75,000, the respective indices would be $591.72 and $468.75. This indicates that the XYZ package would provide more than the minimum functional requirements and almost equal coverage of these requirements as the alternative DSS software package but at considerably less cost per requirement.

Additional Selection Requirements   The matrix scores are not necessarily the determining factor for selecting a particular DSS generator. The matrix should be used as a decision tool—a means for organizing and summarizing the significant quantity of information that the project team has collected. The highest score on the evaluation matrix may not always indicate the best DSS generator. The matrix scores may not accurately reflect certain intangible factors such as the cosmetic appearance of reports and screens, how easy it will be to use the DSS software, etc.

TAILORING.   The matrix may not indicate how much time or the level of technical expertise needed to "tailor" the DSS generator. Tailoring can be either costly if it is relatively extensive, or difficult if the internal structure of the software is complex. The importance of the technical processing architecture will depend on how much tailoring is anticipated. Furthermore, the architecture of the DSS generator also determines how much modification is even possible.

DOCUMENTATION. A decision to use a particular DSS generator should not be made on the basis of functional requirements alone. The DSS software's documentation is a very important nonfunctional factor. Its accuracy and level of detail can affect the time it will take to evaluate and modify the package.

Comparing documentation is sometimes very difficult at this stage of the evaluation process due to differences in format, style, etc. Still, it is important to review the vendors' documentation and to reconfirm that the information collected on maintenance and support, for instance, is accurate and correct. At this stage, the vendor should be able to refer the project team to current users of his software. The comments of these customers should prove invaluable. Site visits and demonstrations of the DSS software in operation may be helpful.

Specific DSS Design

Assuming that DSS software which is anticipated to provide satisfactory performance has been selected (see Figure 13.2), the project team is ready to confirm the selection by developing some specific DSS prototypes based on the chosen generator. The primary reasons for this stage are to ensure that the DSS package can be used effectively and to provide one last chance to reconsider the DSS software design.

It is often difficult to determine the degree of user satisfaction until the design process has begun for specific applications utilizing the selected DSS software. Therefore, this stage involves the design of demonstration prototypes of specific DSS built from the DSS generator [11, 19]. Such prototypes can provide significant benefits before finalizing the selection decision [1, 11, 12, 13]. These benefits afford much information for the evaluation and selection process [19], including: (1) estimates of programmer productivity; (2) measures of computer resource utilization; (3) personnel requirements for the DSS software; (4) performance of the documentation under actual working conditions; and, (5) experience with the iterative development process using the DSS generator for building specific DSS applications.

In addition to prototyping specific DSS with the selected DSS software before actual purchase, Meador and Mezger [19] suggest conducting "benchmark evaluations" which would be undertaken during this stage of the proposed evaluation and selection process. A benchmark evaluation is a series of simulated tests for a comprehensive set of the DSS software's features. The simulations attempt to determine the level of computer system resources utilized by the various capabilities of the DSS package. Resources include CPU cycles, main memory, input/output activity, and response time. The programs or models to be tested are specifically designed to execute the features or capabilities of the DSS generator, rather than to solve specific DSS application problems.

Alter Functional Requirements Based on the capabilities of the selected DSS generator as experienced in the prototyping exercise of specific DSS and benchmark testing, the definition of user requirements might be altered to include package features not previously considered, or to change or eliminate others. The modified requirements should be reviewed with the users. The effect of DSS software deficiencies perhaps can be minimized by altering user procedures or postponing the implementation of some requirements until generator enhancements could be made.

DSS Software Modifications and Supporting Programs   Typically, the specific DSS being developed requires certain functions and interfaces not provided by the software. If a DSS generator does not meet all the functional requirements of a system, the following alternatives should be considered: (1) persuade the vendor to include additional features; (2) develop supplemental software; and, (3) modify the vendor's software. The chosen alternative will depend on the extent of the DSS generator's deficiencies, the potential costs and benefits of altering the software, and the size and technical skills of the programming staff.

VENDOR-SUPPLIED ENHANCEMENTS.   If possible, the vendor should be persuaded to do the modification for the purchaser. This is often the best alternative, since the vendor will usually update and maintain the software on a routine basis.

SUPPORTING PROGRAMS.   Developing software to supplement the vendor's DSS package is often the most practical alternative. The vendor will normally continue to service the DSS generator; but if this alternative is selected, the supplemental software should conform to the standards used by the vendor in developing the DSS generator.

ALTER CODE.   Modifying a DSS generator is usually not recommended. If the software is modified, the vendor may be reluctant or may even refuse to service the package. Updates to the software may not be compatible with the modifications effected.

In some cases, this may not even be an option, since the purchaser of the DSS generator does not have (or cannot get at any price) a copy of the source code. In this instance, all that the purchaser can do is to build a front end or back end to the software package.

Finalize DSS Generator Selection   It is not unheard of for an organization to complete the last stage of the evaluation and selection process for DSS software, only to realize that the DSS generator selected is not the best choice. Perhaps too many compromises have been made and users are no longer satisfied. Possibly, the tailoring effort has become so extensive that a custom DSS (i.e., specific DSS application built from tools) would be a better choice (see Figure 13.2). Therefore, a final commitment to using a particular DSS generator should be avoided until the design of specific DSS using the potential software package has progressed to the point where user satisfaction is ensured.

The following section provides an illustrative example of how the DSS software evaluation and selection methodology works. It uses a real-world case, the Wildlife and Fisheries Department, to demonstrate the applicability of the proposed methodology.

CASE EXAMPLE: THE WILDLIFE AND FISHERIES DEPARTMENT

The Wildlife and Fisheries Department (WFD) is a state government office responsible for developing a strategy to manage its state's deer population. Each year, the

Department chooses to either maintain, increase, or decrease the deer population in each county. Population regulation may be achieved through the selective issuance of hunting permits. Therefore, it is essential that WFD be able to accurately predict deer population levels within each of the state's counties.

Case Background

Deer hunting regulations require that each successful hunter reports his kill to a check station within 24 hours. Within the state of Indiana, for example, there are approximately 240 such check stations. When a hunter brings his deer to a check station, the deer is tagged and the hunter is required to fill out a form listing the county of kill, date of harvest, and the sex of the deer taken. A copy of this form is then forwarded to the WFD on a weekly basis for the duration of the hunting season.

Once the WFD receives the data, it must sort it by county. Certain statistical analysis, such as the percentage of yearling, must also be calculated. Once the data is adequately prepared, it is ready for use in a predictive model. With data, such as population fecundity and survivorship by age class, a spreadsheet model could produce estimates of the state's deer population. The harvest number can then be varied to show its effects on the deer population within each county of interest. In this way, the WFD can determine the number of permits to issue within each county. The spreadsheet output along with recommendations for management are then incorporated into an annual report which is presented to the WFD's "administrator" who makes the final decision.

The professional construction and presentation of the report may also influence the "administrator." Therefore, it is to the advantage of the WFD staff to have its report neatly processed. For illustrating the calculated trends in the deer population, graphical and tabular summaries should also be incorporated into the report.

DSS Generator Screening

While practically any spreadsheet program could perform the mathematical requirements of the population forecasting model, the production of the complete report requires additional software capabilities. A functional and technical analysis of the procedures to be used by the WFD revealed the following list of requirements (i.e., screening criteria).

IBM-PC COMPATIBILITY. This was essential for interfacing with the corresponding systems of neighboring states which would provide relevant input data. As a base level operating system, DOS 3.0 was identified.

DATABASE. The database must be large enough to incorporate all of the data from the approximately 50,000 individual kill reports received each year. One hundred characters were needed for each record. Also, the maintenance of a five-year database was recommended.

STATISTICAL ANALYSIS. Functions such as mean, standard deviation, relative percentages and to a lesser extent regression analysis, were necessary for the data analysis.

SPREADSHEET. The dimensions of the spreadsheet should be large enough to accept data from all 92 state counties and perform the necessary computations. In addition, the spreadsheet functions must link individual county spreadsheet models into a comprehensive statewide summary.

WORD PROCESSOR. This component required both spelling and grammatical checks to assist the biologists in preparing their reports.

GRAPHICS. The software had to produce good quality line, grouped line, and bar charts for showing trends and supporting quick information assimilation by the WFD users.

FILE IMPORT/EXPORT. In addition to exchanging files from other computer programs, the chosen software package must be able to accept data from existing files which contain a significant amount of needed historical data. The acceptance of this material by the new system without major modification would allow for considerable savings in time and money.

DOCUMENTATION. The documentation had to be detailed, organized and precise. Both external documentation (books, manuals, videotapes) and internal (on-screen help) should be available. On-line documentation should be context sensitive, and external documentation might include videotape sessions.

Two classes of potential "commercial" DSS software, namely basic and integrated spreadsheets, were identified by the WFD. It should be noted here that these packages are commercially-available products which might differ from the "ideal" DSS generator defined in the first section of this reading. The list of spreadsheet packages available in this market is very long, ranging from the most simplistic to the very sophisticated. A preliminary list, based on the two potential classes of DSS software, follows. From this roster, a short list of three DSS generators was developed by applying the aforementioned screening criteria (i.e., functional and technical criteria, etc.) and eliminating those packages which were not considered adequate for more detailed inspection.

BASIC SPREADSHEETS	INTEGRATED SPREADSHEETS
Lotus 123	Enable
Visicalc	Symphony
Quattro	Framework
Excel	Smart
Multiplan	Electric Desk
Supercalc	Get Organized

A brief evaluation of the main characteristics of the basic spreadsheets uncovered the following attributes: (1) good features in terms of mathematical abilities; (2) lack of graphical components (except in Lotus and Quattro); (3) none of them has a word processing component; and, (4) none of them can handle the necessary database size.

The functional and technical environment described earlier in this section documented the crucial nature of the graphical, word processing, and database capabilities. Consequently, the basic spreadsheet packages were eliminated and would not be included in the final evaluation. While separate software products may be combined into one DSS to perform the necessary functions, the number of possible combinations was too large to consider.

The further matching of screening criteria against the list of integrated spreadsheet packages eliminated all but the following potential DSS generators: Symphony (Lotus Development), Framework (Ashton-Tate), and Enable (Software Group). The other potential DSS generators failed to be included in the short list since they did not meet one or more of the screening criteria (i.e., database size or spreadsheet linking functions).

DSS Generator Evaluation and Selection

Based on the aforementioned list of screening criteria, a scheme for the detailed evaluation and selection of the generator software was based upon the following categories: (1) technical criteria; (2) functional criteria; (3) documentation criteria; and, (4) vendor criteria.

TECHNICAL CRITERIA.   The primary technical requirement for the WFD computing environment is IBM and DOS compatibility. A version of DOS 3.0 or higher was also considered a necessity.

FUNCTIONAL CRITERIA.   The functional requirements of the WFD application include the database, statistical, spreadsheet, word processing, graphics creating, file handling and exchange, and documentation criteria which were listed in the initial phase (DSS Generator Screening).

For purposes of evaluating the three commercial DSS generators listed before, the preceding criteria were weighted according to their relative importance to the WFD operations. The following scale was used: "3" expressing a crucial function; "2" meaning significant; and "1" noting optional. Table 13.4 describes the relative importance assigned to each criterion.

In addition to the weighting scale, a rating system was used to indicate the respective software's performance on each of the criteria. This rating was based on a four-point scale (3 = good, 2 = fair, 1 = poor, and 0 = not available).

Table 13.4 depicts both the weights and the total scores (weights multiplied by rating scores) developed for each DSS generator. The matrix totals give Enable the edge over the other DSS software packages evaluated. However, the tabulated scores were rather close (i.e., Enable = 91, Framework = 85, Symphony = 76).

While scores were close, Enable was the best performer in the most critical areas. Of the criteria considered to be the most crucial, Enable received a perfect (3) rating in four of them. Perhaps the most important criterion was database size. Enable was the only DSS generator capable of handing the required 50,000 records. Enable was also superior in both internal and external documentation, which was critical since non-computer personnel would be directly involved in the operation of the DSS software. However, Enable was relatively inferior in two areas, namely its spreadsheet linking function and its vendor reputation (i.e., lack of market prominence compared to the other vendors).

Overall, Framework had the best word processing features, Enable offered the most useful database module, and Symphony's spreadsheet capabilities were exception-

TABLE 13.4   WFD Case: Evaluation Matrix for DSS Software

CRITERIA	WEIGHT	DSS GENERATOR SCORES		
		SYM-PHONY	FRAME-WORK	ENABLE
Technical				
IBM Compatibility	3	9	9	9
Functional				
Database Size	3	3	3	9
Basic Statistics	3	9	9	9
Regression Analysis	1	0	0	0
Spreadsheet Size	3	3	6	6
Spelling check	2	0	6	6
Grammar Check	1	0	0	0
Graphics	3	6	6	6
Spreadsheet Linking	2	6	6	4
File Import/Export	2	2	6	6
Combine Graphics and Text	2	2	4	6
Menu Dialog	2	6	6	6
Common Dialog	2	4	2	6
Documentation				
External Documentation	2	2	4	6
On-Line Help in Context	3	9	9	9
Vendor				
Reputation	3	9	9	3
Total		76	85	91

al. However, the superior package at providing comprehensive functionality in spreadsheet, database, and word processing in a single package was Enable.

Specific DSS Applications

At this point in the evaluation and selection process, specific DSS applications were constructed with Enable, the chosen DSS generator. Representative prototypes were built to evaluate the DSS software's ability to handle not only functional requirements but also appraise its operating efficiency. If satisfactory performance was achieved by the DSS generator, then multiple copies would be purchased or a site license acquired. In the event that performance was less than satisfactory, the methodology prescribes construction of the specific DSS application from tools as needed to achieve the application requirements and user expectations.

Case Summary

It is important to note that no package provided a perfect fit for the WFD case. For example, none of the software offered regression analysis as a standard feature. A grammar check was also not available in any package.

As described by Sprague [26], an "ideal" DSS generator does not likely exist. The ideal generator would be developed over a long period of time in a fairly narrow problem domain. In practice, however, most specific DSS applications are being developed with general purpose DSS generators such as FOCUS, IFPS, and Lotus 1-2-3 [31, p. 205].

THE IMPACT OF DSS SOFTWARE ON SPECIFIC DSS DEVELOPMENT

Because DSS software can reduce the costs of developing specific decision support systems, organizations should investigate the possibility of using DSS generators during the systems planning process. Obviously, this may increase the personnel requirements of systems planning. However, such an investigation is valuable even if a custom approach to developing specific DSS from tools is determined to be more appropriate.

The evaluation process will help familiarize personnel with the functional requirements of proposed DSS applications. Furthermore, the availability of good DSS packages may have a significant effect on the organization's hardware and software strategy. Although the evaluation of DSS products can increase the cost of systems planning, the use of a DSS generator can clearly reduce overall development costs for specific DSS.

The following subsections discuss the effects that DSS software may have on developing specific DSS applications. In particular, the impact on system analysis and design, installation, and operating support is assessed.

DSS Software Impact on Systems Analysis and Design

DSS software selection often precedes the design of a specific DSS since the latter will be based on the chosen DSS package(s). Therefore, DSS software evaluation and selection is usually an additional effort that would not be required (or at least not to the same extent) for building specific DSS from tools.

While using DSS generators will often reduce the time and effort needed to complete the preliminary design, this reduction is frequently offset by the amount of work involved in evaluating and selecting a DSS package. Therefore, the overall effort for systems analysis and design may remain fairly constant regardless of whether users decide to use DSS generators or develop specific DSS from tools.

User Requirements and Application Design   The systems analysis activity for developing specific DSS determines whether or not the user's requirements are met by DSS software. While the effort needed to define these requirements is not reduced when a DSS generator is used, specific DSS design usually requires fewer personnel than when a specific system is custom developed from tools.

If user requirements are not satisfied by a DSS software package, the investment in time and effort depends on the amount of analysis and design that is necessary to meet the user's needs. This might involve developing manual procedures, interface capabilities, as well as additional software modules.

Technical Design   The work required for technical design is significantly reduced when DSS software is used. This is apparent because the technical architecture, database, and system processes for the DSS generator have already been defined by the vendor. However, what is necessary here is a confirmation by the project team that the architecture of the DSS package is compatible with the organization's technical environment.

The personnel requirements for designing security and control mechanisms will vary according to the particular DSS software package being used. For many packages, however, security and control is a weak area that requires additional work.

The operating performance of the system can be affected by the use of DSS software. It may suffer especially if many options are used, since the generalized software logic could require longer execution times than specific DSS developed from tools. Therefore, operating performance should not be overlooked during systems design just because DSS software is being used. This underscores the need for benchmark testing as previously mentioned.

DSS Software Impact on Systems Installation

Clearly, the greatest savings in developing specific DSS from a DSS generator are realized during installation. When a DSS package is installed, detailed systems design, programming, and debugging should require less effort than they would in the installation of a custom developed, specific DSS. Computer programs have already been designed, and coding and testing completed when DSS software is utilized.

Detailed Design and Programming   The primary purpose of using DSS software is to reduce the work performed for detailed design and programming. If the user requirements are not completely met by the DSS generator, some tailoring may be necessary. Any modification at this point needs thorough documentation which should be made available (by the system support group) for on-going maintenance of the DSS software.

Even if no program code changes to the DSS software are necessary, there is usually some detailed design, programming and testing required. Other production systems (e.g., transaction processing) might need to be changed, or interface programs be developed. Data conversion facilities are commonly needed to load the initial production (raw) files.

Systems Testing   The reduction of effort in detailed design and programming does not imply that system testing is less critical when DSS software is used. It is just as important as for specific DSS built from tools, if not more. A combination of conditions could be unique to a particular user and may not have been system tested by the vendor.

Some additional effort is required to perform physical installation of the DSS package. The project team should verify that the software delivered by the vendor is complete and operates in the company's technical environment. Some vendors provide a limited test case to be executed during what is often called the "acceptance test." All other segments of systems installation are still required and usually are not materially affected by DSS software.

Operating DSS Software Support

The amount of support work involved with installed DSS software usually depends, to a large degree, on the quality of the vendor support. DSS generator packages are more difficult to maintain if vendor support is poor.

The type of necessary maintenance also determines the extent of the impact DSS software has on supporting installed decision support systems. Maintenance of a DSS generator is categorized as follows: (1) maintenance of the code performed by the vendor, including new releases, temporary program fixes in response to bugs or code changes requested by the user; (2) maintenance of the code performed by in-house personnel, which refers to modifying the DSS software's program code; and, (3) maintenance of existing parameters and selected options (i.e., most parameter-driven software is designed to be maintained by the user).

When vendor modifications are implemented to an installed DSS generator, it is very important to maintain a listing of updates made to the DSS software, and to keep track of specific modifications and who made them. It is very useful for the vendor to know the status of the software when he is asked to investigate problems.

When implementing new vendor releases, several levels of modification and testing may be necessary: (1) acceptance testing of the new release; (2) modification of the new release to reflect prior user changes and parameters; (3) testing the modified release with acceptance data; and (4) testing the modified release with a system model. The net effect of installed generator effort varies with the particular package, the quality of vendor support, and the extent of maintenance. With a DSS generator, the number of necessary maintenance changes is often fewer than for custom-built specific DSS.

If the DSS software is well designed, it incorporates additional functions that can be activated as needed. The activation and testing effort required in this case would be far less than the effort to add the same functions to a specific DSS built from tools. If the DSS generator is well coded and tested, the number of bugs occurring immediately after conversion should be substantially fewer than with custom-developed specific DSS.

CONCLUDING REMARKS

Using DSS generators for the development of specific decision support systems will reduce personnel requirements and development costs. Conducting the evaluation of DSS software increases the effort necessary for developing specific DSS, but this undertaking is offset by the advantages of using a generator package. Despite the promises offered by DSS software, the performance of some DSS generators is much less than expected. Weak or nonexistent selection procedures may explain most of this poor implementation record. The methodology proposed in this reading will hopefully reduce the risks associated with decision support systems software and facilitate success in developing specific DSS from generators.

The most critical phases of the methodology are the first (the development of a short list) and the third (design of specific DSS with the selected generator). Initially, the screening process determines whether a generator is feasible and reduces the number of DSS software packages to be evaluated in detail. Finally, the development of specific DSS with the selected generator ensures that the DSS software can be used effectively and provides a last chance to consider building specific DSS from tools.

As stated in the first section of this reading, while prior work provided partial guidelines for DSS software evaluation and selection, no unified and comprehensive methodology (as presented herein) was suggested. It is the author's belief that this methodology is quite easy to use and pragmatic. Its intent is to efficiently choose a DSS generator that meets the application needs and user expectations from the employment of packaged software.

QUESTIONS

1. What is the purpose of the DSS software screening phase of the methodology? Give some examples of the criteria used in this phase.
2. The second phase of the methodology, which evaluates DSS generators, uses an evaluation matrix. What is the purpose of this matrix? What are its rows and columns?
3. The third phase of the methodology calls for the development of some specific DSS. Is this a proper part of the selection process for a DSS generator? Why or why not?

REFERENCES

1. ALAVI, M. "An Assessment of the Prototyping Approach to Information Systems Development," *Communications of the ACM,* 27, no. 6 (June 1984), 556–563.
2. ARIAV, G., AND M. J. GINZBERG "DSS Design: A Systemic View of Decision Support," *Communications of the ACM,* 28, no. 10 (October 1985), 1045–1052.
3. BERST, J. "The ABC's of Evaluating Packaged Software," *Interface Age* (February 1983), 35–38.
4. BRESLIN, J. *Selecting and Installing Software Packages.* Westport, CT: Quorom Books, 1986.

5. COURBON, J. C., J. GRAJEW, AND J. TOLOVI, JR.   "Design and Implementation of DecisionSupporting Systems by an Evolutive Approach." Unpublished working paper, University of Grenoble, France, 1980.

6. CURRY, J. W., AND D. M. BONNER   *How to Find and Buy Good Software: A Guide for Business and Professional People,* Englewood Cliffs, NJ: Prentice-Hall, 1983.

7. DECISION SUPPORT SOFTWARE, INC.   *EXPERT CHOICE User's Manual.* McLean, VA, 1983.

8. EXECUCOM SYSTEMS CORPORATION   *IFPS User's Manual.* Austin, TX, 1982.

9. GRAY, C. D.   *The Right Choice: A Complete Guide to Evaluating, Selecting, and Installing MRP II Software.* Essex Junction, VT: Oliver Wight Limited Publications, 1987.

10. HOGUE, J. T., AND H. J. WATSON   "Current Practices in the Development of Decision Support Systems," *Proceedings of the Fifth International Conference on Information Systems,* 117–127. Houston, TX, 1984.

11. JANSON, M.   "Applying A Pilot System and Prototyping Approach to Systems Development and Implementation," *Information And Management,* 10, no. 4 (1986), 209–216.

12. KEEN, P. G. W.   "Adaptive Design for Decision Support Systems," *Data Base,* 12, no. 3 (1980), 15–25.

13. KEEN, P. G. W.   "Value Analysis: Justifying Decision Support Systems," *MIS Quarterly,* 5, no. 2 (1981), 1–15.

14. KLEIN, G., AND P. O. BECK   "A Decision Aid for Selecting among Information System Alternatives," *MIS Quarterly,* 11, no. 2 (June 1987), 177–185.

15. LAUER, T. W., AND M. T. JELASSI   "PREFCALC—A Multi- Criteria Decision Support System: A User Tutorial," Indiana University Institute for Research on the Management of Information Systems, Working Paper #714, December 1987.

16. LYNCH, R. K.   "Implementing Packaged Application Software: Hidden Costs and New Challenges," *Systems, Objectives, Solutions,* 4, no. 4 (1984), 227–234.

17. LYNCH, R. K.   "Nine Pitfalls in Implementing Packaged Applications Software," *Journal of Information Systems Management,* 2, no. 2 (1985), 88–92.

18. MARTIN, J., AND C. MCCLURE   "Buying Software off the Rack," *Harvard Business Review,* 61, no. 6, (November–December 1983), 32–47.

19. MEADOR, G. L., AND R. A. MEZGER   "Selecting An End User Programming Language For DSS Development," *MIS Quarterly,* 8, no. 4 (December 1984), 267–281.

20. NAUMANN, J. D. AND S. PALVIA   "A Selection Model for Systems Development Tools," *MIS Quarterly,* 6, no. 1 (March 1982), 39–48.

21. REIMANN, B. C.   "Decision Support for Planners: How To Pick The Right DSS Generator Software," *Managerial Planning,* 33, no. 6 (May/June 1985), 22–26.

22. REIMANN, B. C. AND A. D. WAREN   "User-Oriented Criteria for the Selection of DSS Software," *Communications of the ACM,* 28, no. 2 (February 1985), 166–179.

23. SAATY, T.   *The Analytic Hierarchy Process.* New York, NY: McGraw-Hill, 1981.

24. SAATY, T.   *Decision Making for Leaders.* Belmont, CA: Lifetime Learning, 1982.

25. SANDERS, B. L., P. MUNTER, AND R. O. REED   "Selecting A Software Package," *Financial Executive,* 50, no. 9 (September 1982), 38–46.

26. SPRAGUE, R. H., JR.   "A Framework for the Development of Decision Support Systems," *MIS Quarterly,* 4, no. 4 (June 1980), 1–26.

27. SPRAGUE, R. H., JR., AND ERIC D. CARLSON   *Building Effective Decision Support Systems.* Englewood Cliffs, NJ: Prentice-Hall, Inc., 1982.

28. SUSSMAN, P. N. "Evaluating Decision Support Software," *Datamation,* 30, no. 17 (October 15, 1984)., 171–172.

29. THOUGHTWARE, INC. *LIGHTYEAR User's Manual,* Coconut Grove, Florida, 1984.

30. TIMMRECK, E. M. "Computer Selection Methodology," *Computing Surveys,* 5, no. 4 (December 1973), 199–222.

31. TURBAN, E. *Decision Support and Expert Systems.* New York, NY: Macmillan Publishing Company, 1988.

32. WAREN, A. D., AND B. C. REIMANN "Selecting DSS Generator Software: A Participative Process," *Policy and Information,* 9, no. 2 (December 1985), 63–76.

33. WELKE, L. A. "Buying Software," in *Systems Analysis And Design: A Foundation for the 1980's,* edited by W. W. Cotterman, J. D. Couger, N. L. Enger, and F. Harold. New York, NY: Elsevier North Holland, Inc., 1981, 400–416.

34. YOUNG, O. F. "A Corporate Strategy for Decision Support Systems," *Journal of Information Systems Management,* 1, no. 1 (Winter 1984), 58–62.

14

THE MEAD CORPORATION

Ralph H. Sprague, Jr.,
Barbara McNurlin

Mead Corporation, with headquarters in Dayton, Ohio, is a paper and forest products company. It has over one hundred mills, offices, and distribution centers throughout the United States and Canada. Since the mid-1970s, Mead has also been in the electronic publishing business, with NEXIS, its news information retrieval service, LEXIS, its on-line legal research service, and several other on-line and database services. The company is highly decentralized, with four operating groups—forest products, consumer and distribution, specialty, and Mead Data Central. Each group has one or more divisions.

INFORMATION SYSTEMS ORGANIZATION—PRE-1980

In the 1960s, Mead's corporate information systems department provided all Mead divisions with data processing services. By 1967, the department's budget had become so

Reprinted by permission of Canning Publications, Inc., from Sprague and McNurlin (eds.), *Information Systems Management in Practice* (Prentice Hall, 1986), and the *EDP Analyzer*, June 1985.

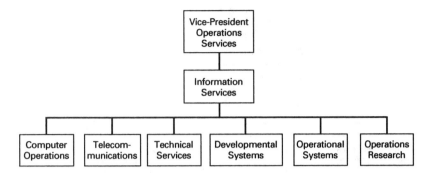

FIGURE 14.1   Mead Corporation's Pre–1980 Information Services
Department (from Mead Corporation)

large that management decided to spin off some of the functions to the divisions. Divisions could establish their own data processing and process engineering groups if they so desired. Or they could continue to purchase data processing services from the corporate information services department. Many of the divisions did establish their own information systems departments, but all continued to use the corporate data center for their corporate applications.

In the late 1970s, the corporate information services department had six groups, as illustrated in Figure 14.1. The director reported to the vice-president of operations services, and under the director were the following:

- Computer operations—responsible for managing the corporate data center
- Telecommunications—responsible for designing the telecommunications network and establishing standards
- Technical services—responsible for providing and maintaining systems software
- Developmental systems—responsible for traditional systems development
- Operational systems—responsible for maintaining systems after they become operational
- Operations research—responsible for performing management science analysis

CURRENT ORGANIZATION

In 1980, management realized that the existing organizational structure would not serve the needs of the rapidly growing end-user computing community. In addition, in order to become an "electronic-based" organization, management needed to build a corporate-wide network. Thus, they reorganized into three departments, as shown in Figure 14.2. In this new structure, the corporate information resources group not only creates the hardware, software, and communication standards for the entire corporation but runs the corporate data center and operates the network. All the divisions use the network and corporate data center. They follow the corporate standards, and some operate their own small distributed systems as well, which link into the corporate network.

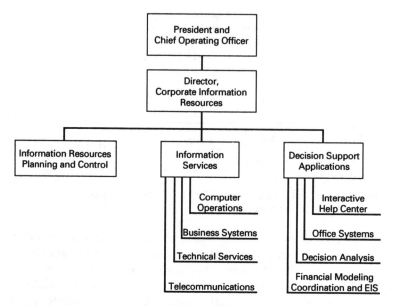

FIGURE 14.2   Mead Corporation's 1980–1984 Corporate Information Resources Group (from Mead Corporation)

The director of the corporate information resources group now reports directly to the company president—not through the vice-president of operations, as in the former structure. This change signaled an increase in the importance of information resources to the company. There are three departments within the new group:

- Information Resources Planning and Control—responsible for planning future information systems and technology
- Information Services—responsible for most of the traditional information systems functions from the previous information services department
- Decision Support Applications—responsible for "marketing" and supporting end-user computing

The Information Resources Planning and Control Department

The information resources planning and control department grew out of the company's strong planning culture. The decentralization of the 1970s pointed out the need for a coordinating body for information systems planning. Although it is a small department, it plays two important roles. First, it takes the corporate perspective for information systems planning to ensure that Mead's information resources plans mesh with the business plans. Second, it acts as planning coordinator for the various groups and divisions, helping them to coordinate their plans with corporate and information resources plans. The information resources planning department is currently concentrating on planning in six areas: networking, office automation, end-user computing, database management, manufacturing systems, and automating the system development process.

The Information Services Department

The information services department handles the traditional computing functions for Mead. It manages computer operations and traditional system development of corporate-wide systems. It also provides technical services—database administration, system software support, and technical support for end-user computing, such as creating micromain-frame communication links. The department also provides all the telecommunications services to the company.

The question of database management required special consideration. At the time of the 1980 restructuring, Mead believed it needed a separate function to provide centralized database administration. The value of centralized data became apparent in 1978 when a takeover attempt required Mead to combine and analyze divisional data rapidly. However, further investigation revealed that there was little need for data sharing between the divisions on a day-to-day basis; consequently, there was little need for permanent corporate databases. The database administration function, therefore, was left within technical services. Their role is to guide the use of standard data definitions throughout Mead. Thus, data from the many divisions can be pulled together on an ad hoc basis when needed.

Most divisions develop their own applications, following the guidelines created by the information services department. The *EDP* steering committee—composed of the president and group vice-presidents—has established the policy that applications should be transportable among the various computing centers and accessible from any Mead terminal. The company's telecommunications network sets the guidelines for making this interconnection possible.

The Decision Support Applications Department

The decision support applications (DSA) department provides all end-user computing support for the company. The corporate information resources director sees it as the "marketing arm" of his group. The DSA department "sells" and trains Mead employees on end-user computing, whereas the information services department provides the technical support for the end-user systems.

At the time of the 1980 reorganization, DSA had no users, no products, no common-use applications among its multiple locations, and only five staff members in operations research and two in its office systems support group. In 1985, this department was serving fifteen hundred users in some thirty Mead locations, with ten people in its own department. DSA offers fourteen products and eight corporatewide common-use applications. Its purchased products include SAS, IFPS, PROFS, APL, and Focus. An example of a proprietary common-use system is its corporate planning resources mode, which is used to cost-justify projects and purchases.

DSA consists of four groups that provide end-user computing support:

- Interactive Help Center
- Office Systems
- Decision Analysis
- Financial Modeling Coordinator/*EIS*

Mead's *interactive help center* provides the "customer relations" type of on-going support for end-user computing. It focuses on introducing end-user computing to Mead employees at various types of company meetings. One main function is to hold an annual user group conference. It also evaluates new end-user computing products, provides training for the various end-user products, and offers consulting and hot-line assistance to end users.

The *office systems group* provides services to end users who are interested in using IBM's Professional Office System (PROFS) or Four Phase's dedicated word processing systems. It also provides consulting to groups contemplating putting in an office system. Divisions are free to select any office system, but most of them have followed the recommendations of this group to ensure corporatewide interconnection.

Mead sees PROFS as the "gateway" through which users can access all other end-user computing products. PROFS runs on an IBM 4341 under the IBM VM/CMS operating system and is menu-driven. It allows users to create on-line calendars and tickler files, view others' calendars to schedule meetings and conference rooms, perform limited word processing and electronic filing and retrieval, and send electronic mail—both formal documents and informal messages. Mead has enhanced PROFS by creating an on-line telephone directory, writing various enhancements to the calendar and scheduling systems, and adding an executive information system, which we describe shortly.

The *decision analysis group* uses operations research tools to develop linear programming models and simulations for users needing such sophisticated analysis tools. It has also built a number of companywide decision support systems, such as a corporate budgeting model and a graphics software system.

The *financial modeling coordination group* is in charge of Mead's integrated financial system. It also supports executive computing. This support takes two forms. First, this group supports the IBM PCs that are used by corporate executives. Second, it has developed an executive information system (EIS), which is accessed through PROFS. EIS was developed exclusively for use by top management. The first version was developed in 1982 as an easy-to-use system to introduce top management to potential managerial uses of computers. Using menus of commands and questions, executives can retrieve monthly summary operating reports, financial statements, forecasting data, and so forth.

Mead had few requests for personal computers before 1985, because employees found the company's systems met their needs. Since 1985, Mead has gradually introduced PCs, where they are cost-justified. The group generally recommends PCs be able to communicate with their network.

Mead's new structure presented both benefits and problems. It separated the more people-oriented activities under DSA from the more technical activities under the information services department. Professional staff in each department spent more time doing what they did best—technical people developed and managed the technology, and DSA people worked with end users. The technology was better managed, and relations with users improved. However, this split in responsibilities caused two problems. One, traditional programmers and system analysts felt that the DSA group was receiving all the new and exciting development work. The second problem was coordinating the two departments.

A matrix arrangement has evolved at Mead to handle both problems. Most projects now have both information services and DSA people on project teams; staff from both groups now work on all kinds of projects. For example, a version of the executive information system required the services of a traditional programmer. The programmer was involved with both the system development and the unveiling presentations made to top management.

The new structure has been in place since 1984, and despite the coordination problems that it presented, the company is pleased with the corporate-wide view it is giving to information resources.

CURRENT ORGANIZATION—1985 TO PRESENT

The departmental organization that was put in place from 1980 to 1984 has remained essentially intact through 1988, with two main changes. In early 1988, the vice-president of information resources began reporting directly to the chairman and chief executive officer of Mead. And, two, the DSA group has been reorganized, as shown in Figure 14.3.

In 1985, as users became more computer literate, the focus of the DSA group began to shift from marketing products to supporting end users. As the needs of the users became more sophisticated and less generic, the department found itself creating small groups with expertise in specific areas. So their support groups have become more specialized and focused. They now serve over 5,000 users corporate-wide in three ways—service center help, application development consulting, and local area experts.

The *service center* people continue to introduce new users to technology and provide telephone hot-line assistance to experienced users.

The *application development* consultants help users develop more sophisticated applications. They also get involved in guiding maintenance of user-written applications, which has become a noticeable problem. They are also updating traditional applications to permit access to data for end user systems.

The *local area experts* work out in the departments and support users in their area. They report directly to their area manager and indirectly to the information resources department. Due to the growing number of user-written applications, they, too, have become more involved in helping users keep their applications up-to-date.

Their most dramatic new development in end-user computing has been the introduction of a natural language for database query. It has been very popular and has become the platform for developing their executive information systems.

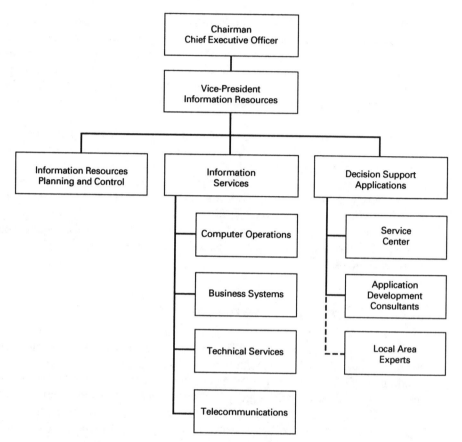

FIGURE 14.3   Mead Corporation's Current Corporate Information Resources Group

So, from 1985 to the present time, Mead has found its end-user computing focus shifting from introducing new technology to making more effective use of the technology already in place. Mead is concentrating on harvesting its investment in information technology by using it as a lever to change the way it does business.

QUESTIONS

1. Describe Mead's pre-1980 information systems organization.
2. Describe Mead's 1980–1984 information systems organization.
3. Discuss the factors that have caused Mead to change the information systems organization structure over the years.

PART 5

Executive Information Systems

Executive information systems (EIS) are one of the fastest growing applications in organizations today. They provide senior executives with current status information about events internal and external to the firm. This information is typically related to the executives' critical success factors—those things that must be done right if the executives and the organization are to be successful. Most EIS contain additional features such as E-mail or decision support system capabilities that further support the performance of executives' job responsibilities.

Although EIS offer great potential, they are high-risk systems. There is a myriad of potential organizational, development, and technical problems that have to be overcome. For example, they serve users who often have little previous computer training and experience, have been successful without using computers in the past, and may feel that they have little need to use computers now. Developers may have a limited understanding of executive work and information needs, little prior experience in developing applications of this kind, and typically must work with new technology.

A successful EIS, however, can generate a variety of benefits. It can provide information that is timely, accurate, relevant, concise, and in an attractive format. It can support strategic business objectives such as improving the firm's competitive position or improving the quality of goods and services provided. It may even facilitate downsizing the organization.

The four EIS readings in this part should enhance your understanding of what EIS are, how they are developed, current organizational practices, and their potential benefits.

One of the oldest and most successful EIS is used by seventy executives at Lockheed-Georgia. George Houdeshel and Hugh Watson describe this EIS in "The Management Information and Decision Support (MIDS) System at Lockheed-Georgia" (Reading 15). They discuss how it is used; how it has evolved over time; its component parts, features, and capabilities; its benefits; and the keys to its success.

Hugh Watson, Kelly Rainer, and Chang Koh, in "Executive Information Systems: A Development Framework and a Survey of Current Practices" (Reading 16), provide a development framework consisting of a structural perspective, which covers the key elements of an EIS and their interactions; the development process; and the user–system dialog. They also present survey data collected from fifty organizations in order to describe current EIS practices.

Hugh Watson, in "Avoiding Hidden EIS Pitfalls" (Reading 17), describes an EIS development effort that ends in failure after what seems to be a promising start. He describes what went wrong and what actions systems developers should take in order to avoid a failure in their organization.

Lou Wallis, in "Power Computing at the Top" (Reading 18) describes interviews with the CEOs at Xerox, Beneficial, and Quaker Oats. These executives discuss how they use their EIS and the benefits it provides.

15

THE MANAGEMENT INFORMATION AND DECISION SUPPORT (*MIDS*) SYSTEM AT LOCKHEED-GEORGIA

George Houdeshel,
Hugh J. Watson

INTRODUCTION

Senior executives at Lockheed-Georgia are hands-on users of the management information and decision support system (MIDS). It clearly illustrates that a carefully designed system can be an important source of information for top management. Consider a few examples of how the system is used.

- The president is concerned about employee morale which for him is a critical success factor. He calls up a display which shows employee contributions to company-sponsored programs such as blood drives, United Way, and savings plans. These are surrogate measures of morale, and because they have declined, he becomes more sensitive to a potential morale problem.

Reprinted by special permission of the *MIS Quarterly,* Volume 11, Number 1, March 1987. Copyright 1987 by the Society for Information Management and the Management Information Systems Research Center. It was revised in 1992 to describe the ongoing evolution of the MIDS system.

- The vice president of manufacturing is interested in the production status of a C-5B aircraft being manufactured for the U.S. Air Force. He calls up a display which pictorially presents the location and assembly status of the plane and information about its progress relative to schedule. He concludes that the aircraft is on schedule for delivery.

- The vice president of finance wants to determine whether actual cash flow corresponds with the amount forecasted. He is initially concerned when a $10 million unfavorable variance is indicated, but an explanatory note indicates that the funds are en route from Saudi Arabia. To verify the status of the payment, he calls the source of the information using the name and telephone number shown on the display and learns that the money should be in a Lockheed account by the end of the day.

- The vice president of human resources returns from an out-of-town trip and wants to review the major developments which took place while he was gone. While paging through the displays for the human resources area, he notices that labor grievances rose substantially. To learn more about the situation so that appropriate action can be taken, he calls the supervisor of the department where most of the grievances occurred.

These are not isolated incidents; other important uses of MIDS occur many times a day. They demonstrate that computerized systems can have a significant impact on the day-to-day functioning of senior executives.

The purpose of this article is to describe aspects of MIDS which are important to executives, information systems managers, and information systems professionals who are the potential participants in the approval, design, development, operation, and use of systems similar to MIDS. As a starting point, we want to discuss MIDS in the context of various types of information systems (i.e., MIS, DSS, and EIS), because its positioning is important to understanding its hands-on use by senior Lockheed-Georgia executives. We will describe how it was justified and developed, because these are the keys to its success. While online systems are best seen in person to be fully appreciated, we will try to describe what an executive experiences when using MIDS and the kinds of information that are available. Any computer system is made possible by the hardware, software, personnel, and data used and these will be described. Then we will discuss the benefits of MIDS. An organization considering the development of a system like MIDS needs to focus on key factors of success, and we will describe those factors that were most important to MIDS' success. As a closing point of interest, future plans for the evolution of MIDS will be discussed.

MIDS IN CONTEXT

Management information systems (MIS) were the first attempt by information systems professionals to provide managers and other organizational personnel with the information needed to perform their jobs effectively and efficiently. While originators of the MIS concept initially had high hopes and expectations for MIS, in practice MIS largely came to represent an expanded set of structured reports and has had only a minimal impact on upper management levels [11].

Decision support systems (DSS) were the next attempt to help management with its decision-making responsibilities. They have been successful to some extent, especially in regard to helping middle managers and functional area specialists such as financial planners and marketing researchers. However, their usefulness to top management has been primarily indirect. Middle managers and staff specialists may use a DSS to provide information for top management, but despite frequent claims of ease-of-use, top managers are seldom hands-on users of a DSS [4, 5].

With hindsight it is understandable why DSSs have not been used directly by senior executives. Many of the reasons are those typically given when discussing why managers do not use computers: poor keyboard skills, lack of training and experience in using computers, concerns about status, and a belief that hands-on computer use is not part of their job. Another set of reasons revolves around the tradeoff between simplicity and flexibility of use. Simpler systems tend to be less flexible while more flexible systems are usually more complex. Because DSS are typically used to support poorly structured decision-making tasks, the flexibility required to analyze these decisions comes at the cost of greater complexity. Unless the senior executive is a "techie" at heart, or uses the system enough to master its capabilities, it is unlikely that the executive will feel comfortable using the system directly. Consequently, hands-on use of the DSS is typically delegated to a subordinate who performs the desired analysis.

Executive information systems (EIS), or executive support systems as they are sometimes called, are the latest computerized attempt to help satisfy top management's information needs. These systems tend to have the following characteristics which differentiate them from MIS and DSS:

- They are used directly by top managers without the assistance of intermediaries.
- They provide easy online access to current information about the status of the organization.
- They are designed with management's critical success factors (CSF) in mind.
- They use state-of-the-art graphics, communications, and data storage and retrieval methods.

The limited reportings of EIS suggest that these types of systems can make top managers hands-on users of computer-based systems [2, 10, 12]. While a number of factors contribute to their success, one of the most important is ease-of-use. Because an EIS provides little analysis capabilities, it normally requires only a few, easy to enter keystrokes. Consequently, keyboard skills, previous training and experience in using computers, concerns about loss of status, and perceptions of how one should carry out job responsibilities are less likely to hinder system use.

MIDS is an example of an EIS. It is used directly by top Lockheed-Georgia managers to access online information about the current status of the firm. Great care, time, and effort goes into providing information that meets the special needs of its users. The system is graphics-oriented and draws heavily upon communications technology.

THE EVOLUTION OF *MIDS*

Lockheed-Georgia, a subsidiary of the Lockheed Corporation, is a major producer of cargo aircraft. Over 19,000 employees work at their Marietta, Georgia plant. Their current major activities are production of the C-5B transport aircraft for the U.S. Air Force, Hercules aircraft for worldwide markets, and numerous modification and research programs.

In 1975, Robert B. Ormsby, then President of Lockheed-Georgia, first expressed an interest in the creation of an online status reporting system to provide information which was concise, timely, complete, easy to access, relevant to management's needs, and could be shared by organizational personnel. Though Lockheed's existing systems provided voluminous quantities of data and information, Ormsby thought them to be unsatisfactory for several reasons. It was difficult to quickly locate specific information to apply to a given problem. Reports often were not sufficiently current, leading to organizational units basing decisions on information which should have been the same but actually was not. This is often the case when different reports or the same report with different release dates are used. Little action was taken for several years as Ormsby and information services personnel waited for hardware and software to emerge which would be suitable for the desired type of system. In the fall of 1978, development of the MIDS system began.

The justification for MIDS was informal. No attempt was made to cost-justify its initial development. Ormsby felt that he and other Lockheed-Georgia executives needed the system and mandated its development. Over time, as different versions of MIDS were judged successful, authorization was given to develop enhanced versions. This approach is consistent with current thinking and research on systems to support decision making. It corresponds closely with the recommendation to view the initial system as a research and development project and to evolve later versions if the system proves to be successful [7]. It also is in keeping with findings that accurate, timely and new kinds of information, an organizational champion, and managerial mandate are the factors which motivate systems development [6].

A number of key decisions were made early in the design of the system. First, an evolutionary design approach would be used. Only a limited number of displays would be created initially. Over time they would be modified or possibly deleted if they did not meet an information need. Additional screens would be added as needed and as MIDS was made available to a larger group of Lockheed-Georgia managers. Ease-of-use was considered to be of critical importance because of the nature of the user group. Most of the Lockheed-Georgia executives had all of the normal apprehensions about personally using terminals. In order to encourage hands-on use, it was decided to place a terminal in each user's office, to require a minimum number of keystrokes in order to call up any screen, and to make training largely unnecessary. Response time was to be fast and features were to be included to assist executives in locating needed information.

Bob Pittman was responsible for the system's development and he, in turn, reported to the vice president of finance. Pittman initially had a staff consisting of two people from finance and two from information services. The finance personnel were used because of their experience in preparing company reports and presentations to the corporate headquarters, customers, and government agencies. Their responsibility was to determine the system's content, screen designs, and operational requirements. The information services personnel were responsible for hardware selection and acquisition and software development.

Pittman and his group began by exploring the information requirements of Ormsby and his staff. This included determining what information was needed, in what form, at what level of detail, and when it had to be updated. Several approaches were used in making these determinations. Interviews were held with Ormsby and his staff. Their secretaries were asked about information requested of them by their superiors. The use of existing reports was studied. From these analyses emerged an initial understanding of the information requirements.

The next step was to locate the best data sources for the MIDS system. Two considerations guided this process. The first was to use data sources with greater detail than what would be included in the MIDS displays. Only by using data which had not already been filtered and processed could information be generated which the MIDS team felt would satisfy the information requirements. The second was to use data sources which had a perspective compatible with that of Ormsby and his staff. Multiple organizational units may have data seemingly appropriate for satisfying an information need, but choosing the best source or combination of sources requires care in order that the information provided is not distorted by the perspective of the organizational unit in which it originates.

The initial version of MIDS took six months to develop and allowed Ormsby to call up 31 displays. Over the past eight years, MIDS has evolved to where it now offers over 700 displays for 30 top executives and 40 operating managers. It has continued to be successful through many changes in the senior executive ranks, including the position of president. MIDS subsystems are currently being developed for middle managers in the various functional areas and MIDS-like systems are being implemented in several other Lockheed companies.

MIDS FROM THE USER'S PERSPECTIVE

An executive typically has little interest in the hardware or software used in a system. Rather, the dialog between the executive and the system is what matters. The dialog can be thought of as consisting of the command language by which the user directs the actions of the system, the presentation language through which the system provides the response, and the knowledge that the user must have in order to effectively use the system [1]. From a user's perspective, the dialog *is* the system, and consequently, careful attention was given to the design of the dialog components in MIDS.

An executive gains access to MIDS through the IBM PC/XT on his or her desk. Entering a password is the only sign-on requirement, and every user has a unique password which allows access to an authorized set of displays. After the password is accepted, the executive is informed of any scheduled downtime for system maintenance. The user is then given a number of options. He can enter a maximum of four keystrokes and call up any of the screens that he is authorized to view, obtain a listing of all screens that have been updated, press the "RETURN/ENTER" key to view the major menu, access the online keyword index, or obtain a listing of all persons having access to the system.

The main menu and keyword index are designed to help the executive find needed information quickly. Figure 15.1 shows the main menu. Each subject area listed in the main menu is further broken down into additional menus. Information is available in a variety of subject areas, including by functional area, organizational level, and project. The user can also enter the first three letters of any keywords which are descriptive of the information needed. The system checks these words against the keyword index and lists all of the displays which are related to the user's request.

Information for a particular subject area is organized in a top down fashion. This organization is used within a single display or in a series of displays. A summary graph is presented at the top of a screen or first in a series of displays, followed by supporting graphs, and then by tables and text. This approach allows executives to quickly gain an overall perspective while providing backup detail when needed. An interesting finding has

FIGURE 15.1 The MIDS Main Menu

MIDS MAJOR CATEGORY MENU

▮ TO RECALL THIS DISPLAY AT ANY TIME HIT 'RETURN-ENTER'KEY.
▮ FOR LATEST UPDATES SEE S1.

A   MANAGEMENT CONTROL
　　MSI'S; OBJECTIVES;
　　ORGANIZATION CHARTS;
　　TRAVEL/AVAILABILITY/EVENTS SCHED.

CP CAPTURE PLANS INDEX

B   C-5B ALL PROGRAM ACTIVITIES

C   HERCULES ALL PROGRAM ACTIVITIES

E   ENGINEERING
　　COST OF NEW BUSINESS; R & T

F   FINANCIAL CONTROL
　　BASIC FINANCIAL DATA; COST
　　REDUCTION; FIXED ASSETS; OFFSET;
　　OVERHEAD; OVERTIME; PERSONNEL

H   HUMAN RESOURCES
　　CO-OP PROGRAM, EMPLOYEE
　　STATISTICS & PARTICIPATION

M   MARKETING
　　ASSIGNMENTS; PROSPECTS;
　　SIGN-UPS; PRODUCT SUPPORT;
　　TRAVEL

O   OPERATIONS
　　MANUFACTURING; MATERIAL;
　　PRODUCT ASSURANCE & SAFETY

P   PROGRAM CONTROL
　　FINANCIAL & SCHEDULE
　　PERFORMANCE

MS MASTER SCHEDULING MENU

S   SPECIAL ITEMS
　　DAILY DIARY; SPECIAL PROGRAMS

been that executives prefer as much information as possible on a single display, even if it appears "busy," rather than having the same information spread over several displays.

Executives tend to use MIDS differently. At one extreme are those who browse through displays. An important feature for them is the ability to stop the generation of a display with a single keystroke when it is not of further interest. At the other extreme are executives who regularly view a particular sequence of displays. To accommodate this type of system use, sequence files can be employed which allow executives to page through a series of displays whose sequence is defined in advance. Sequence files can either be created by the user, requested by the user and prepared by the MIDS staff, or offered by MIDS personnel after observing the user's viewing habits.

All displays contain a screen number, title, when it was last updated, the source(s) of the information presented, and a telephone number for the source(s). It also indicates the MIDS staff member who is responsible for maintaining the display. Every display has a backup person who is responsible for it when the primary person is on leave, sick, or unavailable for any reason. Knowing the information source and the identity of the responsible MIDS staff member is important when an executive has a question about a display.

Standards exist across the displays for the terms used, color codes, and graphic designs. These standards help eliminate possible misinterpretations of the information provided. Standard definitions have also improved communications in the company.

The importance of standard definitions can be illustrated by the use of the word "signup." In general, the term refers to a customer's agreement to buy an aircraft. However, prior to the establishment of a standard definition, it tended to be used differently by various organizational units. To marketing people, a signup was when a letter of intent to buy was received. Legal services considered it to be when a contract was received. Finance interpreted it as when a down payment was made. The standard definition of a signup now used is "a signed contract with a nonrefundable down payment." An online dictionary can be accessed if there is any question about how a term is defined.

Color is used in a standard way across all of the screens. The traffic light pattern is used for status: green is good; yellow is marginal; and red is unfavorable. Under budget or ahead of schedule is in green; on budget or on schedule is in yellow; over budget or behind schedule is in red. Bar graphs have a black background and yellow bars depict actual performance, cyan (light blue) is used for company goals and commitments to the corporate office, and magenta represents internal goals and objectives. Organization charts use different colors for the various levels of management. Special color combinations are used to accommodate executives with color differentiation problems, and all displays are designed to be effective with black and white hard copy output.

Standards exist for all graphic designs. Line charts are used for trends, bar charts for comparisons, and pie or stacked bar charts for parts of a whole. On all charts, vertical wording is avoided and abbreviations and acronyms are limited to those on an authorized list. All bar charts are zero at the origin to avoid distortions, scales are set in prescribed increments and are identical within a subject series, and bars that exceed the scale have numeric values shown. In comparisons of actual with predicted performance, bars for actual performance are always wider.

Comments are added to the displays to explain abnormal conditions, explain graphic depictions, reference related displays, and inform of pending changes. For example, a display may show that signups for May are three less than forecasted. The staff member who is responsible for the display knows, however, that a down payment from Peru for three aircraft is en route and adds this information as a comment to the display. Without added comments, situations can arise which are referred to as "paper tigers," because they appear to require managerial attention though they actually do not. The MIDS staff believes that "transmitting data is not the same as conveying information" [8].

The displays have been created with the executives' critical success factors in mind. Some of the CSF measures, such as profits and aircrafts sold, are obvious. Other measures, such as employee participation in company-sponsored programs, are less obvious and reflect the MIDS staff's efforts to fully understand and accommodate the executives' information needs.

To illustrate a typical MIDS display, Figure 15.2 shows Lockheed-Georgia sales as of November 1986. It was accessed by entering F3. The sources of the information and their Lockheed-Georgia telephone numbers are in the upper right-hand corner. The top

FIGURE 15.2   Lockheed-Georgia Sales

| M5 | PERU/AF
 ———
 REP: DICK SIGLER | | | | SOURCE | BUD LAWLER
 JIM CERTAIN | 5431
 2265 |

REP: LOCATION IF AWAY

	MON	TUE	WED	THR	FRI	SAT	SUN
				CARACAS, VENEZUELA – – – – – – – –			

FORECAST - THREE L-100-30s   PREV, HERC, BUY – – – 8

NEXT EVENT
 FINALIZE FINANCING

KEY PERSON – – CERTAIN

SIGN-UP – – – – · NEXT MONTH

PROBABILITY – – GOOD

ROM VALUE – – – · $60M

A/C DELIVERY: 4TH QTR

AS OF TODAY: MEETINGS CONTINUE AMONG POTENTIAL LENDING INSTITUTIONS, INSURERS, AND GELAC'S INTERNATIONAL MARKETING/FINANCE/LEGAL TEAM TO DISCUSS REQUIREMENTS AND CONDITIONS FOR FINANCING. GELAC REPRESENTATIVES WILL BE IN LIMA MONDAY TO LAY GROUNDWORK FOR FINAL NEGOTIATIONS. NO PROBLEMS EXPECTED.

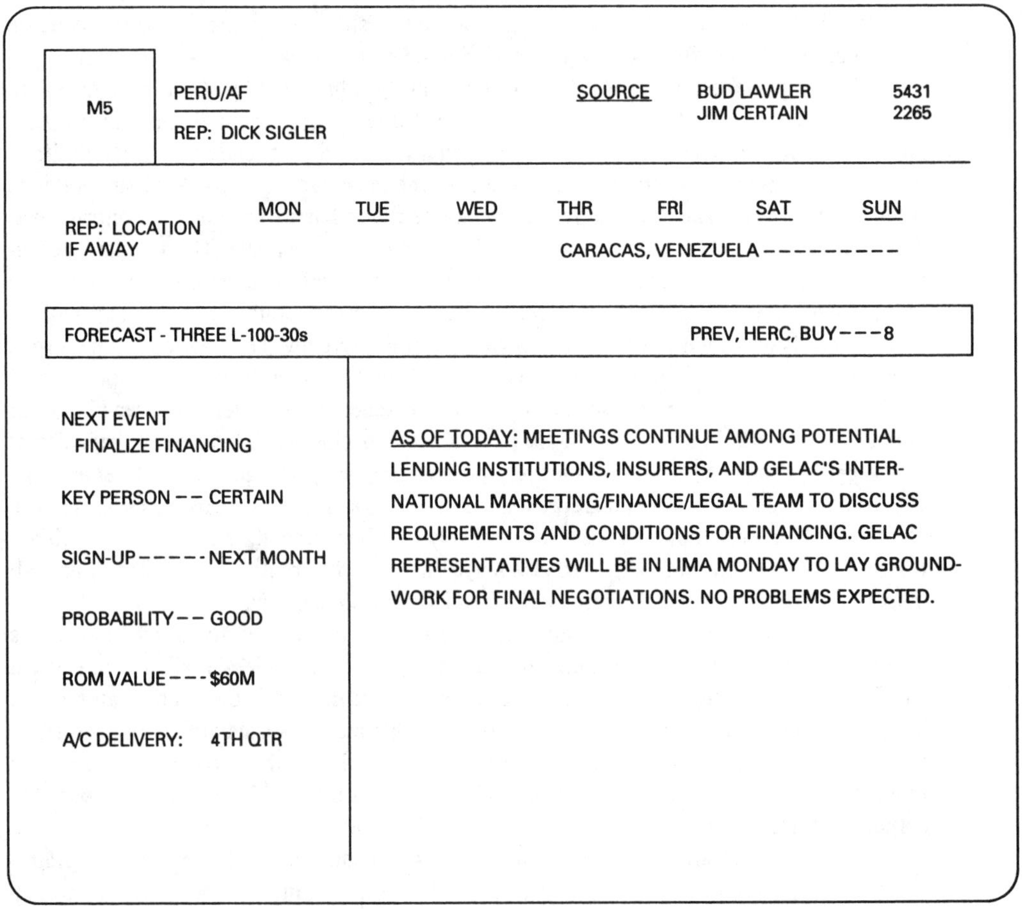

graphs provide past history, current, and forecasted sales. The wider bars represent actual sales while budgeted sales are depicted by the narrower bars. Detailed, tabular information is provided under the graphs. An explanatory comment is given at the bottom of the display. The R and F in the bottom right-hand corner indicates that related displays can be found by paging in a reverse or forward direction.

Executives are taught to use MIDS in a 15 minute tutorial. For several reasons, no written instructions for the use of the system have ever been prepared. An objective for MIDS has been to make the system easy enough to use so that written instructions are unnecessary. Features such as menus and the keyword index make this possible. Another reason is that senior executives are seldom willing to take the time to read instructions. And most importantly, if an executive has a problem in using the system, the MIDS staff prefers to learn about the problem and to handle it personally.

The IBM PC/XT on the executive's desk is useful for applications other than accessing MIDS displays. It can be used off-line with any appropriate PC software. It is also the mechanism for tying the user through MIDS to other computer systems. For example, some senior executives and even more middle managers want access to outside reference services or internal systems with specific databases. Electronic messaging is the most common use of the IBM PC/XTs for other than MIDS displays. The executive need only request PROFS from within MIDS and the system automatically translates the user's MIDS password to a PROFS password and transfers the user from the DEC 780 VAX host to the IBM mainframe with PROFS. After using PROFS' electronic mail capabilities, the transfer back to MIDS is a simple two keystroke process.

THE COMPONENTS OF *MIDS*

A number of component parts are essential to the functioning of MIDS: hardware, software, MIDS personnel, and data sources.

Hardware

A microcomputer from Intelligent Systems Corporation was used for the initial version of MIDS. Each day MIDS personnel updated the floppy disks which stored the displays. As more executives were given access to MIDS, it became impractical to update each executive's displays separately, and the decision was made to store them centrally on a DEC 11/34 where they could be accessed by all users. Executives currently interact with MIDS through IBM PC/XTs tied to a DEC 780 VAX. Next year MIDS will be migrated to an IBM 3081 as part of Lockheed's plan to standardize around IBM equipment. Because an objective of MIDS was to reduce the amount of paper, the generation of hard copy output has always been minimized. The only printers are in the MIDS office and include four Printronix 300 (black and white, dot matrix) and Xerox 6500 (color copier, laser unit, with paper and transparencies) printers.

Software

At the time that work on MIDS began, appropriate software was not commercially available. Consequently, the decision was made to develop the software in-house. Even though commercial EIS software such as Command Center and Metaphor are now available, none of it has justified a switch from what has been developed by the MIDS staff.

The software is used for three important tasks: creating and updating the displays; providing information about the system's use and status; and maintaining system security.

Creating and Updating the Displays   Each display has an edit program tailored to fit its needs. Special edit routines have been developed for graph drawing, color changes, scale changes, roll-offs, calculations, or drawing special characters such as airplanes. These edit functions are then combined to create a unique edit program for each display. This approach allows MIDS personnel to quickly update the displays and differs from off-the-shelf software which requires the user to answer questions for all routines, regardless of whether they are needed.

The edit software has other attractive features. There are computer-generated messages to the information analyst advising of other displays which could be affected by changes to the one currently being revised. Color changes are automatically made to a display when conditions become unfavorable. When the most recent period data is entered, the oldest period data is automatically rolled off of all graphs. The edit software has error checks for unlikely or impossible conditions.

Providing Information about the System's Use and Status   Daily reports are generated at night and are available the next morning for the MIDS staff to review. A daily log of system activity shows who requested what, when, and how. The log indicates everything but "why," and sometimes the staff even asks that question in order to better understand management's information needs. The log allows MIDS personnel to analyze system loads, user inquiry patterns, methods used to locate displays, utilization of special features, and any system and/or communication problems. Another report indicates the status of all displays, including the last time each display was updated, when the next update is scheduled, and who is responsible for the update. Yet another report lists all displays which have been added, deleted, or changed.

Weekly reports are generated on Sunday night and are available Monday morning for the MIDS staff. One report lists the previous week's users and the number of displays viewed by each executive. Another report lists the number of displays with the frequency of viewing by the president and his staff and others.

A number of reports are available on demand. They include an authorization matrix of users and terminals; a count of displays by major category and subsystem; a list of users by name, type of terminal, and system line number to the host computer; a list of displays in sequence; a list of display titles with their number organized by subject area; and a keyword exception report of available displays not referenced in the keyword file.

Maintaining System Security   Careful thought goes into deciding who has access to which displays. Information is made available unless there are compelling reasons why it should be denied. For example, middle managers might not be allowed to view strategic plans for the company.

System access is controlled through a double security system. Users can call up only displays which they are authorized to view and then only from certain terminals. This security system helps protect against unauthorized users gaining access to the system and the unintentional sharing of restricted information. As an example of the latter situation, a senior executive might be allowed to view sensitive information in his office, but be denied access to the information in a conference room or the office of lower management.

Personnel

The MIDS staff has grown from five to its current size of nine. Six of the staff members are classified as information analysts, two are computer analysts, and there is the manager of the MIDS group. The information analysts are responsible for determining the system's content, designing the screens, and keeping the system operational. Each information analyst is responsible for about 100 displays. Approximately 170 displays are updated daily by the MIDS staff. The computer analysts are responsible for hardware selection and acquisition and software development. While the two groups have different job responsibilities, they work together and make suggestions to each other for improving the system.

It is imperative that the information analysts understand the information that they enter into the system. Several actions are taken to ensure that this is the case. Most of the information analysts have work experience and/or training in the areas for which they supply information. They are encouraged to take courses which provide a better understanding of the users' areas. And they frequently attend functional area meetings, often serving as an important information resource.

Data

In order to provide the information needed, a variety of internal and external data sources must be used. The internal sources include transaction processing systems, financial applications, and human sources. Some of the data can be transferred directly to MIDS from other computerized systems, while others must be rekeyed or entered for the first time. Access to computerized data is provided by in-house software and commercial software such as DATATRIEVE. External sources are very important and include data from external databases, customers, other Lockheed companies, and Lockheed's Washington, D.C., office.

MIDS relies on both hard and soft data. Hard data comes from sources such as transaction processing systems and provides "the facts." Soft data often comes from human sources and results in information which could not be obtained in any other way; it provides meaning, context, and insight to hard data.

BENEFITS OF *MIDS*

A variety of benefits are provided by MIDS: better information; improved communications; an evolving understanding of information requirements; a test-bed for system evolution; and cost reductions.

The information provided by MIDS has characteristics which are important to management. It supports decision making by identifying areas which require attention, providing answers to questions, and giving knowledge about related areas. It provides relevant information. Problem areas are highlighted and pertinent comments are included. The information is timely because displays are updated as important events occur. It is accurate because of the efforts of the MIDS staff, since all information is verified before it is made available.

MIDS has also improved communications in several ways. It is sometimes used to share information with vendors, customers, legislators, and others. MIDS users are able to quickly view the same information in the same format with the most current update. In the past, there were often disagreements, especially over the telephone, because executives were operating with different information. PROFS provides electronic mail. The daily diary announces major events as they occur.

Initially identifying a complete set of information requirements is difficult or impossible for systems which support decision making. The evolutionary nature of MIDS' development has allowed users to better understand and evolve their information requirements. Having seen a given set of information in a given format, an executive is

FIGURE 15.3   The Status of a Sale

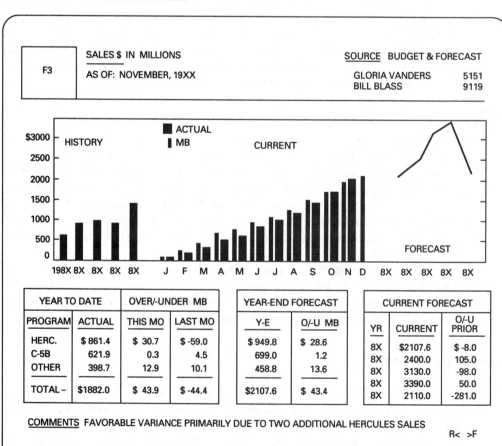

often prompted to identify additional information or variations of formats that provide still better decision support.

The current system provides a test-bed for identifying and testing possible system changes. New state-of-the-art hardware and software can be compared with the current system in order to provide information for the evolution of MIDS. For example, a mouse-based system currently is being tested.

MIDS is responsible for cost savings in several areas. Many reports and graphs which were formerly produced manually are now printed from MIDS and distributed to non-MIDS users. Some requirements for special reports and presentation materials are obtained at less cost by modifying standard MIDS displays. Reports that are produced by other systems are summarized in MIDS and are no longer printed and distributed to MIDS users.

THE SUCCESS OF *MIDS*

Computer-based systems can be evaluated on the basis of cost/benefit, frequency of use, and user satisfaction considerations. Systems which support decision making, such as MIDS, normally do not lend themselves to a quantified assessment of their benefits. They do provide intangible benefits, however, as can be seen in the following example.

Lockheed-Georgia markets its aircrafts worldwide. In response to these efforts, it is common for a prospective buyer to call a company executive to discuss a proposed deal. Upon receipt of a phone call, the executive can call up a display which provides the following information: the aircraft's model and quantity; the dollar value of the offer; the aircraft's availability for delivery; previous purchases by the prospect; the sales representative's name and exact location for the week; and a description of the status of the possible sale. Such a display is shown in Figure 15.3. All of this information is available without putting the prospective customer on hold, transferring the call to someone else, or awaiting the retrieval of information from a file.

When a user can choose whether or not to use a system, frequency of use can be employed as a measure of success. Table 15.1 presents data on how the number of users

TABLE 15.1 MIDS Users, Displays, and Displays Viewed

YEAR	NUMBER OF USERS	NUMBER OF DISPLAYS	MEAN NUMBER OF DISPLAYS VIEWED PER USER/PER DAY
1979	12	69	*
1980	24	231	*
1981	27	327	*
1982	31	397	3
1983	31	441	4
1984	49	620	4.2
1985	70	710	5.5

*Figures not available.

and displays and the mean number of displays viewed per day by each executive has changed over time. The overall picture is one of increased usage; currently an average of 5.5 screens are viewed each day by the 70 executives who have access to MIDS. Unlike some systems which are initially successful but quickly fade away, the success of MIDS has increased over time.

Frequency of use can be a very imperfect measure of success. The MIDS group recognizes that a single display which has a significant impact on decision making is much more valuable than many screens which are paged through with passing interest. Consequently, frequency of use is used as only one indicator of success.

MIDS personnel have felt no need to conduct formal studies of user satisfaction. The data on system usage and daily contact with MIDS users provide ample information on how satisfied users are with MIDS. User satisfaction can be illustrated by the experience of Paul Frech who was vice president of operations in 1979. When MIDS was offered to him, he had little interest in the system because he had well-established channels for the flow of information to support his job responsibilities. Shortly afterwards, Frech was promoted to the corporate headquarters staff in California. When he was again promoted to become the president of Lockheed-Georgia, MIDS had become a standard for executive information and he was reintroduced to the system. He has stated:

> I assumed the presidency of the Lockheed-Georgia Company in June 1984, and the MIDS system had been in operation for some time prior to that. The MIDS system enabled me to more quickly evaluate the current conditions of each of our operational areas and, although I had not been an advocate of executive computer systems, the ease and effectiveness of MIDS made it an essential part of my informational sources.

Because Frech and other senior executives have come to rely on MIDS, middle managers at Lockheed-Georgia and executives at other Lockheed companies want their own versions of MIDS. Within Lockheed-Georgia there is the feeling that "If the boss likes it, I need it." Currently, MIDS personnel are helping middle functional area managers develop subsystems of MIDS and are assisting other Lockheed companies with the development of similar systems.

KEYS TO THE SUCCESS OF *MIDS*

Descriptions of successful systems are useful to people responsible for conceptualizing, approving, and developing similar systems. Perhaps even more important are insights about what makes a system a success. We will identify the keys to MIDS' success here, but it should be remembered that differences exist among executive information systems, organizations, and possibly the factors that lead to success.

1. *A Committed Senior Executive Sponsor.* Ormsby served as the organizational champion for MIDS. He wanted a system like MIDS, committed the necessary resources, participated in its creation, and encouraged its use by others.

2. *Carefully Defined System Requirements.* Several considerations governed the design of the system. It had to be custom-tailored to meet the information needs of its users. Ease-of-use, an absolutely essential item to executives who were wary of computers, was critical. Response time had to be fast. The displays had to be updated quickly and easily as conditions changed.

3. *Carefully Defined Information Requirements.* There has been a continuing effort to understand management's information requirements. Displays have been added, modified, and deleted over time. Providing information relevant to managements' CSFs has been of paramount importance.

4. *A Team Approach to Systems Development.* The staff that developed, operates, and evolves MIDS combines information systems skills and functional area knowledge. The computer analysts are responsible for the technical aspects of the system while the information analysts are responsible for providing the information needed by management. This latter responsibility demands that the information analysts know the business and maintain close contact with information sources and users.

5. *An Evolutionary Development Approach.* The initial version of MIDS success fully addressed the most critical information needs of the company president and strengthened his support for the system. There is little doubt that developing a fully integrated system for a full complement of users would have resulted in substantial delays and less enthusiasm for the system. Over the years, MIDS has expanded and evolved as more users have been provided access to MIDS, management's information requirements have changed, better ways to analyze and present information have been discovered, and improved computer technology has become integrated into the system.

6. *Careful Computer Hardware and Software Selection.* The decision to proceed with the development of MIDS was made when good color terminals at reasonable prices became available. At that time graphics software was very limited and it was necessary to develop the software for MIDS in-house. The development of MIDS could have been postponed until hardware and software with improved performance at reduced cost appeared, but this decision would have delayed providing management with the information needed. Also affecting the hardware selection was the existing hardware within the organization and the need to integrate MIDS into the overall computing architecture. While it is believed that excellent hardware and software decisions have been made for MIDS, different circumstances at other firms may lead to different hardware and software configurations.

MIDS II: THE ONGOING STORY

In 1990, after 12 years of successful MIDS operations, it became necessary to update the hardware technology used with Lockheed's executive information system. This change was required because the Intelligent Systems Company (ISC) graphics computers that were used by the MIDS support staff to design and update the screens were no longer in production and replacement parts were becoming increasingly difficult to find. The MIDS staff faced the real possibility of not being able to maintain the system because of a lack of hardware. Faced with this situation, it was decided to undertake a comprehensive review of the hardware and software options that were available for EIS.

After a review of the software alternatives, it was decided that it was more economical to purchase commercial EIS software than to develop another system in-house. Several commercial products were evaluated and Comshare's Commander EIS was ultimately chosen. This best-selling product offers a large number of capabilities that facilitate the development and maintenance of an EIS; see Table 15.2. Two important changes to the Comshare software were requested, however, before a contract was signed. The changes retained capabilities that were in MIDS but not in Commander EIS. It was deemed important to the MIDS staff that the changes be made to the basic Comshare product and not to just a special version for Lockheed in order to ensure compatibility with later releases of the Comshare software.

The two changes permitted users to operate the system through a keyboard (in addition to a mouse or touch screen) and provided for monitoring the use of the system. Lockheed executives had enjoyed the MIDS system advantage of going from any screen to any other screen without retracing a path or returning to a predetermined point. This capability was retained by allowing executives to enter the number of the desired screen. Monitoring of system usage had always been performed by the MIDS system manage-

TABLE 15.2 Capabilities of Commander EIS

- Support for multiple user interfaces
- Online, context-dependent help screens
- Command files
- Multiple methods for locating information
- Access to external databases (e.g., Dow Jones News Retrieval)
- Interfaces to other software (e.g., Profs, Lotus 1-2-3)
- Integrated decision support (e.g., System W, IFPS)
- Easy screen design and maintenance
- Screen design templates
- Application shells
- Data extraction from existing organizational databases
- Graphical, tabular, and textual information on the same screen
- Integration of data from different sources
- Security for data, screens, and systems
- Support for rapid prototyping
- Support for multiple computing information
- Support for hard-copy output (e.g., paper, overhead transparencies, 35-mm slides)

ment and it had become invaluable in keeping the MIDS system up to date. With these changes, Commander EIS became the development environment for MIDS II.

Even though commercial EIS software was selected for MIDS II, the original screen designs were retained. In fact, when Lockheed asked vendors to prepare demonstration prototypes, they requested screens that looked like those currently in use. Considerable thought and experimentation had gone into screen design over the years, Lockheed's executives were familiar with them, and MIDS II was to continue the look and feel of the original system.

In addition to a new software, hardware improvements were made to take advantage of state-of-the-art technology and to position MIDS II in Lockheed's long-range computing plans. The Comshare software helped make this possible because of its ability to run on a mixed platform of IBM PS/2s and Apple Macintoshes. The executives use PS/2's and screens are developed and maintained on Macintoshes by the support staff. A Novell local area network was installed to improve the system's response time and reliability.

MIDS II was developed and rolled out to users in 1992 and is expected to provide a variety of benefits over the original system: faster response time, easier navigation through the system (drilldown to related, more detailed information), better links to other resources (internal and external databases), reduced maintenance costs (automatic update of some screens), shared EIS techniques with other Commander EIS users, and a state-of-the-art technology platform that permits future improvements and growth within information system's long-range plans. The original MIDS system has served Lockheed very well since 1978 and MIDS II is designed to carry this tradition into the future.

QUESTIONS

1. Why have many senior executives not become hands-on users of a DSS? What raises the hopes for EIS?
2. What screen design features of the MIDS system might be appropriate for any EIS?
3. What methods have been used to document the success of the MIDS system? Are any other methods feasible and desirable? Discuss.
4. What led to the development of MIDS II?

REFERENCES

1. BENNETT, J. "User-Oriented Graphics, Systems for Decision Support in Unstructured Tasks," in *User-Oriented Design of Interactive Graphics Systems,* S. Treu, (ed.), Association for Computing Machinery, New York, New York, 1977, 3—11.

2. DeLONG, D. W., AND J. F. ROCKART "Identifying the Attributes of Successful Executive Support System Implementation," *Transactions from the Sixth Annual Conference on Decision Support Systems,* J. Fedorowicz (ed.), Washington, D.C., April 21—24, 1986, 41—54.

3. EL SAWY, O. A. "Personal Information Systems for Strategic Scanning in Turbulent Environments: Can the CEO Go On-Line?" *MIS Quarterly,* 9, 1, March 1985, 53—60.

4. FRIEND, D. "Executive Information Systems: Success, Failure, Insights and Misconceptions," *Transactions from the Sixth Annual Conference on Decision Support Systems,* J. Fedorowicz (ed.), Washington, D.C., April 21—24, 1986, 35—40.

5. HOGUE, J. T., AND H. J. WATSON "An Examination of Decision Makers' Utilization of Decision Support System Output," *Information and Management,* 8, 4, April 1985, 205—12.

6. HOGUE, J. T., AND H. J. WATSON "Management's Role in the Approval and Administration of Decision Support Systems," *MIS Quarterly,* 7, 2, June 1983, 15—23.

7. KEEN, P. G. W. "Value Analysis: Justifying Decision Support Systems," *MIS Quarterly,* 5, 1, March 1981, 1—16.

8. MCDONALD, E. "Telecommunications," *Government Computer News,* February 28, 1986, 44.

9. ROCKART, J. F. "Chief Executives Define Their Own Data Needs," *Harvard Business Review,* 57, 2, January—February 1979, 81—93.

10. ROCKART, J. F., AND M. E. TREACY "The CEO Goes On-Line," *Harvard Business Review,* 60, 1, January—February 1982, 32—88.

11. SPRAGUE, R. H., JR. "A Framework for the Development of Decision Support Systems," *MIS Quarterly,* 4, 4, December 1980, 10—26.

12. SUNDUE, D. G. "GenRad's On-line Executives," *Transactions from the Sixth Annual Conference on Decision Support Systems,* J. Fedorowicz (ed.), Washington, D.C., April 21—24, 1986, 14—20.

16

EXECUTIVE INFORMATION SYSTEMS: A FRAMEWORK FOR DEVELOPMENT AND A SURVEY OF CURRENT PRACTICES

Hugh J. Watson,
R. Kelly Rainer, Jr.
Chang E. Koh

INTRODUCTION

The target audience for computer support in organizations has evolved over the years. Clerical workers were the first to be impacted as transaction processing systems were automated in the 1950s and 1960s. At the same time, engineers gained access to computers and started what is now recognized as end-user computing. Management information systems (MIS) appeared with much fanfare in the 1960s. While some envisioned them as "central nervous systems" for organizations, in practice they largely expanded the reporting system for lower-level managers. Office automation began two decades ago with the introduction of word processors for secretaries and continues to expand today as a growing variety of support becomes available for office workers. In the 1970s, decision support systems (DSS) provided assistance for specific decision-making tasks. While DSSs can be developed for and used by personnel throughout the organization, they are most

Reprinted by special permission from the *MIS Quarterly*, Volume 15, Number 1, March 1991. © 1991 by the Society for Information Management and the Management Information Systems Research Center at the University of Minnesota.

commonly employed by staff and middle and lower managers. Among the latest developments are expert systems, which capture the expertise of highly trained, experienced professionals in specific problem domains.

As the evolution of computer support for organizational personnel is considered, one group is conspicuously missing: the senior executives of a firm. They have not been omitted by design, and in fact, previous advances were originally thought to potentially serve them (e.g., MID and DSS), but for a variety of reasons, little support has been provided. This lack of support is rapidly changing, however, as executive information systems (EIS) or executive support systems (ESS) are being developed in a growing number of firms (Main, 1989). International Data Corporation, a market research firm, predicts that the U.S. market for EIS is growing at a compound annual rate of nearly 40 percent and that expenditures for EIS software development, including the purchase of software, custom consulting, and in-house software development, will grow to $350 million in 1992 (Alexander, 1989).

Even though EIS support an important clientele and are becoming prevalent, little research has been done about them. The available EIS literature is case study or anecdotal in nature. In order to learn more about current EIS practices, we studied 50 firms that either have an EIS or are well along in developing one. The findings are presented in the context of a framework that can be used to understand and guide EIS development efforts.

The results of this study should be of interest to practitioners who already have an EIS or are planning to develop one. The findings provide benchmarks against which individual company experiences can be compared. The results also should stimulate academicians to do further research. Specific research questions raised by this research are presented later.

The next section defines an EIS, lists EIS characteristics, and distinguishes between EIS and ESS. This is followed by discussion of the failure of previous efforts to support executives. Next, an EIS development framework is introduced and the research methodology of the study is described. Then, the findings of the survey are discussed in the context of the framework. Finally, conclusions are drawn from the study.

EIS DEFINITION AND CHARACTERISTICS

Researchers have used a variety of definitions for EIS (Paller and Laska, 1990; Turban and Watson, 1989). For our purposes, an EIS is defined as a computerized system that provides executives with easy access to internal and external information that is relevant to their critical success factors. While a definition is useful, a richer understanding is provided by describing the characteristics of EIS. Research (Burkan, 1988; Friend, 1986; Kogan, 1986; Zmud, 1986) shows that most executive information systems:

- are tailored to individual executive users;
- extract, filter, compress, and track critical data;
- provide online status access, trend analysis, exception reporting, and "drill-down" (drill-down allows the user to access supporting detail or data that under lie summarized data);

- access and integrate a broad range of internal and external data;
- are user-friendly and require minimal or no training to use;
- are used directly by executives without intermediaries;
- present graphical, tabular, and/or textual information.

The EIS and ESS terms are sometimes used interchangeably. The term "executive support system," however, usually refers to a system with a broader set of capabilities than an EIS (Rockart and DeLong, 1988). Whereas the EIS term connotes providing information, the ESS term implies other support capabilities in addition to information. Consequently, we find it useful to conceptualize an ESS as including the following capabilities:

- support for electronic communications (e.g., E-mail, computer conferencing, and word processing);
- data analysis capabilities (e.g., spreadsheets, query languages, and decision support systems);
- organizing tools (e.g., electronic calendars, automated rolodex, and tickler files).

These additional capabilities are typically made available as options on a system's main menu or by the ability to "hot key" the workstation into a PC mode of operation.

The distinctions between an EIS and an ESS are not particularly important for our purposes other than to recognize that an ESS influences and increases system requirements. For example, many systems include E-mail; hence, E-mail software and a keyboard must be available. The materials provided here apply equally well to EIS or ESS, even though the EIS term is used throughout.

WHY PREVIOUS EFFORTS FAILED

There are many reasons why previous efforts to bring computer support to senior executives have failed. Understanding these reasons is important because they provide insights into what problems must be overcome if an EIS is to be successful.

One of the difficulties involves the executives themselves. Many of today's senior executives missed the computer revolution. Consequently, they may feel uncomfortable using computers, have poor keyboarding skills, or believe that "real" executives do not use computers.

Another difficulty involves the nature of executive work. Previous studies provide a better understanding of what senior executives do and insights into how computer support must be delivered (Isenberg, 1984; Kotter, 1982; Mintzberg, 1975). Executives' busy schedules and travel requirements are not amenable to long training sessions, do not permit much uninterrupted time for system use, and do not allow a system to be employed on a daily basis (Albala, 1988). The result is that senior executives are unlikely to employ systems that require considerable training and regular use to be learned and remembered. Because senior executives have ready access to staff personnel to fulfill their requests for information, any system must prove to be more responsive than a human (Rockart and DeLong, 1988).

Another problem in providing computer support includes technology that is difficult to use, at least from most executives' perspective. Powerful workstations, improved micro-to-mainframe software, high-quality color graphics, and touchscreens are just some of the technological developments that now make it possible to deliver appealing systems to senior executives.

Finally, many previous systems have contained little information of value to senior executives, which is a problem related to a lack of understanding of executive work. This lack was exacerbated by systems designers who often possessed excellent technical knowledge but little business knowledge (Reck and Hall, 1986). This condition is improving as organizations recognize that business skills and the ability to interact with executives are critical.

Three broad guidelines for developing a successful EIS can be gleaned from these failures. First, the EIS must meet the information needs of senior executives. Second, in order to do this, the EIS must be developed by personnel with both business and technical skills. Finally, the EIS must be so easy to use that it might be considered to be "intuitive" or "user seductive." Even though it is challenging to implement an EIS that meets executive information needs and is extremely easy to use, a number of EIS have achieved these objectives (Applegate and Osborn, 1988); (Houdeshel and Watson, 1987).

AN EIS DEVELOPMENT FRAMEWORK

According to Sprague (1980), a *development framework* is "helpful in organizing a complex subject, identifying the relationships between the parts, and revealing the areas in which further developments will be required" (p. 6). It guides practitioners in developing systems and provides insights for academicians in identifying where research needs to be performed. Gorry and Scott Morton's (1971) framework for MIS and Sprague's (1980) for DSS are two of the best known and most useful frameworks. Turban and Schaeffer (1987) suggest the need for an EIS development framework. This article provides such a framework based on the EIS literature, our experiences in developing EIS, and discussions with vendors, consultants, and EIS staff members.

The EIS development framework introduced here is illustrated by the structural perspective depicted in Figure 16.1. With this perspective, there are key elements and interactions among the elements that are important when developing an EIS. The elements include executives, functional area personnel (e.g., line managers, staff personnel, and data suppliers), information systems personnel, vendors, data, and information technology. The interactions are in the form of pressures, human interactions, and data flows.

The development of an EIS is a dynamic process that places the key elements and interactions in motion. In order for this to be successful, an appropriate development process must be used. This consideration is another important part of the framework.

From the users' perspective, the dialog with the system is of fundamental importance. It includes what must be known in order to use the system, how to direct the system's actions, and how the output is presented by the system (Bennett, 1977). The dialog is another important part of the framework.

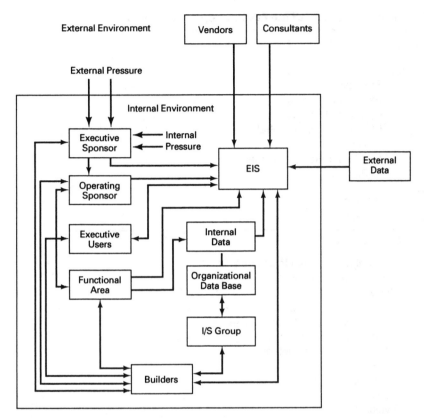

FIGURE 16.1   Structural Perspective of the EIS Development Framework

In summary, the EIS development framework includes a structural perspective, the development process, and the user-system dialog. There are a number of aspects associated with each. Those that are explored in this research are identified in Table 16.1.

THE STUDY

The research study was begun in the spring of 1988 to investigate current EIS practices. The authors mailed a multipart questionnaire to a large sample of geographically dispersed firms. The first part of the questionnaire defined an executive information system. The definition is important because EIS are the most recent computer-based information system to evolve, and, therefore, a precise definition of EIS is not universally accepted among academicians and practitioners. The second part of the questionnaire gathered demographic data on each organization. Finally, the questionnaire sought data concerning the development, operation, support, and capabilities of the EIS in the organization. Suggested changes made after two pretests were incorporated into the final survey instrument.

TABLE 16.1 Aspects of the EIS Development Framework

Structural

Personnel
        EIS Initiator
        Executive Sponsor
        Operating Sponsor
        EIS Builder/Support Staff
        EIS Users
        Functional Area Personnel
        IS Personnel
Data
        Internal
        External

Development Process

        External and Internal Pressures
        Cost/Benefit Analysis
        Costs
                Development Costs
                Annual Operating Costs
        Development Time
        Development Methodology
        Hardware
        Software
        Spread
        Evolution
        Information Provided
        EIS Capabilities

User-System Dialog

        Knowledge Base
                Training
                User Documentation
                System User
        Action Language
                User-System Interface
                System Response Time
        Presentation Language
                Multiple Information Formats
                Color

The survey population was chosen from three groups. The first group attended either the DSS-87 or DSS-88 conferences. One hundred and eighty-five questionnaires were sent to this group. Questionnaires were not sent to attendees from educational institutions or consulting firms. The second group, all of whom received questionnaires, consisted of the 100 firms identified by a *Computerworld* survey as having invested the most effectively in information systems. The authors believed that organizations that are leaders in the use of information systems (IS) are likely candidates to have an EIS. The third group consisted of 19 firms known by the authors to have an EIS but were not included into the first two groups. Each firm was carefully checked to ensure that the firm was not included in more than one group. Because 18 firms appeared more than once, a total of 286 questionnaires were mailed. The survey was not a random sample. Because most firms had not developed an EIS at this point in time, a frame was used that maximized the likelihood of contacting firms with an EIS.

Initially, the authors received 72 usable responses, with 30 of the firms indicating that they had an EIS, and 42 indicating that they did not. Five weeks after the first mailing, another questionnaire was mailed to non-respondents. This follow-up resulted in responses from 20 additional firms with an EIS and 20 with none. The profile of responses from the second group corresponded closely with the profile of the initial responses. A total of 112 usable responses was received for a response rate of 39.1 percent. The number of companies with an EIS was 50, which provides the "n" on which percentages are based when describing current practices in this article. In some cases, the respondents did not answer every question. In such instances, the percentages calculated are based on the number of responses received.

FINDINGS AND DISCUSSION

Demographics

Organizations in this survey represent a variety of industries located in widely dispersed geographic areas (see Figure 16.2). Their total corporate assets average $5.37 billion, with only three firms reporting total assets of less than $1 billion. Forty-eight respondents listed their positions in their firms (see Figure 16.2). The largest number of respondents are IS managers, followed by executives and IS staff members. The respondents averaged 18.74 years of work experience, 13.78 years of IS work experience, and 2.77 years of EIS experience.

Forty-seven firms (94 percent) had an operational EIS, and three firms (6 percent) were far enough along in developing one that they were able to partially answer the questions on the survey. The latter three firms all indicated that they would have an operational EIS in less than one year.

While some EIS date back to the late 1970s (Houdeshel and Watson, 1987), most of them are recent. The survey findings support this statement as 40 firms (80 percent) indicated that their EISs were less than three years old. The average age of an EIS in this survey is two years.

A Structural Perspective

Personnel   Thirty-four firms (68 percent) indicated that a company executive(s) served as the *initiator* of the development of the EIS. Survey respondents were allowed to define the term "executive" in the context of their own organizations. Information sys-

Respondents by Geographical Area

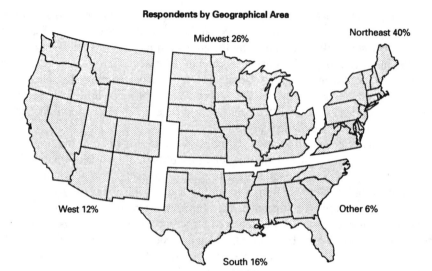

Respondents by Industry

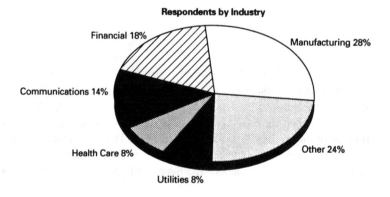

Respondents by Position in the Firm

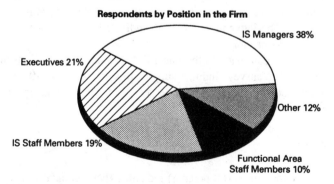

FIGURE 16.2   Respondents by Location, Industry, and Position

tems personnel initiated EIS development in 14 firms (28 percent). Finally, the information center in one firm (2 percent) initiated EIS development.

The finding that IS personnel initiated EIS development in 14 firms is somewhat surprising because the literature indicates that executives initiate EIS development (Houdeshel and Watson, 1987; Stecklow, 1989). However, 11 of these 14 firms (79 percent) had EIS that were less than two years old. Of the 34 firms with EIS initiated by executives, nineteen (56 percent) had EIS that were less than two years old. These numbers suggest that executives motivated EIS development when these systems first evolved. Few IS departments had the confidence of management and/or the risk-taking propensity to push for an EIS. However, as the number of EIS success stories has grown, more IS departments are taking the lead in advocating EIS development by keeping abreast of technological developments and communicating the potential benefits of the technology to senior executives (Volonino and Drinkard, 1989).

EIS development is spurred by a highly placed senior executive who serves as the system's *executive sponsor* (Barrow, 1990; Rockart and DeLong, 1988). This person is typically the president or vice president of the company. Rockart and DeLong (1988) suggest that three major responsibilities of the executive sponsor include making the initial request for the system; staying on top of the system's development and providing direction and feedback about proposed applications; and communicating strong and continuing interest to those with a stake in the system, such as key staff groups and line managers supplying data.

In this study, 42 firms (84 percent) reported having executive sponsors for their EIS. Interestingly, 62 percent of the executive sponsors hold positions other than CEO or president (see Table 16.2). A partial explanation for this finding relates to the scope of the EIS. While it is not explored in this survey, the authors are familiar with a number of EIS that serve a functional area rather than the entire organization. In these situations, it is logical that the executive sponsor would be the vice president from the functional area served.

The executive sponsor typically assigns an *operating sponsor* to manage the day-to-day development of the EIS (Rockart and DeLong, 1988). The operating sponsor is often a senior executive who has an interest in having an EIS for his or her own purposes. An information systems project manager may serve as the operating sponsor. The operating sponsor works with executives, specialized staff, functional area personnel, IS personnel, and vendors in creating the EIS.

TABLE 16.2   Positions Held by Executive Sponsors

POSITION	PERCENT OF FIRMS
Chief Executive Officer	21
President	17
Chief Financial Officer	14
Vice President	42
Controller	6

TABLE 16.3   Positions Held by Operating Sponsors

POSITION	PERCENT OF FIRMS
Manager or Director of IS	50
Manager or Director of Functional Areas	14
Vice President	12
Analyst	10
Staff	7
Consultant	7

Forty-five firms (90 percent) reported having an operating sponsor, and 42 firms listed the operating sponsor's position. The operating sponsor held a variety of positions, the most prevalent being the manager or director of IS (42 percent of firms) (see Table 16.3). This finding is different from what might be expected because the literature suggests that the operating sponsor is typically a senior executive (Rockart and DeLong, 1988).

The *EIS builder/support staff* is responsible for creating and maintaining the EIS (Paller and Laska, 1990; Rockart and DeLong, 1988). The staff may be either newly created or an existing organizational unit given a new charge. For example, a unit that provides specialized information and presentation materials to senior management can be given EIS responsibilities (Houdeshel and Watson, 1987). It is likely that an existing group will require help with technical matters. This lack of technical skills is not the case when IS personnel are responsible for the EIS, but IS personnel are often judged to be out of sync with the needs of senior management or too busy with other activities. Consultants and vendors can also be involved, especially during initial development.

All firms in this survey had EIS builder/support teams, with 37 firms (74 percent) indicating that their group consisted of five or fewer full-time people. The average size of the team was four people. Table 16.4 shows that the four categories of personnel most commonly found on the EIS team are end-user support personnel (58 percent of firms), systems analysts (54 percent), programmers (44 percent), and executive staff support personnel (40 percent). Only seven firms (14 percent) reported using vendor personnel when developing their EIS.

The builder/support team should include personnel with a mixture of business and technical skills because the team must work closely with many different people in the firm (e.g., executives, the IS department, and functional area personnel) (Reck and Hall, 1986; Rockart and DeLong, 1988). The business skills typically come from people who have experience in the company. The technical skills often come from IS personnel, either by virtue of being assigned to the staff or given specific responsibilities for supporting EIS activities.

Respondents were asked to rank the top five skills in order of importance. Five points were awarded to the most important skill, four points to the second most important skill, and so on. The ability to work well with executives was found to be the most neces-

TABLE 16.4   EIS Development Team Members

CATEGORY	PERCENT OF FIRMS
End-user support personnel	58
Systems analysts	54
Programmers	44
Executive staff	40
Executive	22
Vendor personnel	14
Others	14

sary skill for a development team member, followed by knowledge of the business and interpersonal skills (see Table 16.5). Technical skills ranked only fourth.

While it was not explored in the survey, it is worth noting that the EIS builder/support group can have a variety of organizational structures. One approach is to have a centralized group that reports to IS or a functional area. Another approach is to have a small, centralized group with functional area personnel working on a part-time basis performing tasks such as identifying information requirements and supplying data. These tasks are in addition to other job responsibilities. This arrangement matches up well with the skills that the support group needs in order to work effectively with executives.

The executive sponsor, operating sponsor, and EIS staff identify the *users* of the EIS. This group is usually small initially and expands over time. A key to the success of the EIS is identifying the system and information requirements of the executive users (Stecklow, 1989). A variety of methods can be used, including participation in strategic planning sessions, formal CSF sessions, informal discussions, monitoring executive activities, discussions with staff support personnel, software tracking of system usage, and others (Watson and Frolick, 1988).

Functional area personnel are an important source of data for the EIS, and an implementation strategy should be pursued that encourages their cooperation and support for the system. Before implementation of an EIS, much of the needed data are already

TABLE 16.5   Important Skills for the EIS Development Team

SKILL	TOTAL POINTS
Ability to work well with executives	161
Knowledge of the business	143
Interpersonal skills	141
Technical skills	133
Ability to organize data	115
Other	12

being gathered but often only for the executives of the functional area in which the data originate. Two of the major organizational resistances to EIS are staff personnel who feel threatened by the possibility of a diminished role in supplying information to executives and subordinate line managers who fear that their operations will be too visible to top management (Argyris, 1971; Carroll, 1988; Rockart and DeLong, 1988).

Information systems personnel may not lead the EIS project, but their support, cooperation, and assistance are critical (Leibs, 1989). Helping select and install hardware and software, providing maintenance, trouble-shooting problems, and providing access to machine-resident data are some of the support responsibilities that fall to IS personnel. In organizations where IS personnel have the attention and confidence to top management, they may be able to create an interest in the creation of an EIS (Volonino and Drinkard, 1989). This task is accomplished by demonstrating what an EIS is and the kind of information it provides. Possible demonstration strategies include showing a potential executive sponsor an EIS in another company; arranging a vendor-provided demonstration, ideally using company data important to the executive; or prototyping an EIS in-house.

Data   Data play a critical role in an EIS because they are the basis for the information provided (Houdeshel and Watson, 1987; Rockart and DeLong, 1988). The data can come from internal or external sources and can be hard or soft. The EIS can require that new data be collected and stored. Much of the *internal data* is extracted from existing organizational databases that are used by transaction processing systems and functional area applications. This tends to be hard data. The use of this hard data in an EIS is not as straightforward as it might seem, however, because of different reporting and updating cycles, functional area feelings of data ownership, and multiple, incompatible databases (e.g., inconsistent data definitions). Other internal data come from human sources and often are soft in nature and are critical to understanding complex problems (Mintzberg, 1975; Zmud, 1986). Included can be news, rumors, opinions, ideas, predictions, explanations, and plans. Collecting, analyzing, and entering these data to an EIS tends to be very labor-intensive but adds considerably to the richness of the information provided.

Firms in the survey listed a variety of internal data sources. The corporate database is a common source of internal data for most (82 percent) of the firms. Other internal data sources include the functional areas of the firm (62 percent), documents (38 percent), and humans (34 percent). These data indicate the richness and variety of data sources that can be used by an EIS. Further, the data illustrate the extensive data access requirements associated with an EIS.

External data are also important to an EIS (Runge, 1988). Like internal data, they can be hard or soft and can come from existing databases or require special collection efforts. Data sources include external databases (e.g., Dow Jones News Retrieval), published data, customers, and suppliers. External data sources primarily noted in this survey include news services (56 percent of firms), stock markets (46 percent), and trade/industry data (34 percent).

The Development Process

The executive sponsor's interest in the development of an EIS can be the consequence of external and internal pressures (Gulden and Ewers, 1989; Houdeshel and Watson, 1987; Rockart and DeLong, 1988). The *external pressures* come from the firm's external environment and can include environmental turbulence (e.g., rapidly changing costs of raw materials), increased competition, and increased government regulations. *Internal pressures* include the need for new, better, or more timely information; having to manage organizations that are increasingly complex and difficult to run; and the need for more efficient reporting systems.

The study asked respondents to rank order the three most important external pressures and the three most important internal pressures. Three points were awarded to the most important pressure in each category, two points to the second most important pressure, and one point to the third most important pressure.

The most critical external pressure is an increasingly competitive environment. Other critical external pressures, in descending order, include the rapidly changing external environment and the need to be more proactive in dealing with the external environment (see Table 16.6).

The survey findings for internal pressures (see Table 16.6) reveal that respondents consider the need for timely information to be most critical. Other internal pressures include the need for improved communication, the need for access to operational data, and the need for rapid status updates. An interesting finding is that respondents place the need for more accurate information as the least critical internal pressure. This seems to indicate that EIS users already consider the information they receive to be accurate.

Many researchers observe that *cost/benefit analyses* are difficult to perform on EIS because of the difficulty in quantifying many of the benefits (Houdeshel and Watson, 1987; Moad, 1988; Rockart and DeLong, 1988; Rockart and Treacy, 1982). These researchers suggest that there is simply an intuitive feeling that the system will justify its costs. After the system becomes operational, specific benefits and cost savings may be identifiable (Wallis, 1989). Forty-four firms answered this questionnaire item. Their responses support these assertions; forty-two respondents (95 percent) indicate that their firms assessed potential benefits of their EIS through intuitive feelings about improved decision making. Only two firms (5 percent) assessed hard dollar benefits.

Costs

Even though most firms do not measure hard dollar benefits, many firms do consider the costs involved before undertaking EIS development. Most firms estimate software costs (79 percent), hardware costs (68 percent), and personnel costs (68 percent). Fewer firms (32 percent) estimate training costs, perhaps because training costs are anticipated to be minimal.

In conjunction with data on firms that estimated EIS costs before development, this study gathered data on actual EIS development costs and operational costs. *Development costs* are those costs incurred creating the first version of the EIS. Thirty-three firms provided development costs for their EIS. The firms averaged $128,000 on software,

TABLE 16.6   Pressures Leading to EIS Development

EXTERNAL PRESSURES	TOTAL POINTS
Increasingly competitive environment	113
Rapidly changing external environment	59
Need to be more proactive in dealing with external environment	46
Need to access external databases	25
Increasing government regulations	15
Other	8
INTERNAL PRESSURES	
Need for timely information	61
Need for improved communication	39
Need for access to operational data	35
Need for rapid status updates on different business units	34
Need for increased effectiveness	27
Need to be able to identify historical trends	27
Need for increased efficiency	25
Need for access to corporate database	25
Other	17
Need for more accurate information	15

$129,000 on hardware, $90,000 on personnel, and $18,000 on training. These firms also supplied *annual EIS operating costs,* which were found to average $117,000 on personnel, $46,000 on software, $29,000 on hardware, and $16,000 on training. These numbers suggest that an EIS is expensive and, consequently, may be limited to larger firms with considerable financial resources.

Of note is that annual operating costs for personnel appear to be higher than personnel development costs. A possible explanation for this finding is that companies may need additional people to handle increases in the number of users, screens, and system capabilities.

The *time to develop* the initial version of an EIS is important. As with other systems that support decision making, the first version of an EIS should be developed quickly and presented to users for their reactions (Moad, 1988; Runge, 1989). Forty-six firms (92 percent) developed their EIS using an *iterative, prototyping methodology* and four firms (8 percent) used a formal systems development life cycle approach.

The *hardware* and especially the *software* used in developing the first version may or may not be what are used in later versions. At one extreme, a few screens can be designed using existing software to run on workstations already in place (Rinaldi and Jastrzembski, 1986). Information for the screens can be entered manually. This approach minimizes development time and cost. At the other extreme, a commercial EIS package can be purchased and installed. The EIS builders use the package to create the initial screens and to supply them with information. This approach minimizes the difficulties of moving to later versions if the EIS proves to be successful.

There are several hardware configurations possible with an EIS (Paller and Laska, 1990; Rockart and DeLong, 1988). Forty-eight companies indicated the hardware configuration used for their EIS. Forty firms (83 percent) use a mainframe approach. The mainframe approach includes 18 firms (37 percent) that employ a shared mainframe, 17 firms (35 percent) that use a PC network connected to a mainframe, and five firms (11 percent) that employ a dedicated mainframe. Eight firms (17 percent) use a PC network with a file server for their hardware configuration. More vendors have been offering local area network-based EIS products (e.g., Lightship from Pilot) since this study was conducted.

The availability of commercial software has contributed considerably to the growth of EIS. Products from vendors such as Comshare (Commander EIS), Pilot (Command Center), IBM (Executive Decisions), and EXECUCOM (Executive Edge) facilitate the development and maintenance of an EIS. These products support ease of use (e.g., mouse or touch screen operation), access to data, screen design and maintenance, interfaces to other software (e.g., Lotus 1-2-3), and other system requirements.

An EIS can be developed using in-house developed software, vendor-supplied software, or some combination of the two (Paller and Laska, 1990; Rockart and DeLong, 1988). Twelve firms (24 percent) developed their EIS using custom-built, in-house software; 12 firms (24 percent) used vendor-supplied software; and 26 firms (52 percent) used a combination of in-house and vendor software. Of the 38 firms that employ at least some vendor-supplied software, nine firms (24 percent) use Pilot's Command Center, seven firms (18 percent) use Comshare's Commander EIS, five firms (12 percent) use Interactive Image's EASEL, and the remaining 17 firms (46 percent) use a wide variety of other vendor software. These results are not surprising; Pilot and Comshare are generally recognized to be the two leading vendors of EIS software.

Over time an EIS evolves in terms of the number of users, the number of screens, the content and format of the screens, and EIS capabilities (Houdeshel and Watson, 1987; Rockart and DeLong, 1988). In some cases the EIS may be "pushed" on users, but a more desirable approach is to allow "demand pull" to occur. The latter normally occurs as subordinates learn that their superiors have access to certain information and they "want to see what their bosses are looking at." Still, some executives may legitimately have little interest in using the EIS because it contains little information relevant to them, or they have well-established alternative sources of information.

Executive information systems usually spread over time. *Spread* refers to the increase in the number of users who have access to the EIS (Rockart and DeLong, 1988). It can be argued that an EIS that does not spread is likely to fail (Friend, 1990). The survey question about spread referred only to the number of users over time and did not specify that the users be executives. Therefore, the users could include executives, executive staff, and other organizational personnel. This study found that the EIS supported an average of 7.75 users initially, with a steadily increasing number of users over time, as can be seen in Figure 16.3. The "n"s shown in Figure 16.3 are the number of respondents who provided data for the various points in time.

Evolution refers to additional capabilities and information provided by an EIS over time (Rockart and DeLong, 1988). This study gathered data on the number of screens available to users over time. An average of 55.8 screens were available initially, and the number of available screens increased in each time period (see Figure 16.3). This increase implies that users usually want more information as time passes and they become familiar with the system.

Even though the data show that the number of screens consistently increases, outdated screens must be deleted and other screens modified. Adding, modifying, and deleting screens is an important responsibility of the EIS support staff. Software tracking of system use is very helpful in identifying screens that may need to be changed. Screen content and format can change over time. As an example of this change, screens may become denser in content as users become more familiar with them (Houdeshel and Watson, 1987). Information that was spread over several screens may be placed on a single screen, which can result in format changes.

To be most effective in supporting executives, an EIS must *provide information* from many areas (Houdeshel and Watson, 1987; Rockart and DeLong, 1988). It can supply information about the industry in which the firm competes, company information, work unit information, and information that may be of interest to only a single executive. The information can span subsidiaries, divisions, functional areas, and departments.

The surveyed firms reported that their EIS provided information by strategic business unit (88 percent), functional area (86 percent), key performance indicator (71 percent), product (67 percent), and location (53 percent). These percentages demonstrate that EIS are able to supply information for various perspectives, thus allowing users flexibility in the information they can access.

An EIS can have a variety of *capabilities* (Friend, 1986; Kogan, 1986). Eighty-eight percent of the firms in this study state that their EIS provides access to current status information about the company. Other capabilities provided in a majority of firms are electronic mail, external news access, and access to other external databases (see Table 16.7).

Executives may want access to the EIS while at home (Wallis, 1989). Executives who are traveling may also want to access the EIS. This off-site use creates special communications, security, and support responsibilities. This is just one example of a system requirement that can evolve over time.

The Dialog

From the executive's perspective, the dialog with the EIS is the most important component of the system (Zmud, 1986). As was pointed out previously, because of the nature

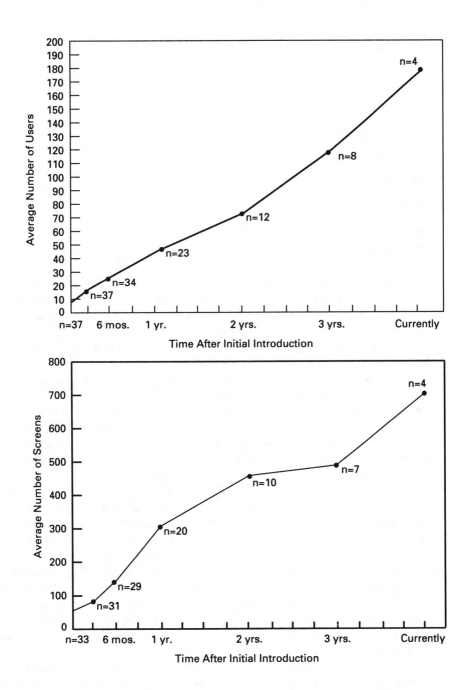

FIGURE 16.3   EIS Spread

TABLE 16.7   Capabilities Available on the EIS

CAPABILITY	PERCENT OF FIRMS
Access to current status	88
Electronic mail	65
Other external database	57
External news access	56
Spreadsheet	37
Word processing	34
Automated filing	22
Other	14

of executives and executive work, the system should be quite user-friendly. It should avoid elaborate logon procedures. Movement among EIS components should be seamless (e.g., E-mail might be a main menu option and not require a separate user ID). The system should provide context-dependent online help. Menus and a keyword index for locating screens should be included to help the executive find information. Sequence or command files should be created that allow executives to page through regularly viewed screens. The inclusion of a "drill-down" capability allows executives to go into more detail when an exceptional situation is encountered. The screens can provide the names and telephone numbers of people who can discuss the information presented.

Training on the use of the EIS should be one-on-one. Any system that requires more than a few minutes of training probably does not satisfy ease-of-use requirements (Carroll, 1988). *User documentation* should not be necessary for a well-designed EIS. If documentation is provided, it should be kept to a single page.

The *system user* of the EIS may be the executive, or it may be operated by an intermediary (Rockart and DeLong, 1988). Forty-eight respondents answered this item on the questionnaire. Forty-three firms (89 percent) report that their executives use the EIS directly, and five firms (11 percent) report that intermediaries operate the system.

In keeping with the fact than an EIS must be highly user-friendly, the *user interface* and *response time* of the EIS are critical (Houdeshel and Watson, 1987; Rockart and DeLong, 1988). Ninety-two percent of the EIS employ a keyboard interface, one-half a mouse, and one-fourth a touch screen. These percentages indicate that there are multiple interfaces available in many of the EIS in this sample. The mean response time of the EIS in this survey was 2.8 seconds, with 42 firms (84 percent) reporting average response times of less than five seconds.

The EIS can provide a variety of capabilities for selecting screens. Keystrokes can be employed to move through menus or to identify particular screens. Even though some executives are adverse to using keyboards, this typically is not a major problem if the required skills are not too great. A keyboardless system can be provided by using a mouse or a touch screen. Most vendor-supplied software offer these methods of system operation as options. Icons are commonly used to make the system more intuitive.

Screens should include graphical, tabular, and textual presentation of information. Most supplied software provides a large variety of screen design capabilities. Standards should be established for any terms used, color codes, and graphic designs (Smith and Mosier, 1984; Tullis, 1981). These standards help to avoid misunderstandings and reduce the amount of mental processing required to interpret information.

Executive information systems should be able to present information to the user in *multiple formats* (e.g., graphical, tabular, and textual) (Friend, 1988; Houdeshel and Watson, 1987; Rockart and DeLong, 1988). Ninety percent of the EIS in this study have graphical formats available, 90 percent use textual formats, and 88 percent employ tabular formats. These percentages suggest that many EIS present information in multiple formats.

Executive information systems make extensive use of *color* in presenting information (Friend, 1988; Houdeshel and Watson, 1987; Rockart and DeLong, 1988). Out of 47 respondents who answered this question, 39 EIS (83 percent) in this study employ color displays and eight (17 percent) do not.

CONCLUSION

This study has presented a framework for the development of executive information systems and data related to this framework from 50 organizations. In most cases, the data support the "conventional wisdom" found in the literature:

- EIS are a recent development.
- EIS development is typically driven by a senior executive.
- An EIS has an executive sponsor, and this person is normally a CEO or a vice president.
- The development of an EIS is approved with little formal cost/benefit analysis.
- EIS development groups include a variety of personnel with a mixture of business and technical skills.
- An EIS obtains data from multiple internal and external sources.
- An EIS provides broadly based information.
- Pilot's Command Center and Comshare's Commander EIS are the two most popular vendor products for creating an EIS.
- The initial version of an EIS is developed quickly.
- Most EIS are mainframe-based.
- An EIS is created using an iterative, prototyping development methodology.
- The number of users and the number of screens of an EIS increase over time.
- Nearly all EIS are used directly by executives without intermediaries.
- An EIS presents information in graphical, textual, and tabular formats.
- Most EIS use color in presenting information.

The study also provides insights about areas where little is previously reported:

- The increasingly competitive environment and the need for timely information are the main external and internal pressures that lead to the development of an EIS.
- On average, the total costs of developing an EIS are $365,000, and the annual costs to maintain one are $208,000. It should be noted that the firms in this study are large, and smaller companies might develop more limited, and therefore less expensive, EIS due to cost considerations.
- The average size of an EIS development group is four people.
- On average, about one-fourth of the EIS are created using in-house developed software, one-half with vendor supplied plus in-house software, and one-fourth with only vendor-supplied software.
- On average, it takes 4.9 months to develop the initial version of an EIS.
- On average, 92 percent of all EIS employ a keyboard interface, one-half a mouse, and one-fourth a touch screen.

And finally, there were a few surprising findings:

- In some firms, EIS development is initiated by IS, and this seems to be a growing trend.
- A vice president is most often the executive sponsor for an EIS.
- An IS manager or director is most often the operating sponsor for an EIS.

While this and other studies provide information about EIS, there is much that still needs to be learned. After reading the MIS literature, one is surprised by how little academic research has been conducted on EIS. Most of the literature only provides glowing descriptions of specific EIS and how they are being used. In conducting this research, a variety of interesting and important EIS research questions surfaced.

- Is the organizational position and level of commitment of the executive sponsor related to EIS success?
- What considerations are most important when selecting an operating sponsor?
- How can the benefits of an EIS be assessed in advance?
- How does the software used in building an EIS affect the development process and system success?
- What level of staffing and organization structure are best for the EIS builder/support staff?
- What methods can be most effectively used to identify executives' information requirements?
- What are the major EIS data management problems and their solutions?
- What impact does the inclusion of soft data have on EIS success?
- What are the major problems associated with EIS "spread" and its evolution?
- How can EIS functionality be increased while maintaining ease-of-use?
- What emerging technologies (e.g., voice, optical disc) can be effectively used with EIS?
- What are the most effective screen presentation formats for an EIS?

Currently, the technology for EIS is evolving rapidly, and future systems are likely to be different from those that are in use today. A number of interesting and promising changes that can be anticipated include:

- Better integration with other applications. For example, better support can be provided by integrating EIS with decision support systems, group decision support systems, and expert systems. A DSS can provide analysis capabilities when problems are identified using an EIS; an EIS can be used to provide information in a decision room setting; and an expert system can be created to help guide executives in using the EIS effectively.
- Better commercial EIS software. Some of the advances to expect include better interfaces to organizational data and other organizational systems, enhanced capabilities for monitoring system usage, industry-specific template screens, and expanded sets of builders' tools (e.g., icons for use in screen development).
- Better executive-system interfaces. While keyboards are required for E-mail and most decision support applications, mouse and touchscreens are attractive alternatives for other types of system use. Animation is likely to be increasingly used to "add life" to information. Television may be available in a window. Voice may be used to direct the system.

An EIS is a high-risk system, and many failures have occurred (Watson and Glover, 1989). By following the EIS development framework, however, the likelihood of having a failure should be reduced. Over time, as more experience is gained, better products emerge, and more research findings are available, the chances for having an EIS success should grow.

QUESTIONS

1. What is the relationship between executive information systems and executive support systems?
2. Why are executive information systems succeeding when most previous attempts to supply senior executives with computer-generated information have failed?
3. Assume that a senior executive has asked you to prepare a summary description of what might be expected if the firm develops an EIS. Prepare such a description based on the study findings presented in the reading.

REFERENCES

1. ALBALA, M. "Getting to the Pulse of the Company," *Personal Computing* (12:10), October 1988, 196–98.
2. ALEXANDER, M. "Executive Information Systems Catch On," *Computerworld*, February 27, 1989, 31.
3. APPLEGATE, L. M., AND C. S. OSBORN "Phillips 66 Company: Executive Information Systems," Harvard Case (9-189-006), Harvard Business School, Boston, MA, December 1988.

4. ARGYRIS, C. "Management Information Systems: The Challenge to Rationality and Emotionality," *Management Science* (17:6), June 1971, B275–292.

5. BARROW, C. "Implementing an Executive Information System: Seven Steps for Success," *Journal of Information Systems Management* (7:2), Spring 1990, 41–46.

6. BENNETT, J. "User-Oriented Graphics Systems for Decision Support in Unstructured Tasks," in *User-Oriented Design of Interactive Graphics Systems,* S. Treu (ed.), Association for Computing Machinery, New York, 1977.

7. BURKAN, W. C. "Making EIS Work," *DSS 88 Transactions,* The Institute of Management Sciences, Providence, RI, 1988, 121–136.

8. CARROLL, P. B. "Computerphobe Managers," *The Wall Street Journal,* June 20, 1988, 21.

9. *Computerworld* "The Premier 100," Special Supplement, September 12, 1988, 9.

10. FRIEND, D. "Executive Information Systems: Successes, Failures, Insights, and Misconceptions," *DSS 86 Transactions,* The Institute of Management Sciences, Providence, RI, 1986, 35–40.

11. FRIEND, D. "EIS and the Collapse of the Information Pyramid," *Information Center* (6:3), March 1990, 22–28.

12. GORRY, G. A., AND M. S. SCOTT MORTON "A Framework for Management Information Systems," *Sloan Management Review* (13:1), Fall 1971, 51–70.

13. GULDEN, G. K., AND D. E. EWERS "Is Your ESS Meeting the Need?" *Computerworld,* July 10, 1989, 85–91.

14. HOUDESHEL, G., AND H. J. WATSON "The Management Information and Decision Support (MIDS) System at Lockheed-Georgia," *MIS Quarterly* (11:1), March 1987, 127–40.

15. ISENBERG, D. J. "How Senior Managers Think," *Harvard Business Review* (62:6), November–December 1984, 81–90.

16. KOGAN, J. "Information for Motivation: A Key to Executive Information Systems That Translate Strategy into Results for Management," *DSS 86 Transactions,* The Institute of Management Sciences, Providence, RI, 1986, 6–13.

17. KOTTER, J. P. "What Effective General Managers Really Do," *Harvard Business Review* (60:6), November–December 1982, 156–57.

18. LEIBS, S. "EIS: It's All Down Hill From Here," *Information Week,* May 1989, pp. 44–46.

19. MAIN, J. "At Last, Software CEOs Can Use," *Fortune* (119:6), March 13, 1989, 77–83.

20. MINTZBERG, H. "The Manager's Job: Folklore and Fact," *Harvard Business Review* (53:4), July–August 1975, 49–61.

21. MOAD, J. "The Latest Challenge for IS Is in the Executive Suite," *Datamation,* May 15, 1988, 43.

22. PALLER, A., AND R. LASKA *The EIS Book,* Dow Jones-Irwin, Homewood, Il, 1990.

23. RECK, R. H., AND J. R. HALL "Executive Information Systems: An Overview of Development," *Journal of Information Systems Management* (3:4), Fall 1986, 25–30.

24. RINALDI, D., AND T. JASTRZEMBSKI "Executive Information Systems: Put Strategic Data at Your CEO's Fingertips," *Computerworld,* October 27, 1986, 37–50.

25. ROCKART, J. F., AND M. E. TREACY "The CEO Goes On-Line," *Harvard Business Review* (60:1), January–February 1982, 84–88.

26. ROCKART, J. F., AND D. W. DELONG *Executive Support Systems: The Emergence of Top Management Computer Use,* Dow Jones-Irwin, Homewood, IL, 1988.

27. RUNGE, L. "On the Executive's Desk," *Information Center* (4:6), June 1988, 34–38.

28. SMITH, S. L., AND J. N. MOSIER "Design Guidelines for User-System Interface," Software Report (ESD-TR-84-190), The MITRE Corporation, Bedford, MA, September 1984.

29. SPRAGUE, R. H. "A Framework for the Development of Decision Support Systems," *MIS Quarterly* (4:4), December 1980, 1–26.

30. STECKLOW, S. "The New Executive Information Systems," *Lotus,* April 1989, 51–55.

31. TULLIS, T. S. "An Evaluation of Alphanumeric, Graphic, and Color Information Displays," *Human Factors* (23:5), October 1981, 541–50.

32. TURBAN, E., AND D. M. SCHAEFFER "A Comparative Study of Executive Information Systems," *DDS 87 Transactions,* The Institute of Management Sciences, Providence, RI, 1987, 139–48.

33. TURBAN, E., AND H. J. WATSON "Integrating Expert Systems, Executive Information Systems, and Decision Support Systems," *DSS 89 Transactions,* The Institute of Management Sciences, Providence, RI, 1989, 74–82.

34. VOLONINO, L., AND G. DRINKARD "Integrating EIS into the Strategic Plan: A Case Study of Fisher-Price," *DSS 89 Transactions,* The Institute of Management Sciences, Providence, RI, 1989, 37–45.

35. WALLIS, L. "Power Computing at the Top," *Across the Board* (26:1-2), January–February 1989, 42–51.

36. WATSON, H. J., AND M. FROLICK "Determining Information Requirements for an Executive Information System," unpublished working paper, Department of Management, University of Georgia, Athens, GA, 1988.

37. WATSON, H., AND H. GLOVER "Common and Avoidable Causes of EIS Failure," *Computerworld,* December 4, 1989, 90–91.

38. ZMUD, R. W. "Supporting Senior Executives Through Decision Support Technologies: A Review and Directions for Future Research," in *Decisions Support Systems: A Decade in Perspective,* E. R. McLean and H. G. Sol (eds.), Elsevier Science Publishers B. V., North-Holland, Amsterdam, 1986, 87–101.

17

AVOIDING HIDDEN
EIS PITFALLS

Hugh Watson

How many things can you find wrong with this true-to-life scenario?

Bill Perry, vice-president of information systems at Genericorp, had advocated the development of an executive information system (EIS) to support the information needs of the firm's senior executives. From trade writings, conferences and conversations with other information systems managers, Perry had heard of EIS successes at firms such as Xerox Corp., Phillips Petroleum and Lockheed-Georgia. Perry believed that besides helping top management, an EIS would also improve the image of the IS department. For too many years, company executives had approved multimillion-dollar budgets without much IS support. An EIS would change that situation, however.

Perry arranged for one of the EIS vendors to present a demonstration to the chief executive officer and other senior executives. The demonstration was very well received. With a touch of the screen, charts and reports quickly appeared in a rich variety of formats and colors. The executives were impressed and, after a brief meeting, authorized the development of an EIS. The project was allotted a budget of $250,000.

The next step was to put together a team of people to develop the EIS. Sam Johnson, who had worked at Genericorp for 20 years in a variety of areas, was recruited to head the project. Johnson was a good choice because of his knowledge of the business, executives, and politics of the organization. Perry also assigned two of his best systems analysts to the project.

After reviewing the software and hardware alternatives, the EIS team chose what they thought would be a good approach. A major EIS vendor's software would be used. The product was designed around the co-processing concept, in which the personal computer performs graphics functions and the mainframe handles data storage. The executives would have IBM Personal System/2 Model 50 machines connected to an IBM 4381 by a Token-Ring network. Most of the hardware was already in place.

Getting the initial set of executive users to specify their information requirements proved to be a problem. The EIS staff found it difficult to arrange time with the executives because of the latters' travel and job requirements. Even when they did meet, the executives were often vague and uncertain about their information needs. Consequently, the executive's staff and secretaries became important sources for determining what should go into the EIS.

Three months later, the initial version of the system was rolled out to five users. The 50 screens provided key financial reports that were previously available only in paper form. The system also provided information on key performance indicators that had been identified in Genericorp's strategic planning processes. The screens were efficiently updated by automatic downloading of data from existing databases.

The executives' initial reaction to the system was generally positive. One executive said, "I've never been able to get my hands on this information this quickly before." Several of the executives seemed proud to finally be able to use a computer. Only one older executive seemed to have little interest in the EIS.

Having delivered the system, the focus turned to maintenance. Johnson was assigned to another project. The systems analysts were given responsibilities for developing a new, important transaction processing application. Two maintenance programmers were assigned the task of handling the evolution and spread of the system to more users, with additional screens and new capabilities.

Little happened with the system during the next few months. It took the maintenance programmers a while to learn how to use the EIS software. Even after they knew how to develop screens, the programmers discovered that this activity always seemed less critical than working on other applications. Besides that, the executives seldom requested additional screens. To some extent, the maintenance programmers viewed the EIS as an "executive toy."

Nine months after the introduction of the EIS, little evolution had occurred. There were no new users, and usage-tracking software revealed that three of the five executives were not using the system at all. Few new screens had been added, and there were no new system capabilities.

At about this time, Genericorp began to encounter financial troubles. To maintain a healthy bottom line, any nonessential expenditures were eliminated. At a key meeting, the executive who had never taken to using the EIS proposed that it be terminated. "We've put a lot of time and money into this system, and I don't see that we have gotten much out of it," he said. "If we are honest with ourselves, all we are getting is the same information that we used to get before—except now it is on a screen with fancy graphs and colors. We can save money by trashing the system and not lose much." After discussion, the executives agreed that the system had turned out to be a disappointment that should be scuttled.

When Perry learned of the decision, he was crushed. The EIS had seemed so promising, and things seemed to have been going so well. What had gone wrong? He'd gotten executive support, assembled a good staff, selected appropriate hardware and software, and quickly delivered an initial version of the system. These were frequently mentioned keys to success. Maybe the executives just weren't ready to use computers. One thing Perry did know, however, was that the EIS experience smeared his reputation, as well as that of his department.

While the scenario and company are fictional, the situation is very much like the EIS experiences of many firms. An EIS is developed with high expectations, but it often ends in failure.

WHAT WENT WRONG?

The Genericorp scenario has many problems in it. The longer you look, the more faults you find. Some problems are not fully appreciated even by experienced EIS developers. Taking a look at the following problems can help you steer your organization away from an EIS failure.

Problem One: Lack of executive support

Conventional wisdom says that an EIS requires an executive sponsor. This person supports the project, makes the necessary resources available, and handles the political problems that occur.

In the early days of EIS (from the late 1970s to the mid-1980s) senior executives tended to drive EIS development. They had a specific information need and thus a strong interest in EIS. More recently, IS managers, sensing a chance for increased visibility and recognition, began initiating interest in EIS. Although they may get executive support, that support is weaker, and as Genericorp learned, there is a difference between support and commitment. Come economic hard times, the system may be abandoned.

There is another reason that an EIS should have a broad base of executive support. More than one EIS has failed after the executive sponsor left the company. The highly touted EIS at Northwest Industries died after Ben Heineman left. When the EIS has multiple supporters, it can better withstand the loss of an executive sponsor. Having a broad base of support requires the creation of a system that meets the needs of many users.

Problem Two: Undefined system objectives

There can be a variety of motivations for creating an EIS. A firm's executives may need information that is more comprehensive, relevant, or timely. An EIS can be used to improve communication within an organization. It may be used to change executives' mental models: for example, how executives view the firm. It might be employed to analyze specific organizational problems.

Many firms fail to clearly define the objectives for their EIS. One outcome is that the system may lack needed features and capabilities. An otherwise excellent EIS that does not serve its intended purposes is likely to fail. At Genericorp, system objectives were never clearly defined, thus contributing to the failure.

Early in the development of an EIS, it's important to assemble key executives and clearly define why the EIS is being developed. A clear purpose suggests the capabilities and features that should be included in the system. Some organizations have used an EIS executive steering committee with good success to not only define system objectives but also provide on-going planning and control for the project.

Problem Three: Poorly defined information requirements

Most organizations know that an EIS should supply relevant information that will aid success. Less obvious are some subtleties and potential problems that need to be understood and addressed when designing an EIS.

There are four basic types of critical success factors: industry, organizational, work group, and individual. In mining, for example, key factors include world demand and price for tin, copper, and other metals. These factors remain relevant over long periods of time. Organizational factors differ by company. These might include the market share for tin or the cost per ton for extracting copper. Such factors are relatively stable over time. Work unit factors apply to the division, group, department, or other organizational unit. Examples might include the number of accidents per month or the number of tons of tin produced per day. Such factors are stable only as long as the responsibilities of the work unit remain the same. They are also unique to the work unit. Finally, individual factors are things that the executive must do well in order to be successful. These factors tend to change relatively quickly as job responsibilities and concerns change and are unique to the particular executive.

Information about industry and organizational success factors tend to be available to all EIS users. (One exception might be sensitive competitive information that only a few executives can access.) Work unit and individual critical success factor-related information is usually of interest to only a few or perhaps even a single executive.

Most organizations take one of two approaches when designing the initial version of their EIS. The first approach is to *focus on the executive sponsor's information needs.* This approach is logical because it reinforces the interest and commitment of this key person. The type of information provided is likely to vary considerably. It will include industry, organizational, work unit, and individual critical success factor-related information. A problem with this approach is that is does not build a broad base of support. Thus, it is critical to expand the information provided by the EIS so that it meets the information needs of more users.

The second and most common approach is to focus on *providing key financial and strategic information.* This was the approach used at Genericorp. Once again, this seems to be a logical approach because it provides information that senior management needs to run the business.

This approach runs the risk, however, of what may be called "the six-month phenomenon." For the first six months, everything seems to be going well, but then executive use of the system starts to decline. As was the case at Genericorp, the system may even be discontinued. The problem is often that the information provided does not grow in depth or breadth. This type of system may not allow executives to drill down to the level of detail needed. It may provide information about only a few of the areas that are important to users. Very little, if any, information is provided about work unit or individual critical success factors. After a while, executives perceive that the EIS is satisfying only a small percentage of their information needs and that it is unlikely that the situation will change. Enthusiasm and interest in the EIS decrease, use of it declines, and the system is terminated.

Even when the EIS support staff realizes the importance of providing individual success factor-related information, there are problems when users are unwilling to commit the time to discuss their information needs. While executive support personnel can provide important insights about what information is required, regular interaction with the executives makes it possible to not only respond to information needs but also to anticipate them.

A portfolio of methods should be used to identify information requirements. Some of the methods involve direct interaction between executive users of the system and the EIS support staff. It is seldom possible to get as much executive time as wanted. Consequently, analysts must use indirect methods, such as discussing executives' information needs with support personnel.

All these methods merit consideration. Those used will depend on factors such as how accessible the executives are, the relationship between the analysts and the executives, whether the information requirements are for the initial or ongoing version of the system, the level of success factors-related information that is needed, and the software used.

It is important to recognize that multiple methods are needed, because no single method is likely to serve all purposes.

Problem Four: Inadequate support staff

A good EIS support staff is critical. Genericorp got off to a good start by naming Johnson to direct the project. He knew the company, the executives and the politics. He was well regarded and had the requisite business, technical, managerial, and interpersonal skills. His staff was also first-rate.

The staffing problems began when people started to think that the EIS could be placed in a maintenance mode, like most other applications. An EIS needs to spread to additional users, accommodate new and changing information needs, and evolve to provide additional capabilities. These requirements demand a permanent staff that promotes the EIS, interacts often and effectively with executives, understands and anticipates information needs, has a vision of what the EIS can be, and is ready and able to overcome problems when they are encountered.

Even though EIS support staffs can be assembled in a variety of ways, three organizational roles must be filled. *Technical supporters* must perform tasks such as testing and installing hardware, handling communications needs, and writing data extraction routines. Such people typically come from IS, whether they are permanently assigned to the

EIS support staff or have a dotted-line relationship to it.

Another role is filled by *business information analysts.* These people perform tasks such as identifying information needs and designing displays. They must work closely with the executives and may even have been the staff that supported the executives before the EIS was created.

The final role is the *data provider.* These people obtain data and enter it into the EIS. This role is often performed by functional area personnel, including secretaries.

In our case, Genericorp created a permanent EIS support staff that was unable to perform the business information analyst role. Their organizational location, training, experience, other job responsibilities, and attitudes made them terrible choices for providing long-term EIS support.

Problem Five: Poorly planned evolution

The initial version of an EIS can take many different forms, depending on the motivation for creating it. The EIS at Genericorp provided financial and strategic information. The initial version may provide information about in important problem. It may focus on communications support. There are many legitimate starting points, depending on the company's needs.

Regardless of the starting point, there should be a plan—or at least a planning process—for the evolution of the EIS. Genericorp had neither. Ideally, an EIS planning committee includes the operating sponsor, executive users, EIS support staff manager and IS personnel. Their purpose is to give direction to the EIS.

To maintain executive interest in the EIS, evolution must occur quickly. Changes and enhancements must be made almost daily. The EIS at Genericorp was in trouble when months passed while the new support staff learned to use the software. Even then, little change was forthcoming.

An important part of the evolution of an EIS is to ensure that it helps address significant needs or problems. The information and capabilities provided should make a real difference in the performance of the organization. Efforts should be made to assess tangible benefits from the EIS. Without this, the EIS is at risk from economic hard times (as was the case at Genericorp), turnover of the executive sponsor and political resistance.

When an EIS is successful, it almost always expands to other users. The spread can be lateral to different areas of the firm or downward to lower organizational personnel. Other people want to have access to information on which important decisions and actions are based. Priorities for the spread of the EIS should be governed by the areas of greatest need.

Ultimately, the EIS may serve everyone in the organization. Having relevant information that is easily accessed is appealing to more than just the senior executives of a firm.

EPILOGUE: IS IT WORTH DOING?

For most organizations, an EIS is a high-risk application. It serves users who have poor computer skills and are skeptical about whether computers can help improve their job performance. Organizations often have little experience in developing applications of this

How to design a system that gets used

Among the many sins in developing executive information systems, probably the biggest is building a system that doesn't meet user needs. The following techniques can be valuable tools in helping you develop EIS requirements:

- **Participating in strategic planning meetings**. Get EIS support personnel active in the organization's strategic planning sessions. This approach—which requires strict confidentiality by the analyst—is especially useful in identifying industry and organizational critical success factors (CSF). If it's not possible for an analyst to attend meetings, a representative from the strategic planning group can brief the EIS support staff.
- **Formal "success" sessions**. This method is often advocated for use with EIS. Sessions are held in which the focus is to identify organizational goals, as well as the underlying CSFs. These sessions can help members explore ways to measure CSFs and devise ways to deliver key information to support these factors. This approach is highly appropriate for identifying organizational CSF-related information requirements.
- **Informal discussions of information needs.** This is probably the most useful method for determining information requirements. Moreover, its usefulness tends to grow over time, as the analyst comes to better understand the executive's job, problems, sources of information, and management style. Placing the analyst as physically close to the executive as possible increases opportunities for executive/analyst interaction.
- **Tracking executive activity.** In this approach, the analyst spends several days with the executive to better understand his job and information needs. Alternatively, the executive or his secretary can keep a log of daily activities and information requirements. This method is especially helpful for understanding individual needs during the early stages of EIS development.
- **Discussions with support personnel.** Because executive time is at a premium, analysts must typically rely on support personnel for insights about information requirements. Secretaries and staff assistants are good candidates.
- **Reviewing computer-generated information**. Most executives receive a plethora of computer-generated information; some is useful, but the rest may be too old, inaccurate, not at the right level of detail, irrelevant, or presented unappealingly. The analyst should meet with the executive to determine what information is useful and what needs to be changed or included.
- **Reviewing noncomputer-generated information**. Most executives use information from newspapers, journals, trade publications, and other sources. It's helpful for executive and support personnel to identify what information is regularly gleaned from these sources.
- **Attending meetings.** Having EIS analysts sit in on areas they support, such as finance or marketing, can help provide a good understanding of the unit and its information needs.
- **Software tracking of EIS usage.** Some custom-built EIS systems and commercial software let analysts monitor executive EIS use. This capability gives analysts the ability to track system usage and problems, which provides insights into how the system could be improved in the future.

kind. An EIS often involves learning, selecting, implementing, and using new technology. Additional data sources typically have to be used. Potential political problems abound.

So a logical question is, is it worth the trouble? For many organizations, the answer seems to be yes. Providing information that is more comprehensive, consistent across the organization, relevant, and timely has value. It lets organizations communicate better, especially when units are separated by time and distance. The perspective and information presented by the EIS focuses attention on those areas that are judged to be important. An EIS can improve the productivity of individuals and groups, thus enhancing the productivity of the organization. An EIS can reduce costs by facilitating the reduction of systems (for example, systems for developing executive-quality presentation materials), staff personnel and management personnel.

IS managers who successfully develop an EIS also benefit. They are afforded the opportunity to work with leading-edge technologies. An EIS provides more visibility with top management than almost any other kind of application. A successful EIS typically results in greater management satisfaction with IS. In some firms, the system has helped IS management join the select group of senior executives who determine the strategic direction for the firm. It could happen to you.

QUESTIONS

1. One of the problems at Genericorp was a lack of executive support. Who is to blame for this—the firm's executives or the EIS support staff? Discuss.
2. Identifying the information requirements for an EIS often proves to be troublesome. Why might this be the case?
3. Assume that you were brought in as a consultant to salvage the EIS at Genericorp. What would you do?

18

POWER COMPUTING AT THE TOP

Lou Wallis

Stories abound about the many senior executives who, while paying tribute to the contributions of computer technology to their companies, break out in a rash when they get within 10 feet of a computer terminal or personal computer.

This resistance is puzzling, since top executives have signed off on billions of dollars' worth of computers for their companies and must realize that their operations would grind to a halt if deprived, even temporarily, of these facilities. But translating that into their own work is another matter. They may note the computer's handling of millions of transactions for payroll, accounting, invoicing, plus word processing and other office automation. But they view their own work as vastly different, not at all susceptible to automation. Their jobs appear fundamentally different from those many layers below them, and they fail to see how their productivity could be improved by a computer system.

For them, productivity may not be the key issue. Jim Carlisle, a consultant who helped develop executive information systems for Xerox Corporation and Westinghouse Electric Corporation, observes: "Anyone who has made senior vice president probably

Reprinted by special permission of *Across the Board,* Volume 26, Number 1&2, 1989. © 1989 by the Conference Board Inc.

can't have his personal productivity improved. However, he can have his vision and comprehension of the business improved."

Others say that many attempts at executive information systems have failed because they do not meet the highly individual needs of top managers. One skeptic is Henry Mintzberg, professor of management at McGill University in Montreal, who has observed that executives "are still forced to conform to the technology's capabilities, rather than being able to tailor it to their own needs. The mistaken assumption is that the technology is based on an understanding of what managers do, and it's not. The technology has simply been superimposed over the work."

Executives make important decisions, a lot of them. But as they grapple for the best outcomes, they can become exasperated, panning the dross and silt of corporate computer data bases, searching for nuggets of information. Too many information systems have been designed for everything and everybody in the company except for the high-level decision-makers, who tend to find them "data rich, insight poor." The problem of providing adequate corporate data for executive decision-makers is similar to that of the provident squirrel who intends to dine on acorns once the winter snows have arrived—that is, saving the treasure isn't the problem, it's finding where it's hidden.

But newer and better systems are designed especially for corporate decision-makers and fit the way they actually work. One type that has worked well for many managers is called an executive support system (ESS). The powerful software is sold by vendors but usually has to be adapted to the needs of each company's top managers. ESS learns what executive users want, allows users to enter information and ask questions in informal English, delivers the results in a meaningful form, and, as far as possible, eliminates the need to make adjustments to the computer itself.

Computer systems have long been able to store and retrieve financial, production, marketing, and other essential measures of company performance. These are the conventional, recognizable output from electronic data processing or management information systems (MIS). The day-to-day output of these systems are garden-variety reports of weekly, monthly, year-to-date results intended for many different people and purposes. "The monthly reports are essentially background music," says Jim Carlisle, managing director of Office of the Future Inc. "They are 10 to 15 days old on arrival. If you're budgeting monthly sales of $50 million and in 15 days you've done $7 million, you need to know now—not 15 days later." With traditional computer systems, a patient analyst can sort and probe the various data bases and standard reports, draw up the comparisons, ratios, increases, and decreases, and, if familiar with the needs of the executive, produce the same kind of quality analyses offered by executive systems.

So, why should a company switch to ESS if traditional systems have worked for years? Some companies have turned to ESS because it is designed to help executives make decisions by giving them immediate access to any information that they deem helpful. ESS takes into account that one executive's needs are not necessarily another's, because analysis, reflection, and decision-making are personal arts. By contrast, little of the costly and imposing structure of corporate computing run by MIS was especially designed for, or is very useful for, making decisions. Rosabeth Moss Kanter, of the Harvard Business School, reminds us: "Information quality requires focusing on what's important, not what's available. Stored information represents potential, but is useless unless it can be actively communicated to those who need it."

Many corporate leaders have tried to do something about the shortcomings of MIS, not just for themselves but for their entire organizations. Determined not to be outflanked by the upwardly techno-mobile, some chief executives have led the charge for installing flexible information systems and convincing people to use them.

Three executives who have had positive experiences with ESS are Paul A. Allaire, president of Xerox, William D. Smithburg, chairman and chief executive officer of the Quaker Oats Company, and Finn M. W. Caspersen, chairman and chief executive officer of Beneficial Corporation. Each has for some time been using an executive support system developed by his company, getting three kinds of support from it: 1) company performance data—sales, production, earnings, budgets, and forecasts; 2) internal communications—personal correspondence, reports, and meetings; 3) environmental scanning—for news on government regulations, competition, financial and economic developments, and scientific subjects.

What follows does not pretend to be a balanced appraisal of executive support systems, but rather conveys how three executives have profited from their use.

WHY XEROX STARTED AT THE TOP

Paul Allaire began by insisting that Xerox would not cram a new system down the throats of executives, telling them, "Use it or else." In 1983, Allaire returned from Britain where he had been managing director of Rank Xerox Ltd. and took over as corporate chief of staff. To begin development of ESS, Allaire brought Kenneth Soha to headquarters from the company's plant in Rochester, New York, where he had directed the information systems group. David T. Kearns, Xerox's CEO, had asked Allaire to reduce the cost of staff work at corporate headquarters and improve its effectiveness; Allaire believed that information technology had a major role to play. He thereby became the executive sponsor of ESS, and Soha became the operational sponsor and director of the system. Allaire describes their early actions: "We hired a consultant, Jim Carlisle, and looked at the state of the art of ESS. Looking at all of the systems that we could find in operation, we concluded that none were much good for us. So we decided to build our own."

In 1983, Xerox embarked on the development of its ESS, which was to serve more than 400 people at corporate headquarters in Stamford, Connecticut. It was to link strategic planning with electronic mail, changing the way top executives communicated and worked with one another. Soha's supporting operation grew to more than a dozen people with an annual budget of $1 million by 1988.

"We decided that ESS had to be evolutionary, not forced," says Allaire, who was promoted to president of the company in 1986. "But we had to start at the top, so we had to prove how it could help [executives] do their jobs. Bill Glavin, our vice chairman, at first said: 'I came from a systems environment, but I'm not going to use the system. I'll give it to my secretary.' " Allaire continues: "We said, 'Fine, we'll put it on your secretary's desk, and if you want a printout of anything, here's how you get it.' " Glavin eventually became one of the system's biggest fans.

"Compared with people, technology is cheap, and one of my objectives every year is to reduce spending on corporate staff," Allaire says. "We have some fairly stringent targets on that." He estimates that for each of the past three years, ESS has helped reduce staff expenses at headquarters by 5 percent. "I felt sure that technology could help reduce staff, the big expense item. But we realized we couldn't just present the system and say, 'Here's the answer to your prayers, and, by the way, take a 10 percent cut in your people.' You have to provide tools and let people decide how to use them most efficiently."

One explanation for the success of ESS at Xerox is that, early on, the principal developers, especially Allaire and Soha, did not just throw money at a vague set of problems. Improving communications and the planning process were always uppermost in their minds. Allaire explains: "Right away, we realized that electronic mail was going to be a big item. Here's an illustration: We have what's called the extended management committee meeting. When I was in Britain, I had to come to the United States for these meetings once a month. The reading material I had for the meeting was supposed to come a week in advance, but sometimes it was only three days. I still needed time to analyze it and comment on it, and have my staff go over it. So I sometimes faced the prospect of reading it in a hotel room the night before the meeting, which was clearly ridiculous. Now, it's all on the ESS. The manager in Britain may actually have the materials before it's available here. The meetings themselves are more productive because the action items that result from decisions go on the system and are likely to be waiting for the British manager upon his return from the United States."

One of the first things put on the system was the management data book, which contains information on sales, customer service, personnel, and finance, including items such as currency rates. Xerox ran into a stumbling block, however, with the data book. Although the data was on the system, executives had to proceed through it page by page, just as with a book. They had to conform their thinking to the structure of the data book, which was the opposite of what Allaire wanted ESS to do. Allaire reports a big breakthrough, just out and not yet generally available, that eliminates this structural problem. "Now, if I'm looking at a profit-and-loss statement and want to zero in on, say, a sales-expense item, I can point with the mouse and get more detail, perhaps geographical or historical, and plot it on a graph. I can look at it any way I want, rather than have a staff person tell me what I should be looking for. I can take a trend that concerns me, bring it up on the screen, put a note on it, and ask my marketing people, 'What's going on here?'"

Part of the pleasure of being president of a company must be to be able to pick up the phone and get anyone on the other end. Is Allaire more likely to use the system, instead of buzzing someone for the information? "Oh yes! In the past, one of the frustrations of managing has been that when you know you need some information and call someone—and we still do—they ask how soon you need the information. I say, 'Right away,' and they say, 'You'll have it this afternoon.' Now that's pretty responsive. But I find that, when you're working on a project this morning and in the afternoon you're out with a customer, then when you return to the office and get the information, you may end up asking yourself, 'What the heck was I thinking of when I asked for this?' So, ESS allows you to work on a project or a decision, complete it right away, and be less reliant on staff support. You have flatter lines of control, and you can be more effective because you have the information you need. You can be more creative as well."

How often Allaire turns to ESS depends on the job at hand. "The fact that it isn't turned on doesn't mean it isn't working," he says. "My secretary's system is on all the time, and she can pick up anything urgent for me. I would say that some days I may not use it at all, but other days I use it most of the day."

Strategic planning at Xerox turned out to be one of the applications of ESS that got executives involved because it performed an essential task better. Shortly after ESS development began, Xerox's new resource management statement (essentially, a five-page summary of each business unit's plan) was put on the system. David Bliss, as executive in Xerox's corporate-strategy office, said that Allaire asked his operation to find a way to improve the planning process and reduce the time spent on it. An obvious target was the different formats each business-unit manager used to present the unit's plans. This made it difficult to compare one plan with another and kept senior executives scrambling to understand the details of each plan (Kenneth Soha describes this as the executives having to play on each unit's home field).

Four of the five pages of the new computer-based planning format consist of a summary of a unit's plan, such as projected sales and earnings, while the final page is reserved for senior management to respond to the plan with decisions or comments. Top management receives the plans on the ESS for a "prereading" three to five days before a scheduled meeting. The pertinent information is greatly condensed, and senior executives can easily compare one plan with another because of the consistent format.

Paul Allaire also developed the business priority list, a 15-item list used by those who report to him. The list keeps Allaire's people focused on important programs and provides progress reports. It is used to set agendas for meetings and is the basis of the direct-action list that prioritizes short-term tasks. Allaire reflects: "The list would be much harder without the ESS. The system permits us to store the items on the list in different ways and follow deadlines. Could we do it without the system? Well, we didn't. It also helps us to discipline ourselves and document meetings immediately."

What has been the impact of ESS on meetings? "I'm not sure we have fewer meetings, but they are more productive," Allaire says. "If we feel that an issue can be decided on material already available, we don't have a meeting. If more information is needed, it's available before the meeting. The result is that we very rarely have a meeting at which we don't have enough information to make a decision."

One benefit of ESS is that when executives must travel they can still use it, wherever they are. "When you travel, it is very valuable," agrees Allaire. "If I need a document, I can tell my administrative assistant and have it sent. The bad part is that you can't hide. People can get messages to you anywhere! I don't use it much at home, frankly. I live only 10 minutes away from the office, and I have to go through a modem to reach the office system. So, if I'm going to work on something, I'll just come in."

The easy flow of information from person to person is another benefit of ESS. But confidentiality of communications is obviously necessary, too—especially at the senior-executive level. ESS has security safeguards to protect that confidentiality. At Xerox, "need to know" is still invoked, and executives see essentially what their bosses want them to see. Nevertheless, since those who report to Allaire are on his system and thus receive similar information, was he worried that he might be second-guessed, perhaps limiting his freedom to make decisions?

"No, that doesn't bother me at all," he replies. "I'm glad to have the information, some that I didn't have before. People have more confidence in the decisions we make, confidence that the decision-makers are using relevant information and aren't up there in an ivory tower, not knowing what's going on in the world."

VISION AND KNOWLEDGE AT QUAKER OATS

"It didn't take any particularly creative thought to realize that executives can enhance their information flow in a way that enhances their decision-making," explains William Smithburg, CEO at Quaker Oats. "All businesses live and die with information, and historically, it's been in a stack of paper somewhere and in files and books."

Smithburg began his initiation into computers in 1982 when he asked that a PC be installed in his office and hooked up to the Dow Jones Service and The Source (an on-line public-access company offering an array of computer data bases and bulletin boards). But, he says, "it eventually took several years to master the idea of computerizing all the information that used to come into our offices on paper. We wanted it in a more digestible and accessible form. I wanted access to all the information without picking up the phone to call my controller. The problem is that the executive wants to describe the end result, 'Give me this, give me that,' rather than delving into the process, which is really what makes it productive in the end."

Smithburg continues: "I remember when one of my business-unit executives came into my office, saw my PC, and asked what I did with it. I proceeded to pull up all kinds of information on his operation, and he was stunned. He rushed back to his information-systems people and said, 'Do you realize what Smithburg has in his office, on his computer? I've got to have the same thing!' Actually, there has been a productive migration of systems, both up and down, within the company."

Using the system didn't come easy at first, Smithburg says. "The main source of slowness was that I had to get up to speed on what I needed. And information systems had to understand better what executives need from a data base; they needed to learn how executives use information to make decisions. The first year or so, my use of the PC was not particularly successful, because all I really used it for was accessing Dow Jones and similar things—valuable, but not worth the cost of putting it in my office. So we needed more. An information-systems person would say, 'Okay, you draw a chart and show us what you want and we'll get it in that box.' But that's not what you want. Then someone said, 'Why don't we ask planning to see what kind of information they want, and maybe we can enhance the flow from them to you.'

"That proved to be very beneficial. The ESS didn't really click until one or two people in information systems clearly understood my personal operating style and what I needed for decision-making. Now they are very client oriented. They say, 'Tell us how you use information and make decisions, and we'll get you a product.' "

An article in *Advertising Age* noted that one of Quaker Oats' strengths was its ability to adapt to change in the marketplace. Frank Morgan, the president, was quoted as saying that Smithburg brought a visionary quality. Had ESS contributed? "I think so," Smithburg says. "I use ESS more for environmental scanning than for management and control. A vision for the future requires knowledge of the present and the recent past, and executives need to be able to get that at will. In days of drought in farming areas, for example, I can get into the ESS and find agricultural information quickly that will influence our costs for raw materials."

With ESS, Smithburg and other senior executives can dig deeply into marketing data to check into, say, sales of Quaker Extra cereal versus sales of Total Oats, a competitor's product. "Sometimes you just feel like wading into the data," Smithburg says. His purpose, however, is to improve his own decisions, not to second-guess another department's. "I might look at more data because curiosity gets the better of me, but not because I want to get involved in managing a business that others run. Quite often I go back and check my assumptions on the ESS, because I can't remember everything I see. I'll look to see if I'm correct and check on a few hunches."

ESS offers two valuable features: compression and freshness of information. Which means the most to Smithburg? "Freshness is important," he replies, "especially for financial data. But for me, compression is the plus. It really helps me focus on the broad issues."

ESS allows the creation and use of graphs to express data visually. Yet, although research has shown that use of graphs instead of numbers increases comprehension, it means a shift in habits for many executives. "Graphs are fine for presentations, but I don't use them on my computer much," Smithburg says. "I know what I'm looking for, and I get the numbers. When I was a brand manager I came up with presentations called super charts. These had everything on them: market shares, advertising expenses, advertising campaigns, and so on. Now I can get that completeness using ESS."

Overall, Smithburg thinks ESS has improved his productivity. "I pick up the phone less, a lot less, than I used to. There are times when you're curious about what's happening, but you don't want to meddle. When important people are freed from this, they can do the more valuable diagnostic work. It makes them more productive. I may be working at home on Sunday night preparing for our management committee meeting on Monday, and I need to check some backup material on products. If I couldn't access my ESS, I would have to phone my controller at home. The vast majority of my time is spent communicating, in meetings, at lunches and breakfasts, on the telephone. It's not reflection time or analysis time. The best time for thinking is at home."

Smithburg agrees that ESS can affect working relationships. "I view the company not as a holding company but an operating entity in which senior executives understand the businesses they run," he says. "I expect them to know what is going on. When I prepare for a meeting, if I can access the right information, I can be more responsive to the upward flow of communications. The presenters see executives who are well informed and up-to-date."

Business leaders must have persuasive powers. Does ESS diminish the need to persuade—do the numbers themselves create agreement? "We used to say that you could make data talk," Smithburg replies. "But there's good data and bad data. The difference now is that we are all looking at the same numbers and the emphasis is on analysis and decision-making. In effect, the data can persuade because they are analyzed well."

Smithburg thinks better information is a competitive asset. "We now ask ourselves: 'Are we competitive with our information systems?' Twenty-five years ago we wouldn't have asked that. It's important now because it is a real asset. I can't pinpoint a decision for which I am sure ESS made a contribution. But I'm sure there are countless examples of when it has. It's become part of our culture. Like the car phone, I don't know how we ever lived without it. ESS is not magic, not a black box, but in general it has exceeded my expectations."

Business has come under heavy criticism for concentrating unduly on the short term, and ESS would seem to make that even easier, but Smithburg doesn't place the blame on the computers. "Business has been criticized for this. Like any fundamental contribution, computers have a dark side, and overemphasis on data has been one result. The information churned out by securities firms can be awesome, and even inhibiting. I was once in a meeting at a securities firm where they had all kinds of computers and began to throw all kinds of data on the screen. It was almost too much. It was approaching 'analysis-paralysis.' But you can't blame the computers, they just do what they're told."

Smithburg thinks the prospects for ESS are very bright. The better that senior executives understand the systems, and the better information systems understand the executives, he says, the better they can work together. "It's really an investment decision. You have to get what's useful and necessary, not pie in the sky," he says. "If you aren't careful, the expenses can go through the roof. You don't need a Rolls Royce to go to the grocery store. I can't overemphasize how necessary prioritizing is to get what you really want and need. It's very hard, very demanding work to do that."

A MILLION-DOLLAR SAVINGS AT BENEFICIAL

"If I get a hard copy of a memo, I send it back. I get 100 to 120 pieces of mail a day, nearly all of it electronic."

Finn Caspersen, the CEO at Beneficial, explains why neither "trickledown" nor "trickleup" ESS implementation was acceptable to him and why personal use of ESS by all of the company's executives is essential to make it work. "The system identifies whether the manager or the secretary answers my memos," says Caspersen. "I simply remind the sender that if I can trouble myself to send a memo, they can trouble themselves to answer it personally. That usually does the trick."

Caspersen admits that initially he underestimated the usefulness of ESS. "I thought it would be a nice tool to contain secretarial costs, but it has now got to the point that I don't think we could operate without it," he says. "I recently came into the office and the computer system was down between 7 and 8 A.M. That was not acceptable to me. You have to educate your systems people that downtime is unacceptable. Three hundred people depend on that system. Now someone comes in at 6 to be sure it's working.

"The system is really just a conduit for information. I don't type 'what-if' scenarios in the wee hours of the morning, and I don't do much primary analysis. The CEO's job is to maintain communication with individuals in the company, move decisions through committees or meetings in a timely fashion, and implement decisions. If I want to ask the senior-management committee for their advice, I only have to type 'SM' on my terminal, type the question, and out it goes to 18 people. I can do the same thing for the board of directors. This has really speeded up communications. Reliability and accuracy have grown tremendously. In only two instances in five years can I remember when a message I sent didn't reach the person intended, and that might have been my fault. I'm not sure."

Outside the office, the system can also be helpful. But Caspersen notes, "I have used the system traveling, and frankly, I've had problems with it. I used a lap-top computer and modem and found it hard to use in hotel rooms. The phone lines are too noisy and sometimes hard to connect. I don't use it that way anymore; I just call my secretary. I do have the ESS in my vacation home and have a dedicated phone line for that, it works fine. And when I visit other Beneficial offices, I often log onto the system."

Users claim that the rewards of networking go far beyond sending an electronic reminder of when the next meeting is going to take place. "ESS is useful in unanticipated ways," says Caspersen. "Let's suppose a broker calls in and says, 'I have a block of 100,000 shares of stock for sale. Would you like to buy it?' There might be five or six people in the company who would be interested. But reaching them by telephone could take half an hour. With electronic mail, we have the answer for the broker almost instantaneously."

Has ESS changed the way companies operate, the way they organize or structure their important functions? In many instances, it has simply automated activities, but in others it has been more fundamental. Caspersen thinks the latter applies to Beneficial. "I do think it has changed the way we do business. The system has an ingrained prejudice against long-winded memos and works best with terse, data-filled content. It has increased our executives' productivity tremendously. Most of them have the system at home, and as a result, they often work in the evening and on weekends. Most of the executives will be on-line with the system at least once each weekend. They can access files and communicate with other executives, who, if you tried to reach by phone, might not be there to receive the call."

The pace of change in today's world has become a cliché, but Caspersen sees a genuine need to make decisions faster "because competitors are making faster decisions." He continues: "The pace of new-product introductions is faster and profit margins are narrower, so the margin of error is smaller. As your business matures, your profit margins can go down and you have to make better decisions. You just can't afford to be the last to respond to important changes. We use the Lexis and Nexis on-line data bases for monitoring changes that can affect us. Lexis is for the legal department, and Nexis is for general news."

Executives invest heavily in meetings, some of which are unproductive. Beneficial uses ESS to eliminate some of the wasted time. "Meetings are more effective because of ESS," says Caspersen. "We have a meeting scheduling system that works well. If you want a meeting with six people who must attend and nine others who it would be nice if they attended, the system will round up their schedules and indicate the date. Not only can all the documents necessary for a decision at a meeting be prepared and distributed, you can tell if each person attending has received the material. You can also choose areas in which you may sacrifice some of the give-and-take of a meeting to make a quicker decision. For instance, I can send out a memo to six people and ask for their thoughts. All respond, and I make the decision. If someone objects, they can append it to the request and then we may have to have a meeting. Obviously, some of the meetings become unnecessary."

Some companies note "soft-dollar" benefits from ESS—such as nonmeasurable increases in the effectiveness and professionalism of their exectutives—but cannot easily document "hard-dollar" savings. Caspersen believes Beneficial realizes real savings. "We have actually decreased the number of secretaries. We had Deloitte Haskins & Sells do a study for us, and they found that there was a $1 million savings in the first year that the system was in operation and a nine-month payback for the cost of the equipment. Now, I'm not sure if that is accurate, and we have spent more since, but I'm sure the system is helpful."

Beneficial is sufficiently convinced of the value of ESS to invest more money. "We are building a new system called Bencom III," Caspersen explains, "which will change the way we do business throughout the company. Not only will it make the field locations more efficient, but by pushing a button, I can inquire about the productivity of a single office if I need to."

Caspersen realizes that since others see a lot of his memos and decisions he is, to an extent, working in a fishbowl. But he sees a brighter side to this. "Some people may want to hide behind the statement that 'I have superior information that you don't have.' But I don't operate that way. I think it's an advantage for all to see the data that decisions are based on. I'd rather have people knock holes in my argument, and if you make a mistake, you make a mistake. The more people that have a chance to speak their piece, the less likely you are to make a wrong decision."

Is old-fashioned persuasion no longer necessary? Not according to Caspersen. "The facts alone won't make the decision or carry it out," he says. "People have to be motivated. As CEO, you have the power to send out a memo to 20 people and say, 'Do this,' and then you can relax and read the *Wall Street Journal.* But if you know someone has a tough job to meet a deadline, you don't just demand cooperation, you call and say it's important and, 'How can I help if you need it?' I find that you really have to lean over backward to avoid saying something in a cold, impersonal way because the system makes it so easy to do that."

Given Caspersen's ESS experience at Beneficial, what would he say to fellow CEO's thinking of acquiring an ESS? "I would tell them it's like getting another three or four secretaries, each with 20 years' experience, and a couple of MBA's thrown in. It's just great. I must admit that I cheated initially, in order to be able to lead and be experienced. I didn't want to look like a fool using it and making blunders. I had a system installed at home three months ahead of the others and worked on it every night until I felt comfortable with it."

If he could have known the benefits of the system beforehand, Caspersen says he would have pushed his managers to adopt the system even faster. "I would be very strict about getting all to use it and insisting that executives use it, not just their secretaries. You don't have to type, I don't type that well. I still believe that it must be done from the top down. There will always be a few who can't change—a secretary who finds long-standing methods comfortable and can't adapt, the executive who deigns not to type on a keyboard. It pays to find that out early rather than several years later. It is absolutely a leadership issue from the CEO on down.

"Those who kept an open mind learned to use it effectively, even if they were at first opposed to it. There's no place for the executive who calls his secretary, presents the document to her, she bows twice, retires, and prepares it. Frankly, we lost a few people who couldn't change, and it's just as well. Although there was both surprising acceptance from some quarters and surprising rejection from others, overall, it went better than I hoped. But it does require firmness. It's an open-and-shut case. There's a natural ambiguity about anything new, but I would probably push it faster if I had it to do again."

CEO-COMPATIBLE SYSTEMS

For executives such as Caspersen, Smithburg, and Allaire, ESS undoubtedly works. But how transferable are their personal and company experiences to others? The answer, some say, lies not just in the technology available or the executives' ability to describe their work and needs, but deeper in the company, in its information systems. To satisfy their ordinary computing requirements, companies have developed systems and attitudes that create inflexible structures, enforce conformity, and are intolerant of ambiguity. These are far from ideal qualities in an ESS. The work of top executives is fairly unstructured and nonroutine; facts are necessary but not sufficient to make good decisions. In addition, a lot of good ESS software is sold by outside vendors such as Execucom, Comshare, Inc., and Pilot Executive Software, which can lead to the not-invented-here syndrome.

Essentially, information systems should see ESS development not as catering to the personal whims of top management but as a means of enhancing their work, to the benefit of the whole company. Giving senior executives the information they need can have greater impact than automating the work of several hundred people below them. Top executives don't want their work to be easier—they thrive on difficulty. But they do want to be more effective, and ESS offers possibilities for doing that.

For some firms, the improved communications from ESS justifies use of the system. It's much harder to prove that better top-level decisions result. In the rarified realm of decision-making, art overshadows science. ESS may not change that. Do shortcomings of current ESS and their rate of improvement justify reluctance to use them now? Probably not.

QUESTIONS

1. What were some of the keys to EIS success at Xerox?
2. William Smithburg at Quaker Oats feels that the EIS has improved his personal productivity. What is the basis for this statement?
3. Finn Caspersen at Beneficial indicates that the EIS has changed the way the company operates. What changes has the EIS brought about?
4. What similarities and differences are there in the EIS experiences at Xerox, Quaker Oats, and Beneficial?

PART 6

Group Decision
Support Systems

Group decision support systems (GDSS) are the newest of the computer-based applications to support decision making. These systems are designed to provide computer support for groups of people who work together on joint endeavors. Because they are often used for purposes other than supporting decision making, they are sometimes referred to as group support systems, collaborative work support systems, or groupware. Actual applications of this technology include strategic planning sessions, focus groups, determining information requirements, and setting budgets.

GDSS products are just now moving from the concept and research-and-development phases and finding their way into the marketplace and business organizations. The five readings in this part of the book should give you a good understanding of what GDSS are, what has been learned about them to date, how they are currently being used, and what their future potential is.

Gerardine DeSanctis and Brent Gallupe, in "Group Decision Support Systems: A New Frontier" (Reading 19), provide an overview of GDSS. They discuss what a GDSS is, the technology used to create it, four scenarios that show how a GDSS capability can be delivered, and design and implementation issues.

Paul Gray and Jay Nunamaker, in "Group Decision Support Systems" (Reading 20), provide a second look at GDSS. After giving background information on GDSS, they consider a specific type of GDSS environment, the decision room, a special facility for GDSS sessions. They describe several decision rooms in current use and what we are learning about this new approach to supporting group activities.

A large American corporation (Boeing) has recently completed a study of the business benefits from using group support technology. Brad Post, in "Building the Business Case for Group Support Technology" (Reading 21), describes this comprehensive evaluation. He covers the growing importance of groups in organizations, the GDSS used (TeamFocus), the process employed to evaluate the technology, the evaluation parameters used, and the results. The findings strongly document the business benefits from using group support technology.

A small but growing number of companies have used GDSS products. David Kirkpatrick, in "Here Comes the Payoff From PCs" (Reading 22), describes how groupware can affect group behavior, the major groupware products that are currently available, specific uses of groupware in companies, and where group support technology is likely to go in the future. The end result is an up-to-date description of what is taking place in organizations in regard to groupware.

Robert Johansen, in "Groupware: Future Directions and Wild Cards" (Reading 23), provides his thinking about the future of groupware. He divides his predictions into "sure things," "probable" developments, and "wild cards," which are low or unknown probability events.

19

GROUP DECISION SUPPORT SYSTEMS: A NEW FRONTIER

*Gerardine DeSanctis,
Brent Gallupe*

INTRODUCTION

During the past decade, much attention has been given to the area of decision support systems by both industry and academia. The concept of a DSS as originally articulated by Gerrity (1971) involves "an effective blend of human intelligence, information technology, and software which interact closely to solve complex problems." In theory this means that either an individual or a group of decision makers might benefit from a DSS. In practice, however, most systems have been designed for use by single decision makers. Although a DSS operating in a mainframe or micro computer environment might be available to many users simultaneously, the software itself accommodates the individual user faced with a particular decision for which he or she is responsible. Support of the individual decision maker undoubtedly is important for effective managerial functioning, but

Gerardine DeSanctis and Brent Gallupe, "Group Decision Support Systems: A New Frontier," *DATABASE*, Winter 1985.

many organizational decisions are made by groups of people, particularly at the strategic or executive level. Moreover, as organizations become increasingly complex, fewer decisions are made by single individuals (Gannon, 1979). Responsibility for organizational actions becomes diffused, resulting in more decision making that involves input from two or more individuals. These group decisions may also benefit from support by a computer-based information system.

A few researchers have acknowledged the need for a group-level focus in DSS (e.g., Hackathorn & Keen, 1981; Keen, 1984; Turoff & Hiltz, 1982). Huber (1984) recently presented some ideas regarding the design of information systems to support electronic meetings. But additional thought must be given to this perspective, particularly with regard to the definition of group decision support and issues related to the design and implementation of computer-based systems for use by groups. The purpose of this paper is to present a conceptual foundation for research and development of decision support systems for group-level decision making. We begin by defining the concept of group decision support systems (GDSS) and outlining the characteristics of these systems. Fundamental features of GDSS technology, including both hardware and software aspects, are described. Four "scenarios," or types of group DSS environments, are proposed. Finally, some specific questions in need of investigation by researchers are identified.

WHAT IS A *GDSS?*

The concept of a "decision support system" has been widely discussed in the MIS literature. Although various definitions have been proposed, there appears to be general agreement that a DSS is an interactive computer-based system which facilitates solution of unstructured problems (Bonczek, Holsapple, & Whinston, 1979; Neumann & Hadass, 1980; Sprague, 1980; Vazsonyi, 1978). The concept of "group decision support" builds on the now well-known idea of a DSS. A group decision support system (GDSS) is an interactive computer-based system which facilitates solution of unstructured problems by a set of decision makers working together as a group. Components of a GDSS include hardware, software, people, and procedures. These components are arranged to support a group of people, usually in the context of a decision-related meeting (Huber, 1984). Important characteristics of a GDSS can be summarized as follows:

1. The GDSS is a specially designed system, not merely a configuration of already existing system components.
2. A GDSS is designed with the goal of supporting groups of decision-makers in their work. As such, the GDSS should improve the decision making process and/or decision outcomes of groups over that which would occur if the GDSS were not present.
3. A GDSS is easy to learn and easy to use. It accommodates users with varying levels of knowledge regarding computing and decision support.
4. The GDSS may be "specific" (designed for one type, or class, of problems) or "general" (designed for a variety of group-level organizational decisions).

5. The GDSS contains built-in mechanisms which discourage development of negative group behaviors, such as destructive conflict, miscommunication, or "group-think."

The definition of GDSS is quite broad and, therefore, can apply to a variety of group decision situations, including committees, review panels, task forces, executive/board meetings, remote workers, and so forth. Appropriate settings for a GDSS range from an executive group meeting which occurs in a single location for the purpose of considering a specific problem (such as a merger/acquisition decision), to a sales managers' meeting held via telecommunications channels for the purpose of considering a variety of problems (such as hiring of sales representatives, product offerings, and sales call schedules). Because the contexts of group decision making vary so greatly, it is useful to think of a GDSS in terms of the common "group" activities which it supports. The basic activities which occur in any group and which, therefore, are in need of computer-based support are: information retrieval, information sharing, and information use (Huber, 1984). *Information retrieval* includes selection of data values from an existing database, as well as simple retrieval of information (including attitudes, opinions, and informal observations) from other group members. *Information sharing* refers to the display of data to the total group on a viewing screen, or sending of data to selected group members' terminal sites for viewing. *Information use* involves the application of software technology (such as modeling packages or specific application programs), procedures, and group problem-solving techniques to data for the purpose of reaching a group decision.

THE TECHNOLOGY OF *GDSS*

A pictorial representative of a typical GDSS is shown in Figure 19.1. In this generalized model, a group of decision makers has access to a data base, a model base, and GDSS applications software during the course of a decision-related meeting. There is at least one computer processor, one input/output device, and one viewing screen. A "group facilitator" coordinates the group's use of the technology, and there is a flexible, friendly user-interface language available for use by the facilitator or each group member. As we shall see later, many different configurations of a GDSS are possible. However, the basic components of any GDSS include hardware, software, people, and procedures. Each of these components is now considered in some detail.

Hardware

Regardless of the specific decision situation, the group as a whole, or each member, must be able to access a computer processor and display information. The minimal hardware requirements of the system include: an input/output device, a processor, a communication line between the I/O device and the processor, and either a common viewing screen or individual monitors for use in displaying information to the group. More sophisticated systems may contain I/O terminals or desktop computers for each group member, several central processors, long-distance communications equipment, and several large viewing

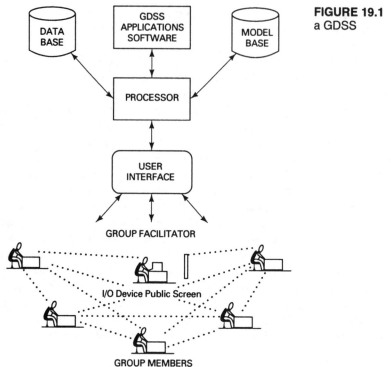

FIGURE 19.1   A Model of a GDSS

screens. A design which allows each participant to work independently of the others, to publicly demonstrate personal work, and to see the work of other individuals and the group as a whole is preferred. Since "keyboarding" is a skill not totally accepted by managerial personnel in organizations, touch-sensitive screens or a facility to input handwritten communication (such as a graphics tablet) or voice communication may be desirable. Preferably, the viewing screen or monitors should be capable of displaying graphics and text, and should have color as well. Graphics can be used to summarize data or to display voting information in the group; color can be used to add attention value to the visuals or text which are displayed (Tullis, 1981). If a public viewing screen is used, it should be large enough to be seen by all members of the group. The screen would facilitate group discussion and take the place of flipchart or blackboard. It also could be used for video conferencing between subgroups in dispersed locations.

The amount of processing power necessary to support group decision making depends on the software being used, the number of members in the group, and the extent to which networking or teleconferencing is used. If the group members have microcomputers or workstations, then central processing can be used to manage communication among them and to store common databases, model bases, or applications software. With regard to communications, the requirements vary according to the setting in which the GDSS is used. In the confines of the traditional meeting room, hardwire links between an I/O device, a central processor, and display monitors or the public screen may be all that is necessary; more elaborate configurations might link microcomputers with one another and perhaps a central processor. For dispersed groups, a local area network, telephone lines, satellite, or microwave relay may be required to allow group members to communicate with one another. Electronic mail, computer conferencing, audio and video conferencing might also be integrated into the GDSS environment.

Software

The software components of the GDSS include a database, a model base, specialized application program(s) to be used by the group, and an easy-to-use, flexible user interface. Some highly specific GDSS systems may not require a database; for example, those that merely collect, organize, and communicate members' opinions about a problem. However, most sophisticated systems will include databases, along with model bases, very high-level languages for program writing, and interfaces with standard managerial-level software (graphics, statistical/OR packages, spreadsheets, etc.). The GDSS software may or may not interface with individual DSS software.

The most distinguishing technological component of the GDSS is specially-developed applications software that supports the group in the decision process. The precise features of this software will vary extensively but may include the following:

Basic Features

- Text and data file creation, modification, and storage for group members
- Word processing for text editing and formatting
- Learning facilities for naive GDSS users
- On-line "help" facilities
- Worksheets, spreadsheets, decision trees, and other means of graphically displaying numbers and text
- State-of-the-art database management which can handle queries from all participants, create subschemas as necessary for each participant, control access to public, or corporate, databases, etc.

Group Features

- Numerical and graphical summarization of group members' ideas and votes
- Menus which prompt for input of text, data, or votes by group members
- Program(s) for specialized group procedures, such as calculation of weights for decision alternatives; anonymous recording of ideas; formal selection of a group leader; progressive rounds of voting toward consensus-building; or elimination of redundant input during brainstorming
- Method of analyzing prior group interactions and judgments
- Text and data transmission among the group members, between the group members and the facilitator, and between the group members and a central computer processor

The GDSS software may be designed to support a specific decision or a class of decisions. In some cases the software will be built around a particular decision-making technique, while in other cases it will be more generalized. At the present time few GDSS software products are available. A great deal of development effort is needed before organizations will have a choice of systems for use in group decision making.

People

The "people" component of the GDSS includes the group members and a "group facilitator" who is responsible for the smooth operation of the GDSS technology when it is in use. The facilitator's role is a flexible one. He or she may be present at all group meetings and serve as the group's "chauffeur," operating the GDSS hardware and software and displaying requested information to the group as needed. On the other hand, the facilitator may be physically located in the MIS department or information center and act only on an on-call basis when the group experiences difficulties in using the technology. When the GDSS is first installed this person can be expected to be relied upon quite heavily to coordinate the group's activities and serve as the interface between the group and the technology. As group members become familiar with the technology and its use in their work, the facilitator's responsibilities may diminish, or even be eliminated.

Procedures

The final component of the GDSS consists of procedures which enable ease of operation and effective use of the technology by group members. These procedures may apply only to the operation of the hardware and software, or they may extend to include rules regarding verbal discussion among members and the flow of events during a group meeting. In the latter case, the GDSS may be designed to accommodate a specific group decision-making technique, such as the nominal group technique (Delbecq & Van de Ven, 1974), brainstorming (Osborn, 1957), the Delphi method (Dalkey, 1972), or social judgment analysis (Cook & Hammond, 1982).

CATEGORIES OF *GDSS*: 4 SCENARIOS

An overview of the types of support systems which are needed for group decision making in organizations is presented in Figure 19.2. This framework emphasizes that the purpose and configuration of a GDSS will vary according to the duration of the decision-making session and the degree of physical proximity of group members. The cells that are shown should *not* be considered as independent of one another but as ends of two continua.

Scenario 1—Decision Room   The first scenario is similar to Gray's "Decision Room" (1981) and may be thought of as the electronic equivalent to the traditional meeting. The organization sets up a room (much like a boardroom) with special facili-

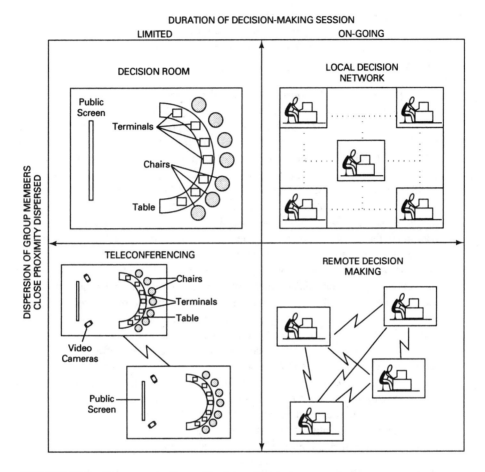

FIGURE 19.2 Framework: Group Decision Support

ties to support group decision making. Each participant is seated around a horseshoe-shaped desk facing a large screen. In a very simple configuration of a GDSS, only the group facilitator would directly interact with the computer. A more typical design would have a display monitor and terminal in front of each participant. Communications may be transmitted verbally or via computer messaging. The public display screen is used to enumerate ideas and to summarize and analyze data. Face-to-face verbal interaction combines with technology-imposed formalization to make the decision meeting more effective and efficient.

To illustrate this type of GDSS, consider a group of high-level managers who must decide on a marketing mix for the coming year. A variety of decision making approaches could be used, such as ordinary group process or nominal group technique, but essentially the process would involve using the GDSS to show the decision makers the current situation in terms of markets and finances, etc., and to facilitate the generation and evaluation of ideas. There is continual interaction among group members, both verbally and through the communication network. Modeling software is used which is capable of being changed to adapt to the group's view of the problem. A number of alternative marketing mix strategies are tested via models and discussed before a specific strategy is selected.

Scenario 2—Local Decision Network The GDSS may take on a somewhat different configuration in a setting in which a fixed group of decision makers, who work in close proximity to one another, must deal with certain problems on a regular basis. Rather than establishing a permanent "decision room" for group meetings, a "Local Decision Network" (LDN) could be developed to support group members as they work in their individual offices. Each decision maker would have a workstation, or what Dickson (1983) refers to as a "managerial support facility," located on their desk or worktable. A central processor would store common GDSS software and databases, and a local area network would provide member-to-member and member-to-central-processor communication. In the LDN environment, group participants communicate via electronic messaging on the local area network. They can access common and private databases or DSS software as required, and view a "public screen" on their own CRT as needed. Decision makers engage in their day-to-day work and set up "group meetings" or conferences as needed. The approach offers greater flexibility in that the one-place/one-time constraint of scenario 1 is removed. There is the disadvantage of removing face-to-face communication, but face-to-face meetings could be held when necessary.

As an example, consider a scenario found at the head offices of a large insurance company where decisions regarding corporate investments must be made on an ongoing basis. Financial managers, investment managers, and analysts are linked together in a local network that enables them to jointly make decisions in an interactive mode. GDSS software enables the group to analyze investments through the use of in-house investment models. The interactive nature of this "local decision network" provides group members with information on what the others are doing.

Scenario 3—Teleconferencing A third type of GDSS is needed for groups whose members are geographically distant from one another but who nevertheless must come together for the purpose of making a decision. In this case two or more decision rooms are connected together by visual and/or communication facilities. For example, suppose that Company X, a large computer vendor with offices throughout the world, has decision rooms located in several major cities. Using teleconferencing technology, meetings could be arranged so that decision making could occur without all of the participants having to be in a single location. The approach is essentially the same as in scenario 1 except that teleconferencing is used to supplement the communication component of the GDSS. Reduced travel costs (time, money, productivity loss), and flexibility in terms of time and duration of holding a meeting are advantages.

Scenario 4—Remote Decision Making The fourth scenario is not yet commonplace but offers possibilities for the near future. Here there is uninterrupted communication between remote "decision stations" in a geographically dispersed organization which has a fixed group of people who must regularly make joint decisions. Part of the problem with scenario 3 is that meetings must be scheduled and coordinated in order to take place. This scenario, along with scenario 2, removes the constraint of meeting location and addresses the needs of decision makers who must work together on a regular basis.

An example of this scenario is a project development team of, say, 5 members which is dispersed in many parts of the country due to facilities at each location (or for whatever reasons that make it inappropriate to bring them all together in one place). Suppose that any changes made by one member will affect other members, and that a group decision is necessary before changes are made. In a remote decision making network, one group member could send a message to the CRT or workstation screens of the other members noting that a decision session is scheduled in, say, 10 minutes. All members are then informed of the problem and decisions to be made. A structured decision technique can be used by the group or a special GDSS application program may aid in the group decision. A long distance communication system, using telephone, microwave, or satellite transmission, would provide communication among the group participants. Eventually, a decision is made by some voting scheme and each member notes the changes that must be made to his or her part of the project.

Summary

This section has presented a framework for categorizing group decision support systems. The precise configuration of a GDSS will vary considerably depending on the type of problem to be solved and the organizational context in which the problem is addressed. Nevertheless, there are design and implementation issues which are common to all categories of GDSS. Several of these are considered in the next section.

DESIGN AND IMPLEMENTATION ISSUES

Existing research on the dynamics of group decision making (Thibaut & Kelley, 1959; Cartwright & Zander, 1968; Bennis & Shepard, 1963; Hackman & Morris, 1975; Shaw, 1971; Guzzo, 1982) has several implications for the design and use of GDSS. Three design implications drawn from the group dynamics literature are first discussed, followed by a summary of implementation options available for GDSS.

First, *an objective of GDSS should be to encourage the active participation of all group members.* An overwhelming amount of research on groups indicates that the major barrier to effective group decision making is any condition which prevents the free expression of ideas in a group (Janis, 1972; Kolasa, 1975; Van de Ven & Delbecq, 1974). A number of events may lead to this problem. For example, group members may feel a strong pressure to conform, thus stifling the input of non-conforming ideas to the decision process, or certain members may regard other members as more competent or higher in status than they are (Hoffman, 1965). The extent to which group members are active in the group is also affected by the group's initial evaluation of the contributions of various members. People whose ideas are initially accepted by the group are likely to increase their participation, while those whose suggestions are rejected may withdraw from the discussion (Oakes et al., 1960; Pepinsky et al., 1958). The implication here is that a computer-based information system should be configured to facilitate group members' communication while reducing bias and prejudice, to enhance participation of all group members. An important feature of a GDSS may be the facility of allowing anonymous input and evaluation of ideas. In addition, GDSS software might have features that actively encourage group members to voice dissident opinions or play a "devil's advocate" role before a critical decision is made.

Second, *special accommodations are needed for groups who have no prior experience working together.* In groups that have never worked together before, members may feel uncertain about the exact goals of the group or their individual responsibilities and expectations. Newly-formed groups usually lack cohesion and a structure for operating (Klein & Ritti, 1980). The GDSS should support the group during the initial phases of group formation. For example, the group meeting room can be set up so that members are in a circle or semi-circle, facing one another. Terminals or other hardware should not obstruct their view or ability to easily interact verbally with one another. Special software might be used to query members on their expectations of how the group should function, and to feedback points of agreement and disagreement among members.

Third, *a useful feature of a GDSS would be to aid high-level management in selecting people to serve as group members for a given decision or problem.* All other things being equal, the quality of a decision made by a group is a function of the skills, abilities, and organizational status of the individual group members (Hoffman, 1965). Data from a human resource information system, or other similar source, could be used along with an appropriate model or selection criteria, to help structure the task of choosing people to serve on committees, boards, panels, or task forces.

Extensive developmental work is needed before decision support systems for groups become widely available and useful to organizations. At the present time only a handful of systems have been developed for in-house use by organizations or are available for purchase (Kraemer & King, 1984). Because of their relative novelty, the importance of careful pilot testing of these systems cannot be overemphasized. Systems which fail to provide useful, easy-to-use facilities will quickly result in negative attitudes toward GDSS on the part of users. The role of attitudes in determining system success has been well documented (DeSanctis, 1984; Lucas, 1975; Robey, 1979; Swanson, 1974). We can anticipate that unrealistic expectations or frustrating experiences with GDSS on the part of even a few individuals could result in negative attitudes and poor use of these systems by decision-making groups.

With regard to installation, three options are possible (Huber, 1984): (1) install the system permanently at the user site; (2) rent the system on an on-call basis from the vendor; and (3) access the system remotely from the vendor site. Option 3 may be the best alternative today since option 1 is very costly and option 2 can be impractical. In years to come, however, option 1 may be the installation method of choice as GDSS systems become more sophisticated, more reliable, and less costly to organizations.

SUMMARY

Computers are increasingly being used in organizations for group communication, and all indications are that this trend will continue (Turoff & Hiltz, 1982). With increasing pressure to use the group as a decision-making body in organizations, there is a need for development and study of computer-based systems to support group decision making. The introduction of decision support technology for groups probably will not occur on a wide scale for quite some time. In this sense, GDSS may be an idea whose time has not yet come. But many of the components of such systems are available currently, and a few GDSS products have been produced. Systems developers and researchers should begin now to consider exactly how much systems can be designed, how they might be used in organizations, and what their impacts will be.

QUESTIONS

1. What is a group decision support system? What are its characteristics?
2. Discuss the components of a group decision support system.
3. Describe the four types of support systems that are needed for group decision making.
4. Summarize the three design implications for group decision support systems that can be drawn from the study of group dynamics.

REFERENCES

BENNIS, W. G., AND H. A. SHEPARD   "A Theory of Group Development," *Human Relations,* Summer 1963, 415–57.

BONCZEK, R. H., C. W. HOLSAPPLE, AND A. B. WHINSTON   "Computer-Based Support of Organizational Decision Making," *Decision Sciences,* 10 (1979), 268–91.

CARTWRIGHT, D., AND A. ZANDER   *Group Dynamics* (3rd ed.). Evanston, Ill.: Row, Peterson, 1968.

COOK, R. L., AND K. R. HAMMOND   "Interpersonal Learning and Interpersonal Conflict Reduction in Decision-Making Groups," in *Improving Group Decision Making,* ed. R. A. Guzzo, 13–72. New York: Academic Press, 1982.

DALKEY, N. C.   *Studies in the Quality of Life: Delphi and Decision Making.* Lexington, Mass.: Lexington Books, 1972.

DESANCTIS, G.   "A Micro Perspective of Implementation," in *Implementing Management Science,* ed. R. Schultz and M. Ginzberg. Greenwich, Conn.: JAI Press, 1984.

DICKSON, G. W.   "Requisite Functions for a Management Support Facility," in *Processes and Tools for Decision Support,* ed. J. G. Sol. Amsterdam: North Holland Publishing, 1983.

GANNON, M. J.   *Organizational Behavior: A Managerial and Organizational Perspective.* Boston: Little, Brown, 1979.

GERRITY, T. P.   "Design of Man-Machine Decision Systems: An Application to Portfolio Management," *Sloan Management Review,* Winter 1971, 59.

GRAY, P., et al.   "The SMU Decision Room Project," *Transactions on the First International Conference on Decision Support Systems,* Atlanta, June 1981, 122–29.

GUZZO, R., ed.   *Improving Group Decision Making,* 13–72. New York: Academic Press, 1982.

HACKATHORN, R. D., AND P. G. W. KEEN   "Organizational Strategies for Personal Computing in Decision Support Systems," *MIS Quarterly,* 5, no. 3 (1981), 21–27.

HACKMAN, J. R., AND C. G. MORRIS   "Group Tasks, Group Interaction Process, and Group Performance Effectiveness: A Review and Proposed Integration," in *Advances in Experimental Social Psychology,* ed. L. Berkowitz, vol. 8. New York: Academic Press, 1975.

HOFFMAN, L. R. "Group Problem Solving," in *Advances in Experimental Social Psychology*, ed. L. Berkowitz, vol. 2, 99–132. New York: Academic Press, 1965.

HUBER, G. P. "Issues in the Design of Group Decision Support Systems," *MIS Quarterly,* 1984.

JANIS, I. L. *Victims of Groupthink: A Psychological Study of Foreign Policy Decisions and Fiascoes.* Boston: Houghton Mifflin, 1972.

KEEN, P. G. W. "DSS & DP: Powerful Partners," *Office Automation: Computerworld,* 19, no. 7A (1984), 13–15.

KEEN, P. G. W., AND M. S. SCOTT MORTON *Decision Support Systems: An Organizational Perspective.* Reading, Mass.: Addison-Wesley, 1978.

KLEIN, S. M., AND R. R. RITTI *Understanding Organizational Behavior.* Boston: Kent Publishing, 1980.

KOLASA, B. J. "Social Influence of Groups," in *Motivation and Work Behavior,* ed. R. M. Steers and L. W. Porter. New York: McGraw-Hill, 1975.

KRAEMER, K. L., AND J. L. KING "Computer-Based Systems for Group Decision Support," unpublished paper, University of California, Irvine, August 1984.

LUCAS, H. C., JR. "Performance and the Use of an Information System," *Management Science,* 20 (1975), 908–19.

NEUMANN, S., AND M. HADASS "DSS and Strategic Decisions," *California Management Review,* 22, no. 2 (1980), 77–84.

OAKES, W. F., A. E. DROGE, AND B. AUGUST "Reinforcement Effects on Participation in Group Discussions," *Psychological Reports,* 7 (1960), 503–14.

OSBORN, A. F. *Applied Imagination.* New York: Scribner's, 1957.

PEPINSKY, P., J. K. HEMPHILL, AND R. N. SHEVITZ "Attempts to Lead, Group Productivity, and Morale under Conditions of Acceptance and Rejection," *Journal of Abnormal Social Psychology,* 57 (1958), 47–54.

ROBEY, D. "User Attitudes and MIS Use," *Academy of Management Journal,* 22 (1979), 527–38.

SHAW, M. *Group Dynamics.* New York: McGraw-Hill, 1971.

SPRAGUE, R. H. "A Framework for the Development of Decision Support Systems," *MIS Quarterly,* 4, no. 4 (1980), 1–26.

SWANSON, E. B. "Management Information Systems: Appreciation and Involvement," *Management Science,* 21 (1974), 178–88.

THIBAUT, J., AND H. KELLEY *The Social Psychology of Groups.* New York: John Wiley, 1959.

TULLIS, T. S. "An Evaluation of Alphanumeric, Graphic, and Color Information Displays," *Human Factors,* 23, no. 5 (1981), 541–50.

TUROFF, M., AND S. R. HILTZ "Computer Support for Group versus Individual Decisions," *IEEE Transactions on Communications,* 30, no. 1 (1982), 82–90.

VAN DE VEN, A. H., AND A. L. DELBECQ "The Effectiveness of Nominal, Delphi, and Interacting Group Decision Making Processes," *Academy of Management Journal,* 17 (1974), 605–21.

VAZSONYI, A. "Information Systems in Management Science," *Interfaces,* 9, no. 1 (1978), 72–77.

20

GROUP DECISION SUPPORT SYSTEMS

Paul Gray,
Jay F. Nunamaker

INTRODUCTION

At the First International Conference on Decision Support Systems, Peter G.W. Keen [12] pointed out that the fundamental model of DSS—the lonely decision maker striding down the hall at high noon to make a decision—is true only in rare cases. In real organizations, be they public or private, Japanese, European, or American, most decisions are taken only after extensive consultation. Although it is possible on occasion for decision makers to go counter to the consensus of their organization, this is not a viable long-term position for them. Decision makers out of tune with the people in their organization either depart the organization or the organization undergoes massive personnel turnover.

In this reading, we consider group decision support systems, usually referred to as GDSS. This is an emerging subfield within DSS in which there has been a marked increase in activity since the mid-1980s. The evolution of GDSS has been rapid. To a

This reading was written especially for this book, and revised in 1992 for the third edition.

first approximation, the evolution can be characterized in terms of a chronology having some very short time intervals (Ahituv [1]):

1982–85	Survey papers and research agendas (e.g., Kraemer et al. [14], Huber [11], DeSanctis and Gallupe [4]).
1981–83	Initial papers describing group decision support systems (e.g., Gray [7], Huber [10], Konsynski [13]).
1982–86	Initial experimentation and experimental results (Kull [15], Gray [8], Lewis [16], Gallupe [6]).
1987–	Building of advanced facilities in universities (DeSanctis [5], Gray [9], Mantei [17], Nunamaker [22, 23], Stefik [24]), and formal experimentation (e.g., Applegate [2], Nunamaker [21], Watson [27], Zigurs [28]).
1988–	Commercial versions of hardware introduced by IBM [19] and other vendors and commercial versions of software introduced by Ventana Corporation of Tuscon, Arizona, and others.

As indicated by this chronology, GDSS was in a laboratory stage throughout the 1980s. In the past, when these systems were installed in industry and government, they often behaved like shooting stars. They were put in by one senior executive and used during his or her tenure. However, as soon as that individual was replaced, the system was dismantled or fell into disuse. The classic "not-invented here" syndrome held sway. As we move into the 1990s, the systems have become commercial in the United States. The move to commercialization became possible because we found out:

- How to use these systems effectively.
- How to design systems so that people (particularly middle-aged executives) do not require any significant training.

There is growing evidence that group decision support systems are able to improve both the efficiency and the effectiveness of organizational group processes.

THE NATURE OF GROUP DECISION MEETINGS

Although most business organizations are hierarchical, decision making in an environment involving choices among alternatives and assessment of risks is usually a shared process. Face-to-face meetings among groups of senior executives (or boards of directors) are an essential element of reaching a consensus. The group may be involved in a decision or in a decision-related task such as creating a short list of acceptable alterna-

This reading is based on portions of three papers: "Group Decision Support Systems" by Paul Gray, which appeared in the *DSS Journal*, 3 (1987); "Computer-Aided Deliberation: Model Management and Group Decision Support" by J. F. Nunamaker, L. M. Applegate, and B. R. Konsynski, which appeared in *Operations Research*, 36 (1988); and "Electronic Meeting Systems to Support Group Work" by J. F. Nunamaker, Alan R. Dennis, Joseph S. Valacich, Douglas R. Vogel, and Joey F. George, which appeared in *Communications of the ACM*, 34 (1991).

tives or creating a recommendation for approval at a higher level. These group meetings are characterized by the following activities and processes:

- The meetings are a joint activity, engaged in by a group of people of equal or near equal status,* typically five to twenty or more individuals.
- The activity, as well as its outputs, is intellectual in nature.
- The product depends in an essential way on the knowledge, opinions, and judgments of its participants.
- Differences in opinion are settled either by fiat by the ranking person present or, more often, by negotiation or arbitration. The results lead to action within the organization.

Another way of looking at group decision meetings is in terms of what groups do. Specifically, groups

- Retrieve (or generate) information.
- Share information among members.
- Draft policies and procedures.
- Use information to reach consensus or decision.

DEFINITION

Definitions of GDSS have been offered by both Huber [10] and DeSanctis and Gallupe [3]. These definitions are more than adequate for our purpose here:

- "A GDSS consists of a set of software, hardware, and language components and procedures that support a group of people engaged in a decision-related meeting" (Huber [10]).
- "An interactive, computer-based system which facilitates solution of unstructured problems by a set of decision makers working together as a group" (DeSanctis and Gallupe [4]).

An important point to note is that the group using the GDSS may not make the ultimate decision. It may be creating and/or reviewing alternatives to be submitted as a short list to the next level in the organizational hierarchy.

GDSS TECHNOLOGY

Although almost all group decision meetings today are face to face, technology is starting to be applied to make it possible for participants to be separated in space and/or time. These electronic meeting systems include computer conferences (either online or extended in time) and audio and video teleconferences. DeSanctis and Gallupe [4] discuss the

---

*However, the use of group systems has proven to be effective as a way of holding meetings whose members cross many levels of an organization.

four combinations of proximity and separation in space and in time. In this reading, we will concentrate on one form of electronic meeting system, the "decision room" in which the participants are in the same room at the same time.

The motivation for creating a decision room comes from the observation that in almost all organizations, office automation had resulted in terminals being ubiquitous in work areas. However, as soon as one stepped into a conference room, the only technology available was a telephone, and high technology was a speakerphone. The personal and online computer capabilities used routinely elsewhere were not available.

In a typical decision room, terminals (or personal computers) are provided at some or all of the seating positions at a conference table. Input to these terminals is by keyboard, mouse, touchscreen, bit pad, or some combination of these devices. Participants can do "private work" at their individual displays. One member of the group (either the group leader or a staff member acting as a "chauffeur") operates the software needed to create the "public" display (e.g., a projection TV) that can be seen by everyone. In some rooms, multiple public screens are provided where one screen is used for the current discussion and the others for reference or slowly changing information.

Because decision rooms are designed for senior managers, they tend to have an "executive feel" to them. Even the experimental laboratories have plush carpeting and quality furnishings.

The computer and communications equipment in the decision room typically includes file servers to act as dedicated storage, local-area networks to interconnect the terminals and the servers, and connection to a central computer (usually a minicomputer) and to peripheral equipment including printers to provide hard copy and (sometimes) electronic blackboards. Whiteboards, overhead and slide projectors, and other audiovisual support are also provided.

The appendix describes the installations at the University of Arizona.

GDSS SOFTWARE

GDSS provide software to support the individual and to support the group. To allow each individual to do private work, the usual collection of text and file creation, graphics, spreadsheet, database, and help routines is provided at the individual workstations. For the group as a whole, in addition to providing information retrieval and display, a GDSS provides software for summarizing group opinion. Thus, for example, the public screen can be used to present a cumulative list of all suggestions (such as from a nominal group technique session) or to show the aggregated results of voting and ranking or ratings of alternatives. Votes and preferences can be either identified by individuals or aggregated so that individuals need not expose themselves if they hold views contrary to the consensus or to those of the senior person present. This last feature allows managers to obtain a truer set of advice, because people need not fear retribution if they do not follow the prevailing group opinion.

As discussed later, introducing GDSS hardware and software into a conference changes the content of the discussions. By being able to do private work, a participant can examine an alternative (e.g., a "what-if") on his or her private screen and, if it is good, send it to the public screen for discussion. However, if the alternative is poor, it can be quietly buried without embarrassment. The recording of information on the public screen reduces the redundancy of the conversation. People do not keep bringing up the same ideas over and over if they are displayed. As a result, communications focuses on what participants know and on the rationale that led them to hold their views. Recording of information also provides group memory by recording all electronic comments.

GDSS COMMUNICATIONS

A GDSS must have a communications base as well as the model base, data base, and interface required in conventional DSS (Bui and Jarke [3]). This is particularly true for a GDSS distributed in time and space. However, even for a decision room where everyone is present at the same time, communications links are required. For example, a participant may want to send you a message "for your eyes only." These links provide electronic mail among participants, access to remote computers, and the ability to send information from a workstation to the public screen via the chauffeur.

GDSS MEETING STYLES

GDSS software and hardware in full-service facilities are sufficiently flexible that they can be used in any of the three styles:

- chauffeured
- supported
- interactive

As shown in Table 20.1, in the chauffeured style, only one person uses the software, either a group member or the meeting leader. A workstation is connected to the public screen to provide the electronic version of the traditional blackboard. The group discusses the issues verbally, with the public screen used as a group memory to record and structure information.

The supported style is similar to a chauffeured style, but differs in that each member has access to a computer workstation that provides a parallel, anonymous, electronic communication channel with a group memory. The meeting proceeds using a mixture of verbal and electronic interactions. Each member is able to enter items that appear on the public screen.

In the interactive style, the parallel, anonymous, electronic communications channel with group memory is used for almost all communications. Virtually no one speaks. Although a public screen may be provided, the group memory is typically too large to fit on a screen and thus is maintained so that all members can access it electronically at their workstations.

In practice, GDSS meetings involve use of two or all three of these styles.

TABLE 20.1 GDSS Meeting Styles

CHAUFFEURED	SUPPORTED	INTERACTIVE
One person enters group information	All group members can enter comments	All Group members can enter comments
Public screen can provide group memory	Public screen can provide group memory	Group memory accessible via workstations
Verbal communication predominates	Both verbal and electronic communications	Electronic communication predominates

A TYPOLOGY OF GDSS FACILITIES

Table 20.2 lists representative GDSS facilities. Such facilities can be characterized by the delivery mode and the range of tasks supported. Delivery modes include the following.

1. *Permanent Installations at the User's Site.* Here a conference room is instrumented with terminals and dedicated to GDSS use. For such a system to be successful, it must be used frequently. Otherwise it is not cost-effective and falls victim to one of the periodic cost-cutting efforts in organizations. Many permanent facilities currently are located at universities. Two corporate installations (COLAB at Xerox Palo Alto Research Center (Stefik [25]) and Electronic Data Systems (Manteii [17])) are developmental systems being used for research.

2. *Portable Installations Brought to the User's Site on an On-Call Basis.* The equipment and the services of support staff to run the meeting are rented from a vendor. The skills of the vendor's staff in facilitating meetings is often as important as the equipment in such arrangements.

3. *Permanent Installation at the Vendor's Site.* Here the group travels to the vendor site to hold its meeting. The vendor supplies the software, hardware, and support staff for a fee. The support staff usually acts as the chauffeur. Such a system is offered by Decisions and Designs, Inc. Some universities also offer this service.

4. *Facilities Designed and Sold by Commercial Firms.* IBM installed over fifty group decision support centers in its own facilities by 1991 and began marketing these facilities to other companies. Two organizations in England, ICL (a computer manufacturer) and Metapraxis (a consulting firm and software house), designed and developed permanent GDSS facilities that they installed at company locations.

The range of tasks supported can be from one or a few to a "full service" GDSS. An example of the former are the rooms provided by Decision and Designs and SUNY-Albany that support primarily interactive decision-analysis sessions that allow users to create decision trees and utility functions and in which the system does the Bayesian statistics. A full-service GDSS contains a broad range of software and the ability to support a diversity of tasks from financial decision making to crisis management to personnel selection to project

TABLE 20.2   Selected Group Decision Support System Facilities

University-Based Facilities

University of Arizona	University of Minnesota
The Claremont Graduate School	Queens University (Canada)
University of Georgia	National University of Singapore
Universitat Hohenheim (Germany)	San Diego State University
University of Indiana	State University of New York at Albany
London School of Economics	Western Washington University

Corporate-Based Facilities

Electronic Data Systems	IBM Corporation
Execucom Systems Corporation	BellSouth
Xerox Palo Alto Research Center	Greyhound Financial Corporation

Commercial Facility Vendors

IBM Corporation	ICL
Metapraxis	Ventana Corporation

For-Hire Commercial Systems—Permanent Installations

Decisions & Design, Inc.

For-Hire Commercial Systems—Portable

Applied Future Inc.	Perceptronics, Inc.
K. R. Hammond	Wilson Learning Systems

review to long-range planning and forecasting. [The decision rooms at the University of Arizona and at the Claremont Graduate School are examples of full-service facilities.]

RELATION OF *GDSS* TO *DSS*

GDSS can be viewed as subsuming conventional DSS within it. That is, the concepts of model base, database, and human interface (see Sprague and Carlson [24]) all apply. Thus, as group size shrinks to one, a GDSS reduces to a DSS. Conversely, in moving from a DSS to a GDSS, some new requirements are introduced:

1. The addition of communications capabilities.
2. Enhancement of the model base to provide voting, ranking, rating, etc., for developing consensus.
3. Greater system reliability.

4. Enhanced physical facilities.

5. Increased setup before use of the system.

The first two have already been discussed. System reliability must be much greater for a GDSS than for a DSS. If a GDSS fails, many people are affected, not just one. Because these people are high-level executives and well-paid, there is a much greater loss, both in terms of financial costs and trusts in the system. A GDSS requires much more setup before the system can be used because both the people and the facility must be scheduled, an agenda must be prepared, participants must be able to prepare for the meeting by seeing its data files and models, etc., and, if necessary, create any additional knowledge bases that are needed.

A GDSS requires capital investment in physical facilities. If the GDSS is located in a decision room, the room has to be elegantly furnished and have the feel of the executive conference room that it is. A GDSS also requires much more display and communications hardware.

APPLICATIONS

GDSS have been used principally for tasks involving idea generation, planning, competitive analysis, and consensus building. For example, Greyhound Financial Corporation used its GDSS for developing a mission statement, strategy formulation, evaluations of senior managers, and information systems planning.

GDSS applications cover a wide range. For example, Gray and Borovits [8] discuss the use of gaming in GDSS environments, with special emphasis on the use of gaming for risk assessment and crisis management. They point out the following:

- Gaming is a form of training that improves both the intuition and skills of a manager in facing real-life situations, particularly high-stress, high-stakes situations such as crises and difficult negotiations.
- The experience and data gained from extensive gaming of a particular situation under laboratory conditions provide a basis for understanding how to cope with "surprise" and with outcomes of low probability.
- Gaming involves highly complex situations in which decision makers respond in novel and unanticipated ways. The iterative nature of the design process for GDSS thus makes it possible to use the results of gaming to increase the ability to handle complex conditions and cope with low-probability events.
- Gaming can assist senior managers both in understanding what consensus exists within their organization and in creating consensus. As such, it provides a basis for decision making that takes into account the internal viewpoint of the organization.

Other applications of GDSS include:

- Supporting negotiations. For example, in international situations, two or more groups that speak different languages and have different cultural backgrounds are negotiating a contract.

■ Supporting business teams involved in design work (the Xerox Palo Alto Research Center facility was used primarily in this way), quality control reviews, and such relatively new tasks as reengineering and concurrent engineering.

■ Supporting visual decisions such as selecting packaging for a new product.

WHAT HAS BEEN LEARNED

Experimentation with the use of decision rooms has been undertaken since the mid-1980s. A number of papers have appeared (e.g., those of Applegate [2], Gallupe [6], Gray [8], Grohowski [9a], Kull [15], Lewis [16], Nunamaker [23a], Watson [27], and Zigurs [28]) that report observations, field research, action research, and laboratory experiments. These papers indicate the high potential for the contribution of computer and communication-based mediation, facilitation, and support in creating effective group decision support. The following summary of what has been learned thus far is based on these and other papers and our own observations.

The research results have underscored the need to review and examine the theories and hypotheses on group decision making that have been developed in the past. There is reason to believe that many previously held assumptions about the conduct of group deliberation are subject to review in the new electronically based forum. Factors such as speed, anonymity, recording of group processes, voting, participation levels, group size, and other facilitated activities change the group environment significantly.

Analysis of the available data shows that using decision rooms can improve group work in many situations because they:

■ Enable all participants to work simultaneously (human parallel processing), thereby promoting broader input into the meeting process and reducing dominance of the meeting by a few people.

■ Provide equal opportunity for participation (through anonymity).

■ Trigger additional points to be made.

■ Enable larger group meetings that can effectively bring more information, knowledge, and skills to bear on the task.

■ Provide process structure to help focus the group on key issues and discourage irrelevant digressions and nonproductive behaviors.

■ Support the development of an organizational memory from meeting to meeting.

In the following sections, we describe these and other findings in more detail.

Group Size and Composition

Groups numbering from three to twenty or more of differing composition have used GDSS facilities to accomplish a variety of tasks. One finding is clear: Individual satisfaction increases with the size of the group. Computer support assists groups in building toward a consensus. Larger groups appreciate the inherent structuring that keeps the group from becoming bogged down or subject to domination by personalities. Small groups find that the fixed overhead associated with using the computer-based systems eats up the gains from using the system. Small groups are less likely than large groups to conclude that the computer-aided support is more effective or efficient than an unstructured face-to-face meeting. The various electronic brainstorming approaches do not work effectively with groups of less than four. Such techniques are more effective for groups of eight or more persons. Many other techniques, such as Stakeholder Identification and Assumption Surfacing, also increase in satisfaction with group size. The implication of this finding is that different tools are required for different group sizes. Work toward this end is currently underway.

The increase in satisfaction with group size is due, in part, to "human parallel processing." That is, in many situations, participants are entering information into the computer simultaneously. They are functioning in parallel rather than in sequence. In a typical meeting that follows, say, Roberts Rules of Order, verbal input is sequential. As a result, if a group of ten meets for an hour, each participant has the floor for only 6 minutes on the average. In parallel processing, the group can finish in 20 minutes and each individual (even slow typists!) has made a larger individual contribution.

Anonymity

The anonymity facilitated through use of nominal group techniques (Van de Ven and Delbecq [26]) and other tools for electronic brainstorming is a positive factor in encouraging broad-based participation. Anonymity is important when sensitive issues being discussed can easily be confounded with personalities in the group. Anonymity also provides a sense of equality and encourages participation by all members in the group, independent of perceived status. Problems of "group think," pressures for conformity, and dominance of the group by strong personalities or particularly forceful speakers are minimized even though the participants are face to face. Group members can contribute without the personal attention and anxiety associated with gaining the floor and being the focus of a particular comment or issue. As a result, issues are discussed more candidly.

Anonymity does tend to heighten conflict within the group because members tend to become more blunt and assertive in their written comments and often are not as polite as when speaking face to face. (However, people are more accepting of written criticism than verbal criticism because it does not carry with it the same level of embarrassment. Written comments become more polite with age and rank in the organization.) Further, in any written medium, the richness of voice inflections and facial expressions is lost, which can lead to misunderstanding. Occasional face-to-face discussions, as well as breaks and social time, are important as issues become more politically charged and sensitive.

Facility Design

The lighting and physical organization of the decision room affect outcomes. Better results are obtained when the facility has aesthetic appeal and provides a comfortable, familiar setting for executives. Carpeting, wall coverings, executive-style furniture, and quality acoustics provide an atmosphere that is well suited to long sessions over a number of days.

Adequate lighting control and arrangement of lights is needed to assure that results are legible on both the public and the individual workstation screens. For example, front screen projector images are "washed out" by fluorescent lighting and can reduce the effectiveness of a meeting.

The decision room should be full-service in order to meet the needs of groups that differ in size and task. The decision room should be designed so to accommodate a range of group sizes and be able to support tasks that range from passive to active. Breakout rooms located adjacent to the decision room that provide computer-based support make it possible to divide a large group into smaller groups and are useful for changing the environment during a meeting.

Multiple Public Screens

More than one public screen increases group productivity. Not all information can be displayed adequately in the standard 25-line-by-80-character format of current computer screens. Windowing on a single screen allows presenting multiple sets of data but further reduces the amount of information that is shown about individual items. In a multiple-screen setup, the group can view both the current information being discussed and reference information (e.g., sales trends, financials) at the same time. They can see the existing version and the proposed alternative side by side. In rank ordering, they can see the unordered and ordered items simultaneously.

Knowledge Bases and Databases

The documentation of meeting activities, the creation of working papers, and the recording of decisions and commitments are particularly useful by-products of GDSS. These outputs are provided without detracting from meeting activities. File servers handle the knowledge bases and databases, facilitate coordination and management of input from individual decision makers, and serve as "organizational memory" from session to session. The file server functions as a knowledge-base repository and provides access to organizational data that are relevant to a particular meeting. A key to effective use of GDSS in supporting planning is the continuity from planning session to planning session provided by an ongoing, expanding knowledge base that is integrated through the output from software tools. This continuity and integration provide the opportunity for analysis from multiple perspectives.

Communication Network Speed

Users become impatient if they must wait more than 1 or 2 seconds for a screen. Experience has shown that users expect to receive subsecond response for all activities. A wide-bandwidth local area network (LAN) is needed to maintain these high levels of network response.

Fixed vs. Customized Tools

In planning, groups usually start with idea generation, followed by the development of alternatives, and conclude by converging on a course of action through forming a consensus. A group can go through this process in either of two modes:

1. It can create a customized methodology from the set of available tools, or

2. It can follow a standard sequence for using the tools.

Some groups prefer to adopt a standard methodology, whereas others feel that their needs are very different from anyone else's and therefore prefer to generate the sequence. Both approaches have given excellent results.

Software Design: Ease of Use and User Friendly

The best GDSS software helps rather than frustrates individual users. It supports a continuum of modes of working ranging from electronically based, self-directed participation to facilitator-directed discussion. However, a minimum amount of instruction and direction is still required. In the system designed by the University of Arizona, for example, it takes less than 5 minutes to explain how to use each software tool. Efforts to increase software ease of use are particularly worthwhile. Techniques that use color, overlays, windowing, consistent interfaces, and on-demand help screens all help the user (particularly the novice and the computerphobic user) to master the software. One or two group members who have difficulty with the software can affect the productivity of the entire group.

Consistency in the dialog interface protocols permits effective dialog management, ease of introduction of participation to new support tools, and ease of tool building. Common keystroke assignments, window layouts, use of color, messaging, and icon semantics facilitate this dialog management.

Screen sharing across, and among, participants opens new opportunities for particular decision tasks. Activities such as local editing of shared screens, help and monitoring activities, and personal messaging create alternative forms of communication. Using the keyboard as an input device has not proven to be an inhibitor of active participation.

Satisfaction

Individual satisfaction is reflected in user reports on the positive aspects of the group decision-making process in a computer-based support environment. Group participants conclude that they are not blocked out of the group and, as a result, they support the group solution with increased confidence.

THE FUTURE OF GDSS

The foregoing discussions were based on the assumption that GDSS is an emerging technology that will become pervasive in many organizations. Certainly, the commercialization of GDSS by IBM and others is an important indicator of its long-term success. People meeting in a group need to have a free flow of ideas and the technology—with its typing, pointing of mice, and other mechanical interruptions—can act as a barrier and a delayer rather than a facilitator of thought. Certainly, the present technology could be made even more user-friendly and transparent. New technologies (such as pen-based systems and voice recognition) should help in this regard. One of the dangers in the development of GDSS is that, like many other computer-based solutions offered previously, it may overpromise and underperform in its early stages, resulting in user expectations that are too high for what GDSS can deliver. The research programs and the commercial experience now underway should increase the long-term viability of GDSS.

What can we expect? Group decision support systems today use relatively standard computer, communications, and display technology. Physically, existing decision rooms look very much like conventional conference rooms with terminals and projection screens added. This is to be expected. When a new technology is introduced into an existing situation, it tends to look like and be used in the same way as the technology it replaces. The early automobile looked like and was used in the same way and over the same roads as the carriage, with only the horse replaced by a motor. GDSS provides an enhanced environment for performing existing tasks and will, in the short term, be used the way conference rooms are used now. As understanding of GDSS develops, the nature of group decision making itself can be expected to change. The idea of human parallel processing is such a change.

One potential new direction comes from the changes going on in the workplace. As large companies decentralize more and more and as computer and communications costs continue to decrease relative to transportation costs, we can expect that many people will "telecommute" (e.g., Nilles [20]) to meetings just as they telecommute to work. That is, they will stay where they are and will be brought into the decision conference electronically—through video and computer conference. It is also possible to use these technologies to call experts on a particular subject into the meeting, obtain their advice, and let them go without their ever leaving their place of work.

Another potential direction of change comes from the expert/knowledge-based system realm. As expert systems become more pervasive, one or more of them will be brought into meetings to assist in deliberations. In effect, they become the $(n + 1)$st person in a meeting of n people. Their role can range from retrieving information to synthesis of new alternatives to helping resolve conflicts of opinions.

The present approach of using the technology to mechanize group processes such as voting, Delphi, and nominal group techniques is relatively crude and rudimentary. We can anticipate that new ways of gaining group interaction and group consensus will be developed that take advantage of the capabilities offered by GDSS.

We are at a very early and a very exciting point in GDSS. The level of activity is building as firms start to explore the possibilities. The 1990s should bring additional innovation and lead to maturity.

APPENDIX: THE UNIVERSITY OF ARIZONA PLANNING LABORATORY

The Planning Laboratory established in 1985 at the University of Arizona's Management Information Systems Department was specifically constructed to aid groups in planning and decision making. The laboratory currently has two decision rooms. The smaller of the two (Figure 20A.1) uses NCR PC4 microcomputers, NCR PC2PC networking, NCR interactive video disk, and Barco large-screen projection technology. As shown in Figure 20A.1, a large U-shaped table is equipped with net-

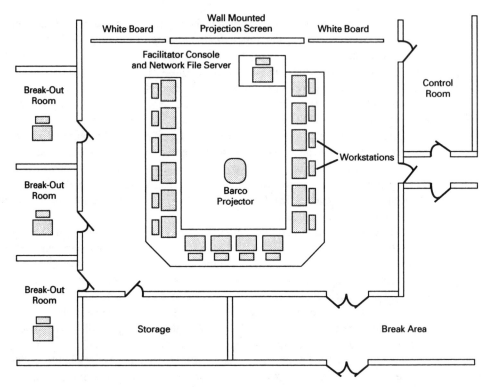

FIGURE 20A.1   University of Arizona Small GDSS Facility

FIGURE 20A.2   University of Arizona Large GDSS Facility

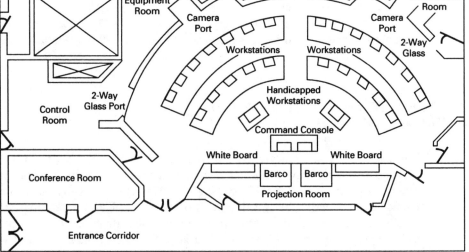

worked microcomputers recessed into the table to facilitate interaction among participants. The public screen is run off the network through a microcomputer. Microcomputer-equipped breakout rooms are used to provide space for working sessions. The second facility (Figure 20A.2) opened in 1987, uses inner and outer rows of PS/2 model 50 workstations and gallery seating. The facility can accommodate up to sixty people at twenty-five workstations. It provides two large public screens. The university installed four additional decision rooms in a new building completed in 1992.

Among the software provided in the Planning Laboratory are facilities for (1) electronic brainstorming, which enhances a form of the nominal group technique; (2) stakeholder identification and analysis, which examines planning issues and looks for discrepancies between stakeholder and organizational interests; and (3) an enterprise analyzer used to determine the relationships among organizational components and to determine the potential impacts that stakeholders have on the organization.

A GDSS software toolkit, known as GroupSystems, was developed at the University of Arizona for use in the Planning Laboratory. The toolkit, shown schematically in Figure 20A.3, is similar to a DSS model base. The toolkit provides tools in the three areas listed on page 323:

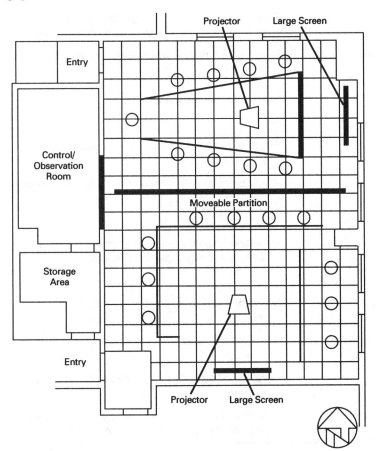

FIGURE 20A.3
Claremont
Facility

TABLE 20A.1   GroupSystems Tools Developed at the University of Arizona

TOOL	FUNCTION
Idea Generation	
Brainstorming	Anonymous entry of new ideas.
Topic Commenter	A set of electronic index cards for simultaneous entry of information on multiple topics.
Group Outliner	Organizing ideas according to a structured outline form.
Idea Organization	
Idea Organizer	Organizing comments from idea generation.
Issue Analyzer	Identifying and consolidating comments from idea generation into issues.
Group Writer	Joint authoring of a document by meeting participants.
Prioritizing	
Vote Selection	Choice of voting method (e.g., yes/no, multiple choice, ranking), voting, and vote result presentation.
Alternative Evaluation	Rating of alternatives according to multiple criteria.
Questionnaire	Electronic questionnaire form.
Group Matrix	Ratings on a two-dimensional matrix.
Policy Development	
Policy Formation	Structured support for reaching consensus on policy statements.
Stakeholder ID	Stakeholder Identification and Surfacing Technique of Mason and Mitroff [18].
Session Planning	
Session Manager	Presession planning, in-session management, and postsession organization of results.
Organization Memory	
Enterprise Analyzer	Structuring and analysis of group information in a semantic net.
Graphical Browser	"Zoom-in" and "zoom-out" on nodes of enterprise analyzer.
Group Dictionary	Develop and store formal definition of terms being used by group.
Brief Case	Immediate read-only access to any stored text file; also provides calculator, notepad, and calendar.

1. Session planning and management.
2. Group interaction.
3. Organizational memory.

The function of each tool shown in Figure 20A.3 is described in Table 20A.1.

At the beginning of 1992, the Arizona GroupSystems toolkit was in use in seventy GDSS facilities worldwide.

QUESTIONS

1. Do you believe that GDSS has high or low potential for use in organizations? Why?
2. What are the various types of GDSS facilities? What are the keys to their success?
3. What has been learned from the GDSS experiments that have been conducted?

REFERENCES

1. AHITUV, N.   Personal communication, 1985.
2. APPLEGATE, L. M., ET AL.   "Knowledge Management in Organizational Planning," *Journal of Management Information Systems* 3 (1987), 20–38.
3. BUI, T., AND M. JARKE   "Communications Requirements for Group Decision Support Systems," *Proceedings of the 19th Hawaii International Conference on Systems Science*, Honolulu, January 1986, 524–533.
4. DESANCTIS, G., AND R. B. GALLUPE   "Group Decision Support Systems: A New Frontier," *Data Base* (Winter 1985), 3–10.
5. DESANCTIS, G., AND R. B. GALLUPE   "A Foundation for the Study of Group Decision Support Systems," *Management Science* (May 1987), 589–609.
6. GALLUPE, R. B.   "Experimental Research into Group Decision Support Systems: Practical Issues and Problems," *Proceedings of the 19th Hawaii International Conference on Systems Science*, Honolulu, January 1986, 513–523.
7. GRAY, P., ET AL.   "The SMU Decision Room Project," *Transactions of the First International Conference on Decision Support Systems*, Atlanta, June 1981, 122–129.
8. GRAY, P.   "Initial Observations from the Decision Room Project," *Transactions of the Third International Conference on Decision Support Systems*, Boston, June 1983, 135–138.
9. GRAY, P., AND I. BOROVITS   "Gaming and Group DSS," *Transactions of the Sixth International Conference on Decision Support Systems*, Washington, D.C., April 1986, 165–175.
9a. GROHOWSKI, R., C. McGoff, D. Vogel, B. Martz, and J. F. Nunamaker   "Implementing Electronic Meeting Systems at IBM: Lessons Learned and Success Factors," *MIS Quarterly* (December 1990), 369–384.
10. HUBER, G. P.   "Group Decision Support Systems as Aids in the Use of Structured Group Management Techniques," *Transactions of the Second International Conference on Decision Support Systems*, San Francisco, June 1982, 96–108.
11. HUBER, G. P.   "Issues in the Design of Group Decision Support Systems," *MIS Quarterly*, 8 (1984), 195–204.
12. KEEN, P. G. W.   "Remarks" Closing Plenary Session, *First International Conference on Decision Support Systems*, Atlanta, June 1981.

13. KONSYNSKI, B. R., AND J. F. NUNAMAKER "Plexsys: A System Development System," in J. Daniel Couger et al., *Advanced System Development/Feasibility Techniques*. New York: John Wiley, 1982.

14. KRAEMER, K., ET AL. "Computer-Based Systems for Group Decision Support," Working Paper, University of California at Irvine, Public Policy Research Organization, December 1983.

15. KULL, D. "Group Decisions: Can a Computer Help?" *Computer Decisions*, 14 (1982) 14.

16. LEWIS, L. F., II "FACILITATOR: A Microcomputer Decision Support Systems for Small Groups." Ann Arbor, Mich.: University Microfilms, 1983.

17. MANTEI, M. M. "Capturing the Capture Lab Concepts: A Case Study in the Design of Computer Supported Meeting Enviornments," Research Paper 030988, Center for Machine Intelligence, Electronic Data Systems Corporation, Dallas, TX., 1988.

18. MASON, R. O., AND I. I. MITROFF *Challenging Strategic Planning Assumptions*. New York: John Wiley, 1981.

19. McGOFF, C., A. HUNT, D. R. VOGEL, AND J. F. NUNAMAKER "IBM's Experience with Group Systems," *Interfaces* (1990), 39–52.

20. NILLES, J. M., ET AL. *Telecommunications–Transportation Tradeoff: Options for Tomorrow*. New York: John Wiley, 1976.

21. NUNAMAKER, J. F., L. M. APPLEGATE, AND B. R. KONSYNSKI "Facilitating Group Creativity: Experience with a Group Decision Support System," *Journal of Management Information Systems*, 3 (1987), 5–19.

22. NUNAMAKER, J. F., A. R. DENNIS, J. S. VALACICH, D. R. VOGEL, AND J. F. GEORGE "Electronic Meeting Systems to Support Group Work," *Communications of the ACM*, 34 (1991), 40–61.

23. NUNAMAKER, J. F., D. R. VOGEL, AND B. R. KONSYNSKI "Interaction of Task and Technology to Support Large Groups," *Decision Support Systems International Journal*, 5 (1989), 139–52.

23a. NUNAMAKER, J. F., A. R. DENNIS, J. S. VALACICH, AND D. R. VOGEL "Information Technology and Negotiating Groups: Generating Options for Mutual Gain," *Management Science* (October 1991), 1325–46.

24. SPRAGUE, R. H., Jr., AND E. D. CARLSON *Building Effective Decision Support Systems*. Englewood Cliffs, N.J.: Prentice Hall, 1982.

25. STEFIK, M., ET AL. "Beyond the Chalkboard: Computer Support for Collaboration and Problem Solving in Meetings," *Communications of the ACM,* 30 (1987), 32–47.

26. VAN DE VEN, A. H., AND A. L. DELBECQ "Nominal Versus Interacting Group Processes for Committee Decision Making Effectiveness," *Academy of Management Journal*, 14 (1971), 203–212.

27. WATSON, R., G. L. DESANCTIS, AND M. S. POOLE "Using a GDSS to Facilitate Group Consensus: Some Intended and Unintended Consequences," *MIS Quarterly*, 12 (1988), 463–478.

28. ZIGURS, I. "Interaction Analysis in GDSS Research: Description of Experience and Some Recommendations," *Decision Support Systems International Journal*, 5 (1989), 233–241.

21

BUILDING
THE BUSINESS CASE
FOR GROUP SUPPORT
TECHNOLOGY

Brad Quinn Post

BUSINESS CASE FRAMEWORK

This reading presents findings from a 1991 field study conducted at a major American corporation concerning the business benefits of group support technology. Both quasi-experimental and qualitative study design elements were used to provide an objective basis for developing a business case evaluation.

The purpose of the study was to produce answers to typical business case questions such as: "What are the measurable benefits of the technology?" "How does the technology improve group work quality?" "What is the return on investment?" "Does the support technology enhance or detract from current business team practices?" These and other similar business issues were addressed in the design and execution of this technology evaluation effort.

Reprinted by special permission of the Proceedings of the Twenty-Fifth Annual Hawaii International Conference on System Sciences, 1992. © 1992 by the Institute of Electrical and Electronics Engineers, Inc.

The professionally operated business demands objective and balanced analysis, as well as dispassionate recommendations. The business case framework is a straight-forward conceptualization and analysis of the concerns that should be considered when attempting to make sound business technology investments, such as group support technologies.

This reading reviews the results of a study involving synchronous group support technology, distinguished by specific business case variables that are important to understanding the effects of collaborative solutions on group performance. The study addresses a research question that has been given little attention: How well does group support technology fare as a business case or proposition in a complex organization? Business case variables include costs, benefits, and qualitative considerations valued by the organization.

This research question makes sense and needs consideration because the business enterprise is the ultimate target customer for the group decision support systems (GDSS) field. Important also is the fact that the field of GDSS is immature and requires extensive empirical exploration (Johansen 1988; VanGundy 1987); DeSanctis and Gallupe 1987; Nunamaker et al. 1989(a) 1989(b); Vogel et al. 1989; Vogel and Nunamaker 1990). Despite its following, this field of inquiry is scattered (Kraemer and King 1988) and will benefit from further conceptualization of its aims. A fundamental purpose of GDSS should be to add value to the organization in at least two ways· heightened group performance from the perspectives of efficiency and effectiveness and second, improved group work quality and process (Pinsonneault and Kraemer 1990). The relevance of business case concepts is given some attention by Tanniru and Jain (1989), who found that most group decisions have to be eventually translated into financial terms before they are meaningful to management.

Group Work and Business

Doing business today means accomplishing group work. The modern organization depends on the participation, and increasingly on the consensus, of its principals, employees, and interested others—all of whom are potential stakeholders in the innumerable business processes and decisions that create success.

While often overlooked, the significance of groups in business has long been accepted—at least in academic quarters. The well-known Hawthorne studies, which began at Western Electric in 1929, led engineers and scientists to ascribe much of the variance they observed in worker productivity to group behavior variables. Prior to these important findings, group work was not given much attention in critical circles of research (Barnard 1938).

Emergence of Business Teams

The salience of business teams in today's business environment is due to many factors, some of which are not well understood. In his authoritative work about business team technology, Robert Johansen (1988) points to a series of driving forces which underlie the pivotal position that groups now play:

- Deregulation

- The downsizing of middle management
- Increased reliance on contract work
- Mergers and acquisitions
- Globalization

Groups now form the bedrock of most business operations and, as such, have emerged as a critical unit of analysis in the ongoing effort to increase the quality of our products and services. Just understanding business group behavior alone cannot produce the results we seek for our organization, our customers, and the community in which we work.

Group Process Model

Effectively harnessing business teams is a question of dynamic social psychology, management science, and technology. The myriad factors shaping the activity and variability of each group effort cannot be readily tamed as in an economist's *ceteris paribus* function equation. Instead, the productivity, quality, and effectiveness of any given business team is a function of a complex model not presently well explained by research or practice (McGrath 1984).

For business, the daunting challenge of developing effective patterns of teamwork can best be viewed in terms of group process characteristics. Initial efforts to describe these processes using business entity models suggest that further work in this area will be valuable in understanding group performance (McGoff et al. 1990). By designing processes that minimize variance in team performance, we will be in better position to conduct business using team resources. Technological leverage applied to teams make these efforts all the more critical.

The Technology Support Group Process Enterprise Model that was employed in this research, shown in Figure 21.1, presents the extended set of entities and relationships that framed this study. The model helped establish a structured basis for contrasting technology supported group work and traditional group work in process-oriented terms. This modeling also provided a useful heuristic for defining our quasi-experimental comparisons, thus helping overcome some of the thorny control and approach problems long prevalent in this field (Lewis and Keleman 1988; Kraemer and King 1988).

GROUP SUPPORT TECHNOLOGY

For nearly three decades, the use of computer-based tools in support of group work has been a vision of futurists, commercial developers, research institutions, and major corporations.

The GDSS focal area grew out of exploratory interest in group work (Gray et al. 1981; Huber 1982) and the concurrent drive to expand the long-standing field of decision support systems (DSS). These emergent group support technologies were timely because of the concomitant rise of the business team (Johansen 1988) in corporate enterprise. Despite their increasing visibility, these technologies are not appropriate for every organizational setting. Organizational boundaries, differing cultural and management structures can limit GDSS utilization (Kydd and Jones 1989). At the same time, a

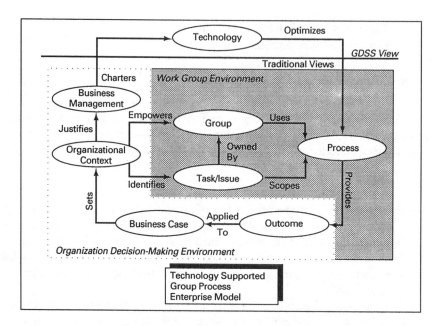

FIGURE 21.1 Technology Supported Group Process Enterprise Model

recent study of 135 randomly selected organizations indicates that GDSS tools are gradually being incorporated into many explicit information system strategies (Beauclair and Straub 1990).

GDSS and "groupware" tools perform functions such as electronic brainstorming, issue organization and analysis, as well as alternative evaluation, voting, and policy formation functions. Tasks supported are far-ranging, but research has demonstrated their impact on mission development, planning and strategy, issue documentation and evaluation, assumption surfacing, stakeholder identification, policy formulation, nominal group work, system requirements, group negotiation, and idea development (Diehl and Stroebe 1987; Campbell 1990; Vogel and Nunamaker 1990). While there are more than a few technologies available, many share closely related features and appear to be based on similar metaphors (Nunamaker 1989; Boose et al. 1992). The scope of these technologies suggest a robust marketplace, however, the evidence is that widespread acceptance is slow in building (Kraemer and King 1988), and that empirical research is needed to better understand their application, limitations, and business value.

GDSS specialists argue that meaningful group support technology research should be clearly tied to both group performance and satisfaction variables, because the purpose of these systems is to promote the overall efficiency and quality of group work.

CREATING AN EVALUATION INFRASTRUCTURE

Planning for this technology evaluation and business case study began with a technical feasibility review of leading GDSS products that supported the company's team collaboration functions. With more than 160,000 employees globally, the company has a rich, diverse infrastructure making its teamwork composition difficult to map in any straightforward categorization. Indeed, it is the vitality and magnitude of the company's group resources and processes that make it attractive from a GDSS research perspective.

Since the company should be characterized as heterogeneous from the standpoint of its team environments, it presents a challenge to the typical field study configuration, where limited access organizationally, functionally, and geographically, might lead to biases or gaps in the selection of groups for study. The organization sponsoring and managing this study is a unique operation, providing management consulting, systems integration, and group facilitation services inside the company. This consulting organization has a history spanning more than twenty years and provides technical and managerial support throughout the company on a world-wide basis. Among the many offerings delivered by this organization, and of particular importance to this study, are these key products and services:

- Group facilitation and consultation
- Process improvement
- Decision support
- Consensus
- Management counsel
- Planning
- Technology deployment

TeamFocus

At the time the study began, this consulting organization was considering the efficacy of acquiring and deploying group support technology in support of its client requirements. As a first phase of the effort, a technical feasibility assessment was conducted. This involved the formation of a small group of specialists who reviewed current research and product literature. They also consulted with Company researchers outside this organization who had kept abreast of GDSS issues and technologies and participated in product demonstrations. Based on this review, they prepared a statement of work to produce a technical feasibility report. This statement of work focused on the narrow objective of reviewing a leading group support technology which would become available commercially within a short timeframe. This technology was TeamFocus, produced jointly by IBM, the University of Arizona, and the Ventana Corporation. The product offering included utilities and eight tools: electronic brainstorming, idea organization, issue analysis, policy formation, alternative evaluation, voting, a data dictionary, and group questionnaire. The product featured anonymous participation (Connolly et al. 1990) and full session documentation. The questionnaire tool provided for evaluation data collection.

Technical Feasibility Review

The technical feasibility review included an evaluation tour of some five IBM TeamFocus facilities in the Washington, D.C., area by two members of the feasibility team—a technical consultant and a management consultant. The technical consultant was primarily concerned with functionality, performance, architecture, documentation, platform, state of software maturity, and maintenance-support criteria. The management consultant areas of interest were product definition from a user standpoint, product life cycle and stability, embedded or methodological neutrality, tool set capabilities, applications currently deployed, early on commercial experience, as well as service capability and program management.

Based on this field tour and follow-on calls to others familiar with this product offering, a technical feasibility report was prepared and presented to the sponsoring organization's management team. The report presented a series of findings as well as recommendations to proceed with a full-scale evaluation of the technology to determine its business case efficacy for possible use within the Company. The scope of the recommended actions included the following key action items:

1. Formation of an evaluation team.
2. Development of a detailed evaluation study plan.
3. Order of magnitude business case estimate.
4. Definition of business case metrics and evaluation methods.
5. Customer acquisition strategy for evaluation.
6. Capital and operating budget for evaluation.
7. Approvals for rapid acquisition of software, hardware, and a technology test facility.
8. Design evaluation across significant group practice areas.

Total elapsed time from the chartering of this feasibility review to the presentation of the report's findings and recommendations was 15 days. The recommended schedule for the evaluation was to develop the study infrastructure and complete the entire evaluation cycle, including the presentation of a business case report at its conclusion, within nine months. This proposal was accepted by the organization's management team and the study was initiated the next day.

Planning and Staffing

An evaluation team was formed by the newly assigned program manager. Members of the team were selected to fill what were initially six positions, but which soon became ten different parttime job assignments. Over a three month period, five facilitators joined the team. Two customer contact positions were assigned to the effort, as was technical manager, and an evaluator. The facilitators chosen all had group session facilitation experience including involvement with the organization's high visibility product offerings called Consensus and Preferred Process.

The customer contact assignees each had extensive professional experience as consultants and as sales force principals associated with both information services and management services. These individuals had specific knowledge of a wide range of internal customer accounts throughout the Company. The technical manager was chosen because of the extensive scope of his skill and relevant experience with the development of technology applications, including local area networks, and hardware and software testing. Similarly, the evaluator was asked to support the team because of his reputation for his structured approach to program planning. The program manager was chosen by the organization's management team because of his early on involvement in the feasibility review, interest, and organizational skills.

Early on tasks of the evaluation program team centered on the development of a plan, the negotiation of a software agreement with the vendor, the acquisition of hardware, facility furnishings, reconstruction of an existing conference room, development of a customer strategy, creation of marketing materials, and the design of business case metrics for the evaluation. Concurrently, the first two facilitators assigned to the team began an extensive training schedule which began with a structured five day course provided by IBM. The training focused on technical briefings and session mock-ups given by instructors highly experienced with TeamFocus software and facilitation methodology. This preliminary education was followed by a deliberately slow-paced series of varied, short practice sessions at the sponsoring organization's newly built evaluation facility.

The evaluation program plan rested on the definition of a business criteria for the research, specific objectives to be met, and application areas to be tested. The metrics important to the business case were closely aligned with these objectives. The agreed upon business objectives for the evaluation were to evaluate TeamFocus technology and associated group support methodology to:

- Determine business benefits and costs
- Assess integration issues with existing services
- Define customer impacts and
- Develop insight about group support technology

Business Case Parameters

High level business case issues were also established from the outset of the study. The business case was built to answer these pivotal questions:

[FLOWTIME]
To what extent does the group support technology help customers make faster decisions?
[QUALITY]
Does the technology significantly enhance the customer decision process with qualification, traceability, and increased exchange of participant knowledge?
[ROI]
What is the documented return on investment?
[VALUE]
How does support technology add value to the customer's business?
[COST-BENEFIT]
Does the technology make the organization a more efficient provider of consulting services?

These business case questions drove the development of indices employed in this study. As part of the staging for the evaluation, a preliminary productivity analysis was prepared. On the basis of this preliminary exercise, final approval was given for funding the business study. The analysis assumed that the evaluation facility would have a 70% utilization rate. The analysis projected a conservative productivity gain for all session participants using the facility averaging 25%. Using authoritative operating and capital budget research, standard six-year life-cycle costs were predicted to be $384,000, with $117,000 of these costs occurring in the first year. With an average operating savings of $175,000 due to productivity, the five-year cash savings was calculated to be $164,000 (present value). The ROI calculation derived from these values was 42.6%—well above the Company requirement of 25% or better.

The Test Facility

The facility was built on a "shoestring" basis to conserve resources. Its configuration included surplus XT workstations, an AT class facilitator workstation, and a 386 file-server. Portable color projection equipment was purchased along with state-of-the-art screengraber technology that allowed screen capture and VGA display of computer screen data. Existing light and furniture was adapted to requirements. The overall result was a low-cost, practical GDSS facility readied in less than a month's time.

Design and Pretesting

In parallel with these infrastructure developments was the definition of an evaluation methodology, data architecture, and comprehensive business case metrics. These efforts initially focused on the latter issue, evaluation indices, and soon thereafter on the procedures for measurement, data collection, analysis, and reporting. To help ensure both sound measurement protocols and criteria, experts outside the team were consulted. The metrics were crafted on a preliminary basis, then alpha tested using team members during mockup sessions conducted primarily as practice for the newly trained facilitators. The results of these alpha sessions led to the improvement and formalization of the measurements as well as the multi-stage data collection process.

Beta tests were then conducted with outside customers who were considered by the team to be "friendlies." Despite this informal labelling, these groups were generally representative of customer segments currently being served by the sponsoring organization. In addition, they were considered to be "experienced" customers who would be open to early involvement with the evaluation program. Like the alpha phase, this phase was conducted to extend team exposure to session work with "live" customers, with emphasis placed on testing the evaluation methodology, facilitation techniques, software behavior, and process mechanics. The beta sessions were useful and led to the final configuration of both the evaluation and general facilitation methods that were initially deployed during the first leg of the evaluation program.

For the purpose of this study, a total of forty-five variables were defined. Among them were thirteen measurements of calendar time, labor, and cost. This set of indices was critical to the business case in terms of quantifying costs and benefits. Additionally,

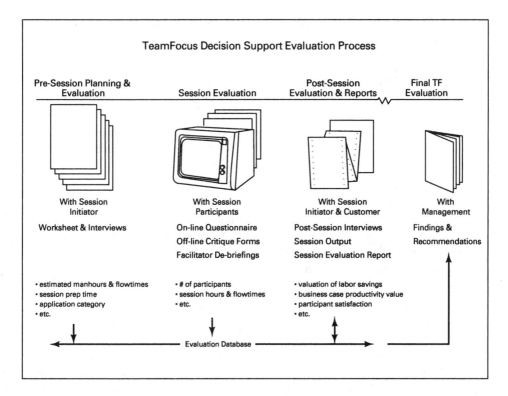

FIGURE 21.2   TeamFocus Decision Support Evaluation Process

the team constructed a set of scaled questionnaire measures that were directed to participants online at the end of the sessions. These measures focused on customer satisfaction, utility, perceptions of quality, ergonomic, and economic questions.

The online questionnaire also contained nominal measures (yes–no values) assessing participant decision making, understanding of session objectives, adherence to the session purpose, and role awareness by the participant. Coupled with the online measurements, essay questionnaires were distributed for completion by group session participants after reflection. These essay questions focused on issues regarding user acceptance of the technology as well as the session process, criticisms of both the technology and process, suggestions for improvement, and an open opportunity to express opinions concerning the strengths of the technology and the session, if any.

As shown in Figure 21.2, the evaluation methodology approved by the team for implementation involved several measurement points. The first of these occurred at the time of the pre-session interviews with customers, where group session requirements were operationalized. This information was documented with session planning worksheets which were also used in the capture of detailed estimates of traditional customer group process metrics such as working day flowtime and labor factors. This traditional group process estimation information was carefully defined in terms of the normal customer requirements for conducting a group process to achieve a specific result. The pre-session planning worksheet establishes the group session information baseline in terms of these key elements:

- Customer identification and category
- Purpose of the session
- Session objectives
- Deliverables (such as a specific decision, plan, recommendation, list of priorities, definition of work statement, solution to problem, and the like)
- Value of session to customer business
- Roles of session participants
- Customer's current group process
- Satisfaction with current group practices
- Customer traditional process estimates for same session/same result
- Session agenda and software tool pathway
- Precise brainstorming questions
- Description of in-depth focus areas

As these evaluation components were fielded, a database application was designed, tested, and fielded for daily use by the evaluator and other team members. The database included the design of data entry screens and reports that ensured efficient and accurate data storage and retrieval operations. An early decision was made by the team to share all session results and business case evaluation data with session customers within three days following each group process event with TeamFocus. Session data was captured, stored, and a data report was produced in graphical and business analytical form.

Following a quality check of each rapidly produced group session report, the facilitator responsible for the session delivered to the customer the data report along with session documentation in a specially bound book. This approach was designed into the evaluation to ensure that all customers were an integral part of the evaluation milieu and therefore could provide the team with a richer set of feedback. The customer was part of the quality consciousness of the method, a concept based on the Japanese business model of customer involvement called Quality Function Deployment (Zultner 1990; Gause and Weinberg 1989; Akao 1989).

Group Session Startup and Process Control

The first leg of the formal business case evaluation carefully staged technology support to customer groups who were solicited to help the team launch the program. Each of these initial groups had legitimate group process requirements and each was accommodated on the basis of full-cycle presession planning, documentation, session facilitation, post-session evaluation, and facilitator followup. Lessons learned during this early stage were significant and were discussed at length on a *post-mortem* basis the day after each session. These deliberations included detailed review of the presession and in-session process mechanics with in-depth attention given to modeling our approaches to enhance future session efficiency and effectiveness. Since each group session was unique, the precise pathway for software tool utilization had to be optimized by the facilitator and customer during the planning and execution stages of each session.

From the outset of the study, serious attention was paid to the software itself, its performance capabilities and shortfalls, as well as captured bugs and agreed upon work-arounds. Bug report forms were completed for each problem encountered by facilitators and other team members. These reports became the data trail for related communications with the vendor over the course of the evaluation. Similarly, hardware and lanware issues were also reviewed, with the technical manager taking the lead in determining the best courses of action. The combined software and hardware technical issues required a series of system adjustments, equipment and component replacements and repairs as well as the proverbial acts of "ghost-busting" less finite problems.

Stabilizing the evaluation process and environment was the critical priority during the first weeks of the evaluation program. A key step in this effort was the development of the TeamFocus Customer Lifecycle Procedures. These standards were the result of the team's efforts to define a cradle-to-grave process for conducting group sessions. While procedural approaches are not customary in group process circles, the function of the Lifecycle Procedures was to minimize variance across the many endogenous and exogenous factors affecting an objective evaluation. The Customer Lifecycle Procedures were spread across five distinct phases of activity:

> Phase 1—Customer Acquisition
> Phase 2—Session Planning
> Phase 3—Session Activities
> Phase 4—Evaluation Administration
> Phase 5—Post-Session Follow-up

This structure helped establish a firm basis for rapid deployment as a business service offering, should the technology evaluation and business case warrant that decision downstream. Throughout the stabilization of the effort, the team was determined to provide a professionally delivered product to all customers during the evaluation so that the "real-world" business benefits of the technology could be clearly recognized.

Customer Acquisition

To ensure the validity and success of the evaluation, it was critical that there were sufficient customers, with substantive group tasks and issues, that were representative of the Company's life blood. This meant that the evaluation served a relatively large number of clients. A minimum of sixty-two session clients was established as a study requirement for statistical reasons. A population roughly similar to Company organizational and functional sectors, including both upper, middle, and lower management strata, as well as staff groups was targeted. These requirements necessitated a relatively focused customer solicitation approach. Educational and marketing aides proved useful in the customer acquisition effort. Since the sponsoring organization and all team members had extensive customer relationships previously established, developing initial leads was not a significant problem. However, it is clear to the team that other GDSS operations, those without similar relationships with customers, may well find the hurdle of finding customers a major challenge.

Several team members took responsibility for developing a customer lead list and contacting them systematically. Daily and weekly reviews were held to assess each qualified lead and how best to involve them as participants within a short period of time. The scheduling of group sessions was problematic from the outset of the program for several reasons:

- Customers wanted relatively immediate session service, despite the team process requirements that called for two weeks lead time, and
- Customers exhibited typical group management behavior by rescheduling or canceling planned TeamFocus sessions late enough so that other sessions could not be substituted.

These problems challenged the conduct of the evaluation and threatened the team's ability to cost-effectively develop a representative customer set. The first response was to express irritation that time was wasted in pre-planning sessions which were too often rescheduled. It was decided that these customers were acting normally since the typical group process included meeting changes. Thereafter, the customer coordination efforts, indeed the entire lifecycle approach to working with customers cradle to grave, was amended in several ways:

1. Initial customer communication was enhanced with messages about the importance of a firm, committed schedule.
2. The difficulty of rescheduling a session with less than two weeks notice was emphasized.
3. The facilitator was assigned to the session immediately after the initial qualifying contact.
4. The facilitator established a "contract" with the customer as well as a direct communication tie, functioning as a risk assessment-abatement loop.
5. The pace and coverage of the customer contact effort was intensified to ensure that a ready stream of customers, which later became a backlog, was preplanned and available for load-leveling of the schedule.

Facilitator Training

The relevance of the facilitator in GDSS settings is dramatic (Phillips and Phillips 1990). Training and developing new facilitators, beyond the original two that started with the evaluation team on Day One, required special effort. Vendor training provided to each facilitator as they joined the team was not sufficient. New facilitators would return from their initial training eager to begin work leading sessions, but were ill equipped to do so. This was true despite their prior group facilitation and consultation experience and demonstrated ability. There were several deficiency patterns tied to this problem.

First, the training provided by the vendor, while certainly useful and necessary, did not emphasize sufficient hands-on practice time with the software. The training lasted five days, but because there were too few participants in the early vendor seminars, facilitator-trainees did not experience full size group dynamics. Also, the vendor training was not "real" enough as it relied too often on insignificant test problems and issues—nothing like the complex and dense issues areas which our facilitators faced in the actual evaluation sessions. Second, the vendor training program did not give the facilitators adequate exposure to varied GDSS techniques.

A series of changes in the training approach were undertaken:

- The vendor was consulted and a large number of improvements were negotiated.
- Seasoned "lead" facilitators were given direct responsibility for giving each new facilitator a graduated series of apprenticeship lessons and experiences.
- New facilitators were asked to conduct mock sessions and lead them using volunteers from within the sponsoring organization.
- New facilitators were given extra attention by the program manager and customer coordinator so that their concerns were understood and met.
- A conscious effort was made to expose new facilitators to as much of the program evaluation infrastructure as practical (metrics, procedures, management issues, budgets, program schedules, events, vendor communications, and the like).

These and other less important changes reduced training and apprenticeship duration from 3.75 months to 2 months. It is envisioned that the learning curve for most facilitators will extend up to 2 years as they develop all the software and GDSS facilitation skills necessary to be effective with virtually any group that comes forward.

EVALUATION RESULTS

The data shown here represents some sixty-four measured group support technology sessions that employed TeamFocus tools and procedures adopted for use in the study. The results suggest that a business case approach to technology evaluation can produce stark findings as well as reinforce existing research. A summary of these evaluation data is shown in Table 21.1. There were 654 persons attending the evaluated group sessions. Mean group size was 10.2 persons. The average session length was 4.7 hours. Mean pre-session preparation time was 16.7 hours, with the customer spending 7.8 hours and the evaluation group spending 8.9 hours of that time. Post-session labor averaged 4.5 hours, with most of this time spent by the evaluation group completing the documentation and meeting with the customer for each session. Savings data shown in the table are discussed later.

The distribution of the sessions by major category included in this study is shown in Figure 21.3. These categories are particularly relevant to the organization sponsoring this evaluation, as they are representative of major work categories considered relevant to this study. The Preferred Process activity area, which is similar to information systems planning, amounted to 11% of the sessions evaluated. The data indicates that one-quarter of the sessions involved planning work. The Consensus activity (11%) is a structured development and problem-solving service provided by this particular organization. Only

TABLE 21.1   Evaluation Data Summary

Session Activity

64 Sessions
654 Participants—Mean of 10.2 per Session
Mean Session Length of 4.7 Hours
Mean Preparation Time (Hours)
   Customer—7.8
   PSO—8.9
   Total—16.7
Mean Post-session Time—4.5 Hours
Current Booking Lead Time—29 Days

Savings to Company

$432,260 Total Labor Dollars Saved
$6,754 Mean Labor Dollars Saved per Session
$1,446 Mean Labor Dollars Saved per Session Hour
11,678 Total Labor Hours Saved (71%)
1,773 Total Days of Flowtime Saved (91%)

two sessions are categorized as management sessions, despite the fact that most of the evaluation events had management participation. The management strategy category was only applied to those sessions composed entirely of managers, whose activity centered on matters of management. Two other areas of significant activity were requirements definition (28%) and survey work (22%). The first of these was a high volume activity for the Company geared to information systems development. The second is a human

FIGURE 21.3   Session Categories

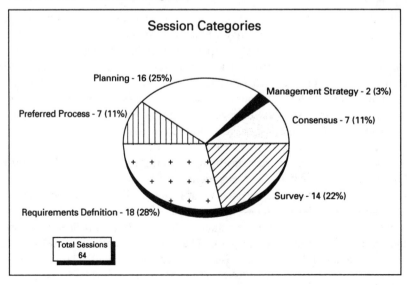

resources function associated with the Company's employee surveys. These distribution data indicate a relatively strong conformity with the average workload distribution of the sponsoring organization.

Measuring the Business Case

The study captured business case (effectiveness and efficiency) data through direct accounting and closely controlled estimation procedures. Direct charging of all labor hours was established for each session. This labor track captured all time spent from the first presession planning event held with a customer, through preparation and staging, actual session activity, and all post-session work attributable to the particular customer. Time accounting included both the evaluation staff and the session participants. Estimation data were gathered through structured interview and presession questionnaire documentation concerning both the flowtime and the labor that would be expended using the customer's traditional group process approach.

These estimates were operationalized in terms of the specific deliverables and session objectives established during the pre-session planning work. Customers were asked to carefully consider the deliverables defined for their particular group session and to calculate the group time in work days and hours for the team members involved if they used their traditional group processes. To ensure extra care, the group manager was instructed to provide conservative estimates. These estimates were also revisited by the customer at the conclusion of the session to provide an estimation validity check.

Efficiency

Perhaps the most dramatic results of these group support technology session evaluations are shown in Table 21.1. These numbers tell much of the business case story. The total flowtime in calendar days saved during the nine month evaluation equaled 1773 or 91%. The mean labor savings per session was $6,754 and totalled $432,260 for the Company. These financial results are compelling, especially when the number of sessions is taken into consideration. Further, since this is a new technology, having all of the inherent "start-up" business burdens, it is significant that this evaluation generated labor savings for the Company during the first stage of an evaluation effort. These data, along with

TABLE 21.2   Business Case Productivity Analysis ($000)

Average Operating Benefits Labor (@ 80% utilization)	1057	71% Productivity Gain
Average Operating Expenses	466	
Average Operating Savings	591	
Investment	348	5-Year Life-Cycle w/Labor
ROI	170 %	

flowtime and other efficiency data points create an optimistic business case picture.

Presented in Table 21.2 is a general depiction of a business case for the technology evaluation. This business case information provides an objective basis for making decisions about the wisdom of deploying group support technology as part of this organization's consulting practice. These calculations show average operating benefits will be $1,057,000, thus providing average operating savings of $591,000, based on a 5-year life-cycle investment of $348,000. The return on investment will equal 170%. These business case findings help Company management make well-founded technology investment decisions.

Effectiveness

All of the 654 persons participating in group session evaluations completed an online questionnaire. These surveys were aimed at measuring the effectiveness of the group support technology and delivery methodology. Scaled questions were designed to elicit participant judgments about each element of this portion of the business case study.

The results of this group participant survey are shown in Table 21.3. As these data indicate, participants rated the technology and delivery methods with relative enthusiasm. All of the means were significantly above the midpoint of each of the satisfaction

TABLE 21.3   Participant Questionnaire Responses

Question	Mean	Std Dev
Improved Channels of Communications	3.82	0.49
Helped Set Clear Objectives	3.63	0.62
Provide Insightful Information	3.90	0.46
Produced More Complete Decision Making	3.69	0.56
Higher Quality or More Valuable Session Results	3.91	0.51
Improved Teamwork and Morale	3.62	0.54
Increased Commitment to Results of Session	3.54	0.61
Enabled Greater Efficiency and ROI	4.02	0.46

Scaling: 1 - No Benefit to 5 - Great Benefit   Participants 654

Question	Mean	Std Dev
Session Well Suited to Group's Objectives	4.04	0.49
Comfortable Using the GDSS Tools	4.14	0.39
Personal Responsibility for Group's Decisions	3.70	0.55
Other Meeting Would Not Have Produced Same Ideas	3.52	0.52
Results Achieved in Much Less Time	4.04	0.51
Willing to Participate in Another TeamFocus Session	4.37	0.46
My Group Could Use TeamFocus on a Regular Basis	3.55	0.56
Comfortable Using the Keyboard	4.06	0.40
Facilitator Beneficial to Session	4.24	0.45

Scaling: 1 - Strongly Disagree to 5 - Strongly Agree   Participants 654 and agreement scales used. Standard deviations indicate fairly homogenous response distributions. Clearly, the highest positive response was the respondents' willingness to participate in another session (4.37). Significant to the sponsoring organization was the high value placed on the group session facilitator (4.24).

Participants reported a high degree of comfort with the software tools (4.14) and the computer keyboard (4.06). These last two variables were considered "trip-wires" in the study because of concerns on the part of some managers over potential "fear of computing" participant responses to the group technology.

Overall, the session participants rated the effectiveness of the technology and the methodology high in terms of enhanced quality (3.91), more insightful information (3.90), and improved channels of communication (3.82). These data point to a strong showing for the technology and its positive impact on the Company's current group business practices.

Quality and Customer Satisfaction

An additional followup questionnaire was systematically administered to the managers of all completed group sessions. These questionnaires were mailed to the group leaders several weeks following their sessions. An overall rate of return of 74% was achieved. The data from this source are shown in Table 21.4.

This instrument utilized scaled questions that sought respondent data concerning quality, utilization, and customer satisfaction variables. The response means show a high level of satisfaction and utility associated with the results of these technology supported group sessions. Of particular interest is that these customers indicated that session products were used by their organizations (4.83), that session objectives and requirements

TABLE 21.4   Followup Questionnaire Responses

Question	Mean	Std Dev
A decision by consensus was reached in session	4.77	1.38
Organization has made use of session output/product	4.83	1.37
TeamFocus improved decision-making and information gathering	5.04	1.07
Required results were obtained from session	4.88	1.08
TeamFocus allowed organization to shorten schedule or reduce resource usage	5.04	1.23
Facilitator and services added value to the *TeamFocus* session	5.54	0.78
Would use *TeamFocus* again	5.38	1.06

Scaling: 1 - Strongly disagree to 6 - Strongly agree   Respondees = 24 were met (4.88), and that the services provided before, during, and after these sessions added value (5.54). Taken together, the results of these post-sessions surveys make it clear that groups and their parent organizations reap significant benefits from using this technology and the attendant delivery services.

CONCLUSIONS

The results of this study demonstrate the value of business metrics in the design of GDSS research, as well as in the development and deployment of the program using these technologies. These variables have *a priori* significance to decision makers throughout the world, whether they operate in large commercial settings, applied research environments, or small entrepreneurial organizations.

Group decision support systems can only be valuable to the extent that they are deployed and integrated with organizational infrastructure elements which are at once both dynamic and complex. The opportunity available to the GDSS industry is in creating value for organizations by providing an effective means of performing group work.

This study raises other concerns that future research efforts should address, such as understanding the costs of information and the costs of decisions in group settings and the relative consequences of group support technologies.

QUESTIONS

1. What are the forces driving the enhanced roles that groups are now playing in organizations?
2. What parameters were used to evaluate the TeamFocus technology? Discuss the appropriateness of the parameters used. What other parameters might have been used?
3. Summarize the results from using TeamFocus.

REFERENCES

AKAO, Y.   "Recent Aspects of QFD on Service Industry in Japan," *International Conference on Quality Control 1989 Proceedings*. International Academy for Quality.

ALLPORT, F.   "The Influence of the Group upon Association and Thought," *Journal of Experimental Psychology*, 3 (1920), 159–182.

BARNARD, C.   "The Executive Function," *The Functions of the Executive*, 215–34. Cambridge: Harvard University Press, 1938.

BEAUCLAIR, R. A., AND D. W. STRAUB   "Utilizing GDSS Technology: Final Report on a Recent Empirical Study," *Information & Management*, 18, no. 5 (1990), 213–220.

BOOSE, J., J. BRADSHAW, J. KOSZAREK, AND D. SHEMA   "Better Group Decisions: Using Knowledge Based Acquisition Techniques to Build Richer Decision Models," submitted to Hawaii International Conference on Systems Sciences, 1992.

CAMPBELL, T. L.   "Technology Update: Group Decision Support Systems," *Journal of Accountancy*, 170

(1990), 47–50.

CONNOLLY, T. L., M. JESSUP, AND J. S. VALACICH "Effects of Anonymity and Evaluative Tone on Idea Generation in Computer-Mediated Groups," *Management Science*, 36, 6 (1990), 689–703.

DESANCTIS, G., AND GALLUPE, R. B. "A Foundation for the Study of Group Decision Support Systems," *Management Science*, 33, 5 (1987), 589–609.

DIEHL, M., AND W. STROEBE "Productivity Loss in Brainstorming Groups: Toward the Solution of a Riddle," *Journal Social Personality and Social Psychology*, 53, 3 (1987), 497–509.

GAUSE, D. C., AND G. WEINBERG *Exploring Requirements: Quality Before Design*. New York: Dorsett House, 1989.

GRAY, P., J. S. ARONOFSKY, N. BERRY, O. HELMER, G. R. KANE, AND T. E. PERKINS "The SMU Decision Room Project," *Proceedings of the Conference on Decision Support Systems*, 122–129. Execucom Systems Corporation, 1981.

HUBER, G. "Decision Support Systems: Their Present Nature and Future Applications," in *Decision Making: An Interdisciplinary Inquiry*, ed. G. R. Ungson and D. N. Braunstein, 249–262. Kent, 1982.

JOHANSEN, R. *Groupware: Computer Support for Business Teams*. New York: The Free Press, 1988.

KRAEMER, K. L., AND J. L. KING. "Computer-Based Systems for Cooperative Work and Group Decision Making," *ACM Computing Surveys*, 20, no. 2 (June 1988), 116–145.

KYDD, C. T., AND L. H. JONES. "Corporate Productivity and Shared Information Technology," *Information & Management*, 17, no. 5 (1989), 277–282.

LEWIS, L. F., AND K. S. KELEMAN. "Issues in Group Decision Support System (GDSS) Design," *Journal of Information Science*, 14, no. 6 (1988), 347–354.

McGOFF, C., A. HUNT, D. VOGEL, AND J. NUNAMAKER "IBM's Experience with GroupSystems," *Interfaces*, 20, no. 6 (November–December 1990), 39–52.

McGRATH, J. E. *Groups: Interaction and Performance*. Englewood Cliffs, N.J.: Prentice Hall, 1984.

NUNAMAKER, J., ET AL. "Experiences at IBM with Group Support Systems: A Field Study," *Decision Support Systems*, 5 (1989a), 183–196.

NUNAMAKER, J., D. VOGEL, AND B. KONSYNSKI "Interaction of Task and Technology to Support Large Groups," *Decision Support Systems*, 5 (1989b), 139–152.

PHILLIPS, L. D., AND M. C. PHILLIPS *Facilitated Work Groups: Theory and Practice*. London: London School of Economics & Political Science, 1990.

PINSONNEAULT, A., AND K. L. KRAEMER "The Effects of Electronic Meetings on Group Processes and Outcomes: An Assessment of the Empirical Research," *European Journal of Operational Research*, 46, no. 2 (1990), 143–161.

TANNIRU, M. R., AND H. JAIN "Knowledge Based GDSS to Support Reciprocally Interdependent Decisions," *Decision Support Systems*, 5, no. 3 (1989), 287–301.

VANGUNDY, A. B. "Idea Collection Methods: Blending Old and New Technology," *Journal of Data Collection*, 27, no. 1 (1987), 14–19.

VOGEL, D. R., ET AL. "Electronic Meeting System Experience at IBM," *Journal of Management Information Systems*, 6, 3 (Winter 1989–90), 25–43.

VOGEL, D., AND J. NUNAMAKER "Group Decision Support System Impact: Multi-Methodological Exploration," *Information & Management*, 18 (1990), 15–18.

ZULTNER, R. E. "Software Quality Deployment: Applying QFD to Software," *Transactions from the 2nd Symposium on QFD*. American Society for Quality Control, 1990.

22

HERE COMES THE PAYOFF FROM PCs

David Kirkpatrick

Ever been in a meeting where ideas start flowing so fast everybody wants to talk at once? Boeing and other companies have found a radical new way to harness that creative energy. Their brainstormers still sit around a table, but instead of shouting, they type their thoughts on networked personal computers using a new kind of software that keeps track of what everyone has to say. Participants can sift through far more material and act faster than they could in an ordinary meeting.

In fact, after years of complaints that investment in desktop computing doesn't pay off in productivity, this new software—called groupware—has produced dramatic results. Boeing has cut the time needed to complete a wide range of team projects by an average of 91%, or to *one-tenth* of what similar work took in the past. In one case last summer, a group of engineers, designers, machinists, and manufacturing managers used TeamFocus software from IBM to design a standardized control system for complex machine tools in several plants. Managers says such a job normally would take more than a year. With fifteen electronic meetings, it was done in 35 days.

Boeing's data come from the largest and most rigorous study yet of the cost-saving impact of groupware—computer software explicitly designed to support the collective work of teams. Productivity gains around a conference table have so far been most obvious. But groupware's ultimate promise is larger—linking departments, or colleagues in different locations, or even entire corporations in ways that vastly improve the efficiency and speed of collaborative projects.

The software has piqued the interest of many company problem solvers because the typical American manager spends 30% to 70% of the day in meetings. The setup that Boeing and others are finding so successful seems absurd at first: a conventional conference room with a computer at every place. "Why can't we just look each other in the eye and talk?" you wonder. The answer: because you seldom elicit all the best ideas, and many potentially valuable contributors remain silent. In many meetings, 20% of the people do 80% of the talking. Those who are shy, junior, intimidated, or just too polite typically shut up.

Meeting software uses several techniques to loosen the lips of the silent majority. Everyone speaks at once, via the keyboard. (In most cases, plenty of outloud interaction happens too.) As you type in your ideas and comments—hunt and peck is okay—they accumulate on your screen alongside everyone else's. Most people can read much faster than they can listen, so they can deal with far more material in a given period. Says Jay Nunamaker, who helped pioneer the concept at the University of Arizona in the early 1980s and is now CEO of Ventana Corp., a Tucson firm that markets systems based on his work: "In a typical hour-long meeting of 15 people, everybody's got an average of only four minutes of air time. With computer support, everybody's got the potential to talk for 60 minutes. That's a big increase in productivity."

Also important, most systems keep the author of a given comment anonymous. That can be a powerful incentive to speak. Go ahead and disagree with your boss. He won't know it was you. Explains a market researcher at a Fortune 500 company who has begun conducting all meetings electronically: "It's generally unacceptable in a culture like ours to say your most private thoughts on a matter. You might be embarrassed or considered silly. But once a thought is on the screen it becomes something to be seriously considered by the group, and otherwise secret thoughts can be very useful. The processes of the mind become open to the group." The software uses a voting system, again anonymous, to rate ideas.

Groupware is already having a major impact on companies willing to move toward the new form of organization futurist Alvin Toffler calls "ad-hocracy," in which individuals decide what needs to be done and form teams to do it. These pioneers—which include Boeing, Dell Computer, GM Europe, IBM, Marriott, MCI Communications, J.P. Morgan, Pacific Gas & Electric, Price Waterhouse, Southern New England Telecommunications, and Texaco—are using technology to push toward flatter, faster, more team-focused organizations.

Proponents believe in what could be called the democratization of data: the flow of knowledge to wherever it is needed. Groupware enables team members to stay abreast of one another's progress whether they are in a meeting room or scattered at PC keyboards from Boston to Bangkok. Companies can more quickly find connections

FIGURE 22.1   Groupware can get Everybody into the act

While groupware generally aimes to help established teams work more efficiently, Lotus's Notes helps create ad hoc teams. It provides interlinked electronic bulletin boards that allow people in a company who have insights or expertise on a particular problem to find one another. At Price Waterhouse a Notes user logs on and sees a screen with lists of different databases (large screen below). Need to know who in the firm is an expert on nonferrous mining? The box called FISP Resumes will tell you. (The initials, which also appear in the Hot Topics box, stand for Financial Service Industry Practice, an internal PW designation.)

The Notes Program differs significantly from electronic mail, where senders must select the recipients of a message. With Notes, anyone with an interest in a subject can read the information. It's not uncommon for a Notes conversation to include people from five or six cities around the world. A query from London may be answered by someone in Toronto, who may be challenged in turn by someone else in Los Angeles. Before Notes, only four members of Price Waterhouse's 15-person senior executive committee used PCs at all. Now they all do.

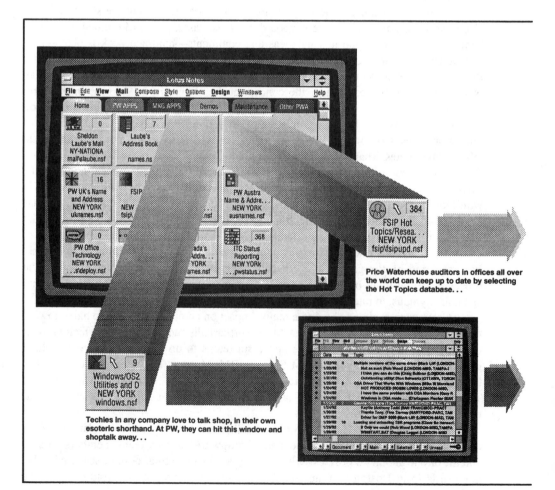

Price Waterhouse auditors in offices all over the world can keep up to date by selecting the Hot Topics database. . .

Techies in any company love to talk shop, in their own esoteric shorthand. At PW, they can hit this window and shoptalk away. . .

among disparate pieces of information and disparate people whose expertise might otherwise be overlooked.

Many of these companies use a unique product from Lotus Development called Notes, which Robert Johansen, a senior fellow at the Institute for the Future in Menlo Park, California, calls "the bellwether groupware product out there." Introduced in late 1989, Notes is starting to show how the remarkable possibilities of groupware go well beyond meetings. Users type into the system vast amounts of their written work, which creates a set of databases that can be organized and searched in whatever way a user finds most convenient.

Price Waterhouse was Lotus's first Notes customer and now has 9000 employees hooked up (see box). Sheldon Laube, who has responsibility for all technology in the accounting and consulting firm's U.S. operations, required virtually everyone to have a PC powerful enough to handle the Notes network. Says he: "This is a revolutionary piece of software that will change the way people think about computers."

... on the Financial Accounting Standards Board (FASB) ...   ... as summarized by Diane Altneu in New York.

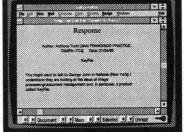

... as described by Tina Tierney in the Hartford office ...   ... and commented on by Anthony Todd in San Francisco.

In many companies, leaders of teams trying to improve customer service have been among the first to embrace groupware. Technology consultants at Boeing used TeamFocus to better identify their customers' needs and to set a strategic direction for themselves. They estimated the process would normally have taken six weeks but with the help of two half-day electronic meetings was finished in one.

At Marriott, human resources executive Carl Di Pietro started using meeting software five months ago. He has run meetings for groups from all across the company, and his enthusiasm is boundless: "In my 30 years, it's the most revolutionary thing I've seen for improving the quality and productivity of meetings. It gets you closer to the truth." A group is able to reach a genuine consensus, he says, and members leave much more committed to decisions than they would have been with conventional methods.

By definition groupware requires groups of PC users wired into a network. That knitting together is happening so fast in the Nineties that Steve Jobs of Next Computer suggests rechristening the machines "*inter*personal computers." Already 38% of corporate PCs are tied into networks, many spanning whole companies.

Computer networks not only connect machines but also make employees feel connected to the organization. Researchers find that electronic mail users are more likely to feel committed to their jobs than do the unplugged. No similar data yet exist for groupware, but anecdotal evidence so far suggests it creates an even more powerful sense of belonging.

Managers have been frustrated for years by their inability to prove that office computing increases productivity. Morgan Stanley senior economist Stephen Roach flatly asserts that there has been *no* productivity payoff. His primary evidence: While service companies spent about $800 billion on information technology in the past decade, service productivity growth over that period has been a measly 0.7%. One problem, Roach says, is that service companies have not made the staff reductions that the new hardware should have made possible.

Others make a similar point about manufacturing. Economist Gary Loveman at the Harvard business school studied comprehensive five-year cost and productivity data for 60 large manufacturing enterprises and found no evidence that information technology improved productivity.

Neither Roach nor Loveman thinks computers are the fundamental problem. "I don't blame the machines," says Roach. "It's a managerial problem. Call it ineptitude. They haven't had the guts to trade machines for bodies." Loveman concurs: "I don't think most organizations have thought about what information does to authority, job structures, decision-making, and allocation of people's time."

Lotus CEO Jim Manzi agrees that evidence of productivity gains is paltry—so far. "Nobody can demonstrate a return on investment for stand-alone computing," he says. (By contrast, CEO Bill Gates of Microsoft argues that productivity gains do exist but are just extremely difficult to measure.) Manzi thinks progress will come with groupware. Says he: "We think productivity can be improved if we use work group computing to integrate people into teambased organizations." He adds that Notes demonstrates the difference between "information processing" and "information sharing."

IBM was the first company to install an electronic meeting room in a real business situation—a manufacturing and development facility in Owego, New York. A team from the University of Arizona led by Nunamaker designed the software and in the fall of 1987 visited Owego to measure its impact. They found that meeting time was cut by 56%. Subsequent research by IBM itself at a corporate administrative center found similar results.

Boeing's study late last year is the most comprehensive followup to the IBM research. It closely replicated the Owego results with a larger sample over a longer period. It also demonstrated cost benefits for the first time. Boeing studied 64 meetings with 1,000 participants, tracking what managers did compared with what they said they would have done without the software. Boeing saved an average of $6,700 per meeting, mainly in employee time. Says TeamFocus project manager Brad Quinn Post, who ran the study, "The data show there are very clear opportunities to use these products to significantly improve business processes, to make our work cheaper, faster, and better."

In 1989, IBM signed a licensing agreement with Nunamaker's Ventana that allowed Big Blue to install more meeting rooms in its own offices and to sell the software to outside clients. IBM now has more than 50 such rooms all over the world. It rents some to outsiders for $2,000 to $7,000 a day, and will license its TeamFocus software—a version of Ventana's system—for one meeting room for $50,000. Ventana charges $25,000 to license its product, called GroupSystems.

One other program is on the market: VisionQuest, developed by tiny Collaborative Technologies of Austin, Texas. IBM has deliberately proceeded slowly, wanting to establish TeamFocus internally and refine the software before pushing it hard on customers. Collaborative Technologies, on the other hand, recently reorganized in order to market its product more aggressively. The company sells a VisionQuest license for $29,000.

All three are elegantly designed and user-friendly. Collaborative Technologies has taken the simplest path: It requires no equipment other than a network of PCs. The competing systems designed and sold by Ventana and licensed to IBM add a big display screen at the front of the room. While a professional meeting facilitator is helpful at any electronic meeting, Ventana and IBM virtually require one. That makes their systems costlier to operate, though they do offer a wider range of features, including a way for groups to collaborate on writing letters or documents.

Some gleanings from the experience of companies already seriously committed to groupware follow.

At Marriott's Bethesda, Maryland, headquarters recently, seven executives from one of the company's large Washington-area hotels sat in a room full of PCs equipped with VisionQuest. None had ever taken part in an electronic meeting. A sign at the front warned: "Enter this room ONLY if you believe the ideas and opinions of others have value."

Their challenge was to find new ways to improve guest satisfaction. After a lot of laughing and a few silly suggestions on screen, the room was silent. Occasionally someone left briefly. The hotel's general manager ate a cookie. After 25 minutes, the group had generated 139 ideas. Then they rated them on a scale of one to five: once according to the likely impact of each idea on guests, and again according to what each would probably cost. A consensus emerged that, among other things, more thorough training of hotel employees was essential.

A market researcher, who asked not to be identified because he doesn't want his competition to start using groupware, has been running all his meetings with VisionQuest for six months. They typically include scientists, product developers, sales and marketing people, and often ad agency staffers. Says he: "While I thought I was a good facilitator, I'm convinced I was actually missing about 75% of the information I could have got out on the table." He installed the software in a room his company had designed for PC training, where 15 networked PCs often sat unused.

Southern New England Telecommunications installed IBM's TeamFocus in an electronic meeting room in its New Haven, Connecticut, headquarters in June 1990 and has just added a second. The company used the rooms to develop a new customer relations strategy in seven weeks that it figures would have taken about a year using focus groups or surveys of employees who deal with the public.

J. P. Morgan installed a handsomely appointed thirteen-seat room equipped with TeamFocus last March. Since then it has been in almost constant use for meetings devoted to strategic planning, organizational changes, auditing, and employee surveys, among other subjects. Morgan will soon install TeamFocus rooms in its Wilmington, Delaware, and London offices. Says Lynn Reed, a vice president in Morgan's global technology and operations group: "The software works best for a meeting that is going to take more than an hour and that is intended to achieve a group decision. It's not beneficial for status-checking meetings, where each participant has to give a report, or for meetings with a single speaker."

Dell Computer started using VisionQuest last May for strategic planning meetings. The company found it could include more people in the process and still finish faster. Says Bruce Ezell, manager of business development: "That went so well we've started using it for any type of project that requires groups of people to work together—like product planning and developing marketing strategies."

In one case, Dell used the system to name a new product. In the past, names were developed by asking product team members to send in suggestions by electronic mail. Then meetings were called to consider lists of names on flip charts. "Whoever screamed loudest would be heard," says Ezell. "It was still up to the product manager to make a decision, but there was no way to get consensus." With VisionQuest, a group of marketing and sales managers met for two hours, proposed and rated 75 names, and reduced them to five finalists. It would have taken two months to get there the old way.

Ezell says groupware is a natural for Dell since everyone in the company has good computer skills. More important, the PC industry is experiencing brutal price cutting and going through faster technological change than perhaps any other industry in history. Says Ezell: "When we detect a major change in the market, we need to pull our management team together immediately. We can't tolerate meetings that hash things out all day and end without consensus." Strategic planning meetings that used to last two days now take four hours.

Di Pietro of Marriott is convinced that meeting software can also enhance cultural diversity, a company priority. "It's a room of nondiscrimination," he says. "You don't know if that idea you're reading comes from a woman or a man, part of the minority or majority, or a senior or junior person. People begin to say, 'Hey, we've got a lot in common with each other.' "

Many experts caution, however, that a repressive boss or a dysfunctional group will probably remain so with or without electronic help. Says Bob Bostrom, who teaches at the University of Georgia and consults with companies on using meeting software: "The technology doesn't make people equal in terms of power but in terms of being heard." Some bosses defeat its purpose by walking around the room glaring at people's terminals or loudly bullying everyone to put in ideas that resemble their own, says Gerardine DeSanctis, a professor of information systems at the University of Minnesota. "The group has to decide it wants to get more out of meetings," she observes. "It's like an alcoholic has to want to stop drinking."

The next step is to enable people to meet without being in the same room—or even the same city. The three meeting software products are all designed to work among distant participants, and a few companies, including Dell Computer, are already reporting early success with this approach. Nunamaker, however, says his research has found obstacles. Without the nonverbal cues and other stimuli that come from seeing others in the same room engaged in a common task, people's attention easily wanders.

Groupware has other potential drawbacks. Notes, for example, may prove threatening to some managers because employees can independently identify and connect with others working on similar tasks. These new working relationships may improve efficiency, but they may also upset organizational hierarchies. Says Natasha Krol, an analyst at the Meta Group, a Westport, Connecticut, consulting firm: "You can start your own subculture in Notes. Managers often have very little to do with that, and the process may even help identify which managerial layers are obsolete."

The flip side of Notes is that putting so much employee activity on the network gives management the potential to monitor exactly what is going on in the organization. At Price Waterhouse, some departments use Notes as a kind of electronic filing cabinet, with all written documents inserted in the database. The boss can see every memo anybody writes.

Some new types of groupware on the horizon could increase management control still further. Later this year NCR expects to release an enhancement to Cooperation, its program that ties together office activities now conducted on different computer systems from PCs to mainframes. The new feature can, among other things, keep track of documents that must be passed from person to person for processing. It will alert managers to logjams or other inefficiencies.

The payoff from groupware could be huge. John Oltman, CEO of SHL Systemhouse, a large Ottawa firm that manages computer systems for clients, predicts that some big insurance companies could reduce their claims-processing work force by as much as 50% over the next five years.

Groupware that allows teams to communicate using video will open entirely new productivity horizons. Researchers are already working on various ways to conduct what they call "virtual meetings," in which videoscreens would allow people in various places to interact as if they were face to face. Jay Nunamaker has a plan that calls for groups of four people to sit at terminals in front of giant screens in four different rooms. The screens create the illusion that all 16 participants are in the same room.

At AT&T Bell Laboratories, researcher Sid Ahuja is working on a way to accomplish the same thing from individual offices. His system would display live video images of each participant on a desktop terminal, and allow them to share software, graphics, and other data as easily as if they were all together.

If Groupware really makes a difference in productivity long term, the very definition of an office may change. You will be able to work efficiently as a member of a group wherever you have your computer. As computers become smaller and more powerful, that will mean anywhere. Paul Saffo, a researcher at the Institute for the Future, thinks networked computing may well lead to drastic population dispersal. Says he: "For the first three-quarters of the century our cities were shaped by developments in transportation and telecommunications, but now the influence is shifting to computers and communications." And all we really wanted was a little boost in productivity.

QUESTIONS

1. What are some of the ways that groupware can affect how people in groups act?
2. Summarize how companies have used various groupware products.
3. What are the potential obstacles to the use of groupware in organizations?
4. Describe a potential use of groupware in an organization that you belong to.

23

GROUPWARE: FUTURE DIRECTIONS AND WILD CARDS

Robert Johansen

INTRODUCTION

"Groupware," like most emerging technologies, is difficult to name. There are competing terms to describe this phenomenon: "computer-supported cooperative work," "interpersonal computing," "shared systems," "cooperative computing," "coordination systems," "team computing," and so on. I use groupware because that is what business users appear to have adopted more than any other term, at least for the moment. After having studied emerging information technologies for nearly 20 years now, I am used to the problem of

The author is grateful to Christine Bullen at the Massachusetts Institute of Technology and Ken Lyon at Procter & Gamble for their help in refining Figure 23.1. This reading has benefited greatly from ongoing research with colleagues at Institute for the Future, particularly the Outlook Project and the Groupware Users' Project. Core team members include Jeff Charles, Richard Dalton, Elliot Gold, Alexia Martin, Robert Mittman, Paul Saffo, David Sibbet, and Stephanie Bardin.

Reprinted by special permission of the *Journal of Organizational Computing,* Volume 2, Number, 1991. © 1991 by Ablex Publishing Corporation.

naming. In fact, if an emerging technology is easy to name, it is probably not worth studying. By that criterion, groupware is certainly worth studying.

Groupware also merits study because it is an emerging technology that is linked to clear and pressing user needs, the needs of business teams. Business teams are small, cross-organizational, time-driven, task-focused, cohesive work groups. Business teams are part of the evolving organization of the future that includes flatter hierarchies, network style, and international flavor.

At Institute for the Future, we are working with a variety of companies to try to make business sense out of groupware. We are an independent nonprofit research group with a goal of mapping emerging information technologies as they appear on the horizon, from a prospective user point of view. Groupware is one in a continuing series of emerging technologies that we are studying.

This article provides my views on where groupware is going, thinking out 5 years or so. My purpose here is not an academic review, but a personal speculation that forces me to be specific about what I *think* will happen.

Before the speculation begins, I want to introduce a basic map that we are using to describe and explore groupware options. Our experience with emerging information technologies is that you need some simple map that can be used quickly by someone who has never thought about groupware before. This map should introduce options and provoke thought about how groupware might be used in the future. Figure 23.1 provides our basic map of groupware options, with some examples of systems that we would classify as groupware. This map provides a basic framework that I will use as I speculate about groupware between now and 1994.

The future of groupware is not predictable, although there are some directions that are more likely than others. Thus, I have divided my thoughts into "sure things" (assuming there are some), "probables," and "wild cards."

SURE THINGS

The surest sure thing surrounding groupware is the importance of business teams. We are entering an age of organizational experimentation and redesign where teams will be a basic—perhaps *the* basic—organizing unit. Flatter organizations will depend on teams to get things done; the remaining hierarchies will still provide basic business functions, but teams will be where the action is in most companies. Peter Drucker's *Harvard Business Review* article "The Coming New Organization" set a new *HBR* reprint record while trumpeting business teams as a wave of the future [2]. Literally millions of business teams have pressing needs for communications and computing support, whether or not the computer and telecommunications industries choose to help them. Of course, while business teams are a sure thing, the reality of the team-based organization is still more public relations than practical experience. We know we will have teams, but we do not know how team-based organizations will evolve.

Meanwhile, the international nature of business is another sure thing—meaning that many teams will cross national boundaries. Furthermore, alliances and customer or supplier links will mean intercompany, as well as international, collaborations.

	Same Time	**Different Times**
Same Place	*Need: Face-to-Face Meetings* e.g. Copyboards PC Projectors Facilitation Services Group Decision Rooms Polling Systems	*Need: Administrative,* *Filing and Filtering* e.g. Shared Files Shift Work Kiosks Team Rooms Group Displays
Different Places	*Need: Cross-Distance Meetings* e.g. Conference Calls Graphics and Audio Screen Sharing Video Teleconferencing Spontaneous Meetings	*Need: Ongoing Coordination* e.g. Group Writing Computer Conferencing Conversational Structuring Forms Management Group Voice Mail

FIGURE 23.1 Business Team Needs and Groupware Solutions.
This map was stimulated by Ref. 1. The present version was modified in discussions with various user groups and other researchers.

Corporate boundaries will often be difficult to draw and even more difficult to protect. Desires for interoperability with other collaborators will be tempered with concerns about security.

On another front, companies will be looking for way to avoid making long-term
commitments to employees wherever possible. Temporary workers, for example, will
continue to grow in number since they allow a corporate work force to be increased or
decreased quickly, depending on business needs. As for health care benefits, there are
strong incentives for employers to shift as many of these costs as possible to employees.
The sure thing here is caution about commitments. For example, *Fortune* magazine concluded an analysis of labor trends in the following way: "The old career-long marriage
between employer and employee is giving way to a series of one-night stands" [3].

The telecommunications and computing infrastructure will continue to improve,
although not in any easy regular fashion. Rather, there will be fits and starts, as well as
disappointments, on the way to the workstation of the future. Thus, it is a sure thing that
the technology will become more powerful and more portable, but it is not clear just
what this will do for users.

In the groupware domain, the connection between same time/same place and different times/different places on Figure 23.1 is the central axis for groupware as it currently exists. The quest here is for the familiarity of same time/same place, with the flexibility of different times/different places. The sure thing is that this connection will remain
central to the evolution of groupware products and services for the foreseeable future.
The most promising electronic infrastructure for groupware is available in the different
times/different places domain [electronic mail, voice mail, local-area networks (LANs),
public networks, and so on], but the cultural familiarity is with face-to-face meetings.

In short, it is a sure thing to expect increases in complexity—with occasional notes
of stability and predictability. Anybody's "sure things" will be debatable. But, most people's list of sure things will have at least one thing in common: it will be short.

PROBABLE DIRECTIONS FOR GROUPWARE

Given this uncertainty and the absence of many sure things, what directions are at least *probable?* Figure 23.2 summarizes my projections, using the map of groupware options as an organizing framework.

Same time/same place groupware will finally come into its own by 1994. There are obvious wins here for most businesses, but there is strong cultural resistance to be overcome. In most U.S. businesses today, conference rooms are decidely low-tech; they may have a flip chart pad, a white board, and an overhead projector. Some rooms have slide projectors, VCRs, or audio conferencing units, but most do not. Furthermore, the people in charge of these austere conference rooms are rewarded for saving money, not for innovating. Businesspeople assume they must meet the old-fashioned way, without technology.

But this belief will give way, gradually, to a recognition of the value of electronic tools. The chief payoffs will come from functions such as having a written record of what was agreed upon during the meeting, anonymous discussions, simultaneous input of ideas, and voting or ranking of alternatives.

Low-tech tools will be most common in the short run, such as the copyboard or personal computer projector systems. A significant minority of rooms, however, will be equipped with terminal devices (ranging from a keypad to a full keyboard) for each participant. The University of Arizona's software (now licensed to IBM) is the first practical example of the range of tools that can be provided within such rooms. A key question is unresolved, however: Is this a product and/or a service? Once this question is answered, such rooms will become practical for many businesses. I think the question will be resolved with the conclusion that both products and services are involved. "High-touch" characteristics will be critical for such rooms, with an emphasis—in the short run at least—on human facilitators. Furthermore, I think such systems are on the verge of becoming practical, and that this emergence will occur over the next five years.

FIGURE 23.2   Probable Future Groupware Developments (circa 1994)

	Same Time	Different Times
Same Place	• Low-tech computer aids for conference rooms commonplace. • High-tech, high-touch computer-assisted rooms finally practical and used, though on a limited scale.	• Team rooms are commonplace, with electronic aids. • Shift work groupware (e.g., international traders, factories) commonplace.
Different Places	• Greatly increased use of conference calls. • Conference calls with PC graphics and image commonplace. • Video conferencing continues gradual growth, with some use of computer aids.	• E-mail and voice mail have evolved to include group features. • "Total Quality" groupware commonplace. • Text filtering and "information refineries" commonplace in a few sectors.

At the other end of the spectrum, different times/different places groupware will build on the considerable electronic infrastructure that is already out there. In particular, electronic mail and voice mail provide very attractive building blocks for group-oriented services. Both electronic mail and voice mail are "horseless carriage" or "paving the cowpaths" products: they simply automate what used to be done with conventional media. Now that large systems are in place, however, it is possible to extend the concept and add group capabilities for communications, project management, and other group functions. Person-to-person systems can evolve into groupware. Given the time demands on most business teams, the flexibility of different times/different places groupware will be attractive indeed.

"Total quality" methods are increasing in U.S. companies, fueled by Edwards Deming, Joseph Juran, Philip Crosby, and others. Such programs emphasize customer orientation, enterprisewide view, emphasis on process rather than outcomes, decisions driven by data, and long-term orientation. Groupware (primarily different times/different places groupware) can assist teams in implementing quality methods. I suspect that a distinct class of groupware products will emerge to service this rapidly growing market.

Text filtering and what John Clippinger has called "information refineries" are also likely within a 5-year time frame, at least within specialized market segments. Large information companies are already using early versions of such systems. Tom Malone's work at MIT on text filtering and his ambitious notions of the Information Lens and the Object Lens are also likely to be translated into commercial products. Such ideas are different times/different places-oriented, but they are certainly beyond the horseless carriage. They imply the ability to do things that previously were not possible: intelligent navigation through large text data bases. Such systems can also serve to link teams with teams and to coordinate the activities of varied teams within an organization.

Over the next five years, the focus of groupware creativity will shift gradually from inside small teams to the complicated connections across teams. I do not expect this shift to occur quickly or easily, but it will occur—beginning with specialized business segments that have pressing needs and the financial resources to experiment.

Same time/different places groupware over the next five years is likely to be "steady as she goes," with large increases in scale of activity, but little change in basic functionalities. Conference calling in North America is already growing rapidly, even with no marketing, and the capabilities of digital conference calling bridges mean much better sound quality and the ability to carry parallel computer images. Conference calling may seem boring to many computer people, but it is a critical building block with considerable momentum. At the high-tech end of the spectrum from conference calling is video teleconferencing, which has been an emerging technology for almost two decades. Finally, however, the installed base of two-way video rooms has grown substantially (over 1,000 rooms in North America) and people are using the medium in practical ways. In addition, the synergies of motion video and personal computing will be kicking in over the next five years, meaning drastic reductions in costs. (Actually, the cost of full-motion video coder-decoders was cut in half during recent years and is still dropping.) In short, same time/different places meetings are crucial to the life of business teams and have a very high probability of success on a large scale over the next five years.

The same place/different times cell is perhaps the most difficult to describe on the groupware map. One obvious use is shift work, where a team of people must hand off to another team to a manufacturing line going, for example, or to continue a process of international currency trading. Team rooms provide an example of same place/different times: they are "club rooms" assigned to teams, often with electronic aids of different sorts to facilitate group memory, chart progress toward team goals, and otherwise assist a team in getting its job done. Over the next five years, I expect that team rooms will become increasingly common (particularly in companies where open offices are the norm) and that many of these rooms will be equipped with various forms of groupware. Furthermore, shift work groupware will be expanded—particularly in high-payoff or high-risk segments such as trading and emergency monitoring.

Looking across the map in Figure 23.2, I suspect that the next five years will see a melting down of divisions among the four cells. In fact, the highest leverage groupware plays will be those that cut across two or more of the cells. For example, same time/same place groupware will be even useful if the discussion can be carried over to the user's different times/different places medium. Or, electronic meetings could be held to connect a computer-assisted meeting room with people who are not able to be present face-to-face. Ultimately, any time/any place groupware will be the norm, building on ultralight computers and cellular networks.

One of my disappointments with the current state of groupware is that people doing the most creative work in each of the four cells on the Figure 23.2 map are often ignorant of work going on in the other three cells. Such overspecialization is understandable in the early stages of a field, however, and it is likely to disappear over the next five years. It is interesting to recall that Doug Engelbart, one of the early groupware pioneers, had a system in the late 1960s (NLS) that had capabilities touching on all of the four time/place cells in Figure 23.1. For same time/same place, Engelbart had a team room where the moderator had a full workstation and each of the participants had a mouse and screen. For different times/different places, there were shared journals and group writing capabilities. For same time/different places, there was a screen sharing and remote multimedia (including audio and full-motion video). Finally, same place/different times capabilities were in place in Engelbart's Augmentation Research Center at Stanford Research Institute so that team members could use the center at any time of the day or night—even if other team members were not present simultaneously. Engelbart's broad vision is now becoming practical.

A final probable forecast: I think the term "groupware" (and the various competing terms) will be obsolete by 1994. Such banners serve a useful function in the short term, helping along the transition to thinking of the "user" as a collaborative group or team. Once this transition has been made, support for teams will be something we simply expect our personal computers and workstations to do. There will be no need for a specialized term.

WILD CARDS

Wild cards are low or unknown probability events (over the next five years) that, if they should occur, would have a major impact on groupware growth. In this section, I have listed events or developments that I think are particularly interesting. This is not an all-inclusive list. In fact, one sure thing is that there will be more wild cards than anyone can anticipate at this time. Here is my current list.

- *Interoperability.* Interoperability, a term I first heard from Mark Stefik at Xerox Palo Alto Research Center, means that systems can work together well—even if they are not fully integrated. Interoperability is a practical dream, but it has not come to pass yet, and I have trouble finding people who can give me convincing estimates of when it will happen. The more interoperability happens, the more groupware will occur on a large scale.

- *Radio LANs.* Local-area networks are an important platform for groupware, but they are also quite awkward to install and difficult to move. Teams, of course, move very rapidly and benefit greatly from flexibility. If radio LANs become practical, groupware for teams could be assembled and reassembled with much greater ease.

- *Free-form speech recognition.* The voicewriter (a machine that translates free-form spoken language into text) would be the obvious winner for groupware. Speaker independence, large vocabulary, and some speech understanding would add great power and open the use of electronic groupware to a wide range of nontechnical (or even technophobic) users.

- *User interface breakthrough.* I am thinking here of something at the level of the icon graphics interface made popular by the Macintosh. Some form of multimedia interface is most likely, probably incorporating voice, though not necessarily with the free-form speech recognition mentioned earlier. The current interfaces for groupware are often burdensome, particularly because of the multiple users that are involved in those applications.

- *"Cultware" becomes popular.* The trend toward business teams and the pressures to produce short-term business results could create a climate where executives are extremely open to quick-fix solutions. In such a climate, one could imagine simplistic groupware-type solutions have cult-like characteristics. Such groups have tended to arise in California, and quickly create loyal followers and great profits. If this wild card afflicts corporate America, expect groupware to absorb some of the bad press.

- *Jump in market demand for groupware.* Although business teams present obvious user needs for groupware, these needs are not yet articulated clearly enough to present a strong and focused market demand. For this to occur, some wild card happening would need to accelerate and focus market demand. A business fad (á la Japanese management styles or the book *In Search of Excellence)* would be one believable possibility. A breakthrough groupware product could also do this (i.e., the groupware equivalent of the spreadsheet). Such a development is a wild card for the next five years because it has an unknown probability of occurrence, but if it did occur, it would have a major effect.

CONCLUSION

Although there are few sure things in this marketplace, the user need (i.e., business teams) is real, and I feel that it is probable that the marketplace will develop strongly over the next five years. Although the probable developments in the 5-year period are quite straightforward, wild card events could speed up the process dramatically. The major growth of groupware is most likely to occur within the 5- to 10-year time horizon, however.

Groupware (or whatever it comes to be called) is here to stay. The primary questions concern how long groupware will take to develop, what development paths will prove most popular, and who will make money from the process.

QUESTIONS

1. Summarize what Johansen predicts are the sure things, probable developments, and wild cards for groupware.
2. What do you think are the sure things, probable developments, and wild cards for future groupware developments? Compare your thinking to Johansen's.
3. Radio (or wireless) LANs are starting to appear in the marketplace. Describe a creative group support application that would be possible or greatly facilitated by radio LANs.

REFERENCES

1. DeSantis, G., and B. Gallupe   "A foundation for the Study of Group Decision Support Systems," *Management Science, 33,* 5 (May 1987), 589–609.
2. Drucker, P.   "The Coming New Organization," *Harvard Business Review* (Jan.–Feb. 1988), 45–53.
3. *Fortune,* April 11, 1988.

ADDITIONAL REFERENCES

Crosby, P. B.   *Quality Is Free: The Art of Making Quality Certain.* New York: Mentor Books, 1979.

Deming, W. E.   *Out of the Crisis.* Cambridge, Mass.: Center for Advanced Engineering Study, 1988.

Juran, J. M., ed.   *Quality Control Handbook.* New York: McGraw-Hill, 1974.

Malone, T. W.   *What is Coordination Theory?* Cambridge, Mass.: Massachusetts Institute of Technology. Paper presented at the National Science Foundation Coordination Theory Workshop, February 19, 1988.

Malone, T. W., K. R. Grant, F. A. Turbak, S. A. Brobst, and M. D. Cohen   "Intelligent Information-Sharing Systems," *Communications of the ACM,* 30, no. 5 (1987), 390–402.

Malone, T. W., K. R. Grant, K. Y. Lai, R. Rao, and D. A. Rosenblitt   "Semistructured Messages Are Surprisingly Useful for Computer-Supported Coordination," *ACM Transaction on Office Information Systems,* 5, no. 2 (1987), 115–131.

Malone, T. W., K. R. Grant, K. Y. Lai, R. Rao, and D. A. Rosenblitt   "The Information Lens: An Intelligent System for Information Sharing and Coordination," in *Technological Support for Work Group Collaboration,* ed., M. H. Olsen. Hillsdale, N.J.: Erlbaum, 1989.

Peters, T., and R. H. Waterman, Jr.   *In Search of Excellence.* New York: Harper & Row, 1982.

PART 7

Expert Systems

Expert systems are computer applications that contain the knowledge, experience, and judgment of skilled professionals. They suggest decisions and often the reasoning behind their recommendations. Whereas many organizations once viewed expert systems as intriguing possibilities, many are now actively developing them. The applications range from complex ones to simple ones such as embedding intelligence in transaction-processing systems. The readings in this part describe what expert systems are, how they should be developed, organizational strategies for introducing expert systems, and several descriptions of expert systems, including the highly innovative CoverStory.

Fred Luconi, Thomas Malone, and Michael Scott Morton, in "Expert Systems: The Next Challenge for Managers" (Reading 24), provide an introductory look at expert systems. They discuss what they are, their component parts and how they function, and a framework for understanding how expert systems fit into the information systems constellation of applications. They also describe their benefits, problems, risks, and other important issues.

The development and implementation of an expert system is a complex undertaking. Dorothy Leonard-Barton, in "The Case for Integrative Innovation: An Expert System at Digital" (Reading 25), argues that an integrative innovation approach should be used. The development of XSEL, Digital Equipment Corporation's eXpert SELling assistant application, is used to illustrate the realities of developing an expert system.

Organizations that want to develop expert systems should have a strategy for doing so. Different strategies can be successfully employed, as discussed by Larry Meador and Ed Mahler in "Choosing an Expert Systems Game Plan" (Reading 26). The experiences of DuPont and Digital Equipment Corporation are used to illustrate how two companies took different approaches. Insights are provided for how a company can develop a strategy appropriate for it.

Bar-code scanners generate millions of records of data of great potential value to marketing managers. The problem is making sense out of the data. John Schmitz, Gordon Armstrong, and John Little, in "CoverStory—Automated News Finding in Marketing" (Reading 27), describe CoverStory, an expert system developed for Ocean Spray Cranberries that serves this purpose.

24

EXPERT SYSTEMS: THE NEXT CHALLENGE FOR MANAGERS

Fred L. Luconi,
Thomas W. Malone,
and Michael S. Scott Morton

Winston defines artificial intelligence (AI) as "the study of ideas which enable computers to do the things that make people seem intelligent."[1] AI systems attempt to accomplish this by dealing with qualitative as well as quantitative information, ambiguous and "fuzzy" reasoning, and rules of thumb that give good but not always optimal solutions. Another way to characterize artificial intelligence is not in terms of what it attempts to do, but in terms of the programming techniques and philosophies that have evolved from it. Specific AI techniques such as "frames" and "rules" allow programmers to represent knowledge in ways that are often much more flexible and much more natural for humans to deal with than the algorithmic procedures used in traditional programming languages.

There are at least three areas in which AI, in its current state of development, appears to have promising near-term applications: robotics, natural language under-

Reprinted from "Expert Systems: The Next Challenge for Managers," by Fred L. Luconi, Thomas W. Malone, and Michael S. Scott Morton, *Sloan Management Review,* Summer 1986, pp. 3–14, by permission of the publisher. © 1986 by the Sloan Management Review Association. All rights reserved.

standing, and expert systems. In this article, we will focus on the realistic potential for the use of expert systems in business. To emphasize our main point about appropriate ways of using these systems, we will exaggerate a distinction between expert systems, as they are often conceived, and a variation of expert systems, which we will call expert support systems.

WHAT DO EXPERT SYSTEMS DO?

Preserve and Disseminate Scarce Expertise

Expert systems techniques can be used to preserve and disseminate scarce expertise by encoding the relevant experience of an expert and making this expertise available as a resource to the less experienced person. Schlumberger Corporation uses its Dipmeter Advisor to access the interpretive abilities of a handful of their most productive geological experts and to make it available to their field geologists all over the world.[2] The program takes oil well log data about the geological characteristics of a well and makes inferences about the probable location of oil in that region.

Solve Problems Thwarting Traditional Programs

Expert systems can also be used to solve problems that thwart traditional programming techniques. For example, an early expert system in practical use today is known as XCON. Developed at Digital Equipment Corporation in a joint effort with Carnegie-Mellon University, XCON uses some 3,300 rules and 5,500 product descriptions to configure the specific detailed components of VAX and other computer systems in response to the customers' overall orders. The system first determines what, if any, substitutions and additions have to be made to the order so that it is complete and consistent. It then produces a number of diagrams showing the electrical connections and room layout for the 50 to 150 components in a typical system.[3]

   This application was attempted unsuccessfully several times using traditional programming techniques before the AI effort was initiated. The system has been in daily use now for over four years and the savings have been substantial, not only in terms of saving the technical editor time, but also in ensuring that no component is missing at installation time—an occurrence that delays the customer's acceptance of the system.[4]

WHAT ARE EXPERT SYSTEMS?

With these examples in mind, we define expert systems as *computer programs that use specialized symbolic reasoning to solve difficult problems well.* In other words, expert systems (1) use specialized knowledge about a particular problem area (such as geological analysis or computer configuration) rather than just general purpose knowledge that would apply to all problems, (2) use symbolic (and often qualitative) reasoning rather than just numerical calculations, and (3) perform at a level of competence that is better than that of nonexpert humans.

Expert systems can, of course, include extensive numerical calculations, but a computer program that uses *only* numerical techniques (such as a complex optimization program) would not ordinarily be called an "expert system." The kinds of nonnumerical symbolic knowledge that expert systems use include component/subcomponent relationships and qualitative rules about causal factors.

One of the most important ways in which expert systems differ from traditional computer applications is in their use of heuristic reasoning. Traditional applications employ algorithms, that is, precise rules that, when followed, lead to the correct conclusion. For example, the amount of a payroll check for an employee is calculated according to a precise set of rules. Expert systems, in contrast, often attack problems that are too complex to be solved perfectly; to do this, they use heuristic techniques that provide good but not necessarily optimum answers.

In some ways, of course, all computer programs are algorithms in that they provide a complete set of specifications for what the computer will do. Heuristic programs, however, usually search through alternatives using "rules of thumb" rather than guaranteed solution techniques. A program might consider many different types of geological formations before deciding which type best explains the data observed in a particular case.

WHAT ARE EXPERT SUPPORT SYSTEMS?

While expert support systems and expert systems use the same techniques, expert support systems help *people* (the emphasis is on people) solve a much wider class of problems. In other words, *expert support systems are computer programs that use specialized symbolic reasoning to help people solve difficult problems well.* This is done by pairing the human with the expert system in such a way that the expert system provides some of the knowledge and reasoning steps, while the human provides overall problem-solving direction as well as specific knowledge not incorporated in the system. Some of this knowledge can be thought of beforehand and made explicit when it is encoded in the expert system. However, much of the knowledge may be imprecise and will remain below the level of consciousness, to be recalled to the conscious level of the decision maker only when it is triggered by the evolving problem context.

COMPONENTS OF EXPERT SYSTEMS

To understand how expert systems (and expert support systems) are different from traditional computer applications, it is important to understand the components of a typical expert system (see Figure 24.1). In addition to the *user interface,* which allows the system to communicate with a human user, a typical expert system also has (1) a *knowledge base* of facts and rules related to the problem and (2) a set of reasoning methods—an *"inference engine"*—that interacts with the information in the knowledge base to solve the problem. As these two components are separate, it makes it much easier to change the system

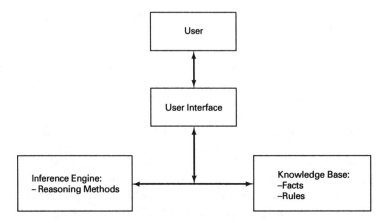

FIGURE 24.1 Expert systems Architecture

as the problem changes or becomes better understood. New rules can be added to the knowledge base in such a way that all the old facts and reasoning methods can still be used. Figure 24.1 shows in detail the elements of the expert systems architecture.

Knowledge Base

To flexibly use specialized knowledge for many different kinds of problems, AI researchers have developed a number of new "knowledge representation" techniques. Using these techniques to provide structure for a body of knowledge is still very much an art and is practiced by an emerging group of professionals sometimes called "knowledge engineers." Knowledge engineers in this field are akin to the systems analysts of data-processing (DP) applications. They work with the "experts" and draw out the relevant expertise in a form that can be encoded in a computer program. Three of the most important techniques for encoding this knowledge are (1) production rules, (2) semantic networks, and (3) frames.

Production Rules Production rules are particularly useful in building systems based on heuristic methods.[5] These are simple "if- then" rules that are often used to represent the empirical consequences of a given condition or the action that should be taken in a given situation. For example, a medical diagnosis system might have a rule like:

If:	(1) The patient has a fever, and
	(2) The patient has a runny nose,
Then:	It is very likely (.9) that the patient has a cold.

A computer configuration system might have a rule like:

If:	(1) There is an unassigned single port disk drive, and
	(2) There is a free controller,
Then:	Assign the disk drive to the controller port.

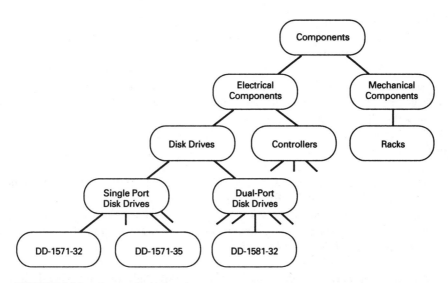

FIGURE 24.2   Semantic Network

Semantic Networks   Another formalism that is often more convenient than production rules for representing certain kinds of relational knowledge is called semantic networks or "semantic nets." To apply the rule about assigning disk drives, for example, a system would need to know what part numbers correspond to single port disk drives, controllers, and so forth. Figure 24.2 shows how this knowledge might be represented in a network of "nodes" connected by "links" that signify which classes of components are subsets of other classes.

Frames   In many cases, it is convenient to gather into one place a number of different kinds of information about an object. Figure 24.3 shows how several dimensions (such as length, width, and power requirements) that describe electrical components might be represented as different "slots" in a "frame" about electrical components. Unlike traditional records in a database, frames often contain additional features such as "default values" and "attached procedures." For instance, if the default value for voltage requirement of an electrical component is 110 volts, then the system would infer that a new electrical

FIGURE 24.3   Frame

Electrical Component	
Part No.	
Length	
Width	
Height	
Volume	
Voltage	

component required 110 volts unless explicit information to the contrary was provided. An attached procedure might automatically update the "volume" slot, whenever "length," "height," or "width" is changed (see Figure 24.3).

These three knowledge representation techniques—production rules, semantic networks, and frames—have considerable power in that they permit us to capture knowledge in a way that can be exploited by the "inference engine" to produce good, workable answers to the questions at hand.

Inference Engine

The inference engine contains the reasoning methods that might be used by human problem solvers for attacking problems. As these are separate from the knowledge base, either the inference engine or the knowledge base can be changed relatively independently of the other. Two reasoning methods often employed with production rules are *forward chaining* and *backward chaining*.

Forward Chaining   Imagine that we have a set of production rules like those shown in Figure 24.4 for a personal financial planning expert system. Imagine also that we know the current client's tax bracket is 50 percent, his liquidity is greater than $100,000, and he has a high tolerance for risk. By forward chaining through the rules, one at a time, the system could infer that exploratory oil and gas investments should be recommended for

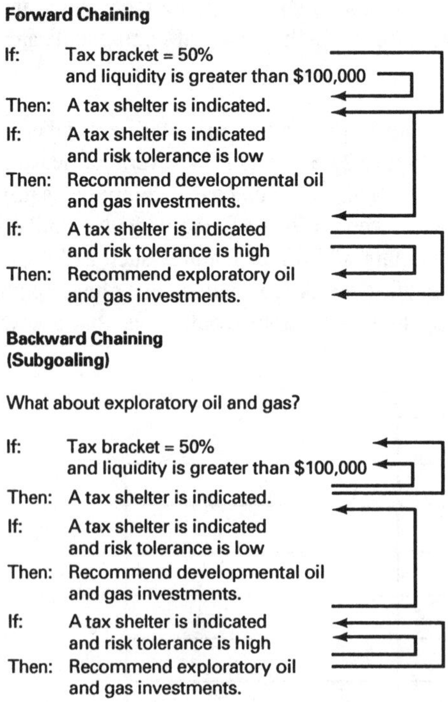

Forward Chaining

If: Tax bracket = 50%
         and liquidity is greater than $100,000
Then: A tax shelter is indicated.

If: A tax shelter is indicated
         and risk tolerance is low
Then: Recommend developmental oil
         and gas investments.

If: A tax shelter is indicated
         and risk tolerance is high
Then: Recommend exploratory oil
         and gas investments.

**Backward Chaining
(Subgoaling)**

What about exploratory oil and gas?

If: Tax bracket = 50%
         and liquidity is greater than $100,000
Then: A tax shelter is indicated.

If: A tax shelter is indicated
         and risk tolerance is low
Then: Recommend developmental oil
         and gas investments.

If: A tax shelter is indicated
         and risk tolerance is high
Then: Recommend exploratory oil
         and gas investments.

FIGURE 24.4   Inference Engine

this client. With a larger rule base, many other investment recommendations might be deduced as well.

Backward Chaining   Now imagine that we want to know only whether exploratory oil and gas investments are appropriate for a particular client, and we are not interested in any other investments at the moment. The system can use exactly the same rule base to answer this specific question more efficiently by backward chaining through the rules (see Figure 24.4). With backward chaining, the system starts with a goal (e.g., "show that this client needs exploratory oil and gas investments") and asks at each stage what sub-goals it would need to reach to achieve this goal. Here, to conclude that the client needs exploratory oil and gas investments, we can use the third rule (indicated in Figure 24.4) if we know that risk tolerance is high (which we already do know) and that a tax shelter is indicated. To conclude that a tax shelter is recommended, we have to find another rule (in this case, the first one) and then check whether its conditions are satisfied. In this case, they are, so our goal is achieved: we know we can recommend exploratory oil and gas investments to the client.

Keeping these basic concepts in mind, we now turn to a framework that puts expert systems and expert support systems into a management context.

THE FRAMEWORK FOR EXPERT SUPPORT SYSTEMS

The framework developed in this section begins to allow us to identify those classes of business problems that are appropriate for data processing, decision support systems, expert systems, and expert support systems. In addition, we can clarify the relative contributions of humans and computers in the various classes of applications.

This framework extends the earlier work of Gorry and Scott Morton,[6] in which they relate Herbert Simon's seminal work on structured vs. unstructured decision making[7] to Robert Anthony's strategic planning, management control, and operational control.[8] Figure 24.5 presents Gorry and Scott Morton's framework. They argued that to improve the quality of decisions, the manager must seek not only to match the type and quality of information and its presentation to the category of decision, but he or she must also choose a system that reflects the degree of the problem's structure.

In light of the insights garnered from the field of artificial intelligence, Figure 24.6 shows how we can expand and rethink the structured/unstructured dimension of the original framework. Simon separated decision making into three phases: intelligence, design, and choice.[9] A structured decision is one where all three phases are fully understood and "computable" by the human decision maker. As a result, the decision is programmable. In an unstructured decision, one or more of these phases are not fully understood.

For business purposes, we can extend this distinction by taking Alan Newell's insightful categorization of problem solving, which consists of goals and constraints, state space, search control knowledge, and operators.[10] We relabel and regroup these problem characteristics into four categories (see Figure 24.6):

	Operational Control	Management Control	Strategic Planning
Structured	Accounts Receivable	Budget Analysis– Engineered Costs	Tanker Fleet Mix
	Order Entry	Short-term Forecasting	Warehouse and Factory Location
	Inventory Control		
Semistructured	Production Scheduling	Variance Analysis– Overall Budget	Mergers & Acquisitions
	Cash Management	Budget Preparation	New Product Planning
Unstructured	PERT/COST Systems	Sales and Production	R&D Planning

FIGURE 24.5   The Original Information Systems Framework

Reprinted from G. A. Gorry and M. S. Scott Morton, "A Framework for Management Information Systems," *Sloan Management Review,* Fall 1971, p. 62.

1. *Data:* the dimensions and values necessary to represent the state of the world that is relevant to the problem (i.e., the "state space");

2. *Procedures:* the sequence of steps (or "operators") used in solving the problem;

3. *Goals and Constraints:* the desired results of problem solving and the constraints on what can and cannot be done; and

4. *Strategies:* the flexible strategies used to decide which procedures to apply to achieve goals (i.e., the "search control knowledge").

For some structured problems, we can apply a standard procedure (i.e., an algorithm or formula) and proceed directly to a conclusion with no need for flexible problem-solving strategies. For example, we can use standard procedures to compute withholding taxes and prepare employee paychecks, and we can use the classical formula for "economic order quantity" to solve straightforward inventory control problems.

In other less structured problems, no straightforward solution techniques are known. Here, solutions can often be found only by trial and error, that is, by trying a number of possibilities until an acceptable one is found. For instance, for a manager to determine which of three sales strategies to use for a new product, he or she might want to explore the probable consequences of each for advertising expenses, sales force utilization, revenue, and so forth. We will discuss the range of these different types of problems and the appropriate kinds of systems for each.

Type I Problems: Data Processing

A fully structured problem is one in which all four elements of the problem are structured: we have well-stated goals, we can specify the input data needed, there are standard procedures by which a solution may be calculated, and there is no need for complex strategies for generating and evaluating alternatives. Fully structured problems are computable and one can decide if such computation is justifiable given the amount of time and computing resources involved.

Such problems are well suited to the use of conventional programming techniques in that virtually everything about the problem is well defined. In effect, the expert (i.e., the analyst/programmer) has already solved the problem. He or she must only sequence the data through the particular program. Figure 24.6 represents pictorially the class of decision problems that can be solved economically using conventional programming techniques. This class is referred to as Type I Problems—that is, problems historically thought to be suited for data processing.

It is interesting to note that the economics of conventional programming are being fundamentally altered with the provision of new tools such as an "analyst's workbench."[11] These tools include professional workstations used by the systems analyst first to develop flow chart representations of the problem and then to move automatically to testable running code. The more advanced stations use AI techniques, thereby turning these new techniques into tools to make old approaches more effective in classical DP application areas.

FIGURE 24.6 Problem Types

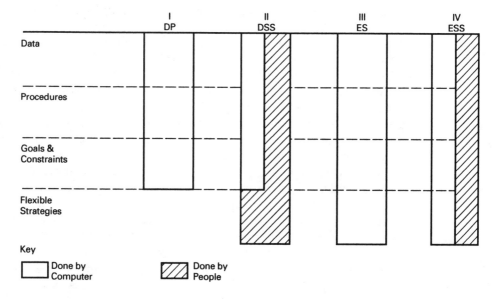

Key
Done by Computer
Done by People

Type II Problems: Decision Support Systems

As we move away from problems that are fully structured, we begin to deal with many of the more complicated problems organizations have to grapple with each day. These are cases where standard procedures are helpful but not sufficient by themselves, where the data may be incompletely represented, and where the goals and constraints are only partially understood. Traditional data-processing systems do not solve these problems. Fortunately, in these cases, the computer can perform the well-understood parts of the problem solving, while, at the same time, humans use their goals, intuition, and general knowledge to formulate problems, modify and control the problem solving, and interpret the results. As Figure 24.6 shows, human users may provide or modify data, procedures, or goals, and they may use their knowledge of all these factors to decide on problem-solving strategies.

In many of the best-known decision support systems,[12] the computer applies standard procedures to certain highly structured data but relies on human users to decide which procedures are appropriate in a given situation and whether a given result is satisfactory. Investment managers, for instance, who used the portfolio management system (PMS)[13] did not rely on the computer for either making final decisions about portfolio composition or deciding on which procedures to use for analysis: they used the computer to execute the procedures they felt were appropriate, say for calculating portfolio diversity and expected returns. In the end, the managers themselves proposed alternative portfolios and decided whether a given diversification or return was acceptable. Many people who use spreadsheet programs today for "what-if" analyses follow a similar flexible strategy of proposing an action, letting the computer predict its consequences, and then deciding what action to propose next.

Type III Problems: Expert Systems

We call the problems where essentially all the relevant knowledge for flexible problem solving can be encoded Type III Problems: the systems that solve them are expert systems. Using AI programming techniques like production rules and frames, expert systems are able to encode some of the same kinds of goals, heuristics, and strategies that people use in solving problems but that have previously been very difficult to use in computer programs. These techniques make it possible to design systems that don't just follow standard procedures, but instead use flexible problem-solving strategies to explore a number of possible alternatives before picking a solution. A medical diagnosis program, for example, may consider many different possible diseases and disease combinations before finding one that adequately explains the observed symptoms.

For some cases, like the XCON system, these techniques can capture almost all of the relevant knowledge about the problem. As of 1983, less than 1 out of every 1,000 orders configured by XCON was misconfigured because of missing or incorrect rules. (Only about 10 percent of the orders had to be corrected for any reason at all and almost all of these errors were due to missing descriptions of rarely used parts.)[14]

It is instructive to note, however, that even with XCON, which is probably the most extensively tested system in commercial use today, new knowledge is continually being added and human editors still check every order the system configures. As the developers of XCON remark: "There is no more reason to believe now than there was [in 1979] that [XCON] has all the knowledge relevant to its configuration task. This, coupled with the fact that [XCON] deals with an ever-changing domain, implies its development will never be finished."[15]

If XCON, which operates in the fairly restricted domain of computer order configuration, never contained all the knowledge relevant to its problem, it appears much less likely that we will ever be able to codify all the knowledge needed for less clearly bounded problems like financial analysis, strategic planning, and project management.

In all of these cases, there is a vast amount of knowledge that is *potentially* relevant to the problem solution: the financial desirability of introducing a proposed new product may depend on the likelihood and nature of a competitor's response; the success of a strategic plan may depend as much on the predispositions of the chief executive as it does on the financial merit of the plan; and the best assignment of people to tasks in a project may depend on very subtle evaluations of people's competence and motivation. While it is often possible to formalize and represent any *specific* set of these factors, there is an unbounded number of such factors that may, in some circumstances, become important. Even in what might appear to be a fairly bounded case of job-shop scheduling, often there are many continually changing and possibly implicit constraints on what people, machines, and parts are needed and available for different steps in a manufacturing process.[16] What this suggests is that for many of the problems of practical importance in business, we should focus our attention on designing systems that *support* expert users rather than on replacing them.

Type IV /Expert Support Systems

Even where important kinds of problem-solving knowledge cannot feasibly be encoded, it is still possible to use expert systems techniques. (This dramatically extends the capabilities of computers beyond previous technologies such as DP and DSS.) What is important, in these cases, is to design expert support systems with very good and deeply embedded "user interfaces" that enable their human users to easily inspect and control the problem-solving process (see Figure 24.6). In other words, a good expert support system should be both *accessible* and *malleable*. Many expert support systems make their problem solving accessible to users by providing explanation capabilities. For example, the MYCIN medical diagnosis program can explain to a doctor at any time why it is asking for a given piece of information or what rules it used to arrive at a given conclusion. For a system to be malleable, users should be able to easily change data, procedures, goals, or strategies at any important point in the problem-solving process. Systems with this capability are still rare, but an early version of the Dipmeter Advisor suggests how they may be developed.[17] The Advisor is unable by itself to automatically detect certain kinds of complex geological patterns. Instead it graphically displays the basic data and lets human experts detect the patterns themselves. The human experts then indicate the results of their analysis, and the system proceeds using this information.

An even more vivid example of how a system can be made accessible and malleable is provided by the Steamer Program, which teaches people how to reason in order to operate a steam plant.[18] This system has colorful graphic displays of the schematic flows in the simulated plant, the status of different valves and gauges, and the pressures in different places. Users of the system can manipulate these displays (using a "mouse" pointing device) to control the valves, temperatures, and so forth. The system continually updates its simulation results and expert diagnostics based on these user actions.

SUMMARY OF FRAMEWORK

This framework helps clarify a number of issues. First, it highlights, as did the original Gorry and Scott Morton framework, the importance of matching system type to problem type. The primary practical points made in the original framework were that traditional DP technologies should not be used for semistructured and unstructured problems where new DSS technologies were more appropriate; and secondly that interactive human/computer use opened up an extended class of problems where computers could be exploited. Again, the most important practical point to be made is twofold: first, "pure" expert systems should not be used for partially understood problems where expert support systems are more appropriate; and second, expert systems techniques can be used to dramatically extend the capabilities of traditional decision support systems.

Figure 24.7 shows, in an admittedly simplified way, how we can view expert support systems as the next logical step in each of two somewhat separate progressions. On the left side of the figure, we see that DSS developed out of a practical recognition of the limits of DP for helping real human beings solve complex problems in actual organizations. The right side of the figure reflects a largely independent evolution that took place in computer science research laboratories. This evolution grew out of a recognition of the limits of traditional computer science techniques for solving the kinds of complex problems that people are able to solve. We are now at the point where these two separate progressions can be united to help solve a broad range of important practical problems.

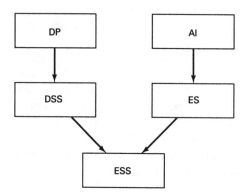

FIGURE 24.7   Progressions in Computer System Development

THE BENEFITS OF *ESS* TO MANAGERS

The real importance of ESS lies in the ability of these systems to harness and make full use of our scarcest resource: the talent and experience of key members of the organization. There are considerable benefits in capturing the expert's experience and making it available to those in an organization who are less knowledgeable about the subject in question. As organizations and their problems become more complex, management can benefit from initiating prototypes ES and ESS. However, the questions now facing managers are when and how to start.

When to Start

The "when" to start is relatively easy to answer. It is "now" for exploratory work. For some organizations, this will be a program of education and active monitoring of the field. For others, the initial investment may take the form of an experimental low-budget prototype. For a few, once the exploration is over, it will make good economic sense to go forward with a full-fledged working prototype. Conceptual and technological developments have made it possible to begin an active prototype development phase.

Where to Start

The second question is "where" to start. A possible beginning may be to explore those areas in which the organization stands to gain a distinct competitive advantage. Schlumberger would seem to feel that their ES used as a drilling advisor is one such example. Digital Equipment Corporation's use of an expert system for "equipment configuration control" is another example. It is interesting that of the more than twenty organizations that we know are investing in ES and ESS, almost none would allow themselves to be quoted. The reasons given basically boil down to the fact that they are experimenting with prototypes that they think will give them a competitive advantage in making or delivering their product or service. Examples of where we can quote without attribution are cases in which an ESS is used to support the cross selling of financial services products (e.g., an insurance salesman selling a tax shelter), or to evaluate the credit worthiness of a loan applicant in a financial services organization.

It is clear that there are a great many problem areas where even our somewhat primitive ability to deal with expert systems can permit the building of useful first generation systems. The development of expert support systems makes the situation even brighter: by helping the beleaguered "expert," the organization will get the desired leverage in the marketplace.

PROBLEMS, RISKS, AND ISSUES

It would be irresponsible of us to conclude without acknowledging that expert systems and expert support systems are in their infancy, and researchers and users alike must be realistic about their capabilities. Already there is an apparent risk that an expert system will be poorly defined and oversold: the resulting backlash may hinder progress.

There is also a danger of proceeding too quickly and too recklessly, without paying careful attention to what we are doing: We may very well embed our knowledge (necessarily incomplete at any moment in time) into a system that is only effective when used by the person who created it. If this system is used by others, there is a risk of misapplication: holes in another user's knowledge could represent a pivotal element in the logic leading to a solution. While these holes are implicitly recognized by the creator of the knowledge base, they may be quite invisible to a new user.

The challenge of proceeding at an appropriate pace can be met if managers treat artificial intelligence, expert systems, expert support systems, and decision support systems as a serious topic, one that requires management attention if it is to be exploited properly. To this end, managers must recognize the differences between Types I and II problems, for which the older techniques are appropriate, and the new methods available for Types III and IV.

CONCLUSION

Although there are some basic risks and constraints that will be with us for some time, the potential of AI techniques is obvious. If we proceed cautiously, acknowledging the problems as we go along, we can begin to achieve worthwhile results.

The illustrations used here are merely a few applications that have been built in a relatively brief period of time with primitive tools. Business has attempted to develop expert systems applications since 1980 and, despite the enormity of some of the problems, has succeeded in developing a number of simple and powerful prototypes.

The state of the art is such that everyone building an expert system must endure this primitive start-up phase to learn what is involved in this fascinating new field. We expect that it will take until about 1990 for ES and ESS to be fully recognized as having achieved worthwhile business results.

However, expert systems and expert support systems are with us now, albeit in a primitive form. The challenge for managers is to harness these tools to increase the effectiveness of the organization and thus add value for its stakeholders. Pioneering firms are leading the way, and once a section of territory has been staked out, the experience gained by these leaders will be hard to equal for those who start later.

QUESTIONS

1. How do expert systems differ from other types of computer applications?
2. What are the component parts of an expert system? Briefly discuss each component.
3. Do expert systems *replace* humans in the decision-making process or *support* humans in decision making? Discuss.
4. What are some of the potential benefits of expert systems to managers?

REFERENCES

1. WINSTON, P. H.   *Artificial Intelligence,* 2d ed. (Reading, MA: Addison-Wesley, 1984), P. 1.

2. R. DAVIS ET AL.   "The Dipmeter Advisor: Interpretation of Geological Signals," *Proceedings of the 7th International Joint Conference on Artificial Intelligence* (Vancouver: 1981), pp. 846–849.

3. J. BACHANT AND J. MCDERMOTT   "RI revisited: Four Years in the Trenches," *AI Magazine,* Fall 1984, pp. 21–32.

4. J. MCDERMOTT   "RI: A Rule-based Configurer of Computer Systems," *Artificial Intelligence,* 19 (1982).

5. WINSTON (1984).

6. G. A. GORRY AND M. S. SCOTT MORTON   "A Framework for Management Information Systems," *Sloan Management Review,* Fall 1971, pp. 55–70.

7. H. A. SIMON   *The New Science of Management Decision* (New York: Harper & Row, 1960).

8. R. N. ANTHONY   "Planning and Control Systems: A Framework for Analysis" (Boston: Harvard University Graduate School of Business Administration, 1965).

9. SIMON (1960).

10. A. NEWELL   "Reasoning: Problem Solving and Decision Processes: The Problem Space as a Fundamental Category," in *Attention and Performance VIII,* ed. R. Nickerson (Hillsdale, NJ: Erlbaum, 1980).

11. B. SHEIL   "Power Tools for Programmers," *Datamation,* February 1983, pp. 131–144.

12. P. G. W. KEEN AND M. S. SCOTT MORTON   *Decision Support Systems: An Organizational Perspective* (Reading, MA: Addison-Wesley, 1978).

13. Ibid.

14. BACHANT AND MCDERMOTT   (Fall 1984).

15. Ibid., p. 27.

16. M. S. FOX   "Constraint- Directed Search: A Case Study of Job-Shop Scheduling" (Pittsburgh: Carnegie-Mellon University Robotics Institute, Technical Report No. CMU-RI-TR-83-22, 1983).

17. DAVIS   (1981).

18. J. D. HOLLAN, E. L. HUTCHINS, AND L. WEITZMAN   "Steamer: An Interactive, Inspectable Simulation-based Training System," *AI Magazine,* Summer 1984, pp. 15–28.

25

THE CASE FOR INTEGRATIVE INNOVATION: AN EXPERT SYSTEM AT DIGITAL

Dorothy Leonard-Barton

The internal development and implementation of technologies is a complex management problem, especially when the technology is on the cutting edge of knowledge and managers must be pioneers. However, companies undertake development of such technologies for good reasons: increased productivity and propriety advantage over competition.[1]

The particular instance of technology development chronicled in this reading illustrates two areas of emerging managerial concern, one specific and one general. The specific topic is the development of expert systems—a state-of-the-art technology in which many corporations are investing today. The more general issue is replacing the old model of "handing off" technology from developers to users with a new paradigm: integrative innovation.

Successful new technology implementation, I suggest, is an interactive process of incrementally altering the technology to fit the organization and simultaneously shaping the user environment to exploit the potential of the technology.[2] Thus it is a process of integration because technology managers must be concerned simultaneously with organizational and technical design. It is innovation because inventive activity is not confined to one period of time (preceding implementation) or one function (R&D), but rather occurs continuously across functions until the technology is totally absorbed into routine—or is discontinued. In the following pages, this paradigm is illustrated by detailed reference to the case of XSEL, Digital Equipment Corporation's eXpert SELling assistant program. The very nature of expert systems technology exacerbates the need for an integrative approach. While other forms of software (notably decision support systems) *can* be developed and implemented using the approaches advocated below, expert systems technology (at least in its current form) *necessitates* using some aspects of an integrated innovation process.[3]

Many of the problems encountered with XSEL do not differ in kind from those faced in the implementation of other technology. However, they are magnified in this case by extreme uncertainty on all fronts: untried software development procedures; lack of clarity about technology uses and users; uncertain organizational impacts. The story of this expert system thus illustrates general development and implementation issues—but in a particularly interesting and difficult situation.

THE TECHNOLOGY

Expert systems, often defined loosely as software programs that mimic the judgment and capabilities of human experts, are the most commercially available form of artificial intelligence.[4] They are usually developed through rapid prototyping (the quick production of a demonstration model in order to obtain corrective feedback from experts and/or potential users.) Since the relationships to be captured in the software often exist only in the heads of human experts, construction of the program usually requires active, ongoing, and the intensive participation by experts other than the developers. Sometimes it has proven easier to train user experts in the programming language than to train knowledge engineers in the task to be automated or aided. Regardless of who does the actual coding, prototyping requires frequent, extensive interaction between two bodies of knowledge: the programming technology and the task expertise.

Digital Equipment Corporation, the second largest computer manufacturer in the United States, first ventured into developing an expert system for internal use in 1979 when the task of configuring the wide range of computer systems traditionally offered its customers had reached almost unmanageable proportions. Literally millions of design possibilities for working configurations existed, since the product line included more than 50 types of central processors and more than 400 core options. Moreover, the number of options was increasing exponentially. With the help of Professor John McDermott of Carnegie-Mellon University, Digital developed XCON, an eXpert CONfiguration program that checks the accuracy of complex computer systems configurations before the configuration information is fed into manufacturing and shipping schedules, to ensure that the system can be assembled and will function as designed—that no vital parts are omitted, no incompatible components paired, and so forth.[5]

Recognizing that many potentially disruptive configuration errors originate early in the order process, Digital managers next conceived of an interactive sales-force aid

(XSEL) that would guide and check designs as sales representatives originated them in response to customers' particular needs. The configurations that emerged from this process could then be submitted in batch form to XCON for a final, detailed check before submission to manufacturing. If Digital were to continue its strategy of tailoring products to customers' needs, two forces would drive an increase in the need for such a system: first, the number of potential configurations was increasing; second, the sales force was increasingly made up of people with general sales skills, but without the technical training and experience that had characterized earlier Digital sales representatives.

Starting in the spring of 1981, McDermott guided the development of the first prototype for XSEL. The original software development group included the knowledge engineer who had begun the coding at Carnegie and had subsequently moved to Digital, as well as a number of knowledge engineers who had worked on XCON.

By 1984, the year in which the research reported here began, XSEL was already a very large system (see Figure 25.1) and was about to be widely disseminated. Over the next three years, data on the XSEL project was collected from unstructured interviews with developers, users, and managers of the computers on which the first releases ran, and from Digital management at various levels—both in manufacturing (where XSEL had been developed) and in sales (where XSEL was used). In addition, a cohort of sales representatives, chosen as a random representative sample in 1984, was interviewed in

FIGURE 25.1 Number of Rules in XSEL

Data courtesy of Intelligent Systems Technology Group, Digital Equipment Corporation.

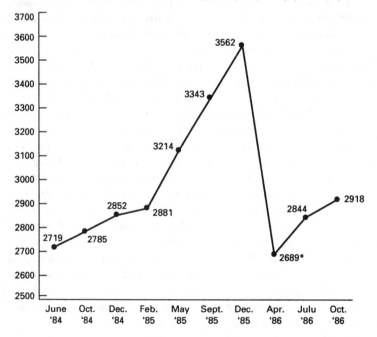

*Drop in number due to extraction of floor layout rules into separate program, which grew from 1606 rule in April, 1986 to 1702 in October, 1986.

the summers of 1984, 1985, and 1986. Notes from numerous meetings and from archival sources supplemented data obtained by interview.

MANAGING INTEGRATIVE INNOVATION

Integrative innovation requires attention to three management domains at once:

- cultivating users as codevelopers;
- creating a support system, including a network of supporters and an adequate delivery system for users; and
- organizational prototyping (i.e., experimentation and planned learning about the integration of the new technology)

To a degree not necessitated by the old hand-off model, these three interactive streams require, housed in one person or one team, diverse skills such as an ability to manage differing perspectives and a capacity to design an organizational learning process. Each of the three domains harbors pitfalls not always obvious at the outset of a project. The initial dip in productivity occasioned by introducing innovations to operations[6] is often traceable to inadequate attention to one or more of these three domains.

USERS AS CODEVELOPERS

Involving users in the development of new software systems is widely recognized as a management strategy that leads to better user acceptance, but evidence that such involvement leads to higher-quality systems is harder to adduce, in part because so many different standards of excellence have been applied.[7] Therefore, not only is there debate about the ultimate utility of involving users in design, but there is considerable ignorance as to the mechanics of user involvement. Thus managing user involvement is a case of "easier said than done."

The model followed by Digital, "participative design, is an extreme form of user involvement in which users actively aid in shaping the original technology specifications as well as in directing reformulation during development."[8] Users are thrust into a proactive rather than a reactive mode; they must understand enough of the technology to explore its potential realistically, and they must give the developers a comprehensive understanding of the environment in which the technology will be deployed.

Involving users as part of the integrative. innovation process necessitates more planning than may be recognized at the outset. This cooperative design process requires the management of a series of paradoxes: user participants in the software development process must typify their community, yet be expert in the task being automated; user participants must develop a sophisticated understanding of the technology, yet retain the perspective of the user rather than the developer; development progress must be visible to users, yet important improvements are often discernible only to the eye of the technical expert. Since to manage these paradoxes one must first understand them, they are illustrated by the following XSEL example.

TABLE 25.1 Development of XSEL

Category of Tasks[*]	Approximate Person Months[**] 7/'82–7/'83	Example	Approximate Person Months 8/'83–7/'84	Example
Checking/ Cataloging	26	Check for order completeness	3	Check cabinet requirements for disk types
Adding to Database	1–2	System "building blocks" (i.e., standard groupings of components)	4	Add "Q-bus" systems-
User Interface	26	Improved ability to edit (add, delete, modify commands)	7	Mini-XSEL for expert users
Internal Efficiency or Maintainability of Program	24	Conversion of OPS^5 from LISP base to BLISS; average large configuration takes 2 minutes	13	Change to compiled database (from 14 hours CPU time down to 4)
Percent of Total Development Activities Rated "Intelligent"[***] 4 or 5 on scale)	25		60	
Percent of Total Development Activities Rated Very "Traditional"[***] (1 or 2 on scale)	29		29	

[*]Does not include administrative, supervisory, training, or all general maintenance tasks. Original interview protocol included seven coding task categories, collapsed here into four.

[**]*Approximate* only; constructed by developers involved, from memory, with archival aids (e.g., release notes, progress reports to user design groups, etc.). Original data are lists of specific tasks, from which examples cited here are drawn. Note also that the four periods are not exactly comparable in length.

[***]"Intelligence" was very specifically defined, for the purposes of this study, as follows:

   5 (Highest): To our knowledge, previously done only by humans

   4 (High): XCON set the example for doing this type of thing in software

   3 (Moderate): Probably done elsewhere with software, but by humans at Digital

   2 (Low): Certainly done elsewhere with software, but by humans at Digital

   1 (Lowest): Previously done at Digital by other software

TABLE 25.1 (Continued)

Category of Tasks*	Approximate Person Months** 8/'84– 5/'85	Example	Approximate Person Months 6/'85– 8/'86	Example
Checking/ Cataloging	1	Defaults altered; check for country requirements	7	Improve accuracy of defaults
Adding to Database	10	Add micro-Vax II	27	Add "standard" systems
User Interface	4–5	Work on linkage with automatic quotation system	8–9	New menu keywords
Internal Efficiency or Maintainability of Program	10	Minor efficiency improvements	1	Bugs fixed for better maintenance
Percent of Total Development Activities Rated "Intelligent"*** (4 or 5 on scale)	31		41	
Percent of Total Development Activities Rated Very "Traditional"*** (1 or 2 on scale)	69		54	

In 1981, the program manager hired to direct the development and deployment of XSEL set up a user design group (UDG) to help formulate the program. His first problem was choosing the members. Proceeding basically by word of mouth, Bruce MacDonald pulled together a diverse group: a few highly experienced, productive senior sales representatives who were also skilled configurers; several less experienced sales representatives, and someone from field services who knew a lot about configuration from experience gained in installing systems for customers. This group's task was to represent the user community in the development process.

At their first meeting in November 1981, the user design group saw a demonstration of the fledgling XSEL program and laid out the objectives they believed the program should meet—a kind of job description for the expert they were to help create. When they returned to their sales offices located around the United States, they were given access through telephone lines to the prototype, which was running on a VAX machine in Massachusetts. Consequently, the developers received immediate feedback in a tight loop from the users, who tried out each new feature as it emerged. The electronic communication was first augmented and then replaced by occasional face-to-face meetings in which users requested additional changes, and developers acquiesced or else explained why that particular change would be delayed or impossible. Out of the approximately twenty original members of this group, only four or five senior sales representatives worked on the system for the next five years; they became de facto members of the development team.

Most of the user input, therefore, came from a few highly skilled, very experienced sales representatives. Their qualifications were important in providing high-quality knowledge for system design, but they were more representative of configuration experts than of typical XSEL users. This bias was difficult to overcome, for from the beginning it was difficult to incorporate new, relatively naive sales representatives into the group. These initiates were intimidated by the highly experienced, vocal representatives, whose expertise increasingly included understanding of expert systems technology as well as configuration skills and sales know-how. The inexperienced sales reps enticed into a user design group meeting tended to sit in the back and say little. Nor were they likely to be members of the group for any length of time.

The resulting clublike atmosphere contributed to a focused development process. The users made fewer "blue sky" requests (one that would entail an enormous expenditure of manpower, or a complete change in system architecture, or were simply beyond the current capabilities of the technology) as they came to understand the bounds of the expert system technology.

As the system matured, users and developers agreed to concentrate on the quality of system performance rather than on improving user friendliness. This meant an emphasis on "accuracy," a term that users employed to refer both to the validity of judgments made by the program and to the inclusion of new products and components to keep the database up-to-date (see Table 25.1). Since ease of use, as interviews revealed, was never one of the major barriers to use and since accuracy was critical, this emphasis seemed appropriate.

However, the composition of the user design group also affected allocation of development resources. For instance, expert users quickly became impatient with

XSEL's initial prompts and queries, which were intended to help with system component selection. Able to construct a configuration from memory and experience, these users wanted to use the system only for verification of their configuration design. In response to this need, the developers constructed a "mini-XSEL" that allowed users to bypass much of the preliminary setup help and go directly to XCON to check their configuration. This addition turned out to be fortuitous when XSEL went to Europe, where experienced users were initially less receptive than those in the U.S.

On the whole, it was probably a useful addition, especially since the inclusion of the mini-XSEL cost the team a relatively minor two person-months of effort. Nevertheless, that it happened illustrates the potential influence of a biased (i.e., nonrepresentative) user design group. The importance of this bias could increase as the Digital Sales force continues to expand and shift away from its traditional technical-skill base so that most sales representatives are relatively inexperienced.

The fact that the users who had invested so many days in development work began to think of XSEL as their invention had other disadvantages. By early 1985 the user design group meetings were relaxed, with little creative tension between users and developers. One program team member emerging from the eighth of these meetings observed, "That was entirely too cozy. They aren't challenging us any more."

By 1986, the four or five expert configurers in the UDG who had worked longest on XSEL had seen their program progress "from about 50 percent accuracy to over 90 percent," one longtime participant estimated. Consequently, these expert user designers were quite pleased with XSEL. However, those sales representatives who were equally expert at configuration but had not been directly involved in designing XSEL were not as satisfied. In 1984 expertise in configuration was either (in statistical terms) unrelated to or tended toward a mildly negative relationship with various evaluation measures. The negative trend intensified over the three years until, by 1986, the more expert the sales representative was in configuration, the less likely he or she was to be satisfied with XSEL's accuracy or its quality as a piece of software.

This increasingly negative trend among users did not hold for sales representatives who were expert in software programming. Initially (in 1984) dubious about XSEL, they became increasingly positive until, by 1986, the relationship essentially disappeared between programming skill and evaluations of XSEL. If anything, skilled programmers were likely to evaluate this expert system positively.

Thus it is difficult to generalize about the opinion of a user population from the few users who are most heavily involved in development. They may or may not reflect general perceptions, not only because of their commitment to the project but also because they may not reflect the shifting composition of the population. Yet people are notoriously vulnerable to the "law of small numbers"[9]—in other words, to generalize from extremely small samples of a given population, especially if the sample is particularly vivid or near. Managers can easily be lulled by the heavy involvement of a few users into the complacent belief that they are in touch with the user community.

To help combat the potential bias introduced by working with the same small group of users, the development team appended a "comment" facility to XSEL. After the program was disseminated to regional machines, anyone using the system was prompted at the end of a session to rate the program and to make any comments or suggestions they wished. These suggestions were forwarded by each system manager to a designated development team member, who scanned and routed them to the appropriate knowledge engineer. Thus the XSEL program team lessened the potential for bias by creating another, nominal UDG—users in the field.

A final paradox in managing interactions with users is that much effort is necessarily expended on nonobvious improvements. Early in the development of XSEL, many hours were invested in refinements that strongly affected the system's internal efficiency. These refinements were largely invisible to the user design group and totally invisible to other, less knowledgeable users (see Table 25.1). The primary complaint of users throughout the three years tracked in this study was slow response time. Changes such as completely shifting how the database was handled sped up the program's internal CPU time and lessened requirements for memory space. However, since the system was growing in size simultaneously (see Figure 25.1), the improvement in efficiency was not noticeable. Thus, even to members of the user design group, large chunks of development work were invisible. Moreover, for reasons detailed below, the hardware delivery system was inadequate. Any improvement in internal speed was lost because of the waiting time caused by overloaded computers and communication lines. As discussed in what follows, the XSEL program team addressed this problem by allotting some managerial time to lobbying for a better delivery system—even though the issue was considered the province of the user community rather than the developers.

CREATING A SUPPORT SYSTEM

The integrative innovation approach requires that users prepare to receive the new technology at the same time it is being developed, rather than after the fact. This parallel process is both social and physical. That is, if the new technology is to move smoothly into use, there must be in place both a network of supporters or advocates and a physical delivery system that makes the technology accessible to potential users. Internally developed technologies falter when responsibility for creating the social network is unclear or when the importance of the physical system is underestimated.[10] Yet it is not always clear who should be responsible for developing these two kinds of support systems. Moreover, managers may reason that implementation is uncertain—so why waste resources on a system that may never be used? This kind of cautious posture can become a self-fulfilling prophecy. Below I discuss first the social support systems and then the delivery systems needed.

The Network of Supporters

A sponsor and a champion provide necessary advocacy for any new idea,[11] but this support is no guarantee of success. In fact, failed projects can have highly visible champions.[12] Champions (and their projects) are successful to the degree that they stimulate support in the right quarters. Creation of this network is, in fact, an internal marketing task. Just as in technical development it is usually necessary to plan for continual design refinements, so in the design of the environment that will receive the innovation it is necessary to continually reexamine assumptions, target new groups of potential allies, and capitalize on serendipitous discoveries. The network is not a rigid structure, but a changing kaleidoscope of social links. The XSEL case demonstrates the importance of support that is visible, carefully timed, and appropriately positioned to address potential bottlenecks.

Visibility   The XSEL team faced special difficulties in setting up a support network because they were part of the manufacturing organization rather than the sales organization. While the Intelligent Systems Technology Group (of which the XSEL project was a part) perceived themselves as serving a corporatewide service function, all their artificial intelligence programs were viewed by others as manufacturing projects.

One of the first and visible advocates for XSEL in sales management at Digital was a vice president impressed by an early prototype. In a September 1982 meeting with the development team, he challenged them to have this new productivity tool "on the desk of every sales representative as a Christmas present." The incident illustrates the way that expert systems magnify common problems in technology implementation. It is not unusual for highly placed managers to set difficult time schedules for new technology and to underestimate the amount of development left to be done. The first prototype of an expert system can seem so "intelligent" that someone unversed in the technology assumes a far greater degree of technical readiness than is justified. In the case of XSEL, it would be fall of 1983—twelve months rather than three—before the product was ready for the field.

Loath to admit their inability to meet the Christmas deadline, the team somewhat reluctantly agreed to try. Spurred by the interest of their vice president, the sales organization agreed to supply a computer in each sales region dedicated to running XSEL. The project thus obtained high visibility with a well-placed sponsor.

Timing   However, the support was not well timed. Expectations were raised that would not be met for a couple of years, and the team members found themselves frequently on the defensive during those two years. "It was as if we had been sloughing off," one team member recalled, "when, really, there was no way we could have met that deadline." In the field, sales representatives were critical of what they regarded as an "over sell." "From what I hear," one representative commented in 1984, "the XSEL team is spending too much time on selling a product they don't even have yet."

Moreover, because even the first release of XSEL was not ready for the field until six months after the machines were in place, space on the "dedicated" machines was quickly upsurped to run existing software. It was difficult to expel these squatter programs once XSEL was ready. Finally, the vice president moved on to another position in the company, and no similar advocate appeared in sales for a couple of years.

As this example illustrates, high visibility can be worse than none at all if the timing is wrong. Part of the delicate business of orchestrating support is considering its timing. In this case, the development team was not really in control, since the technology was being built in one organization (manufacturing) and used in another (sales) over which they had little influence.

Placement   Another similarity between the development and implementation of a new technology and of a marketing campaign is that, as the technology is rolled out, the targets for advocacy shift. That is, different groups hold the power to advance or inhibit the flow of the technology at different times. Often people quite low in the hierarchy of an organization can shut off needed resources[13] or, in contrast, can ease the innovation's passage into widespread use. Therefore, part of management's problem is identifying and working with different groups to develop the needed social and physical support.

For example, when XSEL was first sent to the field in September 1983, the regional machines originally designated to run the software were, as mentioned before, often being used to run other programs such as high-priority electronic messaging. Each of the seven regional machines was managed by a "systems manager" who regulated machine usage and space allotments. For a period of about six months, these seven guardians were especially critical to the dissemination of XSEL. Representatives wanting accounts on the machine to run XSEL applied to them; space allotted to XSEL depended upon their willingness to move other programs around to make room. They were also the most available—sometime the only—XSEL trainers. The seven ranged widely in their interest in XSEL. At one extreme, one manager took the personal risk of creating false files to protect the space needed to run the program, even from the encroachment of her own management. At the other, a systems manager vociferously criticized XSEL as a "kluge" (i.e., a hastily constructed, unsystematic program). He reached this unflattering conclusion because he programmed his computer to display the order in which the software "fired" the rules needed to interact with the user. When he saw that these rules were activated in random patterns rather than in the orderly progression characteristic of a good COBOL or BASIC program, he concluded that the programming was inefficient. His disparaging comments discouraged some users in his region from even trying the innovation.

Bruce MacDonald's team thus had to focus their attention for a time on these seven individuals whose power over the success of the project was totally disproportionate to their organizational titles. The skeptical systems manager has to be educated to understand that what he interpreted as sloppy programming was in fact quite characteristic of a heuristics and rule-based system. Even those systems managers who believed in XSEL felt like isolated and besieged champions and needed the assurance that they would be vindicated by productivity increases. Several meetings were held with these individuals to apprise them of advances in the technology, to prepare them to train users in their area—but mostly to encourage their support of XSEL.

Perhaps the most important group of advocates for XSEL turned out to be the members of the user design group, whose original charter did not include advocacy, but only help in program construction. In summer 1984, XSEL reached a critical point in its history. The program still lacked a highly placed sponsor in the user organization. The first release in the fall of 1983 had so many problems that it was recalled, and a temporary freeze was placed on new software development while the team corrected bugs. By the summer of 1984, the new, corrected releases had been out only a few months, so few people were aware of the improvements. Furthermore, XSEL was meeting the criticism that innovations typically attract during their middle period.[14] Since sales representatives' performance appraisals were not directly dependent on the accuracy of their configurations, the benefits of a program that decreased errors were not readily apparent. Also, many in the company felt that Digital would be moving toward "standard" configurations that would require much less customization and hence would be less complex than those currently handled by XSEL. Finally, users complained that the system was slow and inaccurate. The program seemed in imminent danger of cancellation.

At this juncture, the user design group members enlisted themselves in the battle to preserve XSEL. Convinced of its potential, they asked to meet with a central committee of top sales managers to explain the value of the system. At this meeting, the sales managers were impressed with the UDG members' enthusiasm and with the amount of time and effort already expended on the project by rank-and-file members of their own organization. Moreover, the spokesperson for the UDG were high performers in terms of sales and hence very credible. The project was officially sanctioned to move ahead. Without consciously planning to do so, the XSEL project team had created the needed "pull" in the user organization. The users accomplished what one advocate might not have been able to. As Figure 25.2 shows, usage since that time has increased at a fairly steady pace, although there was a leap during the last quarter of fiscal 1986, followed by a return to previous growth lines. Growth in the number of XSEL output runs roughly parallels that in the number of users, starting at 1,417 runs in April–June 1984 and peaking at 5,090 runs in April–June 1986.

FIGURE 25.2 Number of XSEL Users in the United States
Data courtesy of Intelligent Systems Technology Group, Digital Equipment Corporation.

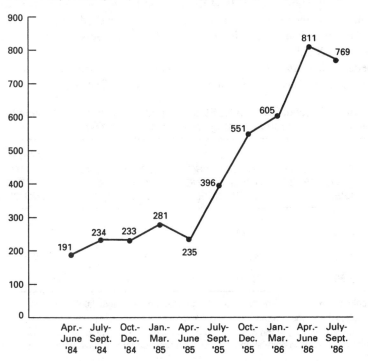

The Delivery System

Technology development teams frequently underestimate the importance of the physical and educational infrastructure with which their invention interacts in the user organization, since this infrastructure is often directly under the management of users. Thus development teams usually relinquish not only management responsibility but also concern about the issue. Such abdication of all interest is potentially very dangerous to the project for three reasons: users are generally unable to distinguish the characteristics inherent in the technology itself from those of the system by which the technology reaches them; a bad initial experience with a new technology can translate into extreme reluctance to try it again, even when conditions have improved;[15] and people with unfavorable experiences are more likely to relate those experiences to acquaintances than are people who have favorable experiences.[16]

Bundled Characteristics   In the case of XSEL, when the computer or communication lines were too burdened to carry the program efficiently (and artificial intelligence languages tend to be machine intensive), all the sales representatives cared about was that the response time was slow. In their minds the slowness of the hardware was bundled together with the other attributes of the software and contributed to a negative evaluation. In all three annual surveys, "slowness" was cited as a key weakness of the system.

Personal and Vicarious Negative Experiences   By 1986, about 75 percent of the sales representatives first interviewed in 1984 had tried XSEL, but only 25 percent were actually using it. Discontinuers tended to be less favorably disposed toward the technology than were those who had never tried it (see Table 25.2). Users, of course, were more enthusiastic about XSEL.

Inadequate delivery systems not only discourage triers from a second attempt to use an innovation, but also create innovation "assassins." The opposite of champions,

TABLE 25.2   Differences in Evaluation of XSEL among 93 Sales Representatives Who Have Never Tried, Discontinued Using, or Are Still Using XSEL

EVALUATION CRITERION	PEOPLE WHO NEVER TRIED XSEL	PEOPLE WHO DISCONTINUED USING XSEL	PEOPLE WHO STILL USE XSEL	SIGNIFICANCE LEVEL OF DIFFERENCES AMONG GROUPS[***]
XSEL as a productivity tool[*]	4.25	3.88	4.92	.02[***]
XSEL as software[*]	4.26	4.50	4.59	.62 (N.S.)
XSEL's accuracy[**]	3.86	3.60	4.05	.09

[*]Measured on a 1–7 scale, where one means "very poor" and seven means "excellent"
[**]Measured on a 1–5 scale, where one means "very poor" and five means "excellent"
[***]This figure represents the probability that the difference might have occurred by chance. Thus, there is only a 2 percent probability that the differences in opinion about XSEL as a productivity tool could have occurred by chance.

innovation assassins advise people *not* to use the new technology. Survey data showed that potential XSEL users who knew such individuals evaluated the new tool significantly less favorably and were less likely to use it than both colleagues who knew an advocate and colleagues who were not influenced either way.

Gradually over the three years studied, the XSEL program office made considerable headway in establishing an effective delivery system. In 1984 the hotline in Colorado that serviced internal users of Digital software packages agreed to support XSEL. In late 1985 XSEL was introduced into the sales orientation and training course for new sales representatives. Finally, and most important, in 1986 the sales organization agreed to purchase enough very powerful VAX machines to support XSEL in the field. This move ensured that at last the limitations on response speed would be determined principally by the software itself instead of by the capabilities of the hardware and communication connections. The XSEL team now had under its control both of the technology attributes of greatest importance to users: accuracy and response time. One of their next tasks would be to advertise this fact and alert past triers that both response time and accuracy were greatly improved.

Organizational Prototyping

Technical prototyping is the preferred method of constructing many radically new software programs, and the only method for constructing most expert systems, because no one can initially lay out the specifications of the entire program. Its ultimate boundaries and capabilities are unknown; the strategy is to discover structure through trial and error. This methodology is often also applicable to designing the organizational environment for new technologies—for precisely the same reasons.

Managers react differently to the concept of prototyping depending upon their orientation toward resolving uncertainty. As researchers studying the deployment of management information systems pointed out recently, there are two kinds of uncertainty: uncertainty in the sense of not knowing what the outcome of a given action will be, and ambiguity, which results from having some idea of outcome, but not of its meaning or value to others.[17]

Building upon this useful distinction, one might observe that the first kind of uncertainty induces a search for more information. Prototyping is a natural response to such uncertainty. The second kind of uncertainty, ambiguity, takes knowledge as a given and induces a search for resolution among differing views and values. Conflict resolution is a natural response to such ambiguity.

Managers are not equally comfortable with these two modes of reaction. Those who are accustomed to voyages of technical discovery (e.g., engineers designing products or knowledge engineers) regard experimentation as a natural road toward certainty. Those who are accustomed to questions for which there is no absolute answer (e.g., general managers dealing with personnel problems) regard negotiation among conflicting views as a natural road to resolution of ambiguity.

In the development and deployment of new technologies, both approaches are necessary. It is important for the technically oriented manager to recognize that a technology does not have an absolute meaning, but differs in profile and value depending upon the perceptions of users. Therefore, the final form of the technology is to be negotiated among multiple sets of users, and the value is to be established for differing sets of supporters through much interpersonal contact. Similarly, the more generally oriented managers need to become comfortable with the concept of experimentation as a legitimate way to manage the gradual shaping of the organizational environment into which the technology is introduced (i.e., organizational prototyping).

The newer the technology, the more likely it is that organizational prototyping will be needed to answer such basic questions as these:

- Who are the real users of this technology? If they are not the originally targeted users, is that cause for concern? Does the switch in users necessitate unanticipated changes in the organization? in the technology?
- How is the technology actually being used (as opposed to how the developers expected it to be used)?
- What is the actual value of this new technology to the corporation and how should that value be measured?

The answers to such questions may appear obvious at the outset of a project, yet even when managers think they know the answers, events may prove them wrong. For example, computer-aided engineering tools intended for use by design engineers may instead be used by technical assistants in some divisions,[18] and electronic mail systems intended for managers used instead by their secretaries. Thus, technologies are sometimes handed down by the targeted users, for whom the technology offers no advantage in skills, to those subordinates whose expertise is enhanced by use of it. Moreover, there is a tendency (noted decades ago by sociologists) for professionals to hand the "dirty work" to employees with less status.

In the case of XSEL, many sales representatives do use the program themselves. However, in some districts, a technical assistant (often someone who was formerly an order-entry clerk) enters the representatives' configurations for them.

The implications of such differing patterns of use are not clear-cut. On the one hand, the fact that engineers earn higher salaries than technicians, managers than secretaries, sales reps than clericals, would argue for the efficiency of the "hand-me-down" trend. On the other hand, in each of these cases the technology may not be fully utilized by the less highly trained employees. Technicians, for instance, in the case of the CAE system, cannot use the simulation capabilities of the system, since they do not usually understand enough about circuitry logic to do so. Moreover, many systems were designed to give the user feedback about performance of a given task. If the technician rather than the design engineer enters the design into the computer system, it is the technician who notes the design mistakes—not the engineer responsible for them. Similarly, if the assistant rather than the sales representative uses XSEL, the assistant, not the representative, learns from the system about common errors such as leaving out certain cables or trying to combine incomparable components.

Therefore, there are both advantages and disadvantages to hand-me-down patterns in technology use. The only way to determine whether these patterns are helpful or deleterious to the organization is to evaluate them (i.e., to treat these different patterns of use as naturally occurring experiments that can be observed and whose outcome can be compared).

The second question, how the technology is being used, can also be answered only by observation, and of course differing situations in the field occasion different use patterns. In the case of XSEL, the annual research-related surveys that I conducted provided some feedback on this issue. In 1986, users reported utilizing XSEL's expertise in the following ways: to select components and guide the configuration from the beginning (17 percent); to complete a partial configuration started manually (21 percent); and to verify a configuration designed entirely manually (62 percent). These surveys were not permitted to cover new entrants into the sales force, so no one is exactly sure if and how XSEL is being used by new recruits. Moreover, such time as the XSEL program team had to conduct its own interviews in the field was necessarily directed to gathering ammunition to save the program from the firing line. Not surprisingly, team members chose to interview enthusiastic users rather than discontinuers. Consequently, there is little information available about which subpopulations are most likely to stop using XSEL after an initial trial—and why.

The final question, about the value of the technology to the organization, is especially important. Regardless of how it is figured, the potential return-on-investment calculation used to justify a new technology project at its outset almost always proves inadequate to the task of generating continued organizational support during development. Targeted stakeholders and users want to see convincing performance data—the more quantifiable the better. Again, an internal test market can demonstrate progress toward the desired goals and identify barriers to achieving more benefits.

Of course, experiments in technology usage often occur naturally during the initial dissemination of a technology. Even in those rare cases in which a manager recognizes the opportunity to learn consciously from a pilot study, however, ad hoc experiments may not generate credible data.

In the case of XSEL, one district manager decided in 1985 to require all his sales representatives to run their quotations through XSEL, since the costs of return authorizations were running at a relatively high three percent of district costs. He attributed the subsequent drop (to about one-half percent) in large part to use of XSEL.

At first, Bruce MacDonald and the XSEL team saw an opportunity to capitalize on this success story. However, the fact that this mandated trial of XSEL had not been set up from the beginning as a real experiment undermined its credibility. First, some skeptics believed the highly visible demonstration was motivated by the district manager's political ambitions within the company, rather than by any real interest in the technology. Therefore, they discounted the reports of dramatic benefits as hyperbole. Second, judging the accuracy of the XSEL output proved problematic.

The district manager's success figures were based on configurations judged correct at the district sales level, but when these same configurations reached the technical editors who checked orders going into manufacturing many were rejected as incorrect. Rumors to this effect further undermined the credibility of the success story. When MacDonald tracked down some of these "incorrect" configurations, he found that most had been rejected not because they were technically incorrect but because some features in the XSEL output format were inconsistent with plant-specific manufacturing administrative practices. If the experiment were to be valid, such nontechnical reasons for rejection would have to be identified separately in the analysis of benefits. The XSEL team had neither the time nor the inclination for such an undertaking. They ceased promoting the midwestern experiment as a demonstration.

In contrast, a limited form of organizational prototyping occurred in Europe. From the time XSEL was introduced in Europe, it was seen as a productivity tool for the technical editors who manually checked configurations, rather than as a tool for the sales representatives. In one Scottish location, the technical editors designed and executed a carefully planned test of XSEL accuracy by conducting 1,000 XSEL runs and collecting a number of metrics on them. They reported a "raw" accuracy of 75 percent for XSEL output using very stringent criteria, that is, rejecting any order as totally incorrect if even one line item was added or deleted incorrectly. Even more important, they found they could raise that percentage to 90 if three relatively minor but common problems, such as inadequate provision for country-specific adjustments to configurations, were corrected. These and other metrics gathered from the same test provided convincing evidence of XSEL's utility.

Another European experiment currently under way may generate insight into the advantages and disadvantages of technical editors versus sales representatives as users. In three Digital offices in England, three different modes of configuration are being used: manual configuration by a technical specialist; configuration with XSEL by a technical specialist; and configuration with XSEL by sales representatives. This situation has real potential as an organizational prototyping exercise.

IMPLEMENTATION AS INTEGRATIVE INNOVATION

The reading has used the XSEL example to illuminate some managerial issues inherent in the development and implementations of any new technology and exacerbated in the case of expert systems. Technology managers need to work very closely with users, as codevelopers rather than receivers of the technology; constantly redefine the necessary support structure in the user organization, identifying and targeting potentially weak links; enlarge their definition of the technology to include the delivery system or other linkages on which the technology is critically dependent; and experiment as consciously and productively with organizational forms wherever possible on experiments occurring naturally in the environment.

With hindsight, it is clear from the XSEL case that these suggestions are deceptive in their apparent simplicity. For instance, experience with the user design group showed both that this kind of group can have more functions than envisioned when it was set up, and that the dynamics of managing such a group are more complex than anticipated. Users who are expert in the task being automated are unlikely to be typical of the population for whom the technology is targeted. In fact, if they are, the system may add little value! Yet typical users do not obtain the same intrinsic satisfaction from building the system as experts do, for it is not their expertise being captured. The system is unlikely to elicit the same feelings of ownership as it does from the experts who see their knowledge being immortalized in the system. Therefore, the interface with typical but nonexpert users has to be motivated and managed differently, either separately from the experts or with some explicit recognition of their vital but different role.

A second point learned from the XSEL experience is that a user design group can be as important in guiding implementation as in development. While top management support for the innovation may lessen the need for the grassroots support that was so essential in the case of XSEL, users can always provide insight into how their own organization functions and therefore help plan the internal marketing of the technology.

Building a network of supporters was especially problematic for the XSEL team because the members belonged to one functional organization and built the system for another. Reflecting on the XSEL experience, MacDonald commented that he would, given the task again, spend more time "working the interface between manufacturing and sales." As the XSEL case demonstrates, the original home of a new technology will always influence the way it is perceived by the rest of the organization. Therefore managers need to choose that site, whenever possible, with an eye to how that choice affects generation of an adequate support structure.

The third issue, inadequate infrastructure, accounts for a surprising number of problems in the implementation of new technologies.[19] This can be an issue of special concern with expert systems because the initial version of large expert systems is often quite machine intensive; currently, micro-based experts systems (usually built using commercially available PC software packages that guide the development process) are limited in size. Therefore, the utility of the expert system can be substantially affected by the resources dedicated to running it.

The final point made about technology development in general—the need for organizational prototyping—is especially true for expert systems. An expert system often turns out to be like a book—it is used differently by various groups of people. The organizational impacts of such systems cannot be simulated or totally anticipated, since there is so little previous experience with them. Therefore the managers of such development projects need to have both the personal skills and the resources to experiment with organizational as well as technical design.

The major point of this reading is this: even if the developers and the users of a new technology work in different organizations within the corporation the development and internal implementation of the technology should be managed as one integrated and continuously innovative effort.

While some technologies, such as the one reviewed here, tend to force that approach, all development projects are likely to profit from it. If an integrative approach is used, technology considerations are not divorced from organizational ones and implementation is not separated from innovative effort. Rather, the development process becomes a series of experimental steps in a predetermined direction both for the technology and the user organization. Unable to foresee the final form of either the technology or the organization with any great precision, managers of new technology projects will increasingly need this approach in order to succeed.

QUESTIONS

1. Describe the applications for which XCON and XSEL were developed.
2. What are the key concepts associated with integrative innovation?
3. Compare and contrast the integrative innovation approach to system development with the system development life cycle.
4. Summarize the major points learned from the XSEL development experience.

REFERENCES

1. SKINNER, W. "The Productivity Paradox," *Harvard Business Review,* July–August 1986, pp. 55–59; M. E. Porter, *Competitive Advantage* (New York: The Free Press, 1985).

2. LEONARD-BARTON, D. "Transferring Technology from Developers to Operations" (Boston: Harvard Business School, working paper #87-049, June 1987).

3. HARMON, P. AND D. KING, *Expert Systems: Artificial Intelligence in Business* (New York: John Wiley, 1985).

4. Expert systems are still in their infancy, and it may well be that the direct mimicry of human expertise is not the most appropriate nor the most powerful application for this technology. However, most of the current systems do attempt to clone human judgment, i.e., to simulate human reasoning. Further discussion of this issue is beyond the scope of this reading.

5. For a history of XCON's development, see D. Leonard-Barton and B. DeLacey, "Skunkworks and Digital Equipment Corporation: The Tale of XCON" (Boston: Harvard Business School, case services #9-687-051); and J. Sviokla, "Planpower, XCON and Mudman: An In-Depth Analysis into Three Commercial Expert Systems in Use" (Boston: Harvard Business School, unpublished doctoral dissertation, 1986).

6. HAYES, R. M. AND S. C. WHEELWRIGHT, *Restoring Our Competitive Edge: Competing through Manufacturing* (New York: John Wiley, 1985).

7. IVES, B. AND M. H. OLSON, "User Involvement and MIS Success: A Review of Research," *Management Science,* 30 (May 1984), 586–603.

8. MUMFORD, E. AND D. HANSHALL, *The Participative Design of Computer Systems* (London: Associated Business Press, 1978).

9. TVERSKY, A. AND D. KAHNEMAN, "Belief in the Law of Small Numbers," *Psychological Bulletin,* 76 (1971), 105–110.

10. LEONARD-BARTON (June 1987).

11. ROBERTS, E. B. "Generating Effective Corporate Innovation," *Technology Review,* October–November 1977, pp. 25–33; A. K. Chakrabarti, "The Role of Champion in Product Innovation," *California Management Review,* Winter 1974, pp. 58–62; R. M. Kanter, "When a Thousand Flowers Bloom: Structural Collective and Social Conditions for Innovation in Organizations" (Boston: Harvard Business School, working paper #87-018, October 1986).

12. ROTHWELL, R. "Some Problems of Technology Transfer into Industry: Examples from the Textile Machinery Sector," *IEEE Transactions on Engineering Management,* EM 25, #1, February 1977, 15–20.

13. DOWLING, A. "Hospital Staff Interference with Medical Computer System Implementation: An Exploratory Analysis" (Cambridge: Sloan School of Management, M.I.T., working paper #1073-79, 1979).

14. KANTER (October 1986).

15. MCERLEAN, D. P. "Diffusion of Innovation within a Large Corporation" (Cambridge: Sloan School of Management, M.I.T., unpublished thesis for master of science degree, 1983).

16. RICHINS, M. L. "Negative Word-of- Mouth by Dissatisfied Consumers: A Pilot Study," *Journal of Marketing,"* Winter 1983, 68–78.

17. DAFT, R. L. AND R. H. LENGEL, "Organizational Information Requirements, Media Richness, and Structural Design," *Management Science,* 32 (1986), 554–571.

18. LEONARD-BARTON, D. "A New CAE System for Shield Electronics Engineers" (Boston: Harvard Business School, case services #9-687-081, 1987).

19. LEONARD-BARTON, D. (June 1987 working paper); R. Walton, *Innovating to Compete: Lessons for Diffusing and Managing Change in the Workplace* (San Francisco: Jossey-Bass, in press).

26

CHOOSING
AN EXPERT SYSTEMS
GAME PLAN

C. Lawrence Meador,
Ed G. Mahler

In the world of baseball, there are many ways to score a run. The brute force of a power hitter can certainly do the job in dramatic fashion. But so, too, can the individual efforts of players working their way down the bases with in-field hits and walks. By the ninth inning, it matters little how each team planned and plotted to rack up its runs. Only the total score—and who came out on top—really counts.

Choosing an expert systems strategy also involves making a series of choices from the beginning of the game. As in baseball, there is no right or wrong approach to winning with expert systems technology. But choosing a strategy that fits your company's culture and structure has a lot to do with your chances for ultimate success.

Five years ago, E. I. DuPont de Nemours & Co. opted to train its end users to develop their own small systems. Today, the more than 600 expert systems installed in DuPont's business units are cumulatively saving more than $75 million per year. By 1991, this expert systems program is expected to contribute more than $100 million annually to the bottom line.

Reprinted by special permission of *Datamation,* August 1, 1990. © 1990 by Technical Publishing

Over the last 10 years, Digital Equipment Corp. has evolved an equally successful program following an entirely different strategy. To begin its expert system efforts organization, Digital established the Artificial Intelligence Technology Center (AITC), in Marlborough, Mass. AITC has become a strategic resource for training highly skilled knowledge engineers. The result is a fast-growing number of operational and strategic systems affecting all its business processes. Digital now has 50 major expert systems in place, contributing $200 million in annual savings.

DuPont and Digital share a fundamental expert systems goal: to improve decision making throughout the corporation by putting relevant information and knowledge into the hands of those making the decisions. But the routes the companies have chosen in achieving this goal are very different.

DuPont uses a "dispersed" approach to expert systems development. End users develop their own systems using standard, low-cost tools.

The "specialist" approach used by Digital typically involves a centralized development center where specially trained programmers or knowledge engineers use custom tools to create systems. Generally, the systems are more complex and are used by more people than those created under the dispersed approach.

Each approach can vary in the way that it's controlled and deployed, and many companies are evolving systems that use elements of both approaches. In choosing an expert system for your company, you should ask questions in the following areas:

Knowledge

What are the critical points of decision-making for the business? Is it critical to share knowledge between departments or is knowledge highly localized?

Resources

What is the state of your company's current information systems infrastructure? What is the computer literacy level of the employees? And what is your company's IS strategy?

At first glance, DuPont and Digital appear to have a lot in common. Both are global, highly decentralized organizations. Both have 120,000 employees and more than 100 plants worldwide. But that's where the similarity ends.

Digital's focus is on a single basic technology and a single architecture, with a primary emphasis on selling computer systems to end users. Dupont is a federation of businesses that produces products in almost every category found in a host of categories: fibers, plastics, chemicals, imaging systems, oil, coal, automotive products, electronics, agricultural products and medical products. DuPont offers an array of product types that are typically several sales away from the end user. For instance the nylon it manufactures may ultimately end up in carpets made by Karastan and sold to the consumer by Sears Roebuck & Co.

THE KNOWLEDGE PROFILE

The term "knowledge profile" describes the patterns of information flow throughout a company. Some companies require a tight integration of information between departments, while others function well with localized wisdom.

Although Digital also has a vast array of products—namely, 43 computer families comprise some 30,000 parts—most of these products must function under the constraints of a single computer architecture. That's a fundamental corporate totem, the basic strategy through which Digital tries to differentiate itself. Each part must plug and play with all the others, and the knowledge possessed by each function must be aligned with the others to create the final product.

Sales, for example, must be able to propose systems that are technically correct, manufacturing must be able to verify that an order can be produced and field service must know how and when to assemble the system at the customer's site.

At DuPont, the distribution of knowledge parallels the organizational structure—both are localized. The knowledge required to manufacture nylon in Seaford, Del., has nothing to do with the knowledge needed to sell Teflon in Hamburg, Germany. Fiber production is a world away from coal mining.

Furthermore, enormous disparity exists within each product line. Most of the company's 1,700 product lines each contain several hundred subtypes. Some, such as the electronics connectors business, range up to 500,000 items. Even within a single plant, the individual assembly lines may differ.

Such dispersed knowledge pushed DuPont to its roll-your-own approach to expert systems. So did the organization's culture. DuPont nurtures fierce independence and technical excellence throughout its federation—a prerequisite for a company trying to stay on the leading edge in so many arenas.

Another DuPont characteristic begs for the dispersed approach. At DuPont, big is not necessarily beautiful. Large problems can be broken into small pieces that an individual expert can tackle. If care is taken to create standard interfaces—in this case, between expert systems—each of those solutions can be linked later to solve bigger problems. In one plant, for example, an expert system for process-control troubleshooting is actually an agglomeration of smaller systems designed for troubleshooting various components.

Understanding the resource profile of an organization is critical to devising a strategy for implementing expert systems, no matter which approach is followed. First, an effective resource profile dictates that the company's information systems infrastructure—the hardware platforms, the networks, the databases—must be in place. The decision makers, the users or user/developers of the systems must also have an adequate level of computer literacy. Without such a foundation, success will take a long time to achieve.

THE RESOURCE PROFILE

Digital's resource profile is blessed with a staff that's largely computer literate. This literacy level contributes to the company's success in spreading the use of expert systems throughout its organization and beyond. AITC has already trained 500 knowledge engineers throughout the world.

Another key aspect of Digital's resource profile is an IS strategy to integrate at all levels—business process, applications and data. Driven by its need to align knowledge across functions, Digital's strategy mandates that expert systems adhere to all data and network standards. Like the products it sells, Digital's expert systems must be able to communicate with each other and with any databases and applications.

DuPont, in contrast, works with various hardware platforms and global networks. A degree of applications and database integration exists at each major organizational level—corporate, department and business unit—with most needs satisfied through four large IBM data centers. For example, an electronic mail system operates across all platforms: IBM mainframes, Digital and Hewlett-Packard Co. minicomputers, and PCs. The Digital VAXs and HP 3000s are used throughout DuPont's engineering and manufacturing facilities. And 15,000 IBM PCs and 15,000 Apple Macintoshes are used in DuPont offices worldwide.

More than 30,000 DuPont managers and professionals are Lotus literate today, a number that will grow to 60,000 before the decade is out. With this supporting infrastructure in place. DuPont's resource profile is naturally more oriented toward PC-based expert systems. More than 1,800 DuPont people are now using expert system shells as readily as they do spreadsheets, electronic mail and other tools.

THE SPECIALIST APPROACH

Being a high-cost/high-payback effort, the specialist approach requires many of the same attributes of any major system development effort: senior management sponsorship, adequate funding and rigorous management control when it comes to project selection, prioritization and development.

The human resource requirements can be a problem with the specialist approach. A knowledge engineer requires a mixture of normal programming skills, expert system language and tool skills and a firm understanding of subject matter. Digital says that, for complex systems, it can take a year before a trained individual is fully up to speed. The company's knowledge engineers are put through an apprenticeship program ranging from 13 weeks to nine months, depending on the business problem and the level of training required. In some instances, AITC consultants may continue to work with the trainees back at their home sites.

The development and maintenance of complex systems require more than a group of knowledge engineers working together. A group at Digital responsible for the XCON and XSEL programs, which are used to configure systems for customers, includes a program manager, software systems integration engineers and various experts providing information in terms of process and data content. For each quarterly release of these systems, Digital consults hundreds of experts in manufacturing and engineering. Moreover, 40% of the rules in the configuration systems change annually.

The possible options for getting started using the specialist approach are:

- Hire an outside firm to develop the first expert systems.
- Experiment internally, but team up with other companies to create a support group.
- Create a specialized shop.

In the late 1970s, when Digital decided on an expert system as the solution to its configuration problems, the technology was in its infancy. So the company joined with an academic artificial intelligence hotbed, Carnegie Mellon University in Pittsburgh, to produce what became XCON. The AI Technology Center grew out of this effort, and subsequently so did Digital's entry into the expert systems market, providing tools, training and consulting for customers wanting to leapfrog steps in the specialist approach.

AI CENTRAL

As its expert systems strategy evolved, Digital discovered that, in some cases, development and maintenance had to be controlled centrally. Yet this didn't prove to be true of the total expert systems program. Nor would the culture and organizational structure of the company allow for vesting such control in a single organization, says Jack Rahaim, manager of Digital's AI marketing and productivity shell programs. "From the beginning, we planned to disperse the technology throughout the organization," he says.

Digital's structure is not a simple one—a functionally decentralized organization integrated at the business process level and run under a matrix style of management. Even though the AI Technology Center is the locus for AI expertise at Digital, it doesn't run the entire expert systems show. Nor does its management plan or control the applications.

The Marlborough facility houses two basic expert systems groups. The first comprises 150 people involved in applications development for configuring systems, field service and manufacturing and engineering. These professionals report to line managers, as do other expert systems developers scattered throughout the company.

The second is the core staff under AITC management—also 150 professionals—who are involved in services and products for both internal and external customers. They are responsible for distributing the technology they develop throughout the organization and to customers via marketing, training and apprenticeship programs. They are also involved in establishing new training centers in Europe, Japan and the United States.

Rahaim emphasizes that line managers and their staffs control the selection of applications, the tools they use for development and even the skills-training process. (AITC offers training, but it's not mandatory for employees to go there.) The only rules are that applications meet the communications and data standards of the company if they are to be integrated at the business process, network and data levels.

In short, although AITC has enormous influence over the Digital program, it does not pull all the strings, a fact that Rahaim feels has contributed to corporatewide acceptance and commitment.

THE DISPERSED APPROACH

The issues involved in implementing the dispersed approach are quite different. The key questions to ask are the following:

- Who will be the target developers—the ultimate end user, the user in concert with an IS professional or a local guru?
- How can you build the user/developer's understanding and commitment?
- How can developers increase their programming skills?
- What standard tools should you select and sponsor, and how many of them will you need?
- How do you avoid reinventing the wheel?
- How do you find and maintain area management support?

The strength of this approach is that expert systems are often developed fast—from days to months—and for costs ranging from a few hundred to a few thousand dollars. At DuPont, training consists of a basic two-day course, plus a number of one-day, specialized courses.

Besides speed and low cost, the dispersed approach fosters user ownership and creates broad organizational support. If it's handled correctly, the successful user/developers will sell the concept to their colleagues.

To succeed in the dispersed mode, a company must move through three stages:

- **Maverick.** A few aggressive pioneers begin to create their own small systems.
- **Experimentation.** The mavericks' successes convince a group or a manager to address certain problems formally for a trial period.
- **Culture change.** A group decides to embrace the development of expert systems for a wide variety of applications.

With so many issues to resolve, don't expect shortcuts to culture change. Culture change means that many existing processes for resolving problems must be thrown out and new ones adopted. To make culture change work, the group must have a vision. And that vision must be supported by successful experiences, a sizable cadre of trained amateurs and a plan that specifies each milestone for achieving a completed system and the rewards at the end of each milestone.

It's taken five years for DuPont to evolve through the maverick and experimentation stages. Eighteen hundred people have been trained to use expert system shells, and several business units are now ready for the culture change that lies ahead. Two of them are developing several hundred expert systems this year.

SUPPORT FROM THE TOP

The dispersed strategy does not mean no corporate guidance or support. Back in 1985, DuPont did not simply scatter a few expert systems shells on users' desks and tell its people to play with them. An AI task force led by coauthor Ed Mahler examined the idea of letting the experts—the decision makers—develop their own systems using existing expert systems shells. The task force approved 40 different packages that would run on DuPont's installed workstations and personal computers.

Although shells were still in their commercial infancy, the task force decided there was enormous opportunity for improving front-line decision making through a dispersed approach. Senior management agreed to experiment and provided $3 million in seed money.

Gradually, a consulting organization was put in place. The corporate AI group was to serve as the catalyst and change agent, selling the concept, selecting the standard tools and establishing training programs. Under this group, a cadre of site coordinators (now numbering 200) have been assigned to user locations, arranging for training and supplying help when needed.

Recognizing the culture of fierce independence at DuPont, the AI Group knew the expert system movement had to grow by word-of-mouth advertising, rather than by edict. Group members began by calling their colleagues throughout the business units and giving talks, and then waited for the word to spread. As the successes piled up, area management support increased.

The standard tools that were selected were not stipulated by law—users could opt to use any tool that would run on their microcomputers or VAX workstations. The initial tools sponsored were Insight + from New York City-based Information Builders Inc. and RS Decision from BBN Software Products, a division of Cambridge, Mass.-based Bolt Beranek and Newman Inc. Because no shell is suited to all applications, the number of standard tools in use today has grown. The only hard and fast rule was that each system had to have a standard interface for linking into the network and the data files.

It didn't take long for results to come in. Typically, trainees developed their first systems within a few weeks. DuPont tried several routes to avoid reinventing the wheel with these systems. The first idea, to create a database of expert systems, was soon discarded. Besides the technical complexity involved, the AI Group recognized that human nature would not cope with the centralized database idea. Could everyone be counted on to enter their expert systems into the central file? Not likely.

But people who were creating new systems could be counted on to find out if anyone had done a similar project. Fortunately, a vehicle for managing this type of fishing expedition was already in place. DuPont's global electronic mail network allows employees to put out a single call to all of DuPont's 1,800 expert systems developers.

The dispersed approach requires a lot of self-help and self-discipline. Novices will make mistakes, and they will sometimes develop systems that are not useful. Yet most mistakes quickly work themselves out, and whimsical projects usually fall into disuse because of the maintenance time involved. Just 50 systems have simply withered away at DuPont, while 600 have proven highly productive.

DuPont's expert systems generally fall into one of the following areas: troubleshooting and selection systems used from development to sales and delivery; production planning and scheduling; and remote process control.

Useful expert systems have been devised to help design products meeting specific customer needs. For example, the Packaging Adviser, used for designing rigid plastic food containers, helped DuPont break into the highly competitive barrier resin market.

The company also tackled a critical problem, chemical spills occurring in transit, by developing a Transportation Emergency Response Planner to guide people in the field through the right procedures for diagnosing, controlling and cleaning up a spill. A Maintenance Finish Adviser is used at trade shows to answer questions on high-performance paints and obtain sales leads. And a Confidentiality Document Adviser is used for preparing sections of legal documents.

Expert systems are widely used throughout DuPont's manufacturing processes for troubleshooting and quality control. So far, the company has developed 50 expert systems for diagnosing and correcting process control problems. A 600-rule expert system, built by two people in concert with the business team, has been integrated into one unit's production planning and scheduling system.

While DuPont continues to decompose large problems into parts addressable through small expert systems developed by individuals, the company realizes that there are economies of scale in creating centers to help tackle generic problems, such as real-time process control and production scheduling. These groups, called competency centers, are composed of IS and network professionals who work with business units wanting to develop such systems.

17,000 RULES

At Digital, the configuration systems today include six systems totaling more than 17,000 rules: XCON, used to validate the technical correctness of customer orders and guide the assembly of these orders; XSEL, used iteratively to assist sales in configuring an order; XFL, for diagramming a computer room for floor layout for the proposed configuration; XCLUSTER, to configure clusters; XNET, for designing local area networks; and SIZER, for sizing computing resources according to customer need.

Among the variety of other expert systems are inventory monitoring (CAN BUILD), truck scheduling (National Dispatch Router), manufacturing planning (MOC) and logic gate design (APES).

Digital's Rahaim notes that although enormous operational savings have been realized through the use of these systems, even greater benefits are evident, although difficult to quantify. "The configuration systems allowed us to pursue and extend our à la carte marketing strategy, which is what differentiates us."

The APES system has resulted in striking productivity gains. "Typically, a senior design engineer can create 200 logic gates per week," say Rahaim. "With APES, the number had gone to 8,000 per day. The first chip we designed this way sped up a computer introduction by six months. How do you quantify the strategic advantage of slashing the time to market?"

Besides day-to-day operational systems, Digital also has expert systems designed for senior management. One such system is called Manufacturing Operations Consultant (MOC), which helps managers examine the impact of major changes—in pricing, in resources, in market demand—on the capacity and work load of their plants worldwide. "That is an example of a strategic system and of a system that must integrate," says Rahaim. "You don't know about the plant in Ireland unless you can tap into the databases there on their production load, the cost structures, etc." MOC is used for short-range planning, but other expert systems are being devised for modeling long-range plans.

Systems integration is extremely important to the evolution of strategic expert systems at Digital. For instance, Rahaim foresees the day when systems such as APES will be integrated with other design systems and business processes so that management can electronically simulate the final product and estimate the manufacturing costs and time to market.

What's the right approach for your organization? There is no simple answer. Analyzing the business environment and the technology readiness of your business are critical steps that can lead to the use of either or both approaches described here. Whatever method is chosen, managing the evolution of the effort must be handled carefully if the program is to achieve broad organizational commitment.

Becoming a world-class organization requires putting world-class knowledge, not just information, into the hands of decision makers. Expert systems technology is far from mature, but we already have the tools, methods and approaches to use expert systems to begin to achieve that goal. Those still mulling over the question of whether to develop an expert system program will be outclassed by those already planning and implementing these systems.

QUESTIONS

1. Describe the strategy that Dupont used to introduce expert systems.
2. Describe the strategy that Digital used to introduce expert systems.
3. Discuss the factors that an organization should consider when developing an expert systems strategy.

27

COVERSTORY— AUTOMATED NEWS FINDING IN MARKETING

John D. Schmitz,
Gordon D. Armstrong,
John D. C. Little

INTRODUCTION

Machine-readable bar codes on products in supermarkets have changed forever the way the packaged-goods industry tracks its sales and understands how its markets work. Although the codes were originally introduced and justified to save labor at check-out, the spin-off data produced by them provide marvelous opportunities for retailers and manufacturers to measure the effectiveness of their marketing programs and create greater efficiencies in their merchandising and promotion. We shall describe how one manufacturer, Ocean Spray Cranberries, Inc., has responded to these opportunities with an innovative decision support system designed to serve marketing and sales management.

Ocean Spray

Ocean Spray Cranberries, Inc., is a grower-owned agricultural cooperative headquartered in Lakeville-Middleboro, Massachusetts, with about nine hundred members. It produces

Reprinted by special permission of the *Interfaces*, Volume 20, Number 6, November-December, 1990. © 1990 by the Institute of Management Sciences and distributes a line of high quality juices and juice drinks with heavy emphasis on cranberry drinks but also with strong lines in grapefruit and tropical drinks. The company also has a significant business in cranberry sauces and fresh cranberries. About 80% of Ocean Spray products sell through supermarkets and other retail stores with lesser amounts flowing through food service and ingredient product channels. Ocean Spray is a Fortune 500 company with sales approaching $1 billion per year.

Until the mid-1980s, Ocean Spray, like most grocery manufacturers, tracked the sales and share of its products with syndicated warehouse withdrawal and retail store data provided by companies such as SAMI and A. C. Nielsen. This data supplemented the companies' own shipments data by providing information on competitive products and the total market. Such databases have formed the cornerstones of useful and effective decision support systems in many companies (Little, 1979; McCann, 1988). For some time, however, it has been apparent that a radically new generation is on the way. By the mid-eighties, the penetration of scanners in supermarkets had reached a level such that data suppliers could put together valid national samples of scanning stores and provide much more detailed and comprehensive sales tracking services than previously. In 1987, Ocean Spray contracted for InfoScan data for the juice category from Information Resources, Inc., (IRI) of Chicago.

InfoScan

IRI's InfoScan is a national and local market tracking service for the consumer packed-goods industry. InfoScan follows consumer purchases of products at the individual item level as identified by the industry's universal product code (UPC). IRI buys data from a nationally representative sample of over 2500 scanner-equipped stores covering major metropolitan markets and many smaller cities. These provide basic volume, market share, distribution and price information. Added to this are measures of merchandising and promotion collected in the stores and markets. These include retailer advertising in newspapers and flyers, in-store displays, and coupons. Most of the measures contain several levels of coding; for example, newspaper ads are coded A, B, or C, according to their prominence. In addition, the InfoScan service provides access to IRI's individual household purchase data collected from approximately 70,000 households across 27 market areas.

Data Explosion

The amount of data is almost overwhelming. IRI adds about 2 gigabytes per week to its master database in Chicago. Compared to the old tracking data, a company buying the InfoScan service receives increased detail by a factor of 4 to 6 because of dealing with individual weeks instead of multiweek totals, 3 to 5 because of UPC's instead of aggregate brands, 4 to 5 because of 50 individual markets instead of broad geographic regions, 2 to 3 because of more tracking measures, and 1 to 3 because of breakouts to individual chains within a market. Multiplying out the factors reveals that 100 to 1000 times as much data is being handled as previously.

Most packaged-goods manufacturers did not initially understand the implications of two to three orders of magnitude more data. And, in fact, this kind of change is difficult to comprehend. In terms of a management report, it means that, if a report took an hour to look through before, the corresponding report with all the possible new breakouts would take 100 hours to look through. In other words, the new detail will not be looked at.

The remarkable advances that have taken place in computing have helped conceal this issue. Today's technology certainly makes it feasible to store and retrieve all the new data and, although the hardware and software to do this are not cheap, they represent a small fraction of the sales dollars involved, so that, if using the data can lead to more effective marketing, a full scale DSS with on-line access to the database is certainly warranted. Indeed, it was clear in advance and even more clear after the fact that the detailed data contain much information of competitive value in running the businesses.

DSS Strategy

Packaged goods companies today have lean staffs. Many have been restructured and lost people. This is in the face of the huge data increases just described. Although Ocean Spray has not been restructured, its roots as an agricultural cooperative have always given it an internal culture of lean self-sufficiency. It has a small IS department for the organization as a whole.

This situation led Ocean Spray naturally to a strategy of a small marketing DSS organization running a decentralized system where the users do most of their own retrieval and analysis. The marketing DSS for syndicated data currently consists of one marketing professional plus the database administrators. The goal is to have a largely centralized database with workstations for sales and marketing in the business units. User interfaces must be easily mastered by busy people whose main jobs are in the functional areas. The role of the DSS organization is to acquire and develop tools with which the end-users can do their own analyses. DSS consults with users to develop appropriate pre-programmed reports to be delivered as hard copy and/or online.

An important characteristic of the system must be growth potential. Not only should retrieval of specific numbers, tables, and graphs be easy now, but the system architecture and computing power should be there for future calculations and analyses that are likely to be much more computationally intensive than simple retrieval.

Ocean Spray's InfoScan Database

Ocean Spray's syndicated database for juices is impressive, almost imposing, considering the change from the past and the level of human resources put against it. It contains about 400 million numbers covering up to 100 data measures, 10,000 products, 125 weeks, and 50 geographic markets. It grows by 10 million new numbers every four weeks. Finding the important news amid this detail and getting it to the right people in a timely fashion is a big task for a department of one.

Hardware and Software

The DSS architecture puts the database and CPU-intensive processing on an IBM 9370 mainframe with ten gigabytes of disk storage and puts user-interface tasks on eleven 386-

level workstations located in the marketing and sales areas. The basic DSS software is IRI's DataServer, which manages data and mainframe computation in the fourth generation language EXPRESS and the user interface in pcEXPRESS. This provides menu driven access to a family of flexible preprogrammed reports available on the workstations.

Unlike some other solutions used by packaged-goods manufacturers, this architecture provides easy access to mainframe computing power from the workstations as is needed, for example, to run applications like the CoverStory software to be discussed.

BASIC RETRIEVAL AND BASIC REPORTING

The basic retrieval, reporting and analytic capabilities of Ocean Spray's DSS are extensive. Any particular fact from the database can be pulled out in a few steps with the help of pull-down menus and picklists. Much of the use comes from standard reports: a company top line report, and four business area reports (cranberry drinks, grapefruit, aseptic packages, and tropical drinks) showing status and trends including changes in share in aggregate and in detail, and changes in merchandising and distribution against a year ago or four weeks ago. Derived measures such as BDI (brand development indices) and CDI (category development indices) are available. Product managers can get a quick update of what is going on with their products. Standardized graphs can be called up and it is relatively easy to construct new ones. Similarly, users can readily construct measures that are ratios, differences, and other combinations of ones already in the database. Usage has been growing steadily since DataServer and the InfoScan database were installed.

Nevertheless, the introduction of the system has required as much learning for the DSS department as the end users. Some people, especially in sales, made little use of the system. Within marketing a few individuals took to the system quickly and did considerable analysis but there was also a feeling that you would not want to have a reputation for spending too much time pushing numbers around. In fact, within sales, the characteristic attitude has been: "Using the computer is not my job. Give me something that is already analyzed. Give me materials that are ready to use and will help me do my job."

In response to this the DSS department has developed (and continues to develop) tools and analyses that will help solve specific user problems. There are a number of approaches; CoverStory to be discussed below is one of the key directions. In addition a variety of reports oriented about selected issues have been developed. For example, reports that rank products and point out Ocean Spray strengths and identify markets where some Ocean Spray product is underdistributed relative to its inherent selling power. The intention is to help sales and marketing people identify market opportunities and product selling points.

FINDING THE NEWS: COVERSTORY

CoverStory is an expert system developed by IRI to tackle the problem of too much data; Ocean Spray has been a development partner and first client. CoverStory automates the creation of summary memoranda for reports extracted from the large scanner databases. The goal is to provide a cover memo, like the one a marketing analyst would write, to describe key events that are reflected in the database—especially in its newest numbers. The project began as a teaching exercise in marketing science—"How would you summarize what is important in this data?" (Stoyiannidis, 1987; Little, 1988)—and has developed into a practical tool.

CoverStory is undergoing continuing development as we gain experience with its use in new situations. We describe the following aspects of the system as it is now being used: (1) the role of marketing models, (2) the basic decomposition steps embodied in the search strategy, (3) the linearization and ranking processes used to decide what facts are most worth mentioning, and (4) methods for generating and publishing the output.

Marketing Models

CoverStory is rooted in the modeling tradition. However, by design, it does not directly present model results at this stage of development, but rather reports only database facts, such as share, volume, price, distribution, and measures of merchandising. The reason is to have the output and underlying processes as transparent and easy to understand as possible. The program assesses the relative importance of these facts, and selects them for presentation by using weights and thresholds which come from marketing models. However, the user is able to inspect and change these values.

Furthermore, in choosing measures of marketing effort for CoverStory to consider, we select a set of marketing variables from the scanner database that model-building experience has shown to be important for driving sales and share. Measures commonly used include:

> *Displays*—percent of stores (weighted by size) that displayed a brand or item.
>
> *Features*—percent of stores (weighted by size) that ran a feature ad on a brand.
>
> *Distribution*—size-weighted percent of store that sold a brand.
>
> *Price cuts*—percent of stores that sold a brand at a price reduced by more than a threshold, such as 10%, from the regular price.
>
> *Price*—Price can be represented by many data measures. CoverStory sometimes uses the overall average price paid at the register but often draws from a finer set of price measures that may include regular price, average merchandised price, and depth of discount. The regular price is the price of an item not undergoing special promotion; average merchandised price is the price of an item in stores where it is being promoted with feature ads or displays. Depth of discount is the difference between these two. In an InfoScan database, we can get even finer measures of price by breaking out average merchandised price and depth of price discount by type of merchandising.

Through a marketing model, we quantify the impact of each of these marketing levers on share or on sales volume and find their relative importance. For grocery items, among the measures described above, we usually (but not always) find the distribution is more important than price, displays, features, and price cuts in that order.

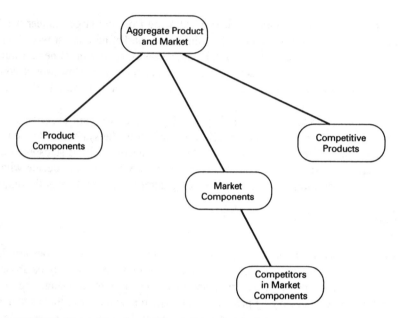

FIGURE 27.1   Structure of CoverStory Analysis

Flow of Analysis and Decomposition

Figure 27.1 shows the general flow of analysis in CoverStory. The central idea is that we will analyze the behavior of an aggregate product in an aggregate market by a series of decompositions or disaggregations. An aggregate product is a product which includes more than one UPC. The UPC (bar code on the package) is the lowest level of product detail available in a scanner database. An example of an aggregate product is Ocean Spray Cranberry Juice and Blends. It consists of many different sizes, package types, and flavors and blends. An example of an aggregate market is the total United States which can be disaggregated into regions or individual cities of even grocery chains within markets.

In doing decomposition, CoverStory follows a style which we have observed in the analytical marketing reports used in many companies. Analysis proceeds by answering the following series of questions. (1) What is going on overall in the aggregate product for the aggregate market? (2) What changes does this reflect in the components of the aggregate product? (3) What changes does this reflect in the components of the aggregate market? (4) What is happening to competitive products? In CoverStory, we go through each of these in turn. Within each of these sections of the analysis, the program follows a standard series of steps:

> Rank the components (markets or products or market/product combinations) by some criteria.
>
> Select the most noteworthy for mention and for further analysis.
>
> Calculate causal factor changes for these top few markets, products, or combinations. Causal factor changes are distribution, price, and merchandising changes.

Rank these causal factors changes then select the top few causal changes to include in the report.

The need to select "the top few" items from different lists is dictated by the size of the scanner database. The number of events that can be mentioned is enormous. Without strictly limiting the amount of information in a report, we found that the news drowned in the detail.

Ranking the Products or Markets

We nearly always rank component products or component markets by share or volume change. When we are looking at size groups within an aggregate product, for example, and we are analyzing share changes, size group ranks will be based on share changes. We have found this to be generally effective with one exception. If there has been a fundamental restructuring of the way a category is marketed, share changes may not be meaningful. (This happened, for example, in the coffee category when packaging switched from multiples of a pound (1-, 2-, and 3-pound cans) to multiples of 13 ounces (13, 26 and 39 ounces). This gave the appearance that a large amount of volume was switching into "new products" and, for a year, volume and share change calculations required special treatment.)

Selecting the Top Few Products or Markets

The top few are the few that are the most noteworthy. We generally calculate which component products or markets are furthest away from average and retain these extremes for mention. Normally, this leads CoverStory to pick winners and losers. In some cases, however, when most of the products and markets are behaving in similar fashion, CoverStory will select only winners or only losers. This approach has been very effective and it closely mimics the way that human market analysts select individual segments of a product line or individual markets for mention.

Calculating Causal Factor Changes

When we point out share or volume changes, we also want to mention possible causes of these share or volume changes. To do so, we calculate the amount of change in marketing support in each of the marketing factors which affects the product. For example, a share change in CranApple sales in Boston may have been partially caused by distribution, price, display, feature, or price cut activity.

Ranking Causal Factor Changes

We can generate a large number of causal factor changes when we decompose the aggregate product and market behavior into components. If there are ten product components, fifty markets, and eight causal factors we are screening, we have four thousand causal changes which are candidates for mention. Trimming this down to a small number for inclusion in the CoverStory report requires a ranking procedure. The procedure we have chosen is similar in spirit to the evaluation functions used in evaluating positions in game-playing programs (Barr, 1981). We calculate a score for each of the causal measure changes. The score incorporates the market in which the change occurred, which causal factor changed, and the magnitude of the change. Symbolically:

Score = Change x Factor weight x Market weight

Change is the amount of change in the causal factor and is either a percent change or raw change depending on the factor. Factor weight is different for each of the marketing factors such as distribution, price, displays, featuring, and price cuts. These factor weights are intended, informally speaking, to make different marketing changes have the same score if their impact on sales is the same. We initialize factor weights based on analysis done outside of CoverStory based on logit models of the type described in Guadagni and Little (1983). Market weight is a term which makes it more likely that an event in a large market will be mentioned than an event in a small market. We originally used market size but found that this was to strong. Only events from New York, Chicago, and Los Angeles would be mentioned and so we have softened the impact of market size. One approach that has proven effective is to use the square root of market size as the market weight.

In all, this scoring method yields a ranked list of causal market changes where such a change can be described in terms of

> What happened? (e.g., price went up by 20%)
> Where did it happen? (e.g., in the Southeastern Region)
> What product did it happen to? (e.g., the 32-ounce bottles)

The events that CoverStory describes are the ones that rank highest using this scoring mechanism.

Presenting the Results

We have experimented with several methods for presenting these results. Our present style is to produce an English- language report in distribution-quality format. This has been an important piece of overall effort and has had a dramatic effect on the acceptability of CoverStory reports to end users. The language generation is usually straightforward; it is based on sentence templates (Barr, 1981). We have considered but not yet implemented context and memory (Schank and Riesbeck, 1981) in our text generation. The use of some randomization of detailed wording through the use of a thesaurus keeps the CoverStory memo from sounding too mechanical. The memo is relatively short and structured so this simple language generation has not been a limitation on CoverStory.

The CoverStory results are published through a high-quality desktop publishing package or a word-processor with desktop publishing capabilities. Variation in typeface, use of graphic boxes, and sidebars are all intended to give the memo visual appeal and highlight the marketing facts which are contained in it.

CoverStory is very much a decision support system rather than a decision making system. The user can adjust all major system parameters such as who competes with whom, what weights to use for the marketing factors, and how much information is to be reported. The final memo is published through a standard word processing package so it can be edited by the user, although this seldom happens. Because the memo is automated and easily set up (and then left alone) to meet the needs of specific managers, the appropriate "news" can quickly be distributed throughout the organizations when new data arrives.

The CoverStory memorandum shown in Figure 27.2 illustrates the output. In this coded example, we present highlights about a brand called Sizzle in the Total United States. The recipient for this memorandum is the Sizzle Brand Manager and the brand management team. The series of decompositions in this report is

Breaking down total Sizzle volume into sales by size groups.
Looking at Sizzle's major competitors.
Looking at submarkets of the United States—cities in this database.
Looking at competitive activity in these submarkets.

FIGURE 27.2   Example of CoverStory Output

To: Sizzle Brand Manager

From: CoverStory

Date: 07/05/89

Subject: Sizzle Brand Summary for Twelve Weeks Ending May 21, 1989

Sizzle's share of type in Total United States was 71.3 in the C&B Juice/Drink category for the twelve weeks ending 5/21/89. This is an increase of 1.2 points from a year earlier but down .5 from last period. This reflects volume sales of 10.6 million gallons. Category volume (currently 99.9 million gallons) declined 1.3% from a year earlier.

Display activity and unsupported price cuts rose over the past year - unsupported price cuts from 38 points to 46. Featuring and price remained at about the same level as a year earlier.

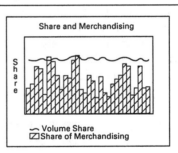

Share and Merchandising

↗ Volume Share
▨ Share of Merchandising

Components of Sizzle Share

Among components of Sizzle, the principal gainer is:

Sizzle 64oz: up 2.2 points from last year to 23.7

and losers:

Sizzle 48oz. -0.6 to 34.9

Sizzle 32oz. -0.1 to 6.7

Sizzle's share of type is 71.3 - up 1.2 from the same period last year.

Sizzle 64 oz's share of type increase is partly due to 11.3 pts rise in % ACV with Display vs. yr. ago.

Competitor Summary

Among Sizzle's major competitors, the principal gainers are:

Shakey: up 2.5 points from last year to 2.6

Private Label +.5 to 19.9 (but down .3 since last period)

and loser:

Generic Seltzer -.7 to 3.5

Shakey's share of type increase is associated with 71.7 pts of ACV rise in ACV Wtd Dist versus a year ago.

Market Highlights

Sizzle showed significant gains relative to

The analysis is based on share change. A sample of a causal change shown by CoverStory is the increase of display activity to support 64-oz bottles of Sizzle.

BENEFITS

Ocean Spray's DSS design strategy has successfully solved several problems. The decision to put users in charge of their own basic retrieval and analysis has generally worked well and, where it has run into problems, the DSS organization has responded by providing increasingly customized tools. The DataServer interface has been easy to learn. Usage on the 386-level workstations located in the marketing area is many hours per week and rising.

The strategy casts the DSS organization in the role of acquiring and building tools to make the users more effective. Consultation with users has led to a set of hard copy reports that are circulated regularly to marketing, sales and top management and to customized reports that can be called up on line and printed locally on laser printers, if needed.

CoverStory is a particularly desirable development because, with very little effort, it provides users with top line summaries and analyzes across a wide variety of situations. Previously this required time-consuming intervention by a skilled analyst. Furthermore the technology is an extensible platform on which to build increasingly sophisticated decentralized analysis for the user community.

The information coming out of Ocean Spray's marketing DSS is used every day in planning, fire-fighting, and updating people's mental models of what is going on in the company's markets. Typical applications include such actions as taking a price increase and monitoring its effect; discovering sales softness in a particular market, diagnosing its causes, and applying remedies; and following a new product introduction to alert the sales department in case of weak results in certain markets compared to others. The DSS is totally integrated into business operations and it no longer seems possible to consider life without it.

Perhaps the easiest way to express the success of the system is that, with the help of marketing science and expert systems technology, the DSS has made it possible for a single marketing professional to manage the process of alerting all Ocean Spray marketing and sales managers to key problems and opportunities and of providing them with daily problem-solving information and guidance. This is being done across four business units handling scores of company products in dozens of markets representing hundreds of millions of dollars of sales.

QUESTIONS

1. In what ways has data generated by bar-code scanners caused both opportunities and problems?
2. Summarize how CoverStory works.
3. Is CoverStory an expert system? Discuss.

REFERENCES

1. BARR, A., AND E. A. FEIGENBAUM, eds. *Handbook of Artificial Intelligence.* Los Altos, CA: William Kaufman, 1981.

2. GUADAGNI, P. M., AND J. D. C. LITTLE "A Logic Model of Brand Choice Calibrated on Scanner Data," *Marketing Science,* 2 (Summer 1983), 203–238.

3. LITTLE, J. D. C. "Decision Support Systems for Marketing Managers," *Marketing,* 43 (Summer 1979), 9–26.

4. LITTLE, J. D. C. "CoverStory: An Expert System to Find the News in Scanner Data," internal working paper, Sloan School of Management, M. I. T. (September 1988).

5. McCANN, J. M. *The Marketing Workbench.* Homewood, IL: Dow Jones-Irwin, 1988.

6. SCHANK, R. C., AND C. K. RIESBECK, eds. *Inside Computer Understanding.* Hillsdale, NJ: Lawrence Erlbaum, 1981.

7. STOYIANNIDIS, D. "A Marketing Research Expert System," Sloan School Master's thesis, M.I.T., Cambridge, MA, June 1987.

Vendors
of Decision
Support Software

A number of companies have developed and marketed a variety of decision support software products. Some of these vendors have university support programs that allow universities to use their products for instructional purposes at a significantly reduced rate. It is also common for them to offer instructional materials, training programs, and hot-line services under favorable terms. Their motivations for offering university support programs include the following: (1) to improve information systems education, (2) to influence future sales of their products, and (3) to expand the number and range of their product applications. The end result is that universities can now offer state-of-the-art training on many of the leading selling decision support products at an affordable price.

The following pages list the vendors, their addresses, and a brief description of their product offerings. The list is not all-inclusive and the information is subject to rapid change. It should provide a good starting point, however, for obtaining decision support software for your university.

Company:	Action Technologies	
Address:	1145 Atlantic Avenue	
	Alameda, CA 94501	
Product:	Coordinator	(GDSS)

Company:	American Information Systems	
Address:	P.O. Box 367	
	Charleston Road	
	Wellsboro, PA 16901	
Product:	RediMaster	(PC EIS)

Company:	Collaborative Technologies	
Address:	8920 Business Park Drive	
	Suite 100	
	Austin, TX 78759	
Product:	VisionQuest	(GDSS)

Company:	Computer Associates	
Address:	711 Stewart Avenue	
	Garden City, NY 11530	
Products:	CA—Super Calc	(PC and mainframe DSS)
	CA—STRATAGEM	(mainframe DSS)

Company:	Comshare	
Address:	3001 South State Street	
	Ann Arbor, MI 48108	
Products:	Commander EIS	(mainframe EIS)
	System W	(mainframe DSS)
	IFPS	(mainframe DSS)
	One-up	(PC DSS)
	Paradigm	(PC DSS)

Company:	Decision Support Software	
Address:	1300 Vincent Place	
	McLean, Virginia 22101	
Product:	Expert Choice	(PC DSS)

Company:	Dickson, Anderson & Associates	
Address:	11301 Fetterly Road	
	Suite 201	
	Minnetonka, MN 55343	
Product:	SAMM	(GDSS)

Company:	Easel	
Address:	600 West Cummings Park	
	Woburn, MA 01801	
Product:	Easel	(PC EIS)

Company:	EPiC Software	
Address:	25 Burlington Mall Road	
	Suite 300	
	Burlington, MA 01803	
Product:	EIS-EPiC	(PC EIS)

Company:	EXSYS	
Address:	1720 Louisiana Blvd., NE	
	Albuquerque, NM 87110	
Product:	EXSYS	(PC EIS)

Company:	Holistic Systems	
Address:	9033 E. Easter Place	
	Suite 20	
	Englewood, CO 80112	
Product:	HOLOS	(mainframe DSS & EIS)

Company:	IBM	
Address:	Contact local sales office	
Products:	Executive Decisions	(mainframe EIS)
	EIS-TRACK	(mainframe & PC EIS)
	AS	(mainframe DSS)
	DIS	(mainframe DSS)
	Personal AS	(PC DSS)
	Expert Systems Environment	(mainframe ES)
	TeamFocus	(GDSS)

Company:	Information Builders	
Address:	1250 Broadway	
	New York, NY 10001	
Products:	FOCUS/EIS	(PC EIS)
	LEVEL-5	(PC ES)

Company:	Information Resources, Inc.	
Address:	200 Fifth Avenue	
	Waltham, MA 02254	
Products:	Express/EIS	(mainframe EIS)
	Express	(mainframe DSS)
	Express/PC	(PC DSS)

Company:	IMRS	
Address:	777 Long Ridge Road	
	Stamford, CT 06902	
Product:	OnTrack	(PC EIS)

Company:	Lotus	
Address:	55 Cambridge Parkway	
	Cambridge, MA 02142	
Products:	Lotus 1-2-3	(PC DSS)
	Lotus Notes	(GDSS)

Company:	Metapraxis	
Address:	900 Third Avenue	
	36th floor	
	New York, NY 10022	
Product:	Resolve	(mainframe DSS)

Company:	Micro Data Base Systems	
Address:	P.O. Box 6089	
	Lafayette, IN 47903	
Product:	GURU	(PC EIS)

Company:	MicroStrategy	
Address:	One Commerce Center	
	Wilmington, DE 19811	
Product:	EISToolKit	(PC EIS)

Company:	Option Technologies	
Address:	1725 Knollwood Lane	
	Mendota Heights, MN 55118	
Product:	OptionFinder	(GDSS)
Company:	Paperback Software International	
Address:	2830 Ninth Street	
	Berkeley, CA 94710	
Product:	VP-Expert	(PC ES)
Company:	Pilot Software	
Address:	40 Broad Street	
	Boston, MA 02109	
Products:	Command Center	(mainframe EIS)
	Lightship	(PC EIS)
	FCS	(mainframe DSS)
Company:	RJO Enterprises	
Address:	4550 Forbes Boulevard	
	Lanham, MD 20706	
Product:	EIS Solution	(PC EIS)
Company:	SAS Institute	
Address:	SAS Campus Drive	
	Cary, NC 27513	
Products:	SAS/EIS	(mainframe EIS)
	SAS	(mainframe DSS)
	PC/SAS	(PC DSS)
Company:	Vantana	
Address:	1430 E. Fort Lowell Road	
	Suite 301	
	Tucson, AZ 85719	
Product:	GroupSystems	(GDSS)

DSS Bibliography

A large body of DSS writings has been published in books, articles, conference proceedings, trade publications, and the like. This diversity can be seen in the varied sources of materials included in this book of readings. To help you find other materials of interest, the following DSS bibliography is provided. Although it contains references to what the authors feel are the most important, interesting, and accessible materials on DSS, it includes only a small percentage of what has been written. There are many other excellent DSS writings, with more appearing daily. This bibliography should provide assistance, however, as you strive to learn more about DSS.

This bibliography includes books and articles. The articles have been categorized by their major topic(s): (1) general overview; (2) relationship with OR/MS and MIS; (3) DSS framework; (4) development process; (5) software interface; (6) model subsystem; (7) database subsystem; (8) integrating the software interface, models, and data; (9) integrating DSS into the organization; (10) evaluation of DSS; (11) applications of DSS; (12) executive information systems; (13) expert systems; (14) group decision support systems; and (15) future of DSS.

BOOKS

1. ALTER, STEVEN L. *Decision Support Systems: Current Practices and Continuing Challenges.* Reading, Mass.: Addison-Wesley, 1980.

2. BENNETT, JOHN L., ed. *Building Decision Support Systems.* Reading, Mass.: Addison-Wesley, 1983.

3. BONCZEK, ROBERT, CLYDE HOLSAPPLE, AND ANDREW WHINSTON *Foundations of Decision Support Systems.* New York: Academic Press, 1981.

4. KEEN, PETER G. W., AND MICHAEL S. SCOTT MORTON *Decision Support Systems: An Organizational Perspective.* Reading, Mass.: Addison-Wesley, 1978.

5. MCCOSH, ANDREW, AND MICHAEL S. SCOTT MORTON *Management Decision Support Systems.* New York: John Wiley, 1978.

6. SCOTT MORTON, MICHAEL S. *Management Decision Systems: Computer Support for Decision Making.* Boston: Harvard University Press, 1971.

7. SILVER, MARK *Decision Support Systems.* Chichester, N.Y.: John Wiley, 1991.

8. SPRAGUE, RALPH H., AND ERIC D. CARLSON *Building Effective Decision Support Systems.* Englewood Cliffs, N.J.: Prentice Hall, 1982.

9. THIERAUF, ROBERT J. *User-Oriented Decision Support Systems: Accent on Problem Finding.* Englewood Cliffs, N.J.: Prentice Hall, 1988.

10. TURBAN, EFRAIM *Decision Support and Expert Systems,* 2d ed. New York: Macmillan, 1990.

ARTICLES

1. ABDOLMOHANNADI, M. J. "Decision Support and Expert Systems in Auditing: A Review and Research Directions," *Accounting and Business Research,* 17, no. 3 (Spring 1987), 173–185.

2. ADELMAN, L. "Involving Users in the Development of Decision-Analytic Aids: The Principal Factor in Successful Implementation," *Journal of the Operational Research Society,* 33, no. 4 (April 1982), 333–342.

3. AIKEN, M. W., O. R. L. SHENG, AND D. R. VOGEL "Integrating Expert Systems With Group Decision Support Systems," *ACM Transactions on Information Systems,* 9, no. 1 (January 1991), 75–95.

4. AKOKA, J. "A Framework for Decision Support System Evaluation," *Information and Management,* 4 (July 1981), 133–141.

5. ALAVI, M., AND J. C. HENDERSON "Evolutionary Strategy for Implementing a Decision Support System," *Management Science,* 27, no. 11 (November 1981), 1309–1323.

6. ALTER, S. L. "Development Patterns for Decision Support Systems," *MIS Quarterly,* 2, no. 3 (September 1978), 33–42.

7. ALTER, S. L. "Why Is Man-Computer Interaction Important for Decision Support Systems?" *Interfaces,* 7, no. 2 (February 1977), 109–115.

8. ALTER, S. L. "A Taxonomy of Decision Support Systems," *Sloan Management Review,* 19, no. 1 (Fall 1977), 39–56.

9.   ARINZE, B.   "A Contingency Model of DSS Development Methodology," *Journal of Management Information Systems*, 8, no. 1 (Summer 1991), 149–166.

10. BAHL, H. C., AND R. G. HUNT   "Decision Making Theory and DSS Design," *Data Base*, 15, no. 4 (Summer 1984), 12–19.

11. BAKER, D. S., S. C. CHOW, M. T. HENNEN, T. P. LUKEN, G. J. ROBINSON, AND H. L. SCHEURMAN   "An Integrated Decision Support and Manufacturing Control System," *Interfaces*, 14, no. 5 (September–October 1984), 44–52.

12. BARBOSA, L. C., AND R. G. HERKO   "Integration of Algorithmic Aids into Decision Support Systems," *MIS Quarterly*, 4, no. 1 (March 1980), 1–12.

13. BEAUCLAIR, R. A., AND D. W. STRAUB   "Utilizing GDSS Technology: Final Report on a Recent Empirical Study," *Information & Management*, 18 (1990), 213–220.

14. BELARDO, S., K. R. KARWAN, AND W. A. WALLACE   "Managing the Response to Disasters Using Microcomputers," *Interfaces*, 14, no. 2 (March–April 1984), 29–39.

15. BENBASAT, I., AND A. S. DEXTER   "Individual Differences in the Use of Decision Support Aids," *Journal of Accounting Research*, 20 (Spring 1982), 1–11.

16. BENBASAT, I., AND R. N. TAYLOR   "The Impact of Cognitive Styles on Information Systems Design," *MIS Quarterly*, 2, no. 2 (June 1978), 43–54.

17. BERRISFORD, T., AND J. WETHERBE   "Heuristic Development: A Redesign of Systems Design," *MIS Quarterly*, 3, no. 1 (March 1979), 11–19.

18. BLANNING, R. W.   "What Is Happening in DSS?" *Interfaces*, 13, no. 5 (October 1983), 71–80.

19. BONCZEK, R. H., C. W. HOLSAPPLE, AND A. B. WHINSTON   "Computer Based Support of Organizational Decision-Making," *Decision Sciences*, 10, no. 2 (April 1979), 268–291.

20. BONCZEK, R. H., C. W. HOLSAPPLE, AND A. B. WHINSTON   "The Evolving Roles of Models in Decision Support Systems," *Decision Sciences*, 11, no. 2 (April 1980), 337–356.

21. BONCZEK, R. H., C. W. HOLSAPPLE, AND A. B. WHINSTON   "Future Directions for Developing Decision Support Systems," *Decision Sciences*, 11, no. 4 (October 1980), 616–631.

22. BRENNAN, J. J., AND J. J. ELAM   "Understanding and Validating Results in Model-Based Decision Support Systems," *Decision Support Systems*, 2 (1986), 49–54.

23. BRIGHTMAN, H.   "Differences in Ill-Structured Problem Solving Along the Organizational Hierarchy," *Decision Sciences*, 9, no. 1 (January 1978), 1–18.

24. BUNEMAN, O. P., AND OTHERS\q>   "Display Facilities for DSS Support: The DAISY Approach," *Data Base*, 8, no. 3 (Winter 1977), 46–50.

25. CANNING, R. G.   "What's Happening with DSS," *EDP Analyzer*, 22, no. 7 (July 1984), 1–12.

26. CANNING, R. G.   "INTERESTING DECISION SUPPORT SYSTEMS," *EDP Analyzer*, 20, NO. 3 (MARCH 1984), 1–12.

27. CARLIS, J. V., G. W. DICKSON, AND S. T. March   "Physical Database Design: A DSS Approach," *Information and Management*, 6 (August 1983), 211–224.

28. CARLSON, E.   "Decision Support Systems: Personal Computing Services for Managers," *Management Review*, 66, no. 1 (January 1977), 4–11.

29. CARLSON, E. D., B. F. GRACE, AND J. A. SUTTON   "Case Studies of End User Requirements for Interactive Problem Solving Systems," *MIS Quarterly*, 1, no. 1 (March 1977), 51–63.

30. CONHAGEN, A. E., AND OTHERS   "Decision Support Systems in Banking," *Bankers Magazine*, 165 (May–June 1982), 79–84.

31. COOPER, D. O., L. B. DAVIDSON, AND W. K. DENISON "A Tool for More Effective Financial Analysis," *Interfaces,* February 1975, 91–103.

32. CRESCENZI, A. D., AND G. K. GULDEN "Decision Support for Manufacturing Management," *Information and Management,* 6 (April 1983), 91–95.

33. CULLUM, R. L. "Iterative Development," *Datamation,* 31 (February 1985), 92–98.

34. CURLEY, K. F., AND L. L. GREMILLION "The Role of the Champion in DSS Implementation," *Information and Management,* 6 (August 1983), 203–209.

35. DAFT, R. L., AND N. B. MACINTOSH "New Approach to Design and Use of Management Information," *California Management Review,* 21, no. 1 (Fall 1978), 82–92.

36. DAVIS, R. "A DSS for Diagnosis and Therapy," *Data Base,* 8, no. 3 (Winter 1977), 58–72.

37. DE, P., AND A. SEN "Logical Data Base Design in Decision Support Systems," *Journal of Systems Management,* 32 (May 1981), 28–33.

38. DENNIS, A., J. F. Nunamaker, and D. R. Vogel "A COMPARISON OF LABORATORY AND FIELD RESEARCH IN THE STUDY OF ELECTRONIC MEETING SYSTEMS," *Journal of Management Information Systems,* 7, NO. 3 (WINTER 1990–91), 107–135.

39. DESANCTIS, G., AND B. GALLUPE "A Foundation for the Study of Group Decision Support Systems," *Management Science,* 33, no. 5 (May 1987), 589–609.

40. DICKSON, G. W., AND M. A. JANSON "The Failure of a DSS for Energy Conservation: A Technical Perspective," *Systems, Objectives, Solutions,* 4, no. 2 (April 1984), 69–80.

41. DOKTOR, R. H., AND W. F. HAMILTON "Cognitive Style and the Acceptance of Management Science Recommendations," *Management Science,* 19, no. 8 (April 1973), 884–894.

42. DONOVAN, J., AND S. MADNICK "Institutional and Ad Hoc DSS and Their Effective Use," *Data Base,* 8, no. 3 (Winter 1977), 79–88.

43. EASON, K. D. "Understanding the Naive Computer User," *Computer Journal,* 19, no. 1 (February 1976), 3–7.

44. EBENSTEIN, M., AND L. I. KRAUS "Strategic Planning for Information Resource Management," *Management Review,* 7 (June 1981), 21–26.

45. EDEN, C., AND D. SIMS "Subjectivity in Problem Identification," *Interfaces,* 11, no. 1 (February 1981), 68–74.

46. ELAM, J. J., AND J. C. HENDERSON "Knowledge Engineering Concepts for Decision Support Design and Implementation," *Information and Management,* 6 (April 1983), 109–14.

47. EL SAWY, O. A. "Personal Information Systems for Strategic Scanning in Turbulent Environments: Can the CEO Go On- Line?" *MIS Quarterly,* 2, no. 1 (March 1985), 53–60.

48. ERICKSEN, D. C. "A Synopsis of Present Day Practices concerning Decision Support Systems," *Information and Management,* 7 (October 1984), 243–252.

49. ETGAR, M., S. LICHT, AND P. SHRIVASTA "A Decision Support System for Strategic Marketing Decisions," *Systems, Objectives, Solutions,* 4, no. 3 (August 1984), 131–140.

50. FARWELL, D. C., AND T. FARWELL "Decision Support System for Ski Area Design," *Journal of Systems Management,* 33, no. 3 (March 1982), 32–37.

51. FERGUSON, R. L., AND C. H. HONES "A Computer Aided Decision System," *Management Science,* June 1969, B550–B561.

52. FINDLAY, P. N. "Decision Support System and Expert Systems: A Comparison of their Components and Design Methodologies," *Computers Operations Research,* 17, no. 6 (1990), 535–543.

53. FRANZ, L. S., S. M. LEE, AND J. C. VAN HORN "An Adaptive Decision Support System for Academic Resource Planning," *Decision Sciences,* 12, no. 2 (April 1981), 276–293.

54. FRIEND, DAVID "Executive Information Systems: Successes and Failures, Insights and Misconceptions," *Journal of Information Systems Management,* 3 (Fall 1986), 31–36.

55. FUERST, W. L., AND P. H. CHENEY "Factors Affecting the Perceived Utilization of Computer-Based Decision Support Systems in the Oil Industry," *Decision Sciences,* 13, no. 4 (October 1982), 554–569.

56. GERRITY, T. P. "Design of Man-Machine Decision Systems: An Application to Portfolio Management," *Sloan Management Review,* 12, no. 2 (Winter 1971), 59–75.

57. GINZBERG, M. J. "Finding an Adequate Measure of OR/MS Effectiveness," *Interfaces,* 8, no. 4 (August 1978), 59–62.

58. GINZBERG, M. J. "Redesign of Managerial Tasks: A Requisite for Successful Support Systems," *MIS Quarterly,* 2, no. 1 (March 1978), 39–52.

59. GORRY, G. A., AND M. S. SCOTT MORTON "A Framework for Management Information Systems," *Sloan Management Review,* 13, no. 1 (Fall 1971), 55–70.

60. GRACE, B. F. "Training Users of a Decision Support System," *Data Base,* 8, no. 3 (Winter 1977), 30–36.

61. GROHOWSKI, R., D. R. VOGEL, B. MARTZ, AND J. A. NUNAMAKER "Implementing Electronic Meeting Systems at IBM: Lessons Learned and Success Factors" *MIS Quarterly,* 14 (December 1990) 369–382.

62. HACKATHORN, R. D., AND P. G. W. KEEN "Organizational Strategies for Personal Computing in Decision Support Systems," *MIS Quarterly,* 5, no. 3 (September 1981), 21–26.

63. HAMILTON, W. F., AND M. A. MOSES "A Computer-Based Corporate Planning System," *Management Science,* 21, no. 2 (October 1974), 148–159.

64. HAMMOND, J. S., III "The Roles of the Manager and Management Scientists in Successful Implementation," *Sloan Management Review,* 15, no. 2 (Winter 1974), 1–24.

65. HASEMAN, W. D. "GPLAN: An Operational DSS," *Data Base,* 8, no. 3 (Winter 1977), 73–78.

66. HEHNEM, M. T., ET AL. "An Integrated Decision Support and Manufacturing Control System," *Interfaces,* 14, no. 5 (September–October 1984).

67. HENDERSON, J. C., AND P. C. NUTT "Influence of Decision Style on Decision Making Behavior," *Management Science,* 26, no. 4 (April 1980), 371–386.

68. HENDERSON, J. C., AND P. C. NUTT "On the Design of Planning Information Systems," *Academy of Management Review,* 3, No. 3 (October 1978), 774–785.

69. HOGUE, J. T., AND H. J. WATSON "Managements' Role in the Approval and Administration of Decision Support Systems," *MIS Quarterly,* 7, no. 2 (June 1983), 15–26.

70. HUBER, G. P. "The Nature of Organizational Decision Making and the Design of Decision Support Systems," *MIS Quarterly,* 5, no. 2 (June 1981), 1–10.

71. HUBER, G. P. "Cognitive Style as a Basis for MIS and DSS Designs: Much Ado about Nothing?" *Management Science,* 29, no. 5 (May 1983), 567–579.

72. HUBER, G. P. "Issues in the Design of Group Decision Support Systems," *MIS Quarterly,* 8, no. 3 (September 1984), 195–204.

73. HUFF, S. L. "DSS Development: Promise and Practice," *Journal of Information Systems Management,* 3 (Fall 1986), 8–15.

74. KEEN, P. G. W. "Adaptive Design for Decision Support Systems," *Data Base,* 12, nos. 1 and 2 (Fall 1980), 15–25.

75. KEEN, P. G. W. "Computer-Based Decision Aids: The Evaluation Problem," *Sloan Management Review,* 16, no. 3 (Spring 1975), 17–29.

76. KEEN, P. G. W. "Decision Support Systems: The Next Decade," *Decision Support Systems,* 3 (1987), 253–265.

77. KEEN, P. G. W.   "Decision Support Systems: Translating Analytic Techniques into Useful Tools," *Sloan Management Review,* 21, no. 3 (Spring 1980), 33–44.

78. KEEN, P. G. W.   "Interactive Computer Systems for Managers: A Modest Proposal," *Sloan Management Review,* 18, no. 1 (Fall 1976), 1–17.

79. KEEN, P. G. W. AND G. R. WAGNER   "DSS: An Executive Mind-Support System," *Datamation,* 25, no. 12 (November 1979), 117–122.

80. KIMBROUGH, S. O., C. W. Pritchett, M. P. Bieber, and H. K. Bhargava "THE COAST GUARD'S KSS PROJECT," *Interfaces,* 20, NO. 6 (NOVEMBER–DECEMBER 1990), 29–38.

81. KING, W. R., AND D. I. CLELLAND   "Decision and Information Systems for Strategic Planning," *Business Horizons,* April 1973, 29–36.

82. KING, W. R., AND J. I. RODRIQUEZ   "Participative Design of Strategic Decision Support Systems," *Management Science,* 27, no. 6 (June 1981), 717–726.

83. KLAAS, R. L.   "A DSS for Airline Management," *Data Base,* 8, No. 3 (Winter 1977), 3–8.

84. KLING, R.   "The Organizational Context of User-Centered Software Designs," *MIS Quarterly,* 1, no. 4 (December 1977), 41–52.

85. KOESTER, R., AND F. LUTHANS   "The Impact of the Computer on the Choice Activity of Decision Makers: A Replication with Actual Users of Computerized MIS," *Academy of Management Journal,* 22, no. 2 (June 1979), 416–422.

86. KOSAKA, T., AND T. HIROUCHI   "An Effective Architecture for Decision Support Systems," *Information and Management,* 5 (March 1982), 7–17.

87. LARRECHE, J., AND V. SRINIVASAN   "STRATPORT: A Decision Support System for Strategic Planning," *Journal of Marketing,* 45 (Fall 1981), 39–52.

88. LITTLE, J. D. C.   "Decision Support Systems for Marketing Managers," *Journal of Marketing,* 43 (Summer 1979), 9–26.

89. LOCANDER, W. B., A. NAPIER, AND R. SCAMELL   "A Team Approach to Managing the Development of a Decision Support System," *MIS Quarterly,* 3, no. 1 (March 1979), 53–63.

90. LUCAS, H. C., JR.   "Experimental Investigation of the Use of Computer Based Graphics in Decision Making," *Management Science,* 27, no. 7 (July 1981), 757–768.

91. LUCAS, H. C., JR.   "Empirical Evidence for a Description Model of Implementation," *MIS Quarterly,* 2, no. 2 (June 1978), 27–42.

92. LUCAS, H. C., JR.   "The Evolution of an Information System: From Key-Man to Every Person," *Sloan Management Review,* 19, no. 2 (Winter 1980), 39–52.

93. MACINTOSH, N. B., AND R. L. DAFT   "User Department Technology and Information Design," *Information and Management,* 1 (1978), 123–131.

94. McCLEAN, E. R.   "End Users as Application Developers," *MIS Quarterly,* 3, no. 4 (December 1979), 37–46.

95. McCLEAN, E. R., AND T. F. RIESING   "MAPP: A DSS for Financial Planning," *Data Base,* 3, no. 3 (Winter 1977), 9–14.

96. McKENNEY, J. L., AND P. G. W. KEEN   "How Managers' Minds Work," *Harvard Business Review,* May–June 1974, 79–90.

97. MEADOR, C. L., AND D. N. NESS   "Decision Support Systems: An Application to Corporate Planning," *Sloan Management Review,* 16, no. 2 (Winter 1974), 51–68.

98. METHLIE, L.   "Data Management for Decision Support Systems," *Data Base,* 12, nos. 1 and 2 (Fall 1980), 40–46.

99. MEYER, M. H., AND K. F. CURLEY   "Putting Expert Systems Technology to Work," *Sloan Management Review,* (Winter 1991), 21–31.

100. MINTZBERG, H. "Managerial Work: Analysis from Observation," *Management Science,* 18, no. 2 (October 1971), B97–B110.

101. MINTZBERG, H., D. RAISINGHANI, AND A. THEORET "The Structure of 'Unstructured' Decision Processes," *Administrative Science Quarterly,* 21, no. 2 (June 1976), 246–275.

102. MOSES, M. A. "Implementation of Analytical Planning Systems," *Management Science,* 21, no. 10 (June 1975), 1133–1143.

103. NAYLOR, T. H. "Effective Use of Strategic Planning, Forecasting, and Modeling in the Executive Suite," *Managerial Planning,* 30, no. 4 (January–February 1982), 4–11.

104. NAYLOR, THOMAS H. "Decision Support Systems or Whatever Happened to M.I.S.?" *Interfaces,* 12, no. 4 (August 1982), 92–97.

105. NELSON, C. W., and R. Balachandra "CHOOSING THE RIGHT EXPERT SYSTEM BUILDING APPROACH," *Decision Sciences,* 22 (1991), 354–367.

106. NESS, D. H., AND C. R. SPRAGUE "An Interactive Media Decision Support System," *Sloan Management Review,* 14, no. 1 (Fall 1972), 51–61.

107. NEUMANN, S., AND M. HADASS "Decision Support Systems and Strategic Decisions," *California Management Review,* 22, no. 2 (Spring 1980), 77–84.

108. NUNAMAKER, J. F., A. R. DENNIS, J. S. VALACICH, D. R. VOGEL, AND J. R. GEORGE "Electronic Meeting Systems to Support Group Work," *Communications of the ACM,* 34, no. 7 (July 1991), 40–61.

109. NUNAMAKER, J. F., L. M. APPLEGATE, AND B. R. KONSYNSKI "Facilitating Group Creativity: Experience with a Group Decision Support System," *Journal of Management Information Systems,* 3, no. 4 (Spring 1987), 5–19.

110. NUNAMAKER, J. F., A. R. DENNIS, J. S. VALACICH, AND D. R. VOGEL "Information Technology for Negotiating Groups: Generating Options for Mutual Gain," *Management Science,* 37, no. 10 (October 1991), 1325–1346.

111. NYWEIDE, J. O. "Decision Support through Automated Human Resource Systems," *Magazine of Bank Administration,* 62, no. 5 (November 1986), 60–62.

112. OSBORN, P. B., and W. H. Zickefoose "BUILDING EXPERT SYSTEMS FROM THE GROUND UP," *AI Expert* (MAY 1990), 28–33.

113. PARTOW-NAVID, P. "Misuse and Disuse of DSS Models," *Journal of Systems Management,* 38, no. 4 (April 1987), 38–40.

114. PRASTACOS, G. P., AND E. BRODHEIM "PBDS: A Decision Support System for Regional Blood Management," *Management Science,* 26, no. 5 (May 1980), 451–463.

115. RECK, R. H., AND J. R. HALL "Executive Information Systems: An Overview of Development," *Journal of Information Systems Management,* 3 (Fall 1986), 25–30.

116. REMUS, W. E., AND J. KOTTERMAN "Toward Intelligent Decision Support Systems: An Artificially Intelligent Statistician," *MIS Quarterly,* 10, no. 4 (December 1986).

117. RICHMAN, L. S. "Software Catches the Team Spirit," *Fortune,* September 1985, 125–136.

118. ROBEY, D., AND D. FARROW "User Involvement in Information System Development," *Management Science,* 28, no. 1 (January 1982), 73–85.

119. ROBEY, D., AND W. TAGGART "Human Information Processing in Information and Decision Support Systems," *MIS Quarterly,* 6, no. 2 (June 1982), 61–73.

120. ROBEY, D., AND W. TAGGART "Measuring Managers' Minds: The Assessment of Style in Human Information Processing," *Academy of Management Review,* 6, no. 2 (July 1981), 375–383.

121. ROCKART, J. F., AND M. E. TREACY "The CEO Goes On-Line," *Harvard Business Review,* 60, no. 1 (January–February 1982), 32–38.

122. ROLAND, R. "A Model of Organizational Variables for DSS," *Data-Base,* 12, nos. 1 and 2 (Fall 1980), 63–72.

123. ROY, A., A. DEFALOMIR, AND L. LASDON "An Optimization Based Decision Support System for a Product Mix Problem," *Interfaces,* 12, no. 2 (April 1982), 26–33.

124. RUCKS, A. C., AND P. M. GINTER "Strategic MIS: Promises Unfulfilled," *Journal of Systems Management,* 33 (March 1982), 16–19.

125. SANDERS, L. C., J. F. COURTNEY, AND S. L. LOY<H>\Q> "THE IMPACT OF DSS ON ORGANIZATIONAL COMMUNICATION," *Information and Management,* 7 (JUNE 1984), 141–148.

126. SCHMITZ, J. D., G. D. ARMSTRONG, AND J. D. C. LITTLE "CoverStory—Automated News Finding in Marketing," *Interfaces,* 20, no. 6, (November–December 1990), 29–38.

127. SEABURG, R. A., AND C. SEABURG "Computer-Based Decision Systems in Xerox Corporate Planning," *Management Science,* 20, no. 4 (December 1973), 575–584.

128. SILVER, M. S. "Decision Support Systems: Directed and Nondirected Change," *Information Systems Research* (March 1990), 47–70.

129. SILVER, M. S. "On The Restrictiveness of Decision Support Systems," *Organizational Decision Support Systems* (1988), 259–270.

130. SIMARD, A. J., AND J. E. EENIGENBURG "An Executive Information System to Support Wildfire Disaster Declarations," *Interfaces,* 20, no. 6 (November–December 1990), 53–66.

131. SPRAGUE, R. H., JR. "Conceptual Description of a Financial Planning Model for Commercial Banks," *Decision Sciences,* 2, no. 1 (January 1971), 66–80.

132. SPRAGUE, R. H., JR. "The Financial Planning System at the Louisiana National Bank," *MIS Quarterly,* 3, no. 3 (September 1979), 1–11.

133. SPRAGUE, R. H., JR. "Systems Support for a Financial Planning Model," *Management Accounting,* 53, no. 6 (June 1972), 29–34.

134. SPRAGUE, R. H., JR., AND H. J. WATSON "Bit by Bit: Toward Decision Support Systems," *California Management Review,* 22, no. 1 (Fall 1979), 60–68.

135. SPRAGUE, R. H., JR., AND H. J. WATSON "A Decision Support System for Banks," *Omega: The International Journal of Management Science,* 4, no. 6 (1976), 657–671.

136. SPRAGUE, R. H., JR., AND H. J. WATSON "MIS Concepts: Part I," *Journal of Systems Management,* 26, no. 1 (January 1975), 34–37.

137. SPRAGUE, R. H., JR., AND H. J. WATSON "MIS Concepts: Part II," *Journal of Systems Management,* 26, no. 2 (February 1975), 35–40.

138. STEFIK, M., ET AL. "Beyond the Chalkboard: Computer Support for Collaboration and Problem Solving in Meetings," *Communications of the ACM,* 30, no. 1 (January 1987), 32–47.

139. STOTT, K. L., JR., AND B. W. DOUGLAS "A Model-Based Decision Support System for Planning and Scheduling Ocean Borne Transportation," *Interfaces,* 11, no. 4 (August 1981), 1–10.

140. SUSSMAN, P. N. "Evaluating Decision Support Software," *Datamation,* 30 (October 1984), 171–172.

141. TURBAN, E., AND P. R. WATKINS "Integrating Expert Systems and Decision Support Systems," *MIS Quarterly,* 10, no. 2 (June 1986), 121–136.

142. VIERCK, R. K. "Decision Support Systems: An MIS Manager's Perspective," *MIS Quarterly,* 5, no. 4 (December 1981), 35–48.

143. WAGNER, G. R. "Decision Support Systems: Computerized Mind Support for Executive Problems," *Managerial Planning,* 30, no. 2 (September–October 1981), 9–16.

144. WAGNER, G. R. "DSS: Dealing with Executive Assumptions in the Office of the Future," *Managerial Planning,* 30, no. 5 (March–April 1982), 4–10.

145. WAGNER, G. R. "Decision Support Systems: The Real Substance," *Interfaces,* 11, no. 2 (April 1981), 77–86.

146. WATKINS, P. R. "Perceived Information Structure:Implications for Decision Support System Design," *Decision Sciences,* 13, no. 1 (January 1982), 38–59.

147. WATKINS, P. R. "Preference Mapping of Perceived Information Structure:Implications for Decision Support Systems Design," *Decision Sciences,* 15, no. 1 (Winter 1984), 92–106.

148. WATSON, H. J., AND M. M. HILL "Decision Support Systems or What Didn't Happen with MIS," *Interfaces,* 13, no. 5, (October 1983), 81–88.

149. WATSON, H. J., AND R. I. MANN "Expert Systems: Past, Present, and Future," *Journal of Information Systems Management,* 5 (Fall 1988).

150. WEITZ, R. R., AND A. DEMEYER "Managing Expert Systems: A Framework and Case Study," *Information & Management,* 19 (1990), 115–131.

151. WHITE, K. B. "Dynamic Decision Support Teams," *Journal of Systems Management,* 36, no. 6 (June 1984), 26–31.

152. WILL, H. J. "MIS—Mirage or Mirror Image?" *Journal of Systems Management,* September 1973, 24–31.

153. WYNNE, B. "Decision Support Systems—A New Plateau of Opportunity or More Emperor's New-Clothing?" *Interfaces,* 12, no 1 (February 1982), 88–91.

154. WYNNE, B., AND G. W. DICKSON "Experienced Managers' Performance in Experimental Man-Machine Decision System Simulation," *Academy of Management Journal,* 18, no. 1 (March 1975), 25–40.

155. WYNNE, B. "A Domination Sequence—MS/OR, DSS, and the Fifth Generation," *Interfaces,* 14, no. 3 (May–June 1984), 51–58.

156. ZALUD, B. "Decision Support Systems—Push End User in Design/Build Stage," *Data Management,* 19, no. 1 (January 1981), 20–22.

CATEGORIES OF DSS ARTICLES

GENERAL OVERVIEW
29, 79, 106, 125, 135, 137, 139, 142, 143, 144, 145, 146, 154

RELATIONSHIP WITH or/ms AND mis
18, 20, 111 137, 139, 151

dss FRAMEWORK
8, 42, 59, 73, 135

DEVELOPMENT PROCESS DESIGN: **17, 33, 46, 52, 74, 93, 118**
User involvement: 2, 6, 58, 82, 84, 89, 94, 119, 156
Organizational variables: 23, 35, 67, 84, 93, 100, 123
Others: 6, 21, 73, 89

SOFTWARE INTERFACE
Impact of cognitive style: 16, 41, 67, 71, 122
Impact on decision making: 15, 85, 90, 122
Others: 24, 78, 84, 135, 139

MODEL SUBSYSTEM
Modeling of decision making: 10, 19, 23, 45, 96, 101
Human information processing: 120, 147, 148
Others: 12, 20, 22, 86, 104, 135, 137, 139, 145

DATABASE SUBSYSTEM
20, 27, 37, 86, 104, 135, 137, 139

INTEGRATING THE SOFTWARE INTERFACE, MODELS, AND DATA
86, 137, 138

INTEGRATING *dss* INTO THE ORGANIZATION
Implementation: 2, 5, 6, 34, 43, 55, 57, 64, 77, 91, 102, 103, 155
Training: 58, 60
Relationship with management: 44, 77, 89, 114, 156
Use of intermediaries: 7, 78, 152, 156

EVALUATION OF *dss*
4, 57, 75, 91, 92, 120

APPLICATIONS OF *dss*
Banking: 30, 132, 133, 136
Transportation/distribution: 83, 140
Financial planning: 31, 95, 132, 133, 134, 144
Corporate and strategic planning: 63, 68, 87, 97, 104, 114, 131
Marketing: 49, 88, 122, 126
Academia: 53
Manufacturing: 11, 32, 66
Others: 14, 25, 26, 29, 32, 36, 40, 44, 50, 51, 56, 65, 79, 80, 107, 118, 130

EXECUTIVE INFORMATION SYSTEMS
2, 116, 130, 141, 149

EXPERT SYSTEMS
2, 3, 52, 99, 105, 112, 116, 141, 149, 150

GROUP DECISION SUPPORT SYSTEMS
3, 13, 39, 61, 72, 108, 110, 117, 138

FUTURE OF *DSS*
18, 21, 25, 142

Index

How to Do Your Dissertation in Geography and Related Disciplines

This book provides undergraduates with a step-by-step guide to successfully carrying out an independent research project or dissertation. The book addresses each stage of the project by answering the questions that a student is likely to ask as the work progresses from choosing the subject area and planning the data collection through to producing illustrations and writing the final report. Most undergraduates in geography and related disciplines are required to undertake individual projects as part of their degree course; this book is a source of constructive, practical advice.

This new third edition continues the tradition of friendly, well-informed but informal support, and continues to focus on answering the specific questions that students typically ask at each stage of the project. The new edition brings the text completely up to date by taking into account changes within the discipline and changes in the ways that students work. New digital media, social networking, mobile technology, e-journals, anti-plagiarism software, ethics approval rules and risk assessments are among the issues that this new edition takes into account. The new edition also broadens the book's appeal by extending its coverage of the wide range of different approaches to geographical research, with expanded coverage of qualitative research, Geographic Information Systems, and new approaches to research design in both physical and human geographies.

Tony Parsons is professor in the Department of Geography at Sheffield University. His research interests are in hillslopes, dryland geomorphology and soil erosion.

Peter G. Knight is a senior lecturer in Geography at Keele University. He carries out research in glaciology based on Arctic fieldwork and laboratory experiments. His research interests also include the relationships between art, science and geography.

How to Do Your Dissertation in Geography and Related Disciplines

Third Edition

Tony Parsons and Peter G. Knight

Routledge
Taylor & Francis Group

LONDON AND NEW YORK

First published 2015
by Routledge
2 Park Square, Milton Park, Abingdon, Oxon OX14 4RN

and by Routledge
711 Third Avenue, New York, NY 10017

Routledge is an imprint of the Taylor & Francis Group, an informa business

British Library Cataloguing in Publication Data
A catalogue record for this book is available from the British Library

Library of Congress Cataloging-in-Publication Data
Parsons, A. J.
How to do your dissertation in geography and related disciplines/
Tony Parsons and Peter G. Knight. – Third edition.
pages cm
Includes bibliographical references and index.
1. Dissertations, Academic. 2. Report writing. 3. Geography – Study
and teaching (Graduate) I. Knight, Peter II. Title.
LB2369.P36 2015
378.2'42 – dc23
2014030173

ISBN: 978-0-415-73235-2 (hbk)
ISBN: 978-0-415-73236-9 (pbk)
ISBN: 978-1-315-84921-8 (ebk)

Typeset in Times New Roman and Franklin Gothic
by Florence Production Ltd, Stoodleigh, Devon, UK

Printed in Great Britain by Ashford Colour Press Ltd,
Gosport, Hants

CONTENTS

FIGURES

TABLES

BOXES

PREFACE TO THE THIRD EDITION

In writing the first edition of this book we hoped that it might prove useful to students who had to write a dissertation, and it turned out that a lot of students found that it was. This was a good thing, of course, but unfortunately it meant that the first edition was still being widely used years later even after we knew that parts of it had fallen out of date. For that reason we revised the text and produced a second edition. After a few years, the same thing happened again, and so now, 20 years after the first edition was published, we are pleased to present this new, third edition. As with our previous revision we have taken advice from users of the book (both students and lecturers), and kept the overall format of the book unchanged. It didn't seem to be seriously broken, so we didn't see any reason to try and fix it (sound advice when you are reviewing your own dissertations). However, we have re-written a number of sections and added some new material. We no longer refer to students using carrier pigeons to keep in touch with their supervisors when they are in the field, or to different ways of sharpening feathers to conserve ink when illuminating your final manuscript. Time has moved on.

During that time we have marked, and supervised, a lot of dissertations. We knew when we wrote the first edition of this book that it was biased towards physical geography. In subsequent editions we have reduced this bias and in this edition give more consideration to a wider range of approaches from across the discipline. We have tried to make it clear when we are giving advice that is specific to one particular branch of the discipline and when the advice is more generally applicable. Perhaps as a result of writing the previous editions, when we've been marking dissertations we have taken greater note of the things we don't like to see. During the decades since we wrote the first edition, we've seen a lot of things that we haven't liked, so we've taken the opportunity to advise against them here!

Some things have changed a lot since we wrote the first edition. For example the internet, electronic journals, and even the virtually ubiquitous use of word processing for student assignments are innovations that the first edition didn't account for. Our advice about employing a typist to produce your text, for example, now seems a little fuddy duddy, and in the new edition has, with other fuddy duddy material that we identified, been gracefully retired in favour of more relevant advice about electronic submission, online resources, social media and issues of that nature. Styles of teaching and examining have also changed. For example, in the first edition we had a number of boxes designed to alert you to some of the searching and difficult questions your examiners could expect you to be able to answer in your viva exam. Vivas are now so much less common than they used to be that we have taken out most of that material.

We are very grateful to the reviewers who made many helpful suggestions about how to improve the book, and we have tried to take all of their suggestions on board. In some areas all the reviewers gave the same advice for this new edition. For example they all suggested that we say more on topics such as mobile technologies and GIS. We have tried to do as they suggested. In other areas, different referees said different things. For example, some of them thought Eric was very helpful whereas others found him nothing but annoying. One thought we should cut out the section on logic in research design, another thought it was one of the most useful parts of the book. In those cases, as you may have to when writing your dissertation, we have accepted that we will not be able to please every reader in every aspect of the book, so we have done our best to make the book as helpful and user-friendly as we can. We hope it works for you.

One thing in particular remains unchanged from the first edition: our sincere hope that if you have to write a dissertation, this book will help. Good luck!

Tony and Peter

ACKNOWLEDGEMENTS

We thank the many students with whom we have worked, especially those whose dissertations provided the basis for the examples used to illustrate this book. For the first edition, colleagues from several institutions, particularly Roy Alexander, Tony Budd, Bob Dugdale, Barbara Kennedy, David Pepper, Neil Roberts, John Wainwright and Steve Williams, generously spared time to give us some insight into the role of dissertations in their undergraduate courses. Denys Brunsden and Derek Mottershead were kind enough to read a draft of the manuscript of the first edition and to provide many helpful suggestions which aided us in preparing the final version. We were helped in preparing the second edition by comments from users of the first edition, obtained by our publishers. We thank Claire Mercer for helpful discussions and, along with Mike Bradshaw and Angus Cameron, for comments on draft chapters of the second edition. For the third edition we greatly appreciate the detailed comments on earlier editions provided by a number of anonymous reviewers, and specialist advice provided by Alex Nobajas and Simon Pemberton.

1

INTRODUCTION

This chapter explains what the book is trying to achieve and how you can use the book to get the most out of it.

The aim of this book

The aim of this book is to help you to do the best dissertation you possibly can, and to help you to get the highest possible mark for it. This book can't write your dissertation for you, but it can help you to write it to the very best of your ability. We think you can probably do better than you expect.

In theory, your dissertation should get you one of your highest marks. It's like an exam where you set the question yourself and have a whole year to find the answer, getting information, help and advice from as many sources as you want. However, some students end up being disappointed with the marks they get for the dissertation, and most students do not do as well as they could. This book is for them.

If you have to write a dissertation, then this book is here to help!

The book is intended to be useful not only for geography students, including those specializing in particular areas of human geography, physical geography or environmental geography, but also for students in related disciplines from across the social sciences, earth sciences and environmental sciences. It is often unwise to try to define the boundaries between these disciplines too precisely, and many of the topics that we will use as examples could be tackled by student projects from all sorts of different degree routes. For example, is a project on rewilding urban areas a biogeography project, or an urban geography project, or an environmental sustainability project? Is a place-hacking dissertation an urban project or a political geography project or a crime geography project? Is a project using art to communicate ideas about climate change through deep time geography, geology or something else entirely? Questions about rewilding, or art–science collaborations, or place-hacking, or any of the other million topics you might chose for your dissertation, can be addressed by students from all sorts of different backgrounds. We take geography as our starting point, but 'Geography and Related Disciplines' covers a very wide area of interests and approaches.

How to use this book

This book will be of help to you from now until the time you finish your dissertation. Don't just put the book away on the shelf after you've glanced through it. Keep it open on your desk, or in the file or box (or pile on the bedroom floor) with the rest of your dissertation material. As your dissertation progresses you should be able to use this book as a constant source of advice. The book is arranged a little bit like a workshop manual or cookery book. After this introductory section, the book takes in turn each stage that you will need to go through in your work – each of the elements of the dissertation – and suggests ways of tackling the job. It is very much a 'how to . . .' reference book.

It would be a good idea to read through the whole book quickly right at the outset. Don't plough through it too diligently at this stage; just skip through it to see what it's all about. Maybe read the summaries at the beginning and end of each chapter. It will help to give you a clear idea of the steps that lie ahead in your dissertation. You'll need to know what's involved in the later stages of dissertation preparation even while you are planning the early stages, and if you have a good overview of the ground you will find it easier to put each stage of your work in context.

We've written this book as a linear narrative: going in turn through each of the steps involved in a dissertation. We have done that because it makes the book easier for you to use. For example, if you want information on writing up your dissertation, we've put it all together in Chapter 9. But actually doing a dissertation isn't such a simple linear process. For example, you cannot wait until after you have written the whole dissertation before you start to think about the format of your reference list. You need to make sure that you have all the information that you will need to format your references correctly (Chapter 9) even as you do the background reading to your study (Chapter 4). Similarly, when you are preparing material for your research proposal (Chapter 6) you should be thinking ahead to how you will be able to re-use that material when you write your methods section (Chapter 9).

Having a quick look through the whole book before you start is probably a good idea.

As you start serious work on your dissertation, you will find a chapter of the book dedicated to each of the tasks you have to do. Re-read the relevant chapter as each stage of your work approaches. Some of the chapters include step-by-step procedures that you can adopt to carry you through sections of the project. Throughout the book, generally at the end of each chapter, we have included 'reminders' or 'instructions' of the type: 'When you've read this chapter, do this . . .' If you are using the book, as we hope, as a manual or guide book, then following these instructions will ensure that everything is going according to plan, and that your work is on target. The idea behind the instructions is that people often find that having specific tasks or checklists forces them to focus their attention more directly than having only general advice.

This book does not replace, supersede or in any way supplant your institutional guidelines. Your department will have its own rules and regulations about dissertations, which you must follow. Your department will allocate you a supervisor or academic advisor, and you must follow your supervisor's advice. If the advice in this book conflicts with the rules of your institution or the advice of your supervisor, then follow their rules and advice. Some of the rules relate to issues like the size of your typeface, the colour of your binding or whether you have to submit both electronic and paper versions of the text, which clearly won't affect the basis of your work and can be sorted out near to the completion of the project. Other rules might be more fundamental. For example, your institution may have particularly strict rules about how long your dissertation must be, or what type of topic you are allowed to choose, or whether you need to collect primary data. Most institutions allow you to ask your tutor to read a preliminary draft of your dissertation (or part of it), whereas others, strangely, do not. You should check straight away what your institution expects and allows. Get hold of the official guidelines as soon as possible. Most departments have a formal handbook for the dissertation, which may be a paper document or something online. If your handbook is online but you are working on your dissertation materials as hard copy it is probably worth printing out key sections of the handbook to keep with your other materials. If you are working entirely electronically, make sure you keep the official handbook (and our e-book!) together in the same folder with your other dissertation work. If you work on several different computers you might consider using a cloud storage account such as Dropbox to keep all of your dissertation work together where you can access it from home, university or on the road. If you do print a paper copy of the handbook, remember to check the online version for updates from time to time. It's really important to make sure that you get a copy of the handbook and to make sure you read it very, very carefully. A surprising number of serious problems can arise if you don't follow the rules. Most lecturers find that their most frequent response to student questions about dissertations is 'That information is in the handbook!' Read it.

We have tried to make the book as 'user-friendly' as possible, and to leave it up to you exactly how to use it.

We've broken the text up into chapters and sections in such a way that you can select only what is relevant to your specific needs at particular times. For example, if you are not doing any fieldwork in your project, then obviously you don't want to wade through the sections about fieldwork. If you are following a positivist critical-rationalist approach to research design, you don't need to dwell on our discussions of qualitative methods in geographical research. Having said that, we suggest that you take at least a quick look at everything – it might give you some ideas that you would otherwise not have considered, and it might help you to decide exactly what you do, and don't, want to do. Each chapter includes a brief summary at the start, so you can check in advance to see if you need to read the whole chapter and you can check afterwards to remind yourself of the key points. We've separated special sections like the 'reminders' out of the main text so that you can easily ignore them if you wish, and we've highlighted key issues with short, clearly signposted, sections of text. Each chapter has a short summary at the end to remind you of the main points of what that chapter is about.

Bear in mind that we've written this book in a pretty informal style, but that your dissertation is a more formal piece of work. We hope that you'll use the book as a source of sound advice, but we don't encourage you to copy our informal tone in your own work!

How to use your supervisor

As well as giving you instructions and guidelines your institution will almost certainly also give you an advisor or supervisor: a member of academic staff who will be on hand to guide, advise and support you. Different institutions organize supervision in different ways, but however your supervision works it will be up to you to make the most of the help and support available. Ensuring that you have an effective professional relationship with your supervisor is really important. Your advisor will certainly be very busy, and will probably not have time to chase after you asking you to rearrange meetings that you have missed. You need to seek out your advisor's help when you need it, and always take up invitations to meetings or workshops. If you turn down your supervisor's help when it is offered, you might find that it is not available later on when you realize that you need it but your supervisor is away at a conference in Detroit or interviewing llamas in the Atacama desert.

Right at the start of your project make sure that you have met your advisor and that you understand the ground rules for what help is available, how often it is reasonable for you to ask for a meeting, what you can expect of your advisor and what your advisor can expect of you. Most supervisors will set up a schedule of meetings for you throughout the period of the dissertation to discuss the various stages of the work. Rather like this book, the meetings may deal with topics in order: deciding on a topic, writing a proposal, doing the research, writing the report and so on. There may be supplementary workshops or classes laid on to deal with common problems or to provide extra help on issues such as statistical analysis or writing critical literature reviews. Some of these meetings may be one-to-one with just you and your supervisor, while others may be group meetings or workshops. You must attend those meetings. Prepare carefully for them: go along with your questions ready and with any problems clearly defined in your mind so that you can explain them to the supervisor and ask for help. Have a notebook with you to write down your advisor's answers. Generally, the students who end up with the best dissertations are the students who made the most effective use of the support available to them through their advisors.

Dissertation supervision is a two-way process. It is not up to the advisor always to feed you instructions about what to do next. It is up to you to feed your advisor questions or information on which you would like feedback. The amount of help you get from your advisor will depend very much on the work that you put into the student–supervisor relationship. It's your dissertation: you need to take the driving seat.

Don't just wait for advice; seek out the advice that you need, when you need it.

Please remember that your supervisor is much better placed than we are to advise you about the specifics of how your institution deals with dissertations. If our advice seems to contradict something your supervisor has said, you should talk to your supervisor about that, work out what is the best thing to do for your particular project, and then follow your supervisor's advice. We hope our book will give you lots of help, but your supervisor is best placed to know the details of your particular project and the requirements of your particular institution.

Getting help from your friends

Doing a dissertation can sometimes feel like a lonely, solitary task, but it is important to remember that lots of other students are going through exactly the same process. You are not alone in this! Your friends and classmates might not have the subject expertise or research experience of your supervisors, but they can still offer support and advice. Be careful not to mistake friendly support for expert advice, but do talk to each other about your dissertations. Share ideas, lend shoulders to cry on, encourage each other to get help from your supervisor when you need it, and motivate each other to do the best work that you can. If your friend has just been to see their supervisor, have a chat and see what they found out. Do the same for your friends when your supervisor gives you any advice.

Our friends Eric and Erica

When you are working on something like a dissertation it's good to have friends to bounce ideas off, to share worries with, and maybe to enlist to help with fieldwork. From time to time in this book we'll mention our friends Eric and Erica; they represent the kind of characters it is sometimes useful to have around. We'll use Eric and Erica to throw up student perspectives or other ways of looking at what we've said, and if we want to refer to whoever it is that you have around to talk to, we'll call your friends Eric and Erica too! They are universal sidekicks. If they get on your nerves, well, people can be like that. Your best bet is to listen to what everybody says, but to remember that it's your dissertation, and that you have to make the decisions.

> **Eric says . . .**
>
> You need all the help you can get!

Dissertations: what this book is all about

Most undergraduate courses in geography and related disciplines include a dissertation as part of the assessment. The precise nature of the dissertation varies a little among institutions (Chapter 2) but the basic requirements are much the same wherever you are studying. Essentially the dissertation is a project of your own. You do some research and you present a report of that research. Your research, as presented in the report, is assessed.

Whether you think of yourself as an arts, humanities, science or social science student, and whether your dissertation deals with a broad geographic topic or something very specific within human geography, physical geography or environmental geography, the same basic issues apply to your work. A dissertation involves investigation, understanding and communication, and your work and your report should be an exercise in the virtues of organization, precision and clarity. Whether you are doing a qualitative or a quantitative study, whether you are using a geological hammer or a historical archive, whether your data are statistical or spatial, whether your approach is ethnographic or ecological, the same fundamental issues will apply to your dissertation: you will devise an interesting question that fits into a framework of previously published research, you will do some kind of investigation to find out something new about that question, and you will present the results of your study in a way that makes it easy for a reader to understand what you have done.

This book is not about all the specific methods or techniques that you might use – we are not going to talk about how to devise a questionnaire or how to lay out a topographic survey. There are plenty of other books that will help you with those things. This book will help you with the basic issues of setting up a project, organizing your work and putting it together into an effective dissertation.

The first important point for us to make before you start is that there are good ways and bad ways of going about research, and there are good ways and bad ways of writing reports. It is very important that you find a good way. You need to go about your research efficiently, and you need to present your report effectively. Unfortunately, it isn't always easy to sort out the good approaches from the bad ones when you are planning your first piece of research, especially since what is considered good in one area of geography might be considered unthinkable in another part of geography, let alone in one of our closely neighbouring disciplines. The right way to design, execute and report qualitative research on war veterans' diaries will not be the same as the right way to design, execute and report quantitative research on sediment transport in rivers.

The dissertation element of a degree course is a test of your ability to negotiate the challenging territories of research design, project execution and report writing. We hope that this book will serve as a guide, and that it will help you to do really well. Regardless of what type of project you are doing we will offer a straightforward body of good advice that we hope you will be able to apply to your work, and where there are major differences between approaches to different types of project we will refer you towards more specialized advice!

Chapter summary and conclusion

- The aim of this book is to help you produce the best dissertation you can.
- Use it as a guide and manual throughout your dissertation.
- Use it in conjunction with the guidelines issued by your own institution.
- Seek the advice of your supervisor as you get started on your project.

What to do after reading Chapter 1

When you've read Chapter 1, before you go any further with your dissertation, make sure that you have a copy of all the instructions and guidelines about dissertations issued by your institution. Your department probably has some sort of 'dissertation handbook' for students. If you haven't received one yet, ask for one or find it online. Before you start your dissertation you must find out exactly what the rules are and what is required of you. When you get the handbook, don't just file it away. Read it carefully, refer back to it as your work proceeds, and check your dissertation web page or online learning environment for updates to be sure that you stay on target. Make sure that you know who your academic advisor or dissertation supervisor is, or when they will be allocated. Arrange a meeting to talk to that person about your dissertation.

GET THE HANDBOOK AND FIND OUT WHO YOUR SUPERVISOR IS NOW!

2

WHAT IS A (GOOD) DISSERTATION AND WHY DO I HAVE TO DO ONE?

This chapter describes what a dissertation involves; explains what distinguishes it from other work you have done; tells you what your examiners will be looking for in a good dissertation; and shows what you can expect to get out of doing one.

What is a dissertation?

A dissertation can be defined as a report on an original piece of research. This definition contains three pieces of information that are important to you.

First, your dissertation is 'a piece of research'. This means that in the course of doing your dissertation you will need to try to find out something. You might try to find out the cause of something, the effect of something or the history of something; you might try to find out what a particular experience involves, or what an old question looks like from a new point of view, or what an old theory looks like in the light of new events.

'Finding out' is a very broad term and can mean different things in different types of geography research, but it is very important because it defines how you will need to go about your dissertation. You are expected to come up with something new at the end of the project that was not there at the start of the project. It won't be sufficient to write what you already know about a topic, or what everybody else knows about it. Your dissertation isn't, therefore, just a longer-than-usual essay. It is fundamentally different from most of the things you will have been required to write during your undergraduate course and is significantly different from any project that you may have done at school. Not surprisingly, it requires a very different approach. This may all sound daunting, but it isn't. Challenging, perhaps, but not daunting. Remember, your dissertation does have to try to find out something, but you don't have to discover something earth shattering in order to produce a good dissertation. Naturally, if you do find out something important that will be great, but a good report on even a minor piece of original research can gain you a first-class mark. (One of the decisions you will have to make will be how big or important a topic you investigate – see Chapter 4.) Equally, you don't actually have to succeed in finding out anything. Many students worry when they discover that their cherished hypothesis comes to nothing and their results support what everybody thought all along. Although this may be disappointing in one way, it needn't affect the quality of your dissertation. A lot of interesting and important research ends up confirming knowledge that has already been discovered. That doesn't mean it wasn't worth checking the old knowledge with new research. We will say more in Chapter 4 about what sort of projects are most likely to be worthwhile, and we will say more in Chapter 10 about how to get the best out of limited results if you do find yourself in that position.

The second point in our definition above is that the research has to be 'original'. Most obviously, this means that your dissertation has to be your own work and not copied from somebody else. Copying other people's work is plagiarism and that will be dealt with very harshly by your examiners. Plagiarism covers everything from lifting your whole dissertation from the work of somebody else to failing to acknowledge a source of data. We'll say more about this, and its consequences, in Chapter 11. The need to be original also means that you can't just repeat a piece of work that somebody else has done. You have either to do something new or take a new approach to something old. Again, this might seem a bit daunting. Here you are, an undergraduate, expected to find out something that the collective endeavours of eminent academics have so far failed to discover. But the world is full of problems to investigate at lots of different scales, and new problems are emerging all the time as disciplines evolve and the world moves on.

Whole new research areas open up year after year, and student dissertations can easily find fresh questions on new topics.

When we wrote the first edition of this book nobody did projects about geographies of online social media, because online social media did not exist then! Now, it is a wide open area for exciting new projects. When we wrote the second edition, unmanned aerial vehicles (UAVs or drones) were not widely used in geography research or available to undergraduates, but now there are many interesting project opportunities involving UAVs: you could use a drone as part of your data collection process, develop a new technique for processing data collected by drones, or consider the application of drones to wildlife conservation, frontier security or crowd surveillance. So don't worry: there are plenty of good topics left for dissertation students to address and get good marks on, and new ones are emerging all the time. We'll have more to say later about the type of problem you investigate. At this point, it's just important to realize that it isn't difficult to be 'original'.

Finally, our definition makes it clear that your dissertation is a 'report'. Because you have carried out a piece of original research, you know something that nobody else knows. Your dissertation is no more than a way of telling people what you have found out. The people you are telling, however, (your examiners) are difficult to convince. You can't simply tell them what you have found out and expect them to believe you. You have to demonstrate that the methods you employed were sound and that your findings are reliable. You can think of your dissertation as a description of the recipe that you followed for finding out what you found out: if your examiners were to follow this recipe they, too, should be able to reach the same conclusions as you have. They won't actually want to repeat your investigation, but they need to be convinced that your recipe makes sense. You want the examiner to read your report and think 'Yes, that makes sense; I see what you did there.'

What makes a good dissertation?

A good dissertation is one in which a soundly constructed and executed piece of research is reported in a clear and logical manner. Your examiners depend on what you have written to decide whether or not what you have done really is soundly constructed and executed, so it is vital that the report that you write is well structured and clearly written, i.e. easy to follow. Your reader (examiner) wants to know what you've done and how you've done it. Tell your story clearly. This may not be easy. You may be unfamiliar with writing such a long document. More commonly, your own close involvement with your dissertation may make it difficult for you to realize just how little the reader will know of what you are doing, and to appreciate the order in which information needs to be conveyed. The best organized research, even if it leads to dazzling discoveries, can be destroyed by poor presentation.

A good dissertation is a clear report on a well-designed piece of research.

Obviously, in writing clearly you will expose the weaknesses of your study just as much as the strengths. This shouldn't worry you too much. First, your examiner will find them anyway and, second, in writing clearly, you may see them first! You may not be able to do anything about them at that stage but you might be able to put up some justification or explanation for them. Better that you should admit and discuss your weaknesses than have the examiner discover them and assume you hadn't even noticed them yourself.

Apart from the quality of the writing, there are many other qualities that distinguish good dissertations from others. All these qualities will be used by your examiners in deciding what mark to award your dissertation, so it is a good idea to know what they are and what your examiners will be looking for. Box 2.1 summarizes the qualities of a good dissertation. As Box 2.1 shows, how you go about achieving some of these qualities is dealt with in some detail in later chapters. For these qualities we'll only have a little to say here. For those not covered in later chapters, we'll say rather more.

Also, be aware that some of what it takes to make a good dissertation might be invisible in the finished product. You might need to do a pilot study, and certainly a lot of reading, and certainly a lot of organizational work that might not actually show up in the final report. Don't neglect those elements. Careful time management, thorough preparation and diligent work will pay dividends even if your examiner is not explicitly marking those things. They will make your dissertation much better. Some of this 'invisible' work may be work that you did in previous modules or previous years of study. Most departments organize their courses in such a way that you will develop skills progressively through the years and then bring them together to complete a major piece of work – such as the dissertation – at the end. This kind of end-of-course project that draws together and demonstrates your abilities is sometimes called a 'capstone' project. You can think of it as a culminating highlight of what you have learned and achieved. Remember, as you are working on your dissertation, that it is an opportunity to bring to bear all the work you did in those research design classes, and in those 1st-year GIS practicals, and in that 2nd-year statistics module. Your dissertation does not stand alone within the course; it is supported upon a framework of previous training.

Box 2.1 The qualities of a good dissertation

A good dissertation:

- addresses a good problem (see Ch. 4);
- is set in its academic, practical, scientific or intellectual context;
- follows a logical research programme (see Ch. 5 and Ch. 6);
- has clearly defined methods;
- contains appropriate and sufficient data analysis (see Ch. 8);
- demonstrates appropriate organization of observation and interpretation;
- is a well-structured and clearly written report (see Ch. 9);
- is a clear demonstration of intellectual achievement;
- reaches valid and sensible conclusions;
- is presented to a good standard (see Ch. 9).

A good problem

A good problem is one that is relevant within your field of study, that you will be able to tackle with the time and resources available to you, that lends itself to exploiting any particular skills, interests or expertise that you have and that can be set into a wider context of intellectual enquiry. This is a tall order! Identifying a good problem is perhaps the most difficult task you will face, and also the most important. We will give much more detailed advice on how to go about it in Chapter 4.

Academic, practical, scientific or intellectual context

Your examiners will want to know why you carried out your particular piece of research and how it fits into existing knowledge. A good dissertation will include a clear explanation of the background to your project. Many dissertations include both a short section in the introduction that succinctly explains the background and a longer section – often a whole chapter – that provides a detailed and critical review of the literature. Both of these sections are important. We will say much more about the literature review later on. You will need to decide, in consultation with your advisor, whether your project needs separate 'background' and 'literature review' sections, or whether it would be better to combine them into one. As long as you achieve both of the goals identified above it does not really matter, but remember when making decisions such as this that one of your main aims is to communicate effectively with the reader. Most readers, in most projects, will benefit from a short explanatory justification or context very near to the start of the report, and from a more detailed review of the history of research on the topic in a dedicated section later in the report. Some institutions are very specific about their requirements for these sections and have clear guidelines about the length of the literature review in particular. Check your handbook.

The succinct introductory 'background' section that typically appears in the introduction is different from the literature review in that the background aims to explain why the project seemed to be worth doing, whereas the literature review provides more detail on the work that has gone before. A background section might focus on an applied aspect of a project:

> Floods have affected this area since the river was diverted, previous research has failed to identify a solution, several options have been proposed but remain untested . . . this project will test option one.

Typically there will be some reference to previous work as part of the background:

> People have studied X since the pioneering work of Jones (1854). In this study Jones argued that . . . More recent investigations by Smith (2014) have suggested that . . . However, it can be argued that . . ., and hence the purpose of this dissertation is . . .

A brief example of how such a context might be established is shown in Box 2.2.

This type of background has two aims. First, you need to demonstrate to your examiner that yours is the sort of dissertation that he or she is going to want to read. Examiners like to read good dissertations, so this is an early opportunity to demonstrate that yours is one of these. You do this by demonstrating your expertise in the topic area. You demonstrate your expertise by showing that you know what has been done before and what is currently being done in this field of research, and that you have a good idea of what needs to be done next. The chances are that at least one of your examiners will be knowledgeable in this field and so will also know the background. It is essential that you convince this person, in particular, that you are somebody whose work is worth reading. Rather than saying you chose a topic just because of some location you had visited or event you had witnessed, you will interest your examiner much more if you can relate your topic to the existing research literature and show that you are familiar with the most important work in that area. All of the major, and some of the minor, contributions to this field should be referred to in this background. It is impossible to specify how large this background should be because it will vary enormously from one field to another, and depend on whether you also include a separate detailed literature review, but reference to a dozen previously published research papers would be a typical minimum for a succinct background. Your thorough literature review will be likely to contain very many more, of course. Your second aim, having convinced your examiners that you are sufficiently

Box 2.2 An example of some background to a study

Much of the research into limestone pavements has been concerned with their formation. In north-west England a major area of controversy centres upon the role of the Devensian glaciation. Clayton (1981) argued that the pavements of north-west England were largely due to stripping of weathered limestone by glaciers down to relatively little weathered bedding planes. However, Pigott (1965) claimed that grikes developed beneath a deep weathering mantle during interglacial times. Williams (1966), on the other hand, believed that the grikes pre-dated the Devensian glaciation and survived through it. Parry (1960) presented a more complex view and proposed the existence of two types of grike. The first type consist of crevasse-like clefts that are long and often curved. These grikes, he argued, are solution-widened joints. The second type of grike consists of smaller and less regular furrows that are entirely solutional in origin and are of recent origin.

In a quantitative analysis, Rose and Vincent (1986) measured grike width on three limestone pavements and claimed that the distribution of grike widths indicated that the grikes were of two ages, thereby supporting Parry's view. However, this conclusion was based upon measurement of grike widths to the nearest millimetre. A preliminary investigation for this dissertation showed that grike width could vary by up to four times within a metre stretch, and that grikes seldom have a sharp edge, so that determination of their widths is, necessarily, subjective. A more appropriate index of grike type might be their depths. Grike depths are both much larger in general, so that any subjective error in measurement will be proportionately less significant, and are less subject to great local variation. The aim of this dissertation is to discover whether grike depth is a better indicator of grike age than is their width. Further, it will compare the implications of width measurements and depth measurements for the claim of two types of grike.

familiar with the literature that your work is likely to be worth reading, is to entice your reader to want to read further. At the end of the background to your study the reader should be intrigued by the apparent paradox or counter-intuitive observation or gap in understanding that you have identified. Having awakened curiosity in your reader's mind, all you have to do now is satisfy it.

A logical research programme

Your research programme is how you go about solving your problem. There are many ways you could do this. Some research designs will be so poor that they could not possibly lead to a solution to your problem. For example, suppose you decide to investigate the relationship between soil properties and slope gradient along a series of hillslope profiles, but choose a site where the upper and lower parts of your profiles are on different rock types. This is a fundamental flaw in your research design, because you have made it really difficult to be sure whether any changes you find in the soil are being controlled by the gradient or by the rock type. You must choose an approach that will allow you to address your question. Making sure that your research programme will lead to solutions to the problems, or answers to questions, that you are investigating and not to solutions and answers to a different set of problems and questions is very important. We will give more attention to that in Chapters 5 and 6.

Clearly defined methods

Your methods are simply the things you do to put your research design into action: measuring things or interviewing people, for example. You need to make sure that you do those things properly and describe accurately how you did them. Again, think of your dissertation as a recipe, or a detailed description for later researchers to follow. Look at the two examples in Box 2.3, which describe how measurements were made of path width and gradient. Clearly, if you wanted to carry out a follow-up investigation to the one being described, you would find it much easier to do so if the original researcher had written a report like Example 2 rather than Example 1. Whether or not you think this is a good way of determining path width and gradient, the writer leaves you in no doubt as to how it was done in this particular study. Your own methods section needs to be equally detailed and clear. The examiner must be able to understand exactly what you did, and precisely how you applied each technique. For some projects the methods might be intertwined with the theoretical framework, so be careful not to oversimplify your recipe. Check with your advisor if you are in doubt, but remember that the point of your methods section is to let your reader see exactly how you went about your project. Don't let the methods section get bogged down in background material that should have gone into your 'background' section!

Box 2.3 Examples of descriptions of methodology. Example 2 is more helpful to the reader than Example 1

Example 1

To determine the differences in path width and gradient, measurements were made of width and gradient at several locations on each path and the averages of these measurements were used as the width and gradient for that path.

Example 2

To determine the differences in path width and gradient, a representative section of each path was identified. This section, which was 2m long, was chosen at a point where the path was straight, had a uniform gradient and where its direction was unaffected by obstacles. Within this section five readings of width were made at 0.5m intervals. Where the edge of the path was obscured by overhanging vegetation, the measurement was taken to the point on the path vertically beneath the overhanging vegetation. The average of these five readings was used as the width for that path. Path gradient was measured using an Abney level as a single value for the full 2m section.

Erica says . . .

Learn how to write a good methods section by looking at papers in respected journals in your discipline. Ask your supervisor to recommend good examples.

Appropriate data analysis

Your research design set out what you need to do to address your question, and your methods section set out exactly how you do those things. You also need to think clearly about the type of data you need to collect, the amount of data you need and what you can do with your data once you have collected them. For example, if you are making measurements and then analyzing the results, you will need to show that you have measured things to the appropriate level of precision and that you have obtained sufficient data for the type of analysis you have undertaken. Did you have a valid sampling strategy and take an appropriate number of samples? If you have the wrong type or amount of data, the analysis won't make sense and your research programme will start to fall apart. Always make sure that you are collecting the right data and analyzing it in the best way for your particular research question, because that is one of the things your examiners will check. We will look at this again, and give you some examples, in Chapters 7 and 8.

Separation of results from their interpretation

The extent to which you need to separate your results or observations from the interpretations that you make of them depends on the type of research you are doing. For example, if you are doing some type of participatory action research or a reflexive ethnographic study then it might be important not to try to separate your observations from your interpretations of them, but to recognize how your own positionality within the study influences both. In a study of that type, the author's interpretations of a situation might be indistinguishable from the author's observations, and it would be unhelpful to set them apart. This kind of research can be thought of as research 'with' rather than 'on' people, so acknowledging your positionality will help you to be explicit about the limits of what you can know. On the other hand, if your research is based on testing hypotheses about your subjects (meltwater lakes, street performers or sustainability policies) by measuring their characteristics (chemical composition, locations or impacts on carbon footprints) then it will normally be important to recognize that what you observe (measurements) and what you make of it (interpretations) are quite separate things.

For instance, in the example given in Box 2.3 the author may have found out that all paths in the area studied had the same width even though their gradients differed. The author might have used this observation to argue that, because path width can be used as a measure of path erosion, path erosion is unaffected by path gradient. The inference (that erosion is unaffected by gradient) that is drawn from the observation (that all paths have the same width even though their gradients differ) is achieved via an argument (that path width can be used as a measure of path erosion). You may disagree with the soundness of the argument, and hence the inference, but that does not affect the validity of the original observation or measurement, which depends for its reliability on the methods used to measure path width and gradient. On the other hand, you might disagree with the inference even though you agree with the argument linking path width to path erosion, because you are unhappy about the way path width was measured. You might think that it would have been better to measure to the edge of ground vegetation cover rather than to the point vertically beneath overhanging vegetation. In that kind of study it is very important that the reader of your dissertation can separate out the stages that you have gone through in reaching your conclusions and be able to evaluate each of them individually, and it is therefore essential that you present them as separate and clearly identifiable sections of text. Dissertations of this type need a section containing measurements or results, and a separate section containing interpretations.

Structure and writing

As we've said before, your dissertation is like a recipe for solving the problem you have set. Just like a recipe, it's important to get things in the right order so that your examiners can follow through the logic of the study. Likewise, you need to write clearly and unambiguously. We'll give greater detail on this aspect of your dissertation in Chapter 9.

Intellectual achievement

In assessing the intellectual achievement of a dissertation, the examiners will be looking for evidence of capabilities for reasoning, analysis and synthesis. In many poor dissertations the results of data collection and analysis are simply presented almost without comment. One good way of demonstrating intellectual achievement is to go beyond the basic answer to your research question and put together a conceptual model that ties together your own findings with the ideas previously published by other researchers. Sections of your dissertation that read something like the example shown in Box 2.4 should be present if you are to do well according to this criterion. This kind of content indicates that you have reached conclusions by putting together a combination of ideas or information in an interesting way.

Valid and sensible conclusions

A good dissertation is one that concludes, rather than just stops. Most dissertations begin with a question or problem, so they should conclude with an answer or solution. In the conclusion you should summarize your findings and set them in the wider intellectual context in which your dissertation was initially set. Your conclusions must match up with your aims. So, you might be able to refer back to your introductory chapter and the existing literature on the subject and show how what you have found out fits into/contradicts/ supports the earlier literature. A conclusion to the dissertation that began with the background shown in Box 2.2 might look like that shown in Box 2.5. The conclusion is also the place to suggest further lines of research or alternative approaches that might be taken to solve your problem. This is particularly useful if your dissertation leads to surprising results, or to no results at all.

Box 2.4 An example of signs of intellectual achievement in a dissertation

The results summarized in Table 5.2 suggest that the spatial organization of work in the music industry in the north of England has changed in much the same way that Hracs and Leslie (2014) described in Toronto. However, the causes of these changes are less clear in the UK case. While the focus-group data confirm that changes in technology and in the organization of the recording industry that were identified in Toronto apply also to Manchester, the GIS analysis of formal and informal aesthetic labour locations in section 5.2 suggests a different response to those changes on the part of independent performers.

Putting together the results of Tables 5.1–5.6 a broader pattern of independent music activity begins to emerge. This behaviour is summarized in the causal linkage model of Figure 7.9. Although this model can only be tentative on the basis of the available information, it does provide a conceptual framework within which an understanding of aesthetic labour in the UK might be developed.

Box 2.5 Concluding material to the dissertation that began with the material in Box 2.2

This study has reported on measurements of grike width and depth on eight limestone pavements, including the three that were examined by Rose and Vincent (1986). The study confirms the preliminary observations of great variability in grike width and, on the basis of comparisons between such measurements made by three independent observers, shows that the measurement of grike width is very subjective. In comparison, it has been shown that grike depth shows much less variation and, using the same three independent observers, is much less susceptible to operator variance. Likewise, the determination of grike age using depth seems to give much more clear-cut results than when these determinations are made from width measurements. It is concluded that grike dimensions can provide a useful tool for identifying the erosional history of limestone pavements (as Rose and Vincent (1986) argued) but that this tool is much sharper if it relies on depth measurements.

Presentation

Your examiners will expect to see a well-presented dissertation. They will expect evidence that you have taken trouble over it and that you have the skills and knowledge to prepare a professional-looking report.

The quality of your presentation can seriously affect the mark you obtain for your dissertation. Check your institution's marking criteria.

If you have taken trouble over the appearance of your dissertation, your examiners are more likely to believe that you have taken trouble over things that are less easy to check on. For example, you may say that you obtained readings of stream discharges every 30 minutes. The examiners have to take your word for this. So if you fell asleep in the sunshine or went off to the pub for a leisurely lunch break with the result that some of your readings were taken late, the examiners won't know. If it turns out that in your dissertation you refer to Table 6 when you mean to refer to Table 5, that the pages are not in order, and that there are typographical errors, then if some of your stream discharge data look a bit peculiar the examiners are likely to wonder whether you were as careless in your data collection as they can see you have been in your writing. On the other hand, if your dissertation is immaculate and there isn't a single spelling mistake, then even if some of your stream data are peculiar, the examiners are more likely to believe that they represent real variations in the discharge of your stream rather than being a result of sloppy work on your part.

Unlike the marks that may be awarded for intellectual achievement, those for presentation are easy to earn. So don't miss out on them. If you put your dissertation through a spelling checker make sure to use the correct version: don't use a US English spell checker if you are submitting your dissertation to a UK English institution! You should use spell check software and you should use grammar check software, but be aware of their limitations. If your word processor suggests you change 'effect' to 'affect' don't automatically assume it knows best. Check the suggestions before adopting them. If you submit a paper copy of the dissertation also do a final check of the print out. Don't assume that it will look OK on paper just because it did on the screen. Printers often do some inexplicable things at the last minute.

Good presentation is very important, but a well-presented dissertation can't make up for sloppy underlying work. Your examiners will have seen a lot of dissertations and read a lot of student work. They will be reassured by an attractive document, but seldom fooled!

Why do I have to do a dissertation?

Your dissertation is not simply a torture dreamed up by your tutors to keep you busy. It has very specific educational aims and there are important benefits to be gained from doing it well. Knowing beforehand what these aims are and how you might benefit from your dissertation should give you extra motivation to do it well and to put effort into it. If you want to go that far, there is even a substantial academic literature about dissertations and other types of final-year projects in geography and related disciplines. Most of that literature is aimed at academic staff more than students, but taking a look at a book such as Healey et al. (2013) could give you an interesting insight into what your tutors are thinking about when they include a dissertation as part of your degree course.

The purpose of doing a dissertation

The reason you are asked to do a dissertation is that it will train you to be able to conduct a geographical investigation and to report on that investigation, and also to be able to judge other people's investigations. This is important because the world needs a group of people who can find things out, and you are quite likely to find yourself in this group. This might be in future academic research or in any of the countless areas of life and work where finding things out is important. It is also important because, if society, civilization or science are not to proceed up a series of false tracks and blind alleys, those who claim to have found things out need to be subjected to scrutiny. People who have tried to find things out themselves are likely to know the pitfalls of doing research and so can more easily identify shortcomings in the apparent findings of others. One aim of your dissertation is to make you competent in evaluating the results of others who claim to have found things out, as well as becoming competent in finding things out yourself. You will be much better at judging research that you see reported in the media if you have learned how to do research yourself.

As well as doing the research, you have to report it – that is, write your dissertation. Another purpose of the dissertation is therefore to train you to convey information. The world needs people who can convey information effectively. You will be familiar with the frequent complaints about official forms that are unintelligible to the average person, and about scientific reports that are impossible even for scientists with different specialisms to understand. They are examples of poor communication. An aim of your dissertation project is to train you so that you don't end up as an author of such an unintelligible form. There is no reason why any piece of information cannot be expressed in a manner that is intelligible. As the physicist Richard Feynman is said to have once remarked, when asked to prepare a freshman (1st-year) lecture on a particular topic: 'I couldn't reduce it to the freshman level. That means we don't really understand it' (Gleick, 1992, p.399).

Almost all people in any profession need to be able to communicate effectively. Whatever you decide to do once you graduate, effective communication is likely to be a valuable skill to have acquired.

In many ways, you can think of your dissertation as the culmination of your undergraduate course. It's where you bring together all the skills you have learned in the course of your degree programme.

Benefits of undertaking a dissertation

If you are successful in your dissertation (and obtain a good mark for it), it will indicate that you have succeeded in meeting the aims described above. You will have become competent at all the steps that are discussed in the remainder of this book. What will that do for you? Who is going to be impressed if you shout out 'I wrote the best dissertation of my year'? Well, you are, for one. Don't underestimate the confidence-boosting benefit of having done something successfully, particularly if you started out thinking that it was unfamiliar, frightening or difficult. If you tackle successfully something about which you had doubts regarding your own ability, you will approach later, seemingly difficult, problems with a bit more confidence. Knowing that you have done everything that was required to put together a good dissertation should give you a long-lasting sense of personal satisfaction and achievement. Being able to do a good dissertation tells you something about yourself.

Your dissertation can:

- train you in research design and execution;
- train you in project management;
- train you to communicate;
- give you self-confidence;
- improve your degree class;
- help you to get a job.

But you (and your friends and family) aren't the only ones who may be impressed. Once you graduate you will want or need to do something else. Maybe you will decide you'd like to undertake postgraduate training, or maybe you will look for a job that pays real money. Either way, a good dissertation can help. Usually the dissertation is carried out and submitted well ahead of finishing your undergraduate course, and is therefore available for you to use to impress those who might employ you or offer you a place on a postgraduate course. Keep a copy of it and take it along to show to anybody who indicates the slightest interest. If it's very good, show it even to those who express no interest! A good dissertation demonstrates more clearly than anything else that you were a good student. If you have done one, tell people about it.

If you are thinking of applying for postgraduate study your dissertation will be particularly important because postgraduate courses involve more research-based activity than undergraduate training, so whether you are thinking about Masters or Ph.D. programmes your dissertation is the best guide as to how well you might do on such courses. For an employer, your dissertation will be a useful guide as to how well you might cope with tasks where you are asked to complete some activity or find out some information and report back on what you have found. A good dissertation demonstrates not only that you were a good student, but that you are likely to be good at other things after you graduate. If you are planning to work in a particular field you might want to choose a dissertation topic relevant to that field, so that it is of even more use in your job hunting. For example, if you want to work in tourism, or environmental education, or regional planning, then doing a dissertation in the area of your intended career will help you to tailor your CV and your academic transcript to suit your future job applications.

> **Eric says . . .**
>
> If you want to spend your life roaming the high seas, then that ethnographic project witnessing life among the pirates might have some value as a way of making potentially useful contacts.

Finally, remember that in many cases you will want to use your tutor as a referee in your applications. Usually, by the time such references come to be written your dissertation is well under way and is quite likely to have been submitted and even marked. This will give your tutor something tangible to say about you even before your final degree results are available. By doing well in your dissertation you can make sure that what the tutor says will be to your advantage. Remember also that your tutor (and referee) will not remember only the final dissertation, but the way you went about doing the project. Was your time management good? Was your background preparation thorough? Did you attend meetings punctually? Throughout the process of doing a dissertation you can develop and display a wide range of important graduate attributes.

A prize-winning dissertation?

A lot of people (not just us) think that dissertations are important. To encourage students to write good ones they have instituted prizes for good undergraduate dissertations. Winning a prize will make you feel even better about your dissertation, and will certainly impress potential employers!

Most departments offer an internal prize each year for the best dissertation. You might see your name in the newsletter or on the roll of honour, and a copy of your dissertation might be lodged in perpetuity in the university library for later generations of students to admire! Many national organizations also offer dissertation prizes. For example, in the UK the Royal Geographical Society offers more than 20 different dissertation prizes associated with different areas of the discipline, including prizes for the best undergraduate dissertations in geomorphology, urban geography, biogeography, rural geography, transport geography, geography of developing areas, political geography, economic geography, quaternary research and geographies of health. The Canadian Association of Geographers presents awards to the most outstanding students graduating in geography programmes at universities or colleges across Canada. The Association of American Geographers offer a variety of different prizes for undergraduate papers through their speciality groups across the breadth of the discipline. An online search of the local Geographical organizations in your home region may reveal prizes for which you will be eligible to apply if you write a great dissertation.

Some of these prizes are restricted to particular parts of the discipline, but others are open to any type of dissertation. If you are eligible for a prize and your tutor thinks you are in with a chance, it's quite likely that your department will enter it on your behalf: they will like everybody to know that they have good students coming through their course, and your advisor will want to be invited to the presentation banquet! If your department doesn't think of entering you, there's no reason why you shouldn't initiate the process yourself. If you have either an institutional or a national prize in your sights as you work on the dissertation it will motivate you to try your hardest. Even if you try hard but don't win the prize, remember that a good dissertation is its own reward!

A good dissertation is its own reward!

If that does not work for you, consider the possibility of publishing your dissertation in an academic journal, or presenting it at a conference, or developing it into a Ph.D. proposal. Some of the national prizes assume that your work will be presented as a conference paper, and even if you are not entering for a prize then presenting at a conference is another way of showing – to yourself and to the world – that your dissertation was of a very high standard. Having your work accepted for a conference or a journal is really the highest level of validation or praise for your work, and is a real feather in the cap – or the CV – for any student considering an academic career. If your dissertation is really good, perhaps that is a career option to discuss with your advisor.

Chapter summary and conclusion

This chapter has explored the things that are important about the definition of a dissertation, described the qualities that go to make up a good dissertation, and demonstrated the aims and benefits of undertaking one. We hope that it has made you realize that the dissertation is important and that it can do you a lot of good.

What to do after reading Chapter 2

Your institution will almost certainly have copies of dissertations submitted in the recent past. Look at some of these. Try to see what is good about them; and what is bad. Imagine yourself as an examiner and see what you would comment on. Write these things down for later reference.

Think seriously about what you want to get out of doing a dissertation: is it just a good mark, or personal satisfaction, or is your dissertation a stepping stone towards a particular career?

As you start to plan your dissertation, keep in mind all the reasons for which you are doing it, and remember how important a part of your under-graduate record it could be.

3

WHEN SHOULD I START AND HOW LONG WILL IT TAKE?

This chapter describes the stages in the life of a dissertation (all the things you have to do), and suggests how to allocate your time sensibly to each task.

Start now

You should start now. It will take longer than you think. One of the most common reasons for students writing disappointing dissertations is that they underestimate how long things will take, and end up in a last-minute panic having to rush, or even miss out, important parts of the job. There are lots of separate tasks involved in producing your dissertation, all the way from deciding what kind of topic you will do to checking the finished article one last time before handing it in. If you want to do as well as you possibly can, then it is essential that you know exactly what needs to be done, that you know how much time needs to be allocated to each task, that you know when you will be in a position to work on each task, and that you plan your schedule of work accordingly. The aim of this chapter is to help you to organize your time as well as possible, and to avoid unnecessary panic and consequent disappointment.

The importance of a timetable

Most institutions allow about a year to do the dissertation, and you may have been given as much as 18 months between the time you had the dissertation explained to you and the time you have to hand it in. Compared to the deadlines you will be used to for your coursework essays or practical assignments, the dissertation stretches unthreateningly into the distant future. Probably you've never been given so much time to do a single piece of work, and it may seem unnecessarily generous. You might think it's just an administrative convenience of some kind for the department to stretch out the dissertation, or some archaic quirk of the academic system, and that in fact you can do it all in the weeks just before the deadline. You're wrong. The length of time that your institution allocates to the dissertation is carefully thought out and based on the length of time that it takes to do the job properly. Depending on the specific requirements of different institutions this is, indeed, about one year.

There are lots of separate tasks involved in producing a dissertation. Some of them can be done simultaneously; others need to be done sequentially. For example, you might be able to start writing your introductory chapters at the same time as you are administering your postal questionnaire, and it might be essential to collect your river velocity data at the same time that you collect your suspended sediment data, but you certainly don't want to collect any data until after you've established the subject of your project, and there's no point printing up your postal questionnaire until after you've analyzed the results of your pilot study. If you do things in the wrong order, or if you try to do two jobs at the same time that should be done one after the other, you'll get yourself in a right pickle. Worse still, try as you might to cover your tracks later, the examiner will be able to spot that you got in a pickle, and won't be impressed. So, it's important to know what things you need to do, and what order to do them in. As we said in the last paragraph, it's also important to get the timing right, so you need to know how long each job, or each group of jobs, will take. Clearly, you need all of this information right at the outset, before you commit yourself to your programme, or else you won't even know where to begin. In other words, you need to worry about this now. The best way to sort out all of this is to make a timetable.

Institutional guidelines and 'the deadline'

Your institution will have its own specific guidelines and regulations about the dissertation. These should include information about how long you should expect to spend on the dissertation, when you might reasonably expect to begin the work, and, most certainly, a specific date by which you must have the work completed and handed in: the deadline. You need to know what your institution's regulations are, and you must know what the deadline is. If you don't already know, then go and find out. You can't organize your time or draw up a timetable if you don't know the deadline. All of your planning depends on that date. Put it in your phone now. Write it in your pocket planner. Scribble it on the bathroom wall.

The deadline is the date beyond which you must not go. There will be a severe penalty if you don't get the dissertation in on time. Some institutions simply do not accept late work, and you will score zero, 0 per cent, nothing. This is a bad thing. In some institutions it means you cannot pass your degree. Other institutions employ systems involving deductions of marks for every hour or day that the dissertation is late. Whatever system your institution employs, you will almost certainly find that being late is a disaster, and you must avoid it at all costs.

Meet the deadline.

If there is any legitimate reason that you might not be able to meet the deadline, such as illness, then consult your tutor at the earliest possible time to see what arrangements can be made. You may be granted an extension, or given some allowance in the assessment. Consult your departmental guidelines, and discuss your situation with your tutor, and do so well in advance. Because you have so long to work on the dissertation, and because the assessment is based partly on your time management and planning, many tutors are very reluctant to offer any extensions, on the grounds that you should have left plenty of emergency time in case anything went wrong.

Your institution may also have intermediate deadlines along the way. You may, for example, have to submit a literature review a few months after you start. Put that date in your phone. There may be scheduled appointments with your tutor that you are required to keep. Put those dates into your phone. Make a note of these intermediate deadlines. Put them all into your timetable!

Constructing a timetable

At this stage you should know at least three things: when the deadline is; how long there is to go between now and then; and how much work, if any, you have already done on the dissertation. Now you are in a position to start putting together a timetable.

Many students are reluctant to spend time drawing up a timetable. They think that having the key dates in their phone will be good enough. They are wrong. Constructing the timetable on paper or on a big whiteboard or on a spreadsheet is a valuable exercise in itself, as it forces you to recognize all the different jobs that you will have to do. You will also have to think about what each job will involve, how long it will take, and how it will fit together with the other jobs.

You may eventually keep your timetable online or on your phone, but in the first instance, as you are building it, there are advantages to using a big sheet of paper. Don't be afraid to go through a lot of scrap paper as you try to get all this stuff out of your head and onto the page. A couple of hours thinking and scribbling at this stage will save you a lot of grief later on. The exercise will also show you something that will crop up over and over again as your project proceeds, namely that your work will not necessarily develop in a linear fashion; as a new idea occurs (or some new disaster befalls your plans), you will find yourself going backwards and forwards through your work readjusting things to keep everything straight. Don't worry, that is supposed to be part of the game; one of the things that the whole business of doing a dissertation is supposed to teach you to deal with. Your handbook may refer to these as 'intended learning outcomes'!

A do-it-yourself timetable kit

It is very easy to start building your timetable. You can do it on paper, you can do it on a spreadsheet on your computer or you could do it on your tablet or phone. These instructions assume you're sketching it out on paper but it really doesn't matter.

1   Take a clean sheet of paper (or open a new spreadsheet page) and write at the bottom: 'Hand in dissertation' and the date of your institution's submission deadline. At the

top of the page write: 'Start work on dissertation' and the date when your institution explained the requirements of the dissertation to you.

All the different tasks that you need to do, the reading, the planning, the fieldwork, the lab work, the writing, and all the rest, then need to be fitted into the blank space in the middle of your page. Straight away you can:

2   Add the months down the side of the page between START WORK and HAND IN.
3   Add an arrow with the word NOW at today's date.

Eric says . . .

Put your timetable into your phone and have a copy pinned to your wall as well!

Set phone alarms to nag you about intermediate deadlines.

If looking at this book and thinking about this timetable are the first things you've done towards the dissertation (which would not be unreasonable!) then your NOW will be immediately underneath your START. If you've already spent some time working at it, then you might be able to put a few things above the NOW to show what you've done so far. For very many students the timetable at this stage looks like Figure 3.1, with START at the point where the department gave the introductory lecture, or gave out the dissertation guidelines, then a long gap of 'did nothing' before the NOW some way down the page. If your timetable looks like this you will recognize already that you have less space than you might like into which to fit your tasks.

4   Screw up this first version of the timetable and move on to version two (Figure 3.2), with NOW at the very top of the page, SUBMISSION DEADLINE at the very bottom, and an encouragingly expansive clean space in between! If you're building your timetable on a spreadsheet you can just delete a few of the redundant rows from the top and insert a few lower down to achieve the same result.

Now all you have to do is fill in the gaps. Read on!

Fitting the jobs into the timetable

As this point you need to think carefully about what exactly lies ahead and how long it will take you to do it. We say 'you' deliberately. Everybody works at their own pace, and you need to produce a schedule that you can achieve, not one for your friends, your tutor or the mythical 'typical student'. Different projects will involve different tasks, but the basic elements are universal. Looking through the later chapters of this book will give you more detail about what is involved, but for the purpose of timetabling you can start

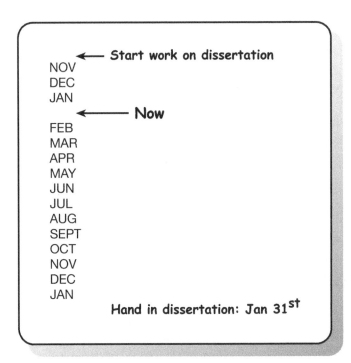

Figure 3.1 First draft of a dissertation timetable

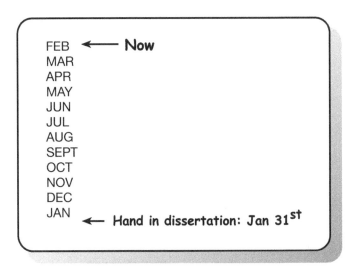

Figure 3.2 Second draft of a dissertation timetable

with a fairly simple list such as that in Table 3.1. For the purposes of your particular project you may need to omit parts of this list, or add new headings to it, but this is a good list to start working with.

Some of the jobs that go onto the timetable will have to be done at specific times, and these are the easiest, and the most important, to fit onto your timetable straight away. For example, your institution might insist that certain forms are filled in at certain times, or that research proposals are presented to tutors before a certain date. Your institution's regulations might include specific limits on the latest time at which you will be eligible to apply for financial support for the dissertation, or the last date at which tutors will be prepared to read drafts of your chapters. Equally, your domestic circumstances can place constraints on the timetable: your fieldwork period might be constrained by dates you have to be at work in the vacation, or by the availability of a friend to help you with the fieldwork, or by the dates of a family holiday. All of these constraints need to be built into your timetable at this stage, along with term and vacation dates, examinations and other commitments. To avoid making your page too messy, things that aren't directly related to the project can be put in a column down the right-hand side of the page.

Table 3.1 An example of the sort of dissertation schedule that can be produced by slotting the jobs to be done into the time available

Job no.	Job description	Time allowed (months)	Schedule
1	Establish schedule and produce timetable	–	Jan
2	Decide what to do it on:	2	Jan/Feb
	(lots of reading and thinking)		
	Specify the TOPIC, PROBLEM, QUESTION		
3	Literature search:	11/2	Mar/Apr
	Read, think and then revise job 2		
4	Research design:	11/2	Apr/May
	How to find out what you asked in (2), bearing in mind what you learned in (3)		
5	Data collection:	1	June
	Fieldwork, questionnaires, lab experiments, getting what (4) required		
6	Data analysis:	1	July
	Sifting ethnographic notes, lab work on field samples, statistical treatment of survey results, etc.		
7	Interpretation:	1	Aug
	Figuring out what (5) and (6) tell you about the question in (2)		
8	Writing:	2	Sept/Oct
	Write the report, draw the figures, check the drafts, etc.		
9	Preparing the report:	1	Nov
	Print final version, attach inserts, binding		
10	Submit report:	–	Dec
	Paper copy, electronic copy, or both		

5   Add the dates of institutional timetable requirements such as term/vacation dates and things like: 'Hand in proposal form to tutor before this time.' Also add other inflexible dates such as: 'Holiday in China with Eric'; or 'Two weeks of exams for car-maintenance night class'; or 'Six weeks for summer vacation job'. Include any key meetings with your supervisor that can be planned well in advance, such as the date for discussing some key section of data analysis, or a date to meet and talk about the results of your pilot study.

It will become clear at this point that there are chunks of time when work on the dissertation will be impossible. For example, you will not make much progress on your study of cinema catchment areas in Milton Keynes while you are in China with Eric.

6   Shade in the areas of the timetable when dissertation work is not possible.

You can also be fairly confident that 'unavoidable constraints' (disasters and emergencies) that you didn't anticipate (never dreamed of) will arise. You will lose all your field notes; your computer will crash and eat your disk; the dog will eat the back-up and the back-up back-up will go into the washing machine in your shirt pocket; you will be sent to jail for a fortnight; loads of good stuff will come on the TV; an unmissable overtime opportunity will come up at work; the central pillar of your statistical analysis will crumble and the whole idea of your project will be rendered obsolete by a publication that appears half-way through your work. Your computer could be stolen, along with the only copies of your dissertation files. (You should have kept a back-up in the Cloud.) Things go wrong. It is a very good idea to allow a few extra weeks in your schedule to cope with all of this. You can do that easily at this stage in your timetabling by artificially bringing forward your deadline. If the real deadline is 1 February, make your personal deadline 14 January, and aim genuinely to have the work completely finished, bound and ready for submission on that date. This gives you a lifeboat, a fire escape and a nail file in the cake. In case of emergency, and only in case of emergency, break into the last two weeks.

7   Add your 'Revised deadline' a couple of weeks above the institutional deadline, and write 'Emergencies' in the little gap between the two. Change the 'Deadline' reminder date in your phone-alert settings.

Eric says . . .

If you've done your timetable on paper, use a pair of scissors to cut the last two weeks off the bottom of the page. Keep the strip of paper in a glass case with a roll of sticky tape. If things go badly wrong, smash open the case and tape the two weeks back into your schedule! If your timetable is on your computer, put the last two weeks on to a CD and keep it in a vault in your Swiss bank, only to be spent on your dissertation as a last resort. Do not plan to use those last two weeks for anything other than celebrating having finished the dissertation.

There are a number of other constraints that can be added at this early stage, too. For example, if you plan to leave all the word processing and assembling of text till the end of the project, make sure that you allow yourself time at the end to do so. Writing up bits of the report as you go along is usually a very good idea so that you don't have a huge typing job waiting at the end of the project; we'll say more about that later (Chapter 9). Remember also that if you have to submit a paper copy it takes a certain amount of time to get your work bound after it is all printed out. How long you need to allow depends on the requirements of your institution. Simple spiral binding can be done on the spot at many high street printers, but you should allow more time if there are any more specialized requirements. If your submission deadline is shortly after Christmas, don't forget to allow for the holiday period when the chap from the binders, on holiday in Orlando, might be remarkably insensitive to your plight. It would also be a good idea to check whether your supervisor has any holidays, research trips or other major absences planned during the year. If your supervisor is away the department should give you a substitute advisor, but it would be a good idea not to be relying on a chat with your supervisor at exactly the time that your he or she has booked passage on a ship through the Gulf of Aden as part of a project on piracy in the Arabian Sea. Discuss your timetable with your supervisor, and check that your supervisor can't see any obvious clashes or omissions.

8   Add 'Start putting final text together' about a month above your 'Revised deadline'.

As you produce your text, of course, you will want someone to look it over for you and check for the silly mistakes that most of us make when we are typing. In many institutions tutors will be happy to read your entire dissertation in draft form. If yours is one of these institutions, take advantage of it; you can get invaluable help at this stage. If your institution is less generous, then at least take advantage of a friend or relative to read through your work. To get any benefit from this process, you will need to give the reader time to read, and give yourself time to do something about their comments. Book your tutor's time well in advance; if you turn up with 9,000 words of text in the middle of a busy week you might have a long wait for any feedback. Allow at least a couple of weeks for anyone to look at your draft and find time to give you feedback.

9   Add 'Give draft of dissertation to Mum/Fred/Dr X for final comments' about three weeks above 'Give dissertation to binder'.

That gets most of the practicalities out of the way, and your timetable at this stage might look something like Figure 3.3. The space that you have left between NOW and 'Final draft manuscript to tutor' is the time that you have to actually carry out your research and draft the report. As your timetable develops, so the time that you seem to have available shrinks! Into your remaining space you now need to insert the major sections of your research programme (as in Table 3.1), and the mini-deadlines by which you intend to complete each section.

Table 3.1 includes a rough estimate of the proportions of your time that you should be thinking of allocating to each of the major tasks involved in the dissertation. You will notice that if you have allowed a complete year to do the work, the numbers in the time-allocation column equate to months. If you have more or less than one year to do the

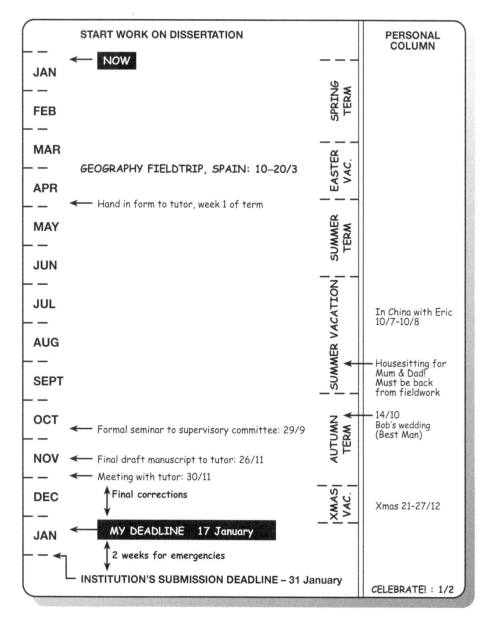

Figure 3.3 What your timetable might look like when you have fitted in all the fixed dates such as terms, administrative deadlines and your safety margins

work, then you can expand or compress this timescale. Different types of project may require slightly different emphases on different parts of the work; the allocations given here are a good guide for most projects, but you may wish to fiddle around with them to suit your own project. If you are indeed out of circulation (in China with Eric, for example) for a month, then you need to accommodate that into your schedule at this stage.

10   Slot the key elements of your programme, as illustrated, for example, in Table 3.1, into the remaining space in your timetable, avoiding clashes with prior engagements and meeting the requirements of your institutional schedule. Add specific dates at the end of each key section to serve as mini-deadlines.

Your timetable should now look something like Figure 3.4. You will notice that in this version the intrusion of a field trip, the summer exams and the trip to China have required

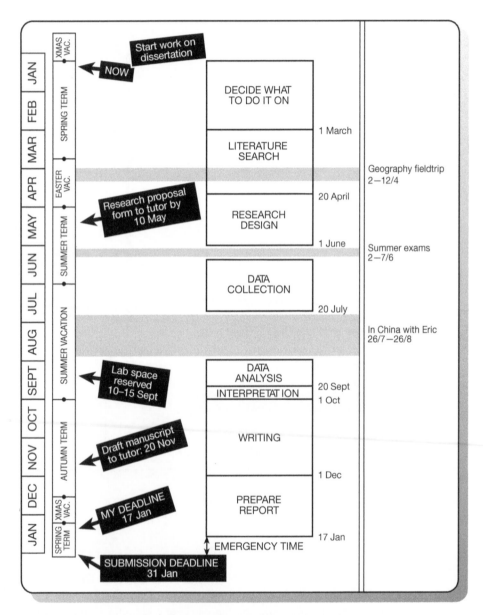

Figure 3.4 An example of what your timetable might look like about a year before your dissertation is due in. More details can be added as you firm up your arrangements later in the year

us to compress the 12 units of time from Table 3.1 into less than the 12 months that we thought would be available. Here we have lopped some time off the interpretation period. You will have to figure out your own solution if you face this problem. Try to avoid the obvious, but risky, gambit of eating into your emergency time.

Your own individual timetable

Bear in mind, of course, that different types of project will need different time allocations. For example, if you need to administer a postal questionnaire then you might need to allow for a much longer period of data collection, but might be able to do another job (like drafting your introductory chapters) at the same time. If you need to create a large number of complex graphics from your GIS data, then you will need more time for preparing the report at the end. Figures 3.5, 3.6 and 3.7 show a variety of timetables drawn up for different types of project. Every project will have its own unique timetabling requirements, so you can't just use one of the timetables that we've drawn up; you need to draw up your own timetable.

One problem that you may encounter at this point is that it can be difficult to construct a detailed timetable before you have decided on the details of your research design (which we will discuss in Chapters 5 and 6). For now, you might have to produce a provisional timetable, and do the fine-tuning after you have sorted out the details of the project later on.

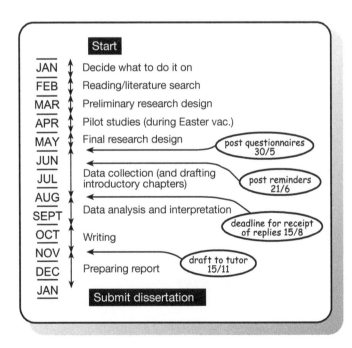

Figure 3.5 An example of a dissertation timetable

Figure 3.6 Another example of a dissertation timetable

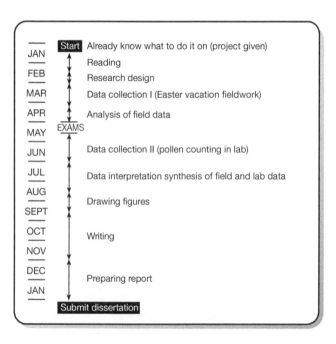

Figure 3.7 A poor timetable. An over-ambitious programme of data collection cuts into both the preparation (reading) time and the time available for analyzing the vast amount of data that might turn up

Another problem is that the whole point of 'things you weren't expecting to happen' is that you have not predicted that those things will happen. Most students, however carefully they plan, find that they have unexpected setbacks and delays through the year that force them gradually to squeeze more and more of the work into the later sections of the timetable. Being realistic, you are quite likely to find yourself busier than you expected in the final third of your timetable. Make sure now that you have left plenty of flexibility in those final few months. Leave yourself plenty of breathing spaces.

Chapter summary and conclusion

It is vital to the success of your dissertation that you allocate sufficient time to each part of the work, and that you do the various bits of the work in the right order. The best way to avoid running out of time or missing out vital bits of the job is to draw up a timetable before you begin. Your timetable should include: all the formal deadlines imposed by your institution; all the constraints on your own time, personal and otherwise; and all the major stages through which you expect your work to progress. Allow plenty of time to deal with unexpected problems. The only way you can produce this timetable is by thinking ahead in great detail about exactly what you need to do, when you will be able to do it and how long it will take. When you have made a timetable, set reminders in your phone or calendar to nag you about key intermediate deadlines. As you move forward with your dissertation, stick to your timetable.

What to do after reading Chapter 3

When you've finished this chapter, make yourself a timetable! Then discuss it with your supervisor and ask whether you have forgotten anything.

At this stage, and throughout the project, if you are afraid that something is going wrong then look at Chapter 10 and talk to your advisor.

As you move forward stick to your timetable, and expect things to put pressure on your time later on.

Start now.

4

WHAT SHALL I DO IT ON?

This chapter shows why the choice of subject for your dissertation is so important; differentiates between topics, problems and questions; discusses ways of choosing the best subject for you; and identifies the qualities of a good dissertation question.

Choosing the right subject

In Box 2.1 we listed 'a good problem' as the first quality of a good dissertation. Deciding on a subject for your dissertation is therefore the first real task you face, and it's by no means a trivial one. In fact, it's the most difficult part of your dissertation. Very often students think that the real work begins after they've chosen their subject. It doesn't. Choosing the right subject, and specifically one that is right for you, can determine whether you write a good dissertation or a poor one. The aim of this chapter is to demonstrate why the choice of subject is important and what issues you need to think about in choosing a subject. More practically, if, when you've read this chapter, you can complete the sentence that begins 'I am trying to find out ...' then you will have made the first significant step towards your dissertation.

> **Erica says . . .**
>
> Don't rush this stage. Choosing what to do it on is difficult and it is important. Don't just do the first thing that comes into your head, and don't just think you'll re-do something you did at school or college!

Topics, problems and questions

Let's begin with some definitions. The topic that you do your dissertation on is some broad area of study. It may be glacial geomorphology, community resilience, landslides, sustainable agriculture, river pollution, land tenure in eighteenth-century England, GIS techniques for monitoring coastal hazards, medical geography, geography of crime or any such branch of the discipline. The problem that you tackle will be a more specific, and smaller, issue within this topic. So, for example, within the field of community resilience you might tackle a problem such as social resilience to the threat of water shortage. Finally, there will be specific questions that you will ask in relation to your problem. Does the Langridge et al. (2006) hypothesis that social resilience to water shortages is primarily determined by access rather than recovery-time apply to a UK case study? What impact do differences in the social resilience of urban and rural communities to water shortages have on migration patterns in southern Africa? In reaching the point at which you can complete the sentence 'I am trying to find out . . .' you will need to select a topic, identify a problem and specify a question.

Selecting a topic

The obvious approach to selecting a topic, and the one which you will often be advised to take, is to choose the topic that interests you the most. This is sometimes a good starting point. For example, it might be that you know for sure that you enjoy doing GIS work and want to do a project involving that, or that you definitely want to do something involving outdoor fieldwork, in which case you are probably in safe territory to begin focusing in from that starting point. However, going straight for the thing you are most interested in is not always the best approach, and is not always as easy as it might sound. In the following paragraphs we identify some of the common pitfalls associated with going straight for the obvious 'interesting' topic, and some of the other opportunities that are available to you.

First, the things in which you are most interested might be things that do not easily lend themselves to a dissertation study, or things that would be difficult for you, personally, to engage with as a research project. Suppose you are interested in the mafia. An ethnographic study of interpersonal territoriality within an organized crime family, interesting though it may sound, might not be a suitable undergraduate dissertation topic. Some things are inherently difficult, dangerous, expensive or time-consuming to study. We will have a lot more to say about ethics and safety later in this book, but you need to think about those issues even before you choose your research topic. Also, your resources of finance and time will be limited and you may have particular personal circumstances to take into account. You are advised to sort out what these are at an early stage. Make a list – some of the personal issues that you need to consider are listed in Box 4.1. Your personal list of constraints and opportunities might help you to narrow down your options.

Second, your institution may have rules about exactly what you are allowed to do. These might be rules concerning ethical issues, rules about overlaps between your dissertation and other modules, or rules about whether you are required to collect primary data. If you are required to use primary data this may mean that you cannot do a study of housing in Detroit unless you actually visit the place. In most institutions, however, it is acceptable to use secondary data, data that somebody else has collected (such as census data or remotely sensed images), provided that you make due acknowledgement of this fact. Check the rules in your own department: they may help you to narrow down your options.

Box 4.1 Your personal list of constraints and opportunities

Things to consider before selecting your topic:

*   Are you free to travel, or is the location limited to a few choices?
*   How much time do you have for data collection?
*   Can you work on the project full time for a period or do you need to do something else for parts of each day?
*   Do you have people who could act as field assistants?
*   Are there physical constraints (e.g. health conditions) limiting what you might do?
*   What transport do you have, and does this limit the size of your study area?
*   Do you have money to spend on this work?
*   Do you have access to unusual data sources, such as a friend in the business?

Third, there may be many things that interest you, so how do you choose which one to study? If you are in this fortunate position then you might be able to combine several different interests. Perhaps you could combine your interests in GIS and organized crime and do a GIS-based crime project using secondary data that avoids the need to embed yourself within a crime family and collect primary field data. Interested in art and in cities? Then how about a project on graffiti? 'Urban Art – Beauty and Blight'? Even if you can't put together a combined project, you could pursue several possibilities simultaneously to begin with, and then focus down as you firm up the different ideas. If you can't decide yet whether you want to look at the effects of volcanic ash clouds on air traffic, on crop yields or on the aesthetic qualities of sunsets, start reading up on all three. In all likelihood, one of them will soon turn out to be more promising and interesting than the others. Perhaps there are topics that would be relevant to your future employment. If you know that you want a career in waste management, then perhaps doing a dissertation on some aspect of the geography of rubbish would be a way both to test the depth of your interest in the subject before you commit your life to it, and to establish some credentials and experience to show to your potential employer when you are called for the job interview. Perhaps there are topics where you might be able to get access to some special data through somebody you know. Do you have a member of your family working in some interesting area who could get you access to a usually restricted site or data set?

Is there something to do with your own part-time employment that could open up a dissertation topic?

Crang (1994) famously used his part-time work in Smoky Joe's restaurant as the source of data for his research looking at how workplace geographies constitute the character of an employment. Crang's research focused on 'performative geographies of display' in restaurant waiting work, and on the ways in which the geographical arrangement of the workplace contributed to the ability of management to maintain surveillance over the waiting staff. Even if you are inspired by Crang's paper, you don't have to research exactly the same topic. For example McMorran (2012) started with a very similar approach – participant observation as a restaurant worker – but shifted the focus of his work more onto the methods of ethnographic study and issues surrounding bodily mobility. You could take the basic starting point of workplace participant observation in your own part-time job and develop your own project idea from there. Perhaps if you work in a supermarket at weekends you could combine food geography, sustainability and waste management in a project using your inside knowledge about what happens to unsold fresh food at the end of the day. There are projects everywhere!

Fourth, the things that you are personally most interested in might not be the things that other geographers are interested in! It is nearly always a good idea to choose a dissertation topic that is current in the research literature. Do your research on something that other geographers are doing research on. The way to find out about those things is by reading: explore the research literature. This sounds like a big job, but there are a lot of shortcuts. You are just looking for ideas. For example, just read abstracts, not whole papers. Look at the figures in a paper to get ideas for data that you could collect. Rather than wading in detail through a few books or papers, at this stage skip quickly over a lot of books and papers. If something is not interesting, don't waste your time on it at this stage. When you find an interesting diagram or map, or a title that sounds fun or a method that looks like something you could try, then slow down and read more carefully. A good way to find out what topics are really hot in any area of research is to look at the list of papers scheduled in a forthcoming conference, or just read the description of what the conference is about. If you already know that you want to do something on glaciers then perhaps look at the details of the next few workshops and conferences being organized by the International Glaciological Society. If you are still trying to narrow down your research area then try the conferences of organizations such as the Association of American Geographers or the Institute of British Geographers or your local equivalent. Read through the list of titles. Look at the abstracts of any that look interesting. If you find one that looks promising, find out more by googling the lead authors and checking out more of their publications.

On the other hand, being advised to do the thing that interests you most might not help if you don't find many things in geography very interesting! Obviously that is unlikely, especially since you have chosen to do a geography degree, but let's consider some other ways of choosing a broad topic area for your dissertation.

Before just picking the first thing that interests you, or if you can't think of anything that is both interesting and suitable, or if you just can't choose between all the interesting opportunities that face you, try turning the problem around. Think about the things outside of geography and your lecture courses that most interest you and see if there is a way in which you could bend the geography to match your interests. You may be a great rock climber. Few geomorphologists are, so there is not a great deal of work done on the geomorphology of vertical rock faces. There is even less work on rock climbing in the human geography literature. Consequently, this is an area in which it is relatively easy to come up with a worthwhile problem (although there may be safety issues that you will need to consider). When you think about it, there is a geographical aspect to most things, so it shouldn't be too difficult to find a topic in even apparently unlikely fields. It's a mistake to separate your geography from the world you live in. The danger is that you may spend more time on the other interest and less on the geography. However, if you don't fall into this trap you should end up with a good dissertation and a greater appreciation of some aspect of your leisure interest. Are you interested in music? Or skateboarding? Or model railways? Or pirates? Then do a dissertation based on one of those.

You don't have to confine yourself to 'traditional' old-fashioned textbook geography topics like shopping centres and footpath erosion. In fact, it is much better if you don't.

As an example of this approach, you might look at *Scotland's Golf Courses* by glacial geomorphologist Robert Price (Price, 1989). The golf courses of Scotland have some very interesting geomorphology, so Price used this book as an excuse to combine his interests in golf and geomorphology. You could do something similar with one of your own hobbies. If you know that you will be spending part of your summer in Portugal with Erica and her friends, do you have an opportunity to undertake your dissertation there at the same time? If so, try looking at the literature on the area to see if a topic suggests itself. Are you part of some interesting sports or social group? Perhaps you could do an ethnographic study based on your participation in that group.

Getting started is always the most difficult stage for most things, and of course you can ask for advice about picking a topic. But a word of warning: don't go into your tutor's office and start with whining about not being able to think of a topic. That will not go down well. Have at least an idea to start the conversation with. Try seeking out, say, the transport specialist in your department and starting off 'I've been thinking about studying Asian railway networks for my dissertation . . .'. This may be surprisingly productive. Equally, you could go to the GIS specialist or the cultural geographer or even the geomorphologist and say exactly the same thing: they would probably show you a whole different way of approaching that same topic! The railways of Tibet would make an excellent topic for an applied periglacial geomorphology project. There might even be a way of combining that with your interest in model railways.

In many departments choosing the topic of your dissertation is regarded as part of the training in research, and your choice of topic is something that the examiners will judge you on.

Student choice and off-the-shelf projects

You may have thought that student choice was something that always worked to your advantage. When you have to choose a dissertation topic for yourself, however, the advantages may be less than obvious. It can be the hardest part of the whole process.

Eric says . . .

Can't somebody else choose my dissertation for me?

Although some departments are prepared to identify a list of project titles or ideas for students to choose from, most are not and expect students to come up with their own dissertation projects. Certainly you should be able to go and talk to appropriate tutors as you are thinking about possible projects, but you should not expect them to give you a ready-made topic. There are good reasons for this. Deciding what to investigate is a very important step in research. If your tutors did this for you it would deprive you of an important part of your research training and experience. In leaving this step to you it is expected that you will learn what constitutes a good topic and what does not, and also that you will learn both how difficult and how important it can be to choose your topic wisely. Consequently, when you have your first conversation with a potentially useful tutor in your department, you might be disappointed to discover that the tutor doesn't simply give you a straightforward suggestion about a good topic, but may start asking you difficult questions about the topic. The aim of this is to make you think more carefully about your chosen topic, and may be to make you realize that this is not a good topic for you to work on. Don't be disheartened if this happens, and happens more than once. If, at the end of this stage, you not only have a good dissertation project but also know the difference between a good project and a bad one, all the hard work will have been worth it and you will have achieved one of the goals of the dissertation process.

In the same way that your tutors will probably not give you a ready-made project, they will probably not encourage you to adopt ready-made projects from other sources. For example, several commercial and scientific organizations offer you the opportunity to combine your dissertation research with an organized expedition as part of their operation. While these organized expeditions do provide a good opportunity to travel to locations that might be difficult for you to reach independently, and therefore open up a whole new range of opportunities for your dissertation, there are also some problems with following this route. The first problem is simply that your institution may not allow it. Check your regulations and talk to your tutor. The more pre-arranged your dissertation seems to be, the less likely your tutor is to allow it. The second problem is that if you choose a topic from a list provided by an external organization, your examiners won't be able to give you any credit for devising a project of your own. A third problem with some organizations is that they offer field support and even project supervision that will effectively turn you into a research assistant – dependent upon the operation for every detail of your fieldwork, and possibly receiving direction that conflicts with the requirements of your dissertation.

We don't mean to sound too negative about organized expeditions because some of them can be very effective and can help you a lot. However, we do mean to warn you to be very careful before paying money and committing your time to an expedition that may not, in the end, provide you with what you need for your dissertation.

Eric says . . .

Maybe my friends and I can organize our own expedition?

Similarly, you might have the opportunity to do a dissertation that is somehow tied to your non-academic work, or to your work placement if you are involved in one of those. These opportunities can be very worthwhile, but, as with the opportunities offered by commercial companies, check that any project associated with an employer or work placement would be acceptable within the rules of your institution. Make sure that you will not be expected to take 'supervision' or instructions from your employer that might conflict with the academic advice of your official supervisor. Make sure that if your employer gives you access to data that they are not expecting anything in return that would breach your dissertation rules or ethics. For example, don't promise to let the employer publish your dissertation if the dissertation is technically the property of the institution. Check your regulations and talk to your supervisor. Finally, make sure that your institution would not consider the support you get from your employer to be inappropriate: remember that it has to be your own independent work that gets marked, not the work of your employer or co-workers. You probably won't be allowed just to hand in a work project and call it your dissertation!

It is probably not a good idea to do a dissertation on the same topic that you used for a project at school or college. Students who try that usually find it hard to make the step up to university standard when they revisit work they did at a lower level. Some students think they already know a lot about the topic, so they are not motivated to read as much as they would on a new topic. Usually what you think you know from school, or 'research' that you did at school, is unlikely to be good enough at university. The whole basis of a university project – founded on cutting-edge research literature – will usually be quite different from the kinds of projects done at school. Forget what you did at school. Grow up. Move on.

Erica says . . .

The more you read, the better your project ideas will be. See your project ideas in a broad intellectual context. Be able to discuss their significance within the academic literature.

Remember the geography

With so many things to think about when choosing a topic, and so many exciting topics to choose from that might overlap with your interests outside of geography, remember that this is, after all, a geography dissertation – or, if you are working in a related discipline, a dissertation in that discipline. Be careful not to let your project drift too far from what is considered relevant to your discipline. It is quite common for students to come along with excellent project ideas only to have the tutor ask 'Is that geography?' and find themselves stuck for an answer. Geography is a very wide and flexible discipline, so it is hard to imagine a topic that could not make the basis of a geography dissertation, but as you develop your ideas make sure that you treat your topic in a geographical way, using techniques and approaches, asking questions and addressing problems that will be relevant to an audience of geographers. Check early on, in a meeting with your advisor, that your topic, your question and your approach are suitably geographical! Whatever topic you fancy, whether it is French philosophers from the last century or glaciers in the next, take that topic and do geography to it! Your dissertation might be about geological structures or about social structures, but it should not be a geology or sociology dissertation if it is part of a geography degree.

Identifying a problem

So, you think you've got a topic. Next, you need to identify the specific problem that you will work on.

Now is the time to do some serious research. Explore the literature.
Read. Then do some more reading. Then read some more.

Identifying a specific problem involves pretty much the same thing as choosing a topic all over again, except that it's on a smaller scale. Say you've decided to do your dissertation on rivers in your local area, or the international Fair Trade system. Just what is it about these rivers or that system that you are going to investigate? Focusing in on a problem requires a different approach from identifying a broad topic. In selecting your topic the emphasis was on what you were interested in and were capable of undertaking. To identify a specific research problem you need to become familiar, if you are not so already, with what other people have done and have found interesting. Your dissertation needs to fit into and grow out of the context of the existing literature on the topic. Now is the time to explore that literature in detail. Visit the library or go online and start looking through the literature. You need to find the specific research problem you are going to work on, and you also need to find out what work has already been done on this problem.

Searching the literature

To find a worthwhile problem within the topic area you have selected, you should explore the literature using several different approaches. You can look through the shelves of books and journals in the library, but you can probably access much more material by searching online either using one of the bibliographic databases, such as the Web of Knowledge, to which your institutional library is likely to subscribe, or going to one of the well-known online research gateways such as Google Scholar. Typing in a few key words will produce a huge list of potential sources. Add a few additional key words, or limit the date range and you will have a manageable number. Take advantage of new technologies for searching and retrieving information as they appear. By the time you read this book there will be useful tools available that had not been invented as we were writing the book, and some of the ones we mention here might have disappeared. If you have not already found out how to use the best databases and literature-search facilities provided by your institution or available online you should do that now. A deep search of the literature is an essential starting point to your project, and that is easier to achieve if you have access to the appropriate sources. Your institution's library or Information Resources web page will almost certainly tell you where to get help. Library staff can be very helpful, and your library may offer specific training in searching literature, if you have not already had that as part of your course.

Eric says . . .

Be open to lots of different ways of finding material: follow relevant organizations on Twitter; sign up to email updates from key publishers; keep your electronic eyes and ears open.

First of all you should check the most recent literature in order to find out what topics are currently being discussed most heatedly; in other words, which are most topical, within this subject. Once you have identified a 'live' topic, you should delve further back into the literature to trace its roots. One way to do this is by going through recent (say, the last five years') issues of the journals that you know cover your topic. Journals that have review articles or progress reports on particular fields of research can be particularly useful at this stage. Both *Progress in Physical Geography* and *Progress in Human Geography* regularly carry review articles and progress reports. Equally you can search online for the relevant key words, or for work by the same authors. Remember to follow links back to older papers from the reference lists of the most recent publications you have found. The previous publications are usually just a few clicks away once you find a good starting point.

At this stage you do not want to get bogged down reading papers in immense detail. You just want to get the key point from each paper quickly, decide if it is relevant, and move on. Even the short abstract to a paper should be enough to tell you whether the paper is worth downloading, getting out of the library or obtaining an inter-library loan to read in more detail. An online or database search will list large numbers of papers relevant to your search terms, and they usually provide at least an abstract for each paper and in many cases links to copies of the whole paper. The trick is to enter appropriate search terms that will call up appropriate references from the database. Abstracts are short and easy to scan quickly for relevant details, so scanning through many pages of article titles and reading a few abstracts of articles that look interesting to you won't take a great deal of time.

Of course, you may be lucky and have a journal almost wholly devoted to your topic area. For example, if you have decided to work on periglacial geomorphology then the journal *Permafrost and Periglacial Processes* is a must. Don't stop there, however. Not all the relevant, or even the best, research is in the specialist journals. Researchers working in a particular field will always want to communicate their findings to fellow workers (the readers of the specialist journals) but sometimes they will also want to reach a wider audience, especially if they have something to report that has wider significance. The journal *Nature* doesn't have many articles on periglacial geomorphology, but any that it does have will probably be very important. So you should check. You can tailor your database search to look only in specific journals. This will help to keep the number of references returned within manageable proportions. Reading the recent papers on your topic, or even just their abstracts, will soon give you an idea of the sorts of problems that are being investigated and the methods that are being used. Some students think the best way to start is with a general internet search using appropriate keywords in a standard search engine such as Google or Yahoo, or going to a well-known online encyclopaedia. However, although this will give you some material, that material is usually the least reliable, because a lot of what is on the web has not been put through any check or review process. Whereas what you read in journals has been checked by people other than the author before it is published and these people have confirmed that what is in the article is worth publishing. This is seldom the case for material on the web.

Remember, any old idiot can put up any old rubbish on a web page.

For this stage of your dissertation, try to find one or two days when you have no other commitments (lectures, tutorials, work, etc.) and spend the entire time searching the literature. Give yourself the opportunity to get to know your topic. Don't be in too much of a hurry to identify your problem. You may think you are spending a lot of time and not getting anywhere, but this will be time well spent. What's more, if you make notes of the things you've read you will find these notes useful when you come to write up the intellectual context part of your dissertation. This is probably the most important period of work on your dissertation, so take your time and do it properly. If you come up with a good problem you will be well on the way to being able to produce a good dissertation. If you don't, you won't.

During this stage of your project you will start to accumulate a collection of references to previously published research. In due course you will use some of these in your final write up, so you might as well collect and file them efficiently from the start. A lot of students waste a lot of time searching for the details of references that they have misfiled or lost, and it can be a frustrating way to delay your completion. At the very least you should write down the complete reference for every item that you use in putting together your project. You may wish to use one of the many bibliographic software packages that are available to manage your reference collection. These not only allow you to store and annotate references electronically, but also interface with your word processing software to allow you to produce reference lists very quickly after you have created your text. Some students find such software useful, but be careful not to waste time on any software unless you really find it helpful. Many people find it just as easy to work from a simple list of all the references they have consulted. You can copy and paste the ones you need into your dissertation as you use them.

At the same time that you record your references it would be a good idea to write a very short summary – perhaps just a couple of sentences or a few bullet points – to note what it is about that paper that is relevant to your project. It might be just a short summary of the abstract, but later on when you are scouring your notes to try to remember which paper it was that put you onto the idea of interviewing supermodels, the summaries in your personal reference database might just get you out of trouble. Trying to remember where you read something, or which paper made a particular point, can be a very frustrating and time-wasting part of the write-up period if you do not keep good notes from the start. Having these notes for each reference will help a lot when you come to write the literature review.

Eric says . . .

A lot of note-taking apps let you tag each item that you clip or bookmark. You can tag each reference you collect with key topics then search your tags when you need them.

Situating your problem within previous literature

At the end of this stage you should be able to state the problem you are going to work on. Reviewing the literature has given you a good picture of what we already know about the world and where the gaps in our knowledge are. Your dissertation will probably be aiming to fill one of those gaps. From your reading you may have come to the conclusion that there are aspects of your chosen topic that are ignored in the literature and that you could undertake a dissertation that would address one of them. For example, looking through the literature on Fair Trade you might decide that the key problem area is not in whether people adhere to the guidelines, but whether the guidelines are themselves actually 'fair'. In looking through the literature on rivers you may notice that there has been little study of the channel geometry of rivers flowing in poorly sorted glacial deposits such as those in the area where you live. So your problem emerges from exploring the previous literature. There are a number of ways in which you can arrive at a problem to investigate from reading the literature, and some of them are listed in Box 4.2.

Box 4.2 Some ways in which you might identify a research problem from reading the literature

- It appears that nobody has investigated this topic – I'll have a go.
- Parsons and Knight (2012) investigated this topic and raised a new question regarding the role of X. I'll investigate the role of X.
- Parsons and Knight (2012) investigated this topic and found out . . . but they ignored the possible effects of X. I'll investigate the effects of X.
- Parsons and Knight (2012) investigated this topic at location X and found out that . . . I'll see if the same is true for location Y.
- Parsons and Knight (1998) long ago investigated this topic and found that . . . I wonder if things have changed since then. I'll repeat their study and compare my results with theirs.
- Parsons and Knight (2012) investigated this topic by method A. I wonder if you get different results by using method B. I'll use method B and compare my results with theirs.
- Since Parsons and Knight (1998) did their study long ago, a new data set has become available. I wonder if the new data supports Parsons' and Knight's conclusions.
- Since Parsons and Knight (1998) did their study long ago, a new paradigm has emerged within the discipline. I wonder if looking at the problem through the lens of this new paradigm casts new light on Parsons' and Knight's conclusions.

The next step is to find out whether somebody else has already tackled this problem. If they have, it doesn't mean you can't still work on it – after all you may completely disagree with their findings. However, it is necessary to know what work has already been done. There are three approaches, and you should consider trying all of them.

The first is to do another literature search focused specifically on the problem you have identified. An online search can be completed quite quickly if you know exactly what you are looking for, which you now do!

The second approach is to talk to your tutor. Now that you know what your problem is, and have read some of the background literature, you will be in a position to have a worthwhile conversation. Your tutor will take you more seriously as a result of your evident knowledge, and you will gain far more from what your supervisor has to say because of what you have already learned. Your tutor might have copies of obscure papers that you would struggle to find on your own, and may have been to conferences and heard papers that have yet to be published. In addition, your tutor may know relevant experts in the field who could offer useful advice.

These experts offer the third approach to finding out what has already been done. You could email, write to or visit these experts. But be warned. Experts in a field are unlikely to be very pleased if they have to deal with ill-informed students with poorly focused problems coming from another institution. If you approach them in this state, not only are they likely to be less helpful than they might otherwise be but you are in danger of making them less willing to talk to the next student who approaches them. It would be a good idea to check with your tutor before you start writing to strangers who might get upset at being pestered by somebody else's students. Receiving an email from some poorly prepared undergraduate in a distant location about their dissertation is not something academics, in general, look forward to!

Don't contact an expert in a field until you have a fair degree of expertise yourself, and check that it's OK with your own tutor first.

To get any worthwhile help it is important that you appear serious about the topic and that you are approaching your expert not because you think he/she will offer a short cut to a good dissertation but because you are already on the way to a good one and are looking to make it outstanding!

Finally, don't be too disheartened if, even at this stage, you discover that the problem you have come up with cannot be investigated within the limits of your dissertation, or even that the topic is not suitable. Keep going, try again, develop a new project or a new version of the project. It is likely to take several attempts to get this just right. As we said at the beginning of this chapter, what you do at this stage will play a large part in determining how good your dissertation is. We'd all like our research to progress smoothly, but it seldom does. Difficulties at this stage are particularly frustrating. You want to get going and you can't even sort out the direction to go in! But it is much better to spend time thinking about it now and getting it right than to set off in the wrong direction and have to turn back much later.

This bit of research is probably the most difficult. Don't feel that you are stupid if you seem to be having problems with it. It's almost certain that you will.

One big issue that holds students up at this stage is that often their project ideas are just far too big and vague to make a good dissertation. 'The Impact of Climate Change on Global Sea Levels' is not a promising start. Neither is 'How Glaciers Move'. 'The Changing Nature of Rural Areas' does not really narrow things down very much or give you a clear focus. If you are thinking of 'Urban Change in the Twenty-first Century' think again. Make your thinking much more tightly focused. Narrow it down to one small aspect of the problem, or how the problem affects a certain area, or something about the problem that has been discussed in recent literature. Go back and look again at Box 4.2.

Specifying questions

Specifying questions is all about how you approach the problem you have decided to investigate. Exactly what do you need to find out in order to make progress on the problem you have identified? You might have identified (the problem) that there is a controversy about whether X or Y is the best method to do Z, but exactly what (question) are you going to specify in order to address that controversy? There are lots of different ways of tackling any particular problem. There are lots of different questions you could ask about any particular topic and the ability to specify the right questions is what distinguishes a good researcher from a poor one. Take the example of the Nobel Prize-winning physicist Richard Feynman who once decided, in his spare time, to investigate the problem of cracking safes (Feynman, 1985). The safes he wanted to crack had combination locks with a sequence of three numbers, each in the range 0–99. One way of cracking the safes would be to try all possible combinations (one million). Feynman realized that he didn't have time to do that, so he wondered 'How accurate does each of the three numbers have to be?' If the correct combination was 23–66–49, would 24–67–48 work? If the safe would still open if you were a little bit off with the numbers then you wouldn't need to try so many different combinations! Feynman discovered that, for the safes he was looking at, being within five either side of the correct number would do, so trying every tenth number (0–0–0, 0–0–10, 0–0–20 and so on) wouldn't take so long because there were only 1,000 possible. Feynman had asked the right question about how far apart he could spread his attempts, and was on his way to becoming a renowned safecracker. Likewise, it has been said that when the apple fell, Newton could have asked the question 'Why did that apple fall just then?' and been on his way to not very much at all. His genius lay in specifying the question 'Why do apples fall?'

Specifying the right questions

So, how do you know what are the right questions? By their answers shall ye know them!

Only bother with questions that look as though they will have interesting answers.

The right questions are ones that have useful answers. These questions lead to new knowledge, or solve a specific problem. In the case of Feynman, if the answer had been that the number had to be spot on, he would have known that if he wanted to be a safecracker, he'd have to find another way of doing it. To discover if this was the case, all he had to do was to try a safe for which he knew the right combination and see if he could be wrong by one digit, two and so on. As it turned out, he discovered that the problem was tractable using the approach he had thought of. The question was easy to answer, had two possible answers, and each led to a significant advance in the problem he was investigating. The problem was how to crack safes. The question was 'Do you really have to try every single number?' That led him to a further question 'How few numbers could you get away with trying and still crack the safe?' If Feynman had discovered that the minimum was 1,000,000 numbers he'd have known that he'd have to try another method. If the set of numbers was sufficiently small then he knew he had a workable method. So, not only had he specified a question but he knew what possible answers the question had and what each of the answers would mean in terms of the problem he was investigating. Questions are the right questions if you know what answers they may have and what these possible answers would mean to you. In addition, questions that are easy to answer, and will allow you to make a significant step forward in your investigation if you do answer them, are even better.

Questions are good for research if you know what possible answers they may have and what these possible answers would mean to you.

Types of question

Because questions are so fundamental to good research, it is worthwhile looking into their nature a bit further. In this section we want to show that, although there may be an infinite number of questions you could ask, there are only a few types of question. The literature commonly refers to three fundamental types of question: descriptive questions that try to find out what something is like; relational questions that deal with connections between things; and causal questions that look for explanations of things. By and large, how you can tackle a question depends on the type of question it is. Consider the questions in Box 4.3. Questions such as these might form part of the problem you are investigating for your dissertation. Although these questions may all appear to be different, in effect they are all of the same type. They are all asking for a description or for an identification of what something is. A very large amount of geographical research can be put into the category of this type of question. We might generalize the question to the form 'What is A?' or, even more succinctly, 'A =?' For example, Question 4 in Box 4.3 can be rephrased as 'What is the number of visitors who use this recreational centre and what are the times at which they use it?' Question 7 really asks 'What are the feelings of the pirates?' These are all essentially 'What?' questions. None of them are asking why or how.

In Table 4.1 we list some other questions that, similarly, could form part of your dissertation. We show a way of grouping these questions into types, and we give the types

Box 4.3 Questions that are all of the same type

Here are a variety of questions that are all of the same type (descriptive):

- What is the boundary of this group's territory?
- What is the vegetational history recorded by this peat core?
- What myths are encoded in the cultural rituals of this group?
- How many visitors use this recreational centre and when do they use it?
- What advantages does the use of conversation analysis bring to research on the geography of homelessness?
- How do those pirates feel about those seagulls?
- What proportion of fields in this area show evidence of soil erosion?

of questions that we identify succinct generalized forms. How you approach answering a question depends, to a degree, on its type, so you need to know what type of question you are dealing with as you start your project. We will refer to our types of question occasionally in the following chapters. These are not necessarily all the types of question that there are: this is just an example of how you can reduce lots of different specific questions to a few specific question types.

You may think, as you look at that table, that you have come up with a question that does not fall into one of our categories. You may be right: we probably haven't thought of everything. But be careful to make sure, before you start to develop a research strategy for a whole new species of question, that it really doesn't fall into one of our categories. Imagine, for example, that you want to do a project on homelessness, and you want to use a particular technique – let's say conversation analysis. The idea of your dissertation is to find out whether this approach throws up new insights compared with alternative approaches. You think your project is very cutting edge (as indeed it may be) and so you think it won't fit into one of our pre-existing categories. Are you sure it isn't an A=? (What are the benefits that derive from using this technique?) Or might you tackle it as an A>B? (Is this method better than other methods?) Whatever your question, it is worth spending some time trying to simplify it in this way, because if you can see your question very clearly you are more likely to see your answers very clearly and write a nice, clear dissertation. Only when you know what your question really is can you decide on a strategy to find the answers. You do not have to fit into our categories, but you do need to be absolutely clear on exactly what your question boils down to.

Erica says . . .

It's surprising how often a poorly-prepared student – even late in the dissertation process – can't give a short answer to the simple question 'What are you trying to find out?'

Table 4.1 Some types of question

Example questions	Generalized form of question	Succinct generalized form of question
What is the boundary of this group's territory?	What's A?	A=?
What new insights on territorial boundaries can be gained by adopting a yyy perspective?	What's A?	A=?
What do pirates feel about seagulls?	What's A?	A=?
What proportion of fields in this area show evidence of erosion by running water?	What's A?	A=?
Are preconceptions of tourists to the UK from the USA and from Japan conditioned by the same literary experiences?	Is A like B?	A=B?
Are the children in all the schools in this town drawn from the same range of economic backgrounds?	Is A like B?	A=B?
Do these two deposits of glacial till have a different provenance?	Is A different from B?	A≠B?
Do the schools in different parts of the city differ in terms of the socio-economic backgrounds of their pupils?	Is A different from B?	A≠B?
Is it better to measure grike width rather than grike depth to characterize their age?	Is A better than B	A>B?
Does the record of annual expenditure on agricultural lime provide a better measure of rural wealth than the record of grain sales in eighteenth-century Shropshire?	Is A better than B	A>B?
Is there a relationship between the number of respiratory deaths in a town and the size of the town?	Are A and B related?	A⟷B?
Do the distributions of oak and holly trees in Britain vary synchronously?	Are A and B related?	A⟷B?
Does mean river channel width increase as discharge variability increases?	Does A affect B?	A→B?
Does the amount of usage of public transport increase as the frequency of the service increases?	Does A affect B?	A→B?
Does increasing the frequency of a bus service cause more people to use the service?	Does A cause B?	A=>B?
Does moving to a larger town increase your chances of dying from a respiratory disease?	Does A cause B?	A=>B?

You might at this stage be thinking 'My research is not really trying to find out anything.' Perhaps your project is about experiencing something or building something. Perhaps the core of your project is an ethnographic act of being there. You will never really know how a pirate feels about seagulls unless you are a pirate, you might say, so your project is to be a pirate and see how you feel about the gulls. Well most of those kinds of projects actually do involve finding something out: perhaps finding out what the experience feels like, or finding out how to build something, or what happens when you try to build it or when you place yourself into a situation. For most undergraduate research dissertations, research will involve some element, probably a very large element, of finding out. Describing, experiencing, building, applying or treating with a new theoretical framework – all of those types of projects require you to think about what you are trying to find out and how you will do that. If you are convinced that there is no 'finding out' involved in your project, talk it over carefully with your advisor.

Types of answer

Different types of question demand different types of answer. This is useful in several ways. For example, if you are having trouble coming up with a good question, try imagining what you would like to say in your conclusion to the dissertation, assume that to be your answer, and work backwards from there to work out what question you need to ask in order to head towards that answer. The fundamental link between question type and answer type is also useful because it means that as soon as you have worked out what type of question you are asking, you will also know what your answer will have to look like. If your question says 'Why?', for example, then your answer will have to say 'Because'. If your question asks 'What causes xyz?' then your answer will have to say 'This does'. This means that you can check constantly, as your project progresses, whether your research is really leading you in the direction of an appropriate answer to your question. Only if you know what your answer is supposed to look like will you be able to judge whether your answer might be fundamentally flawed when you eventually reach it. Making sure that you arrive at an answer that matches the question you asked is one of the jobs of research design, which we will consider in the next chapter. In the meantime, look back at the different types of question that we identified in Table 4.1 and see whether you can work out what would make an appropriate type of answer to each one. And what wouldn't.

Chapter summary and conclusion

This chapter has looked at the difference between a topic, a problem and a question. It has identified the qualities of good questions, and shown that, although there are many questions, there are only a few types of question and they can be represented by succinct, generalized forms. It is really important that you can identify clearly your overall topic area, the particular problem that you are interested in within that broad topic and the specific question(s) that you are asking. Only when you have done that can you think seriously about research design.

What to do after reading Chapter 4

Name your topic.

Define your problem by writing a sentence that begins 'I am trying to find out . . .'

Make a table with three columns. In the first column, list the question or questions that you will ask in order to solve your problem. In the second column, list the possible answers that you can get to each of your questions. In the third column, for each of the possible answers state what you will know if that answer turns out to be the right one. This will allow you to check whether you are asking useful questions, because if none of the possible answers leave you knowing anything useful, you have been asking the wrong question! This is a very preliminary form of research design.

Explain to your Mum, your cell-mate or your neighbour what you are going to do your dissertation on. If you want a real challenge, try tweeting your aim: 140 characters or fewer.

Set up your system for keeping records of what you read, whether that be a simple document file, a reference database or proprietary note-taking software. This is a first step towards your literature review, and will be useful throughout your project.

If you think things are going wrong, look at Chapter 10 and talk to your supervisor.

5

RESEARCH DESIGN 1

What approach should I take?

This chapter discusses different ways of approaching a topic and getting answers to questions, and encourages you to think about the different methodological approaches that might be most helpful to you.

Where to begin?

By the time you get to this stage, you should know what it is you are trying to do. You should have chosen a topic, identified a problem, specified the question(s) that you will tackle and know the type of answer(s) you are looking for.

This can be a very difficult moment. You've done all the planning you can think of and now you have to do the dissertation. It might be difficult to know where to start and the task ahead might suddenly look very big. Lots of people get this feeling. It's a sort of mental barrier – like writing the first word on a clean sheet of paper; not writer's block but doer's block. This is one of the reasons why a lot of students keep putting off the dissertation longer and longer and eventually have to do it all in a rush at the last minute. Don't be like that. You should have left space in your timetable to settle down and sort out in your mind exactly what you have to do. When you can see the steps ahead, progress becomes much easier. So, you know what your question is; now you want to know how to get the answer. That's what research design is all about, and the first part of research design is choosing a basic approach for your project. Are you going to do something involving laboratory experiments and hypothesis-testing, or are you going to some ethnographic participatory research, and will you be using spatial data in a Geographic Information System? Are you going to base your whole project on some particular theoretical background and produce work that is explicitly feminist or Marxist or post-structuralist? Are you going to do some numerical modelling? Are you determined to base your observations on soundscapes and auditory data rather than visual, textual or numerical data? There are lots of different directions in which you could set off. It is a good idea to give this some thought at the very beginning and make sure that you set off in the right direction.

This chapter and the next are intended to alert you to the issues you will need to consider as you set out to obtain the answer(s) to your research question(s). We can't tell you how to do your particular research project, but we can discuss the issues and give some examples that will contain something useful for you, whatever your project. You should take from these chapters the bits of advice that are useful in the context of your particular project, and you should be aware of the general issues that affect all research design, but you should also check to see if there are ideas here about other styles of research that you could somehow transfer to your project.

Some really innovative work could stem from applying techniques usually found in one part of a discipline to a topic usually approached in a different part of the discipline, or even to a topic in a completely different discipline.

A whole dissertation project could be based on exploring the application of a particular method to a particular topic or problem where it has not traditionally been applied. Many of the styles of research used in geography at present have only a short history within the discipline, either because they are relatively new inventions or because they have been imported relatively recently from other disciplines. Old text books may dwell on the use of questionnaire surveys, for example, but can the issues that were traditionally addressed by that method be more effectively addressed now by the use of social media networks, or participatory research, or the ethnographic analysis of blogs or diary entries? Could an approach from one part of the discipline be applied in an innovative way in another part? For example, could a physical geography student find some way of using focus groups or conversation analysis in the study of some geomorphological issue? Particularly in environmental topics, or topics looking at applied issues on the boundary between physical and human systems, this kind of cross-discipline thinking could lead to really interesting project ideas or research designs.

Getting answers to questions

There are lots of ways of getting answers to questions. For example, if you wanted to know how to get to the railway station, you could just ask someone. They would give you an answer, but of course you wouldn't know how much faith to put in that answer. If you wanted an answer that you could be more sure of, you could ask a police officer, look in the A–Z, use your Sat Nav or phone the railway company to ask. If your different sources gave different answers, or to convince yourself thoroughly, you might have to go over to the station and look for yourself. The point is that there are lots of ways of getting answers to any question, but sometimes the different approaches give different answers, and it isn't always easy to judge the reliability of the answers you get. Also, it is not necessarily the case that one answer is right and all the others are wrong. The police officer you asked about the way to the railway station might have assumed you were walking, but your Sat Nav may have assumed you were driving. Both answers may have been right (or wrong) depending on your perspective. When you do your own research project you need to find a way of getting answers that enable you to judge their reliability from a particular perspective. You need to be able to reach conclusions with confidence. It's no good getting an answer to your question if you don't know whether it's the right answer or not. You need to design a research programme that will lead you to a conclusion that is reliable in the context in which your research is set.

The role of theory

All research is underpinned by theory; that is, it is set in a context of previous ideas. That's what enables us to go forward and find out new things. At the most basic level, if your dissertation is concerned with sediment transport on hillslopes it is set in the context of Newton's theory of gravity. If your dissertation is concerned with gender relations represented in post-colonial literature, it may be set in the context of post-colonial theory, feminist theory, literary theory . . . there is always a theoretical background to the work that you are doing and, for a lot of geography projects, that theoretical background can stretch a long way into neighbouring disciplines. For some research topics the underlying theory is so well accepted that your dissertation need only refer to it briefly. In other areas, if theory is controversial or still relatively novel in the context of the discipline, or if your whole project focuses on the theory itself as an object of study, then clearly you will need to pay much more attention to your theoretical underpinnings. Throughout the history of the discipline some geographers, and some branches of geography, have been more interested in theory than others. Geomorphologist Richard Chorley famously wrote that geomorphologists would instinctively reach for their soil augers if anyone mentioned the word 'theory' (Chorley 1978, p.1). That difference between human and physical geographers is no longer so prominent, with much more attention being given to theoretical issues within physical geography than in the past. You cannot ignore the theory behind your work. However, the extent to which you need to include theory in your dissertation will depend on your topic. Your examiners won't necessarily expect you to include lengthy theoretical discussions in topics where theory is well known and uncontroversial.

If we have one generally accepted theoretical foundation for research on our particular topic there's nothing to discuss. On the other hand, if your dissertation is an internet mediated virtual ethnography of feminist chatrooms, in which the theoretical background may be complex, novel and controversial, your examiners will expect a discussion of that theoretical foundation. DeLyser et al. (2010b) described the rise of qualitative geography as being the subject of resistance and controversy, anger and acrimony, as the methods of qualitative research appeared, according to the norms of physical science, to be anecdotal, not replicable and not generalizable. If there is any risk of your theoretical underpinning arousing such strong responses, you should discuss it fully in your research proposal and in your finished dissertation. Writing about a project in which the researcher accompanied police officers on patrol in Los Angeles to explore how the worldview of the police helps to explain their specific actions, Herbert et al. (2005) described how the field data did not map neatly onto any pre-existing theoretical framework because reality was so much more complex than the theories allowed for. Their ethnographic fieldwork was therefore an opportunity to flesh out previously existing but inadequate theory. This would be a challenging mission for an undergraduate dissertation, but illustrates how the discussion of theory can be a major part of some research projects. There are many theoretical foundations that you might adopt to answer your question. You might address your topic from an explicitly critical-rationalist perspective, or from a non-positivist ethnographic participatory perspective, or a feminist perspective, or a Marxist one, and your theoretical standpoint would determine your approach. Some researchers think that the tradition of production of geographical knowledge is underpinned by colonialism and capitalism, and view their research in that light. Others don't. It can make a big difference to how they approach their work and therefore what they end up finding out, and how they present it. In your dissertation, it is important to decide early whether you need to address theoretical issues explicitly in your research or whether the theoretical under-pinnings of your topic are sufficiently uncontroversial that you can take them as given.

Methodology

In the previous section we have discussed the theory that underpins all research. To some extent theory and methodology overlap. You know what you want to find out; the question is how you should go about it. As we've seen in the example of finding the railway station, there are different ways of going about it, and these different ways may lead to different answers. All of them may be equally valid, but the validity of each will depend on the assumptions (or theory) that underpin it. So at this stage you need to give some thought to the overall approach you will take to answering your research question. This approach is sometimes referred to as your methodology.

There are many ways you could go about your research. But, first, you need to check if your institution has any rules that might limit your options. In the past, there was an expectation that a dissertation would involve students going out and doing fieldwork to collect the data they would need to answer their question. With increasing availability of data archives, and remote sensing data, together with more sophisticated methods for data analysis, the emphasis on fieldwork as part of a dissertation has lessened, and the opportunities for taking different approaches to the same question have expanded. Consider the different approaches to the same topic in Table 5.1. In the first study, you might imagine a project that looked at topography, traffic density on streets and so on and then compare different routes according to how far you would have to walk, how many hills you would have to climb, how much car exhaust you might have to breathe and so on. In the second study, you might expect accounts of how the researcher accompanied people to the railway station and observed decisions they took. In the third you might find an analysis of how different factors might lead to different routes to the railway station, or how they affected the time taken to get to the railway station. This study might be different from the others because it might not tell you anything about what does happen, but about what might happen under certain conditions. That third approach would be good for a project that was interested in planning how the local transport network should be developed to cope with likely future changes in population characteristics, for example. Modelling is often a good way of tackling 'What if?' questions. You can expand this table for yourself by thinking of alternative approaches and imagining what they might

Table 5.1 Different methodologies for tackling the same problem

TOPIC: Routes to the railway station	
APPROACH:	MIGHT INVOLVE:
A GIS approach	Putting map data, traffic information etc into a GIS . . .
Participatory research	Accompanying different types of people on their journeys to the station . . .
Gravity modelling	Comparing the catchment areas of different stations . . .
Through the lens of environmental sustainability	(fill in with your own ideas . . .)
	Add more rows of your own . . .

involve. Fill in the blank cells yourself and add more rows of your own. You can then try to produce a similar kind of table for your own specific project. What different approaches might researchers take to your topic? And which of those are you going to choose?

So the first thing you need to do at this stage is decide on the approach you will take. Unless your institution has specific rules about what constitutes a dissertation, this is entirely your choice. Most institutions would not allow a dissertation with the title 'Getting to the Railway Station: A Survey of Recent Literature' because a literature review is not usually sufficient for a dissertation. But check with your supervisor what specific rules apply in your case before you commit yourself to a particular methodology.

As always in these opening stages of the project one way to get ideas is to look at the previous literature in your area. What approaches have other people adopted? Do you want to do the same and make a comparative study? Perhaps you want to try something deliberately different. Either way, your own approach needs to be developed in the context of previous researchers' approaches so you will need to have read about them.

Also read (and think) about what each methodology will actually entail. If you took a participatory approach you might need to spend quite a bit of time walking to the railway station with different people. Do you have the time to do this?

Some approaches might be more useful than others, and that will often depend on the type of question you are trying to answer. Being clear on your question, and its implications for your research design, is really important.

Matching your research design to your question

The research design that you employ, in other words the way you go about your dissertation, depends on what you are trying to find out. That sounds like common sense, but failure to bear it in mind has led to the downfall of many promising projects.

There may seem to be an almost infinite number of different research projects for which you might be trying to design a research programme. You might be trying to find out when a medieval settlement was abandoned, whether the development of a Single European Airspace could help mitigate the transport disruption caused by any future

Eric says . . .

One of the most helpful things my supervisor keeps asking when I get stuck is: 'What are you trying to find out?'

volcanic ash cloud, why a river has changed its course, whether an influx of refugees is likely to have a positive impact on a local economy, how sabotage of oil pipelines reflects indigenous politics, where best to locate a new cinema, how best to apply some particular social theory to some particular problem in post-colonial geography or how to measure beach erosion. You could be trying to find out almost anything when you do your dissertation. However, as we mentioned in Chapter 4, you can reduce this almost infinite list to a very short list if you think not about individual titles but about what type of question you are asking. Are you asking a 'when' question, a 'what' question, a 'why' question, a 'what if' question or a 'how' question? Is it a 'who', or a 'does', or an 'is', or an 'are', or a 'will', or a 'should'? As we emphasize throughout this book, different types of question demand different types of answer. If you are asking 'why?', then your answer should involve an element of 'because'. If you know that you want a 'because' answer, then be sure to ask a 'why' question. Are you looking for a 'yes', a '27', or a 'because the ground was wet'? Do you want a date, or a location? Are you looking for a process? Are you looking for the murderer, the murder weapon, the motive or a judgement of guilt? Do you want a description of what happened in history or a prediction of what will happen in the future? Make sure that your question matches the kind of answer you are looking for.

One of the most commonly used distinctions is among (1) studies concerned with description or narrative (what is the world like?); (2) studies concerned with explanation (why is the world like it is?); and (3) studies that form judgements (should the world be like it is?). Not all projects fit conveniently into those categories and many combine elements of each. Predictive studies, for example, often rely on understanding both what the world is like now, and why, to predict how it is likely to change. Policy studies then use those predictions to propose actions.

Many historical studies, in both human and physical geography, are descriptive. For example: what was the vegetation like here at this point in history? When did agriculture begin at this place? What has been the history of climate change at this place? Many regional studies tend towards narrative description. For example: 'Landscapes of East Anglia' or 'Tin Mining in Cornwall'. Predictive studies can also be essentially descriptive: what will this be like in the future, or what will be the sequence of events if we change this variable? So a 'what if' question is really just a special type of 'what' question.

Explanatory studies are different from descriptive studies in that they tend to look for causal relationships, and therefore are often process-related. For example: why was vegetation like this at that time? What caused agriculture to begin at that time? Why does crime have a geographical dimension? How does increased volcanic activity cause climate to change? Why will the stability of this hillslope be likely to change in response to future agricultural development? There are many philosophical arguments about what constitutes explanation, and this question has led to much discussion in the social sciences (see, for example, Chapter 9 in Cloke et al., 2004) about appropriate ways to identify causal mechanisms for social phenomena, or even, indeed, if causal mechanisms can be identified. If your dissertation question is one that questions why something happens/exists then you need to give some thought to what you mean by explanation. At one level, you might argue that an explanatory study is no more than a sophisticated description (you are describing the relationship between two phenomena, for example, between volcanoes and climate).

The third type of question, about judgements of value, is one that physical scientists would traditionally not generally accept as falling within the realm of scientific research, but one that social scientists would consider as a valid research topic. In many topics in geography, the distinction between the physical and human sides of the discipline breaks down as we start to consider applied geography and look at issues where the whole point of a research topic is to identify possible interventions, which, inherently, imply some kind of a judgement call. Looking for the 'best' way to stabilize an eroding coastline implies that political, social, economic and ethical judgements as well as scientific principles are in play even if the cliff stabilization question is treated, at least superficially, as a 'physical geography' issue. A physical geographer might be more likely to focus on the idea that if you wanted to change the environment in this way, this research provides a method for doing so. For example, a physical geographer might be happy to identify a series of possible responses to climate change but less happy to prescribe a specific social response. A human geographer might be more likely to ask questions about whether we should, or should not, wish to change the environment to make the world a better place, and might more readily engage with the question of what would be the best response to climate change. The physical geographer might feel that deciding what was best fell outside the scope of the work. The human geographer might see that as fundamental to the work.

The distinctions that people (and textbooks) often make between human geography, physical geography and environmental geography are somewhat simplistic, and we encourage you to think beyond disciplinary boundaries of this type. Increasingly, projects like this are being done by researchers who do not think of themselves as either physical or human geographers but as environmental scientists, environmental engineers or something that defies a conventional disciplinary label. This is especially so when projects are of an applied nature, making links between theory and practice in topics where the outcome is of direct relevance to human activity.

At the end of the last chapter you wrote a sentence beginning 'I am trying to find out ...'. Make sure now that you are clear what kind of question you are asking, and

---

Are you a social scientist, a natural scientist or an environmental scientist?

Erica says . . .

All three! I'm a geographer!

what kind of answer it demands. As we said in Chapter 4, it is sometimes helpful to break your question down into an almost algebraic form. Replace all the nouns with letters, leaving only the verbs or interrogatives to define your project. For example, if your project is 'Does forest clearance in Grampian Region cause accelerated soil erosion?' it will become 'Does A cause B?'. If you try this with a number of different project titles, you'll begin to see that all the different projects you can think of fall into only a small number of categories. There are only a small number of types of question. This simplifies the problem of finding the right research design for your project.

Should I model?

Modelling is a term that is used very widely to cover a variety of things. Demerrit and Wainwright (2005) define models as simplified representations or abstractions of reality, which could include physical analogues, scale models, box-and-arrow schematic diagrams and mathematical simulations. We are going to focus on two modelling approaches in particular. First, modelling can be regarded as a technique for finding things out, much like fieldwork. You can use a modelling approach actually to do your dissertation. This can be done in different ways, but many of these can conveniently be put under the headings 'physical modelling' and 'numerical or theoretical modelling'. Second, modelling can be used as a way of simplifying reality to describe how we think the world works. This conceptual modelling can help with your dissertation. For example, when you are trying to sort out your project aims by identifying what is and is not already known, and when you are trying to summarize what your project has actually contributed to the sum of human knowledge when you write your conclusion.

Physical modelling

Much physical modelling can be described as 'analogue modelling', in which you replace the process that you are interested in with something else which, you think, behaves in a similar fashion but which has benefits compared to the original process that make it easier to study. Many landscape processes operate so slowly or over such large areas that it is unrealistic to make direct measurement of these processes. An analogue process that behaves the same way, but which operates much faster or over a much smaller area is, therefore, potentially useful. For example, suppose you wanted to investigate how erosion processes fashion hillslopes. These processes take thousands of years to achieve their effect because the rock and soil of which the ground is composed is relatively resistant to the water, ice and wind which fashion them. So you might decide to look for some more easily erodible material. One such material is ice. You could run water over a block of ice and see how the shape of the ice changed, or more usefully, see if it changed in the way you expected it to change.

Perhaps the most widely used physical models in physical environmental sciences are flumes in which you can model river processes, waves, estuaries, debris flows and a range of other physical processes and environments. Given the readily available data on river discharges, there are good opportunities to compare results from flume studies with real rivers and to use real data to guide you in designing flume experiments. Many physical geographers have specialist laboratories that would allow you to undertake physical modelling. For example, one of us has a low-temperature laboratory and the other has a rainfall simulation laboratory. Others have climate chambers in which you can simulate the processes of weathering. You may well have been introduced to specialist laboratories in your department during your course, but it's worth checking if other facilities exist in your department, or elsewhere in your university, to which you may be given access for your dissertation.

Although physical modelling does enable you to gain some insights into how processes work, it suffers from the limitation of how well the analogue retains the essential properties of the thing you are trying to model. The erosion of ice, which we mentioned above, does not work exactly like the erosion of rock, for example. Consequently, you always have to face the problem of deciding whether your results are telling you about the process you are investigating or about the differences between the analogue and the real thing. Nonetheless, this should not deter you from undertaking a dissertation that employs physical modelling, particularly if it is something you are likely to enjoy doing.

Numerical and theoretical modelling

Numerical modelling provides a very powerful means of testing ideas about how the world works in many areas of geography. Unfortunately, it is an approach that few geography students employ in their dissertations, perhaps because many geography students are reluctant to engage with things mathematical. However, if you don't suffer from such reluctance, undertaking a dissertation that employs numerical modelling is one way in which you might attract your examiners' interest. Paul Krugman won the Nobel Prize for Economics in 2008 for work on trade patterns and the location of economic activity, and the models associated with his work had a major impact on our understanding of economic development and location decisions (Ivanova, 2013). Perhaps your dissertation will lead to a Nobel Prize. In discussing this topic Ivanova (2013) points out that freight transport modelling has lagged behind the development of passenger transport modelling. That's the sort of comment that should make a geography student think: dissertation opportunity?

Numerical modelling can be a form of deductive logic (see Chapter 6). You define the rules (i.e. the processes) in terms of a set of equations that describe how a system seems to work; you see what these rules produce when you run the model; you compare the outcome with reality; and, if the two don't match, you have shown that the rules are wrong. If they do match, then the rules may be correct. You can then go on and do something more: you can change some of the variables in your model while still retaining your validated rules, and run 'what-if' scenarios. What would happen (according to our model) if we increased or decreased population, or rainfall, or transport costs? Much numerical modelling is undertaken by computer simulation so, as well as having a reasonable mathematical background, you are likely to need some ability at computer programming to undertake this type of dissertation. However, some of these topics might be amenable to modelling through GIS software that has built-in tools for geostatistical analysis that don't require high-level computational expertise.

GIS includes built-in, user-friendly geostatistical tools for modelling.

Interestingly, modelling is one area where the physical and human sides of geography meet unexpectedly in the mathematics. For example, the freight or passenger transport systems that we discussed a moment ago are often modelled using what are called gravity models. These models are based not on any behavioural theory but on equations from Newtonian physics, but they have proved very effective in many economic spatial contexts despite the apparent incongruity in underlying theory. We will not provide any comprehensive review here of different approaches to modelling, but there is plenty of useful literature available if you want to go in that direction, including Wainwright and Mulligan (2004) on the environmental side and, if you were interested in those transport examples above, Tavasszy and de Jong (2013), among many others.

To show how numerical modelling can be used to investigate a problem, let's look at how Wainwright et al. (1995) used that approach to investigate the formation of desert pavement. These authors came up with the idea that desert pavement might be formed by the action of raindrops falling on the ground surface. Obviously, there are different ways of investigating this hypothesis. They could have set up an experimental plot and seen what happened to the plot under natural rainfall. However, it doesn't rain a lot in deserts so they may have been waiting a long time for anything to happen and, what's more, the process may take a long time to achieve much. Second, they could have set up the same plot but used a rainfall simulator to solve the problem of the shortage of natural rain. Both of these approaches would have told them whether or not the action of raindrops did cause desert pavement to form. The third approach, numerical modelling, is a bit different. In the first two approaches they wouldn't need to know how raindrops work in order to test the hypothesis, but in the third they would. So the outcomes are a bit different. In the case of the first two (the field investigations) it is possible to discover whether or not the action of raindrops can produce desert pavement. In the case of the numerical modelling, if the simulation leads to the formation of pavement then this outcome may mean that (a) the action of raindrops can form desert pavement and (b) we know how the process works; or it may mean that their equations describing the process are wrong and that desert pavement will form under the operation of these incorrect equations but not under the operation of the correct ones. Conversely, if the simulation shows that desert pavement doesn't form, then it means either that the action of raindrops cannot form desert pavement or that the equations are wrong!

You may think this all sounds a bit pessimistic and inconclusive. You may be wondering why Wainwright et al. would have bothered with the modelling approach. One reason, obviously, is that sooner or later, we are going to need to understand how the processes work if we are to develop a true understanding of the formation of desert pavement (or anything else) and the modelling approach does provide a test of our present understanding. Furthermore, modelling, as we shall see, does provide useful insights that may not easily be obtainable any other way.

To run their model Wainwright et al. needed suitable equations describing the processes of raindrop detachment and splash erosion. Like most modellers, they simply went to the library and found out what equations were available in the existing literature and used these. They also needed some initial surface to which to apply the processes described by their equations. Again, they went to the library and found some descriptions of desert soils. Consequently, they were, in this case, using secondary data for their modelling. With this information they were able to construct their model and produce simulations of the results. They found that desert pavement did form (sort of) but, interestingly, the nature of the pavement varied with the initial soil type. None of the previously existing literature on desert pavement talked of differences in the nature of the pavement in response to the initial soil type so this modelling study had identified something that might be worth looking for in the field.

Simulation modelling, of the type practised by Wainwright et al., is a sort of computer game! Like most computer games, it is very easy to spend a lot of time on it. If you undertake field data collection for your dissertation you are likely to find yourself worrying about having enough data, whereas such problems are unlikely to trouble you in simulation modelling. Change a parameter here, or an exponent there, and you can be off in a whole new set of simulations. The challenge is to know when to stop! Don't swamp your examiners with pages and pages of computer output. If you do, they will almost certainly ignore it and turn to the end of it to find out what you made of it. If the analysis and discussion of it aren't as weighty as the output itself the examiners will probably take a dim view of what you have done.

Don't swamp your examiners with pages of undigested computer output.

GIS can be regarded as a type of modelling, in that you can input different values for specific parameters and see what outcomes arise. What would happen to surface drainage routes if we made these changes to topographic gradients? Would we be able to see this proposed windfarm at location X from our beauty spot at location Y if we planted conifer woodland at location Z? In working these things out, GIS gives you a choice about how much you engage with the mathematics behind the modelling. If you want, you can get deeply involved in the geostatistics behind the GIS, but if you prefer you can let the software do the mathematics for you, as most GIS packages have a user-friendly interface that hides the equations and numerical work behind buttons with easy-to-understand labels. If modelling seems like the right way for your project to go, but you are afraid of getting involved with the maths, then GIS might be the way forward for you. Similarly the results of GIS analysis come out, typically, in an immediately accessible and visual format without the need for complex manipulations. GIS allows you to carry out complex geostatistical analysis of spatial data without feeling that you are doing mathematical modelling, and without the need for an advanced mathematical background or training.

You don't have to create your own model to do a successful dissertation. There are plenty of existing models that you can use as the basis for a project either by applying an existing model to a specific new problem (for example, applying a soil erosion model to a location where changes in land use have been proposed) or by testing a model to try and improve it (for example, by applying it to a type of situation, or at a scale, or over a duration for which it has not previously been applied). Many models in both human and physical geography are widely used in planning and environmental management and could be a good starting point for a dissertation.

Conceptual modelling

A conceptual model that expresses the way we think the world works can be useful in an empirical dissertation both early on, when you are trying to sort out the questions you are trying to answer, and towards the end, when you are trying to tie together the results of your empirical investigation.

A conceptual model can be used to show how the various parts of your study fit together.

To look at how conceptual modelling can assist you in designing your research, let's assume, for example, that your dissertation aims to address the problem of the decline of retail services in rural Nottinghamshire. You might formulate a model for this decline as shown in Figure 5.1. Your model proposes that the decline in retail services is due to a falling demand for such services because of rural–urban migration and that this process provides a positive feedback to cause further decline in retail services. In addition, your model indicates a number of factors that contribute to cause the rural–urban migration. The conceptual model is here being used rather like a complex multi-part hypothesis. This model, therefore, provides you with the questions you need to ask. The most important of these is 'Has there been rural–urban migration?' If there is no evidence for

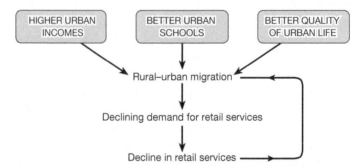

Figure 5.1 Proposed conceptual model for declining rural retail services

this, then your model is falsified (see Chapter 6). If, on the other hand, you do find evidence of rural–urban migration, you might be prepared to accept your model as probably correct and focus upon the causes of the migration. If you investigate income, education and quality of life but find that none of them shows any difference between rural and urban areas, that would not invalidate your model. It would simply show that some other mechanism was responsible for the migration that you had observed. The conceptual model thus allows you to see (and explain) clearly how the various parts of your planned investigation fit together.

Where do *you* fit into doing your dissertation?

Throughout this book, we have emphasized your role in your dissertation – the benefits to you in doing it, how you can use your own interests to select a topic and so on. What role do you, as an individual, have in the doing of it? Would the outcome be just the same if you handed the whole thing over to Erica at this point?

There are three possible answers to this question:

1   It should be just the same if Erica did it, and you should strive to make it so.
2   It wouldn't be the same, and we must reluctantly acknowledge this fact.
3   It shouldn't be the same if Erica did it.

Most physical scientists would think the answer should be (1). Whereas you have an important role in deciding what question to ask, how the question is answered should not depend on your identity. This answer underpins the notion of a repeatable scientific experiment. If you were to drop balls from the leaning tower of Pisa you should get exactly the same result that Galileo did. However, research isn't quite as straightforward as repeating somebody else's experiment, particularly in a field-based subject. No matter how carefully you try to design your research, and no matter how far you think you have a research design that will cover all eventualities, you can be sure that the unexpected will arise. You are likely to find that the method for collecting your soil samples, for example, has failed to provide a procedure for deciding what to do if your sampling point lands on a fallen tree trunk. Inevitably, while actually doing your dissertation, situations will arise in which decisions about procedure have to be made. It's at this point that Erica might make a different decision from yours. You might decide to move the fallen tree trunk, but Erica might set up a rule for choosing a new sampling point when the original one is inaccessible. If they are well thought out in the context of the research question, both your decision and Erica's are equally valid. Provided you document how you dealt with such matters, you are well on the way to having a repeatable experiment. However, just as you may have found unexpected occurrences when you tried to collect your data, so somebody else trying to repeat your work could come across an eventuality that you hadn't encountered and that you therefore hadn't documented a procedure for. So, even if physical scientists might like the answer to be (1), there are good reasons why it might turn out to be (2).

Many social scientists, on the other hand, think the answer should be (3). If you are conducting a piece of research that involves your interaction with a community as part of your study of how that community works (for example, conducting interviews) then your identity and the way you interact with your subject will influence both the outcome of the research and the way you subsequently write up your project. If Erica, rather than Eric, were conducting the interviews she may obtain different responses from those that Eric would obtain (this issue is sometimes referred to as 'positionality'). Even if both Erica and Eric used the same approaches to their analysis, they may well reach quite different conclusions. Some social scientists would argue that because your identity is so closely linked to your research you should involve yourself wholly within your report, writing it up as a first-person account. Others, however, would argue that there is an important distinction between research that recognizes the subjectivity of its findings and research that becomes a personal story told by Eric that may be of no relevance to Erica. At one extreme, then, you might try to exclude yourself from having any influence on the research process, and write your account in an entirely impersonal style, while at the other extreme you might immerse yourself as a participant in the very system that you are studying and write your account as a participant as much as an observer. When we come to think about styles of writing later in this book, this issue will return as we consider whether dissertations should be written in the first person (I, we, our) or in the entirely impersonal style typical of traditional scientific reports. Either way, you need to give some thought to your identity and its implications for your research design. Can YOU, in fact, obtain the answer to your research question? With your specific age, ethnicity and social background will you get honest answers if you try to get data from face-to-face interviews with those particular subjects? Good research design is about making sure that you can reach a reliable answer, from the starting point of your question, via all the obstacles or opportunities presented by your identity, your theoretical background and other constraints.

Chapter summary and conclusion

There are many different ways of approaching research in geography and related disciplines. Even a particular question about a particular topic can be approached in many different ways depending on your theoretical position and methodological framework. It is important that you decide on your approach at this stage in the planning process, before you develop the details of your specific research design. You need to develop a strong research design before you embark on your data collection, and you need to be clear about your overall approach before you set up your research design. At this stage your topic, aim, question and approach should be coming together into a coherent starting point for your project.

What to do after reading Chapter 5

Make sure you are very clear on exactly what your topic is, and what you are trying to find out, and make sure that you have identified a broad approach – a philosophical position or methodology – that is appropriate to your topic, problem, question and aim. Complete the sentence: 'I am trying to find out . . . and my overall approach is . . .' (For example: 'I am trying to find out whether Knight (1989) was correct about the origin of stratified facies basal ice in Greenland and my approach is to use field observations of ice structures in a hypothesis-testing strategy').

Talk about your research idea with as many people as possible, and try thinking it through from different points of view to see whether a different approach might be more appropriate than the one you have in mind.

Keep reading as much as you can about the topic you are working on, and about the different approaches that have been applied previously to research in that topic.

6

RESEARCH DESIGN 2

Exactly how should I do this project?

This chapter discusses the importance of logic in your research, considers different ways of organizing a research strategy, and gives you some suggestions about putting together your first research proposal.

Research design

Research design is critical to any piece of research. It is like the architect's drawings for the builder; it is like the field marshall's battle plan; it is like the explorer's map for the treasure hunter. Without a sound research design your research will get lost, your project will be defeated and your dissertation, if it ever gets built, will fall down. It is hardly surprising, then, that scientists and philosophers have dedicated much effort to the study of research design. However, although there is a substantial literature into which you might delve, no consensus has really emerged as to a universally applicable 'best method' or 'best way of finding out'. Partly because there is such a choice of approaches, and partly because not all researchers have taken as much time as they should to consider those choices, you will be able to find all sorts of different types of research design if you look in the current research journals in your field. You should be able to judge for yourself that some are more effective than others, and that different approaches are valid for different types of research. As we said earlier, there are lots of different ways of getting answers to questions. Your task is to find the best one for your project.

It is very important that your research design is sound, and although all this 'philosophical' background might seem far removed from the business of your dissertation, it is, in fact, central to it. It is worth being familiar with the different sorts of reasoning that you might be using, so that you are in a position to make sure of using them properly and not leaving your dissertation open to painful criticism from the examiners! We said in Chapter 2 that in your dissertation you have to find out something. If you reach the conclusion in your dissertation (as we hope you will) that you have found out X, then you have made a claim to knowledge. Philosophy is partly about the validity of claims to knowledge (sometimes referred to as epistemology). You need to know (and demonstrate to your examiners) that you are aware of the perspective of your claim and the assumptions on which it rests. If everybody was agreed that there was a 'best' way of finding things out and that there was only one perspective from which knowledge could be regarded as valid, you wouldn't have to worry about this in your dissertation. If you ask somebody in the street what time it is, it is assumed by both of you that you mean local time, and not the time in Hong Kong, so you don't need to discuss the issue. But, as we illustrated earlier, if you ask the way to the railway station, there are different perspectives from which you could be asking this question, and you do need to make your perspective clear to the person you are asking.

Typical comments made by dissertation examiners:

1   The critical-rationalist approach you have used is not really appropriate to this sort of project.
2   The logic of the research design was clearly explained.
3   You should have considered a qualitative approach to data collection.
4   It was not sufficiently clear exactly what you were trying to do.

We said in Chapter 5 that there are a lot of different ways of approaching a research project, and discussed the importance of choosing an appropriate approach for your own research. There is a lot of literature on approaches to research and you are almost certain to have come across some of it in your course. We don't intend to discuss all of these approaches here, because that is not what this book is about, but let's look at a few questions and the implications of taking different approaches to address them. Our aim is to encourage you now to think about your research question(s) and about which approach to research design will be best for your particular project.

Sample dissertation question I: Does social group affect tourist behaviour?
You might tackle this topic using a variety of approaches. If you took a behaviouralist approach you might seek to understand how tourist behaviour varied among social groups according to their response to information about the tourist destination that was presented to them. If, on the other hand, you took a Marxist approach to the problem you might seek to explore whether inequality of use of the tourist destination resulted from economic and social deprivation of some social groups. But, equally, you might take a feminist approach in which you could examine how differences in opportunities provided by a tourist destination arose from a gender bias in the way those opportunities were presented to tourists from specific social groups. All of these approaches would lead to insights into the question posed by the dissertation. But they would lead to different insights. The quality of the insight would depend both on how well you had conducted your research and on the relevance of the approach that you adopted.

Sample dissertation question II: How does substrate quality affect the decomposition dynamics of plant residue?
If you took a critical-rationalist approach to this question you would set up hypotheses and seek to falsify them. For example, you might test the hypothesis that a less permeable

substrate accelerates the decomposition dynamics of plant residue. Setting up several such hypotheses may not be an efficient way of answering the question. On the other hand, if you took an inferential approach you would explore the effects without any preconceived hypotheses. This would be a useful approach if you already knew (or were prepared to assume) that the substrate had an effect and you were seeking to quantify it. Such an approach might be a precursor to a subsequent study using your conclusions as its hypothesis.

Sample dissertation question III: What is the role of agroforestry in the UK?
Here you might take a structuralist approach in which you focused upon economic and social frameworks that could influence the role of agroforestry. But you might also take a behaviouralist approach where your focus would be farmers' attitudes to agroforestry and how those attitudes influenced the role of agroforestry. Again, these approaches would lead to different insights into the question posed. We suggested earlier that valuable insights can stem from applying an unexpected approach to your problem. Suppose you tried applying, for example, an ethnographic approach to this question. How might you do that? What insights might an ethnographic study permit that would be unlikely to arise from another approach? Does choosing that approach make you look again at the question and wonder whether it could be set up in a more useful way?

Even from these few examples, we can draw out some key concepts that will help you to sort out your own research and, in particular, how you conduct your research within a particular framework. These are the concept of logic, which needs to be applied to any type of research design, and the concepts of induction (or inductive reasoning) and deduction (deductive reasoning), which in themselves represent specific types of logic or specific types of research design. These are used very explicitly in some forms of research design (such as hypothesis testing) but are important underpinnings to clear thought even if your research design is not of that type.

Logic

Logic is the branch of philosophy concerned with reasoning. From our point of view logic is all about distinguishing good arguments from bad ones, and about ensuring that our reasoning is sound.

Your dissertation, or any piece of research, is an exercise in reasoning, so logic is very important in your research design.

From our everyday experience we are all familiar with 'working things out'. For example, we might have to work out what time to set the alarm clock in order to make a morning lecture, allowing time for breakfast, for walking the dog (unless Eric can come over and walk him for us) and for the vagaries of the bus service. In that situation we would check the bus timetable, ask Eric if he could come over, allow the usual time for breakfast and work out the time to set the alarm. Our powers of reasoning enable us to do that, and our skill in logic enables us to reason soundly. If Eric could walk the dog, we would be able to set the alarm later. If we were late for the lecture and said it was because we had to walk the dog and the alarm didn't go off, our punctuality could be criticized but our logic would be impeccable. If we were late and said it was because Eric walked the dog so we had more time, no one would be able to follow our reasoning. It would be illogical. (NB: this can be a useful technique when trying to excuse your late essay etc.!) With everyday examples it is usually easy to spot 'bad reasoning' or illogical argument. In research, where the subject matter is less familiar and the 'right' answer is less obvious, it isn't always so easy. That's why we always need to be sure that our logic is in order and our reasoning is sound. If they are not, then the conclusions we reach will be invalid (wrong, meaningless, worthless).

In philosophy, logic is often divided into two branches: inductive and deductive. In the literature about research design, the terms inductive and deductive have sometimes been misused, and it is a confusing job trying to match up the descriptions and examples of the two that you might find in different sources. The following points might help.

Inductive reasoning

Inductive logic is concerned with the soundness of making inferences for which the evidence is not absolutely conclusive, and inductive reasoning is the process of reaching those inferences. If a body of evidence points in a particular direction, inductive logic could be applied to judge the strength of the inference or conclusion to which the evidence points. For example, if the accused in a murder trial has motive, opportunity, no alibi, his footprints at the scene and his fingerprints on the strangled victim's neck, inductive logic would lead us, through inference, to suspect the man's guilt. Our inductive logic suggests that the conclusion is probably correct, although the evidence is not incontrovertible. Although there is no conclusive proof that this is the murderer, there is a weight of evidence in favour of that conclusion.

It is characteristic of inductive reasoning that from a series of individual observations (for example, the fingerprints, the footprints, the dodgy alibi) each of which is 'true' but which are not individually conclusive, we put together a body of evidence from which we arrive at a general conclusion.

If we make an observation over and over again, and it always turns out the same way, then we reach a general conclusion on the basis of a number of our individual observations. When Galileo dropped a number of different objects from the top of his tower and found that they all fell at the same rate, he inferred a general truth from his specific observations, and it became a 'law of nature' that all bodies fall with a particular acceleration under the influence of gravity. For all Galileo could say, there might one day be an object that falls at a different rate, just as new DNA evidence might one day turn up to acquit the alleged strangler in our previous case, but the weight of observations so far allows us to infer our conclusion. Suppose someone asks you if a dissertation needs to have a good reference list to get a First Class mark. If you say that all the First Class dissertations you've ever seen have clear reference lists at the end while some of the Third Class dissertations have not, and that you therefore believe that you do need a reference list to get a First Class mark, then you are employing inductive reasoning. You cannot be absolutely sure that your conclusion is undoubtedly correct, but the evidence supports it.

To illustrate an inductive approach to research you might consider Mercer's (1999) study of the role of non-governmental organizations (NGOs) in Tanzania. In this study, Mercer sought to answer the question 'Are NGOs making a difference?' She presented a range of evidence (that NGOs were disproportionately represented in Dar es Salaam and the richer parts of the country, that they were not independent of the state, that attempts were being made to co-opt the local NGO sector into social service provision, etc.), such that she was able to conclude that 'the NGO policy is unlikely to facilitate structural and sustainable changes in state–society relations' (p.252). Many studies in geography employ an inductive approach.

Deductive reasoning

Deductive logic is concerned with the rules for determining when an argument is valid, and deductive reasoning is thus concerned to establish conclusive inferences, or what we might call in common speech 'definite' conclusions. In other words, from our point of view, it's about whether or not your argument can show if something really is true or false.

Deductive logic is not interested in the weight of evidence that leads to an inference, but in the validity or conclusiveness of the argument.

Let's go back to the example of reference lists at the end of the previous section. If you argue that dissertations must adhere to the departmental guidelines in order to get a First Class mark, that the need for a reference list is stressed in the guidelines, and that you therefore conclude (deduce) that you need a reference list to get a First Class mark, then you are employing deductive reasoning. If your premises are correct, then your reasoning soundly and inevitably leads to your conclusion. Whereas inductive reasoning can be said to work from the particular to the general (for example, from the particular instances of objects falling to the general law about falling objects), deductive reasoning can be said to work from the general to the particular. With the example of the reference lists, inductive reasoning begins with the particular instances of dissertations that you have read and works from those instances to an inference about dissertations in general. Deductive reasoning begins with the general rules about dissertations and works from that general framework to the specific issue of your particular dissertation.

Deductive logic seeks to differentiate between valid reasoning and invalid or unsound reasoning. In common usage when someone says 'that's illogical' about something, they usually mean it is deductively unsound. One of the best known forms of deductive reasoning is the syllogism. A syllogism is a formal argument consisting of two premises and a conclusion. For example:

Example 1 (sound reasoning)

Proposition 1 (premise):   All ice-cream sellers wear white hats.
Proposition 2 (premise):   Tony is an ice-cream seller.
Proposition 3 (conclusion):   Tony will wear a white hat.

In Example 1, if the two premises are true, then the conclusion cannot be false, and the argument is therefore valid. Of course, the premises may be false (for example, it might not be true that all ice-cream sellers wear white hats), in which case the conclusion would also be false, although the logic is sound. We could think of the whole argument as being 'If all ice-cream sellers wear white hats, and if Tony is an ice-cream seller, then Tony must wear a white hat.' The conclusion is a prediction based on the premises.

Example 2 (unsound reasoning)

Proposition 1 (premise):   All ice-cream sellers wear white hats.
Proposition 2 (premise):   Tony wears a white hat.
Proposition 3 (conclusion):   Tony must be an ice-cream seller.

In other words: 'If all ice-cream sellers wear white hats, then if Tony wears a white hat he must be an ice-cream seller.' In Example 2, even if the premises are true the conclusion might be false, because other people as well as ice-cream sellers can wear white hats. The argument is clearly unsound. There are all sorts of mistakes that can make an argument unsound. Many, such as circular reasoning (e.g. 'I believe in God because the Bible says He exists and I believe in the Bible because it is the word of God') are familiar in everyday usage and easy to identify. When you are dealing with unfamiliar subjects in your research where the 'answer' is not intuitively obvious, you need to take great care to ensure the validity of your argument. Any good textbook on logic will provide you with a substantial list of logical fallacies that must be avoided in your work.

Here are examples of faulty logic (even though the premises are true, the reasoning is invalid) and of sound logic (even though the premises may be false, the reasoning is valid):

Example 1: Unsound logic

All men are human beings.
All women are human beings
Therefore all women are men.

Example 2: Sound logic

All idiots are happy.
All geographers are idiots.
Therefore all geographers are happy.

You need to be able to recognize good from bad reasoning in your own work and in situations where the right answer is not immediately obvious. How about:

Example 3

Some pearls are not white.
All white things are beautiful.
Therefore some beautiful things are not pearls.

It is often a useful exercise to put your own research arguments into this format and see whether they are really valid. Incidentally, the beautiful pearls example above is unsound.

In constructing an argument where a conclusion follows from premises, your argument must be logical and your premises must be sound. If your argument is logical then the strength of your conclusion depends on the strength of your premises. In your research you will need to accept certain pieces of information as being true without questioning them. This is part of the framework in which your research is set. For example, if your dissertation involves use of the gravitational constant, you will assume that its value is 9.81 ms^{-2}. You would not be expected to test that as part of your project. These are your assumptions, and the strength of your conclusion is limited by the strength of those assumptions. However, your conclusions are also coloured by your theoretical or philosophical standpoint, for example, by your willingness to make value judgements and, if you do so, by your personal or professional values.

Consider the following:

Example 1

Cats kill birds.
People like birds.
Therefore cat-owning should be discouraged.

Example 2

Cats kill birds.
People like birds.
Therefore people should be encouraged to dislike birds.

Example 3

Cats kill birds.
People like birds.
Therefore cats should be discouraged from killing birds.

The same observations can inspire different policy decisions in different observers. It is important to be aware of where the boundary falls between logic and judgement, and whether your branch of the discipline expects research to cross that boundary.

To illustrate a deductive approach to research you might consider Knight's (1989) study of the way that layers of clean ice and debris-rich ice are entrained into the base of a glacier. Knight set out specifically to find out whether the idea that both types of ice were entrained by the same freezing mechanism, which had been suggested in previous literature, was actually right. To do this, he identified a specific characteristic (the isotopic composition) that would be the same in both the clean ice and the debris-rich if, and only if, both ice types had been formed by the same freezing mechanism. Before he even collected the data, Knight could say that if, and only if, his measurements showed isotopic differences between the ice types, then the idea that they formed in the same way could be thrown out. They did, and it was. Many studies in geography and in other disciplines employ a deductive approach.

Designing your own research

By now, we hope, you are beginning to see that getting an answer to your question, or doing your research, involves more than just making some measurements and hoping they 'give you an answer'. If you design your research badly, someone (the examiner) will say 'You can't reach that conclusion from that evidence.' We've already explained that your research design depends on your question, so now it might be helpful to look at an example of how a specific research design might be applied to a particular question. In a short book like this we don't want to cover every possible approach to every possible question. We simply want to demonstrate that research design is important.

At this point, you should ask yourself what branch of logic you will be using in your dissertation. For example, do you aim to measure some things and then see what the evidence leans towards, or do you plan to start with a hypothesis and make specific measurements that will test it? Or is logic not really part of your plan? If you go for that last option, think very carefully and talk to your tutor before going too far. There are too many examples of different approaches to research design in geography for us to be able to treat all of them in detail here, and you will find strategies appropriate to your own project by exploring the research literature in your area, but we thought we should give you an example rather than simply turning you loose into the wider literature on research. An example might at least encourage you to think about whether you need to explore that literature!

An example: the hypothesis-testing approach

The philosopher Karl Popper (Popper, 1959) drew together some of the points that we've been talking about in the last few sections into a framework for research which some geographers, especially physical geographers, have found useful. On the other hand, some geographers have said it is a terrible approach, so don't rush into it without making sure that it is appropriate for your project! It is referred to variously as 'critical rationalism', 'the hypothesis-testing approach' and 'the hypothetico-deductive method'. The background to the approach is the idea that inductive reasoning cannot provide conclusive arguments of the type that some types of research demand. According to the critical rationalists, scientific research in particular relies on deductive reasoning, where conclusive arguments are possible.

One of the best-known examples used to defend and explain the critical-rationalist position involves the question 'Are all swans white?' One way of answering the question (one research design) would be to look at all the swans you could find and observe their colour. The more white swans you found the more convinced you would be that all swans were white. When you had seen enough swans, or when you ran out of time or funding, you would conclude that since you had seen lots of white swans and none of any other colour, all swans were indeed white. We can recognize that approach to be what we called inductive reasoning earlier in the chapter. We have not conclusively shown that all swans are white because we have not seen all swans, but we have a substantial number of confirming instances: a body of evidence which supports the conclusion.

Nevertheless, if we had to answer definitely 'Yes' or 'No' to the question 'Are all swans white?' we could not do it on the basis of our research. We could only say 'probably' or 'the evidence so far strongly suggests that might be true'. In effect we have made no progress because we knew it might be true before we started. On the other hand, if we were to find a black swan, we would know for sure that not all swans were white: that single observation allows us to reach a definite answer to the question. We could never get a definite 'Yes' unless we looked at every single swan in the world. For most research problems we could never be sure that we had looked at every subject so it is impossible ever to answer 'Yes'. By contrast it is possible to reach a definite 'No' if we find just one piece of evidence that falsifies the hypothesis.

The implication is that it is a waste of time designing a research programme to find evidence in support of an idea because no amount of supporting evidence can 'prove' a point.

The sensible thing is to design a research programme that tries to find evidence against your idea. If you don't find evidence against the idea then you are in a position, like the inductivist's, of having to say 'may be'; except that your 'may be' could be stronger than theirs if you have made a positive effort to look for black swans while they just looked at any old swans and wondered if a black one would turn up. If you do find the black swan, which you are more likely to do if you have gone out to look for one than if you haven't, then you are in a very different position. You can then say with confidence that the answer to the question is 'No, not all swans are white.' People who like that approach argue that at least their method gives the possibility of reaching a definite answer, even if the definite answers are always falsifications, rather than verifications of an idea.

The logic involved in the falsification is deductive. If all swans are white, goes the argument, then we should not be able to find any swans of any other colour. In fact we have found a swan of a different colour, therefore we conclude that the premise is wrong and not all swans are white. Rather like the syllogisms we discussed earlier we can recognize a formal structure to the argument. First, there is a hypothesis. This is a possible answer to the question; in our case the hypothesis would be that all swans are indeed white. Second, there is a prediction. If all swans are white as we hypothesize, then we will not find any non-white swans. This allows us to formulate a test of the hypothesis: go looking for non-white swans. Third, there is the observation: 'Look, a black swan in Australia!' Finally, there is the conclusion: the result of the test is that the observation falsifies the hypothesis so the answer is 'No'. The alternative result of the test would be the observation that we could only find white swans and couldn't find any non-white swans. In that case our conclusion would be that, indeed, all swans might be white, but we couldn't be absolutely sure.

Popper's approach works well for some questions. 'Are all swans white?' Definitely not. But it works rather less well for others. 'What colour are swans?' for example, or 'What time is it?' So for some dissertation questions this approach might be useful. For others it will be no use at all. That's really the point of this chapter: to help you realize that different research designs are appropriate for different projects. For example, Karlstrom et al. (2014) were investigating competing hypotheses about the age of the Grand Canyon: was it formed by rivers in the past 5–6 million years as suggested by some previous research, or was it created entirely by rivers in the same location as much as 70 million years ago? They set out to date sections of the canyon by a variety of methods, and the starting point of their research design was that 'If any segment is young, the old canyon hypothesis is falsified' (Karlstrom et al. 2014, p.239). Their problem was very suitable for a hypothesis-testing approach. Their dating indicated that while some sections of the canyon were old, others had been cut recently, so the idea that the canyon as a whole was a very ancient feature was falsified, and their evidence supported the alternative hypothesis that some older canyon sections had more recently been linked up by the development of new sections in the last six million years. Not all of the questions that geographers ask can best be addressed in this way, but some can. If your project is using participant diaries to explore how personal mobilities define perceptions of the city, hypothesis testing may not be the way to go. You need to find the approach that is best for your question.

When you have found the approach that is best for you, you then need to work out a detailed plan of action – a very specific research design. In a book of this size we cannot give you detailed examples of all the different types of research design you could use. We will just give you an example to illustrate the kind of detail in which you should be thinking. There are other, specialist books that focus on different specific research design strategies, so you might want to refer to those as you start to add detail to your particular plan. The titles of general books such as *Research Methods in Geography* (Gomez and Jones, 2010) and *Key Methods in Geography* (Clifford et al., 2010) and of more specialist texts such as *Qualitative Research Methods in Human Geography* (Hay, 2010), *Research-ing the City* (Ward, 2013) and *Participatory Action Research Approaches* (Kindon et al., 2010) should make it easy for you to find material to help you with whatever kind of research design you adopt.

We hope our book is a big help to you, but we hope it is not the only book you read!

If you decide that the hypothesis-testing approach is suitable for your project, then you can use the following guide to lead you through the stages of your research. If you decide that this approach is not suitable, then thinking about why it isn't so should set you on the path to a more suitable research design. Whatever research design you adopt, you need to think through the stages as carefully as we go through the steps in this example.

Eric says . . .

There are many different approaches to research design. Make sure the one you choose is appropriate for your project. Finding the right research design to fit the project is at the core of your dissertation.

A worked example of the hypothesis-testing approach

Step 1: What am I trying to find out? (The question)

A lot of geographic research can be broken down into three stages: discovery, description and explanation. First someone finds something new, be it a country, a physical feature, a process or a relationship. Second, we say exactly what the new discovery consists of. Third, we explain it. For dissertation writers, explanation is generally the most interesting part of the investigation to take on board. It's the 'How?' or 'Why?' part of finding out. 'Why is this like it is?'

Step 2: What is it like? (The preliminary description)

In order to start explaining why something is as it is you need to know exactly what it is like; in other words you need to know exactly WHAT you are trying to explain. For your own preparation, and in your report, you will need to describe your subject (the feature, process or whatever). The nature and detail of your description will depend on the nature and complexity of the subject. You might use maps, diagrams, photographs or statistical data as part of your description. The aim is to give yourself, and eventually your readers, a clear (detailed and unambiguous) idea of what it is you are trying to explain.

Step 3: How can I begin to explain? (The hypothesis)

The way to begin is to come up with some possible answers to your question, in other words some hypotheses. In many cases, your hypothesis is no more than a re-ordering of the words of your research question. To go back to the examples we gave in inductive and deductive logic, Mercer's hypothesis was 'NGOs aren't making a difference', and Knight's hypothesis was 'debris bands are entrained by the same freezing process as the clean layers of ice'. You might be able to come up with hypotheses from your own imagination, but it is important also to explore the existing literature on your topic. Find out what other researchers have suggested about your question. It might be that someone has published what they think is 'The Answer', or a number of researchers might have put forward several different hypotheses. It is very important that your dissertation considers hypotheses that exist in the literature, to set your work clearly into an existing context, even if you also move on to consider new hypotheses that have not been proposed before. At this stage it is a good idea to come up with several alternative hypotheses.

Step 4: How can I test these hypotheses? (The predictions)

Predictions take the form: 'If that is true . . . then this must follow.' Every hypothesis, or possible answer to your question, has a set of implications, or expectations, associated with it. For example, if you wonder what a particular room in the Geography Department is used for, and you suspect (hypothesize) that it might be a lecture room, then you would expect (predict) that if you put your head around the door you would see rows of seats facing a stage or a lectern. If your question is about the origin of a scattering of boulders on a hillside, and your hypothesis is that the boulders are a rockfall deposit, then your prediction might be something like: 'If this is a rockfall, I would expect the largest boulders to be at the bottom of the slope and the smallest ones at the top.' In order to arrive at your prediction, you need to know something about the kind of feature you are interested in. In our examples, the predictions rely on us knowing some of the typical characteristics of lecture rooms and rockfall deposits so that we can compare our observed feature (Room 207 or the scree slopes at Wastwater, for example) with our theoretical model. For the subject of your dissertation, you will probably need to do a lot of background work in the library to enable you to come up with sensible predictions. Bear in mind, of course, that to be useful for your research your prediction has to be testable. It's no good predicting what the room will look like if you can't look inside to check, for example, and it's no good predicting boulder size distributions if you can't go out and measure the boulders.

Step 5: Will any testable prediction do? (Risky predictions)

Some predictions are more useful than others. For example, if we argue that 'If it is a lecture room there will be chairs in it', and if we find that there are indeed chairs in the room, we still won't be sure that it's a lecture room because other types of room also have chairs in them. What we need is a prediction that will be true only if the hypothesis is true. You should try to identify 'risky' predictions. These are predictions that are very unlikely to occur unless your hypothesis is correct. You might find that you can think of no single characteristic of your hypothesis that could furnish a risky prediction to test. It might be that you need to consider an assemblage of characteristics. For example, lots of rooms have chairs in them, but only lecture rooms have chairs, a lectern and a slide projector. In some circumstances you might have to consider situations where there is no single characteristic that is always true of the feature you are interested in. Statistical analysis might help here. If you construct your prediction with specific statistical tests in mind, you might be able to test your hypothesis on a probabilistic basis.

Step 6: What do I do with my risky, testable prediction? (The test)

Once you have a good prediction, go and test it. This will involve making some kind of observation. In our examples, it could mean looking into the room or measuring boulder sizes on the hillside. Your observations might take the form of fieldwork, laboratory experiments, GIS analysis or documentary searches, but will certainly involve some sort of data collection. It is very important that you know before you start your data collection what observations or results are possible, and that you know exactly what each of those results would mean for your hypothesis. For example, your earlier library work might have indicated that all rockfalls have the biggest rocks at the bottom. You will then be able to say before you do your fieldwork that if the biggest rocks are not at the bottom of your hillside then your feature is not a rockfall. You will also know before you start that if the biggest rocks are at the bottom then your feature might be a rockfall. Therefore you should know, before you make any observations, exactly what you need to measure.

Step 7: What if I falsify the hypothesis? (Try another!)

If you falsify your hypothesis, this means that it was not the right answer; the room is not a lecture room or the slope deposit was not a rockfall. This is progress. In everyday life there is a tendency for us to be disappointed if our ideas turn out to be wrong. This is not the case in academic research. Finding out that an apparently reasonable answer is in fact incorrect is a major achievement. However, at this stage you must be quite certain that your observation falsifying your prediction really has falsified the hypothesis. Check once again that the prediction had to come true for the hypothesis to be verified. Is there any chance that the hypothesis could be true even though the prediction was not? Could the cleaner have moved the chairs out of the room, or could the rocks have been disturbed by human activity? Of course, you should have thought of that when devising the test (Step 5, above). If you are confident that you have falsified the hypothesis, and if you still have time, the next thing to do is to return to Step 3 (above) and develop a new hypothesis to work on.

Step 8: What if I fail to falsify the prediction? (Try again!)

If you fail to falsify a hypothesis, that means that you might have the right answer; the hypothesis might be true. On the other hand, as we explained when we were talking about deductive logic earlier, it might be that your hypothesis is in fact incorrect but that the test you used was unable to show it. A rockfall is not the only process that produces deposits with the largest rocks at the bottom, so finding that your deposit has the largest rocks at the bottom doesn't prove that it must be a rockfall. Therefore the next thing to do is to think of another test of your hypothesis, to try again to falsify it. Think of another risky, testable prediction based on your hypothesis, and return to Step 4 (above). If you have trouble thinking of another good prediction, remember that you can use assemblages of related predictions; none of the predictions independently might be 'risky', but taken as a group they might be.

Step 9: Is there no way to progress beyond Stage 8?

When you falsified your hypothesis we sent you back to try a new one, and when you failed to falsify that hypothesis we sent you back to try again. It might seem as if this method of research leads you round and round in circles with no satisfactory conclusion. In fact there will come a point where you run out of sensible hypotheses to test, and where you run out of good tests to apply to the hypotheses that you have failed to falsify. At this point, all your hypotheses will have been either falsified or tested until you run out of tests. We have already said that falsification represents a sort of progress, but what about the hypotheses that you have been unable to falsify?

Step 10: If my hypothesis isn't false, is it the right answer?

Even if you have made a number of risky predictions and they all turn out to be true, you still cannot be completely sure that your hypothesis is correct. Remember the swans: however many white ones you see, you can't be sure that they're all white. This is not as depressing as it might seem. The whole of scientific 'knowledge' is made up of nothing more than hypotheses that have not yet been falsified. If you have tried very hard to disprove an idea, and not been able to do it, then you might well be happy to accept the idea for the time being. Perhaps one day someone will think of a new prediction, or new technology might permit a new test, and your 'answer' will then be rejected. The physics of Isaac Newton was accepted for nearly 300 years before Einstein falsified it! Much of Einstein's physics is still accepted, and seems to 'work', but may one day be falsified and superseded. That's the nature of scientific progress. If, at the end of your research, you retain an unfalsified hypothesis, then you might let it stand as your 'best' provisional answer, and put it forward as a tentative explanation.

Other types of research design

The sequence of steps that we described above for our hypothesis-testing research design might seem quite strict and formal, and you might think that it places inappropriate constraints on the way you might do your research. You may be right. There are different ways of designing research, each appropriate for particular researchers doing particular types of project. Writing about ethnographic research, where a researcher might have collected a vast range of field notes, digital recordings, images and records of conversations, and might be trying to draw an overall picture from all that information, Fetterman (2009, p.10) writes:

> unexpected insights are often the result of allowing the mind to wander and consider unusual combinations of thoughts. The researcher must of course back-track to see whether the data will support these new ideas or invalidate them, but he or she will rarely achieve them through linear, methodical work alone.

Similarly, Herbert et al. (2005) refer to arriving at a conclusion in ethnographic research through a protracted process of moving backwards and forwards between field notes and theoretical work. There are many different ways of designing and doing research.

At first glance a typical ethnographic study might appear to have a less rigid, unidirectional pattern than the hypothesis testing approach. The ethnographer rarely makes such a big deal about using that kind of fixed sequence of observation, comparison of observation against expectation, and logical deduction. Often the data collection and analysis in an ethnographic study occur at the same time, and incoming data informs the data collection immediately and in situ. Subsequently, data in a wide range of formats is sifted, reanalysed and compared against the researcher's own preconceptions and theoretical position en route to the formation of new theory, or the presentation of a new view of the situation being studied. It is not a rigid research design strategy, and is open to adjustment in light of changing circumstances in the field. It is also open to adjustment and reinterpretation by researchers with different intentions or backgrounds. Ethnographic research typically proceeds in an inductive fashion, drawing conclusions from evidence amassed during often extended periods of field observation. Whereas the critical rationalist might pinpoint a specific 'necessary observation' and design a field expedition with surgical precision as an information strike of the shortest possible duration, the ethnographer is more likely to spend a long time becoming embedded within the study community and may not know at the start of the fieldwork what will turn out to be the most important observations. Referring back to previous examples, 'grab and run' might have been a good approach for finding out the isotopic composition of ice in a Greenland glacier, but not so much for finding out how those pirates felt about the seagulls!

Nevertheless, we can draw out some common ground even between such apparently distant cousins as the ethnographers and the hardcore critical-rationalist hypothesis testers! Both begin with a problem, or question or topic of study that has to be clearly identified in the context of underlying theory and previous research. Both approaches involve making observations or collecting data in a way that will permit the researcher to say something worthwhile about the topic at the end of the study. Both involve the analysis of observations from an acknowledged theoretical or methodological standpoint. Both have opportunities for the researcher to reframe their question in the light of observations before making further observations. Both arrive at conclusions or outputs that can be traced back to specific observations or evidence. As Fetterman (2009, p.8) explains, an ethnographic research design is a 'blueprint or road map that helps the ethnographer conceptualize how each step will follow the one before to build knowledge and understanding'. That description could apply equally well to the hypothesis-testing approach or to any other of the research-design strategies that might be used in an undergraduate dissertation in geography, earth sciences, environmental subjects, social studies ... in fact any subject that includes a research element! Fetterman (2009, p.8) goes on to say that an ethnographic research proposal should include 'background information, including historical information and a literature search, specific aims, rationale, methods and significance, as well as a timetable and budget'. Again, this description could apply to any research design in an undergraduate dissertation. Although 'geography and related disciplines' is a very wide area with a huge number of different styles of research, they do all have a great deal in common, so even if you don't find details of a specific approach for your project here, the basic ideas that we are illustrating still apply to your project.

Whatever kind of dissertation you are doing, you should have a problem, or question or topic of study that you can clearly identify in the context of underlying theory and previous research.

There are many different types of research problem that you might choose to tackle in your dissertation. We have already argued that most of these can be reduced to a very small number of types of question. In the same way, there are many different approaches to research design. For example, you may have learned about the differences between qualitative and quantitative research, or between historical and contemporary studies, or between positivism and realism. Some geographers treat their research as an experimental science, and search for the laws of how things work. Others treat it as an interpretative search for meanings that cannot be identified by scientific methods but require qualitative approaches. Just as the range of research questions can be reduced to a small number of basic types, so the range of research approaches can be reduced. If you were to compile a list of all the approaches available to geography researchers it could seem overwhelming. As you firm up your specific project you may well need to read more deeply into cultural relativism or the specifics of the hermeneutic model or the critical-realist approach to conscious subjects or the critical-rationalist approach to hypothesis testing. However, this book is not the place to go into those details. The essence of any research design is an approach to finding something out. You might be trying to find out how it feels to live the life of a pirate, or you might be trying to find out what caused a rockfall or what would be the most sustainable approach to designing a food distribution system, but, in the broadest sense, research is about finding things out. Therefore it is essential, whatever your approach, to identify your question ('I am trying to find out ...'). Whether you are adopting a qualitative or quantitative approach you will need to collect data to answer your question, so you will need to know what data to collect ('In order to find that out, I need to know ...'). For many projects, whatever the details of your study, a framework of question, evidence and logical reasoning will serve you well. It may not necessarily be the same framework that we used in our example, but you will either have a logical framework of some type or, if not, you will be able to explain very clearly why not.

One sensible approach to research design is to base your own design on something that previous researchers have found successful. You can accommodate differences in the style of your data or the context of your question quite easily while retaining their structure to keep you on course. For example, with our hypothesis-testing example you can pick and choose the parts that are relevant to you: if you are doing a purely descriptive study, then you need only use the first few stages of the approach. As you read more deeply into these issues be careful to distinguish between specific methods, such as particle size analysis of sediments or participant observation within a community, and broad methodology or approach, such as hypothesis testing or ethnography, within which specific methods will be appropriate. Some examiners are quite strict about the difference between methods and methodology, so be careful to write, and think, precisely.

Remember, the purpose of your research design is to ensure that your work leads not just to an answer, but to an answer (to the question you asked) which is sound and valid. Be sure to follow a design that will do that.

Writing a research proposal

Professional researchers applying for money to carry out a piece of work are normally required to put forward a substantial research proposal explaining in detail what they plan to do. Most institutions require dissertation students to produce something similar, but on a much smaller scale, as an early indication of what their dissertation is going to be about. In some institutions this research proposal is assessed either as part of the dissertation or as part of a research training module. Even if your institution does not insist on you writing a proposal it would be a really good idea for you to do it anyway. You will almost certainly find it helpful. If your institution does insist on you writing a proposal, now is the time to get started on it. Even if the official one is not due in yet, or if it takes a different format from what we suggest here, use our exercise as a practice.

It will be very useful for you to produce a detailed research proposal at this stage, before you start your data collection.

Thinking through your plans in your head is OK, but most of us are very good at fooling ourselves into thinking that we are better prepared than we really are. The only way to be sure that you really know what you are going to do, and that you have avoided the major pitfalls, is to produce a coherent written plan. To ensure that professional researchers have done their planning and research design properly, grant-giving bodies usually have special research proposal forms to be filled in. Your institution may have a form for you to fill in, in which case you should practise with their headings, but in case your institution does not do that we are going to give you a set of headings that you can use to make your own form. We suggest that you try to keep your proposal at this stage to just a page or two of text. You can do a longer proposal, with a more detailed literature review, for example, later on. Box 6.1 shows the headings that you might use in a preliminary proposal:

Box 6.1 Headings that you might use in a preliminary research proposal

1   Title of project
    (What is the dissertation called? This is just a label, not necessarily a question.)

2   Aim of project
    (What are you trying to find out?)

3   Background and justification
    (Why is this important and what work has been done on it before?)

4   Methodology and specific methods
    (How are you going to do it? Describe both your overall research design and your specific techniques.)

5   Timetable of research
    (When are you going to do what?)

6   Location of data sources
    (Are you going to use a record office? Which one? Remotely sensed data? Who will provide it? Fieldwork? Have you permission to access the site?)

7   Ethical issues
    (Will you need to get any special approvals, for example, to work with children?)

8   Risk assessment
    (Are there any safety issues that might affect you, your subjects or the public?)

Depending on your specific project or the context of your institution you could change the headings a bit. For example, different versions could include the headings: 'Data required', 'Data sources' and 'Data collection' methods. You might want an additional heading 'Literature Review' after the 'Background' section if you are ready at this stage to describe in detail how the previously published work in your area provides a context for your project.

If you really know what you are doing, you should be able to make a coherent and convincing case for your project on one side of A4 paper. Indeed many institutions may require you to do this. Keep redrafting your research proposal until everyone you show it to can understand what you are doing and why you are doing it, and believes that your approach will work. Also, this will help to ensure that *you* know what you are doing and that *you* believe that your approach will work! Don't start your data collection until you've got this bit right. Check whether your institution has a form of its own, and make sure that you can fill it in. There may also be special forms relating to safety, risk assessment or ethics approval. Make sure you know about any forms that you are going to have to complete, and even if your institution doesn't have special forms make sure that your proposal considers any important safety or ethics issues.

When you have drafted your proposal show it to your supervisor and ask for feedback. When your supervisor gives you that feedback, consider it very carefully.

Ethics and safety issues

Ethics and safety are important parts of the research planning process, and we mention them repeatedly throughout this book to remind you to pay attention to them. You cannot do research that is unsafe, illegal or ethically unsound. This is the stage in the dissertation process where you need to look at your plans and identify any potential safety or ethics issues. In all forms of research your own safety and the safety of your subjects or participants, your assistants and the general public is always of paramount importance. Most institutions will specifically require you to complete some kind of risk assessment and some kind of ethics assessment of your project. These are important both for their own sake and because poor ethics or safety planning will probably affect the mark you get for the dissertation. Some projects have very obvious ethics or safety issues. If you are collecting data in remote or inhospitable environments, or working with hazardous materials then clearly you need to take special safety precautions. If you are working with children or vulnerable adults, or hoping to use sensitive private data, then clearly there are ethical considerations to be taken into account. However, safety and ethics reviews are important for all dissertations not only because it is important for you to learn that these reviews are a standard part of the research process but also because some ethics and safety issues are not as obvious as you might expect. A convenient review of ethical practice in geographical research is provided by Hay (2010), and Bullard (2010) provides a summary of issues relating to fieldwork safety. Make sure that you familiarize yourself with the safety and ethics requirements of your institution, and pay particular attention to the safety documentation for the specific type of work that you are doing, for example, in a laboratory or in an extreme environment. Also be aware that what you consider ethical and what your government considers legal might not be the same thing. Bradley Garrett carried out an ethnographic study of a group of urban place hackers, and accompanied them on their explorations of off-limits locations (Garrett, 2013). Unfortunately, what they called 'exploration' the police considered 'trespass', and Garrett was arrested and prosecuted. That whole case raised a lot of issues about academic freedom that might themselves make for an interesting dissertation, but it also serves as a reminder that your dissertation is not only an academic exercise but can have real-world repercussions.

Chapter summary and conclusion

There are lots of different ways of finding things out and doing research, and different projects need different research designs. Not all designs will work for all projects, so you need to choose carefully.

You need to know exactly what you are trying to find out before you start. If you are not trying to find something out, what are you doing? Understand exactly what kind of question you are asking, and be sure you know what the answer should look like. Are you looking for a description or explanation? Is your answer going to be a history, a reason, a narrative account, a prediction or a policy statement . . .?

Follow a logical procedure for reaching the answer to your question. If you adopt the hypothesis-testing approach, for example, follow the sequence of question, hypothesis, prediction, observation. For other approaches, follow the appropriate sequence of investigation for the approach you have chosen.

Suggestions for further reading

The following list provides a flavour of the different types of book that are available, some covering the general topic of approaches to geographical and related research, others focusing specifically on particular research environments or techniques.

Best, S. (2003) *A beginner's guide to social theory*. Sage, London, 280pp.

Clifford, N., French, S. and Valentine, G. (2010) *Key methods in Geography* (2nd ed.). Sage, London, 568pp.

DeLyser, D., Herbert, S., Aitken, S., Crang, M. and McDowell, L. (eds) (2010) *The SAGE handbook of qualitative Geography*. Sage, London, 372pp.

Fetterman, D.M. (2009) *Ethnography: step-by-step* (3rd ed.). Sage, London, 200pp.

Flowerdew, R. and Martin, D.M. (eds) (2005) *Methods in Human Geography: a guide for students doing a research project.* Pearson, Harlow, 366pp.

Gomez, B. and Jones, J.P. (2010) *Research methods in Geography: a critical introduction.* Wiley-Blackwell, Chichester, 480pp.

Hay, I. (2010) *Qualitative research methods in Human Geography* (3rd ed.). Oxford University Press, Oxford, 464pp.

Inkpen, R. and Wilson, G. (2013) *Science, Philosophy and Physical Geography* (2nd ed.). Routledge, Abingdon and New York, 238pp.

Kindon, S., Pain, R. and Kesby, M. (eds) (2010) *Participatory action research approaches and methods*. Routledge, Abingdon and New York, 288pp.

Kitchen, R. and Tate, N.J. (2000) *Conducting research into Human Geog*raphy. Prentice Hall, Harlow, 330pp.

Knight, J. and Whalley, B. (in press) *Handbook of research methods in Physical Geographical sciences.* Routledge, Abingdon and New York.

Montello, D. and Sutton, P. (2013) *An introduction to scientific research methods in Geography and Environmental Studies* (2nd ed.). Sage, London, 328pp.

Phillips, R. and Johns, J. (2012) *Fieldwork for Human Geography*. Sage, London, 240pp.

Rhoads, B.L. and Thorne, C.E. (eds) (1996) *The scientific nature of Geomorphology*. John Wiley & Sons Ltd, Chichester, 481pp.

Ward, K. (2013) *Researching the city: a guide for students*. Sage, London, 184pp.

What to do after reading Chapter 6

Write a research proposal and discuss it with your advisor. This is really important.

Find out whether you will have to complete a formal risk assessment or ethics assessment as part of your formal dissertation procedures. If you will, then find out exactly how those assessments work.

Talk about your research design with as many people as possible. Talking through your plans will help you to think clearly through the issues, and you might also get useful feedback from surprising sources!

Keep reading as much as you can about the topic you are working on.

If you think things are going wrong, look at Chapter 10 and talk to your supervisor.

7

WHAT KIND(S) OF DATA DO I NEED AND HOW DO I GET THEM?

This chapter explains the relationship between the problem you are investigating and the type(s) of data needed to solve it. It looks at issues associated with data collection, including the reliability of data collected in different ways. It distinguishes between primary and secondary data, and assesses the advantages and disadvantages of each.

Data, data analysis and data quantity

The type of data that you will need to undertake your research, what you will need to do with the data you have collected and the amount of data you will need to collect are three interrelated issues that you need to consider together. For simplicity we have chosen to deal with these issues separately in this and the following chapter. However, we should stress that you need to address them all simultaneously and not sequentially.

What kind of data do I need?

Once you have reached this stage, and you have completed your research proposal, you should know the data that are required in order to answer the question, test the hypothesis or complete the task you have set yourself. You should know whether the data you will need will be qualitative, quantitative, spatial or some combination of those. Fundamentally, the type of data you will need will depend on the approach you are taking to your dissertation. Are you doing fieldwork and collecting your own primary data? Are you analyzing samples in a laboratory that somebody else has already collected? Are you using remote sensing data? Are you using existing climatological data? Are you undertaking a modelling study?

It is vital that before you start collecting any data you are absolutely certain that you are collecting exactly the data you need.

You should know at this stage whether you need measurements of wind speed (quantitative data), narrative accounts of residents in a town (qualitative data), evidence of an event in the past that you think may have caused a present-day distribution of vegetation (could be either qualitative or quantitative) or the distribution of Anglo-Saxon buckets (spatial data). You should know whether you need your data to test a hypothesis or parameterize a model or contribute to an ongoing historical record. You will know what your data will be used for after you have collected them, and what kind of analysis you plan to do – the data you plan to collect must be appropriate for the kind of analysis you anticipate. Are you hoping to plug your observations into a GIS-based model? Are you planning to carry out a content analysis based on coding of key themes from a focus group? Are you expecting to use your data to test a hypothesis and to evaluate its significance statistically? You will also know whether your dissertation is going to involve you in fieldwork, laboratory experiments, questionnaires, participant observation, computer modelling, GIS work, collection of data online or in a record office, or whatever. Take some time now to check that you do, in fact, know all this. Good research projects can come to grief here. It's all too easy to think that the data will give you the answer you need when, in fact, they won't. In Chapter 4 we asked you to list the questions you were going to ask and also to list all possible answers to those questions and what those answers would tell you. At this stage it is a very good idea to imagine that you have all the data that you plan to use in your dissertation. Will these data give you (or lead to) the answers to those questions? Are these all the data you will need? Do you need all of them? Think through what you will do at this stage in your dissertation, and check that you can, in fact do it.

A typical examiner's comment:

> I wonder why the student felt the need to collect samples of Y when they had already measured the extent of X. It was not necessary. They should have collected Z instead.

If you are unsure of the answers to any of those questions, this and the following chapter may help you to sort things out. You may also have realized that there may be more than one sort of data you could use to answer your question(s) and you may be wondering which sort to use. In this chapter we will look at the different types of data and the advantages and disadvantages of each. This is not a statistics or methods textbook, so we will only be giving you pointers here. We will not be upset if you go and look up details in more specialist books. In fact, we will be worried if you don't!

Obtaining your data

Before we start talking about obtaining your data we may as well clear up an issue that crops up a lot with data. 'Data' is the plural of 'datum'. So, in correct usage, data should always be referred to in the plural (as we do here). You will find many instances where data are referred to as though they were singular, e.g. 'the data shows', instead of 'the data show'. Some people won't be too fussy whether you get this right or not. Your examiners, on the whole, will be.

As we have already mentioned, data come in all shapes and sizes: qualitative, spatial, quantitative and so on. By now, having gone through your research design process, you should know which kind(s) you need. So the next question you face is how to obtain them. Data are often divided into primary and secondary. Like most things, this division is not as straightforward as it might appear. For our purposes we will define primary data as data that you collect yourself. So, for example, measurements that you make of stream velocity in the field, questionnaires that you administer to visitors to a beach and measurements of infiltration into soil samples in a laboratory are all primary data. Secondary data, on the other hand, are data that somebody else has already collected and that you will use for your own purposes. So, the age structure of the population of a parish that you obtain from somebody else's published work or stream discharges that you obtain from a national hydrological organization such as the Environment Agency in the UK are secondary data. One distinction between the two is that for primary data you will have first-hand information that will help you assess the reliability of your data, whereas for secondary data you may have no idea of the conditions under which data were collected or of the diligence of the collector. Be careful to use secondary data only from appropriate and reliable sources.

The distinction between primary and secondary data is flexible, even within geography. In historical geography, for example, public records, parish registers, etc. are regarded as primary data. Historical geographers think of getting information from a pile of old registers the way that geomorphologists think about getting information from a pile of old gravel. In historical geography the term secondary data is used to refer to data that you may obtain from other studies that are contemporary with the data. For example, data from the 1850 census is primary data for a historical geographer, while data obtained from a book about agriculture that was written in the 1850s, although originally based upon a survey at the same time, would be regarded as secondary.

You should have checked before you reached this stage of your project whether your institution has specific data requirements for the dissertation. Some institutions, particularly in the past, have insisted on students undertaking some primary data collection, so that even if many of the data that you need can be acquired from secondary sources, it may be necessary for you to collect some original data yourself. For example, you could administer a questionnaire to supplement census data, or carry out a river survey to supplement hydrological data provided by the Environment Agency. With more secondary data becoming available from such sources as remote-sensing satellites, data archives and more extensive censuses, and an increasing emphasis on the role of a dissertation in evaluating analytical skills, the strict requirement for primary data collection is becoming less common. Nonetheless, you need to make sure. You don't want to have all your hard work downgraded and miss out on a prize because it falls foul of some archaic rule that even your tutor had forgotten about.

If you are not sure about the rules of your own institution regarding primary and secondary data, find out now. Read the handbook. Check the web page. Ask your supervisor.

Many dissertations will use both primary and secondary data even if, in some field-based projects, the secondary data amount to no more than using a map to locate the sites. Whatever type of data you use, you will need to give some consideration to their reliability.

Data reliability

An assessment of the reliability of your data is important because it affects the validity of the conclusions you may reach. In many areas of geography little regard appears to be given to the issue of data reliability. It is just assumed that the data are reliable. For example, it is not common to find discussion of this topic in research reports in physical geography, unless there are special circumstances that may have significance for the reliability of the data. On the other hand, historical geographers, for example, are very concerned about the issue and it will usually merit substantial discussion in papers on historical geography. However, even if there is little public discussion of the topic in your particular branch of geography, that doesn't mean you can ignore it in your dissertation. In whatever branch of the discipline you are working, it is a good idea to make an objective assessment of your data before you draw conclusions. In modelling studies, for example, it is expected that you will show some assessment of the uncertainty associated with model output. Much of this uncertainty will depend on the accuracy of the input.

In historical geography, for example, two issues are important. The first concerns the veracity of the data. Is the document you are using a forgery? The second issue arises from the fact that in historical geography greater use is made of surrogate measures than in other parts of the discipline. For example, if you wanted to study the effect of land ownership on the use of agricultural fertilizers in the nineteenth century, you might decide to use records of land tenure and sales of agricultural lime. This would not be a perfect measure of what you wanted to investigate so you would need to discuss its shortcomings.

Each type of research that you might consider for your dissertation has its own issues concerning data reliability. In ethnographic research where you might be concerned with unique or idiosyncratic behaviours in situations that cannot be replicated, for example, data cannot be checked in the same way as in a laboratory study where an experiment can be repeated under identical conditions on multiple occasions. Geographers sometimes distinguish between 'closed system' research where external variables can all be controlled, as in a laboratory experiment, and 'open system' research where there are so many uncontrollable external influences that we cannot adopt that same type of traditional 'scientific' approach.

Primary data

Advantages

The main advantage (see Table 7.1) of collecting primary data is that you will have an intimate knowledge of the data. That includes knowing how unreliable some of the data may be. All data are subject to measurement error of one sort or another. On the whole, however, we don't say much about the errors and there is a danger that you may think that everybody else's data are much better than yours. They may be! But there's nothing like trying to make the measurements that somebody else has reported making to discover just how error prone they are. Such an attempt can give you new insight into the conclusions that have been reached on the basis of the measurements! In Chapter 2 we used the example of a dissertation that examined grike depths and showed that because of the student's own experience of the difficulty of obtaining reliable width measurements the student had concluded that the existing literature, which was based on measurements of width, may be unreliable.

An important difference to clear up at this stage is the difference between errors and mistakes. As we said, all measurements are subject to error. This is because of the limitations of measuring equipment. Try measuring the width of your room with a tape measure, giving the answer in millimetres. Do you always get the same answer? Almost certainly not. If you make the measurement many times, the answers will cluster around some central value, which is generally assumed to be the 'correct' value. A distinction is drawn between precision and accuracy. Precision refers to the repeatability of a measurement; accuracy refers to whether the answer is correct or not. So if you measure your room with a tape measure and always get an answer to within 2mm then that is the precision of your measurement. But if your tape measure had been badly made, all of the answers could be inaccurate. One thing you will need to think about is how precise you need your answers to be. Generally, the more precise the answer the longer it takes to obtain it. So, thinking about your room, you could look at it and estimate its width at 3.6m. If you ask Erica she may estimate 3.4m. Both of you could give this answer in seconds, but to measure it with a tape measure will take several minutes. If you need hundreds of measurements for your dissertation, will estimates do, or do you need to more precision? It's always tempting to go for more precision but, as we will say in the next chapter about amounts of data, more is not necessarily better.

Measurements are also subject to mistakes. You may simply write the wrong number down in your notebook, or the instrument you are using may malfunction. Often these mistakes show up in the analysis stage as some rogue point in a plot of the data. If so, you may be able to correct the mistake, or simply throw the data away. What is more worrying is if mistakes don't show up later and your conclusions are based on them. But that is a problem everybody faces, not just you and your dissertation.

Knowing the relative (un)reliability of various sets of data that you have collected can be very useful when you come to analyze them. If things don't seem to make sense it may be because one set of data just isn't good enough for the purpose you need it for.

Table 7.1 Some advantages and disadvantages of primary and secondary data

PRIMARY DATA	SECONDARY DATA
Advantages	*Advantages*
Specific to the problem	Potentially large data set
Intimate understanding of reliability	Often in computer-compatible form
	Quick to obtain
Disadvantages	*Disadvantages*
Small data set	May not be exactly what you want
Time consuming to collect	No information on data quality
	May have restricted access/use

There is a danger that once your field data get into your notebook, or, worse still, into a computer spreadsheet, you will think of them as wholly reliable. Thinking back to the conditions under which they were collected can help a lot. Imagine the case in which your questionnaire survey seems to indicate that most of the population in your study area is retired, yet the census data claim that the number of retired people in your area is below the national average. The notes you made in your field notebook on the day of your survey show that it was a weekday morning, which you now realize was when many employed people would have been at work, when children would have been at school and when the street would have been disproportionately occupied by retired people because the local supermarket café was offering a discount to pensioners that day! That detail might explain why you cannot relate your census and questionnaire data, and highlights an unfortunate weakness in your research methodology. Such a realization might be a disaster for the project you had originally designed, but all may not be lost (see Chapter 10). It's very easy to see where you have overlooked something, but much less easy to anticipate all the problems in advance.

There is danger in thinking that your data are wholly reliable.

A second major advantage of primary data is that (within the constraints of what is technically and logistically possible) you can get exactly what you need for your project. One of the problems of using secondary data is that you might have identified a specific question but the existing data might not have been collected in such a way that they can be used to answer that specific question. They may have been collected too infrequently, at the wrong time or for the wrong administrative units.

Disadvantages

The main disadvantage of primary data is the time often required for data collection. Data collection is, on the whole, extremely slow. It takes time to make measurements. It takes time to collect samples. It takes time to conduct interviews. It takes time to record the day-to-day activities of pirates on the high seas. Furthermore, there is usually a marked learning curve so that initially data collection will be particularly slow and inaccurate. You are quite likely to discover that once you start, things aren't as you imagined they would be. Your planned data collection programme may not work. This may not become apparent for some time, so that you find yourself throwing away the first day's data because by the end of the day you have realized that the methods you are employing are not sufficiently consistent. Added to this, your inexperience may well lead you to make mistakes. For example, you may be undertaking some surveying with a new piece of equipment and fail to realize that, whereas the GPS equipment you used in class recorded some information automatically, the equipment you have in the field requires the user to record that information manually. When you get back to the lab you realize your mistake and need to organize a new field day! Everybody who collects primary data, even the most experienced researcher, encounters these problems. If it happens to you, don't feel that you are unusually stupid. The trick is to know it will happen and allow time accordingly. If you are exceptionally lucky and everything does go according to plan, it will just mean that you may have some time to spare. Take a holiday.

One way to try to overcome this disadvantage is to undertake a pilot study. Again, of course, this takes time. But it is likely to be time well spent. So, whatever your data collection involves, decide first on your method of collection. Then go out on the first day and collect data in this way, expecting things to go wrong. If you can, it is also a good idea to do some preliminary analysis of the data. Even if this is not possible, go through the steps you know you will need to perform and check that they will work. If your project involves using your field data to calculate something, have you measured everything that is needed? It will soon become apparent where the faults are. You may find that it's simply a matter of not having enough hands to hold all the equipment you need, and that you can solve the problem by hanging some of it around your neck. But you may find that your plan leaves a vital piece of information missing, or that you need to arrange for an assistant to come with you into the field.

A pilot study can help identify any problems with your proposed method of data collection.

A second disadvantage of primary data is that data collection can be tedious. Often, you will find yourself doing the same thing over and over again. While it's not quite true to say that when you've measured one infiltration curve you've measured them all, the benefits to you and your project from subsequent measurements very soon start to seem disproportionately small compared to the time taken. There is nothing that can be done to mitigate this problem. All that can be said is that if the research problem exists and the data to solve it don't there is no choice but to collect the data yourself. Be professional and get on with it.

Finally, and largely as a result of the two previous disadvantages, using primary data means that you may end up with a data set smaller than you had planned to have. It is important that you know the relationship between the amount of data you actually have and the amount you will need (see Chapter 8). Otherwise, you may find that, although the data you have are of exactly the right quality, you just don't have enough of them to enable you to answer your question(s).

Fieldwork

Much primary collection involves fieldwork, whether this is undertaken in a city, under a forest canopy or on a glacier. Your fieldwork might be a short excursion to make a very specific measurement or collect a very specific sample, or it might be an extended period of living with, and living like, the group of people who are the subject of your study. There are issues of safety, ethics and data protection that can be associated with data collection, and guidelines on these issues have been produced by a number of agencies. In addition, your own institution will probably have its own documents regarding safety and ethics in fieldwork. Make sure you have read these documents and that you take the necessary precautions. We said something about ethics and safety in Chapter 6. You are likely to be required to complete a risk assessment form and an ethics evaluation form and to have these forms checked and approved by your tutor. There are ethical issues involved particularly when people or animals are the subject of your investigation, but even if you are only studying rocks and plants you need to be aware that many countries have strict regulations about collecting geological samples or removing any organic matter from their territory. In the UK, for example, it is illegal to pick wild flowers. Environmental ethics are very important. Collecting any archaeological material opens up a whole extra set of ethical and bureaucratic paperwork. Your university is likely to have an ethics committee that needs to approve your research. Check whether your proposal will need to be checked by such a committee. Your department should at least have an ethics form for you to sign. Pay particular attention to the matter of data protection. If you collect data about people in such a way that they can be identified in your data set, then they have a right of access to those data. Again, your tutor should know about the rules governing data protection and should be able to advise you.

By definition, fieldwork means you are away from your base and away from advice, technical back-up, spare parts, etc. Fieldwork therefore requires some careful planning both for what you intend to do and what you will do if things go wrong. Make lists of the equipment you will need in order to carry out your fieldwork. Identify those things that are essential and work out what you will do if they break, or if you run out. This doesn't mean that you need to take along two spare total stations! It does mean that you should have a plan of what you will do if your total station breaks – even if this plan is no more than to come back and fetch a replacement! Certainly for small items such as digital sound recorders or hand-held GPS units it might be worth packing a spare. If any of your equipment requires batteries or memory cards or a solar charger remember to take those with you. Low-tech back-ups can be useful in remote areas: take a sketch pad and pencil in case your camera freezes or falls in the river. Take a notebook in case the pirates whom you are trying to interview seize your digital recorder. It is important to think through, before you go, exactly what equipment will be appropriate for your particular fieldwork. For example, if you are planning to interview members of that mafia family or pirate group, they may not be willing to have the interview recorded, so you might need to use old fashioned pencil-and-paper field notes. If you were planning to give members of your pirate group digital cameras with which they could document their own daily routines as part of your project, make sure you choose cameras that pirates find easy to use. Don't expect your research participants to spend a week studying the instruction book before they start.

Eric says . . .

And, as we are talking about pirates, crime families and the high seas, remember never to put yourself or anyone else in any kind of dangerous situation. Your institution should probably stop you from doing a pirate or mafia dissertation!

You might be able to organize all the separate tasks you have planned for the period of fieldwork in such a way that if something does go wrong with the equipment needed for one of them you can work on something else in the meantime. It's always good if you can divide up your tasks in such a way that you can be working on one thing while waiting for conditions to be suitable for another. Think about the weather. Even if you are quite happy to work in the rain, the people you want to interview on street corners might not be. Likewise, large changes in river discharges following rainfall might be unacceptable for your research design. If you are planning coastal research think about the tides. You don't want to get involved with the coastguard or rescue services unless they are part of your research question! A list of some things to think about before setting out on fieldwork is given in Box 7.1.

Box 7.1 Planning for fieldwork

Things to check before setting out on fieldwork:

- Prepare a list of equipment.
- Make sure you have spare/back-up equipment.
- Does your equipment work? Do you know how it works?
- Write a plan of action (including timetable, logistics and transport arrangements).
- Write an alternative plan of action for when things go wrong.
- Do you have any necessary permissions?
- Do you have appropriate insurance?
- Have you checked (as appropriate) the tides, weather, timetable or TV guide?
- Will you need an assistant, partner or chaperone?
- Have you checked your plans for health, safety and personal security?
- Have you had your supervisor check your plans?

If fieldwork is carried out a considerable distance from your base then you may have to assume that there will be no opportunity to return. Any data you fail/forget to collect will not be collected and your project will have to manage without them. If you took the wrong equipment you might not be able to change it for what you need. Plan carefully and expect things to go wrong.

Foreign fieldwork

Everything that we have said about fieldwork generally applies to foreign fieldwork, but more so. There are disadvantages. Not only are you isolated from your base but you may be in a remote setting where you have no idea what the Spanish for 'water-permanent marker pen' is, even if you could find somebody to sell you one. There may also be cultural sensitivities of which you need to be aware. For example, the way you might dress to go out in hot weather at home might be considered very inappropriate by people where you are doing your fieldwork. Don't take it for granted that it will be acceptable to wear shorts and a T-shirt, or to be seen working on a Sabbath day, or to have the flag of your home nation sewn onto the outside of your rucksack. Before you visit some exotic location, talk to other people who have worked there before, and take their advice. Read about the culture even if your dissertation is about the soil. Similarly, read about the climate even if your dissertation is about the culture. You are not going to fit in very well with the local population if you are dressed for the wrong hemisphere!

Eric says . . .

If you choose to do fieldwork in a foreign location, be sure to prepare culturally as well as physically. Training for work in remote mountain villages might involve fitness training, language training and cultural sensitivity training!

Some of what we said in the previous paragraph might have reminded you of the final section of Chapter 5, where we introduced the idea of positionality and talked about the fact that some kinds of research inevitably work out differently depending on who is doing the research. Most people will react differently and provide different responses if interviewed by their best friend, a police officer, a tax official or a prescribing pharmacist. When you go into some field situations and start looking for answers, simply wearing a hat (or not wearing a hat) when you approach somebody could make a huge difference to the response you get from them. It is very important when planning any kind of research to be conscious of your own positionality, but it can become critically important when planning foreign fieldwork and it can become the central issue in your research design if you are doing certain kinds of research with certain groups of people in particular locations. Think back to our examples of mafia families and pirate ships. Eric, Erica and their friends Big Lou and Jack the Patch would each be likely to have a very different experience doing research with those groups. It is essential that you take account of that as you think about the data you are likely to be able to collect or the observations that you are likely to be able to make.

You can't make direct observations in situations that you are not allowed to enter.

If you do decide to undertake foreign fieldwork you will need to make more careful arrangements than if your fieldwork is more local, and you will need to be prepared to spend more time sorting things out when they go wrong. But if all this sounds off-putting don't despair; there are also advantages. You are a geographer: getting out and about and exploring other parts of the world is exciting! If you find your project more exciting, that is likely to come through in a more interesting dissertation. Going into the field may enable you to tackle a really interesting problem that could not easily be studied from home. You may want to study coastal processes although you live in a land-locked country. You may be city-based but want to study rural issues. Studying locations other than the place where you live is a big part of geography, so it is inevitable that a lot of appealing geography research topics are going to involve you in studying a far-away location. Many students study courses on topics involving development and the Global South. Unless you are based in the area you want to study, foreign fieldwork may be the only way you can undertake a dissertation on such a topic. As well as these academic benefits there are personal ones. Foreign travel is a valuable experience. You may be able to have a holiday in your field area before or after doing the fieldwork. You could try to organize a group of your friends to travel to a joint fieldwork location, sharing logistics, making travel safer by being in a group and helping each other with field-assistant tasks. You are more likely to be able to get a group of friends together for an exciting trip to an exotic location than for an outing to some dull place that you all know from school trips. Imaginative projects or a group of related projects that are to be undertaken in a foreign location could also attract funding from some source.

Funding for fieldwork

If you want to carry out fieldwork in an exotic location and need to raise funds to cover your costs, there are several options that you might try. The first possibility is that your institution might provide funds for students to undertake fieldwork as part of their dissertations; some do, but most do not. Even if your institution does not officially offer any funding, less obvious sources of funding might exist. For example your tutor may be involved in a funded research project to which your dissertation work might be able to contribute. Or you could get a free trip to some location to work as a field assistant on your supervisor's other project, but then stay on afterwards to work on your own, saving transport costs. If there is no funding through the institution, a second approach would be to look for charitable organizations that fund research of particular types. These might be based in your home town, aiming to help local students, or they might be based in your proposed field area, aiming to encourage work there. Even if there is no organization willing to fund you, you might be able to raise money through some sponsored events. Alternatively, there may be commercial organizations interested in the results of particular types of market research. If you really want to work on a project that is going to be expensive, it may be worth spending some time looking for funding. However, you have a limited amount of time to spend on your dissertation, so delaying a decision on what you will do while you wait for a decision about funding cannot be allowed to take up too much of your time. Don't use it as an excuse for not getting started.

Permissions, ethics and safety

Wherever you undertake fieldwork, you are likely to need to have access to somebody else's property. Wherever you need permission you must obtain it. Most people are quite happy to give permission in response to a polite request. They may be less accommodating if the request comes after the owner has already discovered you trespassing on the land. If you are thrown out half way through a week's data collection you will have wasted a lot of time. For fieldwork in some areas (especially national parks in many countries) a permit may be required from the local or national authorities. If you need access to restricted areas such as government buildings or corporate offices it may take some time to get all the clearances and appointments that you need. Contact the appropriate offices in good time. You are already probably underestimating what we mean by that. If you want access to a secure facility or you want to interview the chief executive on site, this could take months to set up. Never assume that you will be able to get somewhere, or meet somebody, without checking and re-checking. Getting your core data is important, so you don't want to find out too late that you can't access it.

As soon as you consider doing fieldwork you also have to consider ethical issues and safety. We have already mentioned ethics and safety (in Chapter 6, when you were thinking about your research design), and you need to keep these things in mind at all times. Refer back to the ethics and safety forms that you completed as part of the research design process. Check that you are taking account of all the issues you considered when you completed those forms, and think again to check whether any new ethics or safety issues are appearing now that you have moved the project forward. Your ethics and safety documents should be kept current. You need to review and update them as your project develops. If you decide to visit a new field site you need to complete a new risk assessment. If you decide to change your interview strategy or talk to a different group of people you need to review your ethics assessment. If you make any substantial changes to the plans that were previously approved by your supervisor you will need to have them re-approved.

Ethics documents and risk assessments might seem like a tedious chore, but they are an important part of the research process.

To do certain types of work, for example, if you want to work with young people or vulnerable adults, you might even need to have an official criminal records check. The policies and procedures on criminal records checks vary from country to country, so find out about your local regulations. In the UK, for example, you might need to undergo a criminal records check if you want to work with children. These checks involve a certain amount of bureaucracy and take time to complete.

Look back at the comments we made in Chapter 6, and check out the references we suggested such as Hay (2010) on ethics and Bullard (2010) on field safety.

Laboratory work

Not all primary data need be collected in the field. For some types of project the data collection can be done largely or wholly in a laboratory. Again, two words of warning: first, if you plan to base your dissertation on laboratory work, check that your institution allows this; second, just as with fieldwork, there are safety issues and potential ethics issues associated with working in a laboratory. Check with your institution. There may be regulations affecting the times and conditions under which you can have access to a laboratory that will restrict the type of laboratory work you can undertake. For example, you may not be allowed to monitor experiments overnight or at the weekend. You might not be allowed to use particular chemicals without a licence. The lab might only be available for certain parts of the year.

In some instances, laboratory work will be associated with fieldwork as part of your data collection. For example, you may have collected a peat core from a field site and then need to spend time analyzing the core, or you may have collected soil samples and need to undertake physical or chemical analyses of these samples. In both these cases, the time you will need to spend in the laboratory will be considerably greater than that in the field. Alternatively, you could undertake your entire project in a laboratory. You might be analyzing samples as secondary data sets collected by somebody else, or you might be developing experiments to explore physical processes entirely in the controlled environment of the laboratory. For example, you might be doing experiments on how suspended silt can be entrained into ice during the freezing of supercooled water. It is not easy to observe that process in the field, so a laboratory approach might be more convenient.

Computer laboratories

Not all laboratory work involves people walking around in white coats and safety goggles. Just as laboratory measurements and experiments are as valid as fieldwork for solving problems, so are computer modelling, GIS, digital analysis of remotely sensed data or any number of other IT-related tasks. A great deal of geography-relevant computing power is now available to most students on their own devices, but for specialist software you may well need to use facilities in your institution's IT suite or computer lab. If you have a particular interest in computers and/or have good programming skills, you might consider a dissertation that is strongly based on numerical modelling. Even if you decide to base your dissertation around numerical modelling, you can still include some fieldwork.

Field data can provide an input to GIS or modelling, and you may like to undertake a dissertation that combines the two. A lot of great geography research crosses boundaries that used to exist between different styles of research, whether that be between 'human' and 'physical' topics or between different methods in the lab, in the field, in the archive or on social networks and in the cloud. There are lots of ways of doing geography and lots of ways of combining them.

Other primary data sources

The data sources available to projects in geography and the related disciplines that we are thinking about are many and varied, and do not all fit conveniently under headings such as fieldwork or laboratory experiments. For example, many students embark on projects based on the collection of data by questionnaires administered not directly in the field but remotely by post, by telephone or online. Apart from the fact that you are doing this work from 'home' rather than on a stranger's doorstep or up a mountain, this kind of data collection has many of the characteristics, and raises many of the same issues, as those raised by other types of primary data collection. There are still ethics issues to be considered, there is still the need to think in advance about precisely what data you need, and you need to be sure that your equipment and techniques are fit for purpose. For example, don't rush into carrying out a postal questionnaire based on open-ended questions when what you really need are yes/no answers.

Erica says . . .

Don't try to administer your questionnaire via Facebook if you are hoping to assess your respondents' body language.

Remember that your choice of survey method will affect the validity of your sample population: a Facebook survey will only get responses from people on Facebook, which might bias the age or social profile of your sample. Students sometimes throw in a questionnaire as part of their research proposal thinking that it will be a simple way of generating data, often as a supplementary element in a project involving other fieldwork. This is a mistake. Do not underestimate the subtleties and complexities of any methods you plan to use, but especially don't underestimate the subtleties and complexities of questionnaire surveys. McLafferty (2010) provides a very brief introduction to some of the issues.

Secondary data

Advantages and disadvantages

To a large extent, the advantages and disadvantages of secondary data are the converse of those for primary data: see Table 7.1. Secondary data have the major advantage of being (often) more readily accessible (you don't have to go out and measure rivers or interview people), and typically can provide you with large data sets relatively quickly (you can access data that took a huge organization a long time to collect, and that would have been far beyond the scope of your own primary data collection). In some instances, secondary data will still involve you in some tedious data gathering, or transcribing of data from an original source document into your spreadsheet or database, or coding of information to convert it from the original data into something you can use. So you may spend almost as long in a library or record office as you would in the field or laboratory collecting primary data. Increasingly, however, many data sets other than obscure historical records can be accessed directly in digital form. Nevertheless, you may find that, although the data do exist in digital form, there is a hefty price to be paid for data in that form. You may also find that, the benefits of modern technology notwithstanding, you are still stuck in an archive copying numbers or dates!

Such close contact with the data isn't a bad thing. As with primary data, some 'feel' for data quality and reliability is useful and may be obtainable from original records where it is not from a digital record. As we have already said, it is particularly important in historical geography to be able to assess the reliability of your data. The original records may contain useful clues. Other clues may come from reading the work of others who have used the data and who may have had better access than you may have to the original sources. In addition, there may be reports that go with the data which will tell you something about the accuracy and reliability. For example, if you use data collected by a remote sensing satellite, the data will have undergone some pre-processing before you receive them. Such pre-processing aims to make the data more readily usable by most of the user-community. If the sensor had a tendency to miss out some data, these data may have been 'interpolated' from neighbouring data. Without access to information that tells you this is so, you will not be able to tell the difference between a 'real' value and an 'interpolated' one. Likewise, censuses contain interpolations where full data sets were not available. These interpolations are made to make the census more useful to the people for whom the census data have been collected. You are not among the most significant of the users of census data, so your needs won't have been paramount when the interpolation methods were devised!

So far, we have discussed secondary data that have been collected with a view to their use by a third party, for example census data. Other secondary data might not be designed for public access. However, because of the expense of collecting data, and the fact that often public money has been used to fund data collection, there is an increasing requirement for data archives to be made available. Large research organizations and projects typically have websites where, with a bit of digging, you can often find the sort of data you might need for your dissertation. Your supervisor is likely to know of possible sources of data, and a day spent trawling through websites could easily provide you with just what you need for your project. On the other hand, you might find some data which, though not quite what you had in mind, could form the basis of a slightly different project. Don't be afraid, even at this stage to modify your project. If a more interesting line of enquiry, or approach to the problem presents itself, take it! But don't think of these data sources as being just an easy way out of days spent on a cold, windswept hillside. Such data may have been collected by an individual for a particular research project and now you want to use the data for some other purpose. Treat such data with particular care. Where data have been collected with a user-community in mind, some serious attempt will have been made to make sure the data are as consistent and reliable as possible. Likewise, there will probably be some documentation on the data. For data that you might extract from the appendix in somebody's thesis or journal article, no such safeguards are likely to exist. Bearing in mind that the original researcher did not have your project in mind when the data were collected, and may, anyway, have been reluctant to draw attention to weaknesses in the data, you may well find that this apparent short cut to your data proves to be a time-consuming sidetrack.

If you are developing a project that will rely on secondary data, make sure that you will be able to access data of sufficient quality and reliability, and in sufficient quantities, to achieve your goals.

Check out your likely data sources before you get too far into the project.

For example, if you are doing a UK-based social science dissertation then the Understanding Society data set from the UK Data Service (ukdataservice.ac.uk) is a likely source of information for you. Their whole purpose is to provide good access to data sources for social and economic research. This means that they essentially had people like you in mind as they assembled and presented their resources. That means that you are likely to find the resources helpful and easy to use compared to resources that you might find via other organizations that were not worrying about your particular requirements. If you think you might use the UK Data Service check in advance that the particular data you need are openly available or whether you would need some special access licence. In many online data sets you will find the most recent data is embargoed and unavailable to you, or available only at a high cost. Older data might be freely available. This could affect the way you choose to frame your question and design your research, so you need to know about data availability as early as possible. Delaying a visit to the data source until the last minute could be catastrophic. Check early. Check now.

Permissions (ownership of sites/copyrights)

There may not be free public access to secondary data and, even if there is, there may be restrictions regarding what can be done with them. In particular, publication of secondary data may not be allowed without permission. You will need to check on any restrictions of use that may apply. As we said above, check early. Check now.

Foreign data

Access to foreign secondary data has in the past been much more difficult than access to data in your own country, but that difficulty is diminishing with better international communication and the globalization of information via the internet. Different types of data are likely to be available in different places, and the data may be of a different standard (either better or worse) than that you are used to at home. Just because you have good public-access mapping and accurate census data where you live, don't assume that the same data will be available in your target location abroad. For example, you might be familiar with using data from the UK census, or resources that you have accessed online from the UK Data Service, and you might be planning to do a comparative study looking at how ethnic diversity varies between cities in the UK and another European country. You might be feeling very confident about your project, having assimilated lots of data about country of birth of UK residents from the UK data, but you could come very unstuck when you discover that equivalent country-of-birth data are not available for your other European study location. Check. Checking things such as data availability is relatively easy online and with a few polite emails to likely suppliers.

However, you still may not have the same information regarding the format and structure of the data source as you would have for a source in your own country. The organizations or individuals supplying your data will not know the requirements of your project, and if you are dealing with a country very different from your own they may not even understand the nature of a geography dissertation, and so cannot be expected to recognize exactly what are the best data for your needs. Unless you have a reliable route to secondary data in a foreign country, either from personal contact or through your tutor, it is very risky to trust the success of your dissertation to a foreign secondary data source. Just be careful, and do your homework.

Chapter summary and conclusion

This chapter has described some of the different types of data that you may use for your dissertation, considered some of the differences between primary and secondary data and looked at advantages and disadvantages of each from the point of view of undertaking a dissertation. It is important to think carefully about exactly what data you need and to think early on about how you will access them. You should consider the amount of data you need and what you plan to do with your data at the same time that you are thinking about what data you need, because the data you need will depend on what you plan to do with the data.

What to do after reading Chapter 7

Check the availability of the data that you plan to use.

Read Chapter 8.

8

WHAT AMOUNT OF DATA DO I NEED, AND WHAT CAN I DO WITH MY DATA?

This chapter explores the relationship between the amount of data you collect and your ability to answer different types of question. It also looks at issues of data quality, and what you can do with the data you have collected.

Different amounts of data are needed for different things

You can do many different things with your data, and the amount that you need depends on what you plan to do with them. Different types of analysis require different amounts of data. If you are collecting presence/absence data to test a simple hypothesis you may be able to design a project that requires very few, but if you are collecting data to make into an extended narrative in a project that adopts a storytelling approach you may need a great many.

There are those who will tell you that you can't have too much data. They're wrong, both because they should say 'too many' rather than too much, and because, well, you can have too much (or, rather, too many)! Just as there is no point collecting more precise data than you need, there is no point collecting a greater amount of data than you need. You need the amount of data required to solve the problem, answer the question or carry out the mission that you have set yourself – and no more. Any more data means that you have been wasting your time somewhere and, given that the time you have is finite, losing time somewhere else. The big question is what amount of data do you need to answer your particular question? The answer, of course, is that it depends on the question. It also depends on the kind of data you are using – although that, too, is likely to depend on your question. Are you using quantitative data, qualitative data, spatial data or some combination of those? We will have something to say about each of those, and you will need to be clear in your own mind what kind of data you are using, and what you are trying to achieve in your project, in order to decide which parts of our advice apply most closely to your project. If you are doing six months of ethnographic fieldwork embedded with a band of maritime pirates your data are likely to be substantially different from the data of another researcher doing a one-day hike-and-grab measurement of streamwater chemistry.

Whatever type(s) of data you are dealing with, it is unlikely that raw data will directly answer your research question(s). Collecting the data rarely leads you directly to the answer that you need, and you will usually need to carry out some kind of analysis. For example, if your dissertation sought to test the hypothesis that new manufacturing industry was preferentially located in small, rather than large, towns and your study showed that all the small towns you investigated had higher rates of growth than any of the large towns you studied, then it might seem that the answer to the question would be immediately apparent and no further data processing would be necessary in order to answer that particular question. However, it would only answer the question about the particular towns that you studied. Anyway, few data sets will be so unequivocal and, even if they are, you might wish to explore the question further (for example, could this answer be true of all small and large towns). Or, in this example, you might want to see if the relationship between new manufacturing and town size is stronger than simply big/small and less/more. Is there a linear relation between growth of manufacturing industry and town size, or is there a threshold of size below which growth is rapid and above which it is slow? Or perhaps you got a personal impression about some of the towns in your study that some-how contradicted the data: how could you test the validity of this personal impression?

One way or another, therefore, you are likely to need some processing of your data. Regardless of the methods you use and the type of data you have, all data processing has the same purpose: it moves you forward towards providing the answer to your research question. The amount of data that you need depends partly on the kind of analysis that you are going to carry out. If you are carrying out statistical analyses, then particular statistical techniques require particular amounts of data, so you will need to find out about those before you finish collecting your data, to make sure that you have collected enough, and of the right sort.

Eric says . . .

You need to know before you collect your data what statistics or other analyses you will apply to them.

The first thing to realize is that the size of your data set is only an issue if you wish to make (general) inferences from your (specific) data, and that size is particularly important if you want to apply specific statistical tests to your data. If you are asking a question about a single person or feature, you don't necessarily need to study more than that one person or feature. If you are asking a question about all the examples of that kind of person or feature around the world, then you will need to look at more than one, and have sufficient data so that you can start making inferences about the whole world from your small sample.

Making inferences about large populations from small samples

Whether you need to worry about sample sizes depends on whether you are interested only in the data you have collected, or interested in saying something about a larger (perhaps infinite) population of which your data are a only small part. Are you using your

200 interviews just to find out about the 200 people you interviewed or to reach a conclusion about people generally? Are you using your temperature measurements at three locations just to find out the temperatures at those locations, or are you going to input those three sites into a GIS model that will make inferences or interpolations about the temperatures at positions between those sites? The way you defined your question in Chapter 4 will have determined which of these is the case. It is a good idea now to make certain you are sure of this. In many forms of data processing, exactly what you do will depend on being clear about this point. Don't form the impression, which you can easily do from reading books on statistics, that it's somehow better or more normal if your study is about a sample of a larger population. Much of statistical theory was developed for such situations, and so many books on statistics tend to assume it to be the case, but many perfectly valid research questions don't work that way. Some excellent dissertations are based on studies of the unique, rather than of the general. As with some other sections of this book, and with other books that you use, select from what we say below the sections that are relevant to your particular project.

There are two reasons why you might want to make inferences. First, you may want to use a limited data set that you have collected in your study to draw wider conclusions. For example, you may measure a sample of the total population because the total population is too large, and then make inferences that you hope will apply to the whole. Second, even if you can measure every member of the population (for example, the age of every occupant of a village) you may still find that the total number is too small to give you a conclusive answer to your particular question, so you may need to make statistical inferences from your limited data.

Consider an example in which you are studying the business lifespan of shops that have ceased trading in a particular shopping complex and only 10 shops have closed down since the shopping complex was opened. Even if you study all 10 of them your study will tell you only about these 10 businesses, and, strictly speaking, no more. You may want to make some qualitative inferences from your study in which you suggest that your study may be representative of failed businesses in general. But, given the way in which you set up your study, namely that you deliberately chose to study a particular shopping complex, any such inferences would have no statistical validity. Depending on your overall aim and strategy this may or may not matter to you, but you do need to be aware of it.

Now consider a similar project on a much bigger, older shopping complex. In this shopping complex 150 businesses have ceased trading since the complex opened. This number, you decide, is far too large for you to research them all. One approach would be for you to decide on a few specific businesses you want to study and for you to conduct your study on them. This project would be similar to the previous one. The result you obtain will apply only to those businesses you have studied and any wider inferences you draw from your study will be of a qualitative nature. There is nothing wrong with this approach, as long as you realize the limitations of what you can do with your results.

A different approach would be for you to decide that you want to study 150 businesses by taking a sample from which you will make inferences about all 150. The question of how big this sample needs to be then arises. This is a very common situation for geography dissertation students to find themselves in, so we will say a bit about how you answer this question.

The amount of data you need depends on the type of problem you are tackling and the type of approach you are taking to the problem.

The reasons for making inferences, the inferences you can make and the amount of data you require depend partly on the nature of the question(s) you are asking. Even if you are in the situation of studying all 10 shops that have failed in a particular shopping complex you need to understand that the fact that there are only 10 such shops has implications for the types of question you can ask. Suppose you are considering what factors led these shops to close down and you want to evaluate the relative importance of these factors. Say you think that the previous business experience of the owner may have been a factor. So you plan to compare the experience of the owners of your 10 failed shops with that of the owners of 10 others that are still open. You may also think that the age of the owner is important so you look at that too. Then you realize that older people are likely to have more business experience than younger ones simply because they've had more time, so you plan to do a two-way analysis of variance. Now you will discover, when you come to check up on the appropriate statistical tests, that you have insufficient data for such an analysis. Those 10 shops are not enough in this case to answer the questions in the way that you have chosen to do so. If you want to use inferential statistics there are very explicit criteria that your data must satisfy. We don't want to discuss those criteria here, but simply to point out that if you choose to take a particular approach to solving your problem you need to be aware of the constraints that apply to that approach.

If your research design involves making inferences about one group or individual on the basis of another, you need to beware both the 'ecological fallacy' and the 'exception fallacy'. These two logical pitfalls basically mean that you can't make an assumption about an individual just because you know something about the group of which they are part, and you can't make an assumption about a whole group just because you know something about an individual within it. Just because Tony is part of an organization that includes many ice-cream sellers we cannot assume that he is one, and just because Peter is a model railway enthusiast we can't assume that any club of which he is a member must be full of other model railway enthusiasts.

Consider another example. In this case you are testing the hypothesis that, in a particular locality, east-facing hillslopes are steeper than west-facing ones. Now, if you measure one east-facing hillslope and one west-facing and it turns out to be true that the east-facing one is steeper, what does that tell you? Not a lot! You need more data. If we ignore the possibility that the slopes were identical, one of them had to be steeper than the other. It could just as easily have been the west-facing one as the east-facing one. The number of measurements you need here is a question of probability. It's the old coin-tossing problem where east-facing hillslopes are heads and west-facing hillslopes are tails. To identify bias in the coin, or to establish a difference between east-facing and west-facing hillslopes, you have to get a result that would be unlikely if there were no genuine bias. Statisticians usually say that something has to have a probability of less than 5 per cent before the result is considered sufficiently unlikely to have occurred by chance. So, if you measure three pairs of hillslopes and find that the east-facing slope is steeper in every case, there is still a 12.5 per cent chance that this could have occurred by chance and there is no real difference between east- and west-facing slopes. You would have to measure at least five pairs of hillslopes and find all of the east-facing ones to be steeper to obtain a result that would support or refute your hypothesis. If one west-facing hillslope was steeper you'd need six out of seven steeper east-facing hillslopes for it to be deemed unlikely to have occurred by chance. Of course, if there is some geomorphological process that operates differentially to make east-facing hillslopes steeper than west-facing ones, it is unlikely to be the only process operating. Some other process affecting hillslope gradient may be making the west-facing hillslopes steeper or locally steepening hillslopes from time to time irrespective of their location. Thus, in the real world, measuring five pairs of hillslopes is unlikely to give a conclusive result.

So, going back to the question of how many pairs you would need to measure, it becomes clear that the less important the process(es) causing east-facing hillslopes to be steeper, the more pairs you will need to measure to discover if it has any effect. If the driving process is really strong and dominates the landscape, then you might get a conclusive result with fewer observations, but five will be the absolute minimum.

The bigger the effect something has, the fewer observations you will need to identify it. A very biased coin is easier to identify than a slightly biased coin.

In the case of the coin, if it is very biased then it may come down heads every time, but if the bias is only slight it will come down heads only slightly more than 50 per cent of the time. If you are able to bet heads every time then a slight bias may be so small that your fellow gambler may not notice it, but it will be enough for you to have a certainty of coming out ahead in the long run. So with the hillslopes, if the process causing east-facing hillslopes to be steeper is only a very small contributory factor to their overall steepness, then you will need to measure a lot in order to discover if it is operating. This may sound depressing but, in fact, it can work to your advantage. If you discover the bias even with a very small sample then it implies that the process making east-facing hillslopes steeper is very important in controlling their overall steepness. If it turns out not to be very important then you might ask whether it is worth investigating anyway!

If you are using GIS, then tools for making spatial inferences (such as interpolating predicted values between known data points) will be available within the software, but those tools will work differently depending on how many known data points you actually have. The geostatistical analysis may be hidden behind the scenes in GIS, but the same basic statistical principles apply.

We spent some time on the coin, hillslope and shops examples because they demonstrate a key point: that the amount of data you need depends on the type of problem you are tackling and the question you are asking. In addition, they show that for quantitative data analysis it can often be quite easy to specify the minimum data that you must have in a best-case scenario, but that the actual amount of data you will need to reach a conclusion in your own real-world scenario as it emerges later in your project may be more difficult to specify. But you also need to think about the converse. If you are trying to show two things are different and you have lots of observations, but the stats don't show a significant difference, that still tells you something. Statistical tests are a formal way of agreeing on things. They are not usually an answer to a research question, but a measurement of the reliability, transferability or some other characteristic of your answer or the data that contributed to it.

Simple statistical tests are not designed to investigate causation. However, with good research design you can use the statistical tests that recognize relationships as a part of your investigation into likely causes. For example, if you use a hypothesis-testing approach and realize that if A caused B there would need to be a relationship between C and D, and you then found statistically that C and D were not related, then your statistical test for relationships would have contributed to your investigation of causes. As with so many things in your dissertation, research design is all-important.

There are two issues that you will need to think about if you are assembling data for statistical analysis. One is the relatively simple issue of identifying the minimum amount of data necessary to perform particular statistical tests. The other is the more tricky issue of identifying the amounts of data that are actually likely to be sufficient for your project, which might be more than the minimum that the statistics textbook tells you that the test requires. You can look up what test does what, and how they work, in any of the many basic geography statistics textbooks that will no doubt be available in your institution's library. We are not going to try and cover that here. For each of the types of question that you may be asking, there will be statistical techniques that will allow you to assess your data, identify relationships between them and measure the reliability of inferences that you make from them. These tests will allow you to put some numbers against your opinions of the data. They will enable you to say, for example, that there is a 99 per cent probability that a relationship is real, rather than just having to say that you think it looks as though there might be a relationship. If you want to describe something having measured only a part (a sample) of it, there are tests for that. If you want to assess whether two sets of values (areas, hours of sunshine, pirate incomes) are really different from each other, there are tests for that. If you want to see whether there is a relationship between two sets of data (slope gradient and soil erosion rates, for example), then there are tests for that, too. For each technique there will be a necessary minimum amount of data without which you cannot use the technique.

To get a statistically significant answer to the question 'Is this coin biased?' you would need to toss it a minimum of six times.

When planning your project you may be tempted to take that minimum amount as the amount that you think you need to collect. Think again. Sometimes the amount of data that you need for a test to be useful in your particular situation is more than the minimum required simply for the test to be carried out.

How many data do I really need to answer my question(s)?

The minimum amount of data necessary to perform a statistical test is not likely to be the same as that you will require to answer the question you are investigating. Consider the example in which you are investigating the possibility that hillslope gradient affects pH of the soil. In order to perform a statistical test of such an effect you know that you need a minimum of three pairs of observations of hillslope gradient and soil pH. The result of such an investigation is shown in Figure 8.1(a). There is a relationship but it is considered to be too weak to be statistically significant (as is shown by the probability, under the null hypothesis of no difference, of obtaining the given t value). Now look at

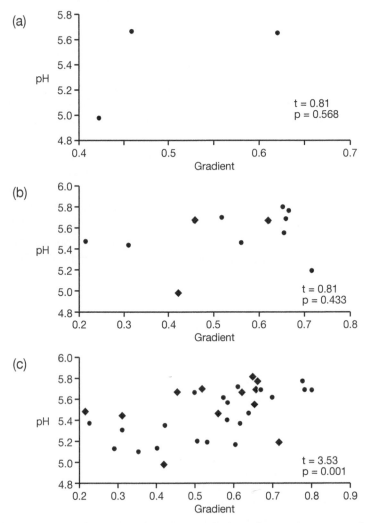

Figure 8.1 The outcome of a statistical test is strongly dependent on the amount of data you have. Where relationships between variables are weak or subject to a lot of scatter because of other influences, you need quite a large data set to obtain a statistically significant result

Points that are common in 8.1 (a), (b) and (c) are shown as ◆

Figure 8.1(b). Your data set is larger. In this case (by chance), the value of the t statistic is the same but the probability of obtaining this value, under the null hypothesis of no effect, is less. This probability is still not sufficiently low for you to reject the null hypothesis of no effect. Now look at Figure 8.1(c), which illustrates a case where your sample is even larger. The probability of t is now less than 5 per cent and you can reject the null hypothesis. So, it seems you can reach a different conclusion depending on the size of your data set. This may be true. However, what is also true is that if you don't have the minimum amount of data you can't reach any conclusion. So, is it just a case of getting past the minimum to perform the statistical test and then you have whatever conclusion you want? Not quite!

If your coin always lands heads up then you could be reasonably certain that it is biased after you had tossed it six times. But if it landed heads up only three-quarters of the time you would need to toss it 20 times to be reasonably certain of bias.

It is the case, however, that the bigger the sample the smaller the difference or the weaker the relationship between A and B needs to be for it to be statistically significant. Whether you should choose a sample size like that shown in Figure 8.1(a) or (b) or (c) depends on what you want to know. A sample size that is close to the minimum for a statistical test would be appropriate for the question 'Does B have a very strong influence on A?', whereas a large sample size (such as that shown in Figure 8.1(c)) would be appropriate for the question 'Does B have any influence at all on A?' It might seem, at first sight, that the second of these questions isn't very important and that what you should be interested in is strong relationships and differences that can be identified from small samples. This will depend on the complexity of the problem that you are investigating. It might be the case that A isn't affected very strongly by anything at all, and this, in itself, is significant.

Figure 8.2 shows the relationships between distances moved by painted stones on a desert hillslope over a 16-year period studied by Abrahams et al. (1984). The results, showing relatively weak relationships between these distances and particle size, gradient and hillslope length, make it possible to discriminate among hypotheses regarding the mechanism causing their movement. If these particles were moved by gravitational forces alone then we would expect to find a strong relationship between the distance moved and the hillslope gradient (since this determines the downslope component of gravity) but no relationship between the distance moved and hillslope length or size of particle, because gravity is the same everywhere and, as Galileo showed, different masses are affected by it equally. If, on the other hand, the particles were moved by overland flow alone we would expect to find direct relationships between the distance moved and gradient and length of the hillslope and an inverse relationship between distance moved and particle size, because the amount of overland flow available to move the particles will be a function of hillslope length and its velocity will be a function of gradient, and smaller particles

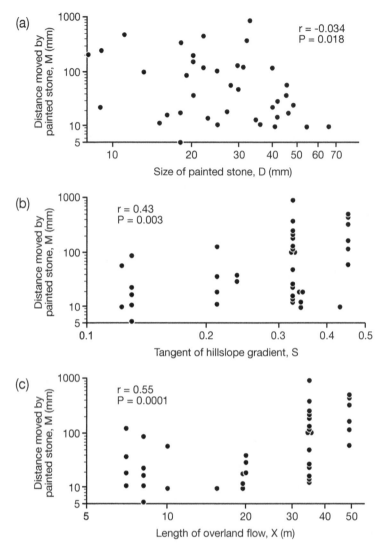

Figure 8.2 Relationships between distances moved by painted stones and (a) stone size, (b) hillslope gradient and (c) overland flow length. The strength of these relationships together with which of them is strongest makes it possible to discriminate among various hypotheses regarding the processes responsible for the movement of the stones

Source: After Abrahams et al., 1984

will be more readily entrained by the flow. That such relationships do exist allows us to reject the hypothesis of gravitational processes acting alone, but the results are consistent with the hypothesis that the particles are moved by overland flow alone. However, the results are also consistent with the hypothesis that the particles are moved by a combination of the two processes. If this were so, and the gravitational processes were stronger, we would expect to find that the strongest relationship would be between distance moved and the hillslope gradient, since this factor affects both sets of processes but is the only factor affecting gravitational processes. As this is not the case we can also reject the hypothesis that the particles move by a combination of processes in which gravitational processes are dominant. Thus, we can conclude from the strengths of the three relationships that the particles are moved dominantly or wholly by overland flow. In this case the fact that a particular relationship was weak and that others existed at all provided the information needed to test the hypotheses. We did not need to look for strong relationships.

Once again we see that exactly what you do, and exactly what data you need, depends on exactly what your question is.

Quantities of data for qualitative analysis

As we have seen, the amount of data you need for statistical analysis of quantitative data is determined by generally accepted rules. You can use fewer data than the rules specify (at least down to the point below which the statistics can't be calculated), and people often do, but if you do this you need to be careful about the interpretation of your results. However, deciding the amount of data you need to answer your question (as opposed to just performing statistical tests which may help you answer your question) is much less straightforward.

For qualitative data analysis you have exactly the same problem. Many research projects involve qualitative data. The data may come, for example, from interviews, observations, diaries or novels. In its raw form, your data might consist of pages of text (transcripts of interviews and so on). The task is to extract from the raw data something meaningful in the context of your research questions. Generally, this task involves some sort of coding of the data. Your coding should enable you to use your data to answer your research questions. Do not assume that because your data are qualitative your research questions are limited to A=?. The question 'Do young people of different ethnic backgrounds have different attitudes to community identity?' (A≠B) can be answered equally well with qualitative data as it can with quantitative data. We would argue that all the types of question we have used as examples previously could be addressed using qualitative data, though, as with quantitative data, causation is the most difficult to address. Likewise, there is no reason why you should not use qualitative data in a hypothetico-deductive framework.

In some research projects, qualitative data are analyzed using statistical methods. If you follow this approach, then the same rules apply as if you were using quantitative data. However, some research projects that use qualitative data use a wholly qualitative approach to the analysis. If you follow this approach then the rules are less clear about how many data you need. This fact makes life more difficult for you because you have to decide, and be able to defend, the amount (and nature) of the data you collect. Qualitative researchers sometimes refer to 'thick' or 'rich' data to indicate the amount or quality of data they have, but those terms do not have clear, universally accepted definitions. You can easily look up the universally agreed answer to the question of how many observations you need in order to get a statistically significant result to a particular numerical test, but you can't look up a universally agreed answer to the question of how many unstructured interviews with pirates you would need to conduct before your data was considered thick or rich. Some people suggest that you should keep conducting interviews until you reach 'data saturation' or redundancy – the point where further interviews stop revealing additional information. Some people say you should stop when three consecutive interviews add no further useful information. Some people say that 10 is a good number. Others say there is no minimum. Others say that there is no maximum and that you should keep going until you run out of time. These different pieces of advice (we won't call them rules) make dissertation planning quite difficult. Whereas with quantitative data you can plan the time to be allocated to your fieldwork knowing what is the minimum amount of data you must have and having a fair idea of a reasonable amount for the question, this is less true for qualitative data. While collecting your data you will need to be continually reflecting on the data and its relationship to your research question. For example, what you need to do after your first unstructured interview with a homeless person in Birmingham may well depend on what that person said during the interview, so you won't have been able to finalize all your planning in advance of starting the data collection. Reflection on your data as you acquire them may allow you to conclude the data collection sooner than you'd expected, but on the other hand it may lead you to conclude that you need to do an extra week of work or that an answer to your question may not even be possible in the time you have available for data collection. You may find that you reach data saturation very quickly in one part of your investigation, but have to continue the interviews because other lines of interest are still developing. Thinking about these things while collecting your data will avoid a nasty shock when you have your first meeting with your tutor after your fieldwork. In fact, if you go into that meeting ready to discuss such reflection, rather than with just a pile of scruffy notes you wrote up after your interviews, your tutor is likely to be impressed by the maturity of your approach.

An important difference between qualitative and quantitative data is that for the latter there are agreed ways of doing things. So, if you report in your dissertation that you used a particular test on your quantitative data, everybody will know the rules of the test and you won't need to say any more, so you can jump straight to the result of the test. Because the 'rules' for analysis of qualitative data are not always so well established you may need to give a more explicit account of how you processed or analyzed your data before going ahead with the explanation of what the analysis showed.

Spatial data

The research questions asked by geographers usually have a spatial dimension to them, so it is unsurprising that geography research projects deal with spatial data. How does soil pH vary downslope? Do distributions of diseases vary with patterns of local economic inequality? The significance for data analysis is that you may need to use additional methods to those we've talked about so far if you want to examine some of the spatial properties of your data. Discussions of spatial data processing sometimes distinguish between geostatistics and GIS, but the two are not really exclusive; you may well want to use both, and in fact GIS is really (among other things) a convenient way of doing geostatistics. In geostatistics the emphasis is on the statistical analysis of the spatial properties of data. If you have data for a few specific points within an area, and you want to interpolate between those points to 'fill in' your map (for example, if you know the temperature at three weather stations but want to infer from those what the temperature would be at a point between them) then geostatistics is how that kind of analysis is done. GIS software typically includes user-friendly tools for carrying out spatial inference and other geostatistical techniques, and provides a convenient way for those of us who lack geostatistical expertise to engage with those kinds of problems. In GIS there is a strong emphasis on the visualization of these spatial properties. The kinds of visualizations associated with GIS, which commonly involve maps, satellite images or other geographic base layers, are especially convenient for representing spatial data. For example, if you have data that essentially lists cities against values such as their economic wellbeing or property prices, you could present that data as a list, or perhaps as a bar chart. On the other hand you could present it as a map, recognizing that the cities are in different locations, adding significantly to the value of the data and making it possible to see spatial patterns in your data.

A map of variation across a space is usually more helpful than a bar chart.

In geography projects this spatial component is normally at the heart of the research, so spatial analysis really matters.

Data quality

So far we've focused on the amount and types of data you may need. But are all data the same? Do you need to think about the quality of your data in relation to the amount? We'd all like to think that the data we have (particularly those we've personally collected through hard work in the field) are wholly reliable. But, really, we all know that's not true. What about that measurement of stream depth you obtained hanging from the branch of a tree? Is it as good as the one you got standing on the bridge? Did you get the feeling that this interviewee was just making up a story for fun? You may have a sufficient number of interviews, but were they sufficiently detailed, and did the interviewees have sufficient opportunity to think about the questions before you hurried them for an answer? Certainly if you are conducting qualitative research, then the quality of your data is at least as important as the quantity. If you know, even as you are collecting them, that some of your data are less reliable than others, you should make a note of that at the time. You can use these notes during your data analysis. If some of your data seem a bit odd and your notes say that you had doubts at the time, you can use these notes to justify any decision to be selective about which data you use and which you reject as flawed.

Without these notes, you can't throw out some data just because they don't fit your ideas of how things should be. If all of your data are measured with less precision than you would have liked (if your shear vane is graduated in kPa but you need measurements at 0.1 kPa so you have to estimate the decimal point, for example) then this lack of precision introduces noise into your data. You need to be aware of your data quality, and your dissertation needs to make the reader aware of it as well. It is particularly important that if your examiner thinks the data are flawed you have covered yourself in the write-up by identifying and discussing those flaws yourself.

Some data are better than others.

Either because you have some dodgy data to throw out, or because there's a higher level of noise in your data than you would like, you will sometimes need more data than you thought. So it's a good idea always to collect a bit extra than the bare minimum you need to answer your question, as insurance.

What can I do with my data?

This is not really a question that you should be asking at this stage, although many students do. The question of what you do with your data was bound up with your previous questions about the kind of data you need and the amount of data you need. If the way you organized your dissertation was to assemble loads of data and then start to think what you might do with it, then you might want to have a look at Chapter 10! Rather than collecting data then wondering what you can do with them, you should start by thinking what you want to do, then assemble the data that you need to do it! You should know what your data are intended for before you start collecting them.

Broadly speaking, data are the evidence that you use to answer your question or solve your problem. Data can feed into a model that you have designed to predict the future; data can be used to perform a test that will potentially falsify your hypothesis; data provide the content with which you can populate your narrative. Data are the ammunition for your analytical arsenal.

Different projects use and produce data in different ways. In the sort of hypothesis-testing project we used as an example earlier, data (observations or results) can be applied simply as tests of predictions to evaluate a hypothesis. You may observe that a section of glacier ice contains no debris, and from that observation deduce that your hypothesis about debris entrainment must be false. The data lead quickly to your final conclusion. In other types of project data come into play at different stages. For example, in a modelling project you might need data as input to calibrate or establish your model before you can then use your model to produce further data that will lead you towards your conclusion. We said more about modelling in Chapter 5. Many projects go through multiple stages of data collection, application and analysis on their way to a final conclusion. In some projects the data make up a fairly small part of the total dissertation, both in terms of time spent collecting them and the space allocated to them in the report. It does not take long either to observe or to report that there is no debris in a piece of ice. In such projects the data may be concise but the interpretation of that data can lead into interesting discussions of their implications. In other projects, for example a project where narrative reporting of extended observation or participation within a social group makes up a substantial part of the data, then that narrative – which is essentially a record of what happened or, basically, your data – can make up a major part of the project. It is useful in your own project to be clear about whether your data are stepping stones towards some goal that lies beyond them (for example, a hypothesis that you will test using those data) or whether the data are themselves the ultimate goal that you are trying to reach (for example, an extended description of a series of events). Different projects use data in different ways.

It is very important that you work out how you are going to use your data before you start collecting them. In your timetable and in your research proposal the different stages of data collection, and the precise types and amounts of data that you need, should be clearly specified.

Chapter summary and conclusion

This chapter has examined why the amount of data you have matters and suggested that the amount of data you need depends partly on what you plan to do with it. It has considered the amounts of data that are necessary to perform statistical tests, and shown how you may well need more than that minimum if you want to answer a particular type of question. This chapter should have helped you to determine the amount of data you will need to collect for your project.

What to do after reading Chapter 8

Look at lots of examples of research papers published in your field of interest, to see what amounts of data the authors used in their analyses and exactly how they used their data. We are not saying that you necessarily need as many as they might have used, or that you can get away with as few as some of them might seem to have used, but it will be a useful exercise to give you an indication of how data are used in your kind of research. If your reading does seem to give you mixed messages about the amount of data you need, then that will give you something with which to start the conversation at your next supervision meeting, and something to include in the literature review and discussion sections of your dissertation.

9

HOW SHOULD I WRITE UP MY DISSERTATION?

This chapter explains how to produce an effective research report, and describes the structure and presentation of a good dissertation.

The dissertation: a report of your research

Your dissertation essentially involves two elements: the research project and the research report. The purpose of the report is to tell people about the research that you have done. The examiners' assessment of the dissertation will be based partly on the quality of the research and partly on the quality of the report. However, the examiners have to base their assessment of the research on what they see in the report; they don't have much else to go on! This means that you can make a mess of a perfectly good project by writing a duff report on it. However good the quality of your research, you rely on your report to communicate that quality to the reader. A weak or careless write-up could waste all the effort that you put into the earlier parts of the project. The aim of this chapter is to help you to make the very best of your project by producing the best report you possibly can.

The longer you give yourself to write the report the better it is likely to be. As a general rule, it is worth trying to write up some of your dissertation as you go along. If your institution requires a literature review or research proposal to be submitted early in the dissertation process you will be able to look back at this and use it as a starting point when you come to produce the final version of the early chapters of your dissertation. You will also find it useful to reflect on what you wrote back then in the light of your subsequent research. Writing up your methodology as you go along is also useful. It's much easier to write down what you are doing than to try to remember what you did six months ago.

The rules of your institution

As in previous sections of this book, we have to remind you first of all that your own institution probably has its own specific rules and regulations about the presentation of the dissertation. These probably include specific instructions about the length of the dissertation, the size of type and the line-spacing at which it is set out, whether it should be submitted electronically or as hard copy, the way in which any hard copy should be bound for submission and the file-type required for any electronic submission. The instructions might also be specific about the content of the report: how long the abstract should be, whether appendices are allowed and what style of referencing is preferred, for example. Where your institution has specific guidelines it is essential that you follow them. Be sure that you have received and read all the instructions that should have been issued. If you are uncertain about any of the instructions, seek advice from your tutor as soon as possible. Don't waste marks by failing to follow instructions. If the advice that we give in this chapter conflicts with the requirements of your institution, remember that it won't be us who mark your dissertation! Have a look at the mark scheme for your institution's dissertations. Some institutions emphasize the importance of an extended literature review or a wide-ranging discussion. Others might emphasize the quality of data presentation. Before you start writing the dissertation make sure you know what the examiners will be looking for. That will help you to put your effort where it will pay greatest dividends. Many institutions have specific suggestions about how long each section should be. For example, a dissertation of 12,000 words might be expected to have a literature review of about 3,000 and a discussion of similar length. Check your institution's guidelines and take a look at Chapter 11 to see our comments on how your dissertation will be marked.

Typical examiner's comment:

> We'd love to give a higher mark, but the regulations are such that . . .

Writing good English

An essential element of your dissertation is communicating your work to someone who reads your report. An essential element of communicating your work to someone who reads your report is writing in a way that the reader will understand. You may or may not be specifically penalized for errors of spelling, punctuation, syntax or grammar (check your institution's guidelines), but such errors will make your report more difficult for the reader to understand, and might cause the examiner to misunderstand or misinterpret your meaning. This could affect your mark for better or worse. Probably worse. When we produced the third edition of this book we were asked by our referees – people just like those who will be marking your dissertation – to put this section in a more prominent position near the front of this chapter. We have done exactly that, because we agree with them that this is an important matter.

Students' frequent whine:

I thought this was supposed to be a geography exam, not an English exam.

Examiners' frequent lament:

1   This looks like a 2.1 project, but we can't give a 2.1 grade to someone with this standard of English.
2   The research might have been OK, but I couldn't make much sense of the report, so I don't know.

Errors of spelling, punctuation, syntax or grammar will make your report more difficult for the examiner to read. This will irritate the examiner, and may make the examiner angry. An irritated or angry examiner is probably going to be a mean examiner.

Eric says . . .

Don't irritate the examiner. Correct, clear English can make the difference between a good dissertation and an excellent one.

There is not room in this book to include a course in English, but it is important that you are able to write in a way that avoids irritating the examiner or making your report hard to read. If you have been told in the past that your English needs work, then it is worth giving it some. We talk a little more about how to write well in the sister volume to this book, *How to do your Essays, Coursework and Exams in Geography and Related Disciplines* (Knight and Parsons, 2003). If you struggle specifically with issues of word choice and phrasing then a book such as *The Student Phrase Book* (Godfrey, 2013) might be the sort of book that could help.

Your dissertation should be written in a fairly formal style. This book is written quite informally, and should not be used as a model! Avoid contractions (don't use 'don't'; 'isn't' ain't good either). Avoid colloquialisms (slang sucks).

Even if you think your English is OK, it is important to watch out for serious (and surprisingly common) errors such as the following:

- spelling mistakes;
- punctuation errors;
- sentences without verbs;
- sipmle typnig errors;
- random variations in tense.

Many serious and mark-damaging errors are made through simple carelessness. Students who can write perfectly good English sometimes submit work with the most appalling blunders. You should read through your work many times before you hand it in, checking for errors. Because you will be familiar with it, it will be difficult to avoid skipping ahead and missing small errors that the examiner, slowly and carefully bumbling through the report, will stumble across. Reading it out loud can be a good way of spotting errors or poor expression.

> ### Erica says . . .
>
> Get family or friends to read the dissertation before you hand it in . . . but check whether your institution has a proof reading policy or requires you to make a declaration about who has read drafts!

When writing a dissertation you do need to write in a professional style appropriate to the discipline, and this may include specialized technical or academic terminology. You need to use this correctly where it is required, but you also need to avoid using jargon gratuitously. Using big fancy technical words for the sake of it will not impress the examiner. The examiner will be impressed if you write clearly, precisely and succinctly using specialized terminology only where it is necessary. Even some professional geographers need a reminder sometimes that using big, difficult, unnecessary words does not help to communicate their ideas.

Most dissertations are written largely in the past tense, because the dissertation is a report on work that has been carried out before the report was submitted and read. Thus, for example, one might write 'The aim of the project was to find out . . .' or 'Data were collected between July and September . . .'. It would not normally be appropriate to write the methods section in the future tense, even though you decided on the methods before you carried out the work. You would still write in the past tense 'The following method was used, and measurements were collected using this equipment . . .'. However, it can get complicated when you start writing the closing sections. It might seem strange to be writing 'These conclusions showed . . .' when you are really writing about what you think they presently show. A strategy that can work well is to frame the whole dissertation as though the report is being finished in the present tense (so, for example, 'These conclusions demonstrate . . .') but being written about work that was conducted in the recent past (so, for example, 'These conclusions demonstrate that my research methods were deeply flawed . . .'). The guiding principle here is to be careful how you write, and to seek advice if you get confused.

Structure and presentation

The purpose of your report is to communicate your project clearly to the reader. The essential elements of a good report are therefore the essential elements of clear communication: structure and presentation. The structure of the report is its organization; the way in which its various parts are put together. A sound structure involves a logical sequence of clearly defined parts. The presentation of the report includes both the overall 'look' of the work in terms of layout and neatness, and the clarity of the writing in terms of correct and effective use of English.

In any discipline, one element of the student's education is a familiarization with certain conventions that exist within the field. An architect, for example, must know the conventional symbols for use in drafting; a surveyor must know the conventions for recording field measurements in such a way that a cartographer could understand and interpret them. In subjects where written reports are an important element of professional work, the student must know the conventions attaching to the writing of reports. The reason that conventions exist is to facilitate communication. If we all expected different things of our reports and if we each tried to achieve our goals in completely different ways, we would find each other's work difficult to understand. Following the conventional styles is rather like speaking the standard language; it may seem restrictive in some ways, but it makes it possible for others to understand your work.

Conventions exist in various areas of geographical report writing. Most obvious are conventions about referencing, writing abstracts and distinguishing observation from interpretation. In the following sections we will alert you to the most important conventions as we take you through each stage of the report. Of course, it is important to remember also that conventions can be ignored, if there is good reason. Our comments are intended as sound advice, not as binding rules.

Bear in mind that even though your dissertation will be marked by somebody who is probably quite expert in your area of research, you should not assume that they will take all the basic information that underpins your work for granted. You need to tell the whole story. Also, you need to appreciate that your dissertation may also be read (and marked) by people who are not as expert as your supervisor. Therefore you need to make sure that you provide all the information necessary for a non-expert reader to understand your work, and you need to write in a style that is both professional and accessible. Telling a clear story that is accessible to expert and non-expert readers alike will depend both on the style of your writing and on the organization of your report. It is sometimes useful to have a friend or relative who knows nothing about the subject read through your project, just to check that it makes sense to a non-expert reader.

Dissertation structure

To decide on the structure of your report you need to be sure of what it is trying to achieve. Any research presentation, be it a talk or a paper, should be made up of a small number of basic elements. There are many stories of learned professors standing up at the end of talks by younger colleagues to make comments along the lines of 'I didn't understand a word you said; will you please tell me in just a few words what you did, why you did it and what it means.' The point of the story is that a research report has some basic tasks to complete and that it should complete them as clearly and succinctly as possible. To explain your work you need to answer the following questions:

1   What is the aim of the work?
2   Why is this important?
3   How does it fit into a broader academic context, e.g. previously published work?
4   How do you set out to achieve your aim?
5   What observations do you make?
6   What do these observations tell you?
7   What, therefore, do you conclude?

These are the questions to which your report should provide answers. The list could be re-written like this:

1   What were you trying to find out?
2   Why?
3   How did you do it?
4   What did you find?
5   What does it mean?

You will notice that the questions follow on from one another in a sequence. The answers to each question in turn build up into a sort of story. The story goes like this: 'I set out to answer [this question], which is important [for these reasons]. I set about it [using these methods and this framework] and I made [these] observations. These observations indicate [this], so I conclude that the answer to my question is [this].'

The story runs like an argument, in a series of logical steps. Each step is clearly separated so that the reader can consider and judge each in turn, but the steps connect fluently together. In the previous paragraph we put bits of the story in square brackets. If you replace the content of the square brackets with your question, your methods, etc. you will have your abstract. Try it! See, also, Box 9.7.

Your dissertation should be a clear, logically constructed story.

The clarity of the story depends on its clear and logical structure. If you try to jumble up the components into different orders, or if you mix the different stages into one another, you will find that the story becomes more difficult to follow. You could try: 'I used these methods and the topic is important for these reasons. I reached this conclusion, which is an answer to this question. These were the observations I made.' At least the main components are there but the order is unhelpful so no convincing argument is developed. If you miss out any of the key stages altogether, or if you add in too much spurious, unnecessary material, the situation deteriorates further. Chaos theory may have made its mark in the geographical literature, but chaos has no place in the structure of your dissertation.

The precise structure of your dissertation will depend to some extent on your particular project and approach. The structure of the report commonly mirrors (for better or worse) the structure of the research on which it is based.

Research is a process of several stages, like a military campaign. Napoleon had to worry about mobilizing troops, assembling an armoury, attaining a strategic position for his flanking divisions, engaging the enemy at a distance and then moving in for close combat. You have had to worry about selecting topics and questions, assessing their wider significance, collecting background material, conducting a pilot study, collecting data, analyzing data, relating your data to your question and reaching conclusions. One of the first tasks in drawing up a research design, or battle plan, was to assemble the elements of your research into a list and assign relative importance and proportion to each part of the list. We discussed this in Chapter 3. This enabled you to see the 'shape' of your project at a glance. Kennedy (1992) referred to the 'wine glass' and the 'splodge' as contrasting types of research plan, and the same distinction can be applied to different styles of report (Figure 9.1). The wine glass represents a well-structured project where the specific research being carried out is set into a wide context and its implications considered fully. The splodge is a poorly designed project where the research is given little context and where the wider implications of the research are largely ignored. Does your project look more like the elegant glassware or the dumpy splodge?

Eric says . . .

Don't let your project be a dumpy splodge!

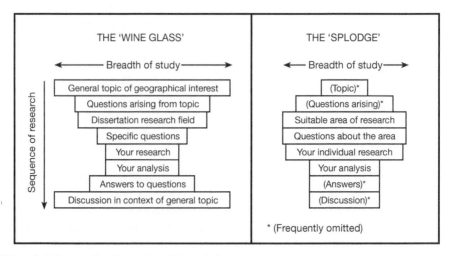

Figure 9.1 Two contrasting styles of dissertation

Source: After Kennedy, 1992

Although the character of your research will influence the structure of your report, some elements of sound structure are almost universally applicable, and we will emphasize these in the following sections.

Your report needs to be structured as a coherent argument, consistent with the conventions of geographical writing, so that you can communicate effectively with your reader.

Dissertation chapters

The main part of your dissertation needs to tell the sort of coherent story that we described in the section above. This is normally achieved by splitting the report into a series of chapters, each one dealing with one stage of the argument, or one of the questions in the lists above. Each chapter is commonly subdivided into a number of subsections, each dealing with a particular issue. A dissertation structured as a single, undivided unit would be unconventional to say the least.

The most common chapter headings include Introduction, Results, Discussion and Conclusion. Methodology, Academic Background, Literature Review and Field Area are also common, but in many cases are relegated to sub-headings within the Introduction. As well as these central chapters, most institutions require an Abstract at the front of the dissertation, and you will also need to include a reference list and a list of contents. Box 9.1 shows the main elements of the typical dissertation or research report. You can look for other examples in the layout of papers in academic journals.

Box 9.1 The main elements of a dissertation

The main elements of a dissertation or research report:

1 Title page
2 Abstract
3 List of contents/figures
4 Introduction (aims, background)
5 Literature review
6 Methodology
7 Observations/results
8 Analysis of observations
9 Discussion
10 Conclusion
11 Reference list
12 Appendices (if required)
13 Acknowledgements

In the following sections we will explain the purpose of the different parts of the report, and offer advice as to how best to produce them.

The title page

Most institutions have clear guidelines as to what your title page should include. In general, most institutions require that a page at the very front of your dissertation should contain:

- the title of the dissertation;
- the name of the candidate (you);
- the date (year) of examination;
- the examination (e.g. BA) and subject (e.g. Geography).

You may be required to include:

- a formal declaration.

The form, and in some cases the exact wording, of the declaration will be stipulated by your institution. You may have to write it into the dissertation yourself, or you may have to fill in a form provided by your institution. You might have to click a button as part of the online submission. Check the guidelines. The idea of the declaration is that you confirm that the dissertation is all your own work, and not somebody else's! A typical form for the declaration would be: 'Except where otherwise acknowledged, I certify that this dissertation represents my own unaided work.'

The title of the dissertation is important as it is the label by which your work will henceforth always be known. Make it a good one. A good title should be accurate, clear, comprehensive and concise. You should not clutter the title with phrases like 'A Dissertation on . . .' or 'A Geographical Analysis of . . .', and you need to strike a balance between being too vague and too detailed. Calling your project 'Cloud Mapping' does not really give much indication of what you are doing. Calling it 'Developing a Graphical User Interface for a Cloud-based Social Mapping Application for Mobile Devices Using Apple iOS' certainly gives more useful information, but is a bit of a mouthful. There may be a word or letter limit in your regulations (check). Consider the examples in Box 9.2. Some typical layouts for effective title pages are shown in Figure 9.2.

The contents page

First impressions are undeniably important, and the contents page is likely to be one of the first parts of the dissertation that a reader will look at. It is also a section that readers will refer back to over and over again as they progress through the dissertation. If they lose the thread of your argument, if they want to check back to a point you made earlier and need to locate it quickly, or if they want an overview of the structure and layout of the whole report, the contents list is where they will turn. A badly constructed or unhelpful contents list will spoil not only the first impression, but the overall impression that the

Box 9.2 Dissertation titles

A selection of dissertation titles, good and otherwise:

- Shopping in Swindon (*Too vague*)
- Cloud-based Mapping (*Too vague*)
- A Dissertation on Shopping in Swindon (*No better*)
- An Application-based Cloud Mapping Project (*No better*)
- Swindon as a Regional Shopping Centre (*Slightly better*)
- Developing User Interfaces for Cloud Mapping (*Slightly better*)
- Swindon's Sphere of Influence in Regional Shopping Patterns (*OK*)
- A New User Interface for Cloud-based Social Mapping Apps (*OK*)
- A Questionnaire Analysis of Swindon's Sphere of Influence in Regional Shopping Patterns (*A bit too much?*)
- Developing a New Graphical User Interface for Apple iOS Cloud-based Social Mapping Applications (*A bit too much?*)
- A Postal Questionnaire Study of Swindon's Sphere of Influence in Southern England and its Effect on Shopping Patterns Among Young Women (aged 18–35) in the Region in Mid-2014: A Qualitative Geographical Analysis (*Too much!*)
- A Project to Develop a New Graphical User Interface for a Cloud-based Social Mapping Application for Mobile Devices Using Apple iOS Operating Systems (*Too much!*)

reader has of your report. It is worth taking care to produce an informative and reader-friendly list of contents.

The purpose of the contents page is to list the various parts of the report. On one level it provides the examiner with a summary overview of your structure. On another level it helps the reader to locate particular sections of interest. It must be designed to fulfil both of these roles.

The most simple contents page is a straightforward list of chapters, as shown in Box 9.3. This is easy to construct and quick to read, but does not offer a great deal of detail to readers trying to find their way through your work. At the other extreme of detail, the contents page could include not only the chapter headings, but also each of the sub-headings within chapters, and even the minor headings within sub-sections of the chapter. As shown in Box 9.4, such a comprehensive contents list could even include brief chapter summaries.

The disadvantage of such a detailed list is that the structure of the report as a whole can easily become hidden in the morass of detail, so while the list is useful for locating specific items it is less useful for showing the layout of the report.

The most effective contents lists fall between these two extremes, usually listing the chapter headings and the major subdivisions of each chapter, as shown in Box 9.5.

Figure 9.2 Some different ways of formatting a title page

There is much to be said in favour of restricting the list to a single page, so that the layout of the report is visible at a glance. Careful use of a hierarchical numbering system, sub-headings of different orders printed in different styles (UPPER CASE, underlined etc.) and indentation can help the clarity of the page enormously. For example, compare the two lists shown in Box 9.6.

Box 9.3 A simple contents page

A simple contents page might look like this:

Contents		Page
Abstract		1
Chapter 1:	Introduction	2
Chapter 2:	Methodology	14
Chapter 3:	Results	24
Chapter 4:	Discussion	40
Chapter 5:	Conclusion	55
Reference list		59

Box 9.4 A comprehensive but unclear contents page

A very detailed contents page can sometimes be rather unclear, like this:

Contents	Page
Abstract	ii
Contents list	iii
List of figures	iv
Acknowledgements	v

CHAPTER 1: INTRODUCTION   1
An introduction to the project including a statement of the aims
and objectives, a description of the field area and an outline of
the techniques used.

Aims:	1
Background:	2
Field area:	9
Methodology:	14
Field techniques:	14
Modelling techniques:	22

CHAPTER 2: LITERATURE REVIEW   26
A description of the major work previously carried out in this field.

Literature on hillslopes:	26
Hillslope form:	26
Hillslope processes:	30
Literature on South Wales:	42
Literature on mathematical modelling:	49

CHAPTER 3: FIELDWORK RESULTS   53

etc . . .

Box 9.5 An effective contents page

A clearly set out contents page might look like this:

Contents	Page
Abstract	i
Acknowledgements	ii

Chapter 1: Introduction

Aims	1
Background	2
Specific objectives	5
Previous research	6

Chapter 2: Methodology

Geomorphological mapping	14
(i) Ground survey	14
(ii) Feature recognition	19
Sampling strategy	19
Sediment analysis	22
(i) Particle size	25
(ii) Mineralogy	25

etc . . .

Box 9.6 Two different layouts for the same contents page

The layouts below show the importance of clear structure and presentation:

Version A

Chapter 1: Introduction
Aims
Background
Literature review
Field area

Chapter 2: Methodology
2.1 The qualitative approach
2.2 Data sources
2.2.1. Interviews
2.2.2. Archival sources

Chapter 3: Results

etc . . .

> ***Version B***
>
> Chapter one introduction
> Aims
> Background, literature review
> Field area
> Chapter two methodology
> The qualitative approach
> Data types and sources
> Interviews
> Archival research
> Chapter three results
>
> etc . . .

You may find that the word processing software that you use to produce your dissertation provides a facility for producing a contents list automatically from your text. It does this by recognizing different levels of heading and sub-heading in your text and using those as items in the contents. This can be very useful, but make sure that you impose your own rules on the contents list that is produced: don't let the software produce a microscopically detailed list if you had decided that a less detailed list would be better. Use the software but don't let it make your decisions for you!

The abstract

The abstract is a short section of text that summarizes the whole of your project. Just as abstract art aims to abstract the essence from its subject, so your abstract should abstract the essential elements of your work and report them in summary form. The regulations set out by your institution probably stipulate a maximum length for the abstract. Between 200 and 500 words is typical. The abstract is normally placed right at the beginning of a report, even before the contents list. When the reader opens up your report, the abstract is the first piece of text that appears. Remember, first impressions count. The abstract is very important.

The abstract is very important.

The abstract serves several purposes. First, it enables the reader to find out what the project is all about before reading the whole report. This means that when the reader moves on through each of the following chapters the thread of the argument will already be clear, and it will be easier to assimilate and to judge the material that is included. Second, the examiner will refer back to your abstract while reading the report if there is any confusion or inconsistency in the text. Also, having read the whole report the examiner can refer to the abstract to check that the project has indeed done what the writer claims, and to check that the writer (you) has a clear grasp of the implications of the work. The abstract announces what you think are the salient points of your story, so the examiner can judge how well you appreciate your own work! Third, an abstract will be read by many people who will not read any other part of the report. This is true particularly of published reports; the abstract acts as a sort of trailer for the paper as a whole. For this reason it is particularly important that the abstract is entirely self-contained.

Given the prominence of your abstract at the front of your project, and the fact that the examiner will read the abstract carefully several times, and the fact that some readers will base their opinion of your work almost entirely on the abstract, it is important that you write a good one.

A good abstract has all the elements of good structure that we described earlier for the report as a whole. Your abstract should explain, in a clear logical sequence: your aims; the background to those aims; your methods; your observations; your interpretation of those observations; the conclusions that you reach on the basis of those observations; and the implications of those conclusions. It should be a self-contained summary not only of your results but of your whole project. That is quite a lot to squeeze into a few hundred words, which is one of the reasons why good abstracts can be difficult to write.

One way of approaching the task is to write a series of one-sentence answers to the list of questions that we produced earlier when we were discussing structure. If you string the series of sentences together, you will have the basis of a sound, if perhaps rudimentary, abstract. If you try it, you will come up with something like the example in Box 9.7.

You can increase the level of sophistication of this abstract by separating out the key sections of the structure into separate short paragraphs. The first paragraph will be introductory and background material: the aim of the project, why it is important and the scientific background. The second paragraph might be the methodology: how you set

Box 9.7 A model abstract

An example of a stylized, simple model abstract:

The aim of this project is to (find out) . . . This is important because . . . This follows from earlier research on this topic in that . . . The research was carried out by (field/lab/documentary methods) . . . It was observed that/found that . . . This suggests . . . It is therefore concluded that . . .

out to do the research and the techniques you used. In some cases this might fit into the first paragraph as introductory material. The next paragraph should be your observations or measurements; the data that you collected yourself. As in the report itself, it is often useful to keep the data separate from the background material and from the interpretation sections (we will discuss this more fully later in this chapter). Your final paragraph might cover the interpretation of your results, your conclusions and some comment on the broader scientific implications of your findings (what it all means).

This paragraph structure within the abstract should reflect the structure of your research. If your project dwells at length on methodological issues, then the abstract might reflect that with a paragraph devoted to methodology. If the methodology in your research is standard, then it might be absorbed into the introductory paragraph of the abstract.

Go to the journals for examples of how to write an abstract, but bear in mind that you will find bad examples as well as good, even in the published literature. The good ones will have a clear, effective structure. Study them, and you will see that they provide clear answers to the questions we have used to help our structure.

> *Eric says . . .*
>
> To make a start on your abstract, try writing up your own project using the seven sentences in Tony and Peter's Box 9.7.

The introduction

The introduction to your report is not just 'the stuff you have to put at the beginning before you start'. It is an essential part of the logical argument that your dissertation puts forward. The purpose of the introduction is to explain to the reader what your research is about and what it aims to achieve, why it is important, what work has been done on the topic by previous researchers, precisely what you are trying to do or to find out and how you are going about it. These roles are indicated by the titles of the sub-sections into which the introduction is commonly divided, as in the example below:

- overall aim of project;
- academic/scientific background;
- previous work/literature review;
- specific objectives of project;
- methodology.

In some cases, some of these sections can be presented as chapters in their own right. 'Literature review' and 'Methodology' are frequently used as chapter headings rather than sub-headings. Sometimes the academic background and literature review are combined into a single section. The approach that you adopt for the organization of your introductory material will depend on several things, for example:

1   Institutional guidelines: some institutions require a literature review chapter.
2   Your material: you may or may not have enough to say on a topic to warrant a whole chapter, and you may or may not want to place so much emphasis on any of these sections in the context of the report as a whole.
3   The style of your argument: for example, you may or may not wish to lead the reader gradually through the development of your ideas by separating the general background to your topic from the specific literature relating to your precise aims.

We will take each section in turn and consider what it should include, whether you produce it as a whole chapter or as part of a chapter.

Overall aim of the project

It is important to make it clear right at the outset what you are trying to do. It is very difficult for the reader to get involved in a report, or to follow an argument, if it is not clear where the story is leading. A bold, clear statement of aim will be a big help to your readers. The examiner will also be impressed to see that you can articulate your aims clearly. It is a common failing of undergraduate dissertations that the student does not seem to be very clear about what the project is really trying to achieve. The 'Aims' section, as long as it is well written, can prevent this problem.

If in doubt what to write, begin with: 'The aim of this dissertation is to . . .'

At this point you should not be so specific in your aim that only an expert in the field will know what you are talking about. If this section comes right at the beginning, remember that the reader will not have seen your 'background' section and may be largely unfamiliar with your subject area. For example, if you write something like: 'The aim of this dissertation is to correlate the fabric of the upper and lower Twiddlecoombe tills with respect to the regional diagenetic glaciotectonic structures of the Late Devensian' the non-expert reader will not be very much wiser after they read the aim than before.

Likewise you should not be too vague. Something along the lines of: 'The aim of this project is to study the tills of the Twiddlecoombe Valley' does little to convince the reader that you know what you are doing. You need a statement that is broad enough to convince the non-expert reader, but specific enough to convince the expert. Consider the following example:

The aim of this dissertation is to identify the extent to which subglacial till deformation occurred in the Twiddleton region during the Late Devensian glacial period by comparing the sedimentological characteristics of two glacial tills in the Twiddlecoombe Valley.

There is no single formula for the 'right way' to state your aims, but your statement needs to be accurate, clear, precise and direct.

Background, theoretical framework and justification

Having explained broadly what you are trying to do, you are ready to explain in more detail what the work is all about and why it is worth doing. Some people like to see the 'Background' section in advance of the 'Aims'. Others, including us, feel that it is easier to get the full benefit out of reading the background if you already know what the aim of the work is.

The 'Background' section is there to fill the reader in about the details of the topic. For example, if you have just announced in your 'Aims' that you intend to examine the food supply/black market system in the city of Harare, you need now to explain a little about urban food supply and black market economics in general, and perhaps about the special case of Harare in particular. If your aim was to make a geomorphological identification of a glacial limit on the Isle of Skye, you will need to explain something about the geomorphology and glacial history of the area. This section is your opportunity to demonstrate to the examiners your wide expertise in the field and your familiarity with a broad range of material that relates to your topic, as well as your chance to set your specific research into its wider academic context.

As we indicated in Chapter 5, it may or may not be necessary to provide a background to the theoretical framework in which your work is set. If you are taking a Marxist-feminist approach to food supplies in Harare you will need to provide a justification for this approach and an indication of the particular insights that this approach will give you. Similarly, you may want to argue why a critical-rationalist approach to the examination of the glacial limit on Skye is a particularly effective approach to the question you are asking.

From the background material should emerge the reason for your study; in other words the justification. Part of the justification will always be that we do not already know whatever it is that you are trying to find out. Thus, an 'unknown' element should arise from your background discussion. You might argue that the location of the glacial limit remains unknown, for example, or that there is controversy about a particular element of the food supply system. This 'unknown' leads you directly and conveniently to the next stages of your argument. If something is unknown, finding it out seems like a sensible objective.

Specific objectives of the project

When you wrote your 'Overall aim' section you had to bear in mind that your reader was not necessarily familiar with your subject area, and so you avoided too much specific detail. If you place your 'Specific objectives' after your 'Background' you can be more confident that the reader has some knowledge: the knowledge that you have provided!

This section therefore aims to explain in specific terms, with reference to the issues identified in the previous section, exactly what you propose to do. At this stage you must be very precise. It is easy to state your objective as one thing when what you have actually done is something subtly but distinctly different. That is a disaster; the examiner will chop your argument into little bits and send it back in a bin liner.

An examiner's favourite question:

'What exactly was the aim of this research?'

(If you have written one thing in your 'Objectives' and done another in the project, the examiner will experience acute disappointment.)

It is often convenient to identify a number of specific objectives which build together to achieve the overall aim of the project. This can help you in the planning and execution of the research by breaking the overall aim into convenient chunks, and it also demonstrates to the reader the logical structure of your work. It also makes it possible to rescue the project relatively easily if bits of the research don't work as well as you hoped (see Chapter 10 for more details).

For the food supply/black market and glacier-limits examples that we used earlier, appropriate 'Specific objectives' might be as follows (these are rather ambitious projects, by the way):

- Title:
  Informal food-supply networks in Harare.

- Overall aim:
  To identify food production and distribution structures in the informal economy in Harare, Zimbabwe.

- Specific objectives:
  To map the distribution of urban agricultural sites in Harare, to identify landowners, food-growers and food consumers for each site, and to identify food sources (formal and informal) for a sample of the urban population.

- Title:
  Geomorphological evidence for the extent of Loch Lomond glaciation on the Isle of Skye.

- Overall aim:
  To identify the maximum extent of glacier advance on the Isle of Skye during the Loch Lomond stadial.

- Specific objectives:
  To identify the distribution of till, the locations of moraines and the limits of periglacial weathering features on the island, and to produce a geomorphological map on which glacial limits can be recognized.

The key points about both examples are that the specific objectives are indeed specific, that they are clear and that they contribute directly to the overall aim that was stated previously. (They are typical of many dissertation proposals also in that they are hopelessly ambitious, and achieving the objectives will not necessarily help to achieve the aims!)

Having read your specific objectives the reader ought to know exactly what you are trying to achieve. This means, of course, that the reader will be in a strong position to judge what you do achieve!

The literature review

Having explained exactly what you are trying to do, your next job is to explain what work, if any, has been done on your topic by previous researchers. The term 'literature review' is commonly used to refer both to the process of finding and studying previous literature and to the product that you put together on the basis of that process. We said a little about the process in Chapter 4 when you were deciding on a topic, problem and questions for your dissertation. The work that you did then, and that you should have been continuing throughout the period that you have been doing the dissertation, will pay dividends again now as you put together the literature review section of your report. This might be included as a big section within the Introduction chapter, but more commonly it will deserve a chapter of its own: the 'Literature review'.

If your topic is worthwhile, it is probable that some previous research will have been carried out on it. Your own work will, presumably, have been devised with these previous contributions in mind. The aim of your own work should be to build on what knowledge already exists. It is necessary, therefore, to explain this existing knowledge and to mention the work that has led to it. That is what the literature review is for.

If your dissertation has both a literature review and a separate 'background' section, the difference between the two should be that the background provides the broad context of your work, whereas the literature review focuses specifically on previously published work and on previous literature that is directly related to your project. This might be work that has attempted exactly the same goals as your own, or has worked in the same field area, or used the same techniques.

If the aim of the background was to give the readers enough information to be able to understand your overall aim, then the aim of the literature review is to give the readers the information they need to see both your overall aims and your specific objectives in a detailed context.

> **Eric says . . .**
>
> The literature review is also an opportunity to fatten up the reference list!

As we will discuss more fully in Chapter 11, one of the things that the examiners will be looking for in your dissertation is some evidence that you have become, to some extent, expert in your chosen field of study. One element of expertise is a detailed familiarity with and understanding of the published research in your field. One function of the literature review in the dissertation is to allow you to display this side of your expertise. You should take advice from your tutor as to how much emphasis your examiners will place on the literature review, but it is generally expected that you should demonstrate that you are very well read in your field. The exact length of your review will depend not only on the institutional requirements but also on your precise field of research. A thorough literature review in a broad field will be much longer than an equivalent review in a narrow field, and a review in a field where a great deal of work has been carried out will cover more items than a review of an obscure, little-researched field. There are also different expectations in different fields. In social sciences there is an expectation that the literature review will be extensive, both in the breadth of the subject-matter context in which your research is set, and in the exploration of the theoretical framework of your dissertation. In physical sciences, by contrast, the context is usually much narrower, and there is sometimes less exploration of the theoretical framework. So, in the social sciences you might devote a whole chapter of your dissertation to a literature review, whereas dissertations in the physical sciences sometimes regard the scientific background and the literature review as the same thing.

The literature review is much more than just a list of relevant publications. It is not even just a list of relevant publications accompanied by a commentary, or review, of each publication that you have listed. Something like that would be called an annotated bibliography, and is not at all what you need in your dissertation. Of course, you may well be asked to write an annotated bibliography as an assignment at some point in your studies, but this is not that point.

Your literature review should not look like a list or catalogue.

Look at the literature reviews in a selection of academic papers in your subject area. You will see that, instead of going through paper by paper talking about each publication in turn, literature reviews normally identify a series of important themes or topics within the subject area and discuss how the previously published literature has addressed those topics. You can think of the literature review almost as an essay within the dissertation, with a title such as 'Evaluate the work that has previously been published on the topic addressed by your dissertation'. The literature review will then comment on the previous literature both in a very general way (for example, identifying whether there is a great deal of literature, discussing whether it has a long history and considering whether writers from different parts of the discipline or from different geographical regions have addressed the subject in different ways) and in very specific detail (comparing how different papers have addressed particular aspects of theory or methodology and reviewing the different conclusions of different publications on the specific issues that your own work will address).

You may divide the literature review into sections with sub-headings to help the reader navigate. You might begin with an introductory section covering the general points and then have a section looking at literature that relates to your specific methods, then a section on work based at your particular study location, then a section on work that has addressed your specific research question. Depending on your project you may well need sections on the history of research in your topic, the current state of research and gaps in the existing literature. That last section is likely to form the basis of the justification for your own project. By the end of the literature review you should have presented a picture of how we currently think that a little part of the world – one small topic area – works, and identified those things that we are still unsure about, or the things where we still have unanswered questions. You might even be able to draw up some kind of flow chart or cartoon of the system and point out the missing connections or blank spaces in our picture. You could then revisit that model in your discussion chapter and consider how far your own work has gone towards filling in the gaps. That can also be a convenient way of specifying your aim. Remember: your aim, literature review, methods, observations, discussion and conclusion all have to tie together.

Erica says . . .

I am building a conceptual model of how we currently see the world, gaps and all, into the end of my literature review.

As with many of the things we talk about in this book, there are different ways of doing a literature review. Most undergraduate geography dissertations have a single literature review chapter somewhere in the early part of the report, but if your research involves several distinct parts or a series of individual research case studies it might be more appropriate to break up the literature review and present parts of it in different chapters alongside the parts of the project to which those parts refer. There might, for example, be a short literature review in the introduction to the dissertation, then further short literature reviews at the start of each of the case-study chapters. That approach is more common in longer dissertations or theses at higher levels, but might be appropriate in some undergraduate projects.

In many degree courses a literature review is set as an independent assessment item, and you may already have received some training and had some practice. There is more to be said about literature searching and reviewing than we can fit in here. If you have not done a literature review before (or even if you have) it would be wise to look at some other books that will give you more detailed advice. A book such as Ridley (2012) would be a good place to start.

Methods

Having told the reader what you are tying to achieve, and why, you now need to explain how you are going to go about it. The purpose of the methods section is to explain the procedures that you followed in carrying out the research. This explanation should be sufficiently clear and comprehensive that if somebody wished to repeat your work in the future they could use your methods section as an instruction manual as to how to proceed. Your explanation is likely to include references to previous research that has used similar (or different) methods in addressing related topics, or reference to standard texts that provide basic descriptions of standard methods that you are using or adapting for your own research. You may find yourself referring again to work that you have mentioned in your literature review, so be careful not to be repetitive, but also careful to include the appropriate details in the appropriate chapter. It is usually acceptable, if necessary, to write something such as: 'See Chapter 3 (literature review) for further details on this work.' In your dissertation, the methods section also serves to convince the examiner that you really knew what you were doing and that you knew how to do it properly. Readers will also judge your results and conclusions on the basis of the quality of your methodology. If you've used a faulty or inappropriate method, your readers will be able to judge that your results are less useful than if you had used a better method. It is important that you acknowledge any weaknesses in your methods. Your examiners will certainly spot them, and will penalize you if you appear not to have recognized them.

What the examiner may be wondering:

> Why does the report not explain why it was not necessary to use distilled water in the experiments? The methods chapter was unclear on this point.

The methods section commonly covers the following issues.

Methodological or philosophical approach

You may have talked a bit about how you have approached the research in your background chapter, since your approach will be closely tied to the background from which your project arises. However, even if you think your approach is obvious, you should explain the philosophical basis and the procedural requirements of your approach formally within your methods chapter. For example, is your study quantitative or qualitative? Does it adopt a hypothesis-testing approach, or an ethnographic approach or something else? Is it derived broadly from the thinking of French philosophers, German sociologists or Belgian ice-sheet modellers? What types of information are required to fulfil the project's aims and objectives? What are the characteristics of your research design? We have dedicated a lot of space to research design in this book, and we hope you dedicate a lot of time and effort to research design in your project. This would be the place to explain your research design to your readers so that they are absolutely clear (i) how your research is designed and (ii) that you understand how research design works. Writing about research design, of course, leads you directly into writing about the specific methods that you employed in your data collection and analysis (see below) so you should be able to make your methods chapter into a fluent, coherent story.

Methods and problems of data collection

You should explain the precise details of your data collection procedures, including the measures taken to overcome problems that you encountered. Depending on whether your study involves field, laboratory or library research, this might require detailed description of experimental equipment, of field survey or sampling procedures or of questionnaire design and implementation. Look in published academic papers in your area of research to see examples of how other researchers have organized this material and what they have included. If you are using technical equipment, refer to its instruction manual or manufacturer's web page: they might provide a useful description that you can quote or a diagram that you could use.

Methods and problems of data analysis

You should explain the reasons for selecting particular analytical techniques, the nature of the techniques chosen, the practical effectiveness of the techniques and any problems experienced in their application to your project. It is especially important to describe any modifications that you have made to standard procedures. If there are different ways of doing things you will need to explain why you selected one way rather than another. It is very important to set your methods in the context of methods others have used, and it is often useful to refer back to previous work that you may have mentioned in the literature review or the background section.

The following examples show you some of the different sorts of material that can be included in the methods section of different types of dissertation:

Example 1

Dissertation title:
Swindon: local centre, regional sphere.

Sub-headings within methods section:
3.1   Retail outlet mapping
3.2   Questionnaire survey
    3.2.1   Design

3.2.2   Implementation
3.3   Computer modelling

Example 2

Dissertation title:
A geomorphological reconstruction of the Loch Lomond glaciation of the Isle of Skye.

Sub-headings within methods section:
3.1   Geomorphological mapping
    3.1.1   Use of air photos
    3.1.2   Field observations
    3.1.3   Feature recognition
        3.1.3.1   Glacial features
        3.1.3.2   Periglacial features
3.2   Till fabric analysis

The results (observations) section

Most dissertations should include a clearly identifiable section, be it a chapter or a series of chapters, which simply reports the data that were collected by means of the procedures previously described in the methods section. This section is often separate from the previous sections, which explain the background to the project, and separate from the subsequent sections, which analyze and interpret the data. There are exceptions to this rule, such as dissertations based on particular types of ethnographic or qualitative research, but in most cases, and certainly if you are unsure, then you should probably follow the conventional practice and let the data stand alone in a section of their own. Future readers of your research can then distinguish easily between what actually happened in the field or in the lab and what you thought it meant. If your methodology was faithfully recorded and was satisfactory, future researchers might trust your observations even if they are not interested in your interpretation. If your results are clearly presented, the reader should be able to assess them and to evaluate the conclusions that you draw from them. The reader might choose to reach a different conclusion from the same results, but at least the results will have been identifiable and useful! On the other hand, if your whole project hinges on the positionality of the observer, then it would make less sense to isolate the observations and the interpretations, which in that case would be inextricably bound up together. We said a little more about positionality in Chapter 5 when we were talking about research design and how you as the researcher fit into your own project.

Results can be presented in a variety of ways, depending on the nature of the study and on the methodology used. Results of water analysis will be presented differently from the results of conversation analysis. A good way of getting ideas about how to present your data is to look through published work that uses similar types of data. See if you can adapt for your project any of the styles of presentation that you see in the literature.

Remember, it's usually a good idea to know how you will present the data even before you start to collect them, as the intended style of presentation might have implications for the style of collection.

One mistake to avoid is presenting raw data without any explanation or descriptive text. When we said that you might want to keep your results separate from your discussion, we did not mean that your results chapter should just be a series of data tables or graphs. You need to lead the reader through your data with a textual commentary or description even if the data are themselves straightforward and numerical. Of course, if your data are in the form of a narrative account then you will need plenty of space to deliver that account, but even if you present your data as a simple set of numbers or a few charts and photographs you need to spend some time telling the reader what those numbers, charts and photographs are. Work on the assumption that a reader will only look at your data table if the text says 'See the data table.' Your results chapter may include many short sections of text along the lines of 'Table 5.1 shows the values of . . . and the locations from which the samples were taken are indicated in Figure 5.2.'

The analysis of results

If you have collected data, they may well require some sort of analysis before you can effectively discuss what they mean. For example, if you have collected numerical data in an attempt to assess the impact of aspect on soil type at a range of different altitudes, you will probably need to carry out some statistical analysis on your data before you can tell what the data actually show. The data analysis usually has to be separate from the data presentation as we have already indicated, and the analysis has to come in advance of the discussion and conclusion (obviously), so a separate chapter may be appropriate. This will certainly be the case if the analysis is complex and extensive. For example, if you have collected data in the field on percentages of cover of particular plant species, but the focus of your research question is on the spatial characteristics of plant distributions, you will need to devote quite a bit of your research effort into deriving the geostatistics that you will need before you can reach your conclusion. In this case a separate chapter will certainly be warranted. On the other hand, if your analysis is limited to simple statistical tests on your data you may be able to have a chapter that incorporates the analysis into the discussion.

Eric says . . .

Should I ever merge the results, analysis and discussion?

We say . . .

That depends on the exact nature of your project, but keep them separate unless you have a good reason for merging them.

The discussion

The purpose of the discussion is to bridge the gap in the story between your observations and your conclusions. In this chapter you need to make very explicit the way in which the observations or measurements that you have made relate to the aims, background and scientific structure of your project. In your results chapter you said 'This is what I saw.' In your conclusion you will say 'This is the answer.' One of the main jobs of the discussion is to fill in the 'therefore'. You will also have to include and explain any 'notwithstanding', 'conditional upon', or 'level of confidence' messages that you wish to use to temper the final conclusion. In telling this story you will almost certainly need to mention previously published work that you already referred to in the literature review and methods sections, or to introduce some new references to elaborate on where your dissertation has brought you. It is perfectly acceptable, indeed probably essential, for you to do that.

Although, as we said before, it is normally important to keep your discussion clearly separate from your results, there are exceptions to this 'rule' in some types of geographical research, especially where you have used an ethnographic approach or data that depends on your own positionality. As with all the rules that we put in this book, feel free to break them if you, and your advisor, are confident that for your particular project our rules do not apply.

Eric says . . .

Be a rebel. But only if rebellion is the best approach. Do things differently. But check before you embark on your innovative path that different isn't just wrong.

There are many different ways of structuring the 'Discussion' chapter. If your dissertation has involved several distinct elements, for example, a fieldwork component and a laboratory experiment component, then the structure of the discussion might be determined by the need to discuss the two components separately. It may also be appropriate to include an assessment of any flaws or weaknesses that you recognize in your project. The following examples show a couple of different ways in which discussions can be organized.

Example 1

Dissertation title:
    Informal food supply in Harare.

Sub-headings in discussion:
    (a)   Limitations of data sources
    (b)   Synthesis of results
    (c)   Implications of results

Example 2

Dissertation title:
   Extent of glaciation, Cader Idris.

Sub-headings in discussion:
   (a)   Discussion of geomorphological data
   (b)   Discussion of palaeoecological data
   (c)   A model of former ice cover

   You should also use the Discussion chapter to demonstrate the 'intellectual achieve-ment' that we talked about in Chapter 2 when we were describing the characteristics of a good dissertation and the things that examiners would be looking for. One way of doing that is to bring together the results of your study into some kind of conceptual model: a simplified picture of how the world now seems to work once your own findings have been incorporated into the previously existing sum of human knowledge. This could tie back to a conceptual model (with gaps in it) that you presented in your introduction, but with some of the gaps now filled in.

Producing a conceptual model out of the results of your empirical investigations is one way of demonstrating intellectual achievement in your dissertation.

   Consider the example of the empirical investigation of the relationships between runoff and erosion rates and ground-surface characteristics conducted by Abrahams et al. (1988). These authors found correlations among runoff, erosion rates and ground-surface characteristics as shown in Table 9.1. From these correlations they produced the causal diagram shown in Figure 9.3 in which it is argued that surface roughness and surface-particle size jointly control infiltration which, in turn, determines runoff. Runoff and gradient jointly control the erosion rate. Finally, both surface roughness and surface particle size are related to each other and to gradient, but causal relationships among these three cannot be determined from the empirical observations. In this conceptual model Abrahams et al. sought to extend their empirical observations into a more general statement about runoff and erosion on desert hillslopes. This type of conceptual model is one way in which you can demonstrate the type of intellectual achievement that examiners will be looking for.

Table 9.1 Rank correlations of runoff and erosion rates with ground-surface characteristics

	Spearman rank correlation coefficient	
	Runoff coefficient	Erosion rate
Gradient	−0.77*	−0.31
Surface particle size	−0.49	−0.14
Surface roughness	−0.66	−0.26

*Denotes a statistically significant correlation

Source: After Abrahams et al., 1988

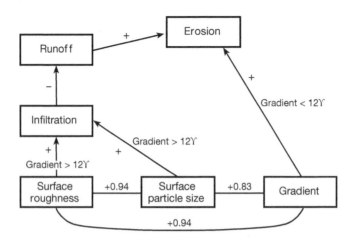

Figure 9.3 Conceptual model for controls of runoff and erosion on desert hillslopes

Source: After Abrahams et al., 1988

The conclusion

The conclusion is the final stage of the logical argument that your dissertation has presented. It is the final position that your story arrives at.

The conclusion is where you say:

> 'Given the evidence presented in the results chapter, and bearing in mind the issues considered in the discussion chapter, this is the answer to the question that was asked at the start of this dissertation.'

Your conclusion need not be very long, and indeed will do its job more effectively if it is concise and to the point. The main part of its job is to list the principal findings of your research. These can be divided into several types. First, and usually most important, are the points that answer the specific questions that your project was investigating. In addition, there may be methodological or other findings that arose as a by-product of the principal line of research. Third, there may be issues concerning the nature of the research itself that warrant coverage as items of conclusion. Finally, you may have material to include under the general heading of 'Future research'; some institutions allocate specific credit to dissertations that identify avenues for the future development of the topic studied.

The conclusion is one of those sections, like the abstract, the contents list and the statement of aims, that the reader will refer to more than once. People who don't want to read the whole report might just look at your conclusion. The examiner will read it especially carefully. You need to be sure that the message of the conclusion is clear and easy for the reader to extract.

Unless the rules of your institution specifically recommend against it, it might be worth listing your conclusions in point form instead of (or as well as) using a conventional paragraph style. This makes it easy for the reader to see the major points without getting lost in superfluous wordage. The following examples illustrate two different ways of presenting conclusions succinctly and effectively:

Example 1

Conclusion

> The mapping of landforms on Cader Idris suggested that the corries were formed before the Loch Lomond readvance, and that the landforms showed only the last position of decaying glaciers, not the maximum extent of ice during the stadial period. The limits for the maximum extent of the advance were probably much further away . . . etc . . .

Example 2

Conclusion

> Three main conclusions arise from this study.
>
> 1   The corries in the Cader Idris range were formed before, not during, the Loch Lomond readvance.
> 2   The Glacial deposits in the area do not reflect the maximum extent of glaciation, but a recessional position.
> 3   etc., etc., . . .

Very often, institutions expect you to identify weaknesses and/or limitations to your study. Do not do this in the conclusion. The conclusion is your opportunity to say what you have found out. This is not the place to be mealy-mouthed and self-effacing. Certainly you do need, somewhere in your dissertation, to acknowledge that there are shortcomings to your methods, that your sample is rather limited, or whatever. But there's a right and a wrong place to do it. The conclusion is the wrong place. The methods or discussion chapter would be a more appropriate place.

Eric says . . .

Go out with a bang, not a whimper.

Don't spend the conclusion explaining what you did wrong.

The reference list

The purpose of the reference list is to provide full details of all the published material that you have mentioned in your report. A reference list is not the same as a bibliography. A bibliography is a list of publications that are relevant to your subject. A reference list contains only those items specifically mentioned in your report. These are items that you have 'referred to' in the sense of 'mentioned', not in the sense of 'looked at'. You should build up your reference list as you build up your text, adding references to the list as you mention them in the text. It is a difficult job to create a list only after you have written the text, and you are likely to make errors if you try to do it that way. One problem that can arise is that you might lose the details of an item that you used in the early stages of writing, and if you can't find the details you won't be able to use the item in your final text! Of course, you might have avoided this problem by using a reference-managing software package, but even without software a well-organized student should be able to keep track of all their references if they manage their work carefully. Manage your work carefully!

The idea of the reference list is that if your reader wants to find a copy of something that you have mentioned in your report, your list will provide all the necessary publication details for them to find it online or in the library. Your reference list is therefore a reader service and an essential follow-up to the text.

In your dissertation, of course, the reference list serves another function. Inasmuch as your dissertation is an opportunity to demonstrate your expertise in the subject, the reference list is an opportunity to indicate how thorough you have been in your preparation for your research. When the examiner has a preliminary glance through the dissertation, a sick-looking list of less than a dozen references is usually taken as a reliable early warning that this is not going to be an expert piece of research.

We spoke earlier of the way in which well-known conventions in writing enable the reader to understand the writer. The reference list is a particularly good example of this. In the reference list you want to communicate a substantial amount of information – what the item is, who wrote it, when it was published, what journal it was in, etc., etc. – in as compact but readable a form as possible, while being certain that the reader will be able to understand what you have written. To facilitate this there are a number of standard methods, or conventions, for listing references. The most commonly used in geography dissertations are the Harvard system and, to a lesser extent, the Numerical or Footnote system. Check your institution's regulations to see whether there are specific instructions about which method you should use.

The Harvard system

This system involves a very brief mention of (reference to) a publication in the text of the dissertation, and an alphabetical list at the end of the text giving full publication details of all the items referred to. The in-text reference includes only:

1   the surname(s) of the author(s);
2   the year of publication;
3   the page(s) from which any direct quotation is taken.

You do not need to include any other details such as the authors' initials or the title of the publication. Save those details for the reference list. The following examples show you what text references should look like.

Without direct quotation

> . . . several authors, including Smith (2015), Brown (2015) and Thompson and Jones (2015), have discussed the way . . .

> . . . this has sometimes been considered a beneficial effect (e.g. Smith, 2015; Brown, 2015) and sometimes detrimental (Thompson and Jones, 2015).

With direct quotation

> . . . Smith (2015, p.75) refers to 'natural order of chaos'.

> . . . but the idea of 'a natural order of chaos' (Smith, 2015, p.75) . . .

When you wish to refer to more than one publication written by a particular author in a particular year, differentiate between the items by labelling them 'a', 'b', etc.

> . . . as discussed by Smith (2015a) and Brown (2014). Smith (2015b) considers the problem of . . .

In the reference list at the end of the text, you need to include the full details of each item. These should be produced in a style similar to the following:

1   For a book:

> author(s) surname(s);
> author(s) initial(s);
> year of publication (in brackets);
> title of book (underlined or italicized);
> name of publisher and place of publication (in brackets).

> For example: Brown, A.B. (2015) *My Research in Chaos.* (Big Book Co., Littlehampton).

2   For a paper in a journal:

> author(s) surnames(s);
> author(s) initials(s);
> year of publication (in brackets);
> title of paper;
> name of journal (underlined or italicized);
> volume (and issue number) of journal;
> page numbers of paper.

For example: Brown, A.B. (2015) Experimental development of laboratory chaos. *Journal of Biochaotics* 27 (2), 129–134.

3   For an article or chapter published in a book (e.g. in a collection of essays):

author(s) surname(s);
author(s) initial(s);
year of publication (in brackets);
title of article
'in'
surname(s) of book editor(s);
initials of book editor(s);
title of book (underlined or italicized);
name of publisher and place of publication (in brackets);
page numbers of article.

For example: Thompson, A. and Jones, B. (2015) Recent progress in chaotic research. In Jackson, P. (ed.) *Trends in Geography.* (GeoPub., Georgetown), 276–282.

You don't need to put the publication date after the name of the editor, as it will inevitably be the same as the date you've given for the paper itself.

4   For a professional report:

author(s) surname(s);
author(s) initials(s);
year of publication (in brackets);
title of report;
name of report series (underlined or italicized);
report number, if any;
place of publication (in brackets).

For example: Brown, A. (1999) Ongoing research in chaotic states. *Institute of Chaotic Science Reports,* Report no. 94–8 (New York).

5   For a web page or internet site:

author(s) surname(s) (if available);
author(s) initials(s) (if available);
the words 'online' (in brackets);
year of creation or last update (in brackets) (if available);
title of page or site (underlined or italicized);
url (http address);
'accessed:' (date that you accessed the site).

For example: Routledge Books (online) (2014) *Information for Authors.* http://routledge.com/info/authors/ accessed 28 September 2014.

The main point is that the reader should be able to trace your material, so, if in doubt, give more details rather than fewer in your reference. For other sources, such as newspapers, you can adapt the examples given above.

For more details and examples of this and other systems, refer to the reference lists in books and journals in your field. Many journals give explicit instructions in their 'guide to authors', often printed inside the cover. As always, check the rules in your own institution and follow the system that is required for your dissertation. Follow it carefully.

Appendices

Include appendices only if you really need them. You will need them if you have material that needs to be included in the dissertation but does not fit into any of the sections in the main body of the text. If you have a lot of data, such as transcripts of interviews, that the reader may need to access in order to confirm your analysis, you should not break up the text with pages of undigested data. Rather, you can put a summary in the text, and put additional data into an appendix. Make sure you mention the appendix in the text, so that the examiner knows it is there and at what point he/she should think about looking at it. Do not include material in the appendix just because you have collected it and don't want to see it go unused! For example, just because you have a thousand pages of interview transcripts, you do not need to include them in your appendix. The summary, highlights and key extracts that you provided in the text of the dissertation are probably sufficient. At most, you might include a page of transcript from the interview as an illustration of what your transcripts looked like. The examiner does not want to see them all. Appendices do not normally count towards the word count of your dissertation, so if you are running up against the word limit of your institution you might think that moving material from the text into an appendix can be a useful tactic. Bear in mind that your examiner may not even look at the appendices, so do not put anything there that is crucial to your argument. Also remember that the examiner is well aware of the cunning tactic of putting excess text into the appendix when challenged by the word count!

Presenting text, figures and other materials

Your institution may have regulations about what you can and can't include with your dissertation, and how you have to include specific types of material. Check your regulations before you follow our advice. For example, don't post some of your supplementary material online, with just a web address provided in your text, if your institution requires the dissertation to be an entirely self-contained paper document.

The main principle behind your presentation of the text, the figures or any other materials in your report should be clarity. Your aim is to help the reader to understand what you are presenting. You can make a lot of progress just by writing good clear English, but the layout and appearance of text and figures are crucial. For a start, they are the 'body language' of the report; they help to signpost what is going on and where the reader is. Also they are the medium of contact between you and the examiner. It's like getting a TV programme on a fuzzy old TV set – however good the programme might be, the duff reception ruins the effect.

Text

> ***Eric says . . .***
>
> Text is talk. Speak clearly. Talk sense.

We have already discussed the layout of text in terms of dissertation structure, but text appearance is important also at a small scale. Each page should look neat. Each page should look like it is related to the other pages through a common format. Your institution no doubt insists on word-processed text, so neatness really should not be a problem. If for some reason you have somebody else do the word processing for you, make sure the person knows what you are trying to achieve and has read the institution's guidelines.

Word processing is a very useful tool. It is easy to make everything look neat and tidy and it is easy to rearrange and correct text after you have typed it. This means that you should be able to produce faultless text, and that you can rearrange the work at the last minute in response to advice from anyone who reads your draft.

Caution:

If you use a word processor spellchecker, be sure it is correctly set to English (UK), or English (US), as appropriate to your location!

When preparing the text pay close attention to your institution's guidelines. These are usually very specific about:

- size of lettering;
- width of margins;
- line spacing;
- weight (thickness) of paper.

Figures

Many figures can be produced to a professional standard using the basic drawing packages that you probably have on your computer. It is worth taking the time to learn how to use one of these simple packages, even if it is only the drawing tool supplied within your word-processing software. If you require specialist diagrams such as sedimentological cross-sections you may want to use more sophisticated software. In some projects, for example, those involving GIS analysis, diagrams may be produced as part of the output of the analysis. Make sure that you take control of the content and style of these, rather than allowing a software program to make all the decisions. The same is true if you use a mapping provider: don't just accept what they provide. Commercial mapping, for example, might include a lot of excess detail, or unnecessary labels. Or it might lack something that would be really useful to your readers. Try to adjust the map or diagram to 'personalize' it to your particular needs.

Remember the key point: figures, like text, are a way of presenting information. Present only the information you need to present, and do so clearly and simply.

Some figures can be produced easily as part of word processed text. Simple tables, for example, can just be typed into the text. Other figures can be produced via computer graphics in association with the data analysis stage of your work. For example, statistical analysis packages on computers will allow you to produce hard copy of graphs and other material. If you use this approach, beware of three things:

1   Make sure that the quality of the output is equal to, or better than, the quality of the rest of your dissertation. It looks very bad if an otherwise nice report is spoilt by a series of graphs presented in faint, smudgy, poorly aligned print on mis-matched paper.
2   Do not fall into the trap of including figures in your report just because the computer has given you figures. Examiners are on the look out for undigested computer junk. Include only what your dissertation requires and benefits from.
3   Don't automatically accept the decisions made by the software about how to present the figure. For example, make your own choices about how to label axes, whether to box the outline of the figure, whether to label every data-point and so on. Your computer may have its own idea of what a graph should look like, but your computer doesn't actually know what your dissertation is trying to achieve. You do. So you should decide what does and doesn't go on your graph. The examiners will quickly spot situations where you have left decisions about your diagrams or maps to a software package or online mapping organization! Personalize your maps, especially by cutting out irrelevant data. Do you really need a full topographic map showing roads and railways as your basic location map? Include only what you need.

If you resort to drawing some of your figures by hand, remember that you do not need to be a professional draughtsman to produce a satisfactory illustration, as long as you keep it simple, go carefully, and follow some basic rules. However, the days of hand-drawn figures in student dissertations are pretty much gone, and we do not recommend this approach except in very unusual circumstances. If you do use hand-drawn figures, for example, if drawings made by participants or research subjects are part of your data, then rather than including the original drawings you should scan them and incorporate them into your work electronically. Be aware that any hand-drawn diagrams that you include will be marked alongside the ultra-smooth computer-drawn figures in your fellow students' dissertations. If you have pencil-drawn sketches with labels scribbled in ballpoint pen and bits of sticky paper glued on, the examiner will be unimpressed unless your project is specifically about hand-made representations of the world!

Remember, your dissertation is supposed to look like a professional piece of work, not a nursery-school project.

Photographs

You may wish to include photographs in your report, and it's usually a good idea. Check your institution's guidelines for any rules about this, but if there are no specific constraints from your institution, remember the same basic point that applied to other illustrations: clarity. Make sure that every photograph illustrates a specific point that is clearly identified in its caption and refers to a point that you've made in your text. Don't include photographs that don't show anything. Do annotate and caption photographs to make the most of what they do show. Adding a clearly labelled line drawing showing the key features from the photo can sometimes help to make your point clearer, especially if the photograph is of a very complicated scene that includes many distractions from your key features. Photographs of complex geological exposures, for example, often benefit from an accompanying diagram.

The best way to include photographs is to embed them within your text electronically. The days of sticking photoprints into your dissertation with sticky tape or glue are, thank goodness, well behind us now. Remember to reduce the size of the image file to something appropriate when you include a photograph that you have taken on a digital camera, and if you scan images from hard copy make sure that you scan them at a suitable resolution. A dissertation with lots of 12MB images could become hard for your computer to deal with, especially if you try to print it on a central machine at your institution at the same time that 200 other students are trying to do the same thing.

Once you have electronic versions of your photos you can easily add labels or annotations to help make your information clearer. Although the days of sticking photographs into the dissertation are gone, it might still sometimes be appropriate to use overlays on your diagrams. These were traditionally a transparent sheet with text or annotations bound into the dissertation as an extra page in such a way that it can be overlaid or lifted back to reveal the photograph. If your dissertation is submitted only as a hard paper copy this could still be effective, but if your dissertation is to be marked as an electronic document make sure that you have a suitable digital solution to the old-fashioned but effective overlay technology!

There are lots of ways you can use photos, but the important thing is to use them effectively so that they help your dissertation and gain you marks rather than simply loading your dissertation with unhelpful dead weight and losing you marks. Like everything else in your dissertation, photos should serve a specific purpose, not just fill space.

Erica says . . .

If your dissertation is supposed to be submitted and marked anonymously, with only your ID number and no name on the cover, you probably should not use a selfie as your cover image.

Where to put the figures and photographs

Figures and photographs can be built into the text, placed at a point near to where they are discussed (every figure, photograph or table that you include in your dissertation MUST be referred to in the text), or they can be collected in groups, for example, at the end of each chapter. The advantage of the latter is that the reader does not have to search backwards and forwards through lots of pages to find a particular diagram each time it is referred to in the text, but the disadvantage is that the reader has to turn to the end of the chapter to find a picture even if it is mentioned only once. The approach you take will depend on whether most of your figures and photographs are mentioned only once in the text (put individually at the appropriate points) or are mentioned repeatedly in several parts of the report (put them in easy-to-find groups). If you embed photos at appropriate points throughout the text where they are first mentioned (the usual approach) but then need to refer back to a photo later in the dissertation, remember to refer to the page number, as well as the figure number, which will help the reader to find the photo easily.

Figure and photograph captions and their numbering

Every figure and photograph should have a caption; a short piece of text immediately below the figure or photograph that describes what it is. The figure or photograph should also have a number, so that you can refer to it easily in the text. A good way of numbering figures or photographs is to number them sequentially within chapters. Thus, the first two figures in Chapter 3 would be Figures 3.1 and 3.2. Traditionally, tables in the text are numbered separately. They can be numbered with roman numerals; Table I, II, III, IV, etc., or they can be numbered sequentially within chapters, as for figures. Photographs often used to be numbered separately as 'plates' but this can lead to an overly complex system, and most people now choose simply to include photographs among the figures.

Figure and photograph captions should be informative. Consider the following examples:

Example 1

Figure 3.1: Map

Example 2

Figure 3.1: Map of the study site at Nether Wallop, showing the locations of the three sampling sites (A, B and C) and the area affected by the flood of April 1994 (shaded)

Remember, it can sometimes be a useful trick to simplify your figure by transferring information from the figure to the caption. On a densely crowded map, for example, the scale, or parts of the key, could be transferred to the caption.

Can I include a DVD with video, or extra data on CD?

Different types of project call for different types of illustrative material or evidence. You may wish to include an extended data set, video coverage of your subjects, recordings or interviews, or a huge collection of additional photographs to back up what you have included in the text. Be very careful. This is not always a good idea. First of all, your examiner is unlikely to sit down with a cup of tea in the evening looking forward to a two-hour screening of your video epic, and is equally unlikely to set aside an afternoon to enjoy your CD 'Three thousand additional images of the sewer system, vol. 2, Kings Cross'. Just as we recommend thinking twice before shoving in a fat appendix, we suggest you think very hard, and in consultation with your advisor, before including anything that can't be 'read' as part of the dissertation. You could include screen-shots and a transcript of the video, or transcripts of interviews, or a small, representative selection of your photographs. But always remember the general rule: include exactly what you really need, and no more. If you do decide to include additional material beyond what can be presented as text, then also remember the option of putting material online, and including in your dissertation just a link to its location. Again, check with your advisor about how your institution will handle this. There may be digital space available within the institution's system, for example, within the Virtual Learning Environment, for you to submit video. Alternatively they may insist that you include a DVD in a wallet fixed inside the dissertation. Or they may just say 'No'. Check. And check before you commit to making a video, just in case the institution says no after you have done it! Geography is generally an eclectic and broad-minded discipline, so 'unusual' data formats, or styles of presentation that break out of the traditional text-based format should be welcomed, but your institution may not (yet) be so open minded about these things.

How long should my dissertation be?

As usual, the first thing to do is check your institution's regulations. Most departments specify a maximum length that the report must not exceed. DO NOT EXCEED THIS LENGTH. Many departments also specify a minimum length. MAKE SURE YOUR REPORT IS NOT SHORTER THAN THIS MINIMUM. Typically, the sort of length required is between about 6,000 and 12,000 words. Some institutions offer the dissertation as a single module, while others make it a double module and some institutions offer both. Check which your dissertation is supposed to be, as that will probably have a bearing on the expectations that the examiners will have of your work, both in terms of length and intellectual achievement (and the implications of the mark you get for it for the class of degree you are awarded).

If your institution does not specify a length requirement, then you can work out roughly how long your dissertation should be by using the same criteria that the departments with length regulations use to work out their requirement. As we discussed earlier, your dissertation is supposed to do a number of different jobs: it describes your research; it discusses the background to the work; it considers the implications of your findings; it details your methodology and instrumentation; it demonstrates your expertise. It should do these jobs clearly but without undue padding. Depending on the scale of your project and the precise field of study this should take somewhere between 6,000 and 12,000 words.

Eric says . . .

Size is not important.

Of course, Eric isn't strictly correct; size is important in as much as you must fit into the regulations and you will inevitably require a certain number of pages to do all the jobs you need to do. What Eric means is that 'bigger' does not necessarily mean 'better'. It is a common fault in dissertations to include superfluous material.

Typical student's strategy:

> I've done all this analysis and it's turned out not to be relevant, but I'm not going to waste it so I'll put it in as an appendix.

Typical examiner's comment:

> Bloody idiot. What's all this rubbish?

How long should each chapter be?

It's hard to specify the ideal length of each chapter because different dissertations will be organized in different ways. For example, if you are using a novel and complex method in an innovative way, your methods chapter will need to be a lot longer than if you are using a standard method in exactly the way it is described in every standard textbook. However, as a general rule you should think of your dissertation as being a highly focused piece of research that fits into a broad framework of existing literature, so the details of exactly what you did (methods and results) need to be well balanced by details of the previously published research that forms the context for your work and by details of how your own findings relate back to that context. In other words, you need a nice big literature review and a nice big discussion section. As a rule of thumb it would not be far wrong to think that as much as half of your total word count should go on those sections. So a 12,000 word dissertation might have a 3,000 word literature review and a 3,000 word discussion chapter.

In what order should I write my dissertation?

We have worked through the content of your dissertation, chapter by chapter in the order that the sections are likely to appear in your final presentation. However, you need not write the sections in that order. For example, you may wish to delay writing the introduction until after you have completed at least a first draft of the data analysis and discussion sections, so that you can be confident that the questions you are identifying in the introduction really are those that your dissertation eventually answers! Alternatively, you may well find that you can write up large sections of the introduction and literature review while you are waiting for your data to arrive, or even before you go out into the field. Some people like to draft the conclusions first, so that they know where they are heading as they write the other sections. Different approaches will work best for different projects and for different students. Don't feel that you have to write chapter in the 'right' order. Do what works best for you, even if that means starting in the middle and working outwards!

Writing the perfect chapter, or even the perfect sentence, probably won't happen in one go. You need to draft, revisit, get feedback and draft again, often over and over until the whole thing is as good as it can be. This takes time, including the time you need to let a draft 'go cold' before you look at it again, and the time you need to have a meeting with your advisor to get feedback on a draft. Make sure that your timetable includes plenty of space for writing, thinking and rewriting. Knight and Parsons (2003) give lots of good advice on writing.

Proof reading and checking

Before you bind the final version of your dissertation for submission, or before you press 'upload' to submit the whole thing for assessment, pause. Leave a little time – perhaps a few days or a week – and then carefully check everything. Again. It is almost certain that there are at least several, and probably many little typographical mistakes, cut-and-paste errors, incorrect figure numbers, diagrams inserted the wrong way up, pages in the wrong order, spelling mistakes, apostrophes where they are not required, missing apostrophes where they really are required, and many, many other small things that will, in combination, seriously distract, irritate and disappoint your examiner. If you discover them only after you have submitted the work then you, too, will be seriously distracted, irritated and disappointed. Fix them. They can be hard to spot. If you just read through the report you will probably see only a small fraction of all the errors. If you read it out loud, or if you read it a sentence at a time starting at the end and working backwards to the beginning you will spot many more. This is tiresome, but it is important. Don't trust your spellchecker or grammar checker. Never, never trust the autocorrect feature. When you are absolutely sure it is all perfect, just check the abstract, the introduction and the conclusion one more time. Those sections will be looked at most often and most carefully, so they need to be most error-free.

Never, never trust the autocorrect feature.

If you have a willing friend or relative get them to read through the dissertation for you as well. You should not accept academic help from them (your institution might see that as collusion), but most institutions will be happy for you to have a proof reader check for simple oversights. Do check with your tutor, though, just in case there are any rules about having to declare any help of that sort.

Binding and submission

Although most institutions now require an electronic submission of the dissertation, which will be used to check for plagiarism, most also still require paper copy. Make sure you know exactly what you are required to provide. If you do have to provide a bound copy, our advice here is very simple: have your dissertation bound in the style required by your institution, and submit it on time. Allow for things to go wrong when you hand in the paper copy (traffic hold-up on the way into the university) and when you submit the electronic copy (internet crash and file corruption). Leave plenty of emergency time. Hand it in at least a day early.

If there are no specific guidelines as to how you should bind the report, there are many options available. At one extreme of convenience and (im)permanence you could use a simple ring binder. The advantage is that it is quick, easy, cheap and amenable to last-minute changes. The disadvantages are that it looks unprofessional, can be cumbersome to carry and to read and is not at all secure. We do not recommend it. More secure and more professional-looking binding techniques are preferable. Most institutions have rules that will not allow you to use anything as basic as a ring binder. Something like spiral binding or comb binding is the most common approach, and most university campuses have somewhere that students can have this done.

Make sure that you have not printed right up to the margins, so that the holes punched for the binding do not chew sections out of your text or diagrams!

The important points to bear in mind when making your choice about binding are as follows:

- regulations;
- appearance, security and ease of handling;
- cost and convenience.

Geography dissertations can be prone to some particular binding problems, such as the incorporation of oversized maps or figures. Problems can arise if you have fold-out illustrations where one edge is bound at the spine and several layers are folded up between the pages. In such a case, be careful not to have the folded-over sections accidentally bound in so that the illustration is bound up in its folded and concealed state. With fold-outs like this, or if anything is stuck onto pages which are bound into a book, the extra thickness can cause the dissertation to bulge inelegantly. A good binder will overcome this problem by inserting spacers at the spine to accommodate the thickness of the extra items, but if you bind the project yourself take care to deal with these issues.

Chapter summary and conclusion

Your report tells the examiners about your research, and the examiners base your grade on what is in the report. You have to explain in the report what you aimed to do, why it was important, how you did it, what you found and what that means. You need to convince the examiners that you know what you are talking about and that you are 'expert' in your field of study.

There are numerous 'conventions' in the writing of scientific reports, and you should adhere to these conventions so as to facilitate communication between yourself and the examiners. The structure and the style of your report are crucial to its success. There are many pitfalls to be avoided in your writing, and many 'tricks' to effective presentation. A good report can make the most of a mediocre project; a bad report can ruin a good project.

You must follow the rules of your institution, produce your report accordingly and submit it at the right time.

Suggestions for further reading

There are many books offering advice and information on writing and presenting reports. Of course, we like:

Knight, P.G. and Parsons, T. (2003) *How to do your essays, exams and coursework in Geography and related disciplines*. Routledge, Cheltenham, 210pp.

However, don't limit yourself to reading only those that have the name of your discipline in the title: a lot of good advice about academic writing is in more general texts. Some that we have come across include:

Craswell, G. and Poore, M. (2011) *Writing for academic success* (2nd ed.). Sage Publications, London, 264pp.
Bailey, S. (2011) *Academic writing: a handbook for international students* (3rd ed.). Routledge, Abingdon and New York, 320pp.
Godfrey, J. (2013) *The student phrase book*. Palgrave Macmillan, Basingstoke, 232pp.
Gillet, A., Hammond, A. and Martala, M. (2009) *Successful academic writing*. Longman, Harlow, 360pp.

What to do after reading Chapter 9

When you've read this chapter you will have an idea of what your finished report should look like. If you have not yet written your report, then go ahead! If you have written your report, go through it and check whether it meets the general criteria that we have discussed. Does it do all the things that a dissertation report should do? If not, do something about it. Remember, there is a lot of room for variety, but the general criteria that need to be met are quite standard.

If you think anything is going wrong with your dissertation look at Chapter 10, and talk to your supervisor.

Re-read your institution's guidelines periodically as you proceed, to make sure that you follow all the rules. When you have finished, check it. Then check it again.

Then DON'T FORGET TO HAND IT IN!

10

HELP! IT'S ALL GONE HORRIBLY WRONG. WHAT CAN I DO?

This chapter tries to help you sort things out if they have gone wrong. It identifies the sorts of things that can go wrong at the various stages in your dissertation and suggests ways of making the best of the situation you find yourself in. Look at this chapter whenever you feel things might be going wrong. Also look at it before you start the dissertation, to get an idea of the kinds of problems you should look out for and avoid.

STOP!

Have things really gone wrong?

Many students think things have gone wrong when, in fact, they haven't. Before you take any remedial action make sure you are not in this category.

Have things really gone wrong?

Many students think things have gone wrong when, in fact, they haven't. The commonest reason for students thinking things have gone wrong (when, in fact, they haven't) is that they have got different results from what they were expecting or hoping for. Perhaps you were expecting your results to show that a new method of measuring something was better than the traditional method, but in fact you discovered that the traditional method was still the best. Or perhaps you aimed to explore the causes of a relationship between two things, only to discover that the relationship actually didn't exist in the way you expected. These outcomes may be surprising to you, but they should not necessarily be disappointing. You have still found out something about the world, even if it was not quite what you had expected. The problem was probably more to do with your expectations than your findings. You can probably still go ahead and write a perfectly good dissertation. Remember, your examiners will be looking for evidence that you can design and carry out a piece of research, not that you have made a major discovery or that you happened to guess correctly in advance what your results would show. Failure to falsify a hypothesis is not failure of a research project!

If you're not sure whether things have gone wrong or not, talk to your tutor.

What can go wrong, and when?

All sorts of things can go wrong while you are doing a dissertation. Some problems can be so serious that they threaten the completion of the project, others threaten to spoil the quality of the work and hence to lower the mark that you will attain for your dissertation, and others simply make life difficult for you while you are doing your work. With luck you may never need this chapter, but just in case things go wrong it is here to help. It might also be a good idea to read through it before you start the dissertation just to get an idea of the kinds of problems that can arise, so that you can take precautions against them and perhaps prevent them from striking your project.

Problems can strike at any time, and, inconveniently, problems often don't show up until long after you made the error or omission that caused them. It may seem harsh to be blaming you for your problems even at this early stage in the chapter, but it is fair of us to do so because even if you didn't directly cause your problem, you evidently didn't do enough to make sure it couldn't happen, or it wouldn't have! Maybe you have just discovered that the data you collected are inadequate for the statistical analysis you had planned. Maybe you are now standing at your field site and have discovered that the area contains none, or insufficient, of the things you had come to measure. Maybe you are back at your desk writing up your analysis and you have just discovered that your data aren't what you actually need to answer the question(s) you set out to answer. Maybe you've lost your disc and have no back-up. Maybe you just don't think you can make the deadline.

If you are seriously reading this chapter because you have recognized that you have a problem, then you are already well ahead of the other guys who don't even know what a mess they're in.

Most of these problems can be prevented from arising by careful planning in the early stages of the project. Those that do arise can usually be dealt with, and dealing with them effectively can be the key to the success of your dissertation. What we will try to do in this chapter is to identify the main stages at which things can go wrong and what you can do about them. Stay calm.

Fixing the mess when things do go wrong

OK, so you are sure things have gone wrong. DON'T PANIC. Just because things have gone wrong there's no reason why your dissertation shouldn't still turn out well, if you can keep your head. The first thing to do is work out where things went wrong. Then you can either go back and fix the problem, or do something else to undo or disguise the damage.

Problems at the planning stage

This is when the most serious problems are likely to occur. These problems are most dangerous because they are likely to be so fundamental that they undermine your entire project. What's more, if you don't notice these problems right away you could well be far into your project (completed your fieldwork and begun your data analysis) before you become aware of them. This is pretty serious, and the most fundamental of these problems could lead to disaster and a complete re-start. You must guard against them.

Erica says . . .

If only you'd taken things more seriously at the planning stage, and thought ahead more carefully, you could have avoided this situation.

We have put great stress in this book on the need for careful planning and a sound research design. It is because errors in planning or research design are hard to spot as you are making them that it is important that you give a lot of attention to these stages of your work. Planning your dissertation is all about choosing a good topic to investigate and designing a research programme that will lead to unequivocal answers to the questions you have asked. If you don't do these things then problems will be building up ready to strike you much later on. Don't say we didn't warn you.

If you are at an advanced stage in your project and you have just realized that there was a fundamental flaw in your research design that undermines your whole project then you can either face up to the mess and include a frank self-assessment within your report, or retrospectively redesign your project so that what you have actually done seems to match up with your newly invented aim, or go back and start again from some earlier stage in the project where everything was OK. Talk to your advisor, of course, and read ahead in this chapter for further advice.

Problems at the data collection stage

Problems can arise whether you are collecting your data in the field, in the laboratory or in an archive. Fieldwork commonly gives rise to more problems, or it appears to do so because you are likely to feel most vulnerable when in the field without much support. The good news is that these problems can usually be fixed. Some of the problems that may occur at this stage are covered in the following subsections:

Your field site is devoid of the features you hoped to study

This could be a matter of your coastal wildflower meadow having been eroded by a storm surge, you pit-head bath being demolished and redeveloped as a supermarket, the chief executive who you planned to shadow for a week being suddenly unavailable or the glacier where you intended to study subglacial deformation turning out to be resting on bedrock. One option might be to go somewhere else. But this is not usually an option that will be available, particularly if you have made logistical arrangements committing you to a particular site, and especially if you are carrying out your fieldwork in a foreign location. You may be restricted to that locality because that is where you can get cheap accommodation; or because Eric, who is going to be your field assistant, lives there; or because that's where you have gone for your summer holiday and your accommodation is booked for another three weeks! Perhaps you could extend your field area so that it does encompass some of what you need: is there an equally suitable flower meadow just along the coast? If you are stuck with the locality and cannot extend it far enough to reach any of the features you were looking for, then look to see what features it does have. It must have something you can study. You wanted to study the meadow, but the meadow has fallen into the sea, so study coastal erosion instead! If you are in this situation then you are back at Chapter 4! The thing to guard against here is rushing into a project without careful planning. Everything we said in Chapters 4 to 8 applies all over again. If you've got into a mess once, you don't want to make things worse by getting into another, different mess because you're rushing through the important stages of planning. Most of the difficulties in doing a dissertation (or anything, come to that) lie in the unfamiliarity of the task. Once you know what you're doing, things get a lot easier. So, having planned a dissertation once, you should find it comparatively easy to do it the second time around! Try thinking back to some of the other topics you had briefly considered for your dissertation. Could one of them be resuscitated to help you now?

Eric says . . .

If you do have to go back repeat some of the work, at least it should be easier the second time around!

One problem you may well have is that you might not have ready access to a suitable library when you're away from your own institution. But, again, things might not be as bad as they seem. For a start, you might be able to get online access either to your own library's resources from your fieldwork location, or, if not to your own library, then at least to the internet and the wealth of information available through online sources such as Google Scholar, Web of Knowledge and so on. Even if you don't have access through your own personal device, there may be access via an internet café or a local library. Maybe Eric can email you something useful. A bit of exploration and you could well find that there's more available then you expected, even in quite remote locations. Of course, if you are in a genuinely remote and unconnected location, this problem may not be so easy to resolve! If you want to avoid having to read a whole new literature, try to think of a new project that is closely related to the one you had originally planned so that all your earlier reading is not wasted. If you are in mid-ocean carrying out your pirate-ship ethnography and the pirates won't talk to you, adjust your project so that it relies on watching the pirates instead of talking to them.

Your equipment breaks

Once again, you have choices. One will be to try to recover the situation so that you can carry on as planned. You may try to get the equipment repaired or return to your department and get a replacement or see if you can borrow something similar from a new source. If none of these options seems likely to work, then ask yourself if you really need the piece of equipment at all. Can you make do? For example, suppose you had planned to measure gradients along a stream channel using a Total Station electronic surveying system. Could you make do with an Abney level? Could you improvise with a protractor, a piece of string, some chewing gum and a pebble? The question you need to ask is 'Will the reduced level of accuracy be such that my results are meaningless?' If the answer is yes, then obviously you cannot make do with the lower quality data, but often you will still be able to make use of results even if they are less precise or a little less accurate. If you can't repair/replace the equipment and you can't make do, then you will have to think of another project that you can do with the equipment that you do have. As in the previous case, if you are in this situation make sure you design your new project with as much care as you did the first one (see above).

The events you planned to monitor didn't happen

This problem is much the same as going to a field site and finding it devoid of the features you planned to study. Dissertations that are based on a need for things to happen can run into problems when they don't! Perhaps you planned to do a study of visitors to a particular picnic spot but for the whole of the period that you had set aside to collect data it rained and nobody had a picnic. (Didn't you consider that possibility when you were planning? Tut tut!) In fact, for many types of dissertation an inability to recruit enough participants is one of the most common causes of problems in this category. You planned to interview 100 people, but only three showed up. You anticipated 1,000 responses to your online survey but had only 27. Your attempt to interview children outside a school was arrested by the intervention of the local constabulary. It is much the same situation as if you had decided to look at the effect of discharge variation on pollution levels in a stream but throughout your period of fieldwork your stream had a remarkably steady discharge. Or perhaps you were doing experiments with different types of ice that you created in the low-temperature laboratory, but there was a power cut and you ended up with no ice at all. In all those cases the outcome is that you realize you are not collecting the data that you were hoping for. Solutions might include an innovative approach to data collection (for example, try a Facebook survey rather than an on-street interview to get extra respondents), or a decision to retire gracefully and think of another topic. Another solution would be to approach the problem through numerical modelling. You may be able to use a simulation study to come up with a model of how you think the phenomenon should behave. You could, for example, analyze the literature on picnics and develop a model to predict the numbers of picnickers who would visit your site under particular conditions or on certain days. Obviously, a dissertation that did this but then didn't provide any empirical testing of the model wouldn't be as good as one that did, but you could still do very well, particularly if your modelling led to a dissertation that demonstrated most of the attributes we listed in Chapter 2.

Problems at the stage of data analysis

The most likely problem for you to discover at this stage is that your data are insufficient or inappropriate. Despite having what looked like a carefully thought out data set, it turns out, now you come to it, that you can't actually answer your question with the data you now have and it's too late to collect any more. There are several reasons why you might be in this position.

First, perhaps you didn't think through the design of your research as well as you should have done. We hope that this book will have prevented this possibility. What often seems to happen is that the research design was fine, but then the execution of the research was flawed. Perhaps you used the wrong piece of equipment, or measured your population with insufficient precision, or did the right measurement but at the wrong time. In this case you probably have results, but are beginning to realize that they are not as useful or reliable as you had hoped.

Second, perhaps the data collection took even longer than you could have foreseen. Maybe things kept going wrong in the field so that you started collecting data but then things happened so that the data had to be thrown away. For example, suppose you planned to measure variation in infiltration in response to differences in vegetation cover. To avoid complications you want each site to have a similar initial soil moisture but you need several days over which to make the measurements. After a few days it rains so you have to stop work and wait for soil moisture levels to drop back to the pre-rain value. As a result you obtain fewer samples than you had intended so the multi-variate analysis you had planned won't now be valid.

Third, perhaps you have, in fact, changed your question from what you originally intended it to be. This may have appeared a very sensible thing to do. Once you started on your data collection you may have realized that there was more to the problem than you'd initially thought. As a result you modified your questionnaire, but, unfortunately, didn't realize the implications this would have for your analysis. You changed your project to watching pirates instead of talking to them, but then remembered that you were banking on doing a content analysis of your recorded conversations when you got home. That's not going to work now!

Whatever the reason, you now find that your data or samples don't match up with the question(s) you are trying to answer or the analytical techniques that you are trying to use. So, what question(s) can your data be used to answer, and what kinds of analysis are they amenable to? Almost certainly, there will be some variant on the question(s) you wanted to answer that your data will be good for. Perhaps, having only managed to meet one football manager, your dreams of a statistical analysis of managers' attitudes might be lost, but you might still be able to use a more qualitative approach to analyzing your one conversation that could yield dividends. Remember, your examiners will be looking for compatibility among the question(s), the data and the analysis. They don't need to know how you achieved that compatibility! It may be normal to start with the question(s) but you can start with the data and work backwards – and you may have to. Many struggling dissertations have been rescued by seeing what data are available and working backwards from that. It isn't the way you are supposed to do it, but, in an emergency . . . We will say more about this solution later on.

Problems at the stage of writing up

Some problems that you encounter when writing up are in fact problems from earlier stages that you simply never noticed until you came to write up. Others are indeed problems with writing up. It is important to recognize which problem you are facing, because the solutions may be different. If your problem is genuinely related to the writing, then check Chapter 9 to see if we have said anything useful. You may find we said even more useful things in our other book about writing essays and coursework (Knight and Parsons, 2003). However, if your problem is to do with research design, data, literature, equipment or anything of that nature, then your solution probably lies somewhere deeper in the mechanics of the project than in the fine detail of how you organize your text. Nevertheless, careful organization of the way you tell your story can make a lot of difference to the way your readers understand and appreciate the story. At this stage, when problems fundamental to the project emerge while you are writing up, you really do need to go and talk to your tutor. Even if your problems are strictly to do with writing, your tutor should be able to help. It is very, very common for students to have done a splendid piece of research and to have plenty of perfectly good data, but to find it very difficult to get started on the writing. Chapter 9, and your tutor, should be able to help get you started, or to jump-start you if you have stalled.

Can I get an extension?

Given that you have had perhaps a whole year to work on your dissertation, and were advised at the outset to leave plenty of emergency time for dealing with problems if they arose (remember our advice about making a timetable with emergency time built in?) it is unlikely that you will be granted an extension for your dissertation deadline without a really good reason. There are not many reasons that you could produce to which your tutor could not give you one of the standard responses: you should have checked; you should have had a back-up; you should have been more careful; you should have worked harder; you should have left more time in case of problems like that; you should have asked for help earlier (Knight and Parsons, 2003). Nevertheless, if you are really struggling and feel that you are not on target to meet the deadline, it is really important that you go and get help and advice from your tutor. Perhaps you will be offered an extension. Don't bank on it.

If this is the answer, what was the question?

One problem that can emerge either in the data collection, analysis or writing up, and which often has its roots in your initial planning, is that you seem to have measured, observed or worked out something different from what you intended.

Students often turn up in a panic telling their advisor that they set out to explore the interactions between pirates and seagulls but ended up finding out about seagulls and fish instead.

Earlier in this chapter we implied that if your data can't be used to answer the question(s) you set out to answer then you might be able to modify the questions to fit the data. This is very important. You can extend this idea a long way. Unless you have been unbelievably unfortunate or lazy, you will end up getting at least some information about something. In an emergency you can plan your dissertation in reverse by working backwards from whatever data you have managed to end up with.

We have stressed throughout this book the need for good research design and careful planning. But you want the best mark you can get for your dissertation and there may come a point where you can't afford to be too fussy about how you get it. Hence the title of this section. Whatever data you have must address some question. Even the most serious of the fundamental problems that may have arisen from weaknesses in planning might be overcome at this late stage by thinking about what you can do with the data you have. You are unlikely to get a very good mark for your dissertation starting from this position, but the first 40 per cent is much easier to get than the last 40 per cent so even an 'emergency rescue' dissertation will be worth something. Even in this position, if you can work out a logical sequence from your data back to a question, you might achieve a reasonably well-structured dissertation. The weakness will be that you won't have much choice in what the question turns out to be. If you find that your data condemn you to using a poor question then that will affect the overall quality of your dissertation, and its mark.

Facing up to the mess

If it turns out that despite the strategies we have suggested you still don't have very much to say in your dissertation because things have gone wrong, then you should consider how much of the mess you want to admit to. If you've managed successfully to work backwards from the data to a modest, if not great, question you might want to present your dissertation as if nothing had gone wrong. On the other hand, you might think it is a better policy to admit to the problems you had in tackling a really interesting problem and present the work as a bold, innovative, but unfortunately flawed effort. We had a student once who set out to do a project about how to create ice by freezing supercooled water in the laboratory. The student was unable to create any of the ice they were interested in, but was able to write a first class dissertation about the factors that made it difficult to replicate subglacial supercooling in the laboratory. Remember what we said about the reasons for doing a dissertation in the first place (Chapter 2). The primary purpose of your dissertation is to teach you how to go about finding things out and for you to demonstrate that you have, indeed, learned how to do this. Generally, you would expect to do this by achieving success, but a thorough understanding of why you failed might get you quite a long way. Being able to explain to your examiners what went wrong, why and what you would do about it if you had the chance to do your dissertation again can get you quite a lot of credit. You could include a whole section in the discussion or conclusion explaining how your problems affected the project, but only do this if you have intelligent things to say. Don't just put in a section of excuses. The examiner won't be interested unless you show what you have learned. Critical evaluation of your own work is another of the skills that undertaking a dissertation should give you. You will gain credit from your examiners if you demonstrate that you have acquired this skill.

Dissertation stress

Your tutors probably tell you that the dissertation should be no more stressful than any other module, that it should take no more work to complete a 30-credit dissertation module than to complete any other 30-credit module, and that as long as you follow their advice the dissertation should be a challenging but enjoyable and beneficial experience.

Eric and Erica both say . . .

Yeah. Right.

In reality, many students do get stressed about their dissertation. Perhaps it is because the idea of a year-long project without many fixed points of contact or intermediate deadlines is intimidating when you are used to weekly lectures and short-term assessment deadlines. Perhaps it is because this is the first time that a module has really emphasized the importance of your own independent study. Often it is because students try to fit too much 'student life' into each day and cut back on essentials such as good sleep, good food and good exercize. Perhaps it is because people like us write books telling you that you do not need to be stressed. In fact, what your tutors say is true: you should not get stressed about the dissertation. First, there is no need for stress as the dissertation should run smoothly if you are well organized and stick to your timetable. Second, getting stressed usually only makes things worse as it leads to panic or denial, to poor performance and potentially to ill health. If you do feel stressed about your dissertation talk to your advisor, and if you still feel stressed after that then consider talking to a personal tutor, a support counsellor or to whatever form of student assistance your institution provides. In most cases some straightforward academic advice will get you out of trouble, but if not, then do seek further support.

The basic academic advice on dissertation stress is essentially the same as the advice that we have tried to distil into this book. If you plan well, allow extra time for emergencies, have good back-up plans, stick to a sensible schedule and get regular advice from your tutor, then everything should be quite stress free! The majority of cases where students start to feel stressed arise from problems with planning or time management. Even if there are problems with data collection, equipment failure, conflicting deadlines or any of the other myriad difficulties and distractions of student life these should not cause you any dissertation stress as long as you have planned well, allowed plenty of time and kept in touch with your tutor.

Key advice includes the following:

- start early and make a sensible timetable;
- seek advice from your tutor at regular intervals;
- always ask for help when you need it;
- stick to your timetable;
- have a good research design with realistic expectations for your data;
- maintain a good balance between work, life, play and sleep;
- if you fall behind your timetable, seek help and catch up;
- if you encounter problems, don't ignore them: seek help.

Chapter summary and conclusion

This chapter aimed to show that you can get out of trouble if problems have arisen with your dissertation. It has identified the sorts of problems that might arise and suggested ways in which you can deal with them. We hope you don't get into a mess, but if you do then stay calm, get help, and you can probably climb back out of it. The best way to avoid problems is to plan very carefully in the early stages of the project and to leave plenty of emergency time at the end.

What to do if you've had to read Chapter 10!

Don't panic. Keep calm. Sort out exactly what has gone wrong and see what remedies exist. If you need this chapter, then you probably also need to talk to your tutor.

11

HOW WILL IT BE MARKED?

This chapter describes examination and assessment procedures for dissertations, explains what the examiners will be looking for, and offers some advice about making sure you give them what they want.

If you know what the examiners are looking for, it is easier to give them what they want.

Examination and assessment procedures

Each institution has its own assessment scheme, but the procedures for marking dissertations are pretty much standard throughout the system. In a typical scheme your project will initially be read and graded by a 'first marker' who will often be the project supervisor. The project is then read and graded independently by a 'second marker' who does not know what the first marker thought of the work. The second marker is usually someone in the department who has some specialist knowledge of the research area, but who may be less familiar with the material than the first marker. The marks assigned by the two markers are compared, and if they are similar a compromise mark, sometimes an arithmetic average of the two individual marks, will be agreed. If the two markers reach substantially different conclusions about the dissertation, and a compromise cannot be achieved, the dissertation will be sent to a 'third marker'. The third marker studies not only the dissertation but also the comments of the first two markers, and reaches a final decision about the work. The third marker is often an examiner from outside your own institution, and might decide that the only way to adjudicate your work is to interview you. In that case you will be called for a viva. This is an increasingly uncommon approach, but in case you do find yourself in that situation we'll discuss vivas later in this chapter. Some institutions use an internal third marker, and only use the external examiner to adjudicate in exceptional cases. Other institutions routinely send many dissertations for external assessment.

There are exceptions to the general format of assessment described here. For example, some institutions allocate a portion of the marks available for the dissertation to elements of the work other than the final report. Some institutions allocate a small percentage to research proposals prepared in the first few months of the project, or to preliminary reports submitted immediately after the field season, for example. As with all the other aspects of the procedure, you need to know how your institution operates, and how marks will be allocated to your work. Check with your supervisor if you are in any doubt.

What are the examiners looking for?

In Chapter 2 we discussed the purpose of the dissertation and what constitutes a good dissertation. The issues that we covered in that discussion are the sort of thing that the examiner will have in mind when assessing your dissertation. You should keep looking back at that section while you are preparing your dissertation. The key points are:

1   a clear problem set in its academic context;
2   a clearly explained and appropriate methodology;
3   adequate and appropriate data and data analysis;
4   appropriate organization of results and interpretation;
5   sensible and penetrating discussion;
6   logical and relevant conclusions;
7   intellectual achievement and originality;
8   a high standard of presentation, easy to read.

Many institutions provide dissertation markers with clear guidelines in the form of a formal mark-sheet with specific questions and with space for examiners' comments. In some institutions the supervisor is given a particular set of questions about how the student went about the work, as well as questions about the finished report. Looking at the questions on these mark-sheets gives a very clear picture of exactly what the examiner is looking for. The examples in Box 11.1 are taken from the mark-sheets from two UK institutions, and give some insight to the examiners' way of thinking.

Notice the similarities between the points we discussed in Chapter 2 and the headings in Box 11.1. Bear these in mind when you are writing your dissertation. If you can get hold of a copy of the mark-sheet used in your own institution, so much the better!

A marking guide

Whether or not your institution uses formal questionnaire-style mark-sheets, there will certainly be a consensus as to what is required of dissertation students and what sort of mark should be allocated to dissertations of different quality. These standards should be constant not only between the individual examiners within each institution, but also among different institutions. One of the jobs of the external examiner is to ensure that this is so. Not every institution has formalized the grading of dissertations to the extent of producing a formal markers' guide, but such a guide is very useful – not only to the examiners, but (more importantly) to you. Box 11.2 is a markers' guide of the sort that many institutions

Box 11.1 Examples of headings on examiners' mark-sheets

Example 1

Selection of topic:
Quality of literature review:
Methodological overview and critique:
Data collection:
Data analysis:
Results: presentation and interpretation:
Conclusion (insight?):
Presentation:
Overall impression:
Recommended mark (%):

Example 2

(Specifically for an examiner who is also a supervisor)
Description of project:
- conceptual difficulty;
- technical complexity;
- originality.

Conduct of project:
- independence;
- organizational ability;
- methodological awareness;
- perseverence;
- critical ability;
- initiative.

Written report:
- Did you offer advice on writing?
- Did you comment on a draft?
- academic content;
- methods;
- data handling;
- presentation of results;
- quality of results;
- discussion;
- suggestions for future work;
- written expression;
- evidence of plagiarism;
- recommended mark (%).

use. This guide tells you exactly what you have to do to reach whatever grade you want for your dissertation. Most institutions will have a qualitative marking guide that describes what is expected for a first class, upper second, etc. piece of work. This scheme is likely to be given to you in a handbook or published on your department's web pages. If you have been given a copy of such a scheme you will recognize the guide in Box 11.2 as a version of the scheme, specifically tailored for dissertations.

Box 11.2 A markers' guide for undergraduate dissertations

First Class (70–100%)

An excellent dissertation. Interesting aims clearly set in the context of previous literature. Evidence of original and independent thinking. High quality reasoning and organization. Appropriate and clearly explained methodology. Sound and comprehensive data collection. Accurate and appropriate data analysis. Insightful and detailed discussion. Sound conclusions based on logic and data. High quality presentation.

Upper Second Class (60–69%)

A good dissertation, meeting all the dissertation requirements, and meeting most of them at a high standard. Falls short of First Class on only a few criteria. May lack polish and fluency of a first class dissertation, or may be flawed in some minor way(s).

Lower Second Class (50–59%)

Flawed in one or several areas, but nevertheless meeting the basic requirements. The level of detail, reasoning, or presentation may be uneven. The evidence of insight, and breadth of reading may be limited.

Third Class (40–49%)

Does no more than fulfill the basic requirements. Meets few of the criteria of a good dissertation. Reasoning, literature review and data may be weak or patchy. Presentation may be scruffy. There may be little evidence of originality or insight. The work may not be clearly set in a broader context.

Fail (0–39%)

A broad category of marks to accommodate a range of dissertation types. These may include dissertations with evidence of plagiarism, dissertations that fail to meet the requirements of the institution, or dissertations that only meet the requirements at a most basic level. Different institutions will have different benchmarks within the fail category, but if you are reading this book before finishing your dissertation, you should not need to worry about them!

First impressions

Your dissertation is a part of your final examination, and as such it will be assessed carefully and meticulously. Nevertheless, examiners are, believe it or not, human, and their approach to marking will reflect common human traits that you can exploit in your final presentation. For example, it is as true in dissertation marking as in anything else that first impressions are very important. Most examiners will glance through the dissertation quickly before settling down to read it thoroughly, and what they see on that first glance will colour their attitude to what they read subsequently. The marker's approach may vary depending on whether the work is submitted and marked as a hard copy or as an electronic document. For a paper copy typically, at the first glance, the examiner will:

- hold and look at the book as an object;
- look at the title page;
- read the abstract;
- skip through the contents page;
- flick through the pages of text;
- look at the reference list;
- possibly read the conclusion if it is short.

For an electronic copy the basic approach will be similar, but the stage of looking at the physicality of the presented object will be replaced by a stage of judging both the overall look of the electronic document and also the ease of accessibility of the file or files. If you were required to upload the work as a single file, and you upload it as a folder including several documents and a zipped collection of image files, the examiner will not be impressed. That's the digital equivalent of submitting the dissertation unbound in a bin bag.

You need to make sure when you submit your dissertation, not only that your work will stand the close scrutiny of a thorough examination, but that the prominent parts of the work will do a good job of impressing the examiner on first acquaintance. If some of your photographs fall out when the examiner picks up your dissertation, or it is obvious at first glance that your contents page is incomplete, or your text appears to have been printed with a faulty print cartridge, the examiner will inevitably form a poor first impression.

Having read the dissertation, for a reminder of key points and to help finalize a mark, the examiner will probably glance again at the key elements. Commonly, having studied the dissertation carefully, the examiner will finally:

- re-read the abstract;
- re-read the conclusion;
- re-read the contents page.

That will usually be enough to check that the work is well planned and clearly structured and to judge the extent to which it has done the job it set out to do.

Before you submit your dissertation, go through the same routine as the examiner and try to see your dissertation as the examiner will see it. If pages fall out when you flick through the dissertation, do something about it! Ask yourself the questions the examiner will ask. Give your dissertation a mark. Ask yourself what you could do, even if it is a last-minute job, to improve your dissertation. Better still, get a friend to 'mock' examine the dissertation for you. The best time to realize your weaknesses is before, not after, the formal examination!

Plagiarism

When we wrote our first draft of this book, and showed it to colleagues in other institutions to get suggestions as to how it might be improved (just as you should do with early drafts of your dissertation) it was suggested to us that we should be more forceful on the issue of plagiarism. When we revised it again for the third edition, reviewers again consistently raised the issue of plagiarism as something we should continue to address here. The strength with which this message came back to us is a measure of how strongly our colleagues – the people who will be marking your dissertations – feel about it, so take note!

Plagiarism is unacknowledged copying. At one extreme it can involve copying a whole document (a government report, for example) and claiming it as your own work. Less extreme, but no less serious, cases could involve copying sections of reports, articles, maps, books, web pages or other people's dissertations. Even using short passages, or ideas, from other people's work without specifically acknowledging the source, is plagiarism. If you lift anything from anywhere, you must acknowledge the source. You can acknowledge it by means of a conventional reference, and/or in a separate section of acknowledgements. If you are deemed to be guilty of plagiarism there could be serious legal implications, and, of course, the examiners will be singularly unimpressed. Your institution might simply disallow the whole dissertation and give you a mark of zero, so watch out. If in doubt, consult your tutor for guidance. Your institution will almost certainly have guidelines on penalties for plagiarism. These guidelines will apply to your dissertation. Do not be fooled into thinking that your dissertation is so specific that nobody will recognize the sources from which you have lifted material. For a start, your examiners are a very experienced bunch of people: if material has been plagiarized, it's likely that somebody will be able to tell, and might even recognize the source! Even if you fool the reader, you will not fool the electronic plagiarism-detection software that is now routinely applied to submitted work. Most institutions, even if they require a paper copy of the dissertation, require students also to submit an electronic copy for that specific purpose. Even if you think that you can somehow fool both the system and the examiner, it really is not worth the risk.

If you try to cheat, then for the rest of your life, when anyone remembers you, they will remember you as the student who tried to cheat on your dissertation.

Being found out as a cheat is about as bad as it gets in terms of what you might take away from university. Just don't even think about going down that path.

One complicated aspect of plagiarism is the problem of self-plagiarism. This is where an author copies his or her own work (from another publication or assignment) and re-uses it in a new piece of work. This is most likely to affect undergraduate dissertations where you have produced a research proposal prior to doing the dissertation, and then think of re-using sections from that proposal (the literature review, for example) in your finished dissertation. Different individuals and different institutions have different views on this. Some people think it must be OK to use your own work, but other people (and many institutions) will argue that if you have already used a piece of work in an assessment and gained credits for it as part of your degree, you can't expect to get more credits for submitting it again! On the other hand, if you wrote the perfect site description as part of your research proposal, you might think it is silly having to write a new one for the dissertation. It's a tricky area, and of course you need to check exactly what rules your own institution and markers will be applying. To be on the safe side we certainly suggest that you never simply copy and paste work from one assignment into another. If you did some good work in your literature review or in an essay in another module that you think would fit well into the dissertation don't just copy it over, but at least re-work and upcycle it! In re-writing it you will probably find that you can improve it anyway, and certainly you should be able to write it in a way that is more directly tailored for the dissertation. For example, your proposal was probably written in the future tense whereas your dissertation should probably be written in the past tense.

Eric says . . .

You don't want to copy something you wrote a year ago, anyway. You could do it much better now, with that extra year of training and experience behind you!

Plagiarism is one of several different types of academic misconduct that you need to avoid. Another is collusion, which is the term applied to inappropriate sharing of work or ideas between students. If you are supposed to be doing something independently, but you actually do it working together with a friend, that's collusion. Rather than dwell too long here on what is a very unpleasant topic, we suggest that you review the information about academic misconduct that you were almost certainly given by your institution earlier in your course. Take care to follow all the rules. If you follow good academic practice – citing all your sources correctly, acknowledging where you got your data and images, ensuring that quotations are correctly identified and only declaring to be your own work that which is indeed your own work – you will be fine. If, on the other hand, you cheat, then your dissertation and your marks will turn to dust.

In the unlikely event of a viva

In the past, many institutions included a face-to-face meeting with one or more examiners as part of the assessment for the dissertation. That practice, known as a viva voce exam (or just a viva), is now much less common, but since some of you may be in an institution where vivas are held, we thought we should say a word or two about it. And vivas might come back into fashion before we write the fourth edition of this book!

If they give you a viva, the examiners are giving you an opportunity to improve your score. They want you to do well.

You could be called for a viva for any one of several reasons. The viva might relate just to your dissertation, or it might cover your whole spread of assessments. Some institutions viva all students, some viva none at all. In some institutions vivas are given to students whose marks are just below a borderline between degree classes, so that the examiners can judge whether the student deserves to be raised into the higher class. There are also differences between subject areas. While geography, in general, has moved away from the idea of the viva, other subjects in the list of 'related disciplines' that we are thinking about as we write this book still use them routinely.

The viva is like a cross between a tutorial and an interview. There may be one or several examiners, and they may want to talk with you about your exam papers, or your dissertation, or your coursework. Remember, the examiners want you to do well. They are trying to give you the opportunity to score marks. They are not trying to trick you or trap you into losing marks. If you relax, answer the questions that the examiners ask and try to engage in some discussion with the examiners, you will do well.

Remember the list of things that the examiners are looking for, and try to give them exactly those things. You need to come across as a keen, interested student who has worked hard and who wants to do well. You need to demonstrate your ability to recall information from your years of study, to think on the spot about new questions that the examiners will throw at you and to argue logically about issues with which you are familiar, such as the design of your dissertation.

You do not need to defend your dissertation to the death if you know that it was in some way flawed. The examiners will be much happier with a student who sees the weaknesses in a dissertation and can see ways of improving it if given another chance, than with a student who thinks the work was just fine and couldn't be improved. There is always room for improvement.

Go into the viva prepared to explain how you'd do it better if you could do it again.

Honesty is always a good policy. If the examiners ask a question that you can't answer, don't pretend to know more than you do. Fumbling around foolishly trying to bluff your way out of a tight spot looks comical from where the examiner is sitting. The best approach is to admit that you don't know, but then to offer some ideas about how you could work out the answer or what you could do to improve your dissertation depending on what the answer turned out to be. Remember, the examiner isn't just testing what you know, but how you can think and discuss. If you are called for a viva follow the advice in Box 11.3.

Box 11.3 How to prepare for a viva

To prepare for your viva:

1   Be sure that you are familiar with the work that you have done. Read through a copy of your dissertation, and get someone to ask you questions about it.
2   Think about how you could do the dissertation better if you had the chance to do it again. Look back through this book and remind yourself of what you should have done!
3   Talk to your tutor or supervisor and see if they have any advice to offer.
4   Check the library to see if any new work in your field has been published since you wrote the dissertation. The examiner will be very impressed if you demonstrate that you have kept up to date with the literature (especially if he/she has written any of it!).
5   Have a few early nights before the viva!

Chapter summary and conclusion

Your dissertation will be marked independently by several markers, some of whom may be expert in the field and all of whom will be concentrating on the specific criteria by which your dissertation is to be judged. These criteria are embodied in the markers' guides in Boxes 11.1 and 11.2, but more specifically in your own institution's documentation. You need to be aware of these criteria and to make sure that your dissertation meets them. If you are called for a viva voce examination stay relaxed but focused, and remember that the viva is an opportunity to improve your mark.

What to do after reading Chapter 11

If you have not yet finished (handed in) your dissertation, then 'examine' it yourself using the criteria we've discussed in this chapter. Make any improvements you can before you hand it in. Remember to keep a copy for yourself that you can use to prepare for a viva if you have one. If you have been called for a viva, follow the advice in Box 11.3.

12
A FINAL WORD

Dear Reader,

Is your dissertation complete? If you're all finished then it's nearly time for us to say goodbye. We wrote the first edition of this book because we were asked to: publishers recognized that there was a need for a book like this. We agreed to write it because we believed that your dissertation was the single most important piece of work that you would do in your degree programme, that you needed all the help you could get, and that we might be able to help. When we were asked to produce a second edition we decided that you still needed help and that we could still offer it, so we did. When they asked us to do a third edition . . . well, we just thought it would be rude not to. And, yes, we still thought you needed help!

We think that research is an exciting and fun thing to do, and we hope that the way we have presented this book hasn't taken the fun out of it for you. We also think that research is largely based on common sense. We hope that this book has not made it seem more complicated than it needs to be.

Successfully completing a dissertation should give you a lot of things. A module contributing to your degree, of course, but more than that the confidence to know that you can identify a problem, devise a research strategy, carry out a project and produce a final report. Those are skills that you may well need again, long after your dissertation has been consigned to the filing cabinet of history (or, in our case, geography). You may well use those skills in your future career, and you should talk about the experience of doing a dissertation whenever you have the opportunity in a job interview, even if the job does not appear to be directly connected to your specific research topic. In the real world 'research skills' can be applied in many different contexts. The fact that you have successfully completed a dissertation says a lot about you. Well done!

We hope that this book has helped you to grow in confidence, as well as in competence. We hope that it has helped you to enjoy doing your dissertation, and we hope that it helped you to do the best dissertation that you could.

Good luck with your next research project,

Tony and Peter.

REFERENCES

Abrahams, A.D., Parsons, A.J., Cooke, R.U. and Reeves, R.W. (1984) Stone movement on hillslopes in the Mojave Desert, California: a 16-year record. *Earth Surface Processes and Landforms*, 9, 365–70.

Abrahams, A.D., Parsons, A.J. and Luk, S.-H. (1988) Hydrologic and sediment responses to simulated rainfall on desert hillslopes in southern Arizona. *Catena*, 15, 103–17.

Bailey, S. (2011) Academic writing: a handbook for international students (3rd ed.). Routledge, Abingdon and New York, 320pp.

Best, S. (2003) *A beginner's guide to social theory*. Sage Publications, London, 280pp.

Bullard, J. (2010) Health and safety in the field. In: Clifford, N., French, S. and Valentine, G. (eds) *Key methods in Geography*. Sage, London, Chapter 4, pp.49–58.

Chorley, R. J. (1978) Bases of theory in Geomorphology. In: Embleton, C., Brunsden, D. and Jones, D.K.C. (eds) *Geomorphology: present problems and future prospects*. British Geomorphological Research Group, pp.1–13.

Clayton, K. (1981) Explanatory description of the landforms of the Malham area. *Field Studies*, 5, 389–423.

Clifford, N., French, S. and Valentine, G. (2010) *Key methods in Geography* (2nd ed.). Sage, London, 568pp.

Crang, P. (1994) It's showtime: on the workplace geographies of display in a restaurant in southeast England. *Environment and Planning D: Society and Space*, 12, 675–704.

Craswell, G. and Poore, M. (2011) *Writing for academic success* (2nd ed.). Sage, London, 264pp.

Cloke, P., Cook, I., Crang, P., Goodwin, M., Painter, J. and Philo, C. (2004) *Practising Human Geography*. Sage, London, 400pp.

DeLyser, D., Herbert, S., Aitken, S., Crang, M. and McDowell, L. (eds) (2010a) *The SAGE handbook of qualitative Geography*. Sage, London, 372 pp.

DeLyser, D., Aitken, S., Herbert, S., Crang, M. and McDowell, L. (2010b) Introduction: engaging qualitative geography. In: DeLyser, D., Herbert, S., Aitken, S., Crang, M. and McDowell, L. (eds) *The SAGE handbook of qualitative Geography*. Sage, London, pp.1–18.

Demerrit, D. and Wainwright, J. (2005) Models, modelling and Geography. In: Castree, N., Rogers, A. and Sherman, D. *Questioning Geography*. Blackwell, Oxford, pp.206–25.

Fetterman, D.M. (2009) *Ethnography: step-by-step* (3rd ed.). Sage, London, 200pp.

Feynman, R.P. (1985) *Surely you're joking, Mr. Feynman*. W.W. Norton, New York, 350pp.

Flowerdew, R. and Martin, D.M. (eds) (2005) *Methods in Human Geography: a guide for students doing a research project*. Pearson, Harlow, 366pp.

Garrett, B. (2013) *Explore everything: place-hacking the city*. Verso Books, London, 320pp.

Gillet, A., Hammond, A. and Martala, M. (2009) *Successful academic writing*. Longman, Harlow, 360pp.

Gleick, J. (1992) *Genius*. Little, Brown & Co., London, 531pp.

Godfrey, J. (2013) *The student phrase book*. Palgrave Macmillan, Basingstoke, 232pp.

Gomez, B. and Jones, J.P. (2010) *Research methods in Geography: a critical introduction.* Wiley-Blackwell, Oxford, 480pp.

Hay, I. (2010) Ethical practice in geographical research. In: Clifford, N., French, S., and Valentine, G. (eds) *Key methods in Geography.* Sage, London, Chapter 3, pp.35–48.

Hay, I. (2010) *Qualitative research methods in Human Geography* (3rd ed.). Oxford University Press, Oxford, 464pp.

Healey, M., Lannin, L., Stibbe, A. and Derounian, J. (2013) *Developing and enhancing undergraduate final-year projects and dissertations.* Higher Education Academy, York, 93pp.

Herbert, S., Gallagher, J. and Myers, G. (2005) Ethnography and fieldwork. In: Castree, N., Rogers, A. and Sherman, D. (eds) *Questioning Geography.* Blackwell, Oxford, Chapter 8, pp.226–40.

Hracs, B.J. and Leslie, D. (2014) Aesthetic labour in creative industries: the case of independent musicians in Toronto, Canada. *Area,* 46(1), 66–73.

Inkpen, R. and Wilson, G. (2013) *Science, Philosophy and Physical Geography* (2nd ed.). Routledge, Abingdon and New York, 238pp.

Ivanova, O. (2013) Modelling inter-regional freight demand with input-output, gravity and SCGE methodologies. In: Tavasszy, L. and de Jong, G. (eds) *Modelling freight transport.* Elsevier Science Publishing, London, pp.13–42.

Karlstrom, K.E., Lee, J.P., Kelley, S.A., Crow, R.S., Crossey, L.J., Young, R.A., Lazear, G., Beard, L.S., Ricketts, J.W., Fox, M. and Shuster, D.L. (2014) Formation of the Grand Canyon 5 to 6 million years ago through integration of older palaeocanyons. *Nature Geoscience,* 7, 239–44.

Kennedy, B.A. (1992) First catch your hare . . . research designs for individual projects. In: Rogers, A., Viles, H. and Goudie, A.S. (eds) *The students' companion to Geography,* Blackwell, Oxford, pp.128–34.

Kindon, S., Pain, R. and Kesby, M. (eds) (2010) *Participatory action research approaches and methods.* Routledge, Abingdon and New York, 288pp.

Kitchen, R. and Tate, N.J. (2000) *Conducting research into Human Geography.* Prentice Hall, Harlow, 330pp.

Knight, P.G. (1989) Stacking of basal debris layers without bulk freezing-on: isotopic evidence from West Greenland. *Journal of Glaciology,* 35(120), 214–16.

Knight, P.G. and Parsons, T. (2003) *How to do your essays, exams and coursework in Geography and related disciplines.* Routledge, Cheltenham, 210pp.

Knight, J. and Whalley, B. (in press) *Handbook of research methods in Physical Geographical Sciences.* Routledge, Cheltenham.

Langridge, R., Christian-Smith J. and Lohse, K.A. (2006) Access and resilience: analyzing the construction of social resilience to the threat of water scarcity. *Ecology and Society,* 11(2), 18.

McLafferty, S.L. (2010) Conducting questionnaire surveys. In: Clifford, N., French, S. and Valentine, G. (eds) *Key methods in Geography.* Sage, London, Chapter 6, pp.77–88.

McMorran, C. (2012) Practising workplace geographies: embodied labour as method in Human Geography. *Area,* 44(4), 489–95.

Mercer, C. (1999) Reconceptualizing state–society relations in Tanzania: are NGOs 'making a difference'? *Area,* 31, 247–58.

Montello, D. and Sutton, P. (2013) *An introduction to scientific research methods in Geography and Environmental Studies* (2nd ed.). Sage, London, 328pp.

Parry, J.T. (1960) The limestone pavements of northwestern England. *Canadian Geographer,* 16, 14–21.

Phillips, R. and Johns, J. (2012) *Fieldwork for Human Geography.* Sage, London, 240pp.

Pigott, C.D. (1965) The structure of limestone surfaces in Derbyshire. *Geographical Journal,* 131, 41–4.

Popper, K.R. (1959) *The logic of scientific discovery.* Hutchinson, London, 480pp.

Price, R. (1989) *Scotland's Golf Courses.* Aberdeen University Press, Aberdeen, 235pp.

Rhoads, B.L. and Thorne, C.E. (eds) (1996) *The scientific nature of Geomorphology.* John Wiley & Sons Ltd, Chichester, 481pp.

Ridley, D. (2012) *The literature review: a step-by-step guide for students* (2nd ed.). Sage Publications, London, 232pp.

Rose, L. and Vincent, P. (1986) Some aspects of the morphology of grikes: a mixture model approach. In: Paterson, K. and Sweeting, M.M. (eds) *New directions in Karst*, Proceedings of the Anglo-French Karst Symposium, September 1983. Geobook, Norwich, pp.473–96.

Tavasszy, L. and de Jong, G. (eds) (2013) *Modelling freight transport.* Elsevier Science Publishing, London, 268pp.

Wainwright, J. and Mulligan, M. (eds) (2004) *Environmental modelling.* John Wiley & Sons, Chichester, 408pp.

Wainwright, J., Parsons, A.J. and Abrahams, A.D. (1995) A simulation study of the role of raindrop erosion in the formation of desert pavements. *Earth Surface Processes and Landforms*, 20, 277–91.

Ward, K. (2013) *Researching the city: a guide for students.* Sage, London, 184pp.

Williams, P.W. (1966) Limestone pavements with special reference to western Ireland. *Institute of British Geographers, Transactions*, 40, 155–71.

INDEX